THE
ANTIQUES
DIRECTORY
FURNITURE

THE ANTIQUES DIRECTORY FURNITURE

General Editors:
Judith & Martin Miller

Chief Consultant Editor:
John Bly

American Consultants:
Lita Solis-Cohen
Kelvyn Grant Lilley

G.K.Hall & Co.,
Boston,
Massachusetts

The Antiques Directory
Furniture
General Editors: Judith & Martin Miller
Chief Consultant Editor: John Bly
American Consultants: Lita Solis-Cohen
                      Kelvyn Grant Lilley

The Antiques Directory: Furniture was compiled by MJM Publishing
Projects Limited and designed by Mitchell Beazley International Limited,
14-15 Manette Street, London W1V 5LB.

Art Editor: Nigel O'Gorman
Design Assistants: Olivia Thomas
                   Jacqui Turpin
                   Janet Cable
Production: Philip Collyer

Published in the United States and Canada by G.K.Hall & Co.,
70 Lincoln Street, Boston, Massachusetts, 02111.

Library of Congress Cataloging in Publication Data
Main entry under title:
The Antiques Directory. Furniture.

1. Furniture—Directories.   I. Miller, Judith.
II. Miller, Martin.   III. Bly, John.
NK2206.A57 1985   749.2   85-8475
ISBN 0-8161-8748-7

Typeset by Hourds Typographica Limited, Stafford
Colour reproduction by Chelmer Litho Reproductions, Maldon
Printed and bound by Wm. Clowes Limited, Beccles, England

CONTENTS

CONTENTS

INTRODUCTION

The market in antique furniture of good quality has never been stronger. Nor has it ever been so international. Fine French furniture comes up for sale in New York as well as Rome; good English pieces may be found from Sydney to Chicago. And these are not only the museum pieces, but the kind of quality furniture that is the backbone of the middle and upper sections of the market. It is such pieces that are the subject of this book.

THE COUNTRIES REPRESENTED

We have collected illustrations and details of furniture from all the main countries of western Europe and from America; to these we have added a number of Oriental pieces. If there is a bias towards the English-speaking countries it is because Britain in particular produced an enormous amount of excellently made, thoroughly serviceable pieces in the 18th century and the early 19th. Relative political stability has meant that many have survived unscathed, and so the kinds of item illustrated appear regularly in the salerooms. Their quality will always ensure that they command substantial prices, but the numbers available prevent those prices from going sky high.

An example may help to explain the bias in the selection. A good Georgian chest of drawers is a standard item in almost any sale of quality English furniture. It will be as useful as the day it was made and two centuries of care will have rendered it even more pleasing to the eye.

Compare the Georgian chest with a Louis XV commode, its contemporary. That will be a fine piece of furniture – a work of art, if it is a good example, displaying the finest marquetry and mounts. But, curiously, its age may have told against it. If it has retained its original condition it will be a rarity, with a price to match. If, as so many pieces did, it suffered a decline in social status, ceased to be an idle ornament of the ancien régime and entered service in a humbler home it is unlikely to have survived unscathed. Its desirability, alias its price, will be affected accordingly.

There is another factor in considering the furniture production of the main European countries. The great artistic movements – Baroque, Rococo and Neoclassicism – that swept Europe between 1600 and 1800 were interpreted differently in each country. But there is a supra-national quality about the finest models – the Italian Renaissance, Dutch-English Queen Anne, the French Rococo – in which the eccentricities of national taste are subordinated to purity of design. By contrast 18th-century Venetian whimsy, Rhenish corpulence and their contemporary lonely echoes of the Spanish Renaissance were a local taste when produced and have in large part remained so. These tributaries are acknowledged, but it would be misleading to give them equal place with the main torrents.

QUALITY AND QUANTITY

This, then, is a collection of many styles from many periods. What they have in common is quality of design, construction and materials. A few, especially in the colour sections, are of museum standard and are chosen to represent the high points of styles. An approximately equal number are fine pieces of country furniture, as pleasing in their way as their cossetted and curatored cousins.

For the most part, however, the items illustrated are in the mainstream and of types that frequently appear in furniture sales. But just as there is a bias in the proportions of space allotted to different countries, there is a parallel bias in the amount of space allocated to standard furniture types. Chairs, tables and chests receive more attention than beds and polescreens; bureaux are better represented than whatnots. The reason is partly the obvious one – that different kinds of furniture were made in drastically differing quantities – and partly that we wished to be able to afford a facility for worthwhile comparison.

THE VALUE OF COMPARISON

The importance of comparison can scarcely be overstressed. The small differences between generally similar items mark the distinction between pieces that are exactly right and those that just miss – between a top price and a middling valuation.

Comparisons are highly informative too in that they show how, for example, otherwise identical tables can, quite authentically, be differently shod; how chair backs of the same date and style reveal numerous possibilities of the design; or how the arrangement of drawer fronts to a chest can be more or less pleasingly done within almost identical cases.

Accordingly we have selected numerous examples of commoner items such as games tables and dining chairs. At first sight they may appear identical, but each shows some small difference, indicating the range of options open to the maker, the different currents of fashionable taste, the hints of a new style or nostalgia for a period whose time is gone.

Some particularly instructive comparisons can be made from country to country. English and American pieces of the 18th century are especially interesting, as one sees the reinterpretation in New England of the Queen Anne and Chippendale styles. Comparisons between Dutch and English furniture around 1700 are illuminating, or those between Roman and Parisian in, say, the 1790s.

A fascinating, if often obscure, aspect of this kind of comparison is looking for hints of foreign craftsmanship. Whereas now we buy pieces ready made from other countries, until transport of bulky items became relatively easy in the last century it was by no means unknown for wealthy patrons to bring in individual furniture makers or teams of them to execute their commissions. Craftsmen travelled of their own volition as well, criss-crossing Europe to improve their skills or in search of wealthier patrons. Both trends overlay the ancient journeyman system under which, for example, German carvers strayed way beyond the boundaries of their native states.

AN UNPRECEDENTED VISUAL REFERENCE

It is, above all, in the facility to make such detailed comparisons that the raison d'être of this book lies. Nowhere else to our knowledge is it possible to see clearly side by side so many variations on certain standard items. For all those engaged in the handling of antique furniture, whether as collectors, dealers, cataloguers, restorers or appraisers, we hope that we have fulfilled our intention to produce the standard visual reference. Not only should this volume facilitate identification, but we hope it will also assist collectors (or dealers on their behalf) in specifying precisely what they seek to acquire.

A work as large and complex as this could not have been compiled without the assistance of numerous people with different areas of expertise. A full list of acknowledgements appears at the back of the book, but to the numerous individuals and organizations who gave us permission to use their photographs we wish to record our gratitude. For the selection and description of items however we, not they, take final responsibility.

Among the furniture experts who have given us their time, advice and help, the contribution of John Bly has been outstandingly generous. We are also deeply grateful to the following for their various contributions: Dennis Charles, Graham Child, Victor Chinnery, Richard Davidson, Rachael Feild, Mike Golding, Christopher King, Christopher Payne, Pat Robins and Perran Wood; we would also like to thank Lita Solis-Cohen of Philadelphia and Kelvyn Grant Lilley of Chicago for their percipient comments on the American furniture shown.

HOW THE BOOK IS ARRANGED

The first distinction is by country. In the main, the furniture shown under the heading of a given country was made in that country, but occasionally this rule has been interpreted loosely to allow the inclusion of items that may not have been made domestically but which were imported in large numbers and which feature prominently in what is now accepted as the style of the country.

American and French furniture define themselves. The British section includes some Scottish and Irish. Germany and Austria are taken together for convenience and by common custom; to have distinguished all the various states at all the various times in their histories would have been pedantic, and ascribing provenances probably impossible. Italy is another amalgam, of course and the Low Countries is an accepted handle for a group of political entities of which Holland is the most recognizably enduring. Spain and Portugal are taken together, and so are the pieces shown from China, Japan and Korea. Both these condensations reflect mainstream international saleroom practice; specialist sales would be more precise.

Within each country, types of furniture are alphabetically arranged along commonsense lines, thus armchairs are shown under "chair". Each type of furniture within each country is prefaced by a few lines to give the reader who may be wholly unfamiliar with the furniture of that country some sort of orientation. At intervals throughout the book there are text panels in which points are made variously about style, construction, authenticity and so on. Read in conjunction with the introduction to the respective country and the introductions to types of furniture they are designed to provide the reader with some key facts about that country's furniture.

It would be a rare person indeed who would have a good knowledge of the furniture of all the countries represented. It may well prove helpful then to start with the colour sections of countries with which you are unfamiliar. There, some examples of the best quality are gathered and one can quite quickly apprehend the chief features of that country's tradition. Extended captions within the colour sections are intended to help establish some framework of periods, names and styles.

PRICES

Captions throughout the book start with a letter in a box, thus: **D** . This is the price code and there are five of them, with approximate values as follows –

- **A** $75,000 or more
- **B** $37,500-75,000
- **C** $15,000-37,500
- **D** $7,500-15,000
- **E** $7,500 or less

All are necessarily only approximate and apply only to similar examples in good condition at a sale in which their value is recognized but at which there are none of the special factors that can suddenly distort conventional pricing. An outstanding provenance or a very determined buyer could raise many items, particularly in the three lower categories, into a higher bracket. The prices given are at mid-1985 levels.

Some unfamiliar terms are explained in the glossary, part of which is a highly simplified chart put in to relieve those moments when one inexplicably forgets when, exactly, Louis XIV came to the throne . . .

AMERICA

"It might be assumed that American furniture having been modelled on English furniture, is like English furniture. It is not. Many facets of American government are modelled on English institutions. Few would say they are imitations. They are indeed new syntheses. This is also true of American furniture ...." (Charles F. Montgomery, *American Furniture of the Federal Period, 1788-1825*).

There has always been a school of thought which holds that the first generation of American furniture-makers were merely transplanted English craftsmen and therefore not truly American at all. However, even though the early designs may have been identical, some of the materials were different and necessitated changes in construction and, to a certain extent, in proportions.

By the second generation it becomes increasingly evident that while continuing to display its ancestry American furniture design has become authentically indigenous. The description of a leaf-capped cabriole leg terminating in a claw-and-ball foot applies with equal accuracy to American and English chairs of the Chippendale period; visually however the proportions of both are so obviously different as to make the different provenances obvious.

There was no radical change from the gentle curvilinear lines of the first 20 years of the 18th century into the fanciful extravagances of baroque and rococo so popular in England from 1720 to the mid-1750s. While the English found it irresistible to over-decorate, the American taste demanded at all times a combination of the useful and the agreeable.

THE FEDERAL PERIOD

By the time the full impact of the classical movement in England should have reached American shores, the revolutionary war had broken out. While there were certainly exchanges between the beaux mondes of both continents, this period showed less English influence than previously and Federal furniture with its elegant lines and fine inlay work developed as a style on its own.

The later Regency styles took many of the heavier aspects of the current tastes in Europe and relied upon exuberant foliate carving and marine motifs for their impact – the name of Duncan Phyfe springs to mind. As in England, the designs of the Federal period laid the foundations for the heavily ornamented furniture of the later 19th century, which was produced in southern cities as well as in traditional manufacturing centres such as New York.

BEDS 1740-1900

Early American beds of artistic merit are extremely rare, though good ones have been treasured perhaps more than other kinds of furniture as symbolic of families' continuity. By the mid 18th century however, beds of quality were being produced in such numbers as to present us with a fully documented catalogue of subsequent styles.

Four-poster beds

D 1 A Queen Anne mahogany bedstead, 1740-1760; 92 in. high by 83 in. long (252 by 210 cm).

D 2 A Chippendale mahogany high-post bedstead, Newport, Rhode Island, 1760-1780, 82 in. (208 cm) high.

D 3 A carved mahogany bedstead, Philadelphia, 1760-1780, 92 in. (234 cm) high.

D 4 A Chippendale carved mahogany bedstead, Newport, Rhode Island, *c.* 1775; 89 in. (227 cm) high.

D 5 A Chippendale birch and maple high-post tester bedstead, Massachusetts or New Hampshire, 1780-1810, 86 in. (218 cm) high.

D 6 A Chippendale birch tester bedstead, Massachusetts or New Hampshire, 1780-1800.

D 7 A Federal carved mahogany high-post bedstead, Salem, Massachusetts, 1790-1810.

E 1 A miniature Federal mahogany four-poster bed, probably New England, 1790-1810, 14 in. (35 cm) high.

D 2 A Federal mahogany bedstead, Massachusetts, 1790-1810, 63 in. high by 55 in. wide (160 by 140 cm).

D 3 A Federal mahogany four-post bedstead, Massachusetts, 1790-1820; footposts 88 in. high, inside rails 74 in. long, 52 in. wide, (223 by 188 by 131 cm).

D 4 A Federal turned and carved curly maple four-poster bedstead, New England, *c.* 1815, 64 by 56 in. (163 by 141 cm).

C 5 *(above)* A carved cabriole leg from a Chippendale four-post mahogany bedstead, made in Salem, Massachusetts, between 1760 and 1780. The acanthus carving to the knee, below stop-fluted posts, is crisp and strong against a punched and stippled ground.

This bed is in complete contrast to the Federal style – see the posts from a Federal bed, no. 7, right.

D 6 *(below)* A Federal inlaid mahogany high-post bedstead, Massachusetts, 1790-1810, 67 in. high by 57 in. wide (170 by 144 cm).

E 7 Footposts from a Federal birch tester bedstead, New England, 1800-1820. In their refined simplicity, these posts are an excellent example of the Federal style.

Four-Poster Beds

It should always be remembered that the secondary function of any four-poster bed was to display the wealth of the owner, partly through the quality of the decoration to the show wood and partly through the richness of the hangings. The headposts therefore may well be plain by comparison with the footposts, as the former were intended to be swathed with fabric.

The structure of four posters led inevitably to wear and possible damage at the junctions of rails and posts, and restoration at these points should not be considered detrimental provided that it is in no way an attempt to increase the value of the article by additional decoration or camouflage.

All too many tall beds have in the past been cut down. A typical reduction would have been cutting the posts shown in no. 7, left, at the junction of vase and reel, without regard for the proportions.

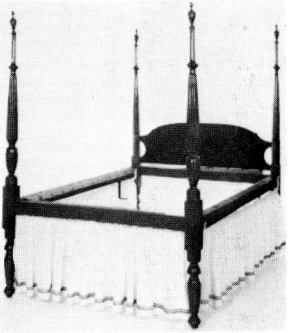

D 8 A Federal birch and poplar tall post bedstead, New England, *c.* 1815; 72 in. high by 55 in. wide, (183 by 139 cm).

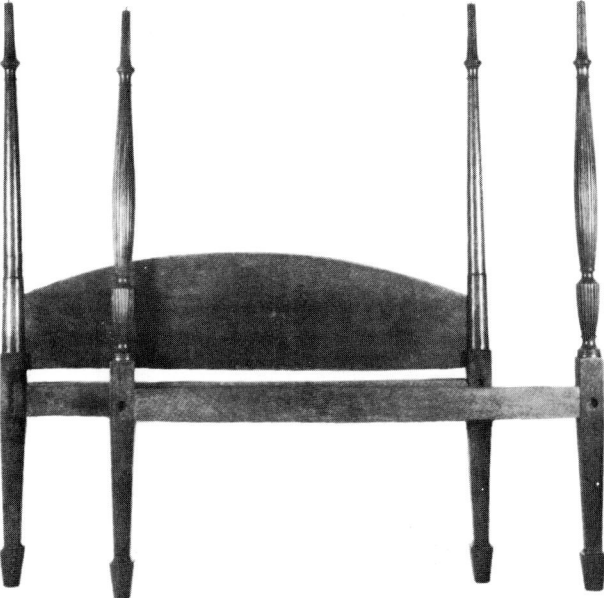

D 9 A late Federal birch canopy bedstead, New England, 1810-1830; 67 in. high (posts) by 54 in. wide (170 by 137 cm).

BOOKCASES
1735-1890

The development of the bookcase or cabinet on a bureau or secretary base was a natural one from late 17th century two-and three-part furniture. Decorative elements such as the shape of the glazing bars, the cornice and the finials are the keys to confirming date and place of origin by basic style.

Secretary bookcases

E1 A mahogany secretary, with double-domed hood and painted niches, with cedar, oak and white pine. New England *c*. 1735.

D2 A Chippendale maple secretary. Massachusetts, 1750-1780; 86 in. high by 40 in. wide (216 by 101 cm).

A3 A mahogany secretary, with blocked shell interior, with acanthus and egg-and-dart moulding, New York, 18th century; 84 in. high by 40 in. wide (215 by 101 cm), writing height 30 in. (76 cm).

A5 A rococo-style desk and bookcase, with curving front, and sides swelling towards the bottom in bombé form, possibly made by John Cogswell, Boston, Massachusetts, 1765-1780.

B4 A Chippendale carved mahogany desk and bookcase, the upper section with dentilled cornice, above two scallop-panelled doors enclosing fitted interior, the lower section with slant-front lid, enclosing drawers and pigeonholes, attributed to the shop of John Townsend, Newport, Rhode Island 1760-1785; 90 in. high by 45 in. wide (228 by 114 cm).

B6 A Chippendale carved cherrywood desk and secretary, the upper section with six drawers on each side, the lower section with slant-top lid, enclosing drawers and pigeonholes, probably Connecticut, 1765-1785; 85 in. high by 35 in. wide (217 by 90 cm).

B7 A Chippendale carved cherrywood desk and bookcase, with triangular dentilled pediment, above a guilloche pattern frieze, over two glazed doors enclosing shelves, the slant front below enclosing a compartmented interior, above four long drawers, on ogee bracket feet, Maryland, 1765-1785; 40 in. (101 cm) wide.

A8 A cherrywood bureau-bookcase of the Connecticut school, *c*. 1780. The deeply scrolled carved swan-neck pediment centres a turned finial and is flanked by two more, over a pair of cupboard doors fielded with scroll borders, flanked by reeded columns, over a fitted slant-front desk and four graduated long drawers, on bracket feet.

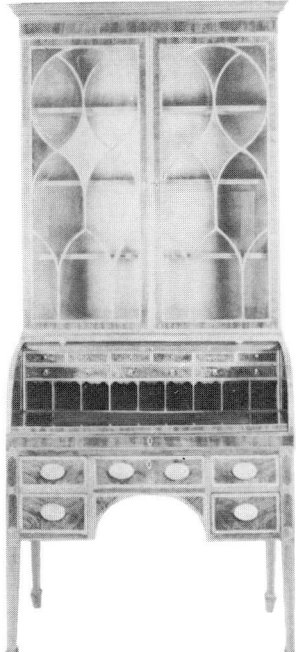

B 7 A mahogany inlaid secretary bookcase, with eagle finials and elliptical lattice glazed doors, possibly from Salem, Massachusetts.

B 1 A walnut desk and bookcase, with broken arched top and turned vase, over two solid doors, with arched fielded panels, the lower part with straight-fronted drawers below the sloping fall, standing on ogee bracket feet, Pennsylvania, 1780-1800.

B 3 A Chippendale cherrywood desk and bookcase, the upper section with scrolled pediment with carved rosettes centring a flame finial, above two shaped panelled doors, concealing three shelves, the lower section with slant lid concealing nine fan-carved drawers over nine pigeonholes, probably Norwich, Connecticut, 1760-1790; 87 in. high by 43 in. wide (221 by 109 cm).

B 5 A Federal inlaid mahogany tambour secretary bookcase, in two sections, the top with double glazed doors, the base with tambour cylinder roll, opening to a slide-out writing board, by John Aitken, Philadelphia, 1790-1800; 87 in. high by 38 in. wide (221 by 96 cm).

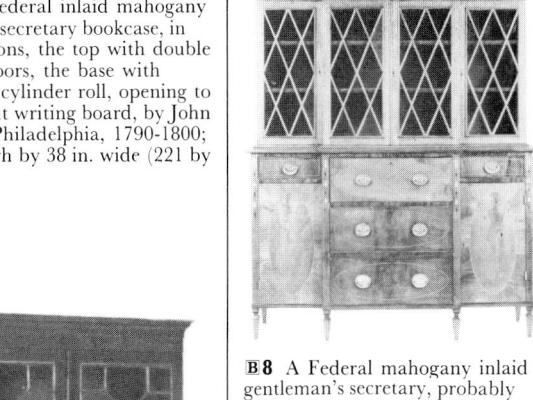

B 8 A Federal mahogany inlaid gentleman's secretary, probably Salem, Massachusetts, *c.* 1800; 90 in. high by 67 in. wide (227 by 170 cm).

B 2 A Chippendale mahogany block-front desk and bookcase, the scrolled pediment with carved rosettes and corkscrew finials, two cupboard doors with serpentine panels, above slant lid concealing pigeonholes and small drawers, on carved knee brackets with claw-and-ball feet, Massachusetts, 1760-1790; 95 in. (241 cm) high.

C 4 A Chippendale cherrywood secretary and bookcase, the upper part with two fielded panel cupboard doors enclosing a fitted interior, the lower section with fall-front desk lid, Connecticut, 1770-1785; 88 in. high, without finials, by 41 in. wide (223 by 104 cm).

D 6 A Federal inlaid mahogany bureau desk and bookcase, in two sections, the upper part with glazed doors opening to shelves, the base with hinged drawer front, forming a writing surface, Massachusetts, 1790-1810; 85 in. high by 43 wide (216 by 108 cm).

D 9 A Federal inlaid mahogany secretary bookcase, with a central drawer revealing a fitted interior; 97 in. high by 67 in. wide (247 by 170 cm).

B1 A Hepplewhite mahogany and satinwood breakfront bookcase, attributed to Nehemiah Adams, Salem, Massachusetts, *c.* 1800; 96 in. (244 cm) high.

C2 A Federal inlaid mahogany ladies' tambour writing desk and bookcase, labelled by Thomas R. Williams, Salem, Massachusetts; *c.* 1800.

C3 A Federal mahogany and bird's-eye maple veneer tambour writing desk and bookcase, Massachusetts; 76 in. high by 33 in. wide (192 by 82 cm).

C4 A Federal inlaid mahogany desk and bookcase, in three parts, the upper with shaped pediment above veneered frieze, the middle section with arched pigeonholes inside, the base with a folding writing surface over two line-inlaid drawers, flanked by line-inlaid stiles, above pattern-inlaid skirt, on square tapering legs, signed on the interior by Charles Douglas, New London, Connecticut, 1800-1820; 83 in. high by 36 in. wide (210 by 92 cm).

E5 A Federal carved mahogany bookcase, in several parts, the removable moulded cornice above six bookcase sections, each with glazed hinged door, the sides fitted with brass carrying handles, the lower section with two long drawers, on square tapering legs, *c.* 1805; 101 in. high by 67 in. wide (256 by 170 cm).

E6 A cherrywood and poplar ladies' writing table, with secretary drawer over three long drawers, on finely tapering legs, the upper part with cupboards flanking a tambour section opening to reveal three manuscript compartments, New England, probably Boston, *c.* 1810.

The quality of this piece illustrates the refinement and skill of the New England cabinet-makers during the Federal period and their interpretation of Sheraton's designs.

D7 A Federal mahogany secretary bookcase, with flat pediment above double arch glazed doors, with ribbed mullions and seven small drawers, the base with a folding writing surface, fitted with a well, above a long drawer and double cabinet doors, flanked by wine drawers, Boston, 1810-1815; 87 in. high by 40 in. wide (220 by 101 cm).

C8 A late Federal mahogany veneer writing desk and bookcase, with two glazed Gothic arch cupboard doors opening to four shelves, above seven arched pigeonholes, with three short drawers above hinged desk top, over five small drawers, probably New York, 1810-1820; 85 in. high by 39 in. wide (216 by 99 cm).

D9 A late Federal tiger maple desk and secretary, in two parts, the upper case with angular cornice above two glazed cupboard doors with moulded glazing bars, the lower case with slant top enclosing pigeonholes, over two small drawers and a central door flanked by two document drawers, above a single cock-beaded drawer, 1820-1830; 77 in. high by 35 in. wide (195 by 90 cm).

E 10 A poplar and pine grain painted bookcase, Middle Atlantic States, first half 19th century; 91 in. high by 43 in. wide (231 by 109 cm).

E 11 A Gothic revival rosewood bookcase, attributed to J. & J.W. Meeks, New York, 1836-1850; 86 in. high by 51 in. wide (220 by 129 cm).

D 12 A "Louis XVI" ebonized inlaid cherrywood bookcase, by Herter Brothers, New York, 1880-1885; 63 in. high by 64 in. wide (160 by 161 cm).

BOXES
1780-1830

It is only during recent years that the value of boxes as repositories of information about our social history has been fully recognized. Work boxes, knife boxes, toilet cases, deed boxes can all tell us a great deal about the requirements of domestic life in other periods and at many social levels – and they are sufficiently numerous to be as collectable as they are interesting.

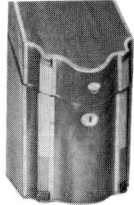
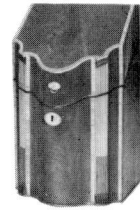

E 1 A pair of Federal mahogany inlaid knife boxes, American or English, 1780-1800; 15 in. (37 cm) high.

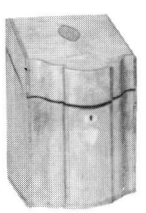

E 2 A pair of Federal birch veneered knife boxes, American or English, 1785-1810; 15 in. (37 cm) high.

E 3 The historical General Thomas Gage official papers box, the leather-covered hinged top with iron nail studded inscription, "SECty OFF/No.5/1768", opening to a double layered partitioned interior, each compartment labelled with a place name, the box interior painted red and with carrying handles, American, c. 1768; 13 in. high by 32 in. wide (33 by 81 cm).

E 4 A William and Mary inlaid walnut box, Chester County, Pennsylvania, 18th century; 6 in. high by 21 in. wide (15 by 54 cm).

E 5 A japanned box, on brass ball feet, painted black with gilt stencilling, American, c. 1825; 4 in. high by 9 in. wide (10 by 23 cm).

E 6 A carved and painted box, with thumb-moulded hinged lid with cleats, all painted black with red, green and yellow details, Pennsylvania, early 19th century; 8 in. high by 12 in. wide (20 by 30 cm).

Boxes
It is important to their value that fitted boxes should retain their interiors intact. Smaller boxes, particularly those for silks and needlework, have been prone to wear and damage; the interiors have frequently been removed. At the beginning of this century it was also fashionable to replace the cutlery fitments of knife boxes with letter compartments.

It has also been common practice to replace some of the exterior fitments such as handles, escutcheons and feet, either because of damage or to substitute more modern versions to give the article an up-to-date appearance. Repairs that restore rather than seek to improve on the original are of course commercially acceptable.

E 7 A small leather and brass trunk, labelled by Haskell Dutch, American, 1800-1820; 8 in. high by 18 in. wide (20 by 46 cm).

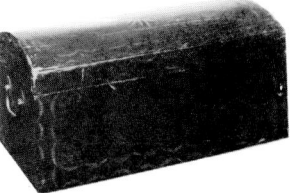

E 8 A painted dome-top box, with initials "S.T." on front, New England, 1810-1830; 6 in. high by 14 in. long (17 by 35 cm).

E 9 A chip-carved walnut box, the top carved in bold relief with two turtles and two seashells, probably American, 19th century; 13 in. (33 cm) wide.

CABINETS
1865-1900

Traditional cabinet styles continued to be made right through the 19th century – see nos 6 and 7, for example – but most of the fine American cabinets were in various revived styles, notably Italian Renaissance. With the assistance of machines, craftsmen were able to turn out substantial quantities of superbly inlaid and mounted pieces, following the overall patterns of originals but not in slavish imitation.

E1 An Aesthetic Movement ebonized corner cabinet, by A. Kimbel and J. Cabus, New York, *c.* 1865; 76 in. high by 30 in. wide (193 by 76 cm).
The single door is mounted with four floral painted tiles and the lower gallery is mounted with two turquoise glazed Aesthetic plaques.

E2 A Renaissance Revival rosewood music cabinet, attributed to Gustave Herter, New York, *c.* 1865; 47 in. high by 35 in. wide (120 by 88 cm).

E3 A Renaissance Revival ebonized and inlaid cabinet, probably New York, *c.* 1870; 62 in. high by 61 in. wide (157 by 154 cm).

E4 A Renaissance Revival inlaid and ebonized parlour cabinet, possibly by Leon Marcotte, New York; 88 in. high by 51 in. wide (222 by 129 cm).

E5 A Renaissance Revival marquetry inlaid rosewood cabinet, *c.* 1875. It is 52 in. high and 64 in. wide (132 by 161 cm).
The superstructure is ebonized and gilded over a single panelled door flanked by ormolu mounted half-columns and concave side panels, the whole inlaid with musical and foliate motifs.

E6 A Victorian bird's-eye maple inlaid wall cabinet, possibly New York, *c.* 1875; 45 in. high by 27 in. wide (113 by 68 cm).

E7 A pine hanging cabinet, second half of the 19th century; 33 in. high, 34 in. wide (82 by 85 cm).

E8 A carved oak and stained glass architectural cabinet, designed by John LaFarge, *c.* 1900; 74 in. high by 59 in. wide (188 by 150 cm).

CHAIRS
1680-1890

While the designs of early American chairs resemble closely their contemporary European counterparts, small details quickly established themselves as the marks of certain localities. It is thus often possible to ascribe accurate provenances to early pieces, and to confirm them from the detailed records of their possessions that many families were in the habit of keeping.

E1 Governor William Bradford's armchair, of Brewster type, Pilgrim Hall, Plymouth, Massachusetts, 1630-1640.

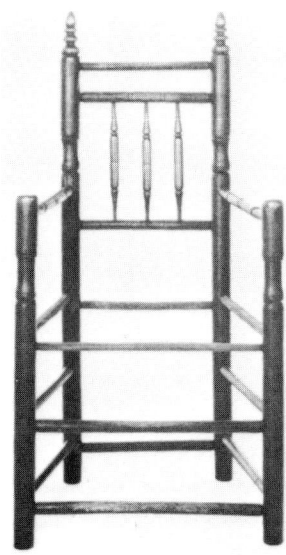

E2 A turned Great chair, New England, late 17th or early 18th century; 45 in. high, 23 in. wide (113 by 58 cm).

E3 A Great chair, New England, 1680-1710, 35 in. high by 22 in. wide (87 by 55 cm).

E4 A turned armchair, Long Island or Connecticut, 17th century; 40 in. high by 23 in. wide (110 by 58 cm).

E5 A William and Mary carved and caned American armchair, New England, *c.* 1700; 51 in. high by 23 in. wide (128 by 58 cm).

E6 A William and Mary painted armchair, probably New England, *c.* 1710; 47 in. high by 24 in. wide (120 by 60 cm).

E7 A William and Mary banister-back armchair, New England, 1700-1720; 48 in. high by 23 in. wide (120 by 57 cm).

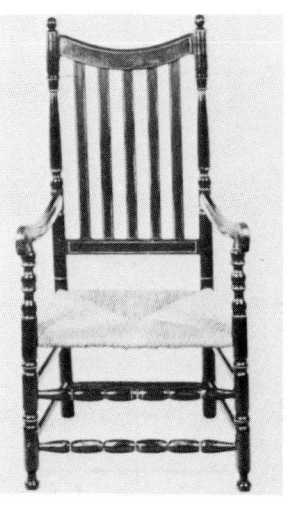

E8 A banister-back armchair, Connecticut or New York, 1710-1730; 48 in. high by 24 in. wide (121 by 61 cm).

E9 A William and Mary banister-back side chair, New England, 1720-1740; 45 in. high by 18 in. wide (114 by 46 cm).

E10 A William and Mary maple slat-back armchair, New England, 1720-1750; 50 in. high by 26 in. wide (127 by 66 cm).

E11 A William and Mary maple banister-back rocker, New England, 18th century; 42 in. high by 24 in. wide (106 by 60 cm).

18th-Century Chairs

One of the most fascinating aspects of early 18th-century chair development is the way that new styles, introduced via expensive examples, were imitated and assimilated by local craftsmen who, lacking access to the latest pattern books, produced versions that took the most prominent features of the new style and grafted them on to vernacular forms – nos 8 and 9 on this page are excellent examples of the process.

During the period from 1750 to 1770 there was a distinct change to the top rail, clearly evident on the facing page. The curvilinear hoop back was swept up in wing form at the corner and carved or left plain according to the commission. Also, following Chippendale's designs, splats came to be pierced.

One of the most popular splat designs of the Chippendale period was the ribbon back, as no. 12 on the facing page. Other forms, more severe but so distinctive as to enable accurate provenancing, are shown in nos. 9, 10 and 11 opposite. In the matter of dating chairs, it is often the splat form that is useful rather than some other apparently important aspects – thus no help can be gained from a Chippendale chair having square as against cabriole legs, since the two styles ran concurrently. The presence or absence of stretchers to square-legged versions is equally uninformative.

E2 A maple ladderback armchair, New England, 18th century; 46 in. high by 24 in. wide (117 by 61 cm).

E3 A William and Mary slat-back armchair, New England, 18th century; 43 in. high by 24 in. wide (110 by 61 cm).

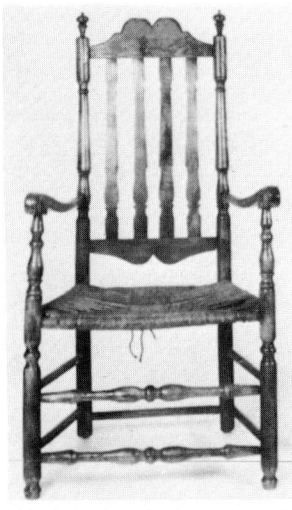

E1 A banister-back maple and ash armchair, Connecticut, 18th century; 45 in. high by 25 in. wide (113 by 63 cm).

E4 A William and Mary maple slat-back armchair, New England, 1720-1740; 45 in. high by 24 in. wide (114 by 60 cm).

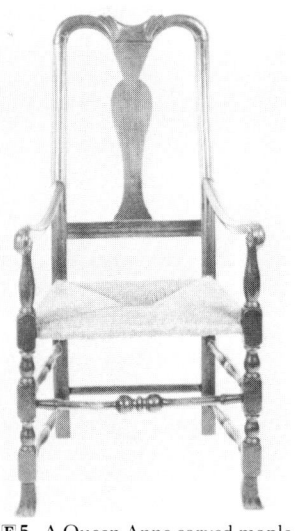

E5 A Queen Anne carved maple armchair, New England, 1725-1750; 41 in. high by 22 in. wide (104 by 56 cm).

E6 A slat-back maple armchair, Delaware Valley, 1750-1800; 44 in. (11 cm) high.

E7 A painted wavy slat-back side chair, Delaware River Valley, 18th century.

E8 A Queen Anne walnut side chair, Boston, Massachusetts, 1730-1750; 42 in. high by 21 in. wide (105 by 53 cm).

E9 A Queen Anne maple side chair, New England, 1730-1750; 41 in. high by 19 in. wide (104 by 48 cm).

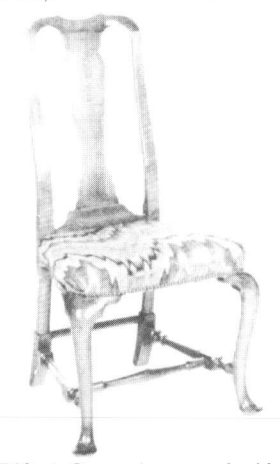

E10 A Queen Anne maple side chair, Massachusetts, 1730-1760; 41 in. high by 21 in. wide (103 by 53 cm).

D 1 A Queen Anne walnut side chair, Rhode Island or Massachusetts, 1730-1760.

D 2 A Queen Anne walnut side chair, Philadelphia, 1735-1745, 41 in. high by 21 in. wide (104 by 53 cm).

E 3 A Queen Anne maple side chair, New England, 1735-1775, 41 in. high by 19 in. wide (104 by 48 cm).

D 4 A Queen Anne carved walnut side chair, New York, 1735-1755; 39 in. high by 22 in. wide (98 by 55 cm).

E 5 A Chippendale carved walnut armchair, Philadelphia, 1765-1785; 41 in. high by 32 in. wide (102 by 80 cm).

D 6 A Chippendale carved walnut armchair, Philadelphia, *c.* 1765.
This is early Chippendale, still made of the traditional walnut, like its fellow immediately above, whereas English models were in mahogany, and it uses the customary Queen Anne splat rather than the pierced splat always associated with this general design.

E 7 A Chippendale walnut armchair, Pennsylvania, 1760-1780; 41 in. high by 28 in. wide (105 by 71 cm).

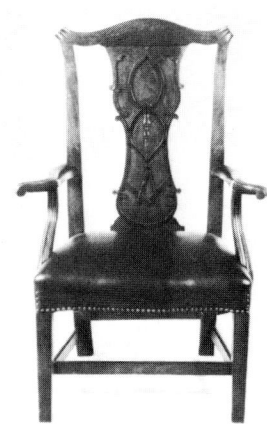

E 8 A Chippendale walnut Masonic armchair, probably Massachusetts, 1760-1790; 51 in. high by 35 in. wide (129 by 88 cm).

D 9 A Chippendale mahogany armchair, possibly Maryland, 1760-1790; 38 in. high by 26 in. wide (97 by 64 cm).

D 10 A Chippendale walnut armchair, possibly Maryland, 1760-1790, 40 in. (101 cm) high. Note the proportions – this chair is not taken from a *Director* design.

E 11 A Chippendale period walnut armchair with the strapwork splat typical of Philadelphia; 42 in. (105 cm) high.

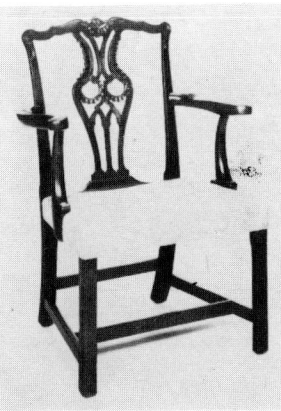

E 12 A Chippendale carved mahogany armchair, Massachusetts, 1765-1785; 37 in. high by 28 in. wide (94 by 69 cm).

Chair Construction

The structural advantages of stretcher rails are obvious, but many fine chairmakers dispensed with their use – as in nos 4 and 9 on this page. Stretcher rails, if retained, did not always conform to the turned variety but occasionally can be found of wavy form, displaying a Dutch influence – see no. 1 opposite.

To complicate any proper chronological cataloguing there are (as with every aspect of antique furniture) examples of earlier styles lingering on, as nos 2 and 3 opposite.

Yet another influence from England is the adoption of straight legs joined with H-stretchers as an alternative to the cabriole, as in nos 10, 11 and 12 opposite. This option was published by Thomas Chippendale in his *Director*, the first edition of which was published in 1754.

Chairs with drop-in seats are prone to damage after being recovered. If the old fabric is not stripped and the new merely tacked over it, the seat becomes wider. The extra width means additional stress to the joints. Provided that this leads only to loosening of the joints – and not to the wood splitting – restoration is both straightforward and in no way detrimental to the chair's value.

D 1 A Queen Anne walnut side chair, Boston, 1740-1760; 39 in. high by 40 in. wide (99 by 101 cm).

E 2 A Queen Anne carved walnut side chair, New England, 1740-1760.

E 3 A Queen Anne walnut side chair, Newport, 1740-1750; 37 in. high by 21 in. wide (94 by 53 cm).

D 4 A Queen Anne carved walnut side chair, Philadelphia, 1740-1760; 42 in. high by 21 in. wide (107 by 53 cm).

D 5 A Queen Anne carved walnut side chair, Newport, Rhode Island, 1740-1760; 40 in. high by 21 in. wide (100 by 53 cm).

D 6 A Queen Anne carved mahogany side chair, Newport, Rhode Island, 1740-1760; 39 in. high by 21 in. wide (99 by 52 cm).

D 7 A Queen Anne carved walnut side chair, Newport, Rhode Island, 1740-1760; 39 in. high by 20 in. wide (99 by 51 cm).

C 8 A Queen Anne carved walnut side chair, Newport, Rhode Island, 1740-1765; 41 in. high by 22 in. wide (102 by 55 cm).

D 9 A walnut side chair, Virginia, *c.* 1745. Of fine quality, this chair shows an intricately carved splat centring a female mask.

D 10 A Queen Anne carved walnut side chair, Newport, Rhode Island, 1740-1760; 40 in. high, 20 in. wide (101 by 51 cm).

E1 A Queen Anne walnut balloon seat side chair, Philadelphia, *c.* 1750.

E4 A Chippendale maple side chair, Pennsylvania, 1750-1780; 40 in. high by 20 in. wide (101 by 50 cm).

E7 A Chippendale shell-carved walnut side chair, Philadelphia, 1760-1780; 37 in. high by 22 in. wide (92 by 56 cm).

E10 A Chippendale maple rush seat side chair, probably Massachusetts, 1760-1790; 38 in. high by 20 in. wide (96 by 50 cm).

E2 A banister-back side chair, Deerfield, Massachusetts, 1750-1800; 43 in. (108 cm) high.

E5 A Chippendale carved mahogany side chair, Philadelphia, 1760-1780; 40 in. high by 20 in. wide (101 by 50 cm).

D8 A Chippendale walnut side chair, Philadelphia, 1760-1790; 40 in. high by 23 in. wide (101 by 57 cm).

E11 A Chippendale figured maple side chair, Philadelphia area or New Jersey, 1765-1785; 37 in. high by 22 in. wide (94 by 55 cm).

D3 A Queen Anne maple side chair, western Long Island, New York, 1750-1780; 41 in. high by 21 in. wide (104 by 51 cm).

E6 A Chippendale walnut side chair, Philadelphia, 1760-1790; 40 in. high by 23 in. wide (101 by 57 cm).

E9 A Philadelphia Chippendale walnut side chair, 1750-1770; 40 in. (101 cm) high.

E12 A Chippendale walnut side chair, Pennsylvania, 1760-1790; 37 in. high by 22 in. wide (92 by 55 cm).

E1 A Chippendale walnut side chair, Massachusetts, 1745-1765, with balloon seat on cabriole legs; 38 in. (95 cm) high.

D4 A pair of Chippendale mahogany side chairs from Boston, between 1755 and 1775, with serpentine crest rails over

pierced splats, on cabriole legs joined with block-and-turned stretchers.

D7 A Chippendale carved mahogany side chair, Philadelphia, 1760-1790; 40 in. (101 cm) high.

E2 A Chippendale walnut slipper chair, Massachusetts or New Hampshire, 1750-1780; 37 in. (93 cm) high.

E5 A pair of Chippendale mahogany side chairs, made in Massachusetts between 1760 and 1780. They stand 37 in. (94 cm) high.
 The form of the splat is almost

identical to that in the chairs immediately above, but on these examples the crest rail is fan-carved and the legs are square, of the Marlborough type.

E8 A Chippendale mahogany side chair, Massachusetts, 1765-1785; 38 in. high, 20 in. wide (96 by 49 cm).

E3 A Chippendale walnut side chair, Rhode Island, 1760-1780; 38 in. high by 23 in. wide (98 by 58 cm).

D6 A pair of Chippendale carved mahogany side chairs, Massachusetts, 1760-1785; 38 in. (95 cm) high.
 The splat form shows little

variation from those directly above, but the form of the stretchers is mixed – a square-section H combined with a turned back stretcher.

E9 A Chippendale mahogany side chair, New York, 1760-1780; 39 in. high by 24 in. wide (99 by 60 cm).

D 1 A Chippendale mahogany side chair, Philadelphia, 1765-1775.

D 4 A pair of Chippendale carved mahogany side chairs, Philadelphia, 1760-1780; 39 in. (99 cm) high.

These chairs are identical to one in the Garvan collection at Yale University, and are probably from the same set.

E 7 A Chippendale walnut side chair, Newport, Rhode Island, 1760-1790; 35 in. high by 22 in. wide (88 by 54 cm).

E 2 A Chippendale carved mahogany side chair, Philadelphia, 1760-1780; 41 in. high by 22 in. wide (104 by 52 cm).

D 5 A pair of Chippendale mahogany side chairs, Philadelphia, 1760-1790; 41 in. (104 cm) high.

The serpentine crest rails are ornamented with central cartouches, the front rails with pendant shells.

D 8 A Chippendale carved mahogany side chair, Philadelphia, 1760-1790; 42 in. high by 21 in. wide (105 by 53 cm).

E 3 A Chippendale-style mahogany side chair, Philadelphia, attributed to Wallace Nutting, *c.* 1930; 41 in. (104 cm) high.

D 6 A pair of Chippendale period mahogany side chairs, in the Philadelphia style; 37 in. (92 cm) high. The splats are carved with leafage and husks under

leaf-carved top rails centring shells, a motif repeated on the front rails; the knees lavishly carved with acanthus.

E 9 A Chippendale mahogany side chair, New York or Connecticut, 1760-1790; 37 in. (94 cm) high.

D 1 A fine Philadelphian carved mahogany chair in the Chippendale style, 1760-1780.

E 4 A labelled Chippendale walnut side chair, by William Savery, Philadelphia, 1760-1770; 40 in. high by 21 in. wide (100 by 53 cm).

E 7 Two Chippendale carved mahogany side chairs, Philadelphia, between 1765 and 1785; 37 in. (94 cm) high. Each has a scroll-carved crest of

pronounced serpentine form centring carved leafage over a Gothic pierced and carved splat, the legs square with similar section H and back stretchers.

E 2 A Philadelphia Chippendale chair of the Gillingham type – with trefoil pierced back – notably finely carved.

E 5 A Chippendale mahogany side chair, Philadelphia, 1770-1790; 39 in. high by 21 in. wide (98 by 52 cm).

E 8 A pair of Chippendale mahogany side chairs, New York, 1770-1790; 39 in. high and 22 in. wide (98 by 55 cm).
    The fluent interplay of the

Gothic splats with the scalloped crest rails is particularly pleasing, and the addition of "Chinese" brackets to the otherwise plain legs adds another touch of quality.

E 3 A Chippendale carved walnut side chair, Philadelphia, 1760-1780; 39 in. high by 24 in. wide (98 by 61 cm).

E 6 A chair with plain legs and stretchers, of the New England type, third quarter of the 18th century.

E 9 A pair of Chippendale mahogany side chairs, 1780-1800; 38 in. (97 cm) high, with ribbon

backs and serpentine front seat rails.

E1 A pair of Chippendale mahogany ladderback side chairs,

Philadelphia, 1775-1790; 38 in. high by 22 in. wide (95 by 54 cm).

E4 A pair of New York Federal-style mahogany side chairs, 39 in. (99 cm) high. The backs are carved with drapery

swags and a stylized Prince of Wales plume over serpentine seats on moulded, square tapering legs.

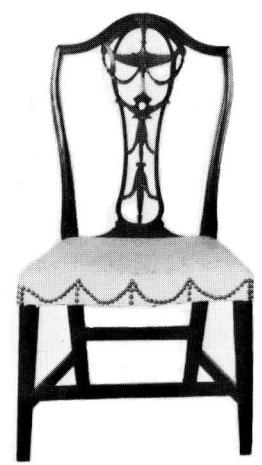   

E2 A pair of Federal carved mahogany side chairs, Newport, Rhode Island, *c*. 1795; 39 in. high

by 22 in. wide (97 by 54 cm). The legs are now tapered, in sympathy with the classically inspired backs.

E5 A pair of Federal carved mahogany side chairs, New York, 1790-1810; 40 in. (100 cm) high. The backs are decorated in the

familiar Federal style with classical motifs, but the flaring legs show a French rather than classical influence.

E3 A pair of Federal mahogany shield-back side chairs, New York, 1795-1800; 39 in. (99 cm) high. The backs are carved with urns,

drapery swags and plumes; the tapered legs are reeded and collared.

E6 A pair of Federal mahogany side chairs, Massachusetts, 1790-1810; 35 in. high by 20 in. wide (89 by 51 cm). Compare

Montgomery, *American Furniture of the Federal Period*, 1966, page 83, for a similar treatment of backs.

The Arrival of Classicism
Following publication, from
1757 onward, of illustrations
showing discoveries at Pompeii
and Herculaneum, new
designs for furniture
throughout Europe used
classical forms and motifs
rather than the traditional
curvilinear shapes. This new
approach became dominant in
America by the Federal
period.

The development is seen
clearly in the differences
between nos 1 and 4 below –
the latter is wholly classical
with its vase-shaped back,
upswept splats and square,
fluted, tapering legs on spade
feet. These features are all
reminiscent of Robert Adam;
an interpretation of the
classical after Hepplewhite is
shown in no. 6 and after
Sheraton in no. 8.

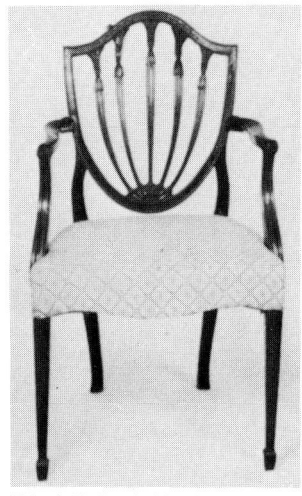

E 3 A Federal shieldback
armchair, Salem, Massachusetts,
1790-1810, with foliate carving to
the toprail and splats.

E 6 A Federal mahogany
armchair, New York, 1790-1810,
in the Hepplewhite manner.

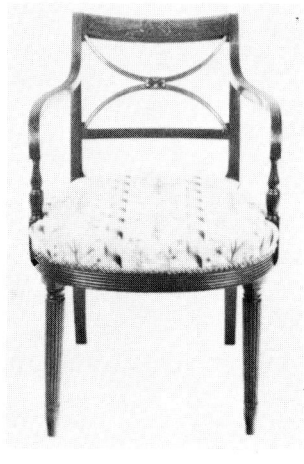

E 8 A Federal mahogany
armchair of classical form on
reeded legs, New York, *c.* 1810;
32 in. (80 cm) high.

D 1 A Chippendale walnut
armchair, Philadelphia,
1760-1790; it stands 40 in.
(100 cm) high.

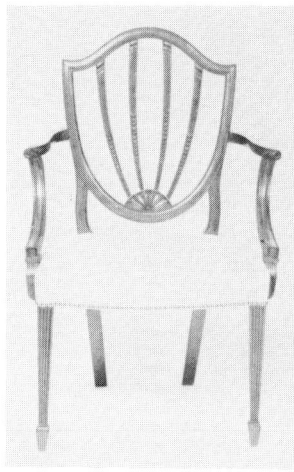

E 4 A Federal carved mahogany
armchair, New York, 1790-1810.
It is 39 in. (98 cm) high and the
legs are reeded.

E 7 A Federal painted armchair,
possibly Baltimore; 1800-1820,
34 in. (85 cm) high.
The tablet crest rail is back
swept and painted over a pierced
horizontal splat; the seat caned on
sabre legs, joined, unusually, by
turned stretchers.

E 9 A Federal carved mahogany
armchair, School of Duncan
Phyfe, New York, *c.* 1810. Note
how closely the lines accord with
those of no. 8 above.

D 2 A period Chippendale
mahogany armchair,
Philadelphia, on square legs;
1765-1780.

E 5 A Federal inlaid mahogany
chair attributed to Jacob Forster,
Charlestown, Massachusetts,
(1768-1810).

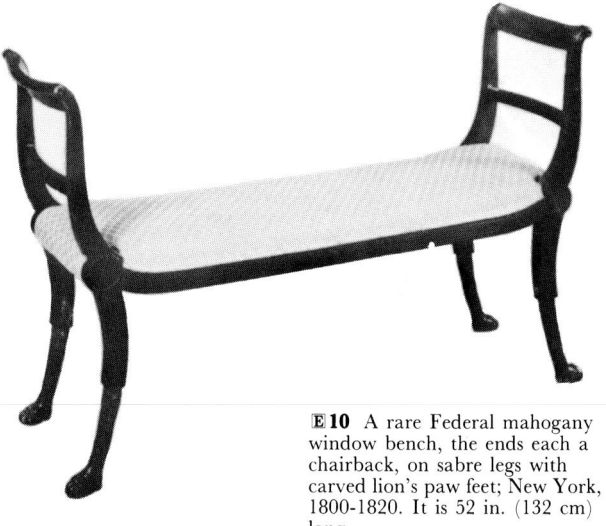

E 10 A rare Federal mahogany
window bench, the ends each a
chairback, on sabre legs with
carved lion's paw feet; New York,
1800-1820. It is 52 in. (132 cm)
long.

E1 A Federal mahogany side chair, New York, 1790-1810; 37 in. (94 cm) high.

E4 A late Federal carved curly maple side chair, with pierced guilloche horizontal splat, New York, 1805-1815.

E7 A painted maple rush-seat side chair, attributed to Samuel Gragg, Boston, Massachusetts, *c.* 1815.

E8 A late Federal mahogany side chair, 1800-1815; 33 in. (83 cm) high. The mount is not original.

D2 A Federal carved mahogany dining chair, possibly by Abraham Slover and Taylor, New York, 1800-1810.

E5 A Federal carved mahogany shieldback chair on moulded square tapering legs, New York, 1790-1810.

E9 A pair of late Federal carved mahogany side chairs, New York, 1815-1825.

The tablet crest rails contain veneered panels over lyre splats with eagle heads on turned rails.

E3 A Federal carved mahogany side chair, attributed to the shop of John and Thomas Seymour, Boston, 1795-1810.

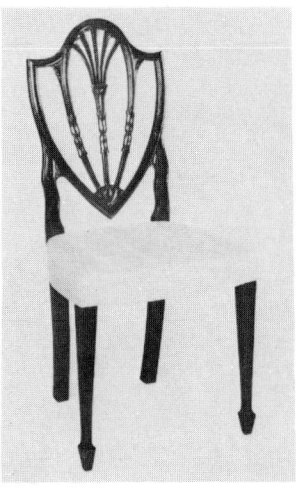

E6 A Federal carved mahogany shieldback chair, the shield deeply pointed, on square tapering legs with spade feet, New York, 1790-1810.

E10 A pair of Federal painted chairs, New York, 1800-1815.
The deep rectangular backs contain painted panels over two horizontal beaded slats, echoed in

the front stretchers. The frames are painted all-over green, with gold banding and a frieze of flowers to the front seat rail.

E 1 A late Federal carved mahogany armchair, the stiles carved with waterleaf, the splat with a cornucopia, New York, 1810-1820.

E 2 A Federal painted and gilt-stencilled armchair, New York, 1800-1820; 34 in. (85 cm) high.

E 3 A Federal carved mahogany side chair, New York, 1810-1820; 33 in. high by 19 in. wide (82 by 47 cm).

E 4 A Federal carved curly maple caned-seat side chair, New York, c. 1820.

E 5 A painted and stencilled fancy chair, New England, c. 1825; 35 in. high by 17 in. wide (87 by 42 cm).

E 6 A fancy painted and stencilled side chair, Connecticut, c. 1830; 35 in. high by 18 in. wide (89 by 44 cm).

E 7 A grained and painted fancy rocker, signed L. Hitchcock, Hitchcocksville, Connecticut, c. 1830; 33 in. high, rocker 24 in. long (82 by 60 cm).

E 8 A Federal mahogany piano stool, New York, bearing later paper label of Sypher & Co., New York; 32 in. (80 cm) high.

E 9 A laminated pierced and carved rosewood rococo revival side chair, Boston, 1850-1860, bearing a Kittredge & Blakes label.

E 10 A Victorian carved walnut lady's armchair, American, mid 19th century; 43 in. high by 21 in. wide (109 by 52 cm).

E 11 A Victorian rococo revival carved rosewood gentleman's armchair, attributed to John H. Belter, New York, 1850-1860; 43 by 24 in. (109 by 61 cm).

E 12 A mahogany framed elbow chair in the French style, 19th century.

E 1 A rococo revival rosewood side chair, probably Boston, *c.* 1855; 36 in. high by 20 in. wide (90 by 49 cm).

E 4 A carved mahogany side chair, probably Boston, 1885-1890; 34 in. (85 cm) high.

Corner chairs

E 7 A Queen Anne walnut corner commode, Pennsylvania, 1735-1755; 33 in. high by 25 in. wide (84 by 63 cm).

E 10 A William and Mary corner chair, probably New York, mid 18th century.

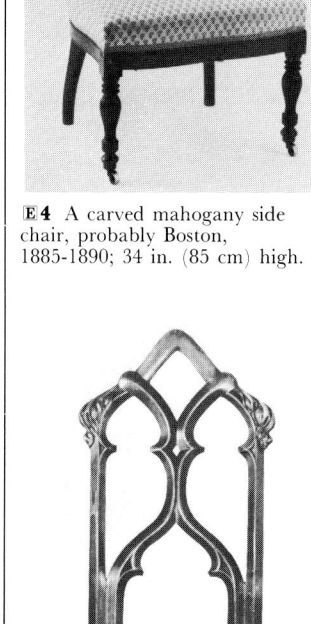

E 2 A rococo revival laminated rosewood side chair, by John H. Belter, *c.* 1855; 35 in. (88 cm) high.

E 5 A rosewood neo-Gothic side chair, designed by A. J. Davis.

E 8 A Queen Anne walnut corner commode, Pennsylvania, 1750-1780; 32 in. high by 28 in. wide (80 by 70 cm).
The front three legs are of cabriole form with trifid feet, the rear leg is turned and terminates in a ball foot.

E 11 A Chippendale mahogany corner chair, Massachusetts, 1760-1780.

D 12 A rare Chippendale mahogany corner chair, New York, 1765-1785, with triangular bow-front seat.

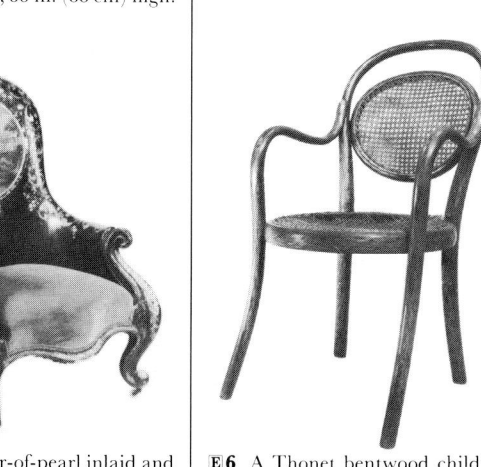

E 3 A mother-of-pearl inlaid and gilt decorated slipper chair, possibly English, *c.* 1860.

E 6 A Thonet bentwood child's chair, "Kinderfauteuil Nr 1" in the Thonet catalogue; also available with a fitted tray.

E 9 A Queen Anne walnut corner chair, Rhode Island, 1745-1765; 32 in. high, 29 in. wide (81 by 73 cm). With shaped crest over two vase-shaped splats; the seat serpentine on four cabriole legs terminating in pad feet and joined by a turned X-stretcher.

E 13 A Chippendale maple corner chair, New England, 1770-1800; 30 in. high by 18 in. deep (76 by 44 cm).

Easy chairs

C1 A Queen Anne walnut easy chair with outscrolling arms on delicate cabriole legs joined by block-and-turned stretchers, Massachusetts, 1735-1760; 45 in. high by 36 in. wide (113 by 91 cm).

C2 A Queen Anne mahogany wing armchair, Rhode Island, c. 1750. The arched crest flanked by shaped wings, with outward scrolling arms on cabriole legs, joined by block-and-arrow-turned stretchers.

C3 A Chippendale walnut easy chair of generous proportions with serpentine-crested back, on stretchered cabriole legs terminating in claw-and-ball-feet, Massachusetts, 1750-1789; 46 in. high by 36 in. wide (116 by 91 cm).

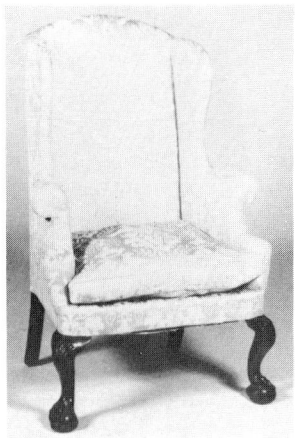

C4 A Chippendale cherrywood easy chair on shell-carved cabriole legs, New York, 1760-1780; 46 in. high by 31 in. wide (115 by 78 cm).

D5 A Chippendale walnut easy chair with the swept-back C-scroll arms typical of Philadelphia, 1760-1780; 47 in. high by 35 in. wide (118 by 87 cm).

D6 A Chippendale mahogany easy chair, Massachusetts, 1760-1780; 47 in. high by 37 in. wide (120 by 92 cm).

E7 A Chippendale mahogany easy chair, New England, 1760-1790; 49 in. high by 35 in. wide (123 by 89 cm). For the relationship of arms and wings compare no. 8 below and no. 10, right.

E8 A Chippendale mahogany easy chair on Marlborough legs with block feet, Philadelphia, 1765-1785; 51 in. high by 34 in. wide (130 by 87 cm).

D9 A Chippendale mahogany easy chair on Marlborough feet, Philadelphia, 1765-1785; 45 in. high by 37 in. wide (114 by 93 cm).

D10 A Chippendale carved mahogany wing armchair, Pennsylvania, c. 1775.
   A generously proportioned chair, this is a fine example of its type, with serpentine crest and outscrolling arms on moulded square legs.

C11 A Chippendale mahogany easy chair with carved knees on claw-and-ball feet, New England, 1760-1790; 46 in. high by 36 in. wide (117 by 91 cm).

E12 A Chippendale mahogany easy chair, Philadelphia, 1765-1785; 45 in. high by 38 in. wide (114 by 95 cm).

E1 A Chippendale easy chair, possibly Massachusetts, 1780-1800; 47 in. high by 33 in. wide (118 by 83 cm).

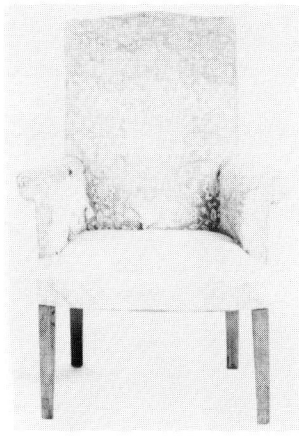

E4 A Chippendale cherrywood upholstered armchair, Massachusetts, 1780-1810; 41 in. high by 29 in. wide (104 by 73 cm).

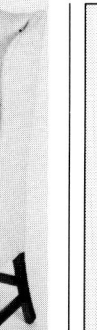

E7 A Federal mahogany easy chair probably New York, 1790-1810; 47 in. high by 36 in. wide (119 by 90 cm).

Wing Armchairs
The fully upholstered wing armchair developed from prototypes introduced during the latter part of the 17th century. The covered part of the frame was invariably made of cheaper timber – and the discovery of a frame totally of primary timber could indicate an open-frame chair covered at a later date.
The change from Queen Anne cabriole to the straight legs of the later Chippendale period apart, the style of wing armchairs changed little during the 18th century or the early 19th, though there was a tendency to make such chairs less generous in their proportions in the Federal period – compare, for example, the Chippendale period chair at no. 10 opposite with no. 10 below.

E2 A Federal mahogany lolling chair, New England, *c.* 1790; 45 in. high by 25 in. wide (114 by 63 cm).

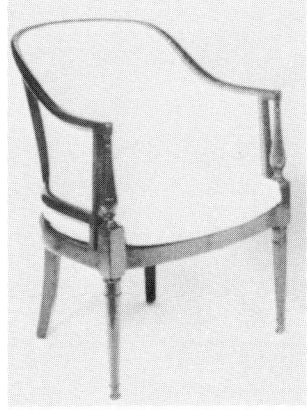

D5 A Federal mahogany bergère-type easy chair, attributed to George Bright, Boston, *c.* 1797; 32 in. high by 23 in. wide (81 by 59 cm).

E8 A Federal mahogany lolling chair, Massachusetts, 1790-1810; 38 in. high by 26 in. wide (95 by 66 cm).
Although it was made in the Federal period, this chair owes little to its era for it is essentially Chippendale adapted.

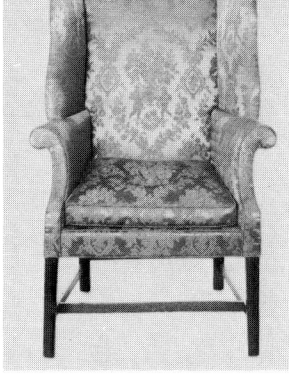

E10 A Federal mahogany easy chair, New England, *c.* 1790-1810; 46 in. high by 33 in. wide (117 by 82 cm).

E3 A Federal mahogany easy chair, Massachusetts, 1790-1810; 49 in. (126 cm) high. Compare no. 2 above.

E6 A Federal mahogany easy chair, probably Massachusetts, 1790-1810; 44 in. high by 30 in. wide (110 by 76 cm).

E9 A Federal upholstered armchair, New England, 1790-1810; 38 in. high by 27 in. wide (96 by 69 cm).

E11 A Federal mahogany easy chair, Massachusetts, 1790-1810; 42 in. high by 28 in. wide (106 by 70 cm).

E1 A Federal cherrywood easy chair, New England, 1790-1810; 41 in. high by 30 in. wide (104 by 76 cm).

E4 A Federal easy chair, New York, 1790-1810; 46 in. high by 30 in. deep (117 by 75 cm).
A finely shaped chair, the serpentine crest finding sympathy in the curved wing tops and the serpentine seat front; the arms are scrolled horizontally, their supports vertically.

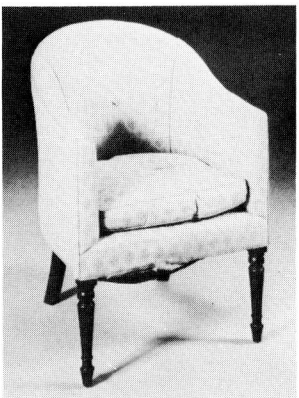

E7 A Federal mahogany bergère probably Massachusetts, 1790-1820; 34 in. high by 24 in. wide (85 by 61 cm).

E2 A Federal easy chair, New York, 1790-1810; 46 in. high by 34 in. wide (117 by 86 cm).

E8 A Federal pine upholstered armchair, New England, 1810-1830; 36 in. high by 22 in. wide (91 by 54 cm).

E3 A Federal easy chair, 47 in. high by 35 in. wide (119 by 89 cm).
The shaped wings have a pronounced outward turn to them, reflecting a rather later tradition than the square Chippendale legs.

E5 A Federal carved cherrywood wing armchair, American, c. 1800. Note the slightly unusual arrangement of the stretchers – to the sides and back only, instead of the more usual H-pattern.

E6 A Federal mahogany lolling chair, Massachusetts, 1790-1815.
Also known as "Martha Washington" chairs (for no ascertainable reason other than tradition), "lolling" would appear to be the older name for this type of comfortable and elegant open armchair, the arms of which are occasionally upholstered, with a fully upholstered back. While based on an English model it has no precise counterpart and was developed independently in New England.

E9 A late Federal mahogany caned armchair, Boston, 1815-1830; 35 in. (87 cm) high.
A very similar chair is illustrated in *Classical America*, The Newark Museum, 1963, at figure 75.

Windsor chairs

E1 A Windsor armchair, possibly New York, 1750-1780.

E2 A turned Windsor bow-back armchair, Rhode Island, *c.* 1780.

E3 A continuous-arm Windsor armchair, Rhode Island, 1780-1800; 36 in. high by 20 in. wide (91 by 49 cm).

E4 A painted Windsor fan-back armchair, probably New England *c.* 1785, the rockers a later addition.

E5 A Windsor armchair by Walter MacBride, New York City, 1792-1796.

E6 A painted Windsor fan-back side chair, Delaware River Valley, 1780-1800.

E7 A fan-back Windsor side chair by G. Gaw, Philadelphia, *c.* 1800; 39 in. high by 23 in. wide (99 by 57 cm).

E8 A brace-back Windsor side chair, Rhode Island or New York, late 18th century; 37 in. high by 16 in. wide (94 by 40 cm).

E9 A Windsor side chair, New England, 1780-1800; 37 in. (94 cm) high.

E10 A bow-back Windsor side chair by William Pointer, Richmond, Virginia, 1780-1800; 37 in. high by 19 in. wide (92 by 48 cm).

E11 A turned and painted Windsor child's sack-back armchair, New England, *c.* 1790.

E12 A painted Windsor sack-back writing armchair, New England, possibly Vermont, 1790-1810. The leather-upholstered writing surface is fitted with a drawer under, a second drawer is fitted to the seat. Compare Santore, *The Windsor Style in America, 1730-1830*, Philadelphia, 1981, figure 176.

E1 A sack-back Windsor armchair, Pennsylvania, 1790-1820; 35 in. (89 cm) high.

E4 A birdcage Windsor side chair, by Jonathan Tyson, Philadelphia, 1808-1817; 36 in. high by 16 in. wide (88 by 40 cm).

D2 A comb-back Windsor armchair, Pennsylvania, early 19th century; 42 in. (105 cm) high.

E5 A painted late Windsor side chair on bamboo-turned legs, New England, c. 1820; 33 in. high, 17 in. wide (84 by 43 cm).

E3 Three bamboo-turned Windsor chairs, 1800-1820; they are 34 in. high and 17 in. wide (86 by 42 cm).
This is a particularly elegant form of Windsor chair with its flaring back, double crest rail and, because they are bamboo-turned, finer than usual legs.

CHESTS
1680-1830

The American chest of drawers developed quickly during the late 17th century. No. 6 below is a fine example of this early period and consists of three drawers, the lower two being deep with applied mouldings. No. 8 shows the rapid transformation into the popular two short and three long drawers arrangement, the drawer fronts being plain.

Chests of drawers

E6 A William and Mary walnut, oak and pine chest of drawers, Boston, Massachusetts, 1690-1710; 40 in. high, 42 in. wide (101 by 106 cm).

E7 A William and Mary grained and painted pine chest of drawers, New England, early 18th century; 47 in. (118 cm) high.

E8 A William and Mary walnut chest of drawers, Pennsylvania, 1710-1730; 40 in. high by 40 in. wide (101 by 101 cm).

E9 A Queen Anne cherrywood and maple chest of drawers on short cabriole legs, Connecticut, 1730-1760; 45 in. high by 39 in. wide (114 by 99 cm).

E10 A Chippendale mahogany reverse serpentine chest of drawers, Massachusetts, 1760-1780; 31 in. high by 35 in. wide (78 by 89 cm).

E11 A cherrywood chest of drawers, Pennsylvania, c. 1760, of serpentine form with quarter-columns and carrying handles on short cabriole legs and claw-and-ball feet.

E12 A Chippendale carved mahogany chest of drawers, New York, 1760-1790; 33 in. high by 43 in. wide (84 by 106 cm).

E1 A Chippendale cherrywood chest of drawers, New England, 1760-1790; 33 in. high, 34 in. wide (82 by 87 cm).

E2 A Chippendale cherrywood chest of drawers, probably Pennsylvania, 1760-1790; 34 in. high by 38 in. wide (85 by 97 cm).

E3 A Chippendale mahogany chest of drawers, Pennsylvania, 1760-1790; 36 in. high by 40 in. wide (90 by 101 cm).

C4 A Chippendale mahogany block-front chest of drawers, Salem, Massachusetts, 1760-1790; 33 in. high by 37 in. wide (83 by 94 cm).

D5 A block-front mahogany chest of drawers, 1760-1780; 31 in. high by 36 in. wide (78 by 91 cm).

E6 A Chippendale curly maple chest of drawers, possibly Pennsylvania, 1760-1790; 41 in. high by 43 in. wide (104 by 109 cm).

E7 A Chippendale walnut chest of drawers, Pennsylvania, 1765-1790; 34 in. high by 41 in. wide (86 by 104 cm).

E8 A Chippendale cherrywood chest of drawers, Connecticut River Valley, possibly Deerfield area, 1765-1780; 40 in. high, 37 in. wide (100 by 93 cm).

E9 A Chippendale walnut chest of drawers, Pennsylvania, 1765-1785; 43 in. high by 40 in. wide (107 by 101 cm).

D10 A Chippendale mahogany chest of drawers with canted corners, Philadelphia, 1765-1785; 37 in. high by 44 in. wide (94 by 110 cm).

D11 A Chippendale mahogany chest of drawers, typically Philadelphian, 1765-1785; 31 in. high by 34 in. wide (79 by 85 cm).

D12 A Chippendale figured mahogany serpentine chest of drawers, eastern Connecticut, 1765-1790; 34 in. high by 41 in. wide (85 by 104 cm).

D13 A Chippendale mahogany reverse serpentine chest of drawers, Massachusetts or Rhode Island, 1765-1780; 32 in. high by 38 in. wide (80 by 95 cm).

D14 A Chippendale mahogany reverse serpentine chest of drawers, Massachusetts, 1765-1785; 42 in. (108 cm) wide.

C15 A Chippendale cherrywood serpentine chest of drawers, probably Massachusetts, 1765-1785; 35 in. high by 39 in. wide (89 by 99 cm).

C16 A Chippendale mahogany chest of drawers with the reverse serpentine front typical of New England, Massachusetts, 1765-1785; 34 in. high by 38 in. wide (85 by 97 cm).

The Restoration of Chests
By the beginning of the 18th century drawers slid on bottom rather than on side runners and it is here, as with all working parts, that damage is encountered and restoration required. The replacement of runners, provided that it is sympathetically executed, is commercially acceptable and is indeed necessary in order to preserve the chest if it is intended for use.

Indeed, specific damage will occur if defective runners are not repaired. When opened and closed the drawer will shake the carcase, loosening the end joints of the drawer frames where they run into the sides. This can cause the veneer to loosen, whereupon it may be struck by the drawer, causing it to chip.

The replacement of handles is necessary when the original pulls have been damaged, but often a new set was substituted in order to give the chest a more up-to-date appearance, particularly during the early 19th century. It is also important that the chest of drawers should retain its original feet, although it may be acceptable for the underside blocks to have been replaced.

D 3 A small Chippendale cherrywood ox-bow chest, Connecticut, 1760-1780; 32 in. high by 35 in. wide (81 by 89 cm).

C 4 A Chippendale mahogany serpentine-front chest of drawers, Boston, Massachusetts, 1765-1785; 33 in. high by 41 in. wide (83 by 102 cm).

D 1 A Chippendale mahogany serpentine-front chest of drawers. Massachusetts, 1765-1785; 31 in. high by 39 in. wide (78 by 99 cm).

C 5 A Chippendale mahogany serpentine-front chest of drawers, Massachusetts, 1765-1785; 32 in. high by 35 in. wide (81 by 87 cm).

E 2 A Chippendale mahogany reverse serpentine chest of drawers, Rhode Island, 1765-1785; 32 in. high by 40 in. wide (80 by 101 cm).

D 6 A Chippendale birch reverse serpentine-front chest of drawers. Massachusetts or New Hampshire, 1765-1790; 32 in. high by 39 in. wide (82 by 99 cm).

D 7 A Chippendale cherrywood serpentine chest of drawers, Connecticut, 1765-1790; 34 in. high by 42 in. wide (85 by 105 cm).

D 8 A Chippendale cherrywood reverse serpentine chest of drawers, Connecticut, 1770-1790; 35 in. high by 36 in. wide (88 by 90 cm).

E 9 A Chippendale walnut chest of drawers, Pennsylvania, 1765-1800; 36 in. (90 cm) high.

D 10 A block-front chest of drawers, New England, 1770-1790, with shell carving and unusual dished top.

E 11 A Chippendale walnut chest of drawers, Pennsylvania, 1770-1795; 36 in. high by 41 in. wide (91 by 102 cm).

E 12 A Chippendale maple blanket chest, New England, 1770-1800.

E 13 A Chippendale figured maple tall chest of drawers, New England, 1770-1800.

E 14 A Chippendale cherrywood chest of drawers, Pennsylvania, 1770-1800.

E 1 A Chippendale mahogany chest of drawers, New York, 1770-1800; 36 in. high, 44 in. wide (91 by 110 cm).

D 2 A Chippendale mahogany serpentine chest of drawers, Massachusetts or Rhode Island, 1780-1795.

E 3 A Chippendale carved maple chest of drawers, New England, 1780-1800; 34 in. high, 43 in. wide (85 by 109 cm).

E 4 A Chippendale inlaid mahogany bow-front chest of drawers, Massachusetts, 1780-1800.

C 5 A Chippendale cherrywood serpentine-front chest of drawers, Hartford area, Connecticut, 1780-1800.

E 6 A Chippendale carved curly maple chest of drawers, New England, *c.* 1785, the top drawer faced to simulate two short drawers.

E 7 A Federal cherrywood inlaid chest of drawers, central or western Pennsylvania, 1790-1810; 39 in. high by 40 in. wide (99 by 101 cm).

D 8 A Federal bird's-eye maple inlaid chest of drawers, probably Massachusetts, 1790-1810; 36 in. high by 42 in. wide (91 by 106 cm).

D 9 A Federal cherrywood and bird's-eye maple bow-front chest of drawers, New England, 1790-1810; 40 in. high by 43 in. wide (100 by 109 cm).

D 10 A Federal inlaid and veneered bow-front chest of drawers, probably New Hampshire, 1790-1810; 37 in. high, 42 in. wide (93 by 106 cm).

D 11 A Federal mahogany and birch inlaid chest of drawers, Massachusetts or New Hampshire, 1790-1810.

D 12 A Federal bird's-eye maple veneered chest of drawers, probably New Hampshire, 1790-1810; 37 in. high by 40 in. wide (95 by 101 cm).

E 13 A Federal mahogany bow-front chest of drawers, Massachusetts, 1790-1810; 39 in. high, 43 in. wide (99 by 109 cm).

E 14 A Federal mahogany bow-front chest of drawers, north-eastern Massachusetts, 1790-1810; 38 in. high by 39 in. wide (96 by 99 cm).

E 15 A Federal inlaid mahogany serpentine chest of drawers, New Hampshire, 1790-1810; 35 in. high by 38 in. wide (90 by 97 cm).

E 16 A Federal mahogany miniature chest of drawers, 1790-1810; 16 in. high, 15 in. wide, 8 in. deep (40 by 37 by 19 cm).

D 17 A Federal bird's-eye maple and figured birch bow-front chest of drawers, Portsmouth, New Hampshire 1790-1810; 36 in. high, 41 in. wide (91 by 103 cm).

E 1 A Federal mahogany veneer bow-front chest of drawers, Massachusetts, 1790-1810; 35 in. high by 41 in. wide (90 by 104 cm).

E 5 A Federal inlaid cherrywood bow-front chest of drawers, Connecticut, 1790-1820; 35 in. high by 38 in. wide (89 by 95 cm).

E 9 A Federal inlaid mahogany bow-front chest of drawers, Massachusetts, 1795-1815; 37 in. high by 41 in. wide (94 by 102 cm).

D 13 A Federal inlaid cherrywood bow-front chest of drawers, Connecticut, *c.* 1800; 34 in. high by 40 in. wide (86 by 100 cm).

E 2 A Federal cherrywood and bird's-eye maple bow-front chest of drawers, New Hampshire, 1800-1820; 41 in. high by 43 in. wide (104 by 109 cm).

E 6 A Federal figured maple bow-front chest of drawers, New England, 1790-1820; 34 in. high by 41 in. wide (85 by 104 cm).

E 10 A Federal mahogany inlaid bow-front chest of drawers, Massachusetts, *c.* 1800; 37 in. high, 37 in. wide (94 by 94 cm).

E 14 A Federal inlaid mahogany miniature sewing chest of drawers, fitted *c.* 1800; 11 in. high by 13 in. wide (28 by 33 cm).

E 3 A Federal inlaid mahogany bow-front chest of drawers, Pennsylvania, 1790-1820; 34 in. high by 36 in. wide (85 by 90 cm).

E 7 A Federal inlaid cherrywood chest of drawers, New England, 1790-1820; 38 in. high by 45 in. wide (96 by 112 cm).

E 11 A Federal mahogany butler's desk, New York, *c.* 1800; 43 in. high by 47 in. wide (110 by 119 cm).

E 15 A Federal carved mahogany bow-front chest of drawers, Salem, Massachusetts, 1800-1815; 40 in. high by 45 in. wide (100 by 113 cm).

E 4 A Federal tiger maple bow-front chest of drawers, Pennsylvania, 1790-1820; 40 in. high by 42 in. wide (101 by 105 cm).

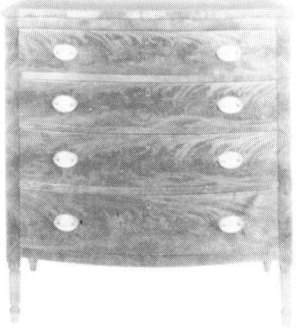

E 8 late Federal mahogany veneer bow-front chest of drawers, New York or Philadelphia, *c.* 1815; 43 in. high by 42 in. wide (109 by 106 cm).

E 12 A Federal mahogany inlaid chest of drawers, attributed to Michael Allison, New York, *c.* 1800; 41 in. high by 44 in. wide (104 by 111 cm).

E 16 A Federal inlaid mahogany bow-front chest of drawers, possibly Natick, Massachusetts, 1800-1815; 36 in. high by 39 in. wide (91 by 99 cm).

E1 A Federal inlaid mahogany bow-front chest of drawers, New England, 1800-1815; 38 in. high by 40 in. wide (96 by 102 cm).

E2 A Federal figured maple bow-front chest of drawers, north-eastern Massachusetts or southern New Hampshire, 1790-1815.

E3 A Federal mahogany and bird's-eye maple chest of drawers, Massachusetts, 1800-1820; 39 in high by 40 in. wide (99 by 100 cm).

E4 A Federal mahogany bow-front chest of drawers, Philadelphia, 1800-1820; 38 in. (97 cm) high.

C5 A Federal cherrywood chest of drawers, Pennsylvania, 1800-1820; 42 in. high by 39 in. wide (106 by 97 cm).

E6 A Federal inlaid walnut small chest of drawers, probably Tennessee or Kentucky, 1800-1820; 29 in. high by 31 in. wide (72 by 78 cm).

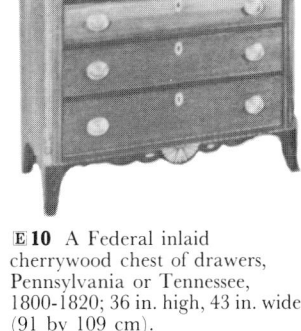

E7 A Federal figured cherrywood bow-front chest of drawers, Kentucky or western Pennsylvania, 1800-1820; 38 in. (96 cm) high.

E8 A Federal inlaid birch and figured maple bow-front chest of drawers, New Hampshire or Massachusetts, 1800-1820.

E9 A Federal inlaid birch chest of drawers, probably New Hampshire, 1800-1820; 38 in. high, 42 in. wide (95 by 105 cm).

E10 A Federal inlaid cherrywood chest of drawers, Pennsylvania or Tennessee, 1800-1820; 36 in. high, 43 in. wide (91 by 109 cm).

E11 A late Federal mahogany bow-front chest of drawers, probably Philadelphia, 1810-1820; 41 in. high by 42 in. wide (102 by 105 cm).

E12 An Empire-style maple and mahogany chest of drawers, Pennsylvania, 1820-1835; 49 in. high by 43 in. wide (124 by 109 cm).

E13 A rosewood chest of drawers with white marble top, stamped "J & J W Meeks N214 Vesey St. New York", 19th century; 37 in. (94 cm) wide.

E14 A Federal mahogany miniature chest of drawers, probably Massachusetts, 1790-1820; 14 in. high by 13 in. wide (36 by 33 cm).

E15 A late Federal mahogany miniature chest of drawers, Massachusetts, 1810-1825; 13 in. high, 10 in. wide, 5 in. deep (32 by 25 by 13 cm).

Coffers

D 1 A Pilgrim Century carved oak "Hadley" blanket chest, the moulded hinged lid opening to a well, with two long drawers below, the rectangular stiles forming the feet, the front carved with volute motifs, Connecticut River Valley, *c.* 1685; 46 in. high by 44 in. wide (117 by 111 cm).

E 2 The Morton family two-drawer "Hadley" chest, probably Hatfield, Massachusetts, *c.* 1710; 42 in. high by 47 in. wide (106 by 119 cm).

E 3 A painted pine blanket chest, probably Milford area, Connecticut, 1704-1735; 28 in. high by 45 in. wide (70 by 113 cm).

E 4 A panelled and painted oak and pine blanket chest with drawer, Massachusetts, *c.* 1720; 30 in. high by 46 in. wide (78 by 117 cm).

E 5 A Chippendale walnut blanket chest, with moulded lifting top above a dovetailed case, with applied mid moulding above two thumb moulded flame figured drawers over a moulded skirt, on bracket feet, Pennsylvania, 1760-1790; 30 in. high by 50 in. wide (78 by 127 cm).

E 6 A Chippendale walnut blanket chest, the top with a thumb-moulded edge lifting above a compartment, over two drawers, Pennsylvania, 1760-1790; 28 in. high by 49 in. wide (71 by 125 cm).

E 7 A Chippendale carved walnut miniature blanket chest, Pennsylvania, 1760-1780; 17 in. high by 23 in. wide (43 by 58 cm).

E 8 A Chippendale carved walnut miniature blanket chest, the hinged lid pierced with a money slot, opening to a well, Pennsylvania, *c.* 1770; 9 in. high by 12 in. wide (23 by 30 cm).

E 9 A Chippendale carved walnut blanket chest, the moulded lid opening to a well with till, the case with three arched panels centring fluted pilasters, the dentil-carved moulded base below continuing to ogee bracket feet, Pennsylvania, *c.* 1770; 24 in. high by 52 in. wide (62 by 132 cm).

E 10 A painted pine blanket chest, Pennsylvania, 1780-1810; 27 in. high by 50 in. wide (67 by 126 cm).

E1 A painted and decorated pine blanket chest, the moulded hinged lid opening to a well with till, the case with three arched panels, above two short moulded drawers, Pennsylvania, dated 1781; 25 in. high by 48 in. wide (64 by 122 cm).

E2 A painted dower chest, with three drawers, Pennsylvania, 1780-1800; 30 in. high by 50 in. wide (76 by 127 cm).

E4 A painted and decorated pine blanket chest, the lid fitted with strap hinges opening to a well with till, the front painted with urns of tulips and flowers in polychrome on a brown ground, with the inscription "GU. & Anna Billch 1789", Pennsylvania, dated 1789; 20 in. high by 50 in. wide (51 by 127 cm).

E3 A painted pine two-drawer blanket chest, probably from Vermont, late 18th century.

Tall chests

C5 A Chippendale bonnet-top cherrywood chest-on-chest, in two sections, the upper with moulded swan's neck pediment centring a flame-carved finial, both parts with various graduated drawers, Connecticut or western Massachusetts, *c.* 1760–1780; 88 in. high by 38 in. wide (224 by 97 cm).

A6 The Van Pelt high chest, Philadelphia, *c.* 1765-1780. Dating from *c.* 1770 this chest has an established provenance beginning with the family of William and Mary King Turner, descending by marriage through the Van Pelts.

C7 A Chippendale carved and figured walnut chest-on-chest, with scrolled broken arch pediment with diamond-pierced fretwork and carved rosettes, centring pierced foliate cartouche and flanked by flame finials, Philadelphia, 1760-1790; 94 in. high by 45 in. wide (239 by 115 cm).

D8 A Chippendale-style mahogany high chest, with pierced and carved swan's neck pediment, flanking an urn and flame finial, with various graduated drawers, the base centre drawer being fan carved, raised on foliate carved cabriole legs; 91 in. high by 40 in. wide (231 by 102 cm).

Tall Chests

Four distinct types of tall chest were made in the last three decades of the 18th century.

They were: the flat-topped double chest, as no. 1 below; the double chest with elaborately carved bonnet-top pediment, as no. 2, right; the tall chest proper, made in one piece as no. 3 on this page, and the chest-on-stand, otherwise known as a high chest or highboy. All forms varied considerably in design – compare, for example, no. 1 on the facing page with three drawers to the lower part, with the pieces shown on pages 44 and 45, all of which have either two shallow or, more commonly, one deep tier.

The arrangement of drawers in the upper part was at least as varied. The top tier may be a single drawer, two or three, and the second tier a single or a pair. This sometimes gave rise to problems in placing drawer pulls – compare the subtlety shown in no. 4 on this page with the result achieved in no. 5 opposite.

Chest-on-chests, unless of the pedimented kind, and tall chests are usually devoid of ornament in the Chippendale period, other than some moulding to the cornice and feet. Quarter columns to the sides are a mark of quality and some pieces are found with chamfered, fluted corners – a Pennsylvania and Connecticut feature. Occasionally the apron will be scalloped, as in no. 9 on the facing page from Pennsylvania.

B2 A cherrywood bonnet-top chest-on-chest, Connecticut, *c.* 1780.

Cherry was a favoured wood among Connecticut cabinet-makers as it has a smooth and close texture and carves well. Time has proved the wisdom of using cherrywood, as it has mellowed to a rich red brown.

The style of finial can be most helpful in establishing the provenance of a piece such as this: the candy twist pattern, for example, was popular in Connecticut, the corkscrew shape in Massachusetts, and the flame in Pennsylvania.

D4 A Chippendale mahogany tall chest of drawers, Philadelphia, 1760-1790; 66 in. high by 43 in. wide (166 by 108 cm).

C5 A Chippendale cherrywood chest-on-chest, New England, 1760-1790; 74 in. high by 39 in. wide (187 by 99 cm).

E6 A Chippendale carved walnut tall chest of drawers, Pennsylvania, *c.* 1780; 60 in. high by 41 in. wide (151 by 102 cm).

C1 A Chippendale walnut chest-on-chest, signed Mahlon Thomas, Mount Holly, New Jersey, 1800; 81 in. high by 45 in. wide (206 by 113 cm).

D3 A Chippendale carved curly maple tall chest of drawers, New England, *c.* 1780; 59 in. high by 40 in. wide (150 by 102 cm).

D 1 A Chippendale carved maple and birch high chest of drawers, New Hampshire, 1780-1800; 77 in. high by 41 in. wide (194 by 104 cm).

C 2 A Chippendale carved birch high chest of drawers, New Hampshire, 1780-1800; 81 in. high by 41 in. wide (204 by 98 cm).

E 3 A Chippendale walnut tall chest of drawers, Virginia, 1760-1790; 54 in. high by 41 in. wide (137 by 104 cm).

E 4 A Chippendale walnut tall chest of drawers, Pennsylvania, 1765-1800; 61 in. high by 41 in. wide (154 by 104 cm).

D 5 A Chippendale carved walnut tall chest of drawers, Chester County, Pennsylvania, *c.* 1770; 58 in. high by 42 in. wide (147 by 105 cm).

E 6 A Chippendale maple tall chest of drawers, Pennsylvania, 1780-1800. It is 55 in. high by 40 in. wide (140 by 100 cm).

D 7 A Chippendale inlaid walnut chest-on-chest, Pennsylvania, 1780-1800; 78 in. high by 46 in. wide (198 by 116 cm).

E 8 A Chippendale inlaid curly maple tall chest of drawers, American, *c.* 1790; 48 in. high by 37 in. wide (121 by 93 cm).

E 9 A Federal mahogany inlaid chest of drawers, Pennsylvania, 1790-1810; 67 in. high by 39 in. wide (170 by 98 cm).

E 10 A Chippendale carved walnut tall chest of drawers, Pennsylvania, 1795-1810; 64 in. high by 40 in. wide (163 by 100 cm).

E 11 A Federal inlaid mahogany tall chest of drawers, probably New York, 1790-1800; 50 in. high by 48 in. wide (126 by 120 cm).

B 12 A tallboy in cherrywood, with carved fans and vine pilasters, Connecticut Valley, *c.* 1780.

High chests

D 1 A William and Mary japanned high chest of drawers, Boston, 1710-1730; 61 in. high by 41 in. wide (155 by 103 cm).

The upper part has a moulded cornice above two short drawers over three graduated long drawers, on a moulded base; the lower part with one short drawer over an arched skirt, flanked by two deep drawers, on trumpet-turned legs joined by a shaped stretcher, on ball feet.

C 2 A William and Mary maple high chest of drawers, 69 in. high by 36 in. wide (175 by 91 cm).

There are essentially two variations on the classic design of the William and Mary tall chest: one, decoration – this piece is of maple show wood with burled walnut veneer drawer fronts, whereas no. 1 above is finished in lacquer, the alternative to veneer; and two, proportion – by comparison with no. 1 this piece is both taller and slimmer, a natural design response to the higher, lighter rooms of the early 18th century.

B 3 A William and Mary highboy, in burl walnut, Massachusetts, *c.* 1725; 66 in. high, 34 in. wide (168 by 86 cm).

A slim and elegant appearance is created by the adoption of simulated short drawer fronts to the three long drawers in the top section. On inspection the maker's ploy is apparent, for the mock centre stiles have had to be widened to accommodate the escutcheons, in contrast to the top tier, in which the (genuine) centre stile is of a purely functional width.

B 4 A Queen Anne double-domed walnut high-chest on carved cabriole legs, Virginia; 78 in. high by 43 in. wide (198 by 108 cm).

B 5 A Queen Anne burl maple veneer high chest of drawers, Massachusetts, 1735-1745, 63 in. (158 cm) high.

C 6 A Queen Anne carved walnut high chest of drawers, Philadelphia, 1730-1750, 72 in. high by 44 in. wide (181 by 110 cm).

C 7 A Queen Anne curly maple high chest of drawers, New England, 1735-1760, 63 in. high by 39 in. wide (160 by 98 cm).

D 1 A Queen Anne walnut high chest of drawers, New England, 1730-1760, 64 in. high by 39 in. wide (161 by 99 cm).

B 2 A Queen Anne walnut flat-top high chest, Massachusetts, *c.* 1740, 68 in. high by 39 in. wide (171 by 99 cm).

C 3 A Queen Anne inlaid and burl walnut veneered bonnet-top high chest, Eastern Massachusetts, 1740-1760, 89 in. high by 38 in. wide (226 by 97 cm).

C 4 A Queen Anne tiger maple high chest of drawers, Newport, Rhode Island, 1740–1760. It stands 82 in. (207 cm) high and is 39 in. (99 cm) wide.

The piece is in two parts, the upper with moulded pediment centering a plinth with corkscrew finial over two short and three graduated long drawers. The lower case has one long drawer over three frieze drawers, on slender cabriole legs with pad feet.

The deeply arched and scalloped skirt is reminiscent of that on a high chest signed and dated 1748 by Christopher Townsend – see Joseph K. Ott, *John Brown House Loan Exhibition of Rhode Island Furniture*, 1965, figure 57.

High Chests

The classic high chest, with or without an elaborate pediment, represents a happy fusion of traditions in 18th-century America. The primary influence was still English rather than Dutch colonial, but the English cabinet-makers of the late 17th and early 18th centuries had taken the style directly from Dutch models. The bonnet top, though the design was mediated through England, never achieved the same level of popularity there that it did in the American colonies. By the same token, the architectural pediment so highly favoured in Georgian England was not as commonly used in America in the same period.

Woods

The favoured woods for chest furniture were mahogany, especially Honduras mahogany which was almost universally used in the latter part of the 18th century, alongside walnut, both black and white, whose chief rival early in the century was maple in both its silver and red forms. Plainly figured maple was much used in New England for underframing fine mahogany furniture; highly figured maple was widely used as show wood. Cherrywood was particularly in demand in Connecticut and New York. Birch was used in combination with maple or, stained, as a substitute for mahogany in country furniture.

C 5 A Queen Anne mahogany high chest of drawers, Massachusetts, 1740-1760, 87 in. high by 43 in. wide (221 by 108 cm).

C 6 A Queen Anne carved cherrywood high chest of drawers, Connecticut, 1740-1770, 92 in. high by 41 in wide (232 by 104 cm).

C1 A Queen Anne carved walnut high chest of drawers, Massachusetts, *c.* 1740-1760; 84 in. (213 cm) high.

C2 A Queen Anne cherrywood high chest of drawers, Connecticut, 1740-1770; 81 in. (205 cm) high.

C3 A Queen Anne cherrywood high chest, *c.* 1740, possibly Connecticut; 64 in. (161 cm).

C4 A Queen Anne maple high chest, New Hampshire, 1740-1760; 79 in. (200 cm) high.

B5 A Queen Anne figured maple high chest, North Shore, Massachusetts, 1740-1760; 73 in. (184 cm) high.

C6 A Queen Ann carved maple high chest, New Hampshire, 1740-1760; 70 in. high, 37 in. wide (179 by 94 cm).

C7 A Queen Anne curly maple high chest, Massachusetts, 1740-1760; 74 in. (186 cm) high.

D8 A Queen Anne walnut high chest, Pennsylvania, 1740-1770; 73 in. high by 40 in. wide (186 by 101 cm).

C9 A Queen Anne maple high chest of drawers, Massachusetts, 1740-1770, 74 in. high, 40 in. wide (186 by 100 cm).

C10 A Queen Anne maple high chest of drawers, Hartford or New London County, Connecticut, 1740-1770; 72 in. (182 cm) high.

E11 A Queen Anne figured maple chest-on-frame, New England, 1740-1760; 57 in. (144 cm) high.

D12 A Queen Anne carved cherrywood high chest, eastern Connecticut or Rhode Island, *c.* 1750; 73 in. (186 cm) high.

D 1 A Queen Anne cherrywood high chest of drawers, 71 in. high, 40 in. wide (179 by 101 cm).

D 2 A Queen Anne birch high chest, New England, *c.* 1750; 72 in. high by 39 in. wide (183 by 99 cm).

D 3 A Queen Anne flat top high chest, New England, 1750-1770; 60 in. high by 39 in. wide (153 by 97 cm).

D 4 A Queen Anne maple chest-on-stand, New Hampshire, late 18th century.

E 5 A Queen Anne cherrywood high chest of drawers, 75 in. (189 cm) high.

D 6 A Queen Anne walnut high chest, Pennsylvania, mid 18th century; 76 in. high by 40 in. wide (194 by 101 cm).

E 7 A Queen Anne birch and pine chest of drawers on frame, New England, 1750-1770; 63 in. high by 36 in. wide (160 by 91 cm).

D 8 A Queen Anne carved mahogany flat-top high chest, Salem, Massachusetts, 1755-1775; 69 in. (175 cm) high.

D 9 A Chippendale figured walnut chest-on-frame, Pennsylvania, 1760-1780; 58 in. high by 40 in. wide (147 by 101 cm).

E 10 A Queen Ann carved maple chest-on-frame, probably Connecticut, *c.* 1765; 50 in. (127 cm) high.

C 11 A Chippendale carved maple high chest, Massachusetts, 1760-1780; 83 in. high, 40 in. wide (210 by 100 cm).

B 12 A cherrywood highboy with broken pediment, shell-carved, on fine cabriole legs, Connecticut, *c.* 1760.

CUPBOARDS
1760-1900

Cupboards fall into two main categories: those that are architecturally inspired and appear to have been built as an integral part of an interior, and those which were made as freestanding pieces of furniture in their own right.

There is then a further subdivision, into those with glazed doors and those with blind panelled doors. Cupboards of the best quality with blind doors frequently open to a carved interior – see no. 4 on this page.

Corner cupboards

E 1 A Chippendale pine corner cupboard, Maryland, 1760-1790; 86 in. high by 48 in. wide (217 by 130 cm).

D 2 An architectural Chippendale corner cupboard, Chestertown, Maryland, 1760-1790; 103 in. by 63 in. (262 by 160 cm).

E 3 A Chippendale pine corner cupboard, American, 1760-1790; 83 in. high by 46 in. wide (210 by 117 cm).

D 4 A cherrywood corner cupboard, Pennsylvania, with shell carved interior.

D 5 A cherrywood corner cupboard, 1770-1800; 77 by 39 in. (195 by 99 cm).

E 6 A Chippendale carved pine corner cupboard, Middle Atlantic States, *c.* 1785; 87 in. high by 60 in. wide (221 by 152 cm).

D 7 A Federal carved walnut corner cupboard, probably Pennsylvania, *c.* 1785; 107 in. high by 54 in. wide (244 by 137 cm).

E 8 A grain-painted cherrywood corner cupboard, probably Pennsylvania, 1780-1810.

E 9 A Federal cherrywood corner cupboard, New England, 1790-1810; 87 in. high by 56 in. wide (223 by 144 cm).

E 10 A Federal cherrywood two-part corner cupboard, with upper glazed door, and two cupboard doors in the lower section; 84 in. high by 44 in. wide (214 by 111 cm).

E 11 A Federal walnut corner cupboard, probably North or South Carolina, 1790-1810; 91 in. high by 42 in. wide (231 by 107 cm).

E 1 A Federal cherrywood corner cupboard, New England, *c.* 1800; 79 in. high by 47 in. wide (199 by 119 cm).

E 2 A Federal cherrywood corner cupboard, probably Connecticut, 1800-1825; 83 in. high by 52 in. wide (212 by 133 cm).

E 3 A Chippendale grain-painted corner cupboard, Pennsylvania, 1810-1830; 88 in. high by 45 in. wide (224 by 113 cm).

E 4 An Empire grain-painted corner cupboard, Pennsylvania, first half 19th century; 91 in. by 55 in. (232 by 138 cm).

E 5 A Federal grain-painted corner cupboard, Middle States, 19th century; 91 in. high by 46 in. wide (230 by 117 cm).

E 6 A painted pine corner cupboard, with glazed door opening to four shelves, 19th century; 83 in. high by 42 in. wide (212 by 107 cm).

D 7 A red gum kas, in two sections, the upper part with fielded panel doors, with moulded frames flanked by two panels with raised moulding, the lower case with cove moulding above two moulded drawers flanked by diamond panels with moulded frames, Queens or Nassau County, New York, 1730-1760; 72 in. high, 65 in. wide (182 by 165 cm).

E 8 A cherrywood kas, with cove-moulded pediment over two panelled doors opening to shelves, decorated with applied bosses, over moulded waisting above a panelled long drawer, on a moulded base and turned bun feet, possibly New Jersey; 71 in. high by 61 in. wide (181 by 155 cm).

Glazed Cupboards
The development of the glass industry in the early years of the 18th century facilitated the use of glass in the manufacture of cabinet furniture. In addition, the solid affluence of the Colonies was no longer exhibiting itself only in the commissioning of fine pieces of furniture but was leading to the acquisition of all kinds of objets d'art and libraries, both of which could be kept safely and displayed in these new glass-fronted cabinets.

Early glazing bars were heavy and plain in form, usually of an astragal section. However, the skill of cabinet-maker and glazier soon enabled the execution of the finest tracery – see for example no. 4 on the facing page.

Linen presses

E 1 A Chippendale cherrywood linen press, New York or New Jersey, 1750-1800; 77 in. (196 cm) high.

D 2 A Chippendale mahogany linen press, Salem, Massachusetts, 1760-1780; 85 in. (215cm) high.

D 3 A painted and decorated walnut schrank, in several parts, the projecting cornice above a pair of panelled hinged doors, two short moulded drawers below, on turned feet, painted and decorated with urns of tulips in polychrome on a brown grained ground, Pennsylvania, 1760-1780; 78 in. high by 67 in. wide (198 by 168 cm).

D 4 A cherrywood press, possibly attributed to Bates How, Canaan, Connecticut, dated 1795.

E 5 A cherrywood linen press, in two sections, the upper part with ogee cornice, above a pair of scalloped-top panelled cupboard doors opening to a shelved interior, flanked by reeded stop-fluted pilasters, the lower section with two short and two long graduated drawers, New Jersey, 1770-1780; 76 in. high by 47 in. wide (194 by 120 cm).

E 6 A walnut linen press, of good proportions and high quality cabinet work, American, 18th century.

E 7 A Chippendale carved walnut schrank, Pennsylvania, c. 1790; 84 in. high by 59 in. wide (214 by 150 cm).

E 8 A pine and poplar schrank, with two fielded panelled doors opening to a shelved interior, over two drawers, Pennsylvania, late 18th century; 84 in. high by 66 in. wide (217 by 167 cm).

Step-back cupboards

D1 A Chippendale walnut step-back cupboard, probably Pennsylvania, 1770-1800; 81 in. (207 cm) high.

E2 Chippendale pine step-back cupboard, Pennsylvania, 1780-1800; 76 in. (193 cm) high.

E3 A painted pine cupboard, American, early 19th century; 110 by 65 in. (278 by 166 cm).

D4 A Chippendale walnut corner cupboard, the projecting moulded and fluted cornice above a pair of arched, glazed, mullioned and hinged doors opening to shelves, the projecting lower section with two short line-inlaid drawers, a pair of line-inlaid cupboard doors below, intersecting similar panels flanking, on reduced feet. Middle Atlantic States, *c.* 1785; 88 in. high by 50 in. wide (223 by 127 cm).

E5 A pine cupboard with shelves, in two parts, the upper part with cove moulding above three shallow shelves wth plate rails, sides fitted into shaped cleats, the lower part with three short drawers over two panelled cupboard doors flanking an open shelf on extended stiles, 19th century; 83 in. high by 61 in. wide (212 by 157 cm).

Later Glazing

At certain periods, cupboards with glazed doors have been considered commercially and aesthetically more desirable than the blind-door type, with the result that the blind panels have been removed and replaced by glazing bars and glass. The quality of the timber used may indicate that this has happened, and the putty is another indicator – if it is original it will be brittle. Partial reglazing of an originally glazed set of doors is quite legitimate if it has been done merely to repair broken panes – this can be ascertained easily by the inconsistency in the age of the putty.

Step-back cupboards, being almost invariably two-part pieces, have been prone to divorce and remarriage – it is always important to check that timber and construction details are compatible.

E6 An Empire pine step-back cupboard, *c.* 1825; 87 in. high by 53 in. wide (219 by 135 cm).

E7 An Empire mahogany step-back cupboard, probably Philadelphia, *c.* 1825; 93 in. high by 61 in. wide (237 by 157 cm).

DESKS
1710-1880

In common with its European counterparts, the American slant front desk developed primarily from the scrutoire or escritoire, which in form is similar to the one illustrated at no. 4. The form gained more refined lines when heightened and set on a cabriole-legged stand, as nos 5 and 6.

But the requirement of portability was diminishing, and portable furniture was no longer fashionable. The logic of using the space below the desk was not to be resisted. A false start was made with starting to fill in the stand with drawers, as no. 5, but the real solution as cabinet-making skills developed was to set the desk on top of a chest of drawers.

Fall-front desks

D 1 A William and Mary maple slant front desk, Massachusetts, 1710-1730; 37 in. high by 34 in. wide (94 by 87 cm).

E 2 A curly maple slant front desk, New England, 1720-1740; 40 in. high by 37 in. wide (101 by 94 cm).

E 3 A Queen Anne slant front desk-on-stand, New England, 1720-1750; 43 in. high by 29 in. wide (109 by 73 cm).

E 4 A William and Mary carved and turned walnut desk-on-frame, Southern, 1730-1750; 39 in. high by 44 in. wide (99 by 110 cm).

D 5 A Queen Anne maple desk-on-frame, Rhode Island, 1735-1765; 42 in. high by 36 in. wide (105 by 90 cm).

D 6 A Queen Anne walnut desk-on-frame, American; 43 in. high by 41 in. wide (109 by 104 cm).

E 7 A Queen Anne inlaid walnut slant front desk, Salem or Boston, Massachusetts, 1740-1760; 46 in. high by 48 in. wide (115 by 122 cm).

D 8 A Chippendale walnut slant front desk, Massachusetts, 1755-1785, 43 in. high by 39 in. wide (110 by 99 cm).

E 9 A Chippendale figured maple slant front desk, probably Rhode Island, 1755-1785; 41 in. high by 36 in. wide (103 by 89 cm).

B 10 The John Brown Chippendale mahogany block front, shell-carved kneehole desk, Goddard or Townsend Shop, Newport, Rhode Island, c. 1770.

D 11 A Chippendale maple slant lid desk, Rhode Island, 1760-1780; 42 in. high by 38 in. wide (107 by 96 cm).

D 12 A Chippendale mahogany reverse serpentine slant front desk, Massachusetts, 1760-1780; 44 in. high by 44 in. wide (112 by 112 cm).

C 13 A Chippendale cherrywood reverse serpentine slant front desk, Salem, Massachusetts, 1760-1790; 44 in. high by 44 in. wide (111 by 112 cm).

C 14 A Chippendale mahogany block front desk, Massachusetts, 1765-1790; 42 in. high by 41 in. wide (106 by 104 cm).

D 1 A Chippendale cherrywood slant front desk, Pennsylvania or New Jersey, 1760-1790; 43 in. high by 43 in. wide (108 by 109 cm).

C 2 A Chippendale carved mahogany serpentine desk, Massachusetts, 1760-1790; 64 in. high by 46 in. wide (161 by 115 cm).

E 3 A Chippendale mahogany slant front desk, Pennsylvania, 1760-1790; 43 in. high by 40 in. wide (109 by 101 cm).

D 4 A Chippendale birch reverse serpentine slant front desk, Massachusetts or New Hampshire, 1760-1785; 44 in. high by 42 in. wide (112 by 106 cm).

E 5 A Chippendale walnut desk, Philadelphia, 1760-1790; 41 in. high by 38 in. wide (103 by 96 cm).

D 6 A Chippendale cherrywood desk, New York, 1760-1790; 43 in. high and 43 in. wide (108 by 108 cm).

E 7 A Chippendale mahogany desk, New York, 1760-1790; 42 in. high by 42 in. wide (108 by 107 cm).

D 8 A Chippendale mahogany reverse serpentine slant front desk, north-eastern Massachusetts, 1760-1790; 45 in. high by 46 in. wide (113 by 117 cm).

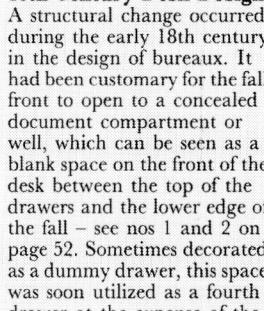

E 9 A Chippendale maple slant front desk, New England, 1760-1790; 41 in. high by 39 in. wide (104 by 99 cm).

C 10 A Chippendale carved cherrywood slant front desk, Connecticut or Massachusetts, 1765-1785; 41 in. high by 35 in. wide (104 by 87 cm).

C 11 A Chippendale carved mahogany slant front desk, Massachusetts, 1765-1785; 47 in. high by 40 in. wide (118 by 102 cm).
The fitted interior has eight fan-carved valance drawers above six pigeonholes, two banks of drawers and a fan-carved prospect door; the case with fan pendant on short cabriole legs with claw-and-ball feet.

18th-Century Desk Design
A structural change occurred during the early 18th century in the design of bureaux. It had been customary for the fall front to open to a concealed document compartment or well, which can be seen as a blank space on the front of the desk between the top of the drawers and the lower edge of the fall – see nos 1 and 2 on page 52. Sometimes decorated as a dummy drawer, this space was soon utilized as a fourth drawer at the expense of the well.

Another change concerned the feet, which became either ogee brackets, or cabriole legs with claw-and-ball feet, or chunky square-edged brackets, though by the end of the 18th century the splay French foot had gained considerable popularity – see no 13 on page 55.

American desks of the Queen Anne and Chippendale periods resemble very closely their English counterparts in design if not in materials, though there is one important exception – the block front. This was a form of Dutch origin, taken up in America for case furniture of all kinds. Fine examples came from Newport, where they were frequently ornamented with characteristic shells.

D 1 A Chippendale walnut slant front desk, probably Pennsylvania, 1765-1800; 42 in. high, 38 in. wide (105 by 95 cm).

E 5 A Chippendale maple slant front desk, New England, 1770-1800; 44 in. high, 40 in. wide (112 by 100 cm).

D 9 A Chippendale walnut slant front desk, Pennsylvania, c. 1780; 43 in. high by 37 in. wide (108 by 94 cm).

D 13 A Chippendale walnut slant front desk, Pennsylvania, 1780-1800; 45 in. high by 44 in. wide (115 by 112 cm).

D 2 A Chippendale maple slant front desk, Massachusetts, 1770-1790; 42 in. by 36 in. (105 by 91 cm).

E 6 A Chippendale birch slant front desk, New England, 1770-1800; 44 in. high by 40 in. wide (111 by 102 cm).

E 10 A Chippendale walnut slant front desk, c. 1780; 42 in. high by 40 in. wide (106 by 101 cm).

D 14 A Chippendale mahogany serpentine slant front desk, Massachusetts, 1780-1800; 44 in. high by 44 in. wide (110 by 110 cm).

E 3 A Chippendale maple slant front desk, New England, 1770-1790.

E 7 A Chippendale tiger maple slant front desk, late 18th century; 37 in. (93 cm) wide.

E 11 A Chippendale walnut slant front desk, Pennsylvania, 1780-1795; 44 in. high by 38 in. wide (112 by 97 cm).

D 15 A Chippendale carved birch serpentine slant front desk, North Shore, Massachusetts, 1780-1800; 45 in. high by 43 in. wide (114 by 108 cm).

E 4 A Chippendale walnut slant front desk with quarter columns, Pennsylvania, 1770-1790.

D 8 A Chippendale carved mahogany slant front desk, signed Rawson, Providence, Rhode Island, c. 1775; 43 in. high by 41 in. wide (109 by 104 cm).

E 12 A Chippendale cherrywood slant front desk, Connecticut, 1780-1800; 42 in. high by 40 in. wide (105 by 101 cm).

E 16 A Federal figured maple slant front desk, New England, 1780-1810; 43 in. high by 42 in. wide (108 by 107 cm).

D 1 A Chippendale carved mahogany slant front desk, Pennsylvania, *c*. 1785; 43 in. high by 41 in. wide (109 by 104 cm).

E 5 A Federal mahogany slant front desk, Pennsylvania, 1790-1810; 41 in. high by 47 in. wide (104 by 119 cm).

D 2 A Chippendale mahogany slant front desk, probably New York, *c*. 1785; 44 in. high by 42 in. wide (110 by 107 cm).

E 6 A Federal mahogany slant front desk of about 1800.

C 9 A Chippendale mahogany bureau table, Massachusetts, 1765-1785; 33 in. high, 37 in. wide (84 by 94 cm).
The piece is of good colour and traditional design, with cockbeaded drawers and original brasses.

D 12 A Federal mahogany tambour desk, line inlaid, the upper part having a central inlaid cupboard door over three graduated long drawers, 1790-1810.

E 3 A Federal cherrywood slant front desk, Middle Atlantic States, 1785-1800; 43 in. high by 45 in. wide (109 by 113 cm).

E 7 A Chippendale curly maple slant front desk, probably New Hampshire, *c*. 1800; 51 in. high by 31 in. wide (128 by 104 cm).

E 10 A Federal inlaid mahogany writing desk, Salem, Massachusetts, 1790-1802; 34 in. high by 30 in. wide (85 by 75 cm).

E 13 A Federal mahogany veneer desk, New York, 1790-1815; 45 in. high by 45 in. wide (113 by 115 cm). The fall front encloses a fitted interior over three long drawers above a shaped apron on French-style feet.

E 4 A Federal inlaid cherrywood slant front desk, Pennsylvania, 1790-1810; 42 in. high by 40 in. wide (106 by 101 cm).

D 8 A Federal inlaid cherrywood slant front desk, Middle Atlantic States, *c*. 1814; 48 in. high by 40 in. wide (120 by 101 cm).

D 11 A Federal inlaid mahogany tambour writing desk, Massachusetts, 1790-1810; 44 in. by 37 in. (111 by 93 cm).

Writing Desks

Period desks by their very nature are complicated pieces of furniture, frequently containing many moving parts – small drawers, secret drawers as well as cylinder and tambour mechanisms. Being required essentially by the well-to-do, they were usually executed to a high standard and should therefore be of fine quality.

Not to be confused with slant front desks, those illustrated here are predominantly of secretary form, wherein the drawer pulls out and its front falls to form the writing surface and disclose the inner fitments. The drawer is sometimes camouflaged to look like other drawer-fronts and sometimes treated as a feature, with oval panels or exotic veneers – as in no. 9 on this page.

D 1 A Federal cherrywood lady's desk, New England, 1790-1815; 67 in. high, 38 in. wide (170 by 97 cm).

D 2 A Federal inlaid mahogany writing desk, probably Massachusetts, 1795-1810; 52 by 43 in. (132 by 109 cm).

E 3 A Federal inlaid cherrywood bureau desk, 41 in. high by 46 in. wide (104 by 115 cm).

E 4 A Federal inlaid mahogany butler's desk, attributed to Michael Allison, New York, *c.* 1800.

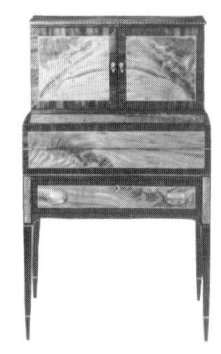

D 5 An inlaid mahogany lady's writing desk, eastern New England, *c.* 1800; 49 in. high by 30 in. wide (123 by 76 cm).

E 6 A Federal cherrywood tambour desk, northern Massachusetts or south-eastern New Hampshire, *c.* 1800; 48 in. (198 cm) high.

E 7 A Federal mahogany secretaire, Massachusetts, 1795-1815; 57 in. high by 40 in. wide (145 by 100 cm).

D 8 A Federal mahogany and figured birch inlaid writing desk, north-eastern Massachusetts, *c.* 1800.

E 9 A Federal inlaid mahogany butler's desk, New York, 1800-1815.

D 10 A Federal inlaid mahogany roll-top desk, Pennsylvania or Maryland, 1800-1815.

D 11 A Federal inlaid mahogany cylinder top desk, Baltimore, 1800-1815; 45 in. (113 cm) high.

E 12 A Federal inlaid mahogany lady's desk, Massachusetts or New Hampshire, 1805-1820.

E 13 A Federal mahogay tambour desk, New England, *c.* 1810; 45 in. high by 35 in. wide (114 by 87 cm).

E 14 A Federal mahogany tambour desk, Salem, Massachusetts, 1800-1820; 54 in. (136 cm) high.

E1 A Federal mahogany and maple tambour desk, 1800-1820; 45 in. (113 cm) high.

E2 A Federal bird's-eye maple and mahogany secretaire, Massachusetts, 1800-1820; 55 in. (139 cm) high.

E3 A Federal mahogany tambour secretaire, New England, *c.* 1820; 63 in. high by 46 in. wide (160 by 115 cm).

E4 An Empire cherrywood and birch butler's secretaire, New England, *c.* 1825.

E5 An Empire mahogany secretaire, American, *c.* 1825; 62 in. high by 40 in. wide (156 by 101 cm).

E6 A classical carved mahogany and satinwood secretaire, stamped John Van Bosre, New York, *c.* 1825.

E7 An American mahogany desk, *c.* 1860; 56 in. high by 52 in. wide (142 by 132 cm).

E8 An American cherrywood desk, *c.* 1879, New York; 31 in. high by 27 in. wide (78 by 68 cm).

D9 *(above and right)* A walnut and burr-walnut desk, by the Wooton Desk Company, Indianapolis, *c.* 1880. It is 55 in. high and 37 in. wide (138 by 93 cm) when closed.

These deceptive desks, far from being the cylinder tops they appear, actually open to a fall-front writing flap with elaborately fitted interior.

E10 A walnut Wooton-shape cylinder top desk, American, late 19th century; 32 in. (81 cm) wide.

D11 An architect's table, finely designed in the Chippendale style by Thomas Jefferson.

MIRRORS
1730-1890

Frames for looking glasses were created in fashionable styles in America from the early 18th century, but until the end of the century the glasses for them were for the most part imported.

As in Europe, mirror plate was considered a luxury item and was treasured by successive generations who – understandably, but to us somewhat confusingly – had the plates reframed to keep them up to date.

Dressing mirrors

E1 A Federal inlaid mahogany dressing mirror, *c.* 1800; 27 in. high by 20 in. wide (69 by 51 cm).

E2 A Federal mahogany dressing glass, early 19th century; 24 in. high by 18 in. wide (59 by 45 cm).

E3 A late Federal mahogany dressing glass, 19th century.

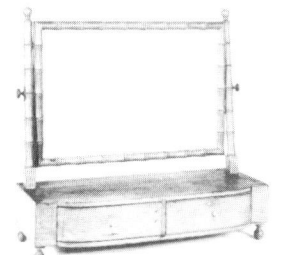

E4 A pine bow-front dressing mirror, probably New England, 1790-1815.

Wall mirrors

E5 A Queen Anne walnut mirror, 1730-1750; 65 in. high by 20 in. wide (165 by 51 cm).

E6 A Queen Anne walnut mirror, American, 1730-1750; 58 in. (146 cm) high.

E7 A Queen Anne walnut veneer and gilt mirror, 1740-1760; 53 in. high by 20 in. wide (134 by 51 cm).

E8 A Queen Anne carved and parcel-gilt walnut mirror, mid 18th century; 38 in. high by 19 in. wide (95 by 49 cm).

E9 A Chippendale carved and parcel-gilt mahogany mirror, American, 1750-1770; 31 in. high by 17 in. wide (77 by 44 cm).

E10 An unusually ornate Chippendale carved wood and gilt mirror, 1750-1780; 40 in. high by 22 in. wide (102 by 55 cm).

E1 A Chippendale mahogany mirror, 1760-1800; 37 in. high by 20 in. wide (93 by 51 cm).

E4 A Chippendale mahogany and gilt mirror, labelled Bittle & Cooper, Boston, 1760-1780.

E7 A Chippendale mahogany and gilt mirror, American, 1760-1780; 35 in. high by 19 in. wide (88 by 48 cm).

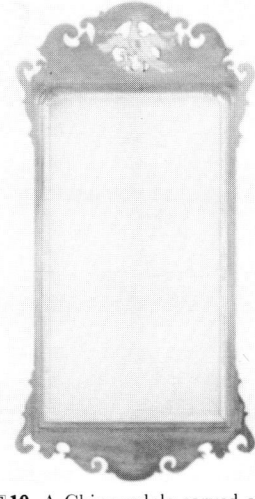

E10 A Chippendale carved and gilt mahogany mirror, 1760-1790; 41 in. high by 22 in. wide (104 by 54 cm).

E2 A Chippendale mahogany and gilt mirror, 1760-1790; 41 in. high by 21 in. wide (104 by 53 cm).

E5 A Chippendale carved and gilded mahogany mirror, 1760-1790; 34 in. high by 19 in. wide (86 by 49 cm).

E8 A Chippendale mahogany and gilt mirror, 1760-1790; 37 in. high by 20 in. wide (93 by 50 cm).

E11 A Chippendale mahogany veneer and gilt mirror, 1760-1790; 42 in. high by 23 in. wide (105 by 57 cm).

E3 A Chippendale mahogany mirror, American, 1750-1780; 47 in. high by 23 in. wide (108 by 59 cm).

E6 A Chippendale mahogany mirror, American, 1760-1790; 36 in. high by 19 in. wide (92 by 48 cm).

E9 A Chippendale gilt and mahogany veneer mirror, 1760-1790; 40 in. high by 21 in. wide (101 by 52 cm).

E12 A Chippendale mahogany veneer and gilt mirror, American, 1760-1790; 47 in. high by 27 in. wide (119 by 68 cm).

The Manufacture of Mirrors

The process of manufacturing mirror glass involved the making of blown cylinders of glass, which were split open and flattened on a stone, then polished and silvered by floating mercury over tin foil. Because of the limitations of this process, mirrors until the 1770s were either relatively small or made up of two or more plates – see nos 5, 6 and 7 on page 58.

The development in England in 1773 of an existing French process of casting glass led to the production of much larger plates than had hitherto been regularly available, and these were used for pier glasses, large overmantels and soon for cheval or dressing glasses.

The predominant styles of mirror frame until the end of the 18th century were those of the Queen Anne and Chippendale periods, joined during the 1790s by frames with deeply scrolling swan-neck pediments. They were made of mahogany and walnut veneers heightened with gilding on to carved wood and gesso, the popular ornaments being the shell and the phoenix or eagle. The slip that ran between frame and mirror was usually gilt.

The border to curvilinear mirror frames was sometimes gilt, but numerous examples – such as nos 2 and 3 on this page – show an apron of plain veneer with a highly fanciful carved edge that incorporates stylized scrolls and foliage.

E 1 A Chippendale gilt and mahogany veneer mirror, American, 1760-90; 37 in. high, 20 in. wide (94 by 49 cm).

E 2 A Chippendale mahogany mirror, probably American, 1780-1800; 36 in. high by 18 in. wide (90 by 44 cm).

E 3 A Chippendale gilt and mahogany mirror, American, 1760-1790; 48 in. high by 23 in. wide (122 by 58 cm).

D 4 A Chippendale mahogany and gilt mirror, American, 1760-1780; 54 in. high by 23 in. wide (136 by 58 cm).

D 5 A Chippendale mahogany and gilt mirror, American, 1760-1780; 57 in. high by 26 in. wide (144 by 66 cm).

The broken pediment centres a phoenix.

D 6 A Chippendale gilt and mahogany mirror, 1760-1790; 58 in. high by 26 in. wide (146 by 66 cm).

The swan's neck pediment, carved with rosettes, centres an urn raised on a plinth and containing flowers.

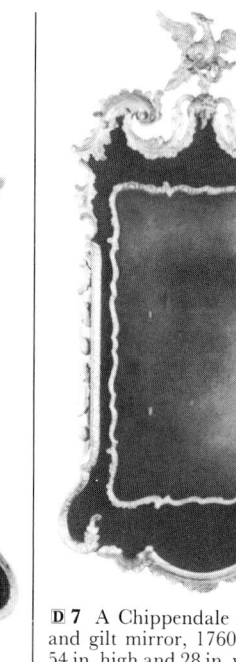

D 7 A Chippendale mahogany and gilt mirror, 1760-1780. It is 54 in. high and 28 in. wide (137 by 70 cm).

The carving of the scrolls, leaves and phoenix to the crest is particularly lavish, making a fine impression. Compare Helen Comstock, *The Looking Glass in America 1700-1825*, New York, 1964, figure 23.

D 8 A Chippendale carved gilt and walnut veneer mirror, 1760-1790; 55 in. high by 30 in. wide (140 by 76 cm).

The moulded broken-arch pediment is carved with trailing leafage and egg-and-dart, a motif that is repeated in the entablature and in the pendant bottom.

D 1 A Chippendale carved and gilt mirror, American, 1760-1790; 61 in. high by 29 in. wide (153 by 72 cm).

D 2 A Chippendale walnut ornately carved and gilt mirror, 1760-1790; 58 in. high by 27 in. wide (146 by 69 cm).

D 3 A Chippendale gilt mahogany mirror, American, 1770-1800; 45 in. (113 cm) high.

D 4 A Chippendale carved mahogany and giltwood mirror, New York, 1790-1800; 44 in. (111 cm) high.

D 5 A Federal inlaid mahogany gilt and églomisé mirror, 1790-1810.

E 6 A Federal inlaid mahogany and gilt mirror, 1790-1810, 53 in. high, 23 in. wide (134 by 58 cm).

E 7 A Federal mahogany and églomisé mirror, American, 1790-1810; 54 in. high by 23 in. wide (137 by 59 cm).

D 8 A Federal inlaid and gilt mahogany mirror, New York, 1790-1810; 57 in. high by 22 in. wide (144 by 55 cm).

D 9 A Federal mahogany and gilt églomisé mirror, Boston or New York, 1790-1810.

E 10 A painted pine dressing mirror, 18th century; 19 in. high by 11 in. wide (48 by 28 cm).

E 11 A Federal giltwood mirror, 1790-1810; 45 in. (114 cm) high.

E1 A Federal gilt mirror, American, 1790-1810; it is 35 in. high and 16 in. wide (88 by 40 cm).

E4 A Federal gilt and églomisé mirror, New York, 1790-1810; 45 in. high by 26 in. wide (114 by 66 cm).

E3 A Federal gilt and églomisé mirror, Albany, New York, 1790-1810; 51 in. high by 20 in. wide (129 by 49 cm).

E2 A Federal giltwood mirror, New York, 1790-1810; 42 in. high by 22 in. wide (105 by 54 cm).
 The black, white and gilt églomisé panel under the moulded cornice is surmounted by an eagle standing on a rosette-carved plinth.

E5 A Federal carved giltwood mirror, New York or Albany, 1790-1815; 61 in. high by 26 in. wide (154 by 65 cm).
 The eagle grasps a laurel wreath in its beak over an églomisé-mounted plinth, with églomisé panels also to the cornice, the sides and heading the capitals.

E1 A Federal gilt and églomisé mirror, New York, 1790-1810; 53 in. high by 28 in. wide (133 by 71 cm).

E2 A Federal giltwood wall mirror, 1790-1815, labelled Bernard Cermenati, Newburyport, Massachusetts.

E3 A Federal gilt and églomisé mirror, American, 1790-1820; 45 in. high and 24 in. wide (113 by 61 cm).

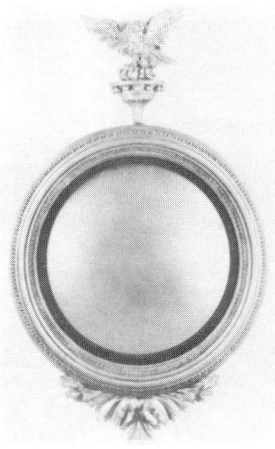

E4 A late Federal gilt convex mirror, American, 1815-1830; 52 in. high and 31 in. diameter (132 by 78 cm).

The glass is mounted within an ebonized, reeded slip inside the moulded gilt frame decorated with egg-and-dart and acanthus leaves.

E6 An Empire carved and gilt mirror, 1815-1830; it is 34 in. high and 31 in. wide (84 by 78 cm).

The crest – composed of anchor, flags, starburst and olive wreath – is supported by two writhing dolphins. The crest motifs – those of naval victory and ensuing peace – suggest that this mirror may be an English import.

E5 A gilt and ebonized girandole mirror, American, 1820-1830; 39 in. high by 73 in. wide (99 by 185 cm).

This mirror is a good example of the application of increasingly elaborate decoration to the convex mirror as the period progressed.

Mirrors in the 1800s

Carved and gilded frames, particularly in the delicate styles of George Hepplewhite, were popular in the early 1800s and were still being imported in the 1820s. However, the architectural columnar mirror frames incorporating a verre églomisé panel at the top were soon taken up and examples as early as 1800 are known – see no. 4 on the facing page and the four mirrors following it.

The girandole or convex mirror first recommended by Thomas Sheraton in England in 1803 but known in France since the middle of the 18th century produced a novel effect in the rooms in which it hung – rather like that of a fish-eye lens. Fine examples were retained in elaborate frames incorporating gilt balls, surmounted by eagles and finished at the base with foliage, often supporting a pair of candle branches – see no. 5 on this page.

The eagle was, of course, a popular cresting motif in England well before it was adopted as the symbol of the newly born United States. Eagles are thus found on American mirrors of all periods, before and after the Revolution.

A crest of wire flowers is more helpful as a guide to dating, as it was an essentially classical feature not appearing before 1780.

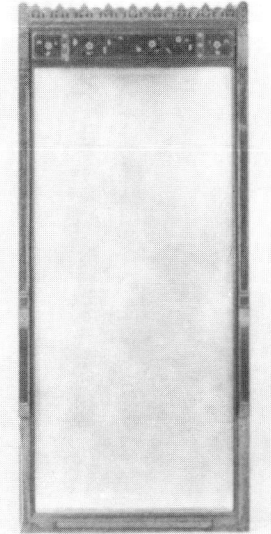

E7 A carved and inlaid mahogany hall mirror in the Aesthetic style, New York, c. 1880; it is 81 in. high and 37 in. wide (245 by 92 cm).

SCREENS
1730-1810

The American resistance to highly elaborate carving in the rococo style is rarely better evidenced than in the design and execution of tripod-base pole screens. Those shown here range in date from the early mid-18th century to the first decade of the 19th and show no major decorative change, whereas a mid-century English version of good quality would have been demonstratively carved by comparison with later models.

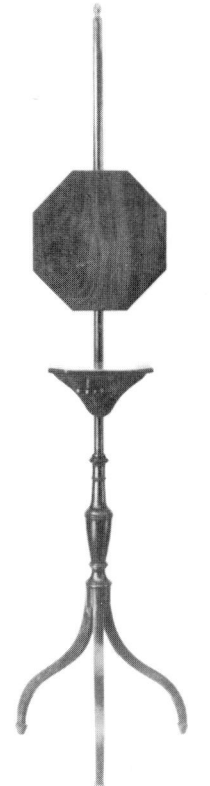

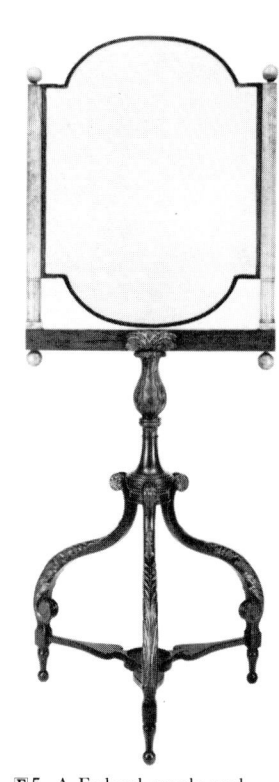

E2 A mahogany tripod pole screen on cabriole legs terminating in shod slipper feet, 1730-1750; 66 in. (167 cm) high.

E4 A mahogany pole screen on an elegant umbrella-form tripod base – the hinged shelf below the banner adds considerably to the aesthetic and commercial value, 1795-1810.

E5 A Federal maple and mahogany firescreen of rare and exuberant form, the carving to the base reminiscent of the work of Samuel McIntire, the design after Sheraton's "horse fire screen"; Salem, *c.* 1800.

E1 An early Federal cherrywood firescreen stand with corkscrew finial, New England, 1780-1800; 62 in. (156 cm) high.

E3 A Federal pole screen, the tripod base of umbrella form, supporting a banner of classical vase shape, 1800-1810.

E6 A painted two-leaf leather screen, the upper panels painted with American scenes, the lower with a pattern of exotic birds, peonies and trailing foliage in a Chinese-inspired stye, early 19th century; it stands 75 in. (190 cm) high.

B1 Chippendale carved mahogany high-post bedstead, Philadelphia or Newport, Rhode Island, 1770–1790. It is 87 in. high, 54 in. wide and 79 in. long (218 by 135 by 198 cm).

The leaf-carved balusters are closely related to those on a bed at Winterthur, by tradition from Philadelphia. However, the Winterthur bed has reeded footposts similar to those on a group of beds from Newport; the stop-fluting of this bed is also typical of Newport furniture.

C2 A George III carved rosewood campaign bedstead, of the late 18th century; 90 in. high, 62 in. wide, 78 in. long (225 by 155 by 195 cm). The posts are in two parts, joined by screws at the base of the columns, and the side rails are hinged in the middle to permit folding in half.

Franklin family tradition has it that this bed was owned by George Washington, who used it as a field bed.

C3 *(below)* An important classical brass-mounted mahogany, giltwood and gesso bed, labelled and stamped Charles Honoré Lannuier, New York, *c.* 1812. It is 43 in. high, 57 in. wide and 93 in. long (108 by 143 by 233 cm). The headboard supports are brass inlaid and surmounted by gilt eagle teminals; at the lower end they finish in pressed brass repoussé portrait busts. The scrolled footboard's supports are inlaid with brass and ebony.

The bed bears two printed Lannuier labels – one in French, one in English – and the Lannuier stamp at each interior corner of the frame, together with the impressed name J.B. Cochois, who, it seems, was working as a journeyman in Lannuier's shop at the time the bed was made. The bed formerly belonged to Alfred Seton, partner of John Jacob Astor.

D4 A Federal mahogany and painted wood bedstead from Massachusetts, 1790–1810; 99 in. high, 63 in. wide (248 by 158 cm).

According to the Franklin family this bed was once the property of Oliver Wendell Holmes. The curtains were designed to hang inside the valance rail.

C5 A Federal inlaid and carved mahogany and giltwood four-post bedstead, school of Duncan Phyfe, New York, *c.* 1820; it is 106 in. high, 66 in. wide and 80 in. long (270 by 168 by 203 cm). A similar bedstead is illustrated in McClelland's *Duncan Phyfe and the English Regency*, New York, 1939, plate 111.

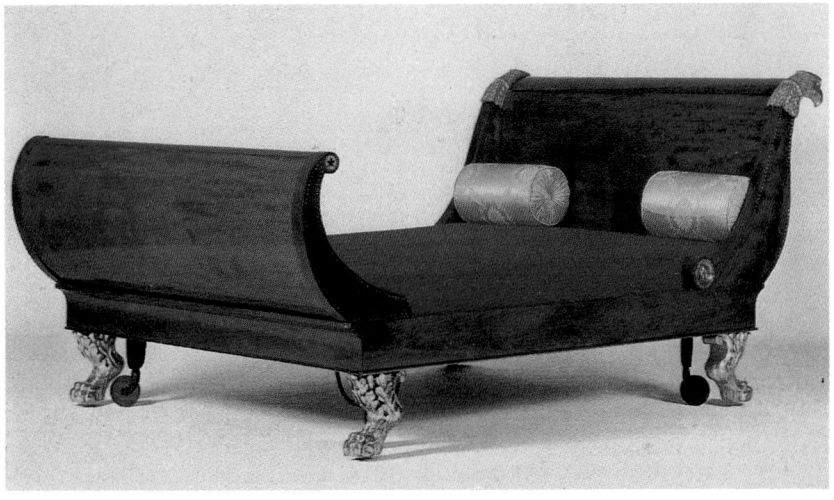

D1 A William and Mary carved walnut child's slant-front desk, New England, 1710–1740; 25 in. high, 21 in. wide, 13 in. deep (62 by 52 by 32 cm). The lid opens to an interior fitted with pigeonholes over small drawers; an interior slide encloses a well behind the dummy top drawer.

C2 *(below)* A fine Chippendale cherrywood desk and bookcase, attributed to Brewster Dayton, Stratford, Connecticut, 1765–1780. It stands 94 in. high and is 43 in. wide (235 by 108 cm).

This piece shows some typical features of furniture made in the Woodbury area of Connecticut: the carved shell on the lower drawer, the sawn profiles of the brackets and the carved paintbrush feet.

C3 A Chippendale carved maple desk and bookcase, Rhode Island, 1750–1780; 82 in. high, 38 in. wide, 19 in. deep (205 by 95 by 48 cm). The piece is in two sections, the fielded panel doors of the upper part opening to a compartmentalized interior.

D4 A Queen Anne curly maple slant-front desk, New England, 1740–1760; 43 in. high, 41 in. wide, 22 in. deep (108 by 105 by 55 cm).

The thumb-moulded lid opens to an interior fitted with ten scallop-valanced pigeonholes above a frieze of five short drawers over two short drawers and an open compartment with two half-pilaster fronted document drawers.

The discolouration of the wood around the handles, suggesting polishing over a long period, is a reasonable indicator of an authentic period piece. The depth of colour is important – whether it is dark or pale is not important – to show the markings of the wood, as is evident here. The slant-front, first and third drawer fronts were made from the same piece of timber: this might not have been so evident when the piece was made.

C5 *(above)* An important Chippendale carved mahogany serpentine fall-front desk, attributed to William King, Salem, Massachusetts. An inscription in a small drawer dates the piece to about 1785. It stands 42 in. high, and is of the same width (105 cm).

The lid opens to a fitted interior with eight valanced pigeonholes above a double tiered frieze of five short drawers over two long drawers; there is an open compartment and flanking document compartments with pilaster covers.

A6 *(left)* A fine Chippendale carved mahogany block-front bonnet-top secretary-bookcase from Boston, Massachusetts, *c.* 1765. Height: 96 in., width: 40 in. (242 by 102 cm). Details of the carving – the corinthian capitals, fluted pilasters and foliate device beneath the bonnet – relate to a similar, larger piece in the Winterthur Museum.

D4 A Federal carved and inlaid curly maple and walnut fall-front desk, Pennsylvania, *c.* 1800. It is 47 in. high, 41 in. wide and 21 in. deep (120 by 103 by 53 cm). The lid bears an oval panel of inlay.

The inlaid valanced tambour doors open to short drawers. The prospect section has its original mirrored interior with curly maple columns and, with the flanking document drawers, fronts three secret drawers.

C1 A Federal inlaid mahogany lady's secretary, in two parts, Boston, Massachusetts, 1790–1810; 85 in. high, 33 in. wide, 20 in. deep (213 by 83 by 49 cm).

C3 A fine Federal inlaid mahogany and birch veneer secretary, New Hampshire, 1789–1815; 88 in. high, 42 in. wide, 20 in. deep (220 by 104 by 51 cm). The upper part has adjustable shelving. Note the French-style splay feet.

C2 A Chippendale walnut serpentine-front fall-front desk, by John Shearer of Martinsburg, Virginia, *c.* 1800; 48 in. high, 46 in. wide (122 by 117 cm).

The centre part is a pull-out prospect section with three small locking drawers. The backboard of the prospect section is marked "Martinsburg" in chalk.

C5 A Federal inlaid mahogany tambour writing desk and bookcase, signed by Timothy Douglas(?), probably from Connecticut, dated 1805; 81 in. high, 43 in. wide, 21 in. deep (203 by 108 by 53 cm).

The piece is made in three sections. The upper cupboard doors open to bookshelves (the section was originally compartmentalized). The tambour doors open to short drawers above ogee valanced pigeonholes, and the lower case consists of a folding writing surface over three long line-inlaid drawers. The signature appears on the interior of the lower case.

B1 An important Queen Anne triple line-inlaid walnut armchair, Newport, Rhode Island, 1730–1750. An interesting feature is the inlay, which was to become a popular decorative device later in the century.

C2 A fine Queen Anne walnut side chair from Philadelphia, 1745–1765.

The shell-carving to the crest rail and knees is particularly fine, so too are the stocking-carved trifid feet. Combined with the tightly carved scrolls to the crest rail, splat and brackets, and the overall colour, such features denote undoubted quality.

C3 *(right)* A Queen Anne tiger maple corner chair, Rhode Island, 1740–1760. Three ring-and-baluster turned legs and one cabriole leg ending in a crisp pad and disc foot. The chair is fitted as a commode.

A4 *(below)* A rare pair of Chippendale carved mahogany side chairs of the Goddard/Townsend school, Newport, Rhode Island, *c.* 1765. They are probably from the same set as a side chair in the Metropolitan Museum – the dimensions of all three are identical, as are the details of carving and construction. See John T. Kirk, *American Chairs, Queen Anne and Chippendale*, New York, 1972, pages 135 and 185.

The overall sturdy character of these chairs is enhanced by the finely turned H and back stretchers to the legs. The carved stop-fluted petals on the knees are an extremely rare feature, and are usually found only on block-and-shell carved case furniture from the Goddard/Townsend workshops.

C5 *(right)* A Chippendale carved mahogany side chair, Philadelphia, *c.* 1770. The convex fluted shell at the centre of the crest rail is flanked by acanthus carving with shell terminals. The crest motif is repeated in the decoration of the vase-form splat and in the carving to the legs. The shell device is repeated on the front rail.

An identical side chair, probably from the same set, is in the Henry Francis du Pont Winterthur Museum; it is illustrated as fig. 124 in Joseph Downs, *American Furniture, Queen Anne And Chippendale Periods*, New York, 1952.

B1 A Chippendale carved mahogany armchair, Philadelphia, 1765–1785.

The scrolls that terminate the crest rail are neatly echoed in the handgrips, and the leaf carving at the centre of the crest rail runs over the joint to the splat and is echoed on the carved skirt.

Of particular interest is the fine pale colour, which is somewhat unusual in mahogany chairs of this period.

D3 A Federal painted and decorated side chair, Philadelphia, *c.* 1795. The legs have been cut down.

This chair was ordered by Elias Hasket Derby for his house in Salem, Massachusetts, and may be one of a set of 24 he bought from Joseph Anthony and Company in 1796. Other examples from the set are in the Winterthur Museum, the Museum of Fine Arts, Boston, and the Metropolitan Museum, New York.

C5 A Queen Anne mahogany easy chair, Massachusetts, 1749–1760,

Apart from the vertically scrolled arm supports and the block-and-turned stretchers it has no decoration and relies entirely for its undoubted quality on proportion.

A2 A Chippendale period mahogany chair by Benjamin Randolph, Philadelphia, 1770–1772.

Of truly outstanding quality, it used to be thought that this chair was of English manufacture. Modern research into Philadelphia chair-making and the work of Randolph has however demonstrated that the piece could certainly have been made in America and the use of white cedar as the secondary timber confirms its origin.

C4 One from a set of six Chippendale carved mahogany side chairs by Samuel Walton, Philadelphia, 1765–1785.

The splat is pierced and carved in simple Gothic style, which creates an interesting contrast to the curvilinear crest rail but is in harmony with the brackets. The legs are beaded, but the stretcher is entirely plain.

B6 A fine Chippendale carved mahogany easy chair, probably from Philadelphia, 1760–1780.

The C-scroll arms and the acanthus-carved knees, together with the secondary woods of oak, pine and poplar, suggest Philadelphia as the source, but the block-and-turned stretchers are more typical of New England. An easy chair with similar stretchers is illustrated in William Macpherson Hornor, *Blue Book of Philadelphia Furniture*, 1977, as plate 376.

C1 A Queen Anne burr walnut-veneered flat-top highboy, Boston, Massachusetts, 1740–1760, in two parts; 77 in. high by 39 in. wide (195 by 98 cm).

B3 A fine Queen Anne carved walnut high chest of drawers, Massachusetts, 1740–1770; 89 in. high by 41 in. wide (223 by 103 cm).

C5 A Queen Anne carved cherrywood high chest of drawers, Connecticut, 1750–1780; 88 in. high by 40 in. wide (220 by 100 cm).

B2 The Danforth family Queen Anne carved curly maple flat-top highboy, North Shore, Massachusetts, *c.* 1745; 69 in. high by 39 in. wide (175 by 99 cm).

C4 A Queen Anne carved walnut bonnet-top highboy, attributed to Joseph Armitt, Philadelphia, *c.* 1755; 86 in. high by 42 in. wide (219 by 107 cm).

A6 A fine Queen Anne walnut high chest of drawers, attributed to the Townsend/Goddard shops, Newport, Rhode Island, 1740–1760; 87 in. high by 39 in. wide (218 by 98 cm).

A1 A Queen Anne mahogany high chest of drawers, Massachusetts, 1750–1770; 84 in. high by 42 in. wide (210 by 105 cm).

C3 A Queen Anne carved birchwood bonnet-top highboy, Connecticut, *c.* 1770; 85 in. high by 39 in. wide (216 by 98 cm).

A5 An important Chippendale carved mahogany chest-on-chest, Philadelphia, 1765–1780; 92 in. high by 45 in. wide (234 by 114 cm).

A2 A fine Queen Anne carved mahogany bonnet-top highboy, Boston, Massachusetts, *c.* 1755; 88 in. high by 41 in. wide (224 by 104 cm).

B4 A Chippendale carved mahogany chest-on-chest, Philadelphia, 1760–1780; 98 in. by 44 in. wide (245 by 110 cm.).

B6 A Chippendale inlaid cherrywood reverse serpentine chest of drawers, Connecticut, 1785–1800; 92 in. high by 41 in. wide (230 by 103 cm.).

C1 A fine Queen Anne figured maple chest of drawers, Pennsylvania, 1750–1770; 40 in. high by 36 in. wide (100 by 90 cm). Of particular note are the fluted quarter columns, the trifid feet and the fine overall colour of the wood.

C4 A small Chippendale mahogany block-front chest of drawers, probably from Boston, Massachusetts, 1760–1780. It stands only 31 in. high and is 34 in. wide (78 by 85 cm). The pendant scallop to the skirt is an attractive feature.

D7 A Federal carved and inlaid mahogany bow-front chest of drawers, Salem, Massachusetts, 1800–1815; 40 in. high by 42 in. wide (100 by 105 cm).

The line-inlaid rectangular panels to the drawer fronts are decorated at each corner with fan spandrels.

D2 A Chippendale carved walnut chest of drawers, Philadelphia, *c.* 1765. It is 36 in. high and almost exactly the same in width (92 cm). Note the fluted quarter columns, original handles and escutcheons.

B5 A Chippendale block-and-shell carved mahogany chest of drawers, Rhode Island or Connecticut, 1765–1780; 34 in. high by 38 in. wide (85 by 95 cm).

The two flanking shell devices to the upper drawer are convex, whereas the central shell is concave.

B8 A Queen Anne carved mahogany block-front kneehole dressing table, Boston, Massachusetts, *c.* 1740; 31 in. high by 36 in. wide (79 by 92 cm).

A single long blocked drawer at the top over the short drawers at the sides. The recessed cupboard with pronounced H-hinges opens to a shelf with a short drawer above.

D3 A Chippendale carved mahogany serpentine-front chest of drawers with widely overhanging top, Massachusetts, *c.* 1770; 32 in. high by 40 in. wide (80 by 100 cm).

C6 A Chippendale carved mahogany small serpentine-front chest of drawers, Salem, Massachusetts, 1770–1790; 34 in. high by 38 in. wide (86 by 95 cm).

Note the particularly fine matching of the veneers and see *American Antiques From the Israel Sack Collection*, 1974, vol. V, p. 1258.

B9 A fine Chippendale walnut block-front kneehole bureau, Boston, Massachusetts, 1760–1780; 30 in. high by 36 in. wide (75 by 90 cm).

The piece is reputed to have belonged to Governor Wentworth of New Hampshire.

A1 A rare Federal inlaid mahogany and bird's eye maple dressing bureau, attributed to John and Thomas Seymour, Boston, Massachusetts, 1794–1816; 75 in. high by 36 in. wide by 21 in. deep (188 by 90 by 53 cm). The square tapering legs are characteristic Seymour.

C2 A Queen Anne walnut dressing table, probably from Portsmouth, New Hampshire, 1740–1770; 29 in. high by 34 in. wide (73 by 85 cm). Of fine colour, with one long drawer over three short.

B3 A Chippendale carved walnut dressing table, Lancaster, Pennsylvania, 1765–1785; 30 in. high by 38 in. wide (75 by 95 cm). Lancaster County dressing tables are very rare.

B5 A Chippendale carved walnut dressing table, Philadelphia, 1760–1780; 32 in. high by 36 in. wide (80 by 90 cm). The front corners of the top are cusped; pierced carving to the centre drawer.

B6 A Chippendale carved mahogany lowboy, Philadelphia, c. 1770; 32 in. high by 34 in. wide (80 by 85 cm).

B4 (left) A Federal inlaid satinwood and mahogany lady's writing desk or bonheur du jour, attributed to Duncan Phyfe, New York, c. 1805; 41 in. high by 25 in. wide (104 by 62 cm).
The piece is in two parts; the upper with tambour slides opening to a fitted interior, the lower with a fold-out writing surface.

B7 (above) A Federal period gilt-bronze mounted mahogany Carlton House writing desk, early 19th century; 66 in. wide (158 cm), with hinged writing flap.

B2 *(below)* A Chippendale mahogany double chair-back settee, Massachusetts, 1760–1780. It is 39 in. high, 61 in. long and 27 in. deep (98 by 153 by 68 cm).

Double chair-back settees are rare in the history of the American Colonies; most of the known examples originated in Massachusetts. They are discussed in an article by Wendy A. Cooper: "American Chippendale Chairback Settees: Some Sources and Related Examples", in *The American Art Journal*, IX (November, 1977) pages 34–5. The settee illustrated here appears as figure 8 in the Cooper article, in which it is related to two similar examples: one of them is in the Winterthur Museum; the other is privately owned.

It may be that the form never took extensive hold in the Colonial period because the shape strikes the eye familiar with the Chippendale armchair as distorted and, perhaps, inelegant. The backs are unduly wide, with an unfamiliarly large space between splats and stiles. And however well the centre stiles are managed, they descend visually to a single leg, raising a certain unease.

A1 *(above)* A Chippendale mahogany sofa, Philadelphia, 1760–1780. It is 41 in. high, 88 in. long and 32 in. deep (103 by 220 by 80 cm).

The Marlborough legs are moulded and beaded, the stretchers completely plain. The brackets are carved and pierced in the rococo style and represent an unusual feature on American sofas of this period.

The serpentine shape to the front seat rail is another indication of fine quality, and reflects the generous sweep to the back. The high, deeply scrolled arms complete the proportion of a fine and important piece of furniture.

Sofas of this size and authenticity are by no means common and are examples of American seat furniture at its best.

B3 *(left)* A rare Federal carved mahogany sofa from Salem, Massachusetts, 1794–1800. It is 29 in. high and 88 in. long (72 by 221 cm).

The moulded serpentine crest is of Cupid's bow form with an elegant dip to mark the central decoration; the rather severely scrolled arms end in elaborately carved rosettes. The square tapered legs are carved with bows and pendant grapes.

This sofa shows American seat furniture in an interesting transitional stage. The design still retains the outlines of the Chippendale style in the sweeping back and scrolled arms. The lines, however, are altogether cleaner and the shape is much lighter, indicating the ideas of Adam and the interpretation of Hepplewhite. The proportions of the legs and front arm supports are still very much in the mid-18th century manner, while their tapering shape and carved decoration show a definite tendency towards the style of the first two sofas on the next page.

B1 *(right)* An inlaid mahogany and birch veneer settee, attributed to John and Thomas Seymour, Boston, Massachusetts, 1794–1816; 37 in. high, 78 in. long (93 by 195 cm).

Fine workmanship is shown in the patterned stringing to the crest and seat rails, the use of birch veneering, which is a difficult timber to lay successfully, and the teardrop-shaped ebonized panels of inlay to the front of the arm supports and legs. The legs have a Grecian curve or sabre-shape and terminate with a collar and spade foot. Such features show certain European influences, particularly English Regency and French during the Empire period.

It is interesting to note that by this period it was popular to have show wood round the entire frame of the sofa.

B2 *(left)* A Federal carved and veneered mahogany small settee, Salem, Massachusetts, 1800–1810. It measures 39 in. high by 58 in. wide (98 by 145 cm).

Sofas of this type show a definite influence of Sheraton, who advised that if carving the top rail were too much work, it could be left plain. Most Salem-made sofas of fine quality will however, like this one, carry such carving and the central panel often shows a basket of fruit. An example with an eagle is illustrated in *American Furniture: The Federal Period*, Charles F. Montgomery, Viking, New York, 1966, plate 270.

A closely related settee is in the Garvan Collection at Yale University Art Gallery.

A3 *(right)* A Federal carved mahogany settee, attributed to Duncan Phyfe, New York, 1800–1810. It is 31 in. high and 74in. wide (76 by 185 cm).

All the front-facing stiles and rails are reeded. The paired cornucopias of the central reserve to the crest rail are repeated in the reserves of the scrolled arm rests and a pair of fine lions' heads terminate the seat rail. The back legs as well as the front have hairy paw feet.

Decorative features such as the cornucopia and hairy paw foot remained in popularity during the first half of the 19th century, but examples dating after the 1820s will show a considerable and increasing heaviness.

The settee shown here is closely similar in form to the New York carved mahogany settee now in the Art Institute of Chicago, which is illustrated in Milo M. Naeve, *Identifying American Furniture*, Nashville, 1981, figure 41.

D 1 The General Knox Chippendale carved mahogany candlestand, Massachusetts, 1769–1780. It stands 28 in. high and is 20 in. wide by 15 in. deep (70 by 50 by 38 cm).

According to tradition, the original owner of this fine stand was Major-General Henry Knox (1750–1806), officer in the Revolution and later Secretary of War.

C 2 A small Queen Anne mahogany card table, Boston, 1740–1760; 28 in. high, 29 in. wide, 14 in. deep (70 by 73 by 35 cm).

Larger Boston card tables with turreted corners are known in greater numbers (see the following piece), but only two other small turret-tops from Boston are known. One, illustrated in Richard R. Randall, *American Furniture*, 1965, as figure 7, is in the Museum of Fine Arts, Boston. The other is illustrated in Israel Sack, *American Antiques*, volume IV at page 1068.

B 3 A Queen Anne mahogany turret-top card table, Massachusetts, 1740–1760; 27 in. high, 34 in. wide and 16 in. deep (68 by 85 by 40 cm).

The English influence on American furniture is never more apparent than in card tables of this type, there being little variation in the proportions. Things to look for are good, bold turrets, and an elegant, strong curve to the leg.

A 4 A Chippendale mahogany circular card table, probably by John Goddard, Newport, Rhode Island, 1760–1780; it stands 26 in. high and its diameter is 36 in. (65 by 89 cm). Note that the forward leg is carved and ends in a ball-and-claw foot, whereas the other three are plain, ending in pad feet.

C 5 A Chippendale mahogany card table, New York, 1760–1780; 28 in. high, 35 in. wide, 17 in. deep (70 by 88 by 43 cm). The corners are prominently square against the marked serpentine waist of the top, and the table is supported on five legs – compare the open card table in the next column.

B 6 A Chippendale mahogany card table, Philadelphia, 1765–1785. It is 28 in. high and 35 in. wide (70 by 88 cm). The carving to the frieze rails is blind fret and is in harmony with the pierced brackets, both being in Chinese Chippendale style. In contrast, but quite contemporary, are the ribbon carving to the edge of the top and the moulded, beaded legs.

B 7 A Chippendale mahogany gaming table, New York, 1765–1785; 28 in. high, 33 in. wide and 17 in. deep when closed (71 by 82 by 43 cm). The table is marked "MWM" and formerly had a secret drawer, hidden behind the swing leg.

A 8 An important Chippendale carved mahogany card table, Boston or Salem, Massachusetts, 1760–1780; 29 in. high, 34 in. wide, 17 in. deep (73 by 85 by 43 cm).

The bottom edge of the apron is carved with an egg and dart border, the knees are star-punched with acanthus carving.

C1 A Chippendale carved mahogany card table, Boston, Massachusetts, 1765–1785; 29 in. high, 32 in. wide and 15 in. deep when closed (73 by 80 by 38 cm). Its delicacy derives from the scalloping of the apron and the intrusion on the apron of the carved knees.

A3 A Chippendale straight-front mahogany "hairy-paw-foot" card table, attributed to Thomas Affleck, Philadelphia, *c.* 1770; 32 in. wide (81 cm). The carving on the legs and frieze edge is particularly fine.

D4 A Federal inlaid mahogany and flame-figured birch veneer card table, North Shore, Massachusetts, 1790–1810; 28 in. high by 37 in. wide opening to 36 in. deep (70 by 93 by 90 cm).

A2 An important Federal carved and inlaid mahogany card table, the carving attributed to Samuel McIntire, Salem, Massachusetts, *c.* 1798. The table is 30 in. high, 49 in. in diameter, and 25 in. deep when closed (75 by 123 by 62 cm).

The carving of glyphs and flower heads on the edge, taken with the fine bead mouldings on the frieze, suggest McIntire, as they are nearly identical to those on a pair of card tables, with carving attributed to McIntire, made for Elias Hasket Derby of Salem and now in the Karolik Collection in the Museum of Fine Arts in Boston. The very fine carved basket of flowers on the frieze shows strong stylistic resemblance to the carving on a chest-on-chest made for Elizabeth Derby for which a bill of sale, dated 1796, exists from McIntire.

D5 A Federal carved mahogany trick-leg card table, New York, 1800–1820; 30 in. high, 36 in. wide (75 by 90 cm).

The top has inset clover-leaf corners with a turned pendant to each; waterleaf carving to the urn-shaped pedestal is repeated (inverted) on the upper part of the legs.

C6 An Empire mahogany veneer, gilt and painted wood card table, New York, *c.* 1825; 29 in. high by 36 in. wide (73 by 93 cm).

The resurgence of the dolphin as a feature on furniture was possibly stronger in Europe than in America during the first quarter of the 19th century.

C1 A Chippendale mahogany single drop-leaf table, Massachusetts, 1760–1780; 26 in. high, 33 in. wide, 33 in. deep when open (65 by 83 by 83 cm).

A related piece appears in Joseph Downs, *American Furniture: Queen Anne and Chippendale Periods,* New York, 1952, no. 310.

C2 A small Chippendale mahogany drop-leaf table with scalloped apron and ball-and-claw feet, Massachusetts, 1760–1780; 28 in. high, 36 in. wide, 36 in. deep with the flaps raised (70 by 90 by 90 cm).

B4 *(above)* A Chippendale mahogany drop-leaf table from the Goddard/Townsend shop, Newport, Rhode Island, 1765–1785. It stands 28 in. high and the top measures 54 by 58 in. (71 by 137 by 147 cm).

Note the open talons to the feet. Three other oval drop-leaf dining tables are known with this feature, one signed by John Townsend.

C5 *(left)* A Federal inlaid mahogany mixing table, Connecticut or Rhode Island, 1790–1810; 29 in. high, 28 in. wide, 21 in. deep (73 by 70 by 53 cm). There is a slide at either end and the legs are decorated with bookend, icicle and line inlay.

B6 *(below)* A Chippendale carved mahogany Pembroke table, attributed to John Townsend, Newport, Rhode Island, 1760–1780; 26 in. high, 35 in. wide, 19 in. deep with flaps closed (65 by 88 by 48 cm). The attribution to Townsend is made on the basis of a similar labelled example in the Winterthur Museum.

B3 A fine Queen Anne mahogany handkerchief table, Massachusetts, 1740–1770; 27 in. high, top 24 in. square with the leaf up (68 by 60 cm).

A similar corner table, now in the collection of Colonial Williamsburg, is illustrated in Barry A. Greenlaw, *New England Furniture at Williamsburg,* 1974, no. 134.

D1 A Federal inlaid mahogany Pembroke table, New York, 1790–1820. It stands 29 in. high and the top measures 22 in. by 28 in. (73 by 55 by 70 cm).

B2 A Queen Anne walnut tea table from Newport, Rhode Island, 1730–1760; 26 in. high, 32 in. wide, 20 in. deep (67 by 82 by 51 cm). The legs are octagonally chamfered down to the octagonal cuffs. The colour is particularly fine.

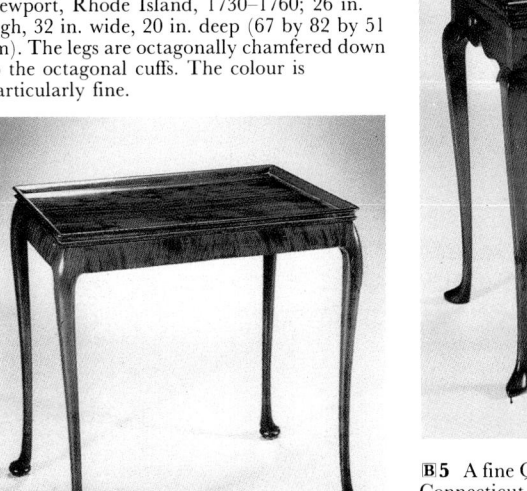

C3 A Queen Anne carved walnut tea table, New York, 1735–1755, 28 in. high, 20 in. wide, 29 in. deep (70 by 50 by 73 cm). The apron is bolection moulded and there is plain relief carving to the knees.

B4 A Queen Anne mahogany "tuck-away" tea table, with two swing legs and two fixed, Boston, Massachusetts, 1740–1765; 26 in. high, 25 in. diameter (65 by 63 cm).

Other examples of this extremely rare form are illustrated in Wallace Nutting, *Furniture Treasury*, 1948, vol. I, figure 1297, and Richard Randall, *American Furniture in the Museum of Fine Arts, Boston*, at pp.116–18. The example illustrated in Israel Sack, *American Antiques*, 1979, vol. VI at p.1450 is also of mahogany and may be from the same workshop.

B5 A fine Queen Anne cherrywood tea table, Connecticut, 1740–1770. It stands 27 in. high and the top measures 23 by 17 in. (68 by 58 by 43 cm).

The squared inward angles of the legs are carried unusually far down towards the slipper feet and the knees too show a sharp rectangular edge, elegantly designed in the cabriole form. There is a candle slide at either end.

B6 The Fisher family Chippendale carved mahogany tilt-top tea table, Philadelphia, *c.* 1770, 28 in. high by 32 in. diameter (71 by 82 cm).

The top revolves above a birdcage support over a ring and flattened ball standard. The underside of the top bears an engraved metal plate recording the first owner, Thomas Fisher, and some of his descendants over nearly two centuries.

B7 A Chippendale tiger maple birdcage tea table from Lancaster, Pennsylvania, 1760–1780. It stands 29 in. high and the top is almost 35 in. in diameter (73 by 88 cm).

The table has a piecrust top tilting over an octagonal birdcage with baluster turned supports. The stem and tripod supports are carved with classical and foliate motifs, terminating in ball-and-claw feet.

B 1 A Federal mahogany work table, labelled Duncan Phyfe, New York, 1800–1820; 31 in. high, 20 in. wide, 13 in. deep (78 by 50 by 33 cm). The astragal top lifts above a fitted interior with hinged work surface (the drawer-front is a dummy), three small compartments (one covered), flanked by two deep demi-lune compartments.

C 2 *(right)* An historical Federal carved wood gilt and églomisé mirror, probably American, from the early 19th century, 56 in. (140 cm) high. The oval panel has the inscription "To The Memory of His Excellency Genl George Washington" surrounding a wreath enclosing a monument and the word "Liberty".

C 3 A Federal inlaid mahogany small sideboard, attributed to Thomas Howard, Providence, Rhode Island, *c.* 1800; 40 in. high, 45 in. wide (101 by 115 cm).

D 4 A small Federal inlaid mahogany sideboard, Baltimore, 1790–1819; 40 in. high, 48 in. wide, 22 in. deep (100 by 120 by 55 cm). Two drawers over a pair of doors flanked by bottle drawers, all doors and drawers line inlaid, as are the canted tapering legs.

C 5 *(above)* A Federal inlaid mahogany marble top commode, probably Boston, 1790–1810; 37 in. high, 45 in. wide (93 by 114 cm). One bow-front drawer over two cupboard doors flanked by hinged cupboard doors ornamented with sham drawer pulls.

C 6 *(left)* A carved and painted pine chest-over-drawer, 32 in. high, 48 in. wide, 18 in. deep (80 by 120 by 45 cm). The date 1703 is inscribed on the top. The channel mouldings and the punchwork used to decorate the front are typical of chests made in the Connecticut River Valley between Wethersfield and Deerfield at about this date.

SETTEES & SOFAS
1780-1870

American-made sofas or upholstered settees are known from the late 17th century. Fine early examples from Philadelphia depended entirely on their handsome lines – swept up backs and deeply scrolling arms.

But ownership of these luxury items appears to have been confined to the well-to-do, even in the Federal period, and it was not until about 1840 that sofas became standard items in ordinary American homes.

C 1 A rare Federal inlaid mahogany double chairback settee, attributed to the Seymour workshop, Boston, *c.* 1805; 35 in. high by 41 in. wide (87 by 104 cm).

Sofas

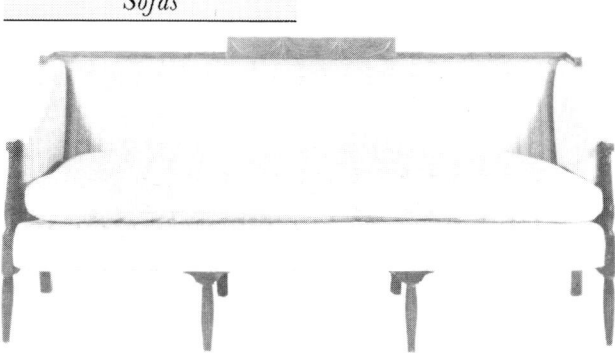

D 5 A Federal carved sofa, New York State, 1780-1800; 34 in. high by 80 in. wide (86 by 203 cm), the seat rail bowed, on four reeded front legs with slightly splayed back legs.

Settees

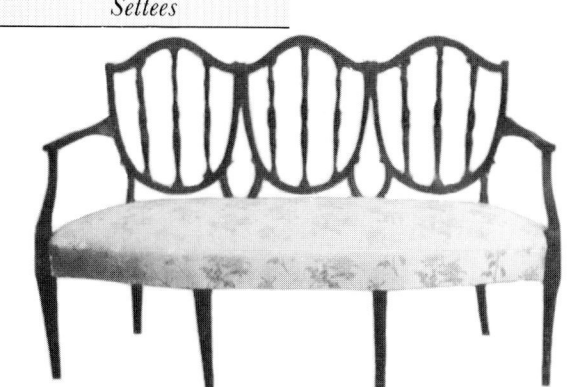

D 2 An American Hepplewhite settee, *c.* 1785. The three shieldbacks are handled with fine grace, with no trace of discord between their verticals and those of the legs.

D 6 A Chippendale mahogany camel-back sofa, probably Massachusetts, 1780-1800; 36 in. high by 86 in. long (91 by 218 cm).

E 3 A Federal fancy painted settee, New York or Connecticut, *c.* 1810-1820; 32 in. high by 79 in. wide (80 by 200 cm). All-over grain painted with gilt highlights.

D 7 A Federal mahogany cabriole sofa on square tapering legs, probably Massachusetts, 1790-1810. It is 30 in. high and 76 in. wide (91 by 193 cm).

E 4 A turned Windsor settee, probably Pennsylvania, *c.* 1800; 83 in. (216 cm) long. The shaped back continues to scrolled knuckle hand-holds on turned supports.

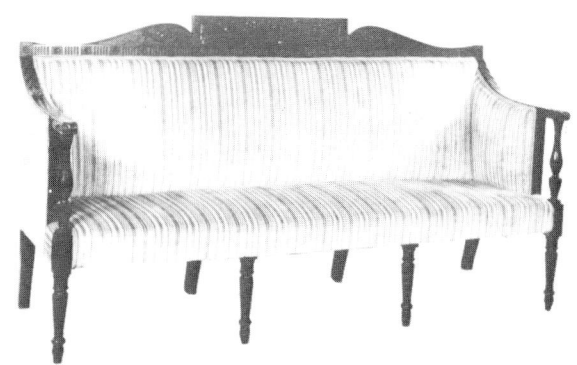

D 8 A Federal carved mahogany sofa, Salem, Massachusetts, 1800-1810; 40 in. high by 76 in. wide (99 by 191 cm).

Compare figure 226 in Patricia E. Kane, *300 Years of American Seating Furniture*, Boston, 1976.

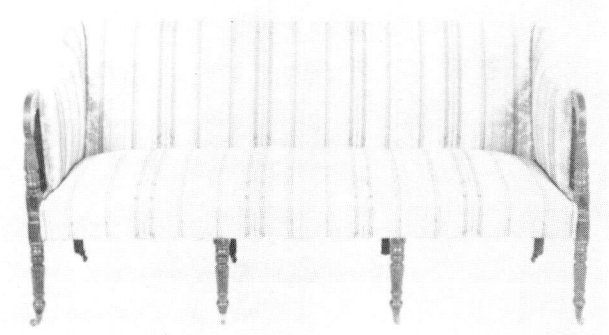

D 1 A Federal mahogany sofa, 1800-1820; 36 in. high by 72 in. long (90 by 181 cm).
The upholstered arms end in down-turned reeded hand-holds on turned and reeded arm supports over similar tapering legs.

D 2 A Federal carved mahogany sofa, attributed to the shop of Duncan Phyfe, New York, 1800-1820; 38 in. high by 81 in. wide (95 by 204 cm). The crest rail with three carved panels centring swags, the rest of the frame reeded and carved on turned legs.

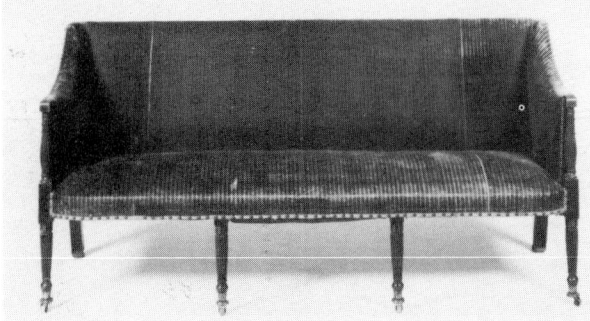

D 3 A Federal carved mahogany sofa, New York or Baltimore, 1805-1815; 64 in. (163 cm) long. The arm supports reeded over similar tapering legs, the stuffed-over seat rail bowed.

D 4 A late Federal carved walnut sofa, New England, c. 1815, the plain roll-back crest continuing to moulded scroll arms on scrolled supports, on turned, reeded legs; 35 in. high, 75 in. wide (89 by 190 cm).

D 5 A Federal carved mahogany sofa, New York, c. 1815, with moulded crest and reeded arm supports on reeded tapering legs; 78 in. (198 cm) long.

E 6 A rare Federal carved mahogany Récamier, New York, 1800-1820; 32 in. high by 89 in. long (89 by 225 cm).

A 7 A Federal carved mahogany settee, attributed to the shop of Duncan Phyfe, New York, 1810-1820; 33 in. high by 62 in. wide (83 by 157 cm).

D 8 A late Federal mahogany sofa, New York, 1810-1820, with carved crest rail and tablets to the reeded seat rail; 34 in. high by 71 in. wide (86 by 181 cm).

D 1 A Federal mahogany sofa, the shaped crest rail carved with acanthus, the scrolling arms finished with flowerheads, the show wood to the front all reeded, with carved tablets heading the cyma-curved legs, *c.* 1815; 72 in. (184 cm) wide.

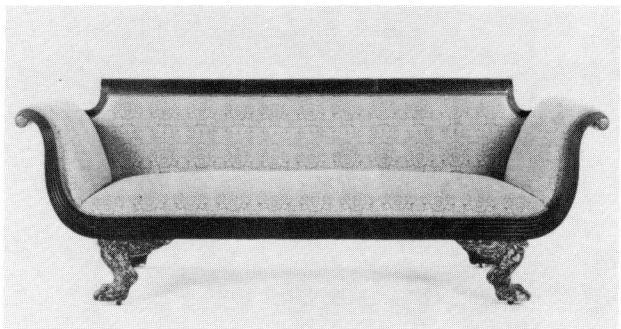

D 2 An Empire mahogany sofa, the back with a panelled crest rail, the arms with scrolling supports, reeded like the apron, on legs carved with spread wings terminating in paw feet, 1810–1830; 92 in. (234 cm) wide.

D 3 A late Federal carved mahogany sofa, New York, 19th century; 34 in. high by 91 in. wide (86 by 231 cm).

E 4 An Empire carved mahogany sofa, probably New York, 1825–1835; 88 in. (223 cm) wide.
The severe restraint of the neoclassical model (see no. 8 opposite) is re-interpreted in a broad, profusely scrolling form with equally lavish carving.

Settees, Federal and Later
The most popular model for Federal settees and sofas was the square type, which can be seen to have originated in the designs favoured by George Hepplewhite and Thomas Sheraton.
After 1802, following the earliest known description of a Grecian chair, Sheraton attempted to describe the style: thereafter the scroll-end sofa and settee, with its obvious reflections of the antique couch, overcame the imagination of American furniture makers. The model was ideally suited to receive increasingly heavy foliate carving as the century progressed, and when strictly antique styles fell from favour the tradition of heavy carving was maintained through the profusion of later 19th-century seat furniture styles. This degree of intricate ornament can be admirable in its own right, but too often it obscured and made ponderous lines that should have been fine, light and graceful.

E 5 An Empire carved mahogany settee, New York, second quarter of the 19th century, profusely carved; 70 in. (177 cm) wide.

D 6 A rococo revival laminated rosewood parlour suite, comprising a settee, a gentleman's chair and two side chairs, attributed to J.J. Meeks, New York, *c.* 1855.

E 7 A rococo revival walnut parlour suite, *c.* 1855, the settee with flaring wings centering an oval back, the chairs with carved crest rails and brackets imitating the shape of the settee arms; serpentine seats to both settee and chairs.

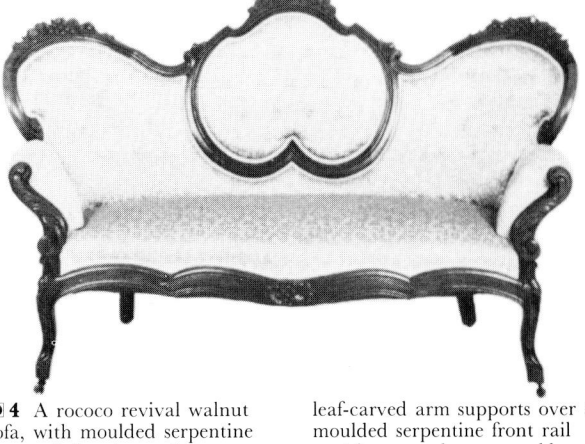

E1 A Victorian rococo revival rosewood sofa, with upholstered back, framed with carved and pierced C- and S-scrolls, with floral and fruit bouquets, the moulded and scrolled arms with upholstered arm pads, leading to serpentine seat rail, on moulded legs with casters, possibly Southern, *c.* 1860; 68 in. (172 cm) long.

D4 A rococo revival walnut sofa, with moulded serpentine crest rail forming a three-part back, each lobe with carved grapes and flowers at crest, continuing to S-scrolled, leaf-carved arm supports over a moulded serpentine front rail centring carved grapes and leaves, terminating in moulded French feet, *c.* 1860; 40 in. high by 66 in. wide (101 by 167 cm).

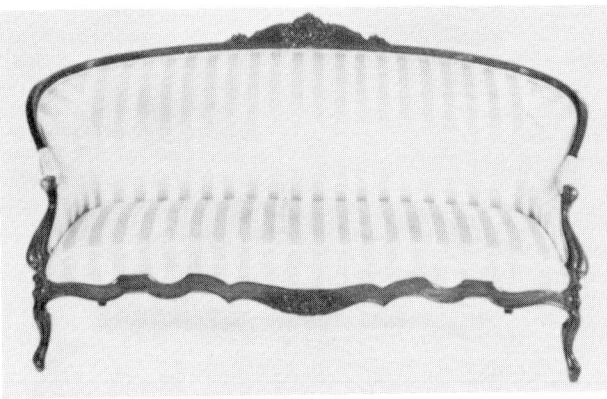

E2 A rococo revival rosewood sofa, with sweeping moulded crest rail centring a panel carved with baroque-style cartouche continuing to moulded serpentine arm supports, above a scalloped serpentine skirt with carved cartouches in the centre and on the knees, above moulded French feet, American, *c.* 1860; 41 in. high by 80 in. wide (104 by 203 cm).

E5 A Renaissance revival walnut sofa, the back in three padded sections, each surrounded by a pierced and carved frame, with a carved scrolling crest rail, separated by pierced quatrefoils, with carved padded open arms, the upholstered shaped seat with incised front rail, with three pendants, attributed to Thomas Brooks & Company, Brooklyn, New York, 1865-1875; 70 in. (178 cm) long.

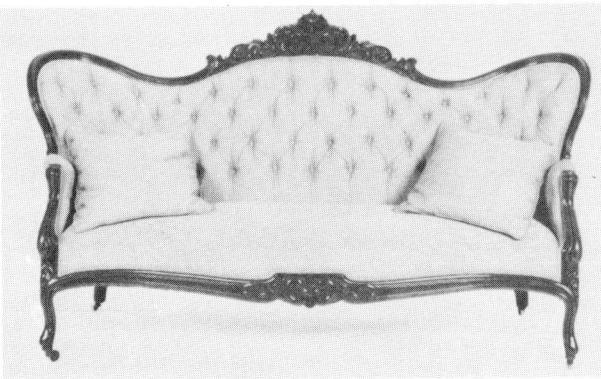

D3 A rococo revival mahogany sofa, with serpentine moulded crest rail centring carved foliate cartouche flanked by acanthus leaves and volutes, the serpentine moulded arm supports above the upholstered seat, the serpentine skirt centring a carved foliate cartouche with scrolls and leaves, continuing to moulded French feet on casters, American, *c.* 1860; 43 in. high by 81 in. wide (109 by 205 cm).

E6 An Eastlake walnut canape, the shaped back with pierced foliate crest centring a female mask, the sides carved with lions' heads and bearded warriors, raised on short turned legs, *c.* 1865; 72 in. (183 cm).

SIDEBOARDS
1785-1830

By the 1780s the sideboard had come a long way from its origins in the medieval dresser, so called because it was used as a serving board upon which food was "dressed". The essential purpose however, was similar, for the sideboard could be used to serve food, and to store the accessories required throughout sometimes prolonged meals.

A significant change occurred in the early 19th century when the cupboard-type sideboard became more popular. In contrast to this the severely architectural pedestal sideboard of the 1830s provided an alternative and was often made *en suite* with a large wine cooler in the space between the pedestals.

D4 A Federal inlaid mahogany sideboard, probably Baltimore, 1790-1810; 40 in. high by 73 in. wide (101 by 184 cm).

E1 A Federal inlaid mahogany sideboard, Virginia or Charleston, South Carolina, 1785-1815; 39 in. high by 72 in. wide (99 by 182 cm).

E5 A Federal inlaid mahogany sideboard, probably Massachusetts, 1790-1810; 41 in. high by 68 in. wide (104 by 171 cm).

E2 A Federal mahogany inlaid sideboard, American, 1790-1810; 42 in. high by 68 in. wide (105 by 173 cm).

E6 A Federal inlaid mahogany sideboard, probably Maryland, 1790-1810; 39 in. high by 72 in. wide (99 by 183 cm).

E3 A Federal inlaid mahogany sideboard, all drawers and doors with figured veneer, with triple line inlaid borders, New York, 1790-1810; 41 in. high by 70 in. wide (104 by 178 cm).

E7 A Federal inlaid mahogany sideboard, probably Southern, 1790-1810; 40 in. high by 72 in. wide (100 by 183 cm).

E 1 A Federal inlaid mahogany sideboard, the upper centre drawer being fitted for writing, Massachusetts, 1790-1810; 41 in. high by 59 in. wide (103 by 148 cm).

D 2 A Federal mahogany sideboard, the drawers and case line inlaid, the legs inlaid with husks, New York, 1790-1810; 40 in. high by 77 in. wide (100 by 195 cm).

E 3 A Federal inlaid mahogany sideboard incorporating a slide over the upper drawers, Massachusetts, 1790-1810; 40 in. high by 70 in. wide (101 by 177 cm).

E 4 A Federal inlaid and veneered mahogany sideboard of kidney shape, Philadelphia, 1790-1810; 74 in. (187 cm) wide.

E 5 A Federal mahogany sideboard with shaped bow-fronted central drawer and two recessed serpentine shaped cupboards, flanked by concave drawers and cupboards, probably Massachusetts, 1790-1810; 65 in. (166 cm) wide.

E 6 A Federal mahogany inlaid sideboard, kidney-shaped, with concave central section centring a shaped horizontal drawer above two shaped cupboard doors, flanked by bowed hinged cupboards; the drawers, door and sides of the case all with line inlay and inlaid urn keyhole escutcheons, Pennsylvania, 1790-1810; 38 in. high by 75 in. wide, (98 by 190 cm).

E 7 A Federal walnut sideboard, with a deep drawer and cupboard door centring a short drawer over a cupboard, on tapering legs, the straight skirt and legs edged with quarter round moulding, Middle Atlantic States, 1790-1810; 33 in. high by 46 in. wide (83 by 118 cm).

E1 A Federal inlaid mahogany sideboard with central long line-inlaid drawer above similar cupboard doors and flanked by short drawers over deep bottle drawers, possibly Kentucky, 1790-1810; 39 in. high by 66 in. wide (99 by 167 cm).

E2 A Federal inlaid mahogany sideboard, with central long drawer over two recessed hinged cupboards, flanked by a deep drawer and a deep cupboard, all inlaid, Middle States, 1790-1810.

D3 A Federal inlaid mahogany serpentine front sideboard, with shaped top and central long drawer above recessed double doors flanked by two cupboards, all with corner fan inlay and string borders, New York, *c.* 1790.

D4 A Federal inlaid mahogany sideboard, with serpentine front, with one long drawer flanked by two cupboard doors, on square tapering line and bellflower-inlaid legs, Baltimore, *c.* 1790; 40 in. high by 72 in. wide (102 by 184 cm).

E5 A Hepplewhite mahogany sideboard, with serpentine front, New York, *c.* 1790; 72 in. long, 39 in. wide (183 by 99 cm).

E6 A Federal inlaid mahogany sideboard, New York, *c.* 1795; 39 in. high by 74 in. wide (99 by 186 cm).

E7 A Federal mahogany veneer sideboard, *c.* 1800; 42 in. high by 72 in. wide (107 by 181 cm).

D8 A Sheraton mahogany sideboard by Thomas Seymour, with finely figured veneer and panelled doors on fluted, reeded and carved legs, Boston, *c.* 1800; 77 in. (195 cm) wide.

E1 A Federal mahogany sideboard, eastern Connecticut, 1800-1815; 42 in. high by 52 in. wide (106 by 132 cm).

E2 A Federal mahogany sideboard, New York, 1790-1810; 39 in. by 77 in. (100 by 195 cm). The concave side drawers flank a bow-front central drawer, the legs inlaid with husks.

E3 A well figured Federal inlaid mahogany sideboard on reeded legs, Massachusetts, 1790-1810; 42 in. high by 71 in. wide (106 by 179 cm).

E4 A late Federal mahogany sideboard, New York, 1810-1830; 51 in. high, 73 in. wide (129 by 184 cm). The brass-galleried top above three drawers over four cupboard doors.

E5 An Empire mahogany veneer sideboard, attributed to the shop of Duncan Phyfe, New York, 1815-1820; 53 in. high by 72 in. wide (134 by 183 cm).

E6 An Empire carved mahogany sideboard flamboyantly veneered and on hairy paw feet, New York, 1820-1830; 46 in. high by 74 in. wide (117 by 188 cm).

E7 An Empire marble top mahogany sideboard, probably Boston, 1820-1830; 40 in. high by 63 in. wide (103 by 160 cm).

E8 A mahogany pedestal sideboard, c. 1830; 89 in. (226 cm) wide. The pedimented top over three cushion drawers on pedestals carved with lobing.

STANDS
1730-1880

The term "stand" has for a long time been used to describe a huge variety of small and occasional tables as well as those pieces made for a specific purpose such as candle, wig or wash stands. The classic candlestand of the type illustrated here could be of fixed-top or tilt-top form, or both tilting and revolving over a bridcage. The presence of a paler conforming patch where the birdcage meets the top is a valuable pointer toward authenticity.

Candlestands

E1 A painted candlestand on trestle base, New England, 1730-1750; 27 in. high by 24 in. wide (68 by 61 cm).

E2 A Queen Anne mahogany candlestand, Newport, Rhode Island, 1740-1770; 27 in. (67 cm) high.

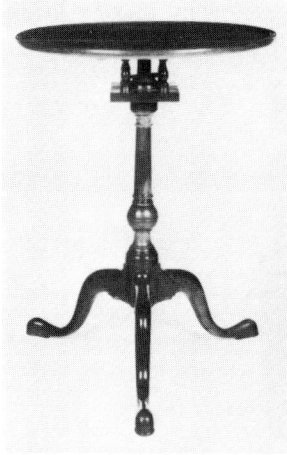

D3 A Queen Anne figured mahogany candlestand, Newport, Rhode Island, 1740-1770; 26 in. high, 21 in. diameter (66 by 54 cm).

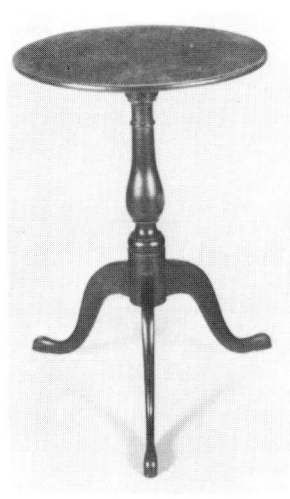

E4 A Chippendale walnut dish-top candlestand, Philadelphia, 1740-1780; 30 in. high, 22 in. wide (76 by 56 cm).

E5 A Chippendale mahogany tilt-top stand, Philadelphia, *c.* 1750-1780; 26 in. high by 21 in. diameter (66 by 53 cm).

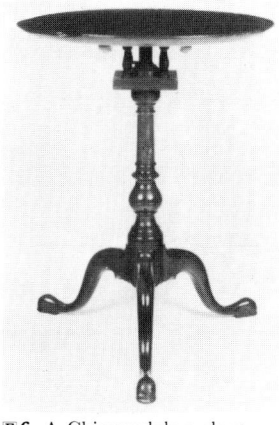

E6 A Chippendale walnut dish-top candlestand, Philadelphia, 1760-1780; 29 in. high by 24 in. diameter (74 by 61 cm).

D7 A Chippendale walnut dish-top candlestand, Philadelphia, 1760-1780; 28 in. high by 22 in. across (71 by 56 cm).

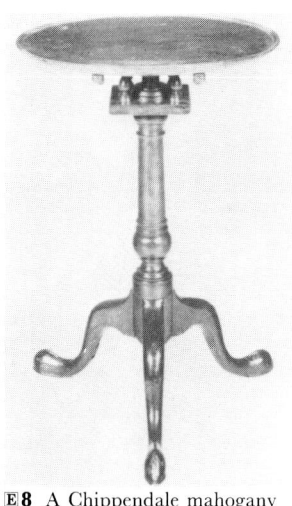

E8 A Chippendale mahogany birdcage candlestand, Philadelphia, 1760-1780; 28 in. high by 21 in. diameter (71 by 51 cm).

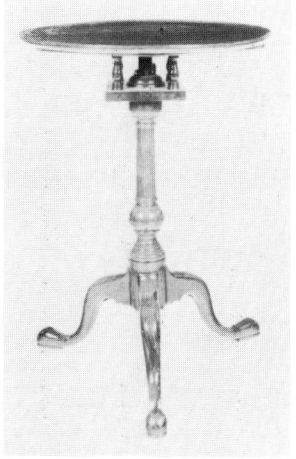

E9 A Chippendale walnut dish-top candlestand, Philadelphia, 1760-1780; 29 in. high by 23 in. diameter (73 by 58 cm).

E10 A Chippendale walnut dish-top stand, Pennsylvania, 1760-1790; 28 in. high by 25 in. diameter (71 by 64 cm).

E11 A Federal mahogany tilt-top stand, possibly New York, 1780-1800; 27 in. high by 22 in. diameter (69 by 56 cm).

The Alteration of Stands

The tops of tripod-based candlestands were often given serpentine edges, oval or octagonal shapes, but the finest 18th-century examples are unquestionably those with a dished top and Chippendale or piecrust border. It is not unknown for plain circular tops to have been dished and carved at a later date – evidence of this may be rows of marks where the dishing has come too close to the fixing screws.

Because of the commercial desirability of such stands, in comparison to the value placed on pole screens earlier this century, the one has often been made out of the other by the removal of the pole and the addition of a top; however the height of the top turning will be greater on a stand than on a pole screen base.

To confuse matters thoroughly, the maker sometimes incorporated a small drawer at the top of the column, as in no. 5 on page 91, and the authenticity of such rare items has to be established by other means, such as patina, signs of use and, of course, compatible timbers.

Tripod tables should always be checked for damage. Any untoward pressure on the top that does not break the junction to the column is transmitted directly to the point where the legs meet and can split the dovetails. A metal plate fitted under the joint may be contemporary, to forestall such damage, or later, securing a repair.

E 2 A Chippendale mahogany candlestand, Massachusetts, 1760-1780; 28 in. high and 19 in. diameter (71 by 48 cm).

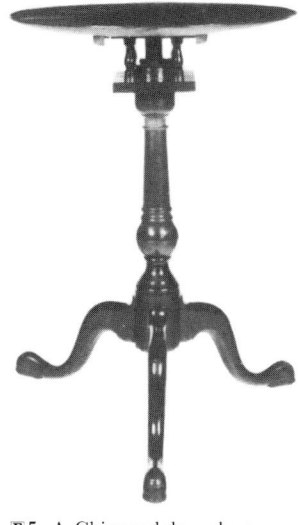

E 5 A Chippendale walnut dish-top candlestand, Philadelphia, 1765-1785; 28 in. high and 22 in. diameter (71 by 56 cm).

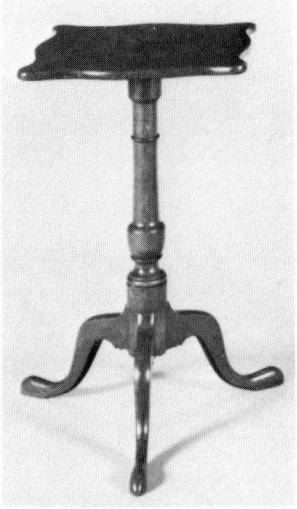

E 8 A Federal cherrywood candlestand, Massachusetts, 1785-1800; 27 in. high by 16 in. diameter (68 by 41 cm).

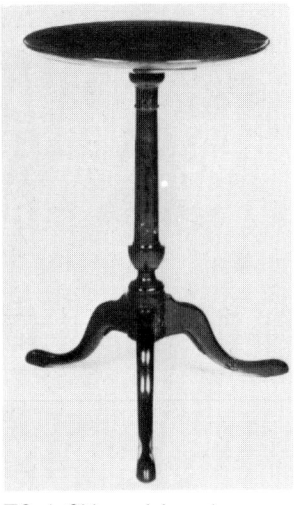

E 3 A Chippendale mahogany candlestand, probably Massachusetts 1760-1790.

E 6 A Chippendale carved mahogany stand, Massachusetts, 1765-1785; 27 in. high by 28 in. diameter (68 by 73 cm).

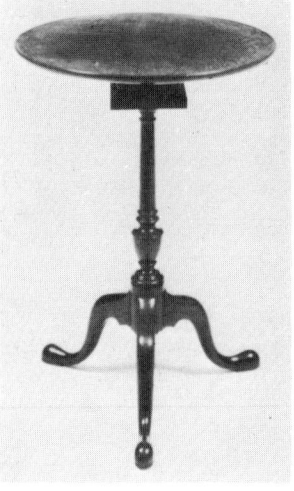

E 9 A Queen Anne carved walnut tilt-top candlestand, Pennsylvania, *c.* 1780; 29 in. high and 22 in. diameter (73 by 55 cm).

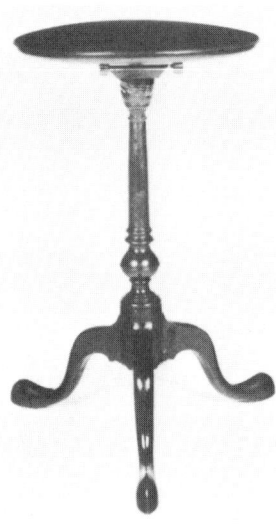

E 1 A Chippendale walnut dish-top candlestand, Philadelphia, 1760-1780; 29 in. high and 18 in. diameter (73 by 45 cm).

E 4 A Chippendale walnut dish-top candlestand, probably Pennsylvania, 1765-1790.

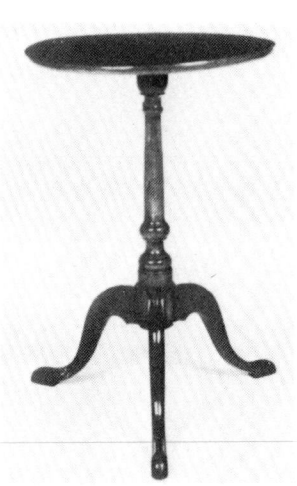

E 7 A Chippendale maple dish-top candlestand, New England, 1770-1800; 27 in. high by 19 in. across (69 by 48 cm).

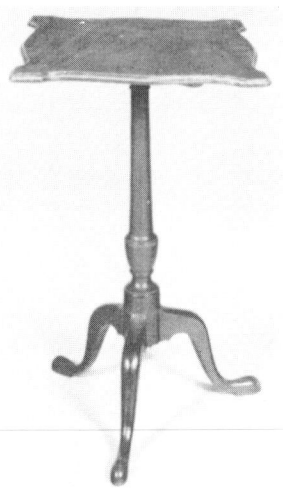

E 10 A Federal mahogany candlestand with serpentine top, Massachusetts, 1785-1810.

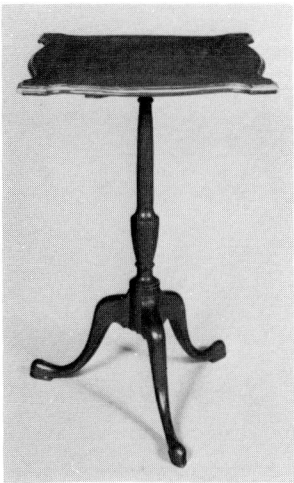

E1 A Federal mahogany candlestand, Massachusetts, 1790-1810; 29 in. high by 30 in. wide (74 by 76 cm).

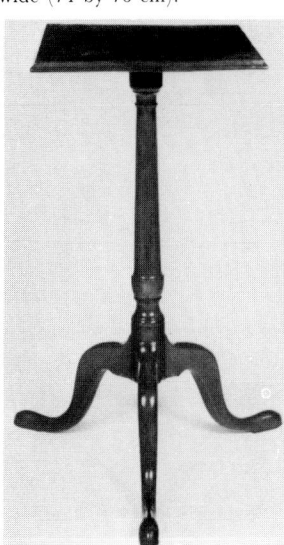

E2 A Federal cherrywood candlestand, New England, 1790-1800; 26 in. high by 14 in. wide (66 by 36 cm).

E3 A Federal mahogany candlestand, New York, 1790-1810; 29 in. high by 23 in. diameter (73 by 58 cm).

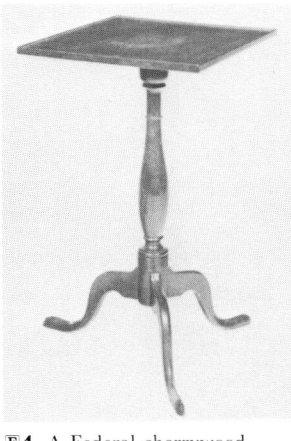

E4 A Federal cherrywood candlestand Connecticut, 1790-1800; 27 in. high by 16 in. wide (68 by 41 cm).

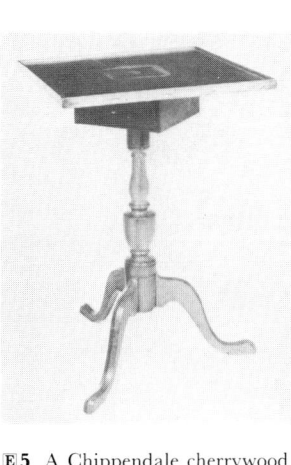

E5 A Chippendale cherrywood candlestand, Connecticut, 1790-1800, the square top with raised edge tilting over a square support fitted with a drawer; 27 in. (68 cm) high, the top 19 in. (48 cm) square.

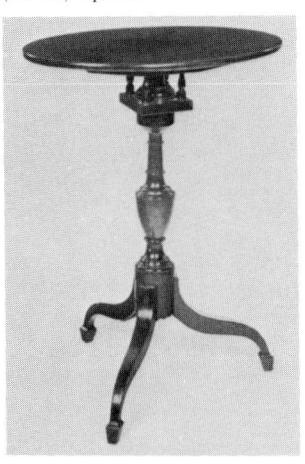

E6 A Federal mahogany stand, probably Massachusetts, 1790-1815; 29 in. high by 16 in. wide (73 by 40 cm). The oval top tilts and revolves on a birdcage support.

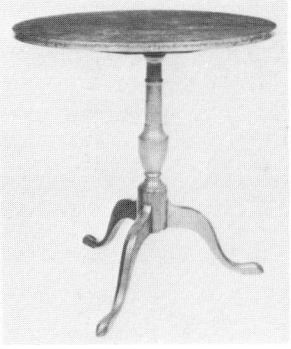

E7 A Federal mahogany candlestand, New York or Connecticut, 1790-1815; 28 in. (71 cm) high.

E8 A Federal turned and carved mahogany tilt-top candlestand, eastern Massachusetts, *c.* 1800.

E9 A Federal curly maple candlestand, New England, *c.* 1800.

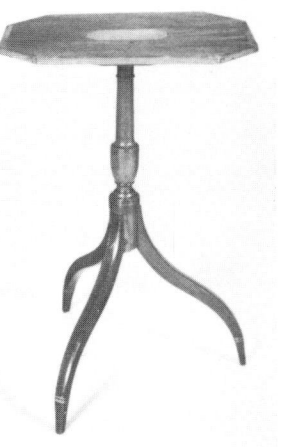

E10 A Federal inlaid mahogany candlestand, Massachusetts, 1790-1810; 28 in. high by 22 in. wide (71 by 56 cm).

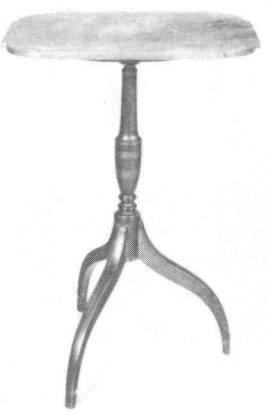

E11 A Federal mahogany candlestand, Massachusetts, 1790-1810; 29 in. high by 23 in. wide (73 by 58 cm).

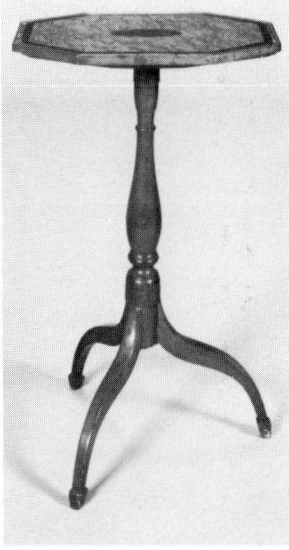

E12 A Federal bird's-eye maple and cherrywood candlestand, Massachusetts, 1790-1810.

E1 A Federal mahogany tilt-top candlestand, New England, 1790-1810; 28 in. high, top 22 in. wide (70 by 55 cm).

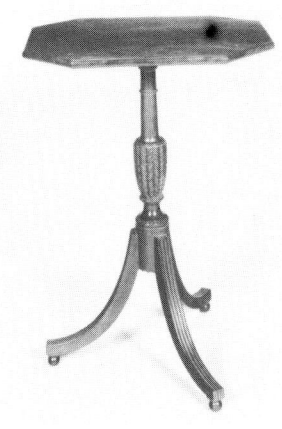

E4 A Federal mahogany candlestand, probably New York, 1800-1820; 29 in. high by 23 in. wide (73 by 56 cm).

E7 A Federal carved mahogany tilt-top candlestand, New England, *c.* 1815; 30 in. high by 20 in. wide (75 by 50 cm).

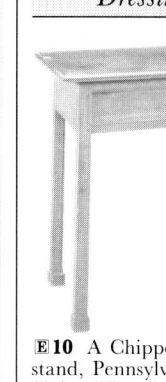

E10 A Chippendale walnut stand, Pennsylvania, 1770-1790; 29 in. (73 cm) high.

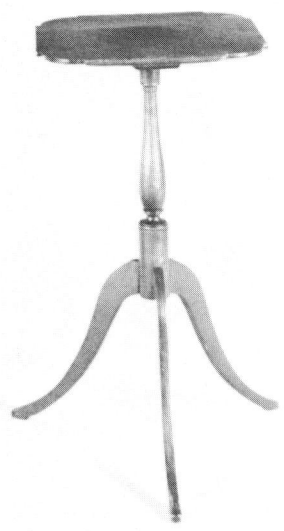

E2 A Federal mahogany candlestand, New England, 1790-1810; 26 in. high by 15 in. wide (65 by 37 cm).

E5 A late Federal curly maple candlestand, New England, 1800-1815; 25 in. high by 21 in. wide (63 by 53 cm).

E8 A Federal carved mahogany tilt-top stand, North Shore, Massachusetts, 1805-1820; 27 in. high, 24 in. wide (69 by 61 cm).

E11 A Federal mahogany and birch stand, Massachusetts or New Hampshire, *c.* 1800.

E12 A Federal birch stand, New England, 1790-1810; 29 in. (72 cm) high.

E3 A Federal mahogany candlestand, New York, 1800-1815; 29 in. high by 24 in, diameter (73 by 61 cm).

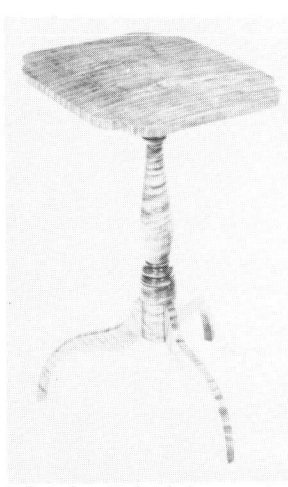

E6 A late Federal tiger maple stand, New England, *c.* 1815; 28 in. high by 23 in. wide (71 by 58 cm).

E9 A Federal birch stand, New England, 1800-1820; 27 in. high, 19 in. wide (69 by 48 cm).

E13 A Federal walnut stand, Middle Atlantic States, *c.* 1800; 29 in. (74 cm) high.

E1 A Federal figured maple stand, 34 in. high, the top 20 in. square (86 by 50 cm).

E4 A Federal mahogany stand, Massachusetts, 1805-1815; 28 in. high by 20 in. wide (73 by 51 cm).

E7 A Federal mahogany two-drawer stand, New England, *c.* 1815; 28 in. high, the top 20 in. by 16 in. (71 by 49 by 40 cm).

Later Candlestands

Later tripod-based candlestands abandoned the knee and pad foot of the Colonial style in favour of the elegant umbrella leg, as in no. 1 opposite, and the splay leg, as in no. 4. Variations on these patterns evolved and after *c.* 1800 the double scroll leg (no. 7) became popular.

18th-century dressing tables, dressing stands or "chamber tables" as they were known in the period, are extremely rare, and were, according to surviving records, expensive beyond their size. The small examples shown on this page were in all probability more used as work tables than for any toilet purposes, but being elegantly conceived and finely made have retained their desirability.

The traditional form of washstand, with its upper platform cut to receive a bowl, has often been modified by being given a solid top the better to fulfil modern requirements.

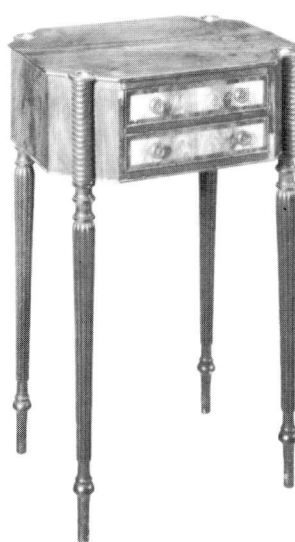

E2 A Federal bird's-eye maple and cherrywood stand, Connecticut, 1790-1810.

E5 A Federal maple stand with two drawers, New England, 1810-1820; 30 in. high and 20 in. wide (76 by 51 cm).

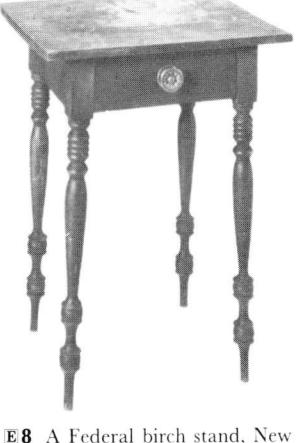

E8 A Federal birch stand, New England 1800-1820; 29 in. high, 22 in. wide (74 by 56 cm).

E10 A Federal bird's-eye maple-inlaid mahogany washstand, Massachusetts, *c.* 1810.

E6 A Federal curly and bird's-eye stand, New England, 1795-1815; 29 in. high and 19 in. wide (73 by 49 cm).

E9 A Federal-style mahogany corner washstand, 39 in. high, 23 in. wide (98 by 58 cm).

E11 A painted washstand, New England, *c.* 1825; 36 in. high by 30 in. wide (91 by 76 cm).

E3 A Federal mahogany and birch veneer stand, Massachusetts, *c.* 1810.

STOOLS
1680-1820

The beginning of the 18th century saw a decline in the popularity of the stool as the chair became the more desirable type of seat furniture for common use. However, in remoter rural areas less subject to the requirements of changing fashion the stool remained a necessary item, constructed to traditional patterns by local turners throughout the 18th and early 19th centuries.

E3 A Federal mahogany piano stool, New York, 1800-1810; 20 in. high by 14 in. diameter seat (51 by 35 cm).

E1 A maple joint stool, New England, 1680-1710; 22 in. high by 17 in. wide (55 by 43 cm).

E2 A painted stick Windsor stool, New England, early 19th century; 22 in. high by 12 in. diameter seat (55 by 29 cm).

E4 A pair of classical carved cherrywood upholstered stools, Massachusetts, *c.* 1820; 19 in. high by 20 in. long (48 by 49 cm).

TABLES
1720-1900

The interchangeable terms "card" and "gaming" table describe tables with fold-over tops, the inner surfaces of which may be lined. The very finest examples display the fashionable characteristics of each period, the most elaborate being those in the Chippendale style, in which such features as carved cabriole legs, dished money wells and candle hollows are much prized.

Card tables

B5 A George II period mahogany card table, with lined top, money wells and candle hollows.

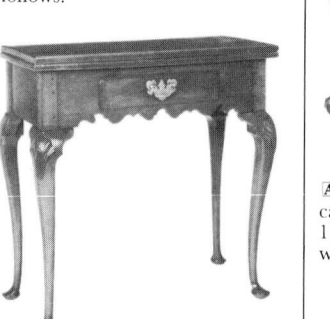

E6 A Queen Anne walnut card table, Philadelphia, 1745-1765; 30 by 31 in. (75 by 77 cm).

B7 A Chippendale carved mahogany card table, Philadelphia, 1755-1775.

D8 A Chippendale mahogany card table, NE Massachusetts, 1755-1785; 29 in. high by 32 in. wide (72 by 81 cm).

B9 A Chippendale mahogany card table, Rhode Island, 1760-1780, 29 in. high by 37 in. wide (72 by 95 cm).

A10 A Chippendale mahogany card table, Philadelphia, 1765-1785; 29 in. high by 36 in. wide (74 by 92 cm).

C11 A Chippendale mahogany circular card table, probably by John Goddard, Newport, Rhode Island, 1760-1780; 26 in. high by 35 in. wide (65 by 89 cm).

C1 A Chippendale mahogany five-legged card table, Philadelphia, 1760-1790; 29 in. high by 36 in. wide (74 by 91 cm).

E5 A Federal mahogany card table, Pennsylvania, 1785-1815; 29 in. high by 36 in. wide (73 by 91 cm). Of pleasingly plain design, the only decoration is the beading to drawer and skirt and moulding to the legs.

D9 A Federal inlaid mahogany card table, probably Massachusetts, c. 1800.

Card Tables
The very substantial value now placed on card tables requires that they be closely scrutinized; any form of decoration denotes quality and should therefore be checked for authenticity.

On pieces of the Chippendale period for example, the carving must appear to stand proud of the outline, the maker having left sufficient timber in consideration of the carver, who created his design to appear as if applied. In contrast, an originally plain piece will have no surplus of timber and the carving will appear within the outline.

In the Federal period the preferred form of decoration was inlay and marquetry. The precision and style of the work must be the first pointers to authenticity, but also the later insertion of marquetry panels into veneer already laid created a difference in height between the two surfaces which may be felt and which will be evident when viewed against the light. A genuinely early piece should have a uniform surface, disturbed, if at all, only by old glue that has seeped up between the panels.

D2 A mahogany card table, Philadelphia, 1760-1790; the secondary woods are oak and poplar.

D6 A Federal cherrywood inlaid card table, New England, 1790-1810; 28 in. high by 36 in. wide (72 by 90 cm).

E10 A Federal mahogany card table of serpentine form with moulded apron on reeded, tapering legs, Rhode Island, 1790-1810; 30 in. high, 33 in. wide (75 by 84 cm).

E3 A Chippendale walnut card table, Philadelphia, 1765-1785; 30 in. high by 36 in. wide (75 by 91 cm).

D7 A Federal mahogany card table, Salem, Massachusetts, 1780-1810; 31 in. high by 37 in. wide (79 by 94 cm).

E11 A Federal inlaid mahogany card table, Baltimore, 1790-1810; 29 in. high by 36 in. wide (72 by 90 cm).

E13 A Federal inlaid mahogany circular card table, New Hampshire, 1790-1810; 30 in. high by 36 in. diameter of top (76 by 91 cm).

D4 A Federal mahogany card table of serpentine form on fluted legs, Rhode Island, 1790-1810; 29 in. high by 33 in. wide (74 by 84 cm).

E8 A Federal inlaid mahogany card table of serpentine form with burl maple and satinwood inlay, Boston, c. 1780.

C12 A Federal carved mahogany card table, Massachusetts or New Hampshire, 1790-1810; 30 in. high by 35 in. wide (75 by 89 cm).

E14 A Federal circular cherrywood card table, New England, 1790-1815; 29 in. high by 36 in. wide (73 by 92 cm).

D 1 A Federal inlaid mahogany card table, Baltimore, Maryland, *c.* 1795; 30 in. high by 36 in. wide (75 by 91 cm).

E 5 A Federal inlaid mahogany card table, north-eastern Massachusetts or New Hampshire, 1790-1810; 29 in. high, 36 in. wide (74 by 91 cm).

E 9 A Federal bird's-eye maple inlaid cherrywood card table, New Hampshire, *c.* 1805; 30 in. high by 35 in. wide (75 by 89 cm).

E 13 A Federal inlaid mahogany card table, Baltimore, 1790-1810; 30 in. high by 36 in. wide (75 by 90 cm).

E 2 A Federal mahogany inlaid card table, Massachusetts, 1790-1800; 19 in. high by 36 in. wide (48 by 91 cm).

E 6 A Federal mahogany veneer serpentine front card table, Philadelphia, *c.* 1800; 30 in. high by 36 in. wide (75 by 90 cm).

E 10 A Federal mahogany veneer card table, Massachusetts, 1790-1810; 29 in. high by 36 in. wide (74 by 90 cm).

E 14 A Federal mahogany card table, Massachusetts, *c.* 1810; 30 in. high by 36 in. wide (76 by 91 cm).

E 3 A Federal mahogany inlaid card table, Massachusetts, 1790-1810; 30 in. high by 36 in. wide (75 by 90 cm).

E 7 A Federal inlaid mahogany card table, Baltimore, Maryland, *c.* 1800; 29 in. high by 36 in. wide (74 by 91 cm).

E 11 A Federal inlaid mahogany card table, Massachusetts, 1790-1810; 31 in. high, 36 in. wide (77 by 90 cm).

E 15 A Federal inlaid mahogany card table, Massachusetts, 1790-1810; 30 in. high by 35 in. wide (75 by 88 cm).

E 4 A Federal inlaid mahogany card table, Philadelphia, 1790-1810; 29 in. high by 34 in. wide (74 by 86 cm).

E 8 A Federal inlaid mahogany card table, Massachusetts, 1790-1810, inscribed in contemporary ink on the underside "H. Toomer"; 29 in. high, 36 in. wide (74 by 91 cm).

E 12 A Federal inlaid mahogany card table, possibly by William Lloyd, Springfield, Massachusetts, 1790-1810, 30 in. high, 35 in. wide (75 by 89 cm).

E 16 A Federal inlaid mahogany card table, probably New York, 1790-1810, 29 in. high by 36 in. wide (73 by 92 cm).

E1 A Federal inlaid mahogany and maple veneer card table, Massachusetts, 1790-1810; 30 in. high by 36 in. wide (75 by 92 cm).

E2 A Federal bird's-eye maple inlaid card table, probably Salem, Massachusetts, 1790-1810; 30 in. high by 35 in. wide (75 by 89 cm).

E3 A Federal inlaid mahogany circular card table, Massachusetts, 1790-1810; 28 in. (71 cm) high, the top is 36 in. (91 cm) across.

E4 A Federal inlaid mahogany card table, probably Massachusetts, 1790-1810; 29 in. high and 36 in. wide (74 by 91 cm).

E5 A Federal inlaid mahogany and birch veneer card table, North Shore, Massachusetts, 1795-1815; 29 in. high by 36 in. wide (74 by 92 cm).

E6 A New York Federal-style mahogany trick-leg card table, by Ernest Hagan, New York; 29 in. high by 36 in. wide when extended (72 by 91 cm).

E7 A Federal carved mahogany card table, New York, 1800-1815; 30 in. high by 36 in. wide (76 by 92 cm).

E8 A late Federal carved mahogany card table, North Shore, Massachusetts, 1810-1820; 30 in. high by 38 in. wide (76 by 95 cm).

E9 A late Federal carved mahogany card table, New York, 1815-1825; 27 in. high by 36 in. wide (68 by 90 cm).

E10 A late Federal carved mahogany card table on spiral turned legs, North Shore, Massachusetts, 1810-1820; it is 30 in. high and 36 in. wide (76 by 91 cm).

E11 A late Federal mahogany card table, by Thomas Needham, Salem, Massachusetts, 1810-1825; 29 in. high by 35 in. wide (74 by 89 cm).

E12 A classical carved and gilt mahogany card table on dolphin standards, probably New York, 1820; 30 in. (75 cm) high.

E13 A Federal carved and brass mounted mahogany card table, coastal New Hampshire, *c.* 1820; 32 in. high by 37 in. wide (80 by 94 cm).

E14 An Empire mahogany veneer card table, attributed to Isaac Vose, Boston, Massachusetts, *c.* 1820; 29 in. high by 36 in. wide (72 by 91 cm).

E15 An Empire mahogany card table, probably New York, 1820-1830; 31 in. high by 36 in. wide (78 by 91 cm).

E16 An Empire gilt-stencilled mahogany card table, New York, 1825-1835; 29 in. high by 36 in. wide (73 by 91 cm).

Centre tables

E1 A William and Mary walnut centre table, Pennsylvania, 1720-1760; 29 in. high by 66 in. wide (74 by 168 cm).

E2 A William and Mary curly walnut centre table, Pennsylvania, 1720-1750; 29 in. high by 60 in. wide (74 by 152 cm).

E3 A walnut centre table, Pennsylvania, 18th century; 29 in. high by 58 in. wide (74 by 146 cm).

E4 A Queen Anne walnut centre table, Pennsylvania, 18th century; 29 in. high by 48 in. wide (79 by 123 cm).

E5 A stained pine centre table, 19th century; 27 in. high by 51 in. wide (69 by 129 cm).

E6 A Federal period brass inlaid centre table in the English style, 36 in. (91 cm) wide.

E7 A curly birch centre table with marble top, by J. & A. Crout, Philadelphia, *c.* 1845; 40 in. (101 cm) wide.

E8 A rococo revival walnut centre table, probably Southern, *c.* 1855; 52 in. (132 cm) wide.

E9 A carved oak library centre table on ornate eagle legs, *c.* 1870.

E10 A mahogany and parquetry centre table, second half of the 19th century; 40 in. (102 cm) diameter.

E11 A Renaissance revival marquetry rosewood centre table, *c.* 1870; 42 in. (105 cm) wide. The oval top is lavishly inlaid with mask heads, scrolls, floral and musical motifs over an inlaid frieze on five fluted columns.

Dining tables

D 1 A Federal inlaid mahogany three-part dining table, Mid-Atlantic States, 1790-1810; 29 in. high by 104 in. long (74 by 263 cm).

D 2 A Federal inlaid walnut three-part dining table, Massachusetts, *c.* 1800; 29 in. high by 126 in. when extended (74 by 320 cm).

D 3 A Federal inlaid mahogany three-part dining table, probably New England, 1790-1815; 28 in. high by 111 in. long (71 by 281 cm).

D 4 A Federal inlaid mahogany three-part dining table, 30 in. high by 170 in. long when extended (77 by 431 cm).

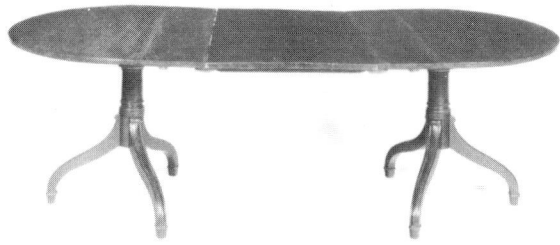

E 5 A two-part Federal mahogany pedestal dining table with two leaves, 19th century; 29 in. (73 cm) high, 52 in. (133 cm) wide, 114 in. (287 cm) long with the leaves in.

E 6 A Federal mahogany drop-leaf dining table, probably from Providence, Rhode Island, *c.* 1810; it is 28 in. (71 cm) high and the top measures 52 in. by 58 in. (131 by 146 cm) with the flaps up.

E 7 One half of a Federal two-part mahogany dining table, each part with a single drop leaf, probably Philadelphia, *c.* 1810; 29 in. high by 41 in. wide (73 by 105 cm), each part 66 in. (167 cm) long with leaf raised.

D 8 A late Federal mahogany two-part mahogany dining table (compare no. 7 immediately above), Philadelphia, 1810-1820; 28 in. high, 48 in. wide, 84 in. long (72 by 122 by 212 cm).

B 9 A three-part Empire mahogany dining table with two leaves, Philadelphia or New York, *c.* 1830; 30 in. high, full length 107 in. (75 by 272 cm).

Dressing tables

D 1 A small Queen Anne walnut veneer dressing table or lowboy, the top and drawers chevron-banded, with deeply arched skirt and pendant finials recalling late 17th-century furniture, on cabriole legs with pad feet; Massachusetts 1730-1750; 29 in. high, 28 in. wide (72 by 70 cm).

D 2 A Queen Anne walnut dressing table, Pennsylvania, 1730-1750; 29 in. high by 34 in. wide (74 by 86 cm).

D 3 A Queen Anne walnut dressing table, Pennsylvania or New Jersey, 1730-1750; 29 by 34 in. (73 by 85 cm).

B 4 A Queen Anne walnut dressing table, probably Virginia, *c.* 1740; 29 in. (72 cm) high.

E 5 A Queen Anne walnut dressing table, Massachusetts, *c.* 1750; 31 by 35 in. (78 by 88 cm).

C 6 A Queen Anne cherrywood dressing table, Connecticut, 1740–1760; 29 by 34 in. (74 by 85 cm).

C 7 A Queen Anne cherrywood dressing table, Connecticut, probably Woodbury area, 1740-1760; 30 by 35 in. (77 by 88 cm).

C 8 A Queen Anne cherrywood lowboy, fan-carved, Connecticut, 1760-1770.

D 9 A Queen Anne carved cherrywood dressing table, possibly Wethersfield, Connecticut, 1740-1770.

C 10 A Queen Anne cherrywood lowboy with four drawers, the central one fan-carved, with pendant finials but, unusually, without shaped skirt, from Connecticut, *c.* 1750.

D 11 A Queen Anne mahogany veneer dressing table, probably Maryland, 1740-1770; 29 in. high by 31 in. wide (72 by 79 cm).

D 12 A mahogany lowboy with canted corners, shell carving to the front and knees, on claw-and-ball feet, Philadelphia, *c.* 1765.

C 13 A small Chippendale carved walnut dressing table, Pennsylvania, 1750-1780; 28 in. high by 31 in. wide (71 by 79 cm).

D 14 A Chippendale mahogany lowboy with shaped and moulded top, carved centre drawer and fine carving to the knees, Maryland, *c.* 1770; 29 in. high, 35 in. wide (74 by 89 cm).

C1 A Chippendale walnut dressing table, Delaware Valley, 1760-1790; 30 in. high by 38 in. wide (76 by 96 cm).

D2 A Queen Anne walnut dressing table, possibly Pennsylvania, 18th century; 30 by 33 in. (77 by 83 cm).

D3 A Chippendale carved mahogany kneehole dressing table, Maryland, *c.* 1770; 29 in. high by 36 in. wide (74 by 91 cm).

E4 A Federal maple dressing table, Massachusetts, 1800-1820; 43 in. high by 34 in. wide (108 by 86 cm).

Drop-leaf tables

E5 A Queen Anne walnut drop-leaf breakfast table, probably Virginia, 1735-1760; 28 by 35 in. (70 by 89 cm).

E6 A Queen Anne walnut drop-leaf breakfast table, 28 in. high by 36 in. wide (71 by 90 cm).

E7 A Chippendale carved maple drop-leaf dining table, northern New England, 1770-1800; 29 in. high by 52 in. wide (73 by 132 cm) extended.

E8 A Queen Anne walnut drop-leaf dining table, Connecticut or Massachusetts, 1735-1760; 36 in. high by 36 in. long (91 by 91 cm).

E9 A Chippendale walnut dining table, Pennsylvania, 1740-1760; 30 in. high by 55 in. wide (76 by 140 cm).

E10 A Queen Anne carved walnut drop-leaf dining table, New England, *c.* 1750; 29 by 58 in. (72 by 147 cm).

E11 A Queen Anne carved walnut drop-leaf dining table, Pennsylvania, *c.* 1760; 29 by 49 in. wide (74 by 124 cm) extended.

E12 A Chippendale mahogany drop-leaf dining table, Massachusetts, *c.* 1770.

E13 A Chippendale walnut drop-leaf dining table, Pennsylvania, 1760-1785; 29 by 48 in. (71 by 121 cm).

Drop-leaf Tables
A number of surviving rectangular 18th-century drop-leaf tables were in fact made to be the centre parts of two- or three-part dining tables. But the preference has long tended to be for round or oval tables and this has led on occasion to early rectangular models, whether made as independent tables in their own right or as inserts to larger tables, being reduced.

Evidence of this kind of reduction is the lack of a uniform darkening to the underside of the top edge, where generations of fingers should have left their marks. Other signs of authenticity are compatible wear to the working parts – the underside of the top where it comes in contact with the top of the swing-out leg – and, a detail that is occasionally found, ring marks around the edge where a lady habitually clamped her sewing frame.

D14 A Queen Anne carved mahogany drop-leaf dining table, Newport, Rhode Island, *c.* 1765.

E15 A Chippendale mahogany breakfast table, 28 in. high by 33 in. wide (70 by 84 cm).

E1 A Chippendale carved mahogany drop-leaf dining table, Massachusetts, *c.* 1770; 55 in. (138 cm) wide.

E2 A Chippendale carved mahogany drop-leaf table, Pennsylvania, *c.* 1770.

E3 A Chippendale carved walnut drop-leaf dining table, Pennsylvania, *c.* 1775.

E4 A Federal carved mahogany drop-leaf table, probably Maryland, *c.* 1785.

E5 A Queen Anne carved walnut drop-leaf dining table, Pennsylvania, 1790-1810.

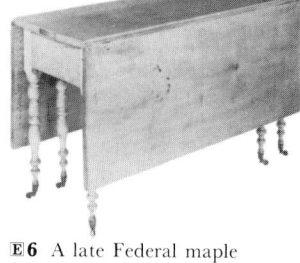

E6 A late Federal maple drop-leaf dining table, 1815-1825; 29 in. high, the top measures 59 in. by 50 in. (74 by 151 by 128 cm).

C7 A William and Mary maple and pine butterfly drop-leaf table, 27 in. high by 26 in. wide (67 by 66 cm).

D8 A Queen Anne mahogany drop-leaf table, Massachusetts, 1740-1760; 27 in. high by 34 in. extended (68 by 85 cm).

E9 A Queen Anne walnut drop-leaf table, New England, *c.* 1750; 29 in. high by 48 in. long (72 by 120 cm).

E10 A Queen Anne mahogany drop-leaf table, Massachusetts, 1740-1760; 28 in high by 55 in. wide (72 by 140 cm).

E11 A Queen Anne mahogany drop-leaf table, Rhode Island, 1740-1760; 28 in. high by 41 in. wide (71 by 103 cm).

E12 A Queen Anne cherrywood drop-leaf table, probably Connecticut 1740-1760; 28 in. high, 40 in. wide (70 by 102 cm).

E13 A Queen Anne maple drop-leaf table, New England, 1740-1760; 44 in. (111 cm) wide.

E14 A Queen Anne cherrywood drop-leaf table, New England, 1740-1770; 41 in. (105 cm) wide.

C15 A rare small Chippendale mahogany drop-leaf table, Massachusetts, 1765-1785; 27 in. high by 30 in wide (69 cm by 75 cm).

E16 A Chippendale fruitwood drop-leaf table, Middle Colonies, 1770-1785; 28 in. high by 45 in. wide (72 by 113 cm).

E17 A Federal mahogany drop-leaf table, New York, 1790-1810; 29 in. high by 34 in. wide (74 by 86 cm).

E18 A Federal mahogany drop-leaf table, New York, 1800-1820; 29 in. high by 36 in. wide (72 by 91 cm).

E19 An Empire mahogany drop-leaf table, New York, 1815-1830; 29 in. high by 41 in. wide (73 by 103 cm).

Gaming tables

E 1 A Chippendale mahogany gaming table, Pennsylvania, 1770-1790; 29 in. high by 37 in. wide (72 by 95 cm).

E 2 A Chippendale mahogany gaming table, Philadelphia, 1770-1785; 34 in. (87 cm) wide.

E 3 A Federal inlaid mahogany games table, Massachusetts, 1780-1790; 34 in. (86 cm) wide.

D 5 A Federal mahogany gaming table, New England, *c*. 1800; 30 in. high by 38 in. wide (74 by 97 cm).

D 6 A Federal carved and inlaid mahogany and maple card table on lyre support, New York, 1810-1820; 31 in. high by 36 in. wide (78 by 91 cm).

D 7 A Louis XVI revival rosewood games table, perhaps by Roux, New York, c. 1850.

D 4 A Federal inlaid mahogany gaming table, Baltimore, 1790-1810; 29 in. high, 36 in. wide (74 by 92 cm). With line inlay to the top and frieze and husks inlaid to the legs.

Gateleg tables

E 8 A turned maple gateleg table, New England, 1700-1730; 27 in. high by 44 in. wide (69 by 112 cm).

D 9 A turned curly maple small gateleg table in the William and Mary style, Massachusetts, 1700-1730; 28 in. high and 40 in. wide (71 by 100 cm).

E 10 A traditional maple turned gateleg table with circular top 48 in. (120 cm) in diameter.

E1 A William and Mary-style maple gateleg table, Rhode Island, 1710-1730; 27 in. high by 43 in. wide (67 by 109 cm).

E2 A turned maple gateleg table in the William and Mary style, early 18th century, 25 in. high by 41 in. wide extended (62 by 104 cm).

E3 A cherrywood oval gateleg table, probably American, early 18th century; it is 42 in. high and 46 in. wide when open (107 by 116 cm).

Library tables

D4 A Federal carved mahogany library table, New York State, 1810-1820; 29 in. high by 24 in. wide (73 by 62 cm) closed.

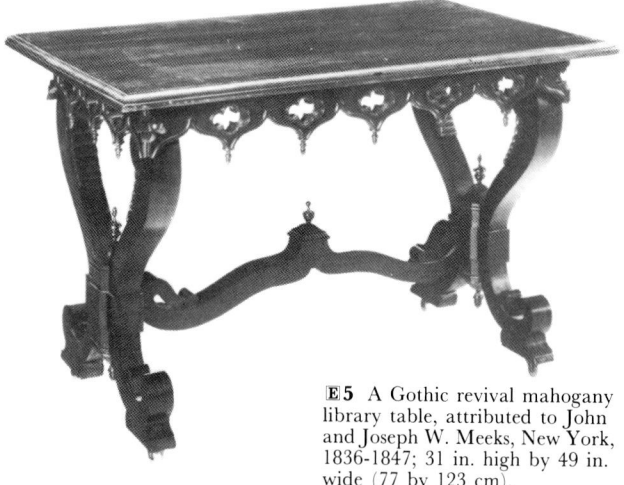

E5 A Gothic revival mahogany library table, attributed to John and Joseph W. Meeks, New York, 1836-1847; 31 in. high by 49 in. wide (77 by 123 cm).

E6 A Renaissance revival rosewood marble-top library table, attributed to Pottier & Stymus, New York, 1865-1875; 30 in. high by 46 in. wide (75 by 116 cm).

Pembroke tables

E 1 A Chippendale mahogany Pembroke table, Rhode Island, 1769-1790; 27 by 33 in. (67 by 84 cm) extended.

E 2 A Chippendale mahogany Pembroke table, probably New York, 1760-1790; 28 in. high by 29 in. (71 by 74 cm) wide.

E 3 A Chippendale carved mahogany Pembroke table, Newburyport, Massachusetts, 1780-1800; 29 by 38 in. (73 by 95 cm) extended.

D 4 A Federal carved curly maple Pembroke table, New England, *c.* 1800; 29 by 36 in. (72 by 90 cm) extended.

E 5 A Federal walnut Pembroke table, New England, *c.* 1800; 29 in. high by 42 in. wide (74 by 107 cm) extended.

D 6 A Federal inlaid mahogany Pembroke table, New York, 1790-1810; 28 in. high by 38 in. wide (71 by 95 cm).

D 7 A Federal inlaid cherrywood Pembroke table, Connecticut, 1790-1810; 28 in. high by 41 in. wide (70 by 103 cm).

D 8 A Federal inlaid mahogany Pembroke table, probably Baltimore, 1790-1810; 29 in. high by 40 in. wide (73 by 102 cm) extended.

E 9 A Federal inlaid mahogany Pembroke table, probably New York, 1790-1810; 28 in. high by 37 in. wide (71 by 94 cm).

E 10 A Federal inlaid mahogany Pembroke table, New York or Connecticut, 1790-1810; 28 in. high by 33 in. wide (70 by 82 cm).

E 11 A Federal inlaid mahogany Pembroke table, Connecticut or Rhode Island, 1790-1810; 28 in. high by 34 in. long (70 by 86 cm).

E 12 A Federal inlaid mahogany Pembroke table, Massachusetts, 1790-1810; 29 in. high by 40 in. wide (72 by 101 cm).

E 13 A Federal inlaid mahogany Pembroke table, Connecticut, 1790-1815; 28 in. high by 28 in. wide (70 by 71 cm).

E 14 A Federal cherrywood Pembroke table, New England, 1790-1820; 27 in. high by 33 in. wide (68 by 84 cm).

Pembroke Tables
According to Thomas Sheraton the name "Pembroke" for these small drop-leaf tables is derived from the lady who first commissioned such a piece – possibly the Countess of Pembroke. Pembroke tables are first mentioned in English accounts during the 1750s, but it was not until the last quarter of the century that they became popular on both sides of the Atlantic.

Pembrokes are essentially drop-leaf tables in which the top is substantial in proportion to the modest leaves; the flaps may be supported on pull-out lopers or on swivelling brackets.

A table with similar stretchers to those in no. 3 on this page appears in Chippendale's *Gentleman and Cabinet-Maker's Director*, 1754, described as a breakfast table; this alternative descripton of a Pembroke table has remained in currency.

E1 A Federal inlaid mahogany Pembroke table, New England, 1795-1810; 29 in. high by 35 in. wide (73 by 88 cm).

E2 A Federal mahogany Pembroke table, 28 in. high by 52 in. wide with flaps up (70 by 130 cm).

E3 A Federal mahogany Pembroke table, Middle Atlantic States, *c.* 1810; 29 in. high by 37 in. wide (maximum) (74 by 73 cm).

E4 A Federal inlaid mahogany Pembroke table, eastern Massachusetts, 1790-1815; 30 in. high by 36 in. wide (76 by 91 cm).

E5 A Federal mahogany Pembroke table, New York, 1800-1820; 29 in. high by 38 in. wide (73 by 96 cm).

E6 A Federal miniature cherrywood Pembroke table, Massachusetts or Connecticut, 1800-1820; 13 in. high by 22 in. wide (32 by 56 cm).

Pier tables

D7 A rare Chippendale carved mahogany pier table, Salem, Massachusetts, 1760-1780; 27 in. high by 33 in. wide (67 by 85 cm).

E8 A classical gilt-metal mounted and stencilled mahogany marble-top pier table, Philadelphia, *c.* 1825; 37 in. high by 48 in. long (94 by 162 cm).

E9 An Empire gilt stencilled and black painted pier table, Baltimore, 1830-1840; 34 in. high by 42 in. wide (87 by 108 cm).

E10 An Empire carved mahogany pier table, Boston or Salem, Massachusetts, 1830-1840; 34 in. (85 cm) high.

E11 A classical carved mahogany marble top pier table, Philadelphia, *c.* 1835.

E12 An Empire mahogany marble top pier table, 1825-1845; 41 in. high by 49 in. wide (104 by 122 cm).

E13 A rococo revival mahogany pier table, *c.* 1855; 30 in. high by 43 in. wide (76 by 109 cm).

Serving tables

E14 A Federal mahogany serving table, Philadelphia, 1790-1810; 36 in. high by 34 in. wide (92 by 86 cm).

E15 A Federal mahogany bowfront serving table, Philadelphia, 1790-1810; 39 in. high by 37 in. wide (98 by 93 cm).

E16 A Federal mahogany veneer serving table, New York, 1800-1820.

D17 A Federal mahogany serving table, North Shore, Massachusetts, 1800-1820.

Side tables

E1 A Chippendale walnut console table, Maryland or Pennsylvania, 1765-1800, with a single drawer over bracketed, fluted legs joined by an X-stretcher; 29 in. high by 34 in. wide (74 by 85 cm).

E2 A Federal figured maple console table, New York, 1810-1820; 35 in. high by 35 in. wide (88 by 89 cm). The rectangular top with rounded corners over a sham long drawer, on C-scroll legs joined by a deep shaped stretcher.

E3 A walnut side table, early 18th century, 30 in. high by 45 in. wide (75 by 113 cm).

E4 A Federal curly maple side table, New England, *c.* 1810; 18 in. (45 cm) wide.

D5 A carved mahogany side table, second quarter of the 18th century, 31 in. high by 54 in. wide (77 by 135 cm).

Tavern tables

E6 A William and Mary figured maple tavern table, New Hampshire, 1720-1740; 27 in. high by 35 in. wide (68 by 88 cm).

E7 A Willliam and Mary pine tavern table, New England, 1720-1750; 25 in. high by 29 in. across (62 by 72 cm).

E8 A Queen Anne cherrywood tavern table, New England, 1730-1750; 26 in. high by 27 in. wide (66 by 69 cm).

E9 A William and Mary birch and pine tavern table, New England, 18th century; 32 in. (81 cm) across.

E10 A Queen Anne maple tavern table, New England, 1730-1760; 26 in. high by 30 in. wide (65 by 76 cm).

E11 A Queen Anne maple tavern table, New England, 1730-1760; 27 in. high by 35 in. across (68 by 87 cm).

E12 A William and Mary painted pine and maple tavern table, New Hampshire, 1740-1770; 27 in. high by 31 in. across (67 by 78 cm).

E13 A William and Mary pine and maple table, New England, 1730-1770; 24 in. high by 27 in. wide (61 by 68 cm).

E1 A pine and maple tavern table, New England, *c.* 1750; 25 in. high by 27 in. wide (63 by 69 cm).

E5 A Queen Anne maple tavern table, New England, 1750-1800; 26 in. high by 30 in. wide (65 by 76 cm).

D9 A Queen Anne mahogany tea table, Massachusetts, 1740-1770; 26 in. high by 19 in. wide (66 by 47 cm).

E13 A Queen Anne walnut tea table, 27 in. high by 31 in. wide (67 by 78 cm).

E2 A Queen Anne maple tavern table, New England, 1730-1760; 27 in. high by 34 in. wide (69 by 86 cm).

E6 A Federal pine splay leg table, New England, early 19th century; 26 in. high by 34 in. wide (65 by 85 cm).

E10 A Queen Anne figured maple porringer-top tea table, Rhode Island, 1740-1760; 27 in. high by 31 in. wide (68 by 78 cm).

D14 A Queen Anne maple and sycamore tea table, Connecticut, 1740-1760; 28 in. high by 25 in. wide (72 by 62 cm).

E3 A Chippendale maple and pine tavern table, 27 in. high by 43 in. wide (69 by 108 cm).

Tea tables

E7 A Queen Anne maple tea table, 1740-1760; 26 in. high by 31 in. wide (65 by 79 cm).

E11 A Queen Anne painted maple porringer-top tea table, New England, 1740-1760; 26 in. high by 24 in. wide (66 by 60 cm).

E15 A Queen Anne mahogany tea table, Newport, Rhode Island, 1740-1770; 28 in. by 32 in. diameter top (70 by 83 cm).

D4 A Queen Anne maple table, with oval top above a straight skirt on flairing turned legs terminating in pad feet, New England, 1750-1780; 27 in. high by 31 in. wide (68 by 78 cm).

E8 A Queen Anne walnut tea table, probably Massachusetts, *c.* 1750; 26 in. by 30 in. (65 by 75 cm).

D12 A Queen Anne mahogany porringer-top tea table, Rhode Island, 1740-1760; 24 in. high by 32 in. wide (61 by 81 cm).

E16 A Queen Anne cherrywood birdcage tea table, Connecticut, 1740-1770.

E1 A George II-style carved mahogany birdcage tea table, second quarter 18th century.

E5 A Chippendale mahogany tilt-top tea table, Massachusetts, 1755-1785.

E8 A sturdy mahogany tea table, Philadelphia, later 18th century.

Tea tables
The earliest type of American tea table was of rectangular form and dates from the early 18th century. The tripod or claw base gained popularity after the middle of the century and at first followed English designs faithfully.

Some tripod tables were made with fixed tops, others with tilt tops and others were fitted with birdcages to allow them to revolve as well as tilt. A table fitted with an original birdcage will always show a paler conforming patch to the underside of the top where it has been closed to the block, inhibiting oxidization. Further, the columns of a birdcage are not stopped but come through to the upper surface of the block and as they will not have shrunk in length but only in width they will protrude through the shrunken block – only fractionally, but enough to cause corresponding bruising to the underside of the top.

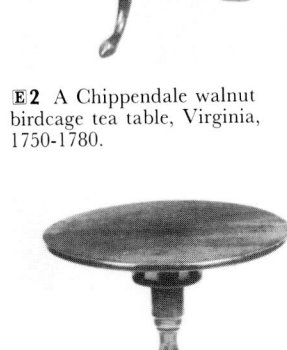

E2 A Chippendale walnut birdcage tea table, Virginia, 1750-1780.

E6 A Chippendale mahogany tilt-top tea table, Massachusetts, 1760-1780; 28 in. (71 cm) high, the top 31 in. (79 cm) in diameter.

E9 A Chippendale carved mahogany tea table, Philadelphia, 1760-1780; 29 in. high by 30 in. diameter top (74 by 76 cm).

E3 A Chippendale cherrywood birdcage tea table, probably Connecticut 1750-1780.

E10 A Chippendale mahogany tilt-top tea table, probably Middle Colonies, 1760-1790; 26 in. high by 32 in. diameter top (67 by 80 cm).

E4 A Chippendale mahogany tilt-top table, western Long Island, New York, 1750-1780.

E7 A Chippendale maple tea table, the top with moulded, scrolling edge tilting over an octagonal birdcage, the standard crisply carved over cabriole legs on claw-and-ball feet, New York or Rhode Island, 1760-1780; the top is 34 in. (86 cm) in diameter.

E11 A Chippendale carved mahogany tea table, Rhode Island, 1765-1785; 29 in. high by 32 in. diameter top (73 by 81 cm).

D 1 A Chippendale walnut dish-top tea table, Philadelphia, 1765-1785; 29 in. high by 34 in. wide (72 by 85 cm).

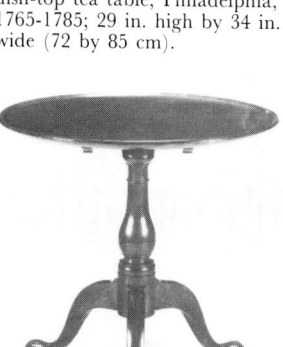

C 2 A Chippendale mahogany tea table, Newport, Rhode Island,1765-1785; 29 in. (72 cm) diameter.

E 3 A Chippendale carved mahogany tea table, probably Massachusetts, 1765-1785; 37 in. (94 cm) diameter.

E 4 A Chippendale mahogany tilt-top tea table, Massachusetts, 1765-1785; 30 in. high by 30 in. wide (76 by 76 cm).

E 5 A Chippendale maple tilt-top tea table, Connecticut River Valley, 1770-1790; 27 in. high by 45 in. diameter (69 by 113 cm).

E 6 A Chippendale carved mahogany tilt-top tea table, New York, *c.* 1775; 28 in. high by 32 in. diameter (71 by 81 cm).

E 7 A Chippendale mahogany tea table, late 18th century; 28 in. high by 30 in. diameter (70 by 75 cm).

E 8 A Chippendale mahogany tea table, late 18th century; 28 in. high by 36 in. diameter (70 by 91 cm).

E 9 A Federal walnut tilt-top tea table, Pennsylvania, 1780-1800; 28 in. high, top 26 in. by 20 in. (71 by 50 cm).

E 10 A Federal mahogany tilt-top table, New England, 1780-1800; 30 in. high by 22 in. wide (75 by 55 cm).

E 11 A rare carved mahogany serpentine top tea table, Salem, Massachusetts 1790-1800; 29 in. high by 34 in. wide (73 by 86 cm).

E 12 A Federal mahogany and satinwood sewing table, eastern Massachusetts, *c.* 1805; 30 in. high by 24 in. wide (76 by 61 cm).

E 13 A Federal bird's-eye maple and painted work table, probably Massachusetts, 1790-1810; 28 in. high by 16 in. wide (72 by 39 cm).

E 14 A Federal mahogany work table, Massachusetts, 1790-1810; 29 in. high by 21 in. wide (72 by 53 cm).

E 1 A Federal inlaid and carved mahogany work table, Salem, Massachusetts, 1790-1810; 31 in. high by 25 in. wide (77 by 63 cm).

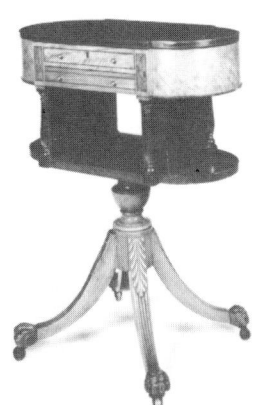

C 2 A Federal inlaid mahogany work table, Baltimore, Maryland, 1790-1810; 32 in. high by 25 in. wide (80 by 62 cm).

D 3 A Federal curly maple and mahogany astragal work table, probably New York, *c.* 1800.

E 4 A Federal mahogany work table, Philadelphia, *c.* 1800.

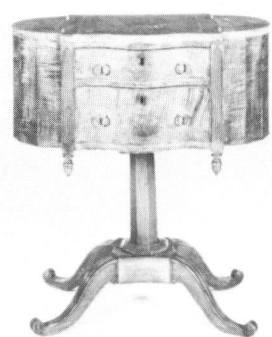

E 5 A Federal maple work table, Boston, 1800-1815; 30 in. high by 28 in. wide (76 by 70 cm).

E 6 A Federal mahogany work table, Philadelphia, 1805-1815.

E 7 A Federal mahogany and bird's-eye maple work table, Pennsylvania (?), *c.* 1810.

E 8 A Federal carved mahogany work table, school of Duncan Phyfe, New York, *c.* 1810; 30 in. high by 19 in. wide (76 by 47 cm).

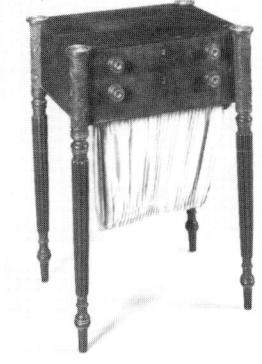

D 9 A Federal carved mahogany work table, Salem, 1810-1820.

E 10 An Empire carved mahogany work table, Massachusetts, *c.* 1815; 29 in. (74 cm) high.

D 11 A late Federal curly maple work table, *c.* 1820.

D 12 An Empire mahogany carved and stencilled work table, New York, *c.* 1830; 30 in. high, 22 in. wide (75 by 55 cm). With one drawer to the side and two to the face, on a stencilled baluster with carved legs and feet.

E 13 An Empire-style curly maple drop-leaf work table, *c.* 1840; 29 in. (74 cm) high, the top 18 in. by 19 in. (45 by 48 cm), over two frieze drawers flanked by columns, on a turned standard with downswept legs ending in scroll feet.

E 14 An Empire mahogany sewing table, by Anthony Quervelle, Philadelphia, *c.* 1840.

BRITAIN

Unlike most European countries England did not suffer the ravages of a war at home for many centuries (those of the Civil War apart) and since the Restoration in 1660 Englishmen's goods and chattels were allowed to survive unscathed except for the depredations of use and the imperatives of fashion. With a less rigid class structure than in many European countries, elements of changing taste filtered through in each period to quite low levels. In this respect, farmhouse furniture of good quality will reveal almost as much about the trends of stylish living as its equivalents in mansion houses.

THE 18TH CENTURY

To view the furniture of the British Isles provincially is inherently misleading. On the one hand there are numerous, relatively minor local differences in the interpretation of major styles – differences that show principally when English furniture is compared with Irish and Scottish. But all three countries shared in the great artistic trends of the 18th century in Europe – the Rococo from France and Germany, the Classical from Italy, the Neoclassical from France – and minor movements too, such as the Chinese and Gothic, found favour.

The period of greatest creativity in English furniture-making was without doubt the 18th century, during which the furniture industry grew in social status and in commercial importance. William Hallett Junior, whose grandfather founded the firm, was a country gentleman who sat for Gainsborough, and in 1786 George Seddon was employing 400 craftsmen in his London workshops and held stock valued at just under £120,000 – compare the £72.0s.0d. that Chippendale charged in 1767 for the library table at Nostell Priory.

The Regency saw fashion rise almost as a political weapon when those architects and designers favoured by the Prince of Wales chose styles in the strongest contrast to those of the establishment loyal to the ailing King. Compare designs by Henry Holland with those of Sir William Chambers and Robert Adam – on the one hand Egyptian, Chinese and French, on the other the established elegance of classical antiquity.

As the Queen Anne period gave visible respite before the excesses of ornamentation of the rococo, so the period of William IV showed a worthy, dignified restraint before the stylistic mayhem associated with machine production gained momentum in the 1840s for the extravagances to come.

BEDS 1500-1900

The traditional form of the English bed is the four-poster, and even quite modest homes sometimes contained a disproportionately grand example. The reason is that when an important 17th-century bed was sold during the 18th century it almost always suffered a drop in social status, for it was rare for an aristocrat to attend the auction sale of another.

Cradles

E1 An oak cradle, on shaped rockers, the body panels carved with fluting; 17th century.

E2 An 18th-century oak cradle, 33 by 38 in. (84 by 96 cm).

E3 An early Georgian period red walnut child's cot, on scroll and rockers.

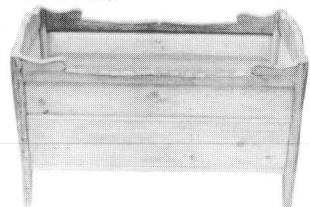

E4 A pine and oak peg-joined cradle, 18th century; 39 in. long by 19 in. wide (99 by 48 cm).

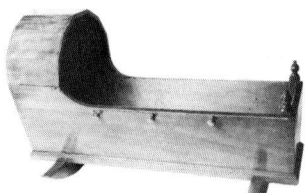

E5 A fruitwood cradle of the early 19th century, 36 in. (92 cm) long.

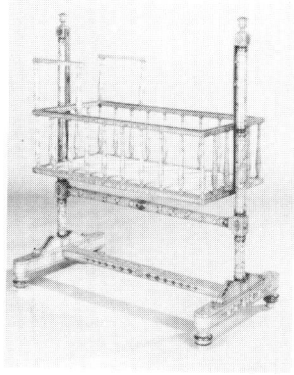

E6 A late Regency painted satinwood cradle, 41 in. (103 cm) wide.

E7 An early Victorian mahogany swing cradle, with arched top rail above two baluster-turned posts, supporting a slatted cradle, 38 in. (96 cm) high.

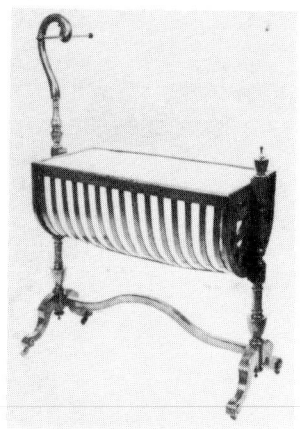

E8 A Victorian walnut cot with slatted body and swan-neck curtain support, on scrolled trestle legs joined by an arched stretcher; 44 in. (112 cm) long.

E 1 An "Old English" Victorian carved oak cradle, with carved canopy on turned supports, on shaped rockers.

E 2 A 17th-century style panelled oak cradle, the body carved with lozenges and flower heads; 30 in. (76 cm) high.

Day beds

E 3 A Charles II day bed, with carved top rail on spiral twist supports; 66 in. (168 cm) long.

E 4 A Charles II walnut day bed, the frame carved with scrolls; 73 in. (185 cm) long.

E 5 A Charles II walnut day bed, with carved head; 66 in. long by 21 in. wide (168 by 52 cm).

E 6 A William and Mary walnut and caned day bed, with adjustable backrest and pierced, carved cresting, late 17th century; 60 in. (153 cm) long.

E 7 A George II large giltwood day bed in the Chippendale style, the padded headboard and moulded edge carved with cabochons, *c.* 1750; 82 in. (208 cm) long.

E 8 A George II-style mahogany day bed, the yoked crest rail above a vase-shaped splat; 68 in. long by 27 in. wide (172 by 62 cm).

Four-posters

D 9 An early 16th-century carved oak bedstead, 70 in. (178 cm) high.

D 10 An oak linenfold carved bed with barleysugar footposts, *c.* 1500; 78 in. (198 cm) long.

C 11 An Elizabethan oak bedstead of the first quality with moulded and carved cornice over a lobed frieze, the headboard superbly carved, arcaded and panelled, the footboard panelled and richly carved under baluster turned cup-and-cover footposts.

C 12 An oak bed of the early 17th century with deeply carved tester over a tiered, panelled headboard with particularly fine arcaded fielded panels in the lower row, the bottom part of the headboard almost plain; the finely turned and carved footposts under Ionic capitals are supported on architectural plinths; 102 in. (258 cm) high.

Four-Poster Beds

17th-century carved oak beds saw a revival during the 1850s, but it was their look and associations that were in demand, rather than the genuine article. Thus a large number of 16th- and 17th-century four-posters were dismembered and rebuilt, the better to fit the Victorian home.

This, to some unforgiveable, butchery continued for more than half a century, when it became the turn of 18th-century beds to suffer an even worse fate. During the 1920s the elegant carved, turned and fluted mahogany posts – footposts in particular, as being more finely decorated than headposts – were reduced in height and given tripod legs and a tray top to form torchères, which are now in demand in their own right.

Authentic four-poster beds from any period prior to the 1850s are thus rare, and it is important to look out for modifications and alterations, as after 50 or even 100 years of being together even ill-matched parts will have assumed a certain deceptive compatibility.

D 3 A small oak four-poster, early 17th century: 84 in. by 56 in. (215 by 142 cm).

C 4 An oak bedstead, carved and inlaid.

B 7 An oak four-post bed, with panelled canopy, the double arcaded head end inlaid with vases of stylized foliage, divided by caryatids, carved with masks and flowerheads, 17th century; 69 in. wide by 98 in. long (175 by 244 cm).

E 1 A Charles I style carved oak tester bed, with later carving, restored and partly made up, *c.* 1640; 51 in. (130 cm) wide.

D 5 An oak four-post bed, the headboard inlaid with marquetry panels, 17th century.

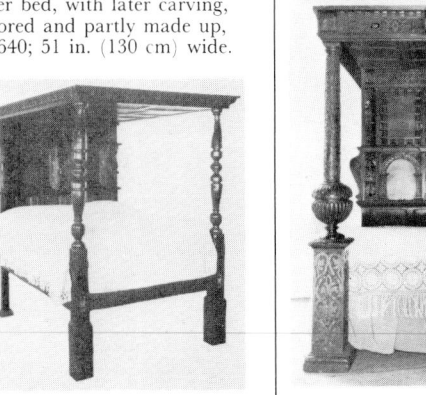

E 2 A James I oak tester bed, with carved moulded cornice, 82 in. by 58 in. (208 by 146 cm).

D 6 A carved tester bedstead, *c.* 1660; 88 in. high by 56 in. wide (224 by 142 cm).

E 8 A Charles II oak tester bedstead, carved with a triad IMP and dated 1664, 96 in. high by 69 in. wide (244 by 175 cm). The arcaded supports to the footposts are later.

E1 A mahogany four-poster bedstead, with moulded cornice and reeded posts, partly 18th century; 88 in. high by 54 in. wide (224 by 137 cm).

D2 A Chippendale mahogany four-post bedstead, the top boldly carved with upstanding shells and acanthus; third quarter of the 18th century.

E3 A George III mahogany four-post bed, with carved canopy, 104 in. (264 cm) high.

E4 A George III mahogany tester bed, 94 in. by 63 in. (239 by 159 cm).

D5 A George III cream-painted four-poster bed, 86 in. (217 cm) wide.

D6 A Georgian mahogany four-poster bed, with pale yellow silk curtain.

E7 A George IV mahogany tester bed, second quarter 19th century.

E8 A George IV mahogany tester bed, second quarter 19th century.

E9 A mahogany single tester bed, second half 19th century; 82 in. by 41 in. (207 by 104 cm).

E10 A George III style mahogany framed four-poster bed, 82 in. by 42 in. (208 by 108 cm).

BONHEURS DU JOUR
1780-1920

The bonheur du jour was first made in France in the middle of the 18th century – its name is said to come from the speed with which it was taken up by the French public – and little time elapsed before it appeared in England. In its purpose – a combined toilet and writing table – and in its form it lent itself admirably to the taste of the period and especially to the decorative styles of the 1770s.

Contemporary references in England are to ladies' writing tables – the French name is a later import – and they were most popular when painted or exotically veneered in the classical manner. Plainer versions were made as well, of course, and if of good quality find a ready market today.

E 3 A Hepplewhite bonheur du jour of exquisite proportion and the finest workmanship.

E 6 A mahogany and satinwood bonheur du jour, in the Sheraton manner, 19th century; 52 in. high by 31 in. wide (131 by 78 cm).

D 9 A Regency brown and gold lacquered bonheur du jour in the manner of John McClean. The superstructure supports an open shelf with gothic-pattern ormolu gallery on turned and chased supports over two drawers; the lower part with a fitted panelled drawer, the whole decorated in the Chinese taste.

E 1 A George III mahogany and inlaid bonheur du jour, 42 in. high by 34 in. wide (105 by 86 cm).

E 4 A satinwood bonheur du jour, of George III design, 18 in. (46 cm) wide.

E 7 A satinwood bonheur du jour, with cedar-lined drawers, 26 in. (66 cm) wide.

E 10 A Regency rosewood bonheur du jour, the lower part of cylinder form, with velvet-lined writing surface, flanked by ten various-sized drawers, 36 in. (92 cm) wide.

E 2 A George III satinwood and purple heart bonheur du jour, 30 in. (76 cm) wide.

E 5 A mahogany bonheur du jour, with satinwood line inlay, 42 in. high by 19 in. wide (106 by 47 cm).

D 8 A George III satinwood bonheur du jour, inlaid with olivewood ovals, 34 in. (87 cm) wide.

E 11 A Regency ebonized and parcel-gilt bonheur du jour, with mirrored back panel, on twisting tapering legs, 28 in. (70 cm) wide.

E1 A Regency rosewood bonheur du jour, in the manner of George Bullock, 37 in. (94 cm) wide.

E2 A Victorian inlaid walnut bonheur du jour with seven drawers and mirrored cupboard, ormolu mounted.

E3 A kingwood and crossbanded ormolu-mounted bonheur du jour, c. 1870; 26 in. (64 cm) wide.

E4 A Victorian walnut-veneered bonheur du jour, c. 1870; 48 by 45 in. (122 by 119 cm).

E5 A burr-walnut bonheur du jour, c. 1870; 48 by 46 in. (122 by 117 cm).

E6 A walnut porcelain-mounted bonheur du jour, c. 1870; 58 by 44 in. (149 by 111 cm).

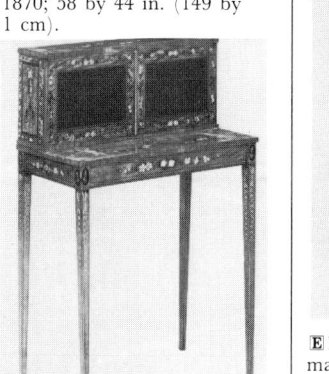

E7 A painted satinwood side bonheur du jour, c. 1880; 40 by 27 in. (100 by 67 cm).

E8 A Sheraton-style satinwood and painted bow-fronted bonheur du jour, c. 1880; 39 in. high by 28 in. wide (100 by 71 cm).

E9 An inlaid rosewood bonheur du jour, c. 1900; 47 in. high by 31 in. wide (120 by 79 cm).

E10 An Edwardian inlaid mahogany bonheur du jour, the superstructure fitted with two glazed cupboards and a mirrored compartment, the frieze fitted with three drawers, on tapered legs.

Bonheurs du Jour

The upper part of the early bonheur de jour was made detachable, often with a hooped carrying handle. It is therefore quite in order to find the entire top surface of the lower part veneered. The portion normally covered by the superstructure is delineated by a simple cockbead. The upper part would naturally have been in place for most of its life and when lifted will give a striking indication of the original contrasting colours of the veneers below.

The platform two-thirds of the way down the legs was an optional extra but has at various times been considered an ungainly feature and therefore removed. There will be marks on the inner sides of the four legs where such a tray existed. It is rare for a platform to have been added where none existed before.

E11 A rosewood and marquetry bonheur du jour, of serpentine form, c. 1910; 43 in. high by 27 in. wide (114 by 68 cm).

E12 A harewood bonheur du jour, crossbanded in tulipwood, 20th century; 41 by 28 in. (104 by 71 cm).

BOOKCASES
1740-1900

It was during the latter part of the 17th century that the possession of a library became the norm among the educated classes. Books were still expensive however, and their presence denoted wealth as well as education. No Georgian gentleman's house was complete without them, and the cabinet-makers who were called upon to create cases for their protection took full advantage of the contemporary improvements in plate glass making for their display.

Breakfront

E1 A George II mahogany and parcel-gilt breakfront bureau bookcase; 58 in. wide (147 cm).

D2 An early Chippendale mahogany bookcase, with graduated drawers on bracket feet.

C3 An early George III mahogany breakfront secretaire bookcase, with shaped bevelled glazed cupboard doors, flanked by outer doors carved with Corinthian pilasters, lower section with secretaire drawer; 106 in. high by 117 in. wide (268 by 297 cm).

C5 A mahogany bookcase; 118 in. (299 cm) wide.

C6 An Adam breakfront bookcase of faded mahogany, 98 in. high, 99 in. wide (247 by 251 cm).

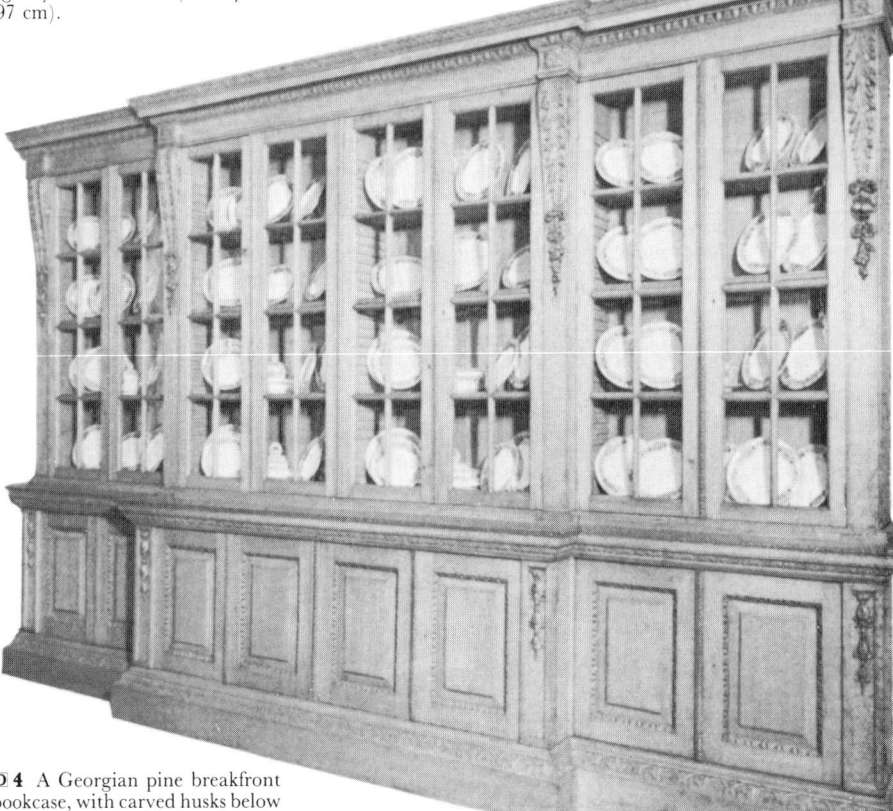

D4 A Georgian pine breakfront bookcase, with carved husks below a carved and moulded cornice, the base with deeply fielded panelled doors, between similar carvings; 111 in. high by 168 in. wide (282 by 427 cm).

D 1 A small Hepplewhite mahogany breakfront bookcase with fretted pediment; 98 in. high by 71 in. wide (248 by 180 cm).

D 2 A small George III breakfront bookcase in mahogany, with finely carved cornice, 1780; 102 in. high by 79 in. wide (258 by 201 cm).

D 3 A mahogany breakfront bookcase, with geometric glazing bars in the upper section, above cupboard doors with applied astragal mouldings, mid 18th century.

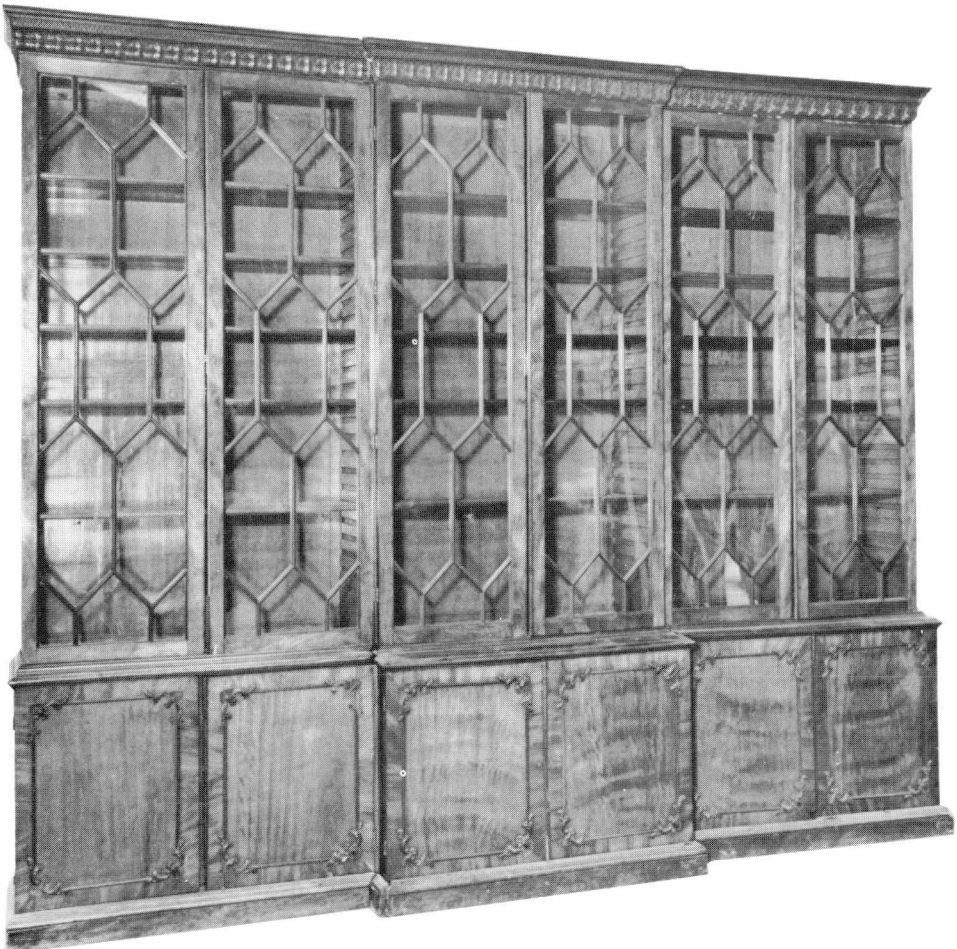

D 4 An early George III period breakfront bookcase, each of the 13-pane doors to the upper part with fine astragal glazing bars, below a carved frieze and moulded cornice, the cupboard doors of highly figured mahogany, with a carved motif at each corner of the door panels, *c.* 1760; 120 in. high by 150 in. wide (305 by 380 cm).

D 5 A Hepplewhite mahogany breakfront bookcase, with finely carved pear-drop cornice, 100 in. (253 cm) wide.

E 1 A Georgian breakfront bookcase in pine with broken pediment over 13-pane glazed doors.

D 2 A mahogany breakfront bookcase, *c.* 1770; 98 in. high by 91 in. wide (249 by 231 cm).

E 3 A mid-Georgian mahogany library breakfront bookcase, probably Irish, 97 by 95 in. (246 by 240 cm).

E 4 A small Irish mahogany breakfront bookcase, 94 in. high by 86 in. wide (240 by 219 cm).

E 5 An Irish Hepplewhite mahogany inlaid breakfront bookcase, the glazing bars of brass, *c.* 1790; 98 in. high, 111 in. wide (248 by 282 cm).

E 6 A Chippendale breakfront bookcase with fine, lavish carving throughout, 105 in. high and 96 in. wide (266 by 244 cm).

D 7 A Chippendale mahogany breakfront bookcase, 93 in. (237 cm) wide.

E 8 A Chippendale mahogany breakfront bookcase, 98 by 108 in. (248 by 275 cm) at cornice.

E 9 A Chippendale mahogany breakfront bookcase, 108 by 81 in. (275 by 206 cm).

D 10 A Chippendale mahogany breakfront library bookcase, 96 in. (244 cm) wide.

D 1 A George III mahogany breakfront secretaire bookcase, 84 in. (215 cm) wide.

C 2 An early George III mahogany breakfront bookcase, stamped T. Wilson, 68 Great Queen Street, London, *c.* 1760.

C 3 A George III mahogany breakfront library bookcase, *c.* 1770; 108 in high by 98 in wide (275 by 249 cm).

D 4 A George III breakfront library bookcase, 111 in. high by 129 in. wide (282 by 328 cm).

D 5 A George III mahogany breakfront bookcase, 95 by 105 in. (240 by 267 cm).

C 6 A George III mahogany bookcase, 87 by 86 in. (222 by 219 cm).

D 7 A George III mahogany breakfront library bookcase, 102 by 110 in. (280 by 285 cm).

C 8 A Hepplewhite breakfront secretaire bookcase, 82 in. (208 cm) wide.

C 9 A Hepplewhite mahogany breakfront bookcase, fitted secretaire, 72 in. (183 cm) wide.

D 10 A breakfront bookcase with secretaire, *c.* 1785; 82 in. high by 60 in. wide (208 by 152 cm).

Breakfront Bookcases

Bookcases are of two main types: the free-standing cabinet and the architectural fitment. Their very purpose necessitates a formal appearance and it follows that their decoration will be of a similar order.

The most important were of breakfront form, the centre part usually standing forward of the two wings, and over the years the sale of such items has led inevitably to the separation of the three pieces. Always bearing in mind the importance of the article it would naturally follow that show wood ends would be of the same material as the front, and not of a secondary timber as would be the case if it were a fitment.

Both cornice and plinth should show a mitred joint at the corner and not one in line with the side of the carcase; the latter feature indicates alteration at some time. It is worth noting that since the 1950s a considerable number of mid-19th century breakfront wardrobes have had their doors glazed to make them into far more desirable breakfront bookcases.

C 11 A mahogany breakfront bookcase of fine quality, well carved, with an unusual and attractive pattern of glazing bars.

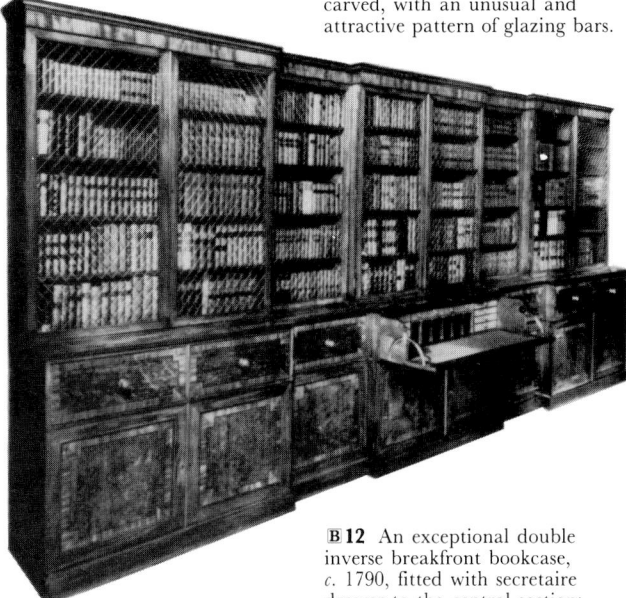

B 12 An exceptional double inverse breakfront bookcase, *c.* 1790, fitted with secretaire drawer to the central section; 192 in. (487 cm) wide.

C 1 A George III mahogany breakfront bookcase; 94 in. high by 94 in. wide (239 by 238 cm).

C 4 A Chippendale breakfront bookcase; 124 in. (315 cm) wide.

D 8 A George III mahogany breakfront bookcase; 94 in. high by 66 in. wide (239 by 168 cm).

D 12 A George III mahogany breakfront bookcase, late 18th century; 99 in. high by 97 in. wide (250 by 246 cm).

C 2 A mahogany breakfront secretaire bookcase glazed in the Gothic style over panelled drawers and cupboards, late 18th century. It is 100 in. high and 70 in. wide (253 by 178 cm). The wings are unusually narrow in proportion to the central section.

D 5 A Chippendale breakfront bookcase; 103 in. high by 69 in. wide (261 by 175 cm).

D 9 A George III mahogany breakfront library bookcase; 97 in. high by 90 in. wide (245 by 229 cm).

D 13 A George III mahogany library breakfront bookcase, *c.* 1780; 101 in. high by 123 in. wide (257 by 312 cm).

C 6 A Chippendale breakfront bookcase; 108 in. (275 cm) wide.

D 10 A George III mahogany breakfront bookcase, *c.* 1790; 96 by 96 in. (243 by 244 cm).

D 14 A late George III mahogany breakfront bookcase; 97 in. high by 101 in. wide (246 by 257 cm).

D 3 A Chippendale period mahogany breakfront bookcase with carved pediment and 13-pane glazed doors, of fine proportion and figuring; 71 in. (178 cm) wide.

C 7 A mahogany breakfront, *c.* 1765; 103 in. high by 96 in. wide (261 by 244 cm).

E 11 A George III mahogany breakfront library bookcase; 92 by 84 in. (234 by 215 cm).

D 15 A George III mahogany breakfront bookcase, late 18th century; 98 in. (249 cm) wide.

D 1 A George III mahogany breakfront bookcase; 90 in. (229 cm) wide.

C 2 A George III mahogany breakfront bookcase; 110 in. high by 154 in. wide (276 by 392 cm).

C 3 A Sheraton breakfront bookcase, veneered mahogany; 102 by 97 in. (258 by 246 cm).

D 4 A mahogany breakfront bookcase; 98 in. high by 80 in. wide (247 by 203 cm).

E 5 A mahogany breakfront bookcase, 18th century; 79 in. high by 44 in. wide (201 by 112 cm).

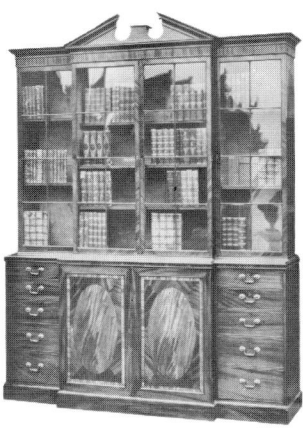

D 6 A late 18th-century mahogany breakfront bookcase with broken pediment and oval panels to the cupboard doors; 81 in. (206 cm) wide.

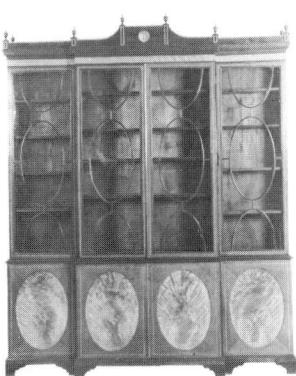

D 7 A satinwood and mahogany breakfront bookcase in late 18th-century classical style, with urns to the frieze, oval glazing panels and ovals to the cupboard doors; 104 in. (263 cm) high.

E 8 A George III mahogany breakfront library bookcase; 67 in. (169 cm) wide.

D 9 A George III mahogany double breakfront library bookcase; 115 by 181 in. (292 by 460 cm).

C 10 A George III mahogany breakfront library bookcase, late 18th century.

D 11 A George III mahogany breakfront library bookcase in the manner of Gillows.

D 12 A George III mahogany breakfront secretaire bookcase, *c.* 1800; 92 in. high by 80 in. wide (234 by 202 cm).

D 13 A finely figured mahogany breakfront bookcase, second half 18th century; 90 in. high by 84 in. wide (229 by 215 cm).

D 14 A George III mahogany breakfront secretaire library bookcase; 91 in. (232 cm) wide.

D 15 A George III mahogany breakfront secretaire library bookcase, *c.* 1800; 105 in. (272 cm) high.

D 1 A Regency mahogany breakfront open library bookcase, early 19th century; 95 in. high by 135 in. wide (241 by 342 cm).

D 2 A Regency mahogany double breakfront library bookcase; 106 in. high by 137 in. wide (271 by 248 cm).

E 3 A mahogany breakfront bookcase, 19th century; 96 in. high by 79 in. wide (244 by 201 cm).

E 4 A Regency mahogany breakfront library bookcase, 99 in. high by 101 in. wide (251 by 257 cm).

D 5 A Regency breakfront bookcase, with broken triangular pediment, centred by a reeded finial, above two pairs of geometrically glazed cupboard doors, enclosing shelves, the base with a fitted secretaire drawer, including maple-veneered short drawers; 101 in. high by 79 in. wide (256 by 201 cm).

D 6 A Regency mahogany breakfront library bookcase with four glazed doors over a secretaire drawer and three long drawers flanked by cupboard doors; 98 in. high, 104 in. wide (249 by 264 cm).

D 7 A William IV breakfront mahogany bookcase, c. 1830; 105 in. high by 84 in. wide (267 by 213 cm).

E 8 A mid-Victorian figured walnut breakfront bookcase, 112 in. high by 138 in. wide (285 by 351 cm).

E 9 A parcel-gilt walnut breakfront bookcase, c. 1840; 86 in. high by 119 in. wide (219 by 302 cm).

E 10 A George III-style library bookcase in figured mahogany, c. 1850; 92 in. high by 90 in. wide (234 by 229 cm).

E1 A mahogany breakfront library bookcase, *c.* 1840; 105 in. high by 87 in. wide (267 by 221 cm).

E2 A Victorian mahogany breakfront bookcase, 96 in. high by 100 in. wide (244 by 253 cm).

E3 A mahogany library bookcase, of double breakfront form, *c.* 1880; 104 in. high by 92 in. wide (263 by 234 cm).

E4 A George III-style mahogany breakfront cabinet bookcase, *c.* 1890; 104 in. high by 92 in. wide (264 by 234 cm).

E 5 An Edwardian mahogany and inlaid library bookcase with three astragal glazed doors, opening to inlaid shelves on breakfront base, 86 in. high by 72 in. wide (219 by 183 cm).

D6 A George III-style red japanned breakfront library bookcase, with rectangular cornice over four glazed doors with octagonal panes enclosing shelves, above four fielded cupboard doors, all decorated in colours with exotic birds and animals, 19th century; 92 in. high, 104 in. wide (234 by 262 cm).

E7 A William and Mary oak double-dome bureau bookcase, *c.* 1695; 36 in. (91 cm) wide.

E8 A small William and Mary oak bureau bookcase in three parts, with fitted interior, on later bracket feet, end of the 17th century; 27 in. (69 cm) wide.

D 1 A bureau bookcase, with candleslides and bookrest, early 18th century.

D 4 A Queen Anne walnut bureau bookcase, 38 in. (95 cm) wide.

C 7 A Queen Anne walnut bureau bookcase, 32 in. (82 cm) wide.

C 10 A Queen Anne elm and walnut bureau cabinet, 84 in. high by 41 in. wide (213 by 103 cm).

E 2 A Queen Anne walnut and crossbanded bureau bookcase, *c.* 1710; 87 in. high (222 cm).

E 5 A Queen Anne walnut bureau bookcase, *c.* 1710; 80 by 36 in. (203 by 91 cm).

C 8 A Queen Anne walnut small bureau bookcase, 69 in. high by 30 in. wide (175 by 75 cm).

E 11 A walnut and marquetry bureau cabinet, *c.* 1700; 89 in. high by 45 in. wide (220 by 114 cm).

C 3 A Queen Anne burr-walnut bureau bookcase, with pewter stringing, by Coxed and Woster.

D 6 A Queen Anne walnut bureau bookcase, *c.* 1710; 95 in. high by 39 in. wide (245 by 99 cm).

D 9 A Queen Anne walnut bureau cabinet, 92 in. high by 42 in. wide (234 by 105 cm).

C 12 A George I walnut bureau bookcase, with enclosed fitted interior, 41 in. (103 cm) wide.

C1 A George I walnut bureau bookcase with crossbanding and double herringbone inlay.

D2 A George I walnut and featherbanded bureau bookcase, *c.* 1720; 87 in. high by 32 in. wide (221 by 80 cm).

E3 A George I walnut bureau bookcase, *c.* 1720; 38 in. (96 cm) wide.

B4 A George I scarlet japanned bureau bookcase, the upper part with moulded broken arch pediment centring an urn above two mirror doors enclosing a well fitted interior with pigeonhole slides and a cupboard framed by fluted pilasters, the centre with sloping lid enclosing a fitted interior above a drawer, the bombé base with three graduated drawers and bracket feet, decorated in raised gilt with chinoiseries, early 18th century; 101 in. high by 44 in. wide (258 by 113 cm).

Bureau Bookcases

Once the escritoire had evolved into the fall-front bureau – by the end of the 17th century – its basic form, subject to the addition of a bookcase or cabinet over, remained unchanged.

The heyday of the bureau bookcase in Britain – in respect of its adornment at least – was the first 40 years of the 18th century. Bureau bookcases were expensive to make, and fine examples were not reluctant to display the wealth that had necessarily gone into their creation.

Exterior ornament, certainly by comparison with examples made on the Continent, was relatively restrained, but as much attention was lavished on the interior as on the outside.

Whereas Continental bureau bookcases were subject to the application of fanciful baroque or rococo ornament, in England classical architecture early became the leading decorative inspiration for library and bookcase furniture. Thus the cabinet surmounted by a broken triangular pediment centring an acrota will be supported on stylized capitals and columns, though the glazing to the doors could reveal a less rigorous taste, with touches of the Gothic, the Chinese and the rustic.

D6 A George I walnut bureau bookcase with two doors fitted with shaped mirror panels over a fall front, two short drawers and three long, *c.* 1725; 90 in. (229 cm) high.

E5 A George I walnut bureau bookcase, 83 in. (211 cm) high.

D 1 A George I walnut bureau cabinet, *c.* 1720; 85 in. high by 43 in. wide (216 by 108 cm).

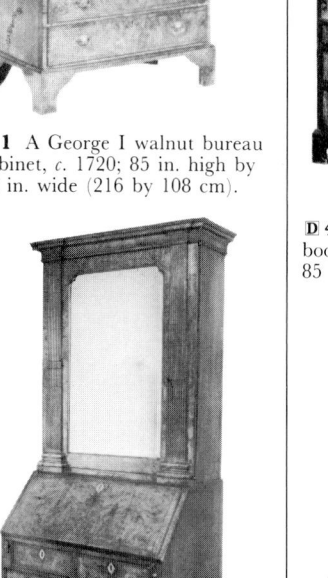

D 4 A George I walnut bureau bookcase, early 18th century; 85 by 44 in. (216 by 112 cm).

C 7 A George III mahogany bookcase, *c.* 1765; 103 in. high by 55 in. wide (260 by 140 cm).

E 10 A George III mahogany bureau bookcase, with well fitted interior; 37 in. (92 cm) wide.

C 2 A George I walnut bureau cabinet, *c.* 1720; 83 by 43 in. (186 by 109 cm).

E 5 A George II Virginian red walnut bureau cabinet bookcase; 42 in. (107 cm) wide.

E 8 A George III mahogany bureau bookcase, *c.* 1770.

D 11 A bureau bookcase, with crossbanded drawers and doors, mid 18th century.

E 3 A George I walnut bureau cabinet; 42 in. (107 cm) wide.

E 6 A George II Cuban mahogany bureau cabinet bookcase; 44 in. (111 cm) wide.

E 9 A George III mahogany bureau bookcase, *c.* 1770; 86 by 42 in. (218 by 108 cm).

E 12 A George III mahogany bureau bookcase, *c.* 1775; 102 by 42 in. (258 by 108 cm).

E 1 An 18th-century oak bureau bookcase.

E 2 A George III mahogany bureau bookcase, *c.* 1770.

E 3 A George III bureau bookcase, *c.* 1770; 80 by 35 in. (203 by 105 cm).

E 4 A George III mahogany bureau cabinet, with fitted interior; 49 in. (123 cm).

E 5 A George III mahogany bureau bookcase; 80 in. high by 42 in. wide (204 by 107 cm).

E 6 A George III mahogany bureau bookcase, *c.* 1780; 93 by 46 in. (236 by 117 cm).

E 7 A George III mahogany bureau bookcase, 46 in. (117 cm) wide. The frieze is carved with blind fretwork over two panelled doors with rosette spandrels, the whole well figured.

D 8 A George III mahogany bureau cabinet; 45 in. (115 cm) wide.

E 9 A Georgian mahogany bureau bookcase, 89 in. high by 44 in. wide (226 by 112 cm).

E 10 A satinwood bureau cabinet, with dentilled cornice, fitted interior.

E 11 A Georgian mahogany bureau bookcase; 38 in. (97 cm) wide.

E 12 A George III mahogany bureau bookcase, *c.* 1780; 94 by 51 in. (237 by 130 cm).

E1 A George III mahogany bureau bookcase, with fitted interior; 41 in. (104 cm) wide.

E4 A mahogany bureau bookcase, early 19th century; 41 in. (104 cm) wide.

E7 A mid-Victorian mahogany bureau bookcase; 97 by 43 in. (246 by 110 cm).

E10 A George III-style mahogany bureau bookcase; 87 by 44 in. (220 by 112 cm).

E2 An oak bureau bookcase, the flap enclosing a fitted interior, late 18th century.

E5 A mahogany cylinder bookcase, early 19th century; 99 by 45 in. (252 by 115 cm).

E8 A twin pedestal cylinder front mahogany bureau bookcase, 19th century; 106 by 60 in. (269 by 152 cm).

E11 A Queen Anne-style burr-walnut bureau bookcase, *c.* 1910.

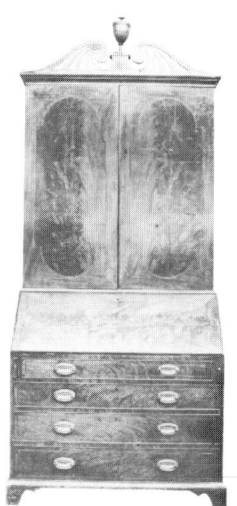

E3 An inlaid mahogany bureau bookcase, the bureau interior well fitted, late 18th century.

E6 A crossbanded mahogany cylinder bureau bookcase, early 19th century; 91 in. (228 cm) high.

E9 A late Victorian mahogany cylinder bureau bookcase, in the Chippendale style; 94 by 42 in. (239 by 107 cm).

E12 A kingwood-banded satinwood bureau bookcase; 78 in. (198 cm) high.

E1 A mahogany bureau bookcase, with fully fitted interior, 19th century.

E2 A small Edwardian inlaid mahogany bureau bookcase; 68 by 30 in. (172 by 76 cm).

E3 A satinwood and kingwood banded bureau bookcase on stand, *c.* 1880; 86 by 34 in. (218 by 85 cm).

Cabinet bookcases

E4 A Charles II oak bookcase, on turned elm feet; 74 in. high by 36 in. wide (187 by 91 cm).

C5 An English oak bookcase, late 17th century.

D6 An English oak bookcase, late 17th century.

E7 An oak bookcase, early 18th century; 46 in. (116 cm) wide.

E8 A Queen Anne walnut bookcase; 78 in. high by 42 in. wide (198 by 106 cm).

D9 A George II inlaid walnut bookcase, *c.* 1745; 102 in. high by 45 in. wide (258 by 114 cm).

C10 A mahogany cabinet or bookcase, first half 18th century.

E11 A George II mahogany bookcase, *c.* 1740; 93 in. high by 55 in. wide (226 by 141 cm).

E12 A George II mahogany cabinet bookcase, *c.* 1755; 89 in. high by 51 in. wide (226 by 130 cm).

E 1 An Adam mahogany bookcase, *c*. 1760; 99 in. high by 39 in. wide (251 by 99 cm).

C 4 A Chippendale bookcase, finely carved, with steeply curved pediment, and of rich, figured wood.

D 7 An Adam mahogany bookcase, *c*. 1775. This was originally the property of H.R.H. the Princess Royal, Duchess of Fife, whose house and furniture in Portman Square were designed by Robert Adam.

E 2 A Chippendale bookcase, 110 in. high by 54 in. wide (280 by 137 cm).

C 5 A George III mahogany bookcase, 100 in. high by 53 in. wide (254 by 134 cm).

E 3 A Chippendale-style mahogany dwarf bookcase, 35 in. (87 cm).

C 6 A Hepplewhite mahogany bookcase with carved scroll pediment centring an ornamented plinth over a carved frieze; 47 in. (119 cm) wide.

E 8 A George III mahogany bookcase, *c*. 1760; 100 in. high by 57 in. wide (253 by 144 cm).

E 9 A George III inlaid mahogany bookcase, with two astragal-glazed doors enclosing a shelved interior to the upper section, three short drawers and two cupboards enclosing shelves and 12 further short drawers below, flanked by reeded columns with waterleaf capitals and on a moulded plinth base, *c*. 1800; 74 in. (188 cm) high.

E1 A George III mahogany cabinet bookcase, *c.* 1800; 85 in. high by 50 in. (215 by 126 cm).

E2 A George III mahogany library bookcase, 40 in. (100 cm) wide.

E3 A George III mahogany bookcase, 94 in. high by 44 in. wide (240 by 112 cm).

E4 A late Georgian mahogany bookcase cupboard, 85 in. high by 47 in. wide (216 by 119 cm).

E5 A late Georgian mahogany bookcase, 113 in. high by 76 in. wide (287 by 193 cm).

E6 A Georgian mahogany bookcase, *c.* 1810; 47 in. wide (120 cm).

E7 A late George III rosewood bookcase, *c.* 1810; 87 in. high by 68 in. wide (220 by 173 cm).

E8 A Georgian mahogany bookcase, with two hinged and one sliding central astragal glazed doors, two drawers, one fitted with writing slope; 82 in. high by 58 in. wide (208 by 147 cm).

E9 A late George III mahogany bookcase, the upper part enclosed by a pair of glazed doors, the two cupboards below with filled panelled doors; 59 in. (150 cm) high.

E10 A Georgian crossbanded mahogany bookcase with fitted interior; 40 in. (103 cm) wide.

D11 A mahogany bookcase, inlaid with marquetry in harewood, satinwood bands and panels, early 19th century; 68 in. (174 cm) high.

D12 A Regency bookcase, with geometrically glazed Gothic cupboard doors flanked by fluted pilasters; 42 in. (108 cm) wide.

C1 A Regency mahogany library bookcase, one of a pair, the upper doors glazed with brass grilles over, the lower doors opening to drawers, front and sides reeded, *c.* 1810; 95 in. (240 cm) high.

E2 A Regency ebony inlaid bookcase, with scrolled pediment over arch-glazed doors, a drawer and grille fronted cupboard below; 104 in. (263 cm) high.

E3 A Regency small oak Gothic revival library bookcase, in the manner of George Smith, *c.* 1820.

E4 A George IV amboyna cabinet bookcase, *c.* 1825.

E5 A George IV mahogany library bookcase, *c.* 1820; 86 in. high by 66 in. wide (219 by 167 cm).

E6 A late Regency rosewood bookcase, with moulded cornice.

E7 A mahogany two-part bookcase, 19th century; 44 in. (112 cm) wide.

E8 A Victorian mahogany bookcase, with ogee-moulded cornice; 48 in. (122 cm) wide.

E9 A mahogany bookcase, with an ogee-moulded cornice, *c.* 1840; 98 in. high by 59 in. wide (249 by 150 cm).

E10 A Victorian oak and pollard oak bookcase, the lancets of the glazed doors echoed in the arches to the panelled doors below; 58 in. (148 cm) high.

E11 A Victorian red mahogany library bookcase; 93 in. high by 72 in. wide (242 by 183 cm).

E12 A Victorian mahogany library bookcase, with carved scrollwork pediment; 102 by 48 in. (258 by 122 cm).

E1 A walnut and marquetry bookcase, 19th century; 51 in. (130 cm) wide.

E2 A Victorian oak library bookcase; 90 by 74 in. (229 by 188 cm).

D3 A walnut bookcase, in well-figured and burr veneers; 84 in. (213 cm) high.

E4 A Sheraton style mahogany and satinwood crossbanded cabinet bookcase, *c.* 1880.

E5 A mahogany narrow bookcase, *c.* 1850; 96 in. high by 55 in. wide (243 by 139 cm).

E6 An Edwardian mahogany and marquetry bookcase, early 20th century; 98 by 55 in. (249 by 140 cm).

E7 A mahogany bookcase, with dentil cornice, 19th century; 72 in. (183 cm) wide.

E8 A George III style mahogany dual bow-front cabinet bookcase, *c.* 1930; 83 in. high by 39 in. wide (210 by 99 cm).

E9 A mahogany bookcase, second quarter 20th century; 87 in. high by 72 in. wide (221 by 183 cm).

E10 A Regency calamanderwood and mahogany dwarf bookcase, early 19th century; 39 in. (99 cm) wide.

E11 A mahogany bookcase, early 19th century; 43 in. high by 34 in. wide (117 by 85 cm).

E12 A Regency rosewood and satinwood low bookcase with glazed doors; 36 by 63 in. (90 by 160 cm).

E13 A Regency rosewood reading pedestal bookcase; 26 in. (64 cm) wide.

E1 A George IV rosewood bookcase, *c.* 1825; 38 in. high by 74 in. wide (97 by 188 cm).

E2 A William IV mahogany bookcase cabinet, stamped M. Willson, 68 Great Queen Street.

E5 A Chippendale secretaire bookcase; 99 in. high by 50 in. wide (251 by 127 cm).

E3 A Victorian rosewood low bookcase, fitted with a pair of plain glazed doors, on turned feet.

E4 A Victorian satinwood and ormolu-mounted bookcase, *c.* 1860; 37 in. high by 36 in. wide (93 by 91 cm).

E6 A Chippendale mahogany secretaire bookcase, the front decorated with carved capitals, fluting and stop-fluting over a secretaire drawer and two panelled, fielded cupboard doors; 100 in. high by 40 in. wide (253 by 103 cm).

E7 A Chippendale period secretaire bookcase, broken pediment and dentil-moulded cornice above two 15-pane doors, the chest base containing a fitted writing drawer over three long drawers and original bracket feet, *c.* 1765.

E8 A Chippendale mahogany secretaire bookcase with carved swan-neck pediment; 87 in. high by 32 in. wide (222 by 80 cm).

E9 A George III mahogany secretaire bookcase, *c.* 1760; 100 in. high by 45 in. wide (253 by 114 cm).

E10 A George III mahogany secretaire bookcase, *c.* 1775.

E11 A George III mahogany secretaire bookcase, *c.* 1780.

Open bookcases

E 1 A George III satinwood and mahogany open bookcase, inlaid with ebonized lines; 48 in. (122 cm) wide.

E 2 A George III mahogany dwarf bookcase; 18 in. (45 cm) wide.

E 3 A Hepplewhite mahogany open bookcase; 48 in. high by 23 in. wide (122 by 59 cm).

E 4 A mahogany open bookcase, c. 1790; 22 in. (56 cm) wide.

D 5 A small late George III mahogany circular revolving bookcase, c. 1800; 42 in. high by 22 in. diameter (107 by 56 cm).

E 6 A Sheraton mahogany open bookcase, c. 1790; 49 in. high by 24 in. wide (124 by 61 cm).

D 7 A Sheraton period West Indian satinwood standing bookshelf.

E 8 A Regency black painted and parcel gilt cabinet, early 19th century; 31 in (76 cm) wide.

E 9 A Regency mahogany dwarf bookcase, the raised superstructure with three shelves; 27 in. (69 cm) wide.

D 10 A Regency inlaid mahogany bookcase, early 19th century; 77 in. (196 cm) wide.

E 11 A Regency rosewood narrow bookcase, the base with an ormolu-panelled frieze drawer.

E 12 A Regency rosewood bookcase, the drawer fitted for writing, c. 1815; 34 in. (85 cm) wide.

D 1 A mahogany open-shelved library bookcase, in the manner of Thomas Hope, 48 in. high by 101 in. wide (122 by 257 cm).

D 2 A pair of Regency rosewood open dwarf bookshelves, with brass mounts on turned supports, 35 in. high by 41 in. wide (88 by 102 cm).

E 5 A Regency rosewood dwarf bookcase, 47 in. (125 cm) wide.

E 3 A Regency mahogany bookcase, with cupboard and fluted columns, 36 in. (90 cm) long.

E 4 A Regency ormolu-mounted rosewood dwarf bookcase, 62 in. (156 cm) wide.

E 6 A mahogany library book cabinet, with ebonized mouldings, c. 1840; 83 in. high by 54 in. wide (211 by 136 cm).

E 7 A Regency rosewood dwarf bookcase, with rectangular top, the frieze and angles inlaid with engraved brass scrolling foliage and flower heads, with adjustable shelves; 54 in. (137 cm) wide

E 8 A Regency rosewood and parcel-gilt dwarf bookcase, with white marble top, 54 in. (137 cm) wide.

D 9 A Regency mahogany revolving four-tier bookcase, 54 in. (137 cm) high.

E 10 A Regency mahogany book case, with gilt metal mounts, the rectangular hinged adjustable top with gadrooned edging, c. 1815; 32 in. high by 21 in. wide (79 by 52 cm).

E 11 A Victorian bamboo framed revolving bookcase, with lacquered bird and floral decoration to top and undertiers, 19 in. (49 cm).

Secretaire bookcases

C 1 A Queen Anne walnut and herringbone writing cabinet.

D 2 A veneered burr-walnut secretaire cabinet, *c.* 1710; 72 in. high by 30 in. (183 by 45 cm).

E 3 A Queen Anne burr-walnut secretaire cabinet, 79 in. by 32 in. (201 by 80 cm).

E 4 A Queen Anne walnut and gold secretaire with Vauxhall bevelled mirror in door.

D 5 A George II mahogany secretaire cabinet, mid 18th century; 45 in. wide by 25 in. deep (116 by 63 cm).

E 6 A George II mahogany secretaire cabinet, *c.* 1750; 76 in. high, 31 in. wide (193 by 78 cm).

E 7 A George III mahogany secretaire cabinet, 89 in. high by 45 in. wide (227 by 114 cm).

E 8 An early George III secretaire cabinet, 44 in. (111 cm) wide.

E 9 A George III secretaire cabinet, fitted with drawers and pigeonholes, 68 in. (173 cm) wide.

E 10 A late George III mahogany secretaire desk, 81 in. high, 40 in. wide (205 by 101 cm).

D 11 A George III satinwood secretaire cabinet, 83 in. high by 38 in. wide (211 by 96 cm).

D 12 A Sheraton rosewood cabinet, with well fitted secretaire drawer, 77 in. high by 34 in. (196 by 85 cm).

BUCKETS
1750-1850

The craft of the cooper combined with that of the cabinet-maker to produce plate pails and peat buckets, both being necessary given the considerable distances in large houses from kitchens and fuel stores to the family rooms. The best examples are in mahogany, brass-bound, sometimes turned, sometimes fretted, a plate pail being distinguished from a peat bucket by its deep slots, designed to allow safe removal of the plates.

E1 A George II mahogany peat bucket, *c.* 1750; 16 in. high by 15 in. diameter (40 by 37 cm).

E2 A circular plate pail, *c.* 1750; 14 in. high by 15 in. diameter (36 by 38 cm).

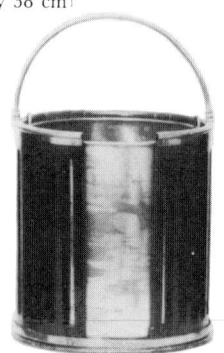

E3 A George II circular mahogany plate pail, *c.* 1750.

E4 A George III mahogany plate bucket, late 18th century; 14 in. by 15 in. (34 by 38 cm).

E5 A George III mahogany peat bucket, late 18th century: 14 in. by 15 in. (35 by 38 cm).

E6 A George III brass-bound plate bucket, 11 in. (28 cm) diameter.

E7 A George III brass-bound mahogany plate bucket, with lift-out copper liner and brass handle.

E8 A George III mahogany plate bucket, 16 in. (42 cm) wide.

E9 A George III mahogany plate bucket, 13 in. (33 cm) high.

E10 A George III brass-bound mahogany peat bucket, with circular tapering body, the carrying handle with copper studs, 16 in. (39 cm) wide.

E11 A George III mahogany oval peat bucket, with brass liner, 12 in. (30 cm) wide.

E12 A George III mahogany plate pail, *c.* 1770; 18 in. (44 cm) high.

E13 A brass-bound mahogany oval bucket, *c.* 1780; 15 in. (37 cm) wide.

E14 A mahogany wall bucket, *c.* 1800; 18 in. (45 cm) high.

E15 A leather fire bucket, painted with the Arms of England, 19th century; 12 in. (29 cm) high.

BUREAUX
1670-1920

The evolution of the two-part escritoire into the single-piece bureau was complete by the late Queen Anne period, though on some later examples a simulated retaining moulding can be seen a third of the way down the carcase at the point where desk and chest meet. Arguably the most attractive bureaux, distinguished for their excellent figuring or fine lacquer work, date from this early period, up to the 1730s.

E1 A Jacobean oak bureau, 42 in. high by 39 in. wide (105 by 97 cm).

E2 A Charles II oak desk, 32 in. (79 cm) wide.

E3 A William and Mary lady's writing bureau.

D4 A William and Mary marquetry bureau, 35 in. high by 36 in. wide (88 by 90 cm).

E5 A William and Mary walnut bureau, 22 in. (55 cm) wide.

E6 A William and Mary oak bureau, *c.* 1695; 38 in. high by 39 in. wide (93 by 99 cm).

D7 A William and Mary walnut bureau, 42 in. by 39 in. wide (105 by 98 cm).

E8 A William and Mary walnut and crossbanded bureau, *c.* 1700; 39 in. by 36 in. (98 by 91 cm).

E9 A William and Mary walnut bureau, in two parts 40 in. (102 cm) wide.

E10 A William and Mary bureau, interior with three secret drawers, 36 in. (90 cm) wide.

E11 A Queen Anne period bureau with oak-lined drawers and well, *c.* 1710; 38 in. by 32 in. (93 by 80 cm).

D12 A Queen Anne walnut bureau, 41 in. (103 cm) wide.

E13 A Queen Anne walnut bureau inlaid with feather-banding, *c.* 1710; 39 in. by 28 in. (99 by 72 cm).

E14 A Queen Anne black and gold lacquer bureau, in two parts, 35 in. (88 cm) wide.

E15 A Queen Anne oak bureau, 34 in. (85 cm) wide.

The Dating of Bureaux
The bureau was by no means an expensive piece of furniture made exlusively for the upper classes, and an extraordinary number dating from the early 18th century are extant in secondary as well as primary woods.

Once established, the shape of the bureau changed little throughout the 18th and 19th centuries, for there was little room for improvement. Precise dating of examples constructed throughout of secondary woods can therefore be difficult and it is to the finer points of construction that one must turn: drawers of the first 30 years of the 18th century will have very thin sides, the tops of which will be of rounded section; the application of a cockbead indicates post-1710; an old bureau originally fitted with bun feet, subsequently replaced, will show holes in the bottom front corners of the carcase base when the bottom drawer is removed and may provide the pleasant surprise of an earlier date than first appearance suggested.

D 1 A Queen Anne scarlet and gold lacquer bureau, 37 in. (94 cm) wide.

E 2 A Queen Anne walnut bureau, 18th century; 29 in. (73 cm) wide.

E 3 A Queen Anne walnut bureau, with sloping crossbanded flap, 30 in. (75 cm) wide.

E 4 A Queen Anne walnut bureau, 36 in. (90 cm) wide.

E 5 A Queen Anne walnut bureau, featherbanded, 36 in (90 cm) wide.

E 6 A Queen Anne walnut bureau, *c.* 1710; 33 in. (84 cm) wide.

E 7 A Queen Anne walnut bureau, *c.* 1710; 40 in. high by 36 in. wide (101 by 91 cm).

E 8 A Queen Anne pale walnut bureau, 36 in. (92 cm) wide.

E 9 A small Queen Anne bureau, of fine colour and patination, *c.* 1710; 24 in. (60 cm) wide.

E 10 A Queen Anne bureau, in finely figured walnut veneer, *c.* 1710; 40 in. high by 38 in. wide (100 by 93 cm).

E 11 A George I bureau, in pollard oak, *c.* 1720; 37 in. (94 cm) wide.

E 12 A George I walnut slant-front bureau, early 18th century; 38 in. (97 cm) wide.

E 13 A George I veneered walnut bureau, with stepped interior, *c.* 1720; 40 in. by 36 in. (100 by 90 cm).

E 14 A George I walnut bureau, inlaid with boxwood stringing, *c.* 1720; 33 in. (84 cm) wide.

E1 A George I burr-walnut slant-front writing bureau, early 18th century.

E2 An early Georgian small oak bureau, enclosing a fitted interior, 31 in. (79 cm) wide.

E3 A Georgian oak and chestnut bureau, with framed slant front bearing moulded bookrest, enclosing interior fitted with drawers, early-to-mid-18th century.

E4 A George I walnut bureau, inlaid, crossbanded and quarter-veneered, the upper drawer concealing a fitted interior.

E5 A George I walnut bureau, distinguished by fine use of veneers and vigorously contrasting banding.

E6 A George I walnut and feather banded bureau, *c.* 1720; 41 in. by 36 in. (105 by 91 cm).

E7 A George I walnut bureau, on bracket feet, *c.* 1720; 41 in. high by 36 in. wide (105 by 92 cm).

E8 A George II bureau, in figured faded oak, *c.* 1740; 39 in. high by 33 in. wide (98 by 81 cm).

E9 A George II walnut bureau, 44 in. high by 42 in. wide (113 by 107 cm).

E10 A George II bureau, in walnut on oak, *c.* 1745; 40 in. high by 36 in. wide (100 by 90 cm).

E11 A George II walnut and yew-wood bureau, 40 in. (100 cm) wide.

E12 A Chippendale period mahogany bureau, *c.* 1760; 43 in. high by 39 in. wide (108 by 98 cm).

E13 A Georgian oak bureau, with mahogany crossbandings, 36 in. (91 cm) wide.

E14 A George III mahogany bureau, probably Scottish, *c.* 1780; 45 in. by 46 in. (114 by 115 cm).

E15 An early George III mahogany bureau, 46 in. (115 cm) wide.

E16 A Chippendale mahogany bureau-on-stand, 31 in. (77 cm) wide.

D1 A George III mahogany bureau with carved corners, mouldings and feet; 42 in. (105 cm) wide.

E2 A Georgian mahogany bureau, fitted interior with secret compartments; 48 in. (121 cm) wide.

E3 A George III oak and elm bureau, the walnut lined flap enclosing a fitted interior, above two short and two long drawers, *c.* 1770; 30 in. (76 cm) wide.

E4 A George III mahogany bureau, the fall front enclosing a simply fitted interior, third quarter 18th century; 41 in. by 36 in. (104 by 92 cm).

E5 A George II chestnut bureau, the fitted interior above four long drawers, on bracket feet, 38 in. (94 cm) wide.

E6 A George III mahogany bureau, the sloping fall front enclosing drawers and pigeonholes, *c.* 1760; 42 in. (105 cm) wide.

E7 A George III solid elm bureau, with fitted interior, *c.* 1770; 42 in. high by 37 in. wide (106 by 94 cm).

E8 A George III mahogany bureau, the fall front opening to reveal a fitted interior including a hinged writing surface, over two short drawers and three long.

E9 A George III burr walnut, tulipwood crossbanded and marquetry bureau; 32 in. (82 cm) wide.

E10 A George III mahogany bureau, with satinwood crossbanded fall front; 44 in. (110 cm) wide.

E11 A late Georgian painted mahogany bureau, decorated with sea battles; 40 in. (100 cm) wide.

E12 A well proportioned mahogany bureau of modest size – 36 in. (90 cm) wide – from the middle of the 18th century.

E13 A small George III mahogany bureau, the interior fitted with drawers, pigeonholes and a cupboard.

E14 A Georgian mahogany bureau, the writing slope enclosing a fitted interior.

E15 A Georgian mahogany bureau, the fittings including secret compartments; 42 in. (105 cm) wide.

E16 A George III oak bureau, the flap enclosing a fitted interior, *c.* 1775; 40 in. high by 37 in. wide (101 by 94 cm).

E1 A George III inlaid and figured mahogany fall-front writing bureau; 47 in. (120 cm) wide.

E2 A George III mahogany bureau, decorated with crossbandings and inlaid stringings, having fitted interior; 36 in. (90 cm) wide.

E3 A small Georgian mahogany bureau, with satinwood and mahogany interior, *c.* 1790; 40 in. high by 30 in. wide (100 by 78 cm).

E4 A mahogany bureau, with inlaid interior fittings; 45 in. (110 cm) wide.

E5 A small oak bureau, with fitted interior, late 18th century; 38 in. (95 cm) wide.

E6 A mahogany slope-front bureau, with well fitted interior, 18th century; 36 in. (90 cm) wide.

E7 A large late Georgian mahogany bureau with inlaid decoration to the interior; 48 in. (122 cm) wide.

E8 A George III well figured satinwood cylinder bureau, in the French style, *c.* 1780; 41 in. high by 43 in. wide (103 by 109 cm).

D9 A George III satinwood and marquetry bureau, in the style of Thomas Chippendale; 34 in. (85 cm) wide.

D10 A George III satinwood cylinder bureau, in the French taste; 41 in. (104 cm) wide.

E11 A George III mahogany tambour bureau, enclosing pigeonholes and drawers; 36 in. (90 cm) wide.

E12 An inlaid roll-top bureau, with fitted interior; 43 in. (107 cm) wide.

D13 A George III satinwood cylinder bureau, enclosing a fitted interior; 39 in. (99 cm) wide.

E14 A George III satinwood cylinder bureau, enclosing a fitted interior with pigeonholes; 37 in. (92 cm) wide.

D15 A George III burr-yew cylinder bureau, with well fitted interior; 36 in. (92 cm) wide.

E16 An inlaid and crossbanded mahogany bureau, fully fitted interior, 19th century; 46 in. (115 cm) wide.

E1 An inlaid mahogany bureau, with well fitted interior, early 19th century; 46 in. (115 cm) wide.

E2 An oak bureau, all carved in high relief with leafage and lions' heads, the sloping front with a fitted interior, 19th century; 38 in. (95 cm) high.

E3 A mahogany bureau, inlaid with shell, foliage and chequered boxwood lines, 19th century; 47 in. (120 cm) high.

E4 A yew-wood bureau, the fall front enclosing a fitted interior, 42 in. by 36 in. (107 by 92 cm).

E5 An Edwardian mahogany inlaid and crossbanded bureau, *c.* 1910; it is 38 in. high and 35 in. wide (96 by 83 cm).

E6 A walnut chevron-banded bureau, with fitted interior, late 19th century; 39 in. (98 cm) high.

E7 A rosewood and satinwood inlaid bureau de dame, fitted with pigeonholes, late 19th century; 30 in. (75 cm) wide.

E8 A small figured mahogany bureau with satinwood crossbanding, late 19th century; 30 in. wide, 40 in. high (76 by 102 cm).

E9 A George I style lady's walnut bureau, *c.* 1920; 26 in. (65 cm) high.

E10 A mahogany and marquetry bureau-on-stand, in the revived Queen Anne style, *c.* 1900.

E11 A William and Mary style walnut and featherbanded bureau, *c.* 1880; 37 in. (91 cm) high.

E12 A George II-design mahogany bureau, with a curved fitted interior; 30 in. (75 cm) wide.

E13 A burr-walnut bureau-on-stand, in George I style, with a fitted interior, *c.* 1920.

Bureau cabinets

E1 A William and Mary walnut bureau cabinet, the mirrored doors enclosing a later fitted interior, the flap opening to a fitted interior with well, *c.* 1770; 80 in. high, 39 in. wide (203 by 99 cm).

C5 A William and Mary walnut double-domed bureau cabinet, enclosing adjustable shelves; 40 in. (100 cm) wide.

C3 A William and Mary burr walnut bureau cabinet, with double-domed top and finely fitted interior, the sloping front enclosing pigeonholes, the wood throughout superbly figured.

E6 A black and gold lacquer bureau cabinet, the interior with pigeonholes and short drawers.

C2 A double-domed mulberry wood bureau cabinet with a fitted interior, attributed to Coxed and Woster, *c.* 1710.

D4 A scarlet lacquer bureau cabinet, the sloping flap decorated with chinoiserie figures; 80 in. (202 cm) high.

E7 A Queen Anne oak bureau cabinet, with considerable modifications to feet, handles and mirrors.

D 1 A Queen Anne walnut bureau cabinet, with moulded double-domed cornice, glazed cupboard doors enclosing a well fitted interior, on turned feet; 82 in. high by 41 in. wide (208 by 104 cm).

D 3 A Queen Anne black and gold lacquer bureau cabinet, the upper part with moulded broken pediment, above two bevelled mirror-glazed doors, enclosing a scarlet japanned interior of nine pigeonholes and six drawers, the inside of the doors decorated with mythical beasts and birds; 41 in. (104 cm) wide.

D 2 A Queen Anne walnut bureau cabinet, the crossbanded doors with bevelled mirrors and enclosing shelves, the lower part with a fitted interior, *c.* 1710; 42 in. high by 43 in. wide (104 by 107 cm).

C 4 A George I walnut bureau cabinet, the cupboard doors enclosing short drawers, racks and pigeonholes above two candle-slides; 103 in. high by 44 in. wide (261 by 112 cm).

C 5 A Queen Anne walnut bureau cabinet, with fitted interior; 87 in. high by 44 in. wide (221 by 112 cm).

C 6 A Queen Anne walnut bureau cabinet, with broken arched cornice above a pair of doors with shaped tops, enclosing shelves, pigeonholes and drawers, *c.* 1700; 93 in. high by 42 in. wide (236 by 107 cm).

C 1 A green and gold lacquer bureau cabinet, the arched broken pediment above mirror-glazed cupboard doors, enclosing a scarlet lacquered interior with pigeonholes and small drawers; 70 in. by 40 in. (229 by 102 cm).

D 2 A George I walnut bureau cabinet, *c.* 1720; 87 in. high by 42 in. wide (220 by 107 cm).

D 3 A walnut bureau cabinet, the front decorated in highly figured burr veneers, the fall front containing compartments and small drawers, above four-drawer base, the doors to the upper part with almost plain rectangular frames, beneath deeply moulded, severe cornice, *c.* 1730; 39 in. (99 cm) wide.

D 4 A George I walnut bureau cabinet, *c.* 1725; 84 in. high by 42 in. wide (213 by 107 cm).

D 5 A George I walnut bureau cabinet, 83 in. high by 41 in. wide (211 by 105 cm).

E 6 A George I walnut bureau cabinet with two arched doors, the fall front inlaid with a vase of flowers, the whole inlaid with chequered lines; 41 in. (104 cm) wide.

Bureau Cabinets

Bureau cabinets are by their very nature structurally elaborate and were therefore expensive when they were made. Most received lavish decoration, either by the application of veneer or lacquer. However, there are a number of contemporary and fashionably correct examples in oak, and it is important to bear this in mind, as in the past this type has sometimes been decorated to enhance its value.

The inside of a drawer front intended to be veneered in walnut would have been made of pine or other less expensive timber, the top edge faced with a piece of oak to match the remainder of the lining visible when the drawer was opened. The inside of the front of a drawer to a cabinet that was intended to have oak as its show wood will also be oak, as the same timber would have been used throughout.

Bureau cabinets have been prone to separation as well as marriage. A bureau intended to take a cabinet will usually have a steeper fall than one made to stand alone – this was to make a larger top for the cabinet to stand on. Also, the retaining moulding should normally be on top of the bureau rather than on the foot of the cabinet – the latter position may indicate a marriage.

E 7 A small walnut veneered bureau cabinet, crossbanded and outlined with feather stringing; 74 in. high by 29 in. wide (188 by 71 cm).

E 1 A late George II or early George III oak bureau cabinet, mid 18th century; 82 in. (208 cm) high.

E 4 A mid-Georgian mahogany bureau cabinet, enclosing a mahogany-lined interior, 86 in. (217 cm) high.

E 7 A George III mahogany estate bureau cabinet, crossbanded in tulipwood, 75 in. high by 47 in. wide (190 by 120 cm).

D 10 A George III fiddleback mahogany bureau cabinet, with well fitted interior, 36 in. (92 cm) wide.

E 2 A George II mahogany bureau cabinet, fitted with drawers, shelves and pigeonholes, 40 in. (100 cm) high.

E 5 A mid-Georgian mahogany bureau cabinet, with triangular broken pediment, 45 in. (114 cm) wide.

D 8 An Irish Georgian walnut bureau cabinet, with moulded double-domed cornice, 37 in. (93 cm) wide.

E 11 A satinwood cabinet in the Sheraton manner, the doors inlaid with ovals and quarter-veneered, c. 1770.

E 3 A mid-Georgian mahogany bureau cabinet, with moulded broken pediment, 45 in. (114 cm) wide.

E 6 An early George III mahogany secretaire cabinet, enclosing fitted interior, 96 in. (244 cm) high.

D 9 A mid-Georgian mahogany bureau cabinet, with well fitted interior, 45 in. (114 cm) wide.

E 12 A red tortoiseshell-veneered bureau cabinet, part late 18th century; 79 in. high by 43 in. wide (199 by 109 cm).

CABINETS
1690-1920

In its earliest known form in England the cabinet was the equivalent of a safe, in which valuables and documents were kept secure. By the time of the grand pieces shown here though, the purpose of the cabinet had changed. Far from being a device to conceal wealth it had become a form of ostentation in itself and was also used to show the owner's prize pieces of *vertu* in the central cupboard, which was often mirrored to enhance the effect.

E1 A William and Mary walnut veneered cabinet-on-chest *c.* 1690; 66 in. high by 42 in. wide (169 by 107 cm). There is a cushion drawer to the frieze and the doors, which enclose an arrangement of 11 drawers and a cupboard, have arched panels and feather banding.

D2 A William and Mary black and gold lacquer cabinet, the cupboard doors mounted with shaped and engraved lockplates, and enclosing various sized drawers, all well decorated, the cabinet on later turned feet, 39 in. (99 cm) wide.

E3 A William and Mary fruitwood and walnut cabinet-on-chest, the cushion frieze above a pair of feather banded doors enclosing a cupboard and small drawers, below are two short and two long drawers, on associated bun feet, *c.* 1690; 67 in. high by 42 in. wide (170 by 107 cm).

C4 A William and Mary walnut and floral marquetry cabinet-on-chest, the doors enclosing 13 drawers and a cupboard, 71 in. high by 43 in. wide (180 by 109 cm).

E5 A brass-mounted walnut cabinet-on-chest with elaborately fitted interior, *c.* 1700 but remodelled *c.* 1890; 71 in. high by 45 in. wide (179 by 114 cm).

E6 A Queen Anne walnut cabinet-on-chest, the upper part enclosing 12 various sized drawers, early 18th century; 44 in. (112 cm) wide.

D7 A Queen Anne walnut veneered cabinet-on-chest, the moulded cornice above a pair of herringbone crossbanded doors, *c.* 1710; 70 in. high by 44 in. wide (178 by 112 cm).

D 1 A rare Queen Anne walnut cabinet, in two parts, the upper part within deep retaining moulding, *c.* 1710.

D 2 A Queen Anne period walnut cabinet, the upper part with several secret drawers, 66 in. high by 42 in. wide (168 by 106 cm).

E 3 A mahogany cabinet with glazed panelled doors in the upper part enclosing small drawers and central cupboard, early 18th century; 76 in. high by 42 in. wide (193 by 104 cm).

C 4 A small veneered walnut cabinet, the upper stage fitted with small drawers and a cupboard flanked by three secret compartments, the lower stage with two short and two long drawers, early 18th century; 48 in. high by 18 in. wide (122 by 45 cm).

D 5 A walnut double-dome gentleman's dressing cabinet, top section fitted with adjustable shelves, *c.* 1730; 83 in. high by 38 in. wide (211 by 95 cm).

D 6 A Chippendale winged cabinet, the underpart fitted for writing, 49 in. (124 cm) wide.

E 8 A Chippendale mahogany cabinet-on-chest, *c.* 1770; 87 in. by 51 in. (222 by 130 cm).

D 7 A Chippendale mahogany cabinet, 96 in. high by 54 in. wide (244 by 137 cm).

E1 A Chippendale mahogany serpentine cabinet with bookshelves above, 53 in. by 30 in. (133 by 76 cm).

E2 A Sheraton mahogany secretaire book cabinet, with satinwood crossbanding, *c.* 1780; 88 in. high by 37 in. wide (224 by 92 cm).

E3 A mahogany cabinet, inlaid with radial boxwood lines, late 18th century; 39 in. (99 cm) wide.

E4 A George III mahogany estate cabinet, with breakfront moulded dentilled cornice and two panelled mirror-glazed cupboard doors, fitted removable interior, various drawers and cupboard, 79 in. high by 52 in. wide (200 by 131 cm).

E5 An Edwardian mahogany cabinet-on-chest, fitted with a pair of figured mahogany doors, inlaid with oval stringing, four crossbanded long drawers, 31 in. (78 cm) wide.

D6 A George III mahogany breakfront cabinet, with later applied carving, the dentilled cornice and fluted frieze above four panelled doors enclosing shelves and drawers, the lower panelled doors enclosing sliding trays and flanked by drawers, on plinth base, *c.* 1800; 96 in. high by 109 in. wide (244 by 277 cm).

E7 A William and Mary design oyster walnut cabinet-on-chest, *c.* 1850; 65 in. by 44 in. (164 by 112 cm).

Divide and Ruin
Two-part furniture has always been prone to marriage and divorce and not always for pecuniary gain. During the 18th century when estates were sold the chattels almost invariably went to houses of a lower standing and often for the sake of convenience, cabinets-on-chests, clothes presses and the like were divided, flat tops being placed on the base parts and feet added to the upper. Furniture left on death was all too often literally divided between the heirs, with the same results.

The traditional arrangement of three short drawers over three long to the tops of tallboys was peculiar to the upper part of a chest-on-chest and was not incorporated in a similar quality chest of drawers until the latter part of the 18th century except, deceptively, in some North Country pieces.

Cabinets-on-stands

E1 A James I black japanned cabinet-on-stand, the doors painted with chinoiserie landscapes, on later ebonized stand, 26 in. (65 cm) wide.

D2 A Charles II needlework cabinet-on-stand, 57 in. high by 38 in. wide (145 by 97 cm).

E3 A James II lacquered cabinet-on-stand, the interior with ten drawers, 63 by 45 in. (160 by 114 cm).

E4 A lacquer cabinet-on-stand, the interior fitted with drawers, *c.* 1680; 66 in. (167 cm) high.

D5 A Charles II marquetry cabinet-on-stand, 45 in. (114 cm) wide.

E6 A Charles II scarlet japanned cabinet-on-stand, *c.* 1665; 66 in. (168 cm) high.

E7 A Charles II japanned cabinet-on-stand, *c.* 1670; 64 in. (162 cm) high.

E8 A Charles II European japanned cabinet-on-stand, the doors with pierced and engraved strapwork mounts, escutcheon plate and enclosing a fitted interior with an arrangement of drawers, on a silvered stand with deep carved and pierced apron, *c.* 1660; 68 in. high by 40 in. wide (173 by 103 cm).

E9 A Charles II walnut veneered cabinet-on-stand, crossbanded doors enclosing an arrangement of 11 drawers, with secret drawers, *c.* 1670; 64 in. (161 cm) high.

E10 A William III walnut and oyster-veneered parquetry cabinet-on-stand, two crossbanded doors inlaid with stringing and enclosing 12 short crossbanded oyster-veneered drawers with central cupboard enclosing a mirrored architectural niche, late 17th/early 18th century, 38 in. (95 cm) wide.

E 1 A William and Mary oyster-veneered olivewood cabinet-on-stand, enclosing a central cupboard with sliding panel at the back, *c.* 1690; 58 in. high, 40 in. wide (146 by 100 cm).

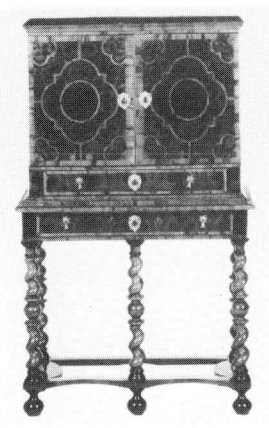

D 2 A William and Mary oyster-veneered olivewood cabinet-on-stand, the doors enclosing eight drawers, *c.* 1700; 56 in. high by 36 in. wide (141 by 90 cm).

E 3 A William and Mary oyster yew-wood cabinet-on-stand, enclosing an interior fitted with drawers, surrounding a central cupboard, *c.* 1690; 51 in. high by 42 in. wide (160 by 106 cm).

E 4 A William and Mary walnut and marquetry cabinet-on-stand, with convex frieze drawer, the two doors enclosing 11 various-sized drawers, 43 in. (108 cm) wide.

E 5 A George I black and gold lacquer cabinet-on-stand, fitted with two cupboard doors decorated in raised gilt with chinoiserie figures and mounted with shaped and engraved gilt-brass hinges, lockplates and angles, enclosing ten various-sized drawers in a well balanced arrangement; 40 in. (101 cm) wide.

E 6 A William and Mary walnut and floral marquetry cabinet-on-stand, enclosing 12 various-sized drawers, 68 in. high by 51 in. wide (173 by 128 cm).

E 7 A Queen Anne black and gold lacquer cabinet-on-stand, the doors highlighted in gold and red, 42 in. (106 cm) wide.

E 8 A walnut cabinet-on-stand, with convex frieze drawer and ten various-sized drawers, the fitted interior enclosed by two doors, the base with a long drawer, early 18th century; 48 in. (123 cm) wide.

E1 A Queen Anne black japanned cabinet on George I stand, 61 in. by 36 in. (155 by 92 cm).

E4 A George III chinoiserie black japanned and gilt decorated cabinet-on-stand, *c.* 1755; 53 in. high by 39 in. wide (135 by 99 cm).

E7 A George III black and gold lacquer cabinet-on-stand, with pierced fretwork gallery, two doors decorated with chinoiserie figures, with shaped and engraved gilt-brass hinges, angles and lockplates, enclosing eleven various sized drawers, the stand decorated with flower sprays on square legs, headed by pierced angle brackets, 39 in. (99 cm) wide.

E2 A George III mahogany collector's cabinet, with lift-top and an arrangement of small drawers, 21 in. (53 cm) wide.

C5 A lacquer cabinet inlaid with pietra dura marble plaques, *c.* 1755; 75 in. high by 38 in. wide (189 by 95 cm).

E3 A George III mahogany cabinet-on-stand, the doors filled with gilt wire, 22 in. (55 cm) wide.

E6 A George I red japanned cabinet-on-stand, with two cupboard doors decorated in gilt with chinoiserie figures, enclosing eleven drawers similarly decorated, the sides decorated with flowering branches.

E8 A George III chinoiserie black japanned and gilt decorated cabinet-on-stand, the legs reduced, *c.* 1755; 53 in. high by 39 in. wide (135 by 99 cm),

E1 A George III black and gold lacquer cabinet, 41 in. wide (103 cm). The doors are decorated in raised gilt and the stand is later.

E2 A black and gold japanned cabinet, 18th century; 39 in. (99 cm) wide. The stand, which is ebonized and parcel-gilt, is approximately contemporary.

E3 *(left and above)* A Regency painted and penwork collector's cabinet; 76 in. high by 41 in. wide (193 by 103 cm).

E4 An oak cabinet-on-stand with two panelled carved doors, late 18th/early 19th century; 43 in. (109 cm) wide.

E5 An oak Gothic revival cabinet, in the manner of A.W.N. Pugin, *c.* 1840; 42 in. (107 cm) high.

E6 A penwork and painted cabinet, 19th century; 49 in. (125 cm) high.

E7 A Victorian pine cabinet-on-stand, in the Renaissance style; 78 in. high by 49 in. wide (197 by 123 cm).

E8 A "George I" walnut side cabinet, *c.* 1920; 48 in. by 31 in. (122 by 79 cm).

E9 A "George I" japanned cabinet-on-stand, *c.* 1920; 60 in. high by 42 in. wide (152 by 107 cm).

Display cabinets

E1 A Queen Anne burr-walnut display cabinet, the base with four graduated long drawers; 76 in. by 38 in. (193 by 97 cm).

E2 A Queen Anne walnut display cabinet, with moulded cornice; 78 in. high by 43 in. wide (198 by 109 cm).

E3 A George II black and gold lacquer display cabinet-on-stand, with gilt brass angles.

E4 A mid-Georgian satinwood and yew-wood display cabinet; 60 in. high by 30 in. wide (152 by 75 cm).

E5 A Chippendale period china cabinet with pierced broken pediment and 13 panels to each door.

E6 A mahogany display cabinet-on-chest, mid 18th century; 83 in. (211 cm) high.

E7 A breakfront cabinet of Judas wood, made from a tree blown down in 1760; 100 in. high by 81 in. wide (253 by 204 cm).

E8 A mid-Georgian mahogany display cabinet; 51 in. (130 cm) wide.

D9 A George II walnut display cabinet, mid 18th century; 88 in. high by 41 in. wide (222 by 103 cm).

D10 An early George III mahogany display cabinet, *c.* 1765; 92 in. high by 43 in. wide (233 by 107 cm).

D11 A George III satinwood display cabinet, with arched pediment crossbanded with rosewood; 80 by 33 in. (202 by 83 cm).

E12 A George III mahogany collector's cabinet, of breakfront architectural form, inlaid, with pierced Isnik gallery, *c.* 1780.

C 1 A Chinese Chippendale carved softwood *Director* show cabinet, 18th century; 84 in. by 38 in. (215 by 95 cm).

E 2 A Sheraton mahogany bow-fronted cabinet, *c.* 1785; 112 in. (285 cm) high.

E 3 An Adam period mahogany china cabinet; 88 in. high by 49 in. wide (224 by 124 cm).

E 4 A satinwood glazed display cabinet, with four adjustable shelves; 60 in. (152 cm) high.

E 5 A Chippendale period mahogany cabinet; 78 in. high by 33 in. wide (198 by 82 cm).

E 6 A Sheraton mahogany display cabinet, the cupboard enclosing sliding trays, *c.* 1785; 84 in. by 42 in. (215 by 105 cm).

E 7 A Sheraton inlaid satinwood china cabinet; 87 in. high by 74 in. wide (222 by 188 cm).

E 8 A Regency lacquered display cabinet, the decorative panels in gold and red lacquer, *c.* 1820; 70 in. high by 39 in. wide (176 by 97 cm).

E 9 A late Regency calamander and gilt bronze display cabinet on stand, by Town & Emanuel; 65 in. high, 40 in. wide (162 by 100 cm). The mirroring to the interior is not original.

E 10 A Regency rosewood display cabinet, inlaid with boxwood lines; 43 in. (108 cm) wide.

E 11 A Regency painted and grained bookcase cabinet, early 19th century; 39 in. (98 cm) wide.

E 12 A Regency rosewood and satinwood crossbanded cabinet, in the manner of Thomas Hope, *c.* 1810.

E 13 A rococo revival painted and parcel gilt serpentine side cabinet, *c.* 1840.

Display Cabinets
The glazed door display cabinet developed as an alternative to the solid or blind door variety during the latter part of the 17th century, when collecting Oriental porcelain became fashionable. The glazing bars were at this time semi-circular (astragal) in section, matching the mouldings around the drawers, and considerable importance should be attached to their style as they may well indicate whether or not the doors were originally solid and subsequently glazed.

Of necessity the panes on early pieces were small and rectangular, but as both cabinet-making and the glass industry developed the glazing bars became finer and the arrangement of glass more intricate. In the 19th century many designs for showcases were distinctly Continental with the most extraordinary shapes of ogee, convex and concave being required of the glass manufacturers.

E3 An ebonized and boulle display cabinet, mid 19th century; 38 in. (95 cm) wide.

E6 A walnut display cabinet, with glazed doors, *c.* 1860; 40 in. by 30 in. (100 by 76 cm).

E9 A Chinese Chippendale-style mahogany display cabinet, with a pagoda canopy over an arrangement of open and glazed cupboards, late 19th century; 90 in. high, 54 in. wide (230 by 137 cm).

E4 A satinwood pedestal vitrine, with chamfered glazed lid and glazed sides, 19th century; 20 in. (52 cm) square.

E7 A mahogany blind fret decorated display cabinet-on-stand, in Chinese Chippendale-style, *c.* 1865; 70 in. high by 38 in. wide (177 by 97 cm).

E10 A Victorian walnut display cabinet, inlaid with ebony and boxwood chequer bandings, 43 in. (107 cm) wide.

E1 A walnut side cabinet with ormolu mounts and crossbanded in thuyawood, 19th century.

E5 A boulle and ebonized slate top serpentined pier cabinet, with ormolu mounts, *c.* 1860; 39 in. high by 29 in. wide (98 by 72 cm).

E8 A mahogany Chinese Chippendale-style breakfront display cabinet, with two pairs of glazed doors enclosing glass shelves.

E11 A Victorian walnut-veneered serpentine side cabinet, applied with gilt brass mounts and with kingwood crossbanding.

E2 A Victorian burr-walnut ormolu-mounted display cabinet, inlaid with boxwood lines, *c.* 1855; 35 by 30 in. (118 by 75cm).

E1 A Victorian serpentine walnut pier cabinet, inlaid with floral marquetry with brass figure mounts, 42 in. high by 44 in. wide (107 by 112 cm).

D2 A fine Victorian figured walnut and floral marquetry breakfront display cabinet, 90 in. high by 76 in. wide (229 by 193 cm).

E3 A wall display cabinet, the glazed cupboard doors flanked by fluted leaf carved columns and concave glazed sides, late 19th century; 37 in. by 32 in. (94 by 80 cm).
The piece is eclectic in combining a pagoda top with classical columns, but its elegant restraint is admirable.

E4 A Victorian carved oak china cabinet, with centre drawer and cupboard to the lower part, the glazed cabinet flanked by carved figures on lion mask plinths, finely carved with face masks, floral and leaf scrolls and fruit; 36 in. (90 cm) wide.

E5 A figured walnut display cabinet with two tall arched glazed doors over two squat inlaid cupboard doors, Victorian; 69 in. (175 cm) tall.

E6 A Victorian ebonized pier cabinet, with amboyna and boxwood inlaid frieze and base, *c.* 1870.

E7 A brass wall display cabinet, late 19th century; 33 by 23 in. (84 by 59 cm).

E8 An ebonized side cabinet, *c.* 1880; 42 in. by 41 in. (107 by 103 cm).

E9 A Sheraton-style mahogany and satinwood display cabinet, late 19th century.

E10 A Regency-style mahogany display cabinet, 75 in. by 58 in. (192 by 149 cm).

E11 A Regency-style mahogany display cabinet, late 19th century; 43 in. (109 cm) wide.

E12 A Victorian marquetry inlaid rosewood corner cabinet, probably English, late 19th century.

E 1 A Victorian inlaid rosewood and marquetry side cabinet. Usually of superb quality, the materials used in such a piece indicate the original cost.

E 2 A Chippendale-style breakfront mahogany china cabinet, the base carved with acanthus and Grecian key motif, 49 in. (124 cm) wide.

E 3 A Victorian painted satinwood display cabinet with rosewood, boxwood and ebony bandings, *c.* 1900; 68 in. by 45 in. (173 by 115 cm).

E 4 A Victorian mahogany and inlaid display cabinet, by Edwards and Roberts, late 19th century; 87 in. by 44 in. (222 by 110 cm).

E 5 A Victorian satinwood display cabinet, *c.* 1900; 74 in. high by 36 in. wide (188 by 90 cm).

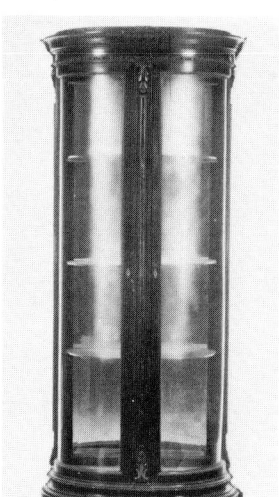

E 6 A stained pine "D"-shaped tall display cabinet, early 1900s; 97 in. high by 47 in. wide (246 by 119 cm).

E 7 A mahogany display cabinet, inlaid with stylized foliage in holly, pewter and copper, the lower part with lead-glazed doors and glazed sides, *c.* 1900; 73 in. by 42 in. (185 by 107 cm).

D 8 A painted satinwood display cabinet-on-stand, of bowed breakfront form, *c.* 1900; 62 in. high by 51 in. wide (158 by 130 cm).

D 9 A pair of mahogany and satinwood crossbanded pedestal display cabinets, *c.* 1900; 48 in. high by 15 in. wide (122 by 38 cm).

D 10 A Sheraton revival mahogany serpentine salon display cabinet, Edwards & Roberts.

E 11 A George III-style mahogany breakfront display cabinet, early 20th century.

E 12 An Edwardian inlaid mahogany serpentine front china display cabinet, 42 in. (104 cm) wide.

E4 An inlaid Edwardian glazed china cabinet. The inlay and fine lines seem to represent Sheraton revival.

E7 An Edwardian mahogany display cabinet, *c.* 1910. Quality of workmanship on such cabinets is most important in determining the price.

E5 A serpentine carved mahogany display cabinet, *c.* 1910; 80 in. high by 56 in. wide (203 by 142 cm).

E8 An Edwardian mahogany and satinwood display cabinet, by Marsh, Jones & Cribb Ltd.

E1 An Edwardian display cabinet, with bevelled glass-fronted cupboards and display stands, with marquetry and bone inlay; 102 in. high by 66 in. wide (258 by 168 cm).

E2 An Edwardian inlaid mahogany display cabinet, with satinwood ribbon and husk decoration.

E3 An Edwardian mahogany display cabinet, two drawers in the frieze with brass knob handles; 69 in. high by 35 in. wide (175 by 86 cm).

E6 A Sheraton-style Edwardian mahogany display cabinet, *c* 1910; 74 in. high by 44 in. wide (188 by 111 cm).

E9 An Edwardian rosewood and satinwood inlaid corner whatnot display cabinet, 78 in. high by 33 in. wide (196 by 82 cm).

Secretaire cabinets

E1 A George III mahogany secretaire bookcase, *c.* 1790; 95 in. high by 50 in. wide (241 by 127 cm).

E2 A Sheraton secretaire and bookcase, 42 in. (105 cm) wide.

E3 A Sheraton secretaire bookcase, inlaid with mahogany and harewood, 93 in. high by 36 in. wide (237 by 90 cm).

D4 A George III mahogany breakfront secretaire bookcase, 120 in. high by 108 in. wide (304 by 275 cm).

E5 An early George III mahogany secretaire bookcase, the lower crossbanded doors enclosing two tray shelves, *c.* 1770; 103 in. (262 cm) high.

E6 A George III mahogany secretaire bookcase, *c.* 1770; 111 in. high by 54 in. wide (281 by 137 cm).

E7 A George III mahogany secretaire bookcase, the lower part with fitted writing drawer, *c.* 1770.

D8 A Georgian mahogany secretaire bookcase, with small drawers and pigeonholes, 29 in. (73 cm) wide.

E9 A George III mahogany secretaire bookcase, with scrolled broken pediment, carved with rosettes.

E10 A George III mahogany secretaire bookcase, the centre with fall-down front, with four drawers, 90 in. high by 46 in. wide (229 by 119 cm).

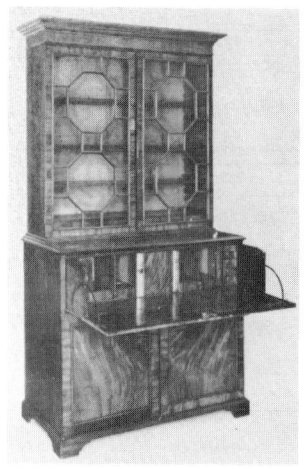

E11 A Georgian mahogany secretaire bookcase, with a fitted interior, 93 in. high by 50 in. wide (236 by 127 cm).

D12 A Hepplewhite secretaire bookcase, veneered with well figured harewood, 78 in. by 34 in. (198 by 85 cm).

E1 A Hepplewhite mahogany bookcase, with secretaire drawer, 37 in. (92 cm) wide.

E2 A small Hepplewhite secretaire bookcase, of faded mahogany, the bookcase top with Gothic astragals.

E3 A George III mahogany secretaire bookcase, with adjustable shelves, *c.* 1790; 93 in. by 48 in. (235 by 122 cm).

E4 A George III mahogany secretaire bookcase, *c.* 1790; 94 in. high by 49 in. wide (239 by 125 cm).

E5 A George III mahogany secretaire bookcase, *c.* 1790; 108 in. high by 59 in. wide (273 by 149 cm).

D6 A small George III mahogany secretaire bookcase, *c.* 1790; 86 in. high by 31 in. wide (219 by 79 cm).

E7 A George III mahogany secretaire bookcase, satinwood crossbanded, *c.* 1795; 90 in. by 47 in. (280 by 119 cm).

E8 A Sheraton secretaire bookcase, of faded mahogany, with drawers and pigeonholes, lined in leather.

E9 A Sheraton mahogany secretaire bookcase 100 in. high by 48 in. wide (253 by 122 cm).

E10 A Sheraton inlaid mahogany secretaire bookcase, with swan neck cornice, 98 in. by 39 in. (248 by 97 cm).

E11 A George III mahogany secretaire bookcase, with shelves and pigeonholes; 89 in. by 44 in. (227 by 110 cm).

E12 A late George III mahogany secretaire bookcase, with drawers and pigeonholes, 100 in. by 53 in. (252 by 135 cm).

E1 A Georgian mahogany secretaire bookcase, with rosewood and boxwood inlaid roundel decoraton, 45 in. (113 cm) wide.

E2 A Georgian mahogany secretaire bookcase, in the Sheraton style, the fitted drawer with crossbanded front, 35 in. (88 cm) wide.

E3 A mahogany satinwood crossbanded and ebony inlaid secretaire bookcase, late 18th century; 43 in. (108 cm) wide.

E4 A mahogany secretaire bookcase, with drawer, early 19th century; 90 in. high by 37 in. wide (229 by 92 cm).

E5 A mahogany secretaire bookcase, well fitted, with two drawers below, on bracket feet.

E6 A Regency mahogany secretaire bookcase, inlaid with satinwood stringing, *c.* 1800; 83 by 44 in. (211 by 108 cm).

E7 A late George III mahogany secretaire bookcase, fitted with pigeonholes and drawers, 91 by 47 in. (232 by 120 cm).

C8 A late George III mahogany and satinwood secretaire bookcase, panels painted with figures of Shakespeare and Milton.

E9 A George III mahogany secretaire bookcase, with fitted interior; 89 in. high by 43 in. wide (226 by 109 cm).

E10 A Georgian mahogany secretaire bookcase.

E11 A George III mahogany secretaire bookcase, with triangular pediment, 86 by 37 in. (219 by 93 cm).

E12 A George III mahogany secretaire bookcase, with a fitted interior, late 18th/early 19th century; 92 by 52 in. (234 by 132 cm).

E1 A George III mahogany secretaire bookcase, with hour-glass shaped glazing bars, early 19th century.

E2 A Regency mahogany secretaire bookcase, with a fitted writing drawer and three other drawers.

E3 A mahogany secretaire bookcase, decorated with satinwood bands and string lines, early 19th century.

E4 A Regency mahogany secretaire bookcase, with a panelled fitted secretaire drawer, *c.* 1820.

E5 A George IV mahogany secretaire bookcase, inlaid with stringing, *c.* 1825; 87 by 43 in. (221 by 109 cm).

E6 A George IV mahogany secretaire bookcase, on splayed bracket feet.

E7 A mahogany secretaire bookcase, fitted with small drawers and pigeonholes, 19th century.

E8 A George IV mahogany secretaire bookcase, inlaid with ebonized lines 90 by 43 in. (229 by 108 cm).

E9 A George IV mahogany secretaire bookcase, with fitted writing drawer, *c.* 1825; 90 by 49 in. (229 by 124 cm).

E10 A William IV mahogany secretaire bookcase, fitted drawer with writing slope and brushing slide.

E11 A mahogany secretaire bookcase, with fitted interior, mid 19th century; 102 by 50 in. (259 by 127 cm).

E12 An oak Gothic revival secretaire bookcase, with a fitted secretaire drawer, late 19th century.

Side cabinets

E1 A Jacobean oak spice cabinet, with four long panelled drawers, *c.* 1660; 16 in. (40 cm) wide.

E2 A seaweed marquetry table cabinet, in the manner of Gerrit Jensen, with 12 drawers, 17th century.

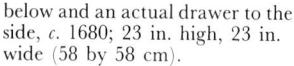

E3 A Charles II oak food and spice cabinet, with moulded cornice above a galleried cupboard, over a shallow divided drawer with three sham drawers below and an actual drawer to the side, *c.* 1680; 23 in. high, 23 in. wide (58 by 58 cm).

E4 A George II mahogany dwarf cabinet, in the manner of William Vile, mid 18th century; 23 in. high by 25 in. wide (58 by 63 cm).

E5 A mahogany or seal cabinet containing 36 trays in various sizes, 18th century; 31 in. high by 23 in. wide (78 by 58 cm).

E6 A dwarf cabinet, in well-figured satinwood, 18th century; 31 in. high by 48 in. wide (76 by 120 cm).

E7 A painted satinwood side cabinet, painted en grisaille with female classical figures.

D8 A Sheraton satinwood dwarf cabinet, with painted panels, "Sacrifice to Cupid" after Angelica Kauffmann.

E9 A George III mahogany and satinwood dwarf cabinet, 36 in. (92 cm) wide.

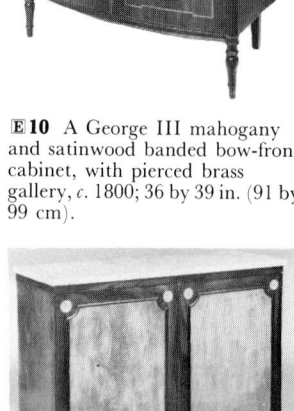

E10 A George III mahogany and satinwood banded bow-front cabinet, with pierced brass gallery, *c.* 1800; 36 by 39 in. (91 by 99 cm).

E11 A George III mahogany and satinwood dwarf cabinet, with mottled white marble top, shaped cupboard doors outlined with ebonized borders; 37 in. (93 cm) wide.

E12 A late George III painted bow-fronted side cabinet, the pink cupboard doors applied with oval prints of Shakespeare scenes *c.* 1790.

E13 A Regency maplewood side cabinet, hinged top banded with rosewood; 37 in. (93 cm) wide.

E1 A Regency rosewood dwarf cabinet, with eared Portor marble top, each door lined with yellow.

E2 A late Regency mahogany side cabinet, the doors filled with pleated silk panels, mid 19th century.

E3 A Regency mahogany side cabinet, the top inlaid with anthemions, 51 in. (129 cm) wide.

E4 A Regency satinwood dwarf cabinet, with bowed breakfront top.

E5 A Regency rosewood dwarf cabinet, with white marble top.

E6 A Regency parcel-gilt and simulated rosewood dwarf cabinet, with carrara marble top, 36 in. (92 cm) wide.

E7 A Regency mahogany side cabinet, 32 in. (81 cm) wide.

E8 A Regency pollard oak dwarf collectors' cabinet, the top outlined with ebonized lines; 27 in. (69 cm) wide.

E9 A Regency bird's-eye maple folio cabinet, with mottled grey marble top inlaid with a figured fossil lozenge; 53 in. (135 cm) wide.

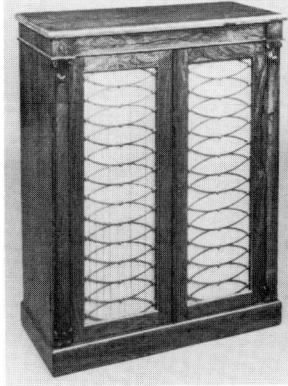

E10 A Regency rosewood dwarf cabinet, with brass-bordered top, doors filled with pleated silk.

E11 A Regency brass-inlaid rosewood and ebonized cabinet, 27 in. (66 cm) wide.

E12 A Regency satinwood dwarf cabinet, the top crossbanded with rosewood.

E13 A Regency rosewood dwarf cabinet, with Siena marble top, doors backed with pleated silk.

Side Cabinets

The side cabinet developed in England in the later part of the 18th century, primarily as an ornamental piece, often designed as an alternative to the pier table and therefore frequently made in pairs. Early examples often show exquisite workmanship.

Once established, the side cabinet remained in vogue, either as a purely decorative item or, particularly in the 19th century, as useful storage furniture, on the top of which ornaments could be displayed.

In the course of the 19th century, a mass produced form of the chiffonier became popular, its lower part being structurally similar to the side cabinet, its upper part consisting of one or two shelves on turned or scrolled wooden supports.

The desirability of Regency side cabinets has led to the alteration of many Victorian chiffoniers by the replacement of blind panels with pleated silk and grills, the addition of classical gilt metal mounts and the removal of the super-structure. Badly marked tops might also have been replaced with marble.

E14 A Regency rosewood dwarf cabinet, with yellow marble top, the doors filled with pleated material behind gilt-brass trellis; 53 in. (133 cm) wide.

E1 A Regency mahogany cabinet, with three-quarter galleried breakfront, rectangular grey and white marble top, early 19th century; 79 in. (201 cm) wide.

E2 A Regency rosewood chiffonier, 46 in. (113 cm) wide.

E3 A Regency mahogany chiffonier, with two open shelves, 37 in. (94 cm) wide.

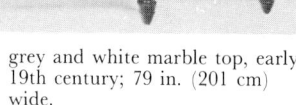

E5 A mahogany chiffonier, early 19th century; 48 in. high by 57 in. wide (121 by 84 cm).

E6 A Regency period concave rosewood chiffonier, *c.* 1810, 50 by 32 in. (126 by 81 cm).

E4 A Regency ormolu-mounted black lacquer chiffonier, 34 in. (87 cm) wide.

E7 A Regency rosewood cabinet with tulipwood crossbanding and brass inlay.

E8 A Regency mahogany dwarf cabinet, early 19th century; 33 in. (84 cm) wide.

E10 A Regency rosewood chiffonier, 48 in. (121 cm) high.

E9 A Regency rosewood chiffonier, with mirror-backed open shelves, 59 in. (150 cm) wide.

E11 A Regency mahogany cabinet, brass-grilled sides and back, 23 in. (59 cm) wide.

E12 A Regency side cabinet, in the manner of George Bullock, 58 in. (147 cm) high.

E 1 A Regency rosewood cabinet, with inlaid panels of kingwood and brass, the top having open shelves with brass galleries.

E 2 A Regency rosewood inlaid-brass cabinet, with ormolu mounts and containing 18 small drawers, c. 1805; 52 in. (132 cm) high.

E 3 A Regency rosewood chiffonier, with pierced brass gallery and column supports; 36 in. (91 cm) wide.

E 4 A rosewood side cabinet, with inverted breakfront green marble top, above a conforming frieze, early 19th century; 39 in. high by 61 in. wide (99 by 155 cm).

E 5 A George IV rosewood veneered side cabinet, with a verde antico marble top, 1820-1830; 37 in. high by 48 in. wide (94 by 122 cm).

D 6 A George IV rosewood side cabinet, of bow-fronted breakfront form, with yellow silk-lined doors, c. 1830; 36 in. high by 48 in. wide (91 by 121 cm).

E 7 A George IV brass-mounted rosewood veneered side cabinet, with mottled beige marble top, c. 1820; 34 in. high by 43 in. wide (87 by 109 cm).

E 8 A George IV mahogany side cabinet, with pair of glazed doors with gilt-wire grilles, c. 1820; 48 in. high by 48 in. wide (121 by 122 cm).

E 9 A George IV rosewood veneered side cabinet, with mottled white marble top, c. 1820; 38 in. (97 cm) high.

E 10 A George IV brass inlaid mahogany side cabinet, c. 1820; 36 in. high by 36 in. wide (92 by 92 cm).

E 11 A George IV rosewood and burr-walnut and calamander and mahogany side cabinet, first quarter of 19th century; 38 by 43 in. (97 by 110 cm).

D 12 A William IV mahogany collectors' cabinet, c. 1835; 51 in. high by 30 in. wide (130 by 75 cm).

E 13 A William IV rosewood combined workbox and collectors' cabinet, c. 1835; 17 in. (42 cm) wide.

E 14 A rosewood cabinet, twin panelled doors with beaded mouldings, 19th century; 47 in. high by 35 in. wide (120 by 88 cm).

E 15 A William IV parcel gilt and rosewood dwarf cabinet, carrara marble top, 49 in. (125 cm) wide.

E1 A William IV rosewood side cabinet, the frieze with three drawers, late 1830s; 37 in. high by 82 in. wide (94 by 207 cm).

E2 A William IV mahogany chiffonier, *c*. 1820; 56 in. (141 cm) high.

E4 A painted bamboo and burr-maple side cabinet, second quarter 19th century; 40 in. high by 38 in. wide (101 by 96 cm).

E3 A William IV pollard elm side cabinet, late 1830s; 72 in. high by 24 in. wide (183 by 61 cm).

E5 An ormolu-mounted ebonized and boulle side cabinet, 31 in. (77 cm) wide.

E6 An ormolu-mounted ash library folio cabinet, with hinged book support, *c*. 1840.

E7 A rosewood side cabinet, the top with rectangular mirror-plate. *c*. 1840; 78 in. high by 68 in. wide (199 by 173 cm).

E10 A satinwood cabinet, the top with arched cornice above glazed doors, 19th century; 32 in. (80 cm) wide.

E8 An ebonized and boulle standing side cabinet, applied with gilt metal mounts and inlaid geometric brass borders, mid 19th century; 54 in. (137 cm) wide.

E11 A Victorian mulberry veneered folio cabinet.
European mulberries, golden brown with darker streaks, hard and durable, were occasionally used from the early part of the 18th century.

E9 A burr-walnut and Tunbridge-ware serpentine side cabinet, the door inlaid with sycamore crossbanding and geometric banding, the central panel with elaborate box foliage on a burr-walnut ground, 42 in. by 71 in. (105 by 180 cm).

E1 A walnut side cabinet, the cupboard applied with foliate fretwork on a damask ground, flanked by velvet-lined open shelves, 1850s; 60 in. by 90 in. (152 by 229 cm).

Formerly with a mirror back, to display Victorian chinaware with different patterns back and front to take advantage of such cabinets.

E4 A Victorian walnut and floral marquetry ormolu-mounted credenza, *c.* 1855; 44 in. high by 80 in. wide (110 by 203 cm).

E8 A Victorian boulle credenza with grotesque ormolu mask mounts, 1850s; 80 in. (202 cm) wide.

E2 A Victorian walnut side cabinet, with two cupboard doors filled with fretwork foliage on a giltwood ground, between two glazed cupboard doors, stamped Seddon London, 36483, 74 in. (186 cm) wide.

E5 A Victorian walnut and ormolu-mounted credenza, *c.* 1855; 48 in. high by 86 in. wide (121 by 217 cm).

E9 A burr-walnut and thuyawood side cabinet, late 1850s; 72 in. (188 cm) wide.

E6 A burr-walnut side cabinet and mirror, with moulded white marble top, *c.* 1855; 70 in. high by 60 in. wide (178 by 152 cm).

E3 A Victorian walnut credenza of finely figured wood with high quality marquetry. The frieze under the moulded top is panelled and inlaid over a quarter-veneered central door inlaid with scrolls, two bow-front glazed cupboards to the sides, on conforming shaped plinth; late 19th century.

E7 A Victorian walnut and inlaid credenza, showing remarkable quality in the execution of the marquetry veneers, *c.* 1855.

E10 A boulle cabinet, in cut brass and tortoiseshell on an ebonized ground with mottled marble top, the door with a convex oval panel with spandrels and the rounded corners with gilt-metal mounts, *c.* 1860; 42 in. by 33 in. (106 by 83 cm).

E1 A walnut side cabinet, in well figured wood, with a pair of doors applied with heavily craqueleur paintings, now with fitted interiors, 1860s; 36 in. by 65 in. (91 by 165 cm).

Some credenzas had no display function but were designed as alternatives to sideboards, being originally fitted with shelves and drawers.

E2 An ormolu mounted burr-walnut and marquetry side cabinet, with curved glazed doors to the sides, *c.* 1860; 43 in. high by 60 in. wide (108 by 183 cm).

The huge popularity of the credenza during the second half of the 19th century led to an infinite variety of decorative and utility features.

E3 A Victorian burr-walnut breakfront side cabinet, applied with gilt brass mounts, outlined with boxwood, tulipwood, satinwood and burr-yew crossbandings, *c.* 1865; 73 in. (185 cm) wide.

Furniture of this period was made to illustrate the imagination of the designer and the skills of the craftsmen.

E4 An ormolu-mounted marquetry side cabinet, of breakfront form, *c.* 1870; 48 in. high by 97 in. wide (122 by 245 cm).

Long four-door cabinets of this type became most popular during the middle of the 19th century and remained in vogue for 40 years.

E5 A walnut side cabinet, with a mirrored centre cupboard, *c.* 1870; 39 in. by 65 in. (99 by 165 cm).
This type of side cabinet with open shelves and mirror backs

became popular during the second half of the 19th century and often had the centre door left blank for a panel of needlework, pleated silk or, as in this case, a mirror.

E6 An ebony veneered inverted breakfront side cabinet, the frieze and doors set with jasperware plaques on a green ground, the frieze inlaid with anthemion

above a mirror backed recess, flanked by a pair of burr-walnut crossbanded arched doors divided by tapering half columns, the bun feet with outset supports inlaid with Greek key, *c.* 1870; 43 in. high by 84 in. wide (108 by 213 cm).

E1 A walnut credenza, the top crossbanded in rosewood, late 19th century.

E2 A cedarwood side cabinet, doors inlaid with ebony stringing within ebonized borders, *c.* 1870; 43 in. by 40 in. (108 by 102 cm).

E3 A marquetry breakfront side cabinet, inlaid with arabesque and walnut banding on ebony ground, *c.* 1870; 46 in. by 66 in. (117 by 168 cm).

E4 A walnut music cabinet, inlaid throughout with boxwood lines, third quarter 19th century; 39 in. by 23 in. (98 by 59 cm).

E5 An Aesthetic influence mahogany music cabinet, 43 in. by 25 in. (109 by 64 cm).

E6 A tulipwood parquetry and marquetry music cabinet, *c.* 1870.

E7 A Henry IV style walnut cabinet, 63 in. high by 53 in. wide (160 by 133 cm).

E8 A bone-inlaid ebonized wood side cabinet, *c.* 1870; 44 in. by 70 in. (110 by 178 cm).

E9 An ebony veneered pietra dura side cabinet, stamped Edwards & Roberts, Wardour Street, London, *c.* 1870; 59 in. high by 36 in. wide (150 by 90 cm).

E10 An ebonized and gilt brass mounted side cabinet, inlaid with brass lines, and set with Sèvres-style porcelain plaques, two bowed glazed doors, late 19th century; 40 in. high by 64 in. wide (100 by 163 cm).

E11 A marquetry and satinwood side cabinet, *c.* 1880; 54 in. by 42 in. (138 by 107 cm).

E12 A Gillows amboyna and porcelain music cabinet, late 19th century.

E13 An Edwardian satinwood and inlaid side cabinet, the top banded with kingwood, fitted with a frieze drawer, above panelled doors with central urn motif, 36 in. (89 cm) wide.

CANTERBURIES
1790-1890

Canterburies appear to have been made first in the latter part of George III's reign. Sheraton attributed their name to a contemporary primate who commissioned such pieces.

Canterburies were designed either to hold music or as plate-holders to stand by the supper table. The relatively large number of 19th century versions now on the market are a consequence of the Victorians' passion for the piano.

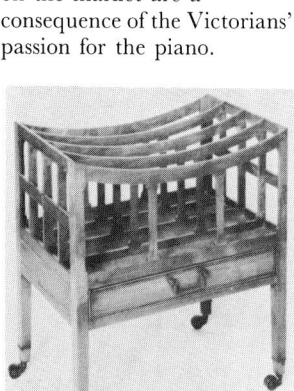

E1 A George III satinwood canterbury, *c.* 1790; 21 in. high by 18 in. wide (51 by 46 cm).

E2 A George III mahogany canterbury, *c.* 1800; 22 in. (55 cm) wide.

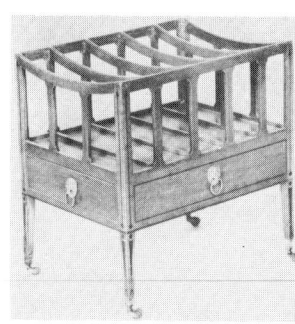

E3 A George III mahogany canterbury, strung with ebony, first quarter 19th century; 21 in. (53 cm) high.

E4 A Regency mahogany canterbury, with one frieze drawer, 24 in. (60 cm) wide.

E5 A Regency rosewood canterbury, with four "X"-frame partitions, 21 in. (52 cm) wide.

E6 A Regency rosewood canterbury, with lyre sides and barley twist supports, fitted with a drawer.

E7 A Regency mahogany canterbury, the brass feet with casters, *c.* 1820; 17 in. (44 cm) high.

E8 A Regency rosewood canterbury and tiered stand, 52 in. high by 13 in. wide (130 by 33 cm).

E9 A George IV rosewood canterbury, *c.* 1825; 19 in. (48 cm) wide.

E10 A rosewood canterbury, *c.* 1840; 19 in. (48 cm) wide.

E11 An early Victorian burr-walnut music canterbury.

E12 A Victorian rosewood music canterbury, 19 in. (48 cm) wide.

E13 A Victorian walnut music canterbury, *c.* 1850; 25 in. (64 cm) wide.

E14 A Victorian walnut canterbury, with inlaid decoration, 27 in. (66 cm) high.

E15 An ebonized canterbury, 19th century.

D3 *(above)* A James I carved oak cupboard, *c.* 1620, though the panels are probably mid-16th century; 59 in. high, 52 in. wide (150 by 131 cm).

The top has a moulded edge above a fluted frieze and is supported on a pair of turned pillars. The panels are elaborately carved with interlacing roundels, the outer two in the upper row forming a pair of doors; in the lower part the upper row of panels has two doors, the lower row one central door. The sides have panels of roundels on a carved and pounced ground.

It is not uncommon to find early furniture of this type constructed using older pieces, especially panels. Careful inspection of the underside of tables, of drawer-linings and inner rails will often reveal crisply carved sections made out of offcuts from room panelling and moulding.

D1 *(above)* A George III painted four-poster bed, *c.* 1780. It is 112 in. high, 84 in. wide and 87 in. long (284 by 213 by 221 cm). The valance is moulded and arched; from it hangs a lambrequin edge surmounted by swagged urns on a simulated satinwood ground.

The continuing movement into classical form by the 1780s is evident here with tapering reeded columns and urn-shaped plinths terminating in tapered feet and castors. The valance is ultimately classical and displays a fine example of the painted decoration so much in vogue during the Adam period.

D2 *(left)* A small James I oak buffet, with three open shelves, *c.* 1620. It measures 44 in. high by 46 in. wide (111 by 119 cm).

The three stages show important features of decoration of the period: the frieze to the top shelf is inlaid, the centre is spirally lobed and the base is arcaded.

D4 *(above)* A Charles I inlaid oak press cupboard, *c.* 1640; 61 in. high, 82 in. wide (155 by 208 cm). It was probably made in or near Halifax, Yorkshire. Keyholes to the upper section have been added irregularly and the piece may have been reduced in width.

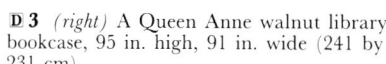

D 3 *(right)* A Queen Anne walnut library bookcase, 95 in. high, 91 in. wide (241 by 231 cm).

This was not originally made as a breakfront – the two side cupboards were added later. The piece would originally have resembled the bookcase on the left (no. 1). Whereas the original has drawers below, the additions have hinged doors, with the latches placed to the side, which makes them incompatible with the centrally placed escutcheons to the drawers. In the same fashion, the doors have no pulls, and the ogee brackets to the side additions are of simpler design than those to the main case. Considering the lack of attempt to disguise the alteration, it is safe to assume that this was undertaken simply to update an outmoded piece of furniture, or it may be that the then owner wished to adapt his existing bookcase to fit in a different place and chose to do so in a more prestigious style.

D 1 A Queen Anne walnut library bookcase of modest size, *c.* 1710; 83 in. high, 50 in. wide, 16 in. deep (211 by 126 by 40 cm). The doors open to shelves above three pairs of drawers behind the fielded panels.

C 4 A fine George III mahogany breakfront bookcase, *c.* 1775; 111 in. high, 125 in. wide (283 by 318 cm).

The glazing bars and applied mouldings to the doors show a definite Gothic influence, combined with certain rococo characteristics – for example the central carved waterfall below each deeply scrolled pinnacle.

D 2 A George III mahogany bookcase, *c.* 1770; 113 in. high, 44 in wide (287 by 112 cm).

The crisply carved detail, especially to the friezes, suggests the work of Sefferin Alken, whom John Cobb employed as a carver.

C1 An early George III mahogany breakfront bookcase in the style of Thomas Chippendale, *c.* 1760; 102 in. high by 86 in. wide (259 by 119 cm). Compare a design for a "Library Bookcase" in Chippendale's *The Gentleman and Cabinet-Maker's Director* (plate LXII in the 1755 second edition).

C3 *(left)* A Regency mahogany breakfront secretaire-bookcase with arcaded cornice, *c.* 1800; 67 in. (169 cm) wide.

The Gothic taste remained popular – as seen here in the glazing bars – throughout the classical revival and was often combined successfully with classical features such as the elegant oval panels to the cupboard doors of this piece. Finely carved pendant moulding to the cornice is another indication of the superb quality of this piece.

C4 A George III mahogany breakfront bookcase, *c.* 1790; 98 in. (249 cm) wide. The foliate clasps ornamenting the panelled doors are very similar to those on an attested Ince & Mayhew piece in the Museum of Decorative Arts, Copenhagen. The overall fine quality of this bookcase would certainly be consistent with an Ince & Mayhew attribution.

Ince & Mayhew are particularly prominent among period furniture makers, not just because of the quality of their work but also because it was unusually well documented, allowing us to attest numerous extant pieces.

D2 A burr-walnut breakfront bookcase by Edwards and Roberts (stamped), 1840s. It measures 108 in. by 112 in. (275 by 285 cm).

The piece is of fine quality, showing careful choice of highly figured timber and the application of machine carving at its best. The design shows a distinct Italianate influence in the mixture of Elizabethan revival motifs, such as applied lozenges and strapwork, the formal applied mouldings to the doors and the deeply carved central cabochons.

Edwards and Roberts, with premises in Wardour Street and Oxford Street, was a fashionable Victorian firm which made, restored and dealt in furniture. Their stamp is to be found on the upper edge of a drawer or door, and is prestigious.

C5 An important rosewood standing bookcase of high-style Regency design, *c.* 1815; 48 in. high, 31 in. wide (122 by 78 cm).

The exaggerated decorations and use of bronzed and gilded carving in contrast to the highly figured rosewood are typical of the best in Regency, and closely resemble the work of George Smith in his *A Collection of Designs for Household Furniture*, 1808.

D1 A Queen Anne black and scarlet lacquer bureau, *c.* 1705; 38 in. high by 28 in. wide (90 by 70 cm).

D2 A Queen Anne walnut bureau, *c.* 1710; 37 in. high, 24 in. wide (93 by 61 cm). The sloping crossbanded flap is inlaid with herringbone bands, which are repeated on the drawer fronts.

D3 A red lacquer bureau on contemporary stand, *c.* 1720; 46 in. high by 37 in. wide (117 by 93 cm).

The use of red lacquer rather than black for this bureau indicates Western provenance.

D4 A Queen Anne brown lacquer small bureau cabinet on stand, early 18th century but restored; 69 in. high, 29 in. wide (176 by 73 cm).

The glazed cupboard doors are decorated with chinoiserie figures and flowering branches.

D5 A William and Mary walnut bureau cabinet, *c.* 1690; 84 in. high, 42 in. wide (213 by 107 cm). The top section with mirrored doors opening to three adjustable shelves; two candle slides below.

D6 A walnut bureau cabinet with double-dome top, *c.* 1700; 86 in. high, 41 in. wide (218 by 104 cm). Mirror panels and bun feet replaced. The doors open to a central cupboard surrounded by drawers; the fall front reveals a fitted interior with a well.

C7 A Queen Anne burr-walnut bureau cabinet, *c.* 1710; 81 in. high, 41 in. wide (206 by 104 cm). The doors with bevelled mirrors open to pigeonholes and small drawers, with two candle slides below.

B2 A Queen Anne black japanned bureau cabinet, *c.* 1710; 91 in. high, 40 in. wide (231 by 101 cm).

The cupboard doors open to a fitted interior with drawers, pigeonholes and a central cupboard flanked by marbelized pilasters concealing pull-out compartments.

B3 A Queen Anne burr-walnut bureau cabinet, *c.* 1710; 88 in. high by 40 in. wide (224 by 101 cm).

The applied moulding immediately above the drawers is a hangover from the earlier practice of making the bureau in two pieces.

B1 A Queen Anne walnut bureau cabinet, *c.* 1710. It stands 92 in. high and is 42 in. wide (234 by 107 cm).

The interior is of serpentine form, the cupboard doors and drawers below being concave, with a dummy escutcheon to the left-hand door and the document pockets at the sides being convex.

Indications of quality abound on this piece of furniture: the elaborate shaping to all divisions in the upper part; finely turned solid walnut free-standing columns surmounted by finials; and the deeply stepped moulding to the double arch, on which the veneer had to be laid in small sections.

An authentic English bureau cabinet of this date will be of veneer over a softwood carcase, which will be readily visible upon removal of the drawers. The upper part should sit within a retaining moulding fixed to the bureau and the bureau top will not be veneered – if it is, the probability is that the piece is made up.

C1 A small Queen Anne single-domed bureau cabinet, *c.* 1710; 64 in. high, 20 in. wide (163 by 51 cm). The upper part consisting of a cupboard with single mirrored door over a candle slide; the bureau with one drawer under; the lower part has a slide over four drawers.

C2 A Queen Anne mulberry, kingwood and pewter-inlaid cabinet, in the style of Coxed and Woster, *c.* 1715. In three parts, with kingwood mouldings to the glazed doors, which enclose pigeonholes and dividers; the slope front with kingwood and pewter banding opening to pigeonholes and veneered drawers.

C3 *(above)* A black japanned bureau cabinet, *c.* 1710. Such pieces sometimes included Oriental panels, whereas the rest of the lacquer-work was European; this may well be the case here, as the two cupboard panels are similar, not paired.

The production of lacquer work in England increased considerably following the publication of *A Treatise of Japanning and Varnishing* by Stalker and Parker in 1688, in which the authors proposed alternative formulae – given that the authentic ingredients were not available – to create Oriental-style effects. Oriental lacquer however deteriorates uniformly, whereas English work is prone to piecemeal degradation.

C4 *(right)* A small Queen Anne burr-walnut bureau cabinet; 76 in. high, 30 in. wide (192 by 76 cm). The glazed door was formerly mirrored. This piece is an early example of cockbeading being applied to the drawers rather than to the carcase.

C3 A small George I walnut bureau cabinet in three parts, *c.* 1720; 67 in. high by 25 in. wide (169 by 64 cm). The mirrored cupboard door is flanked by pilasters with carved Corinthian capitals.

C1 *(above)* An early George I burr-walnut bureau cabinet, *c.* 1715.

This piece shows exceptional quality in the use of carved and gilded finials, gilded capitals to the fluted pilasters that flank the central mirror and the gilded figures that surmount them.

The interior to the bureau has matching pilasters and mirror-door compartment, and all the door and drawer furniture bears traces of original gilding. A further attractive feature, again indicating quality, is the sunburst decoration to the bottom drawer and apron. Here, the front is dished to receive a marquetry panel, the design of which is by origin Dutch.

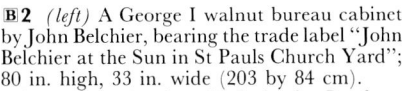

B2 *(left)* A George I walnut bureau cabinet by John Belchier, bearing the trade label "John Belchier at the Sun in St Pauls Church Yard"; 80 in. high, 33 in. wide (203 by 84 cm).

Some records exist, chiefly in the *Purefoy Letters*, of Belchier's work from 1735 until his death in 1753.

C4 A George I walnut and burr-walnut bureau cabinet of small size, *c.* 1725; 79 in. high by 28 in. wide (201 by 71 cm). The piece is of fine colour, and the crossbanding is particularly strongly marked. Note the exaggerated graduation of the drawers and the residual moulding below the top drawer.

D1 A Charles II European japanned cabinet on stand, *c.* 1660; 68 in. high, 40 in. wide (173 by 103 cm).

The chest has the highly elaborate pierced and engraved corner mounts, strap hinges and escutcheon plates typical of the highest quality work of the period. The stand, which is European and contemporary, is silvered.

D2 A William and Mary japanned cabinet, *c.* 1695; 69 in. high, 42 in. wide (176 by 107 cm). The interior has 10 drawers and the stand is contemporary, though restored.

The elaborate stretchering is of exceptional quality.

D3 *(right)* A japanned cabinet with painted decoration of birds and vases of flowers, attributed to Jan Baptist Brueghel, *c.* 1690, on silvered stand.

Elaborately carved stands for Oriental cabinets became popular during the late 17th century. A softwood such as lime or pine was most commonly used and the surface, once carved, was applied with a layer of gesso, which, after being moistened, was applied with metal leaf, either gold or silver. The highlights and polished metal effect were achieved by burnishing the surfaces with a piece of agate or, traditionally, with a dog's tooth.

D4 *(above)* A japanned cabinet with painted decoration, being a companion piece to no. 3 above. These cabinets are probably the finest examples of a European artist working with an Oriental medium to create a stunning effect quite unrelated to the Oriental originals. In fact, Oriental craftsmen were to Westernize their own interpretations in order to compete in an ever-changing market.

B5 *(right)* A William and Mary walnut and seaweed marquetry cabinet-on-cabinet, *c.* 1690; 44 in. (112 cm) wide.

This splendid example of late 17th-century marquetry was formerly the property of King George I, then of George II.

Seaweed marquetry, using only two woods in the most intricate of patterns, is rarer than its floral counterpart and was fashionable in the last decade of the 17th century.

D 1 An early 18th-century japanned table cabinet, *c*. 1700 (the feet are *c*. 1810); 24 in. high, 20 in. wide (62 by 51 cm).

The piece is brass-bound, with pierced and engraved hinges and brackets; the engraving on the escutcheons echoes the painted motifs on the doors. The later feet are European and of cast and gilded brass.

C 2 A Queen Anne black and gold lacquer cabinet-on-chest, *c*. 1710; 42 in. (107 cm) wide. The turned feet are later.

The cupboard doors open to 10 drawers of varying size; the hinges, escutcheons and angles are engraved gilt metal.

The format of a totally Oriental-style cabinet on a European base remained quite popular during the early 18th century, and is evidence of a continuing fascination with the East. So too is the fact that much japanning was done by amateurs, for it became a popular pastime for the upper classes. Such work is easily discernible, lacking as it does both the quality of composition and the quality of execution apparent in the work of experts.

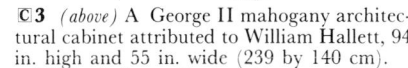

C 3 *(above)* A George II mahogany architectural cabinet attributed to William Hallett, 94 in. high and 55 in. wide (239 by 140 cm).

The basis for attributing this piece to Hallett is the markedly Palladian form and the decorative vocabulary, both of which are very closely paralleled by the only known piece signed by Hallett, formerly in the Colville collection.

Hallett was established in Great Newport Street, London, no later than 1732, and during the 1730s is known to have supplied furniture to Longford Castle, Wilton, Ditchley, Holkham and Cobham. He may later have worked in partnership with Vile and Cobb – he is known to have moved next door to Cobb in St Martin's Lane in 1752.

Hallett died in 1781, having been predeceased by his son, William. The grandson, also William, inherited Hallett's wealth and with his wife was painted by Gainsborough in "The Morning Walk".

D 4 *(left)* A Chinese coromandel lacquer cabinet-on-stand, *c*. 1745; 50 in. high, 31 in. wide (127 by 79 cm). The doors show mountain landscapes and enclose short and long drawers. The sides show peonies on a gilt ground.

C1 A Chippendale period mahogany china cabinet-bookcase, *c.* 1755; 88 in. high, 61 in. wide (224 by 155 cm).

This piece bears the hallmarks of good mid-18th century furniture. Below the moulded dentil cornice a band of blind fret carving surmounts two 13-pane doors. The cupboard doors have attractive D-shaped fielded panels over ogee bracket feet, the knees of which have foliate carving.

D3 An early George III laburnum-wood display cabinet-on-stand, *c.* 1760; 62 in. high, 40 in. wide (158 by 102 cm). The natural figuring of the wood produces a delightful haphazard parquetry effect.

A4 *(above)* An early George III mahogany secretaire cabinet, *c.* 1765; known as the d'Arcy cabinet; 72 in. high, 28 in. wide, 13 in. deep (184 by 71 by 32 cm).

This is a fine example of the eclectic taste of the 1760s running up to the transition from rococo to classical. The fretted upper part is distinctly Chinese, the panelled ends are architectural and the base bears Gothic and foliate decoration below a spirally lobed moulding. At the centre of the upper part a secret folio drawer is camouflaged with carved swags in the Adam manner.

C2 A late George II mahogany writing cabinet, *c.* 1760; 67 in. high, 40 in. wide (170 by 103 cm).

The cupboard doors reveal an interior fitted with a central cupboard and drawers. The top drawer to the bottom part is fitted as a writing drawer, the second drawer down being reduced in width to accommodate the writing shelf supports.

The cabinet may have been made for Thomas Selby of Whaddon Hall, Buckinghamshire.

E5 *(left)* A George III satinwood and padouk collector's cabinet-on-stand, *c.* 1765; 60 in. high by 24 in. wide (151 by 62 cm). The platform stretcher is a later addition.

The use of exotic veneers became fashionable during the transition from curvilinear and rococo designs to the classic antique styles of the third quarter of the 18th century. Leading exponents of the marquetry revival, of which this piece is a superb example, were Chippendale and Haig – a partnership that lasted from 1772 to 1779. The earlier dating of this piece is suggested by the curvilinear style of the panel and by the pierced and carved brackets to the stand.

A3 *(below)* A satinwood and ormolu-mounted cabinet known as the Kimbolton cabinet, made to display a set of 11 pietra dura panels, one of which is signed "Baccio Capelli Fecit Anno 1709 Fiorenza". It was commissioned for the Duchess of Manchester and is now in the Victoria & Albert Museum. It measures 73 in. high by 70 in. wide (185 by 178 cm).

The ormolu mounts are by Boulton and Fothergill of Soho, Birmingham, and the cabinet was made by Ince & Mayhew, of Soho, London.

It was common practice for the English dilettante to return from the Grand Tour with contemporary works of art, which were then mounted or displayed in specially designed pieces of furniture. The detailed invoicing of such pieces gives us an invaluable insight into the costs of making furniture at this time. For example, the gilt metal mounts alone for this piece cost more than Chippendale charged for the well known library table at Nostell Priory.

There is a design, now in Sir John Soane's Museum, London, from Robert Adam's office and dated 1st June 1771, which is so close to that of this cabinet as to be almost certainly a working drawing.

A1 *(above)* An important George III mahogany, sandalwood and boxwood architectural medal cabinet, designed by Sir William Chambers *c.* 1767-1768 and known as Lord Charlemont's medal cabinet. It stands 144 in. high and is 175 in. long (366 by 445 cm).

To either side of the central panel, which bears a medallion carved with a figure of Hercules, are two ranks of fjelded, panelled doors enclosing a fitted ebony interior. The doors below the dado open to 39 various sized ebony drawers in three tiers.

C2 *(above)* A rare George III marquetry writing cabinet, *c.* 1775; 71 in. high, 47 in. wide (180 by 119 cm).

The cylinder front encloses a fitted interior with pull-out reading and writing slide. The glazed doors are faced with gilt bronze quatrefoils, and the mounts to the legs as well as the hoof feet are also gilt bronze. The whole is inset with flower-filled panels on harewood grounds within borders of kingwood, guilloche and Vitruvian scrolls.

C2 *(above)* A George III parquetry lady's cabinet in the French taste, *c.* 1790; 36 in. (91 cm) wide. Compare Sheraton's engraving of a lady's cabinet in the Appendix to his *Cabinet Maker and Upholsterer's Drawing Book*, 1793, plate 16.

C3 *(below)* A George III satinwood and marquetry side cabinet, *c.* 1778, stamped Edwards and Roberts; 40 in. high by 60 in. wide (100 by 154 cm).

A hinged panel in the top opens to a yew interior. The four cupboard doors enclose six short drawers and two long. The marquetry work is of sufficiently high quality to have come from the workshops of Chippendale and Haig.

This piece, formerly in the collection of R.H. Benson, is illustrated in *A History of English Furniture: The Age of Satinwood*, by Percy McQuoid, figure 157. The Edwards and Roberts stamp indicates that this piece was restored or handled by them during the latter part of the 19th century.

C1 *(above)* A small George III satinwood breakfront bookcase, *c.* 1790; 88 in. high, 57 in. wide (224 by 143 cm).

Of the exotic veneers introduced to England in the latter part of the 18th century, satinwood was among the most beautiful and was employed to its best advantage on designs for furniture created by Sheraton. This elegant cabinet is a fine example of the genre and much use is made of contrasting rosewood to the doors and bandings.

Sheraton is best known for his three-part publication *The Cabinet Maker and Upholsterer's Drawing Book* (1791-1794). It was the popularity of this book, rather than any furniture that he made, which caused Sheraton's name to be synonymous with the elegant lines of the classical taste. Indeed, although he was trained as a cabinet-maker, there is to date no proof that Sheraton actually made any furniture to his own designs.

D2 A George III satinwood collector's cabinet, *c.* 1790; 60 in. high, 37 in. wide (153 by 93 cm).

The brass galleried superstructure is supported on turned brass pillars. The brass grille-fitted doors enclose 20 graduated specimen drawers. The top and base are associated.

C3 A small George III mahogany writing cabinet, *c.* 1800; 54 in. high, 38 in. wide (136 by 95 cm). The frieze drawer contains a writing slope, sliding compartments and pen trays.

This cabinet, one of a pair, was reputedly made for Anna Forbes Wilford, wife of General Wilford, and by family tradition the pair were made to house Bell's Poets of Great Britain.

D1 One of a pair of George III painted and gilded secretaire-cabinets, *c.* 1790. It stands 89 in. high, is 48 in. wide and 19 in. deep (226 by 122 by 48 cm).

The glazed doors are satinwood-framed with brass glazing bars. The drawer is baize-lined and has a hinged flap. The cupboard door beneath is mounted with a tole panel of Cupid and Venus in the manner of Angelica Kauffmann. Flanking this central cupboard are two narrow cupboards surmounted by oval paintings of country houses.

The use of paint for decorating furniture well fitted the designs required by Robert Adam and began as a revival during the 1770s. The combination of colours and the design incorporated are distinctly Mediterranean, and furniture so decorated often appears to include a broad mixture of structural features. By the end of the century it was fashionable for artists employed to paint ceilings and walls to be commissioned to paint the furniture as well.

E1 *(above)* A satinwood breakfront display cabinet, second half of the 19th century; 56 in. high, 76 in. wide (142 by 193 cm).

Both satinwood and satin birch were used for fine quality Victorian furniture within finely carved borders that were often gilded to match the applied gilt metal mounts. The inclusion of other decorative media such as porcelain or painted panels or verre églomisé added to the prestige of a piece. Here an allegorical scene is flanked by verre églomisé garlands, at the junctions of which there are two finely carved heads of historical notables.

C2 *(right)* An important Victorian ivory-inlaid ebony cabinet, in the Italian Renaissance style, designed by Alfred Lorimer and made by Jackson and Graham. It is 113 in. high and 81 in. wide (287 by 206 cm). The inlay, apart from the dominant ivory, is lapis lazuli with a little red agate.

This type of furniture became extremely popular after the first Great International Exhibition of Works of Art of All Nations held in London in 1851. The first Great Exhibition was followed by some 19 further international exhibitions staged in Europe, America and Australia before the end of the century. These exhibitions encouraged manufacturers to show the ultimate degree of their skills in design and workmanship, and have left us an inheritance of furniture incorporating the best that man and machine working together can produce.

Styles can be seen to have originated in most major European countries and from most historical periods; thus French, Italian and German influences combine with Gothic, Elizabethan and Romantic styles; the position was made more complicated by the increasing demand for things of Near and Middle Eastern as well as of Oriental taste.

The cabinet shown here is a superb example of English Italian design. Furniture in this category was often fairly close in its resemblance to the model, and for a time it actually cost more.

Jackson and Graham were a prestigious Victorian company who exhibited at the major international exhibitions, including Paris in 1855 and London in 1862.

D 1 *(right)* A Victorian marquetry side cabinet, in the manner of Holland & Sons; 82 in. (208 cm) wide. The top is veneered with a trellis parquetry design and is crossbanded in kingwood.

There is no special reason to believe that this piece came from the Hollands' workshop, but such exceptionally intricate and finely executed marquetry, veneer and applied brass decoration was characteristic of Holland work, although the firm was better known for such skill when it was applied to furniture of a strictly 18th-century English design – which this credenza evidently is not.

The superb fineness of the carving shows admirable use of the relatively new machine-assisted methods of production, following the introduction in 1845 of Thomas Jordan's woodcarving machine.

D 3 *(below)* A Victorian satinwood side cabinet stamped "Wright and Mansfield, 104 Bond Street", third quarter of the 19th century; it is 78 in. high and 96 in. wide (197 by 243 cm).

The firm of Wright and Mansfield did not last for very long and appears to have been in full production only from about 1860 to about 1866. Wright and Mansfield specialized in elaborately inlaid "Adam" furniture, which they produced to a very high standard.

D 2 *(above)* A papier mâché side cabinet, *c.* 1840; 72 in. (182 cm) wide. The mirrors are of a later date.

Papier mâché furniture of this size is comparatively rare and of great interest. The method of production developed in England from 1772, when it was first patented by Henry Clay. It is not in fact papier mâché, but is made by placing wet sheets of paper over a mould before baking them to make the shape durable.

The great age of papier mâché did not begin until the early 19th century; by the 1830s it was a supremely popular material. Early examples are often stamped either by Clay or by Jennens & Bettridge, which firm was responsible for the very finest quality papier mâché.

N.B. The inclusion of mother-of-pearl decoration indicates a post-1825 date, when George Souter, who worked for Jennens & Bettridge, introduced this feature.

E1 *(above)* A painted satinwood side cabinet by James Lamb of Manchester, second half of the 19th century.

James Lamb exhibited in the Paris Exhibition of 1867 and designed several pieces for Manchester Town Hall ten years later.

E2 *(below)* A bone-inlaid rosewood cabinet, designed by Stephen Webb, stamped "Collinson & Lock, London", *c.* 1885; 49 in. high, 45 in. wide (125 by 114 cm).

This cabinet appears to be identical to one designed by Webb, and also made by Collinson & Lock, that is now in the Victoria & Albert Museum.

C3 A Guild of Handicraft oak cabinet, designed by C.R. Ashbee, stamped "The Guild of Handicraft Ltd., Essex House, Bow E", *c.* 1900; 63 in. by 42 in. (160 by 106 cm).

The exterior faces of the cupboard doors are inlaid with fruitwoods, the interiors are satinwood veneered, painted and gilt. The writing slide rests on hinged supports.

E4 *(above)* A Gordon Russell walnut and mahogany fall-front writing cabinet with fine ebony stringing, 1927; 54 in. high, 47 in. wide (136 by 120 cm).

The piece bears a very detailed label: "This piece of furniture design no. 570 was made throughout in The Russell Workshops, Broadway, Worcestershire," and then names the foreman, cabinet maker and metal worker, as well as crediting Russell as designer. The wood is specified as English walnut and white mahogany.

CHAIRS
1550-1920

The classification of chairs is not an exact science, but we have adopted the following broad divisions, each set out in chronological order, in conformity with generally accepted terminology: Armchairs (this page); Open armchairs (p.197); Children's chairs (p.214); Corner chairs (p.214); Country chairs (p.215); Dining chairs (p.216); Hall chairs (p.230); Library chairs/steps (p.232); Porters' chairs (p.232); Side chairs (p.233) and Windsor chairs (p.236).

Armchairs

C1 A walnut wing armchair, with turned and lobed front legs, terminating in braganza feet, joined by a pierced bow stretcher, late 17th century.

C2 A wing armchair, with carved legs terminating in braganza feet, joined with a Dutch bow stretcher, late 17th century.

C3 A William and Mary walnut wing armchair, with turned legs and braganza feet, with shaped stretcher.

E4 A William and Mary walnut wing armchair, buttoned back with shaped wings, stuff-over seat on shaped seat rail, moulded cross-over stretcher.

D5 A William and Mary walnut wing armchair, on finely turned legs, joined with a wavy X-stretcher, *c*. 1695.

D6 A Queen Anne walnut wing armchair with gently arched back on cabriole legs ending in hoof feet, the legs joined by scrolled side and centre stretchers, the back stretcher turned.

D7 A Queen Anne walnut wing armchair with outward scrolling arms on collared cabriole legs carved with scrolls and terminating in shoe feet.

D8 A Queen Anne walnut wing armchair of elegant proportion, the arm supports terminating in outward scrolls, on four cabriole legs, *c*. 1710.

D9 A walnut wing armchair covered in yellow silk, with cabriole legs, carved at the knee with a shell, terminating in pointed pad feet, early 18th century.

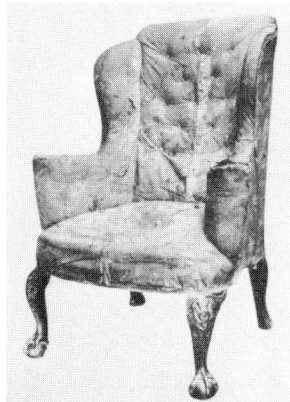

C10 An early Georgian walnut wing armchair, with cabriole legs carved at the knee, terminating in claw-and-ball feet.

D11 A George I walnut wing armchair, with arched eared padded back, outscrolled arms and bowed cushion seat, covered with floral gros point needlework.

D 1 A George I walnut wing armchair, *c.* 1715.

D 2 A George I walnut wing armchair, arched padded back, scrolled arms, *c.* 1720.

D 3 An early Georgian walnut wing armchair on carved cabriole legs.

D 4 A George I carved walnut and upholstered wing armchair, *c.* 1720.

D 5 A George I walnut wing armchair, bowed seat on cabriole front legs, brackets carved with flowerheads, *c.* 1730.

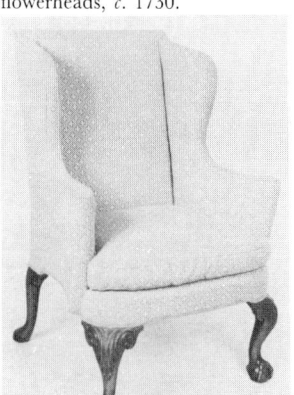

D 6 A George II walnut wing armchair, *c.* 1740; 32 in. (82 cm) wide.

E 7 A George II mahogany large wing armchair, upholstered in green leather, mid 18th century.

E 8 A George II walnut open armchair, rectangular padded back, outscrolled arms.

E 9 A George II mahogany bergère, with leaf-scroll brackets and pad feet, *c.* 1755.

D 10 A George III mahogany bergère, 1760-1770; 36 in. (92 cm) high.

E 11 A George III armchair, in nailed tan hide, *c.* 1770.

D 12 A George III mahogany leather-upholstered wing armchair.

E 13 A George III mahogany caned tub-shaped library bergère, with brass plate for reading equipment and brass candle-arm, *c.* 1790.

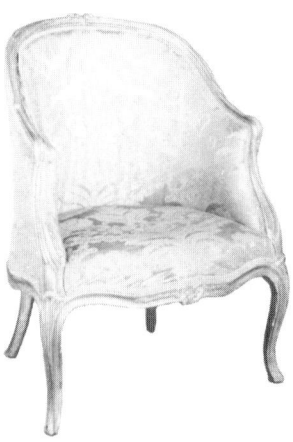

E 14 A George III giltwood bergère, with curved padded back and upholstered seat, covered in blue damask, on moulded cabriole legs.

D 15 A Hepplewhite mahogany high-backed wing chair, covered in green hide.

D 1 A caned bamboo armchair, with rectangular backs, canted sides and arms decorated with pierced panels, octagonal seats above pierced panelled seat rails and legs joined by stretchers, late 18th century.

C 4 A Regency ebonized and parcel gilt bergère, in the manner of George Smith, with tub-shaped back and upholstered seat, the arm rests modelled as lions' masks, on shaped claw feet.

E 7 A Regency mahogany bergère, on reeded tapering legs, with flowerhead bosses.

Armchairs from 1700
The heyday of the classic English armchair (developing earlier Dutch models), with its high back, wings and scrolled arms, was the Queen Anne and George I periods. By the middle of the 18th century French influence was readily apparent – see no. 10 on the facing page – and by the end of the century the old form was almost extinct, though it would be extensively revived within a century. Unless it retains its original upholstery it can be quite difficult to tell an ordinary 18th-century overstuffed armchair from a well made Victorian reproduction without lifting the under canvas and examining the construction.

French influence was strongly maintained and the bergère became popular in England in numerous forms (see no. 6 on this page). "Bergère" was however a confusing term in the 18th century. Introduced in about 1725 and variously anglicized it was used by Ince & Mayhew in their *Universal System* (1759–1763) to describe a couch.

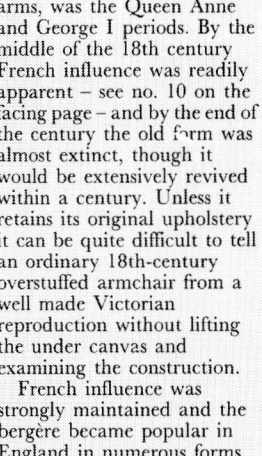

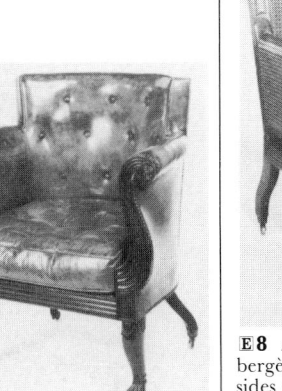

E 2 A Regency mahogany tub armchair, upholstered in brown leather, with square tapering incurved legs with brass casters, early 19th century.

D 5 A Regency mahogany bergère, U-shaped padded back and cushion seat covered in buttoned brown leather, reeded frame on naturalistic claw supports, headed by lotus leaves.

E 8 A Regency mahogany bergère chair, double caned back, sides and seat, *c*. 1815.

D 9 A Regency period rosewood show frame tub-shape armchair, *c*. 1820.

E 11 A William IV patent mahogany library armchair, with adjustable scrolled padded back, in maroon leather.

E 3 A Regency mahogany framed bergère, the scoop shaped back with reeded frame, continuing to slender vase-turned columns, on ring-turned tapered legs.

D 6 A Regency mahogany bergère library armchair, having cane sides, seat and back, reeded scimitar shaped legs, finely carved lion-mask arms.

E 10 A William IV chestnut hide chair, *c*. 1830; 40 by 26 in. (100 by 65 cm).

E 12 A William IV giltwood Gothic bergère, attributed to William Porden, *c*. 1830.

E1 A gentleman's Victorian buttoned back elbow chair, with scrolled carved front supports, scrolled serpentine front rail and snail-shaped feet on casters.

E4 A painted and parcel gilt corner armchair, with moulded frame, buttoned back and seat, and cabriole legs, mid 19th century.
This is one of a set of four similar, which, when placed together, form a centre seat.

E9 A Sheraton-style satinwood and painted cane bergère armchair, the oval back with panel showing classical seated maiden, on turned legs and casters, *c.* 1880.

E2 A rosewood buttonback bergère-type library chair, with scroll arms, mid 19th century.
Of the woods most used for this type of chair – walnut, mahogany and rosewood – the last certainly will indicate top quality.

E5 A rosewood drawing room armchair, *c.* 1850.
Much furniture of this type was made in order to supply a rapid growth in demand, using inferior materials; inspection is advisable.

E7 A walnut armchair, the buttoned back with a moulded leaf-carved top rail, sprung seat, on cabriole legs, *c.* 1850.

E10 A Sheraton revival painted satinwood framed bergère chair, the frame painted with drapery and flowers, 19th century.

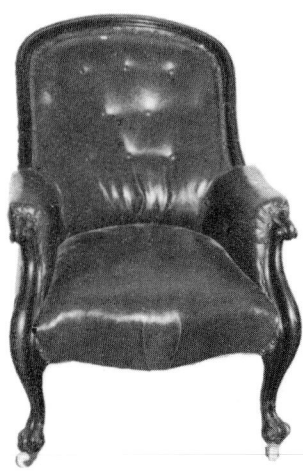

E3 A Victorian mahogany buttonback armchair, with shaped scroll arms, raised on cabriole supports.

E6 An oak buttonback armchair with leaf-carved finials, the sprung serpentine seat on leaf-carved cabriole legs, mid 19th century.

E8 A Victorian rosewood buttoned back armchair, with scrolled arms and serpentine fronted seat, supported on cabriole legs.

E11 A Sheraton revival painted and caned satinwood bergère chair, painted throughout with flowers, *c.* 1900.

Open armchairs

E 1 A small oak and elm turner's chair, 28 in. (71 cm) mid 16th century.

Triangular chairs are among the earliest forms of seating, after the plank-type box seat or stool.

E 2 An Elizabethan turned great chair of highly elaborate form in ash and oak, late 16th century.

D 3 An ashwood bobbin-turned armchair, with elaborately turned framed and railed seat, 17th century.

D 4 A wainscot chair, with floral inlaid decoration and deep carving, late 16th century.

E 5 A carved oak armchair, *c.* 1600.

This distinctive type of chair closely resembles earlier Italian models.

E 6 A James I cupboard base panel back cacqueteuse armchair, attributed to the workshop of Humphrey Beckham, *c.* 1620.

D 7 A Charles I oak chair-table, the three-plank top sliding and pivoting to form the back of the armchair, *c.* 1640; 46 in. by 27 in. (116 by 67 cm).

E 8 An oak armchair, with solid back, carved with decorative motifs, with turned front legs and arm supports, mid 17th century.

E 9 A Charles I oak panel back armchair, the scroll and leaf-carved cresting above a panel of strapwork, centred by a flowerhead, with moulded panel seat, *c.* 1640.

E 10 A Charles I carved oak armchair, with flattened scrollwork toprail, shaped arm supports, *c.* 1640.

E 11 An oak and upholstered sleeping armchair, with adjustable back, 17th century.

D 12 A Charles II carved wing armchair, double S-scroll front stretchers, *c.* 1685.

E 13 An armchair, with straight padded arms, stuffed seat in gros point needlework, *c.* 1680.

E 1 A walnut open armchair, padded seat and back covered in floral damask, with barley twist stretchers, *c.* 1665.

E 4 A Charles II walnut armchair, with rectangular stuffed back, with spiral twist arms, arm supports, legs and stretchers, *c.* 1680.

E 7 A George I mahogany library armchair, with outcurved "shepherd crook" arms, early 18th century.

D 10 A George II mahogany library armchair, with padded back and upholstered seat covered in yellow damask, on cabriole legs headed by overlapping shells and pad feet.

E 2 A Restoration period carved and pierced walnut open armchair, with seat and back of canework panels, decorated with barley sugar twists.

E 5 A Charles II giltwood open armchair, with rectangular padded back and upholstered seat, scrolled legs joined by a pierced and carved scrolling front stretcher and ending in claw feet.

C 8 A George II mahogany open armchair, *c.* 1704. The general lines and carving of this chair illustrate the type of decoration which formed the basis for the high-style rococo of the 1750s. The show wood frame to the back is slightly unusual for this period, and the cushion-shaped seat rails to the sides and front, creating a serpentine line, indicate top quality.

D 11 A George II elbow chair of the mid-18th century French style, covered in contemporary needlework, *c.* 1740. This chair shows a distinct Continental influence in the French feet and line of the arms.

E 3 A Charles II giltwood open armchair, padded back and cushion seat, double scrolled arm-supports, front stretcher carved with putti, flanking a military trophy, lion feet.

E 6 A William and Mary walnut armchair, the back with turned pillars with Corinthian capitals, a caned panel with arched top and base and leafy scroll cresting, *c.* 1690.

C 9 An English Chippendale mahogany armchair, carved in French taste, and with original covering of old petit-point embroidery, *c.* 1750.

D 12 A George II mahogany library armchair, arched padded back and upholstered seat edged with carved arcaded acanthus, on square chamfered legs, with C-scroll brackets panelled with rosettes and Chinese blind fretwork, upholstered in brown velvet brocade, mid 18th century.

E 1 A George II mahogany library armchair, with arched eared padded back, upholstered seat and padded arms, on square legs joined by stretchers, upholstered in red silk damask, mid 18th century.

E 2 A mahogany framed armchair, with an upholstered back and curved, fluted arm supports, on moulded legs, 1740-1770.

D 5 A George III mahogany open armchair, with leather upholstery, *c.* 1760.

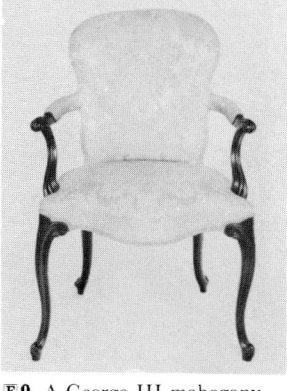

E 9 A George III mahogany fauteuil, upholstered in yellow damask, late 18th century.

D 3 A pair of George III mahogany library armchairs, each with rectangular padded back with serpentine top rail, and padded arms on downcurving blind-fret stumps, the seat raised on blind-fret Marlborough legs with pierced stretchers, on casters, upholstered in later needlework; 39 in. high by 27 in. wide (99 by 69 cm).

E 6 A George III mahogany desk chair, in nailed red leather upholstery.

E 7 A George III mahogany open armchair, in the manner of John Cobb.

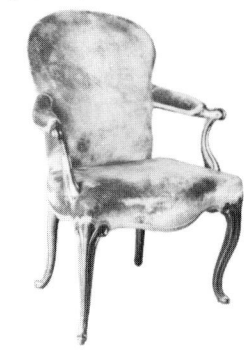

E 10 A George III Chippendale-style mahogany open armchair.

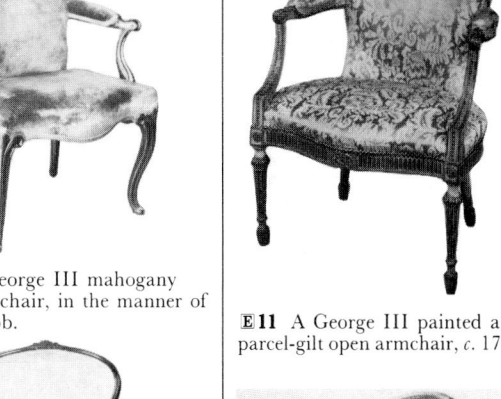

E 11 A George III painted and parcel-gilt open armchair, *c.* 1775.

C 4 A pair of George III mahogany-stained library armchairs, each with shaped upholstered back with serpentine top rail, scrolling upholstered arms on moulded scrolling supports, and upholstered seat with carved and moulded seat rails, sweeping into carved and moulded cabriole legs with scroll feet with casters, each inscribed inside the rear rail TH, *c.* 1769; 28 in. (70 cm) wide.

E 8 A George III mahogany open armchair, in the French taste, with slender cabriole legs, late 18th century.

D 12 A George III armchair, painted white and gilt, *c.* 1770.

E1 A George III armchair, with moulded stick back and carved downcurved arms, moulded serpentine seat rails, on fluted inverted baluster legs, *c.* 1775.

E4 A George III giltwood armchair, moulded cartouche-shaped padded back, on turned front legs with spirally fluted collars, *c.* 1780.

E7 A George III white painted and gilded open armchair with oval ivory silk padded back.

E10 A George III giltwood open armchair, with square padded back and upholstered seat in maroon silk, in plain moulded frame, on fluted tapering legs.

E2 A George III giltwood open armchair, with shaped upholstered back, carved with a bow, the upholstered arms carved with paterae, the upholstered seat with serpentine front, on block feet.

E5 A George III giltwood armchair with shield-shaped back, moulded and carved with husks, *c.* 1785.

E8 A George III green and cream-painted fauteuil, in the French manner, with oval padded back and serpentine upholstered seat in moulded fluted frame, on cabriole legs, upholstered in floral brocade, late 18th century.

E11 A George III beechwood armchair in the French manner, the padded back and upholstered seat in carved moulded frame, late 18th century.

D3 A George III beechwood open armchair, with padded shield-shaped back and bowed seat, upholstered in lime green velvet, inscribed in ink 3071 Hubberd.

E6 A George III mahogany fauteuil with oval padded back and bowed upholstered seat, in yellow silk brocade, late 18th century.

E9 A George III giltwood open armchair, the moulded frame carved with bead-and-reel ornament and coned crestings.

E12 A George III mahogany open armchair, in the manner of Gillows, the upholstered chamfered back bordered with cane, shaped seat on turned and tapering ribbed legs.

E1 A Regency parcel-gilt armchair, concave fluted back, padded arms, *c.* 1820.

D2 A Regency parcel-gilt and green-painted open armchair, manner of George Smith.

E3 A Regency mahogany writing-chair, U-shaped top rail, leather upholstery.

E4 A Regency mahogany library open armchair, early 19th century.

E5 A George IV rosewood library bergère, attributed to Gillows, the curved frame upholstered in buttoned green leather, with scrolled arm supports, on arched legs.

E6 A George IV light oak library armchair, with buttoned leather back and seat, foliate turned legs, the back hinged to form a prie-dieu.

E7 A William IV giltwood chair, in the manner of William Porden, with arched padded back covered in buttoned floral cotton damask, on tapering octagonal legs, headed by clustered foliage.

E8 A Victorian walnut frame spoon back gentleman's chair, on cabriole legs.

E9 A Victorian rosewood open armchair, padded arms and scrolling ends, *c.* 1845.

E10 A Victorian carved walnut and buttoned balloon back chair, bowed seat, *c.* 1855.

E11 A walnut armchair, with padded arms and buttoned back, *c.* 1860.

E12 A walnut drawing room armchair, with a balloon back carved with a rosette, out-turned scroll arms with upholstered pads and scrolling front legs, *c.* 1860.

E13 A walnut armchair, with waisted upholstered back carved with leaves, and circular sprung seat on moulded cabriole legs, *c.* 1860.

E14 A Victorian walnut drawing room armchair, with buttoned upholstered back and sprung seat, on tapering ringed legs, *c.* 1860.

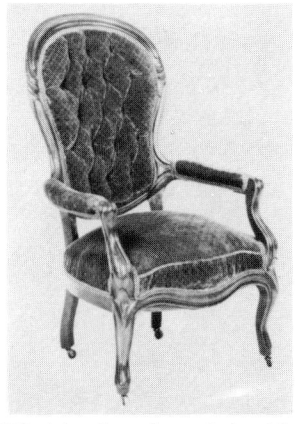

E1 A beechwood armchair, with padded arms and buttoned back, on cabriole legs with casters, third quarter of 19th century.

E2 A Victorian spoon back open armchair, with carved walnut frame with scrolled terminals to the arms, on carved and scrolled legs, upholstered in pale blue.

E3 A simulated rosewood drawing room armchair, with moulded top rails, padded backs and sprung serpentine seat, on moulded cabriole legs, *c.* 1870.

E4 A carved walnut drawing room armchair, with carved and pierced arched top rail, padded back and padded bow seat, on circular tapering fluted legs, *c.* 1870.

E5 A Victorian walnut armchair, the spoon back with moulded top rail, scroll arms on French front supports and pottery casters.

E6 A Victorian rosewood button back chair, the shaped back with carved cresting, the scroll arms with upholstered pads, with carved front legs.

E7 A Victorian rosewood open arm easy chair, on cabriole legs.

E8 A marquetry armchair, frame inlaid with Sheraton-style marquetry, late 19th century.

E9 An inlaid rosewood drawing room armchair, *c.* 1890.

E10 An Edwardian mahogany rocking chair, with carved shield-shaped back.

D11 A Charles II walnut carver, the back and seat with canework panels, with deeply scrolled, carved rails and stretchers, *c.* 1660.

E12 A Charles II armchair, in fruitwood and elm, with spiral twist front stretchers, *c.* 1680.

E13 A Queen Anne fruitwood open armchair, waved top rail, vase-shaped solid splat, early 18th century.

D 1 A Queen Anne walnut open armchair, *c.* 1710.
The graceful lines express the best of the curvilinear style that found favour early in the 18th century.

D 2 A mahogany armchair, with pierced splat, arms dished at the elbow, terminating in a carved eagle's head, with elaborately carved cabriole legs ending in claw-and-ball feet, early 18th century.

E 3 A George I walnut armchair, with boldly modelled arms and pierced ribbon baluster splats, drop-in needlework covered shaped seats, on cabriole legs with claw-and-ball feet.

E 4 A George I mahogany writing chair, with shield-shaped back and shepherd crook arms, *c.* 1720.

E 5 A George I provincial walnut armchair, shaped top rail with solid vase-shaped splat, on plain cabriole legs with pad feet, *c.* 1720.

E 6 A George I walnut armchair, with scroll cresting rail, solid vase-shaped splat and shepherd crook arms, *c.* 1720.

E 7 A George I walnut armchair, *c.* 1725.

D 8 A early George II walnut open armchair, drop-in seat, on cabriole legs, *c.* 1735.

C 9 A George II red walnut hall armchair, in the manner of Giles Grendey, *c.* 1735.

E 10 A George II walnut armchair wth pierced splat, scrolling arms and shaped apron, on cabriole legs.

D 11 A George II mahogany armchair, the scroll cresting rail and pierced and carved vase-shaped splat above a slip-in seat, on cabriole legs with claw-and-ball feet, *c.* 1740.

E 12 A George II mahogany armchair, with pierced leaf-carved Gothic splat, moulded outscrolled arms, stuffed serpentine fronted seat and leaf-carved cabriole legs, on scrolled feet, mid 18th century.

D 13 A George II mahogany open armchair, with moulded waved top rail carved with central coronet, S-shaped arms, drop-in seat on cabriole legs with claw-and-ball feet, upholstered in red silk brocade, mid 18th century.

D 1 A George II mahogany open armchair, in the manner of Robert Mainwaring, leather upholstered seat.

D 4 A George III mahogany open armchair, with waved top rail and pierced interlaced splat, carved with foliage sprays and headed by a C-scroll and rocaille cartouche; 38 in. high by 24 in. wide (97 by 62 cm).

E 7 A George III walnut armchair, serpentine top rail above vase-shaped splat with simple piercing, shaped arms with outscrolled handles, drop-in seat on square moulded chamfered legs, *c.* 1765.

E 10 A George III beechwood "cockpen" open armchair, with drop-in caned seat.

D 2 A George II mahogany masters' armchair, with waved seat rail, on cabriole legs and pad feet.

E 5 A George III mahogany open armchair, with shaped top rail and interlaced-scroll splat, the arms ending in scrolls on downcurved stumps, upholstered seat on moulded Marlborough legs with stretchers, *c.* 1760; 39 by 29 in. (98 by 74 cm).

E 8 An early George III mahogany open armchair, with elaborate carving to the pierced splat and top rail, the arm supports with dished sections, with carved scroll terminals, and serpentine shaped front seat rail.

E 11 A George III mahogany ladder-back dining chair, moulded serpentine top rail carved with leaves, dipped stuffed seats, square chamfered legs, *c.* 1765.

E 3 An early George III walnut carrying armchair, the tall back with baluster splat, on square-section chamfered legs.

E 6 A George III mahogany dining chair, with serpentine top rail and pierced vase splat, with moulded in-curved arms, dipped leather-covered seat and square moulded legs, joined by an H-stretcher, *c.* 1765.

D 9 A George III carved mahogany dining chair, with serpentine crest above an interlacing strapwork splat carved with a shell, leaves and wheat, shaped open arms with spherical hand grips, mid 18th century.

E 12 A George III mahogany open armchair, the waved top rail with concave foliage-and-cabochon crestings, with interlaced scrolled splats and drop-in seat on cabriole legs and claw-and-ball feet.

C1 A Chippendale Gothic dining chair, with triple cluster column back posts, with crocketed pinnacles, c. 1765.

E4 A George III mahogany ladder-back armchair, c. 1775. This type of ladderback is comparatively unusual, being more common to country chairs.

E7 A George III beechwood open armchair. Many beechwood chairs of this period were originally painted.

E10 A George III mahogany open armchair, with arched top rail carved with bellflowers, pierced interlaced Gothic-pattern baluster splats, on square tapering legs.

D2 A Chippendale elbow chair, the open back with Gothic splats and small pagoda capping.

E5 A George III mahogany elbow chair, with finely carved top rail and pierced splat, with square section legs with chamfered inside edge, with H-stretcher, c. 1760.

E8 A George III mahogany framed open armchair, with lobed cresting rail, with pierced vase-shaped splat.

E11 A George III mahogany dining chair, the moulded arched back with pierced baluster splats, with shaped arms, stuffed serpentine seat and cabriole legs, headed by leaves, c. 1770.

E3 A George III mahogany ladder-back dining chair, with pierced serpentine shaped horizontal splat, gros point upholstered seat, moulded square legs, joined by a stretcher.

E6 A George III provincial mahogany dining chair, with gently designed back splat, with moulded front legs, below a serpentine-shaped front rail.

E9 A George III mahogany open armchair, arched back with re-entrant corners and pierced vase-shaped splat, carved with neo-classical motifs, serpentine upholstered seat.

E12 A George III mahogany open armchair, with slatted back, on turned and tapering legs, 1775-1780.

E1 A George III giltwood elbow chair in the French taste, the cartouche shaped back with foliate cresting and pierced radiating wheel splats, padded scroll arm supports and cane seat with squab, on moulded cabriole legs.

E4 A George III mahogany armchair, with moulded arched top rail and pierced vase splat, down-swept arms with stuffed seat, square tapering legs joined by an H-stretcher, *c.* 1780.

E7 A George III mahogany dining chair, shield-shaped back, with finely pierced splat, arms on out-swept scroll supports, with square tapered legs.

E10 A George III country-made walnut armchair, with serpentine top rail above a pierced splat and drop-in rush seat, *c.* 1790.

E2 A George III beechwood armchair, the oval back with three moulded stick splats centred by oval paterae, with stuffed bow-fronted seat, on square moulded tapering legs headed by paterae and ending in block feet, *c.* 1775.

E5 A George III mahogany armchair, the moulded arched top rail with slightly waisted sides, pierced waisted vase splat held by a band of fluting, out-swept arms with moulded supports and stuffed serpentine seat, *c.* 1780.

E8 A George III painted satinwood open armchair with pierced shield-shaped back and waved outscrolled arms, bowed upholstered seat on ring-turned legs.

E11 A George III mahogany open armchair, with shaped top rail, pierced Gothic splat, scrolling arms on in-curved supports, the upholstered seat on Marlborough legs with stretchers.

E3 A George III mahogany armchair, with carved oval back centred by paterae, arms with voluted supports, stuffed serpentine-fronted seat, fluted seat rail faced with paterae, *c.* 1780.

E6 A George III ebonized and painted open armchair, the shield-shaped back with railed splats, downcurved arm supports and upholstered seat on tapering legs.

E9 A George III mahogany armchair, shield-shaped back with pierced and carved splat, moulded arms, stuffed seat, tapering legs, *c.* 1785.

E12 A George III mahogany open armchair, arched back, twin vertical splats, serpentine upholstered seat on square tapering legs with block feet, late 18th century.

E 1 A George III mahogany armchair, the moulded frame with three stick splats, shaped arms, stuffed bow-fronted seat, *c.* 1790.

E 4 A Sheraton mahogany armchair, reeded back supports with paterae, decorated top rail, triple stick back, *c.* 1790.

E 7 A Sheraton period mahogany dining chair, the moulded back with vertical rails with paterae, leaf-carved arms on turned supports, stuffed overseats on front square tapering moulded legs.

E 10 A George III mahogany dining chair, the gabled top rail with pierced tapering splats, upholstered seat, fluted tapering legs on block feet.

E 2 A George III mahogany Sheraton design armchair, with satinwood chevron banding, stuffed seat, tapered square legs, *c.* 1790.

E 5 A George III mahogany Hepplewhite design armchair, *c.* 1795.

E 8 A George III mahogany armchair, Sheraton design, stick splats, stuffed bowed seat, on slender ringed and baluster turned legs, *c.* 1800.

E 11 A George III mahogany open armchair, with stepped top rails, pierced arcaded splats carved with triple plumes, baluster arm supports and upholstered seat on tapering legs.

E 3 A Sheraton mahogany reeded stick-back armchair, slip-in seat covered in striped brocade, on tapered square legs with stretchers, *c.* 1790.

E 6 A George III mahogany dining chair, moulded back with fluted top rail, drop-in seat, late 18th century.

E 9 A George III mahogany framed dining chair, with bowed top rail surmounting three uprights, with arms on curved supports, late 18th century.

E 12 A George III mahogany dining chair, with curved panelled top rail, reeded X-frame splats, drop-in seat, *c.* 1800.

E1 A mahogany dining chair, the shaped rails on reeded uprights above upholstered seats and square tapered legs with spade feet, *c.* 1800.

E4 A George III mahogany open armchair with moulded tablet top rail.

E8 A brass-mounted stained beech armchair with reeded top rail and two shaped crossbars, caned seat on sabre legs and with scroll handles, *c.* 1805.

E11 A George III mahogany dining chair, with concave top rail inlaid with stringing above triple reeded stick splats, outswept arms, stuffed bowed seat, *c.* 1810.

E2 A Sheraton dining chair, the rail back with pierced trellis, stuffed bowed seat above tapered square feet united by X-shaped stretchers, *c.* 1800.

D5 A George III simulated rosewood and parcel-gilt open armchair.

E9 A George III elbow chair, with overhanging panelled top rail, over X-shaped splat, with swept arms on inverted vase supports, on finely turned and tapering legs.

E12 A Regency caned mahogany dining chair, with rope twist top rail and caned crossbars, scroll arms and sabre legs, *c.* 1810.

E3 A George III "bamboo" bergère in beech, with diamond trellis top rail above five spindles, with similar arms and caned seat on straight legs with H-stretchers, *c.* 1800.

E6 A George III mahogany open armchair, top rail inlaid with plum-pudding panel.

E7 A George III mahogany dining chair with down-curved arms, *c.* 1805.

E10 A Regency japanned armchair, the curved top rail painted with a flambeau above trellis crossbars, the arms with turned supports and caned seat, *c.* 1800.

E13 A Regency simulated rosewood armchair, panelled top rails, latticework splats, outcurved arms with bowed caned seat, tapering circular legs, *c.* 1810.

E1 A Regency beechwood armchair, with curved moulded top rail and crossbars, downcurved arms on turned supports, dipped solid seat, *c.* 1810.

E4 A Regency mahogany armchair, with curved top rail, scroll arms, drop-in seat and sabre legs, *c.* 1810.

E7 A Regency mahogany dining chair with figured panelled top rail above rope-twist horizontal splat, on ring turned tapered legs.

E10 A Regency mahogany dining chair, with carved scroll top rail and clasp shaped mid-bar and Trafalgar seat, *c.* 1815.

E2 A Regency mahogany dining chair, with rope-twist over-scrolled back, panelled splat, stuffed drop-in seat and reeded tapering legs headed by flowerhead paterae, *c.* 1810.

E5 A Regency mahogany rail back armchair with pierced scroll mid-bar and Trafalgar seat, on sabre legs, *c.* 1810.

E8 A Regency period rosewood rope back dining chair, *c.* 1815. This model was among the most popular of Regency turned leg dining chairs, particularly in the northern counties.

E11 A Regency mahogany dining chair, tablet top rail and vertical reeded bars with moulded crossbars, upholstered seat on circular tapering reeded legs with ring-turned collars and peg feet, early 19th century.

E3 A Regency brass-inlaid mahogany chair, top rail inlaid with brass stringing, scroll arms and moulded frame with caned seat and sabre legs, *c.* 1810.

E6 A Regency mahogany dining chair, with wide overhanging top rail, ending in a simulated scroll at either end, surmounted by formal drapery.

E9 A Regency mahogany armchair, leaf-carved back support and rail splat, inlaid with satinwood stringing, stuffed seat, *c.* 1815.

E12 A Regency mahogany dining chair, with bowed top rail above an X-back splat centred by a brass sphere, all with reeding and ebony stringing.

E1 A George IV period mahogany open armchair, the wide overhanging top rail swept back over a carved, pierced centre splat with deep scrolling arms, drop-in seat and sabre legs.

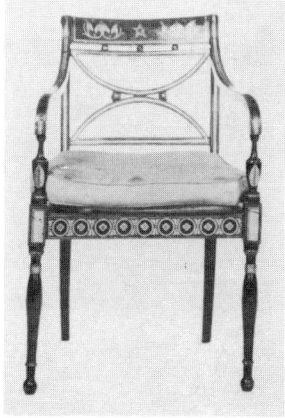

E4 A Regency painted and parcel-gilt chair, with curved top rail, double U-shaped splat, caned loose-cushioned seat, slender turned front legs, decorated in gilt on black ground, eary 19th century.

E7 A Regency ebonized and gilded open armchair, with curved caned top rail, caned seat and down-scrolled arms on in-curved supports.

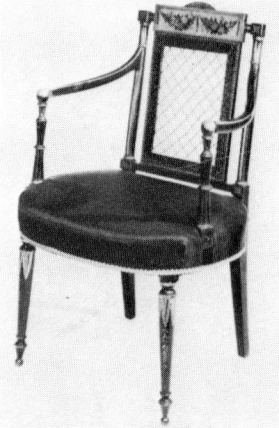

E10 A Regency ebonized and gilded open armchair, with oval horsehair upholstered seat, on tapering legs.

E2 A Regency mahogany dining chair, panelled top rail with trellis and rosettes above pierced interlaced splats, bowed upholstered seat.

D5 A Regency green painted open armchair, in the manner of George Smith, with curved panelled top rail painted in colours, X-pattern splat and down-scrolled arms with paw supports, caned seat and sabre legs.

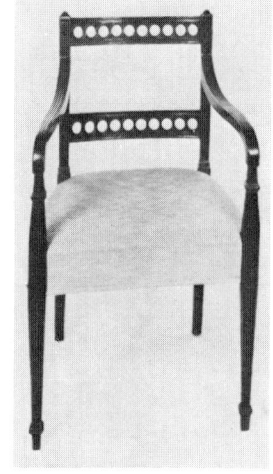

E8 A Regency mahogany open armchair, moulded back with two pierced horizontal bar splats, downcurved arms on square tapering fluted legs with block feet, early 19th century.

E11 A Regency Oriental-style armchair in rosewood, with inside top rail over X-form splat and vase-shaped turned supports to the arms.

E3 A Regency painted satinwood open armchair, the top rail decorated with a grisaille panel, with a trellis pattern splat, the upholstered seat on turned tapering legs.

E6 A Regency ebonized and painted open armchair, with turned shaped top rail above bar splats, centred with tablets, with caned seat on turned tapering legs.

E9 A Regency brown painted open armchair, with pierced vertical splat back inset with a lozenge, with unusual turned hand grips, on turned legs.

E12 A Regency simulated bamboo chair, with rectangular back with X-shaped splat, the rush seat with squab cushion, covered in yellow material.

E1 A Regency armchair, with painted beechwood simulated bamboo frame, pierced and turned spindle rail back and side panels, above a buttoned upholstered seat, on tapering legs with cross stretchers.

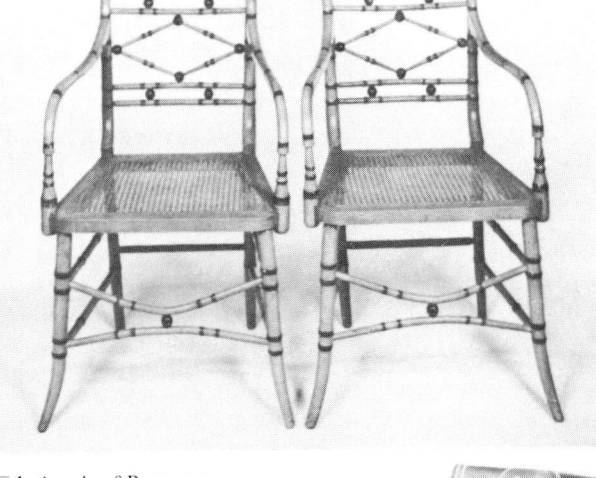

E4 A pair of Regency cream-painted simulated bamboo open armchairs, each with curved pierced trellis splat, caned seats, early 19th century.

E9 A Regency ebonized and gilded armchair, with curved top rail, pierced lozenge-pattern splat and caned seat with squab cushion, on ring-turned splayed legs.

E2 A Regency ebonized painted and parcel-gilt open armchair, with baluster top rail and caned tablet splat edged with reel ornament, scrolled arm-supports, caned seat with squab cushion, on sabre legs.

E5 A Regency painted chair, with caned seat, early 19th century; 33 in. high by 16 in. wide (84 by 41 cm).

E7 A Regency ebonized and gilt armchair, with demi-lune cane panels around painted centres, the swept arms with turned vase-shaped supports and the legs, which are also turned, splay out to the front.

E10 A Regency mahogany armchair, in the manner of George Smith, the fluted crestings above inset caned back and seat panels, with lappeted scrolled downcurved arms ending in carved paws, on sabre legs.

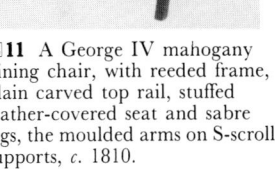

E3 A Regency rosewood and parcel-gilt open armchair, with decorated top rail and foliage between twin turned vase splats, caned seat and scrolled arms on sabre legs.

E6 A Regency painted beechwood dining chair, painted top rail on black ground, above trellis splat, on turned front legs, with gilt highlighting.

D8 A Regency mahogany open armchair, with U-shaped back and upholstered seat in green leather, C-shaped arm supports carved with dolphins and headed by lion heads, on incurved legs carved with lion's paw feet, early 19th century.

E11 A George IV mahogany dining chair, with reeded frame, plain carved top rail, stuffed leather-covered seat and sabre legs, the moulded arms on S-scroll supports, c. 1810.

E1 A pair of George IV mahogany dining chairs, with overhanging top rails and deeply scrolling arms and with turned front legs, *c.* 1825.

The top rails and centre splats are an alternative to foliate carving, with the arms and legs typical of the period.

E2 A George IV carved mahogany rail back chair, with a Trafalgar seat, on turned and reeded legs, *c.* 1825.

E3 A George IV mahogany dining chair, with foliate carved overhanging top rail, centre splat and leaf-capped sabre legs.

E4 A William IV mahogany dining chair, with carved top rail above a scrolled mounted splat, scrolled arms and upholstered seat, *c.* 1830.

E5 A William IV mahogany dining chair, with carved leaf-capped top rail, shell and scroll carved horizontal splat, with scroll arms, drop-in seat and ringed and reeded circular legs, *c.* 1830.

E6 A William IV mahogany framed open armchair, with gadrooned, foliate carved cresting rail, similar crossbar, and upholstered seat.

E7 A William IV mahogany chair, with the effect of an overhanging top rail created by two heart-shaped panels, and the splat similarly formed.

E8 A William IV mahogany rail back armchair, with U-shaped splat and Trafalgar seat, on turned and chamfered legs, *c.* 1835.

E9 A William IV mahogany armchair, with curved top rail, lotus-capped supports, scroll arms and stuffed seat, on circular tapering fluted legs, *c.* 1840.

E10 A William IV mahogany dining chair, the inside top rail spirally lobed above a panel of veneer with a carved, scrolling splat, 19th century.

E11 A walnut framed open armchair in the Continental manner, on cabriole legs with knurl feet, *c.* 1850. The lavish decoration is characteristic of eclectic 19th-century taste.

E1 A Victorian oak open armchair, by Bell & Coupland, with U-shaped carved top rail, with bone and ebony inset, on faceted legs headed by quatrefoils.

E2 A Victorian fruitwood desk chair, with curved top rail, scrolled arms, upholstered seat, *c.* 1860.

E3 An oak dining chair by Thomas Tweedy, with triangular cresting with a carved panel telling the story of Robinson Crusoe, *c.* 1862.

E4 A William IV open armchair, wide overhanging top rail above central splat carved with foliage, deeply scrolling arms, turned and reeded front legs, *c.* 1835.

E5 A Victorian Chippendale-style mahogany dining chair, in the manner of Gillows, with waved and carved top rail.

E6 A mahogany and satinwood crossbanded armchair, with concave top rail, stuffed seat on turned tapering legs.

E7 A George III-style mahogany dining chair, curved back with three splats pierced at top and the base, outscrolled arms and stuffed bowed seat, *c.* 1890.

E8 A Victorian Chippendale-style mahogany armchair, with floral scroll top rail and pierced vase-shaped splat, stuffed seat with carved apron, *c.* 1900.

E9 A mahogany armchair, with manufacturer's label of Cooper & Holt, with serpentine top rail above a two-tier Gothic-pierced splat, outcurved arms, drop-in seat and carved cabriole legs, *c.* 1900.

E10 A walnut dining chair, with a yoke top rail and straight splat, turned legs and H-stretcher, *c.* 1900.

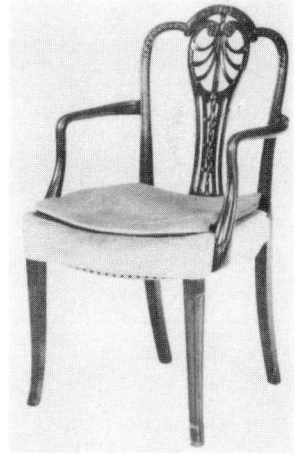

E11 A George III-style mahogany armchair, the arched back with a balloon back pierced and carved, moulded arms with stuffed seat, on square moulded legs with out-set feet, *c.* 1900.

E12 A mahogany armchair, with arched top rail and three stick splats, centred by a panel of fleur-de-lys, padded seat on square tapering legs with H-stretcher, *c.* 1920.

BRITAIN/*CHILDREN'S CHAIRS*

Children's chairs

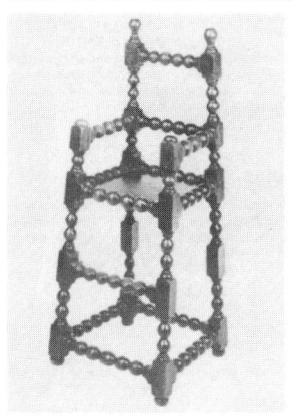

D 1 A high chair with bobbin back, arms and legs and solid seat, 17th century.

D 2 A child's chair in walnut, carved seat and back panel, carved and pierced rails, braganza feet, late 17th century.

E 3 A child's high chair, early 18th century; 34 in. (85 cm) high.

E 4 A provincial oak child's chair, high back, high waved sides, moulded seat on flared base, 18th century.

E 5 A period child's oak high chair of country style, late 18th to mid 19th century.

E 6 A yew child's high chair, shaped pierced splat, elm seat, early 19th century.

E 7 A Regency mahogany high chair, converting to table and chair, *c.* 1815.

E 8 A child's high chair which converts into a low rocking chair, 19th century.

Corner chairs

C 9 An extremely fine early George II period reading chair, the three back splats pierced in the rococo manner.

E 10 An early Georgian oak corner chair, the front leg with carving to the knee.

D 11 A Georgian mahogany cock-fighting chair, with fitting for spurs under left arm.

E 12 A George II mahogany corner commode chair, *c.* 1740.

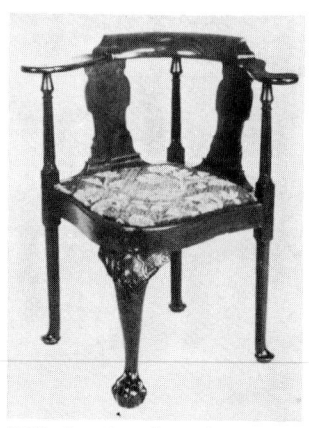

E 13 A walnut framed corner chair, mid 18th century.

D1 A mahogany corner chair, finely carved and turned with claw-and-ball feet, *c.* 1750.

E2 A George III mahogany corner elbow chair, with lift-out seat.

D3 A Chippendale mahogany barber's chair, with distinctive splat, *c.* 1730.

E4 A George III beechwood and fruitwood corner armchair, with open fret splats, mid 18th century.

Country chairs

E5 An elm and ash country ladder-back chair, with American influence, *c.* 1740.

E6 A rush-seated ladder-back chair, with turned legs, 18th century.

E7 A George III elm ladder-back chair, with rush seat on turned legs united by stretchers, *c.* 1790.

E8 A Lancashire spindle back chair, rush seat, turned front stretcher rail on pad, ball feet, early 19th century.

E9 An oak rush seat chair, late 19th century.

E10 A Georgian elm and yew rustic chair, formed from natural limbs and burls, *c.* 1825.

E11 A slat back kitchen chair, 19th century. These solidly made chairs were sold cheaply a generation ago.

E12 An elm smokers bow, *c.* 1900. Designed for tavern use, the smokers bow has been current since at least the 1860s.

E13 A desk chair, *c.* 1900. Usually made in beech or elm, made popular by the Arts and Crafts movement.

Dining chairs

E 1 A Charles I oak side chair, the top rail with a dentilled and moulded cornice, the arch with a carved keystone, *c.* 1640.

E 2 A late 17th-century south Yorkshire back stool, with ornate carving.

E 3 A Yorkshire oak chair, with original colour and patina 41 in. (102 cm) high, *c.* 1670.

E 4 A Charles II walnut ladder-back dining chair, the top rail centred by a crown flanked by putti, stamped RW.

E 5 A Charles II walnut chair, with an oval caned back in a leaf-carved pierced frame, the top rail pierced with two winged cherubs holding a cornet, *c.* 1680.

E 6 A late Stuart stained beech and cane side chair wth pierced scroll cresting over arched cane panel, stamped ET, late 17th century.

E 7 A James II walnut dining chair, with arched caned back in moulded shape frame and caned seat.

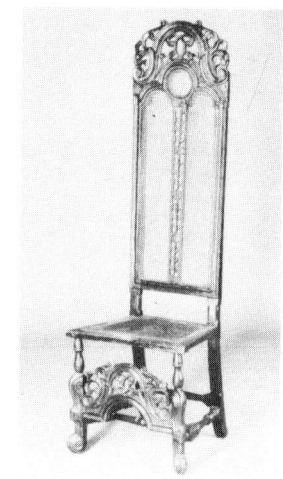
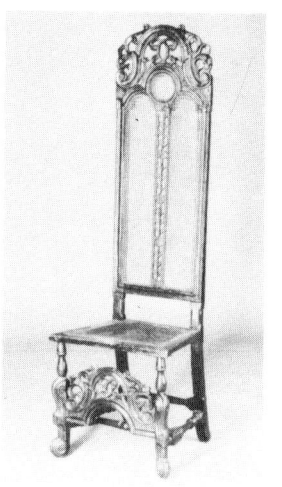

E 8 A James II black japanned side chair, with pierced strapwork cresting decorated in gilt.

E 9 A James II caned walnut chair, with crown and scroll top rail, *c.* 1685.

E 10 A Lancashire chair, with finely carved back, solid seat, turned front stretcher rail and legs.

E 11 A Stuart oak joined chair, Lancashire or Cheshire, mid 17th century; 40 by 19 in. (100 by 47 cm).

E 12 An oak dining chair, with solid seat, all basically 17th century.

E1 An oak joined chair, with scroll-carved top rail, late 17th/early 18th century.

E2 An oak Yorkshire chair, *c.* 1680; 39 in. high by 19 in. wide (97 by 47 cm).

E3 A William and Mary walnut dining chair, with partly caned back, concave top rail and moulded frame.

E4 A William and Mary beech side chair, with an arched crest pierced and carved with stylized leaves, above arched moulding surrounding a caned back panel flanked by column and vase-turned stiles, caned square seat, *c.* 1700.

E5 A William and Mary walnut side chair, with pierced and moulded crest with scrolled ears above arched moulded back centring a caned panel, square caned seat, 1690-1710; 48 in. high by 17 in. wide (120 by 43 cm).

E6 A William and Mary walnut chair, with cane panel to the back and upholstered seat, late 17th century.

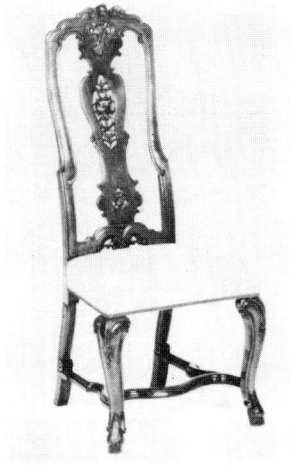

E7 A walnut chair in the manner of Daniel Marot with tall curved back and pierced baluster splat, *c.* 1700.

E8 A Queen Anne walnut chair, with solid vase splat and shaped support, bowed drop-in-seat with moulded seat rail, claw-and-ball feet, *c.* 1710.

E9 A Queen Anne walnut standard chair, with solid spoon back centred by inlaid panels, *c.* 1710.

E10 A Queen Anne walnut chair, with solid vase-shaped splat, slip-in seat, *c.* 1710.

Early English Armchairs
The appearance of the early "backstool" forbade comfort – see no. 1 opposite – but its evolution to the curvilinear design with an upholstered seat and a shaped, albeit solid back – a form much more suggestive of ease – was relatively quick. In between the most important innovation was the use of woven cane.

Cane was imported from China during the first great surge of chinoiserie following the Restoration in 1660. At first interlaced across a frame of walnut or oak to the backs (later to the seats) of chairs, the work was coarse, the holes large and sometimes irregular. By the time of James II however – see no. 6 on the facing page for example – the canework was finer and the holes smaller and more precise.

Cane enjoyed a considerable revival in the latter part of the 18th century, being used for rout chairs as well as bergères and chinoiserie items, and it was of course indispensable during the Victorian Jacobean revival.

E1 A Queen Anne walnut side chair, arched back, baluster-shaped splat, 18th century.

E2 A Queen Anne walnut chair, with solid vase-shaped splat and slip-in seat, on cabriole legs, *c.* 1710.

D6 A pair of George I walnut side chairs, the arched backs with paper-scroll top rail and solid vase-shaped splats, the bowed drop-in seats covered in tapestry pattern material, the plain seat rails centred by shells on cabriole legs, headed by shells ending in claw-and-ball feet.

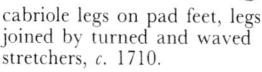

E3 A pair of Queen Anne walnut side chairs, shaped top rail, solid vase splat carving, carved cabriole legs on pad feet, legs joined by turned and waved stretchers, *c.* 1710.

E7 A pair of George I walnut side chairs, with arched backs and solid baluster splats, bowed upholstered seats on cabriole legs headed by scrolls and pad feet, early 18th century.

E4 A George I walnut dining chair, with spooned vase-shaped solid splat back, *c.* 1720.

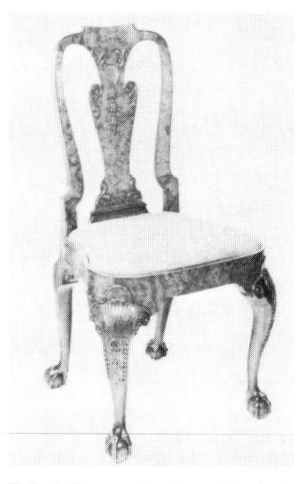

D5 A George I walnut side chair with shaped stiles to saddle top rail over vase-shaped splat, 1725-1740.

E8 A George I red walnut side chair, with shaped top rail carved with drapery, curved stiles and drop-in seat, early 18th century.

E9 A George II walnut side chair, with scroll over uprights joining baluster-shaped splat with panel seat and cabriole front supports.

E1 A George II walnut side chair with pierced and interlaced vase-shaped splat, and lift-out seat.

E2 A George II walnut chair, with pierced deep U-shaped splat with overscrolled top rail, moulded seat rail with drop-in rush seat and raised on cabriole legs with turned H-stretchers, *c.* 1730.

E6 A George II walnut dining chair with paper-scroll top rail, vase-shaped carved splat, and drop-in seat.

E8 A George II walnut dining chair, moulded back with carved dish top rail, slip-in seat, moulded seat rail, cabriole legs on pad feet, *c.* 1740.

E3 A pair of George II mahogany dining chairs with waved top rails and pierced interlaced vase-shaped splats carved with tasselled drapery, drop-in leather seats on cabriole legs and claw-and-ball feet.

E7 A George II mahogany dining chair, with pierced vase-shaped splat, slip-in seat and cabriole legs, *c.* 1745.

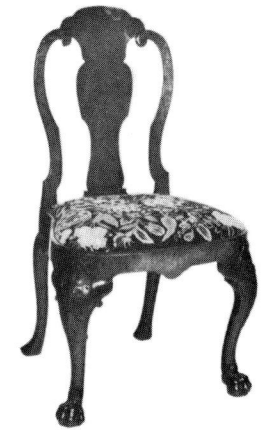

D9 A George II walnut side chair, shaped cresting, vase-shaped splat, curved stile, horseshoe drop-in seat on cabriole legs, mid 18th century.

E4 A George II mahogany dining chair, carved yoke top rail, drop-in seat covered in brown-ground petit point.

E5 A George II red walnut chair, with moulded back and shaped top rail above a pierced splayed splat, bowed drop-in seat on cabriole legs, *c.* 1750.

E10 A pair of George II red walnut dining chairs, with drop-in floral needlework seats, *c.* 1735. The bold pierced splats over shaped seat rails are the hallmarks of George II furniture, as are the cabriole-shaped legs, the upper parts of which are adorned with C-scrolls.

E1 A Georgian beechwood dining chair, with waved top rail and pierced Gothic pattern splats, drop-in seat with plain seat rail on moulded cabriole legs, headed by foliage and claw-and-ball feet.

E2 A Chippendale mahogany dining chair, with carved, eared top rail and pierced ribbon splat on cabriole legs carved with cabochons and leafage, on claw-and-ball feet.

E3 A Georgian walnut dining chair with paper-scroll top rail, pierced vase-shaped splat and drop-in seat, with plain seat rail on cabriole legs headed by acanthus and claw-and-ball feet.

E4 A George III mahogany dining chair with open interlaced splat and carved stiles, mid 18th century; 22 in. (55 cm) wide.

E5 A Chippendale dining chair with fine pierced splat, moulded seat on similar legs, and curved brackets.

E6 A Chippendale mahogany chair with scrolled pierced splat on blind fret carved square section legs, *c.* 1760.

E7 A pair of George III mahogany dining chairs with waved moulded top rails, vase-shaped splats pierced, interlaced and carved, serpentine upholstered seats covered in nailed crimson leather with moulded square legs, edged with beading.

E8 A pair of Georgian mahogany dining chairs, decorated in the manner of Thomas Chippendale, the backs with serpentine crestings, pierced and interlaced splats, seats upholstered in floral needlework raised on square chamfered legs, with plain stretchers and pierced and scrolled angle pieces.

E9 A pair of George II mahogany side chairs, with moulded and carved top rail and pierced scrolling splat carved with acanthus, the upholstered seat with serpentine front rail on moulded square legs, mid 18th century.

E1 A George III mahogany dining chair with waved top rail and pierced Gothic pattern splat, suede upholstered serpentine seats on moulded square legs and stretchers.

E2 A George III mahogany dining chair, attributed to Thomas Chippendale, with slightly tapering backs and arched top rail, and tapering vase-shaped splat, leather upholstered seat on square tapering legs.

E3 A George III mahogany dining chair, with pierced tapering vase-shaped splat, leather upholstered seat on square legs joined by stretchers.

E4 A George III mahogany dining chair, with serpentine top rail and chamfered legs, *c.* 1760.

E5 A George III mahogany dining chair, top rail carved with scrolls, pierced vase-shaped splat on square moulded legs joined by an H-stretcher.

E6 A Chippendale carved mahogany side chair with serpentine crest and carved strapwork splat, 1760-1790; 36 in. by 20 in. (91 by 50 cm).

E7 A George III mahogany chair, slightly rounded top rail with paper scroll ends, dipped stuffed seats, *c.* 1760.

E8 A Chippendale mahogany ladder-back dining chair with bowed seat on square-section legs; late 18th century.

E9 A George III mahogany dining chair with arched open back, pierced with a fretwork splat and bowed upholstered seat, late 18th century.

E10 A George III mahogany "cockpen" dining chair.

E11 A George III mahogany "bamboo" chair with carved seat, *c.* 1800.

E12 A George III mahogany side chair, in Chinese taste, serpentine top rail, open back with pierced pagoda-shaped splat, late 18th century.

E1 A pair of George III mahogany dining chairs, with drop-in seats, serpentine shaped front rail and moulded front legs.

E6 A George III mahogany dining chair, with moulded husk-carved top rail above a pierced moulded carved splat, *c.* 1780.

E7 A Hepplewhite mahogany dining chair, with arched cresting rail and dipped seats, 19th century.

E2 A George III mahogany chair, the serpentine top rail centred by anthemion, with pierced waisted splats, dished stuffed seat and chamfered legs joined by stretchers, *c.* 1775.

E4 A George III mahogany dining chair with arched moulded top rail waisted splat and drop-in seat, *c.* 1780.

E8 A pair of Hepplewhite carved mahogany shield-back chairs, the backs with Prince of Wales feathers, the stuffed seats covered in damask, *c.* 1790.

E3 A George III mahogany dining chair with arched moulded top rail, pierced bar-shaped splat and leather upholstered seat.

E5 A George III mahogany dining chair, *c.* 1780. The splat shows Gothic influence below a demi-lune shape, which became popular during the early classical period.

E9 A George III mahogany dining chair with arched shield-shaped back and pierced splat carved with Prince of Wales plumes.

E10 A George III mahogany chair, moulded shield-back with serpentine top, pierced leafy stick splat and dipped seat, late 18th/early 19th century.

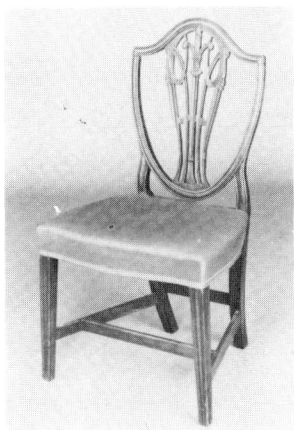

E1 A George III mahogany dining chair, moulded shield-shaped back and pierced interlaced slat, headed by Prince-of-Wales feathers.

E4 A mahogany Hepplewhite shield-back chair with intricate vase-shaped splat back, *c.* 1785.

E7 A George III mahogany dining chair with shield-shaped back, and corresponding shaped splat.

E9 A George III mahogany dining chair, oval back with patera centre and radiating leaf splats, serpentine upholstered seat on turned fluted legs.

E2 A George III mahogany dining chair with shield-shaped back and pierced lyre-shaped splat, carved with rosettes and laurel swag, the bowed drop-in seat on square legs.

E5 A pair of George III mahogany wheelback side chairs, each with moulded oval open wheel-shaped back carved with central patera, serpentine upholstered seat and fluted seat rail on circular tapering fluted legs. Late 18th century.

E10 A painted beech frame chair, with open ladder shield-shape back. 18th/19th century.

E3 A George III beechwood dining chair, shield-shaped back with pierced vase-shaped splat headed by wheatear, serpentine upholstered seat.

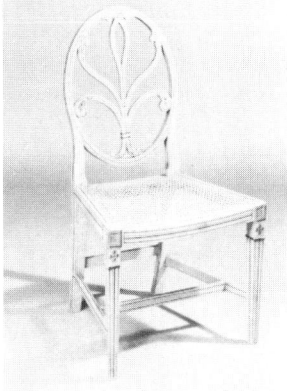

E6 A George III cream-painted dining chair, the oval back with anthemion splat decorated in red and black with lines and foliage, the shaped cane seat on square tapering legs joined by stretchers headed by beads.

E8 A George III style wheel-back chair, the oval pierced back with fluted border and centred by paterae, on square tapering legs joined by H-stretchers.

E11 A George III cream-painted dining chair, the shield-shaped back with pierced lyre-shaped splats decorated with drapery swags and foliage. Rush seats on square tapering legs.

E1 A Hepplewhite mahogany dining chair, showing the formal approach to classicism, *c.* 1785.

E4 A late George III mahogany dining chair with chamfered top rail and railed back with foliate splats centred by roundels, buttoned leather upholstered seat.

E7 A Sheraton carved mahogany chair with reeded stiles and fanned uprights, the arm supports and front legs turned, *c.* 1790. This chair exhibits a most interesting style and tradition.

E9 A George III mahogany dining chair with arched top rail carved with rosettes, tapering splats linked by drapery swags and horsehair-upholstered seats on moulded tapering legs.

E2 A George III mahogany dining chair, the rectangular open back with seven sticks, the padded seat on square tapering legs, *c.* 1790.

E5 A pair of George III mahogany framed dining chairs with rectangular backs, racquet-shaped pierced splats carved with husks, stuff-over seats and on tapering square legs which are joined by stretchers, *c.* 1790.

E10 A George III mahogany chair, the slightly arched back with four leaf-carved and beaded stick splats, with stuffed seat and square tapering legs, *c.* 1780.

E3 A carved mahogany dining chair in the style of George Hepplewhite, with elongated triple vase splat, *c.* 1790.

E6 A Regency oak dining chair in the Gothic style, the block feet carved with rosettes.

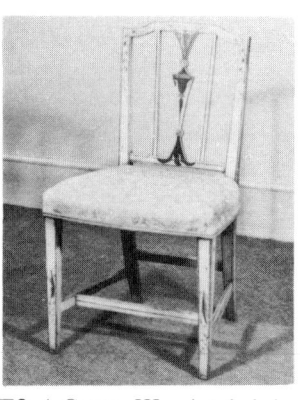

E8 A George III painted chair in classical style, *c.* 1790.

E11 A green-painted dining chair, the top rail with grisaille roundels, with caned seat. This chair reflects an interpretation of classical design.

E1 A Sheraton country chair in oak, with later upholstered seat, 1790-1800.

E4 An Adam mahogany chair, white enamelled, on carved fluted tapered legs, with carved rosette panels, cane seat and back.

E7 A George III mahogany dining chair, with three carved back splats, the frame with tapering square form, with plain legs, joined by H-stretchers.

E10 A Regency mahogany dining chair, the concave top rail inlaid with brass stringing and slightly overscrolled reeded back, with rope-twist splat, *c*. 1820.

E2 A mahogany frame dining chair with trellis back, seat upholstered in black hair.

D5 An Adam-style chair, with cane seat and back, *c*. 1790. Cane became popular again during the late 18th century.

E8 A George IV mahogany chair, the moulded frame with curved padded back above a caned panel, the padded seat on circular tapering legs, *c*. 1820.

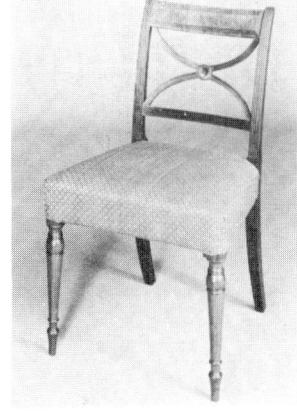

E11 A Regency mahogany dining chair, with shaped plank top rail and X-shaped splats centred by a lozenge on ring-turned legs.

E3 A George III mahogany framed dining chair, with rectangular back and reeded vertical stick splats, *c*. 1800.

E6 A Regency mahogany dining chair, on tapering legs with a bobbin rail back.

E9 A Regency mahogany dining chair, with solid reeded top rail and turned bar splat, with padded drop-in seat on tapering legs.

E12 A Regency mahogany and brass line inlaid rail-back chair, with rope-twist splat and stuffed seat.

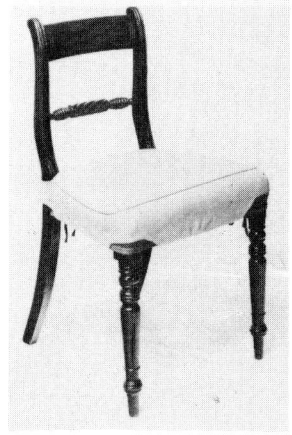

E1 A George III mahogany dining chair, with stuffed seat on turned tapering legs, *c.* 1810.

E4 A simulated rosewood dining chair with cane seat and brass inlay, *c.* 1815.

E7 A Regency painted dining chair with caned seat and curved top rail and scrolled bar splat decorated with polychrome foliage.

E10 A Regency simulated calamanderwood and parcel-gilt dining chair, in the manner of George Smith, covered in lime-green linen.

E2 A Regency chair with cane panel back and seat, with a loose squab cushion in moss green. The frame is simulated rosewood with gilt line decoration.

E5 A George IV ebonized chair, with caned seat, the turned top rail with matching crossbars and turned legs with matching front stretcher, *c.* 1825.

E8 A pair of painted Regency chairs, with outswept backs and deeply scrolled overhanging top rails. The Antique influence on high-style Regency is very obvious in the top rail form.

E3 A Regency simulated calamanderwood and parcel-gilt dining chair in the manner of George Smith, the seat covered in linen.

E6 A Regency parcel-gilt and green-painted dining chair with rope-twist top rail and solid scrolled splat, centred by shell lunette with caned seat on fluted sabre legs.

E9 A Regency solid rosewood chair, with brass inlaid panel, caned seat and squab cushion.

E11 An X-chair in the Greco-Roman style, with Egyptian hieroglyphics on the back. Although a fine example of its type, this combination of X-front legs and curved back legs does appear irregular.

E1 A Regency simulated rosewood Klismos chair, attributed to Thomas Chippendale the Younger, with U-shaped sloping back and D-shaped padded seat on sabre legs decorated with anthemions and lines, *c.* 1820.

E4 A Regency period mahogany dining chair, on four spade legs with drop-in seat and bar back.

E7 A George III mahogany chair with X-shaped splat centred by lozenge, on turned tapering legs, *c.* 1800.

E10 A William IV caned rosewood chair, the arched top rail and crossbar carved with leaves and grapes, the caned seat on circular tapering legs, *c.* 1830.

E2 A Regency mahogany dining chair, the solid top rail strung with satinwood, the shaped splats centred with a diamond lozenge, with upholstered velvet seat on turned tapering legs.

E5 A Regency mahogany dining chair with curved solid cresting rail inlaid with ebony stringing and incised decorations.

E8 A Regency mahogany dining chair, *c.* 1810. This type of chair was very popular at the time, after designs by Thomas Sheraton.

E11 A William IV mahogany chair, the broad convex shoulder rail above centre splat carved with fruit and flowers, the drop-in seat on turned lobed legs.

E3 A George III mahogany dining chair, with shaped bar top rail and moulded X-shaped splats centred by lozenge, the bowed padded drop-in seat upholstered in velvet on ribbed tapering legs.

E6 A Regency mahogany dining chair with drop-in seat which is covered in hand-worked tapestry, *c.* 1810.

E9 A William IV balloon back rosewood dining chair with carved crest rail and splat, *c.* 1830.

E12 A mahogany dining chair with heavily gadrooned over-hanging top rail, the splat similarly carved, in moulded frame, mid 19th century.

E1 An early Victorian mahogany dining chair, with compressed balloon back and horizontal crossbar carved with scrolling acanthus and flowerheads, leather upholstered seat.

E4 An early Victorian carved rosewood spoon-back chair, with clasp-shaped mid-bars, stuffed seat covered in brocade, turned tapering legs, *c.* 1845.

E7 A Victorian dining chair, oval open back with carved decoration of scroll work.

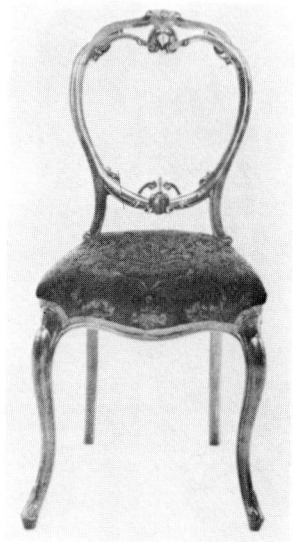

E10 A walnut dining chair with waisted back pierced and carved with scrolls on cabriole legs, *c.* 1860.

E2 An early Victorian dining chair, with stylized scroll horizontal bar.

E5 A walnut side or dining chair, with framework of interlaced leaves and flowerheads, *c.* 1845.

E8 A Victorian rosewood and mahogany balloon-back chair, decorated only with small scrolls to the ends of the splats and turning to the legs.

E11 A Victorian mahogany dining chair, the waisted hoop back with pierced horizontal bar.

E3 A Victorian mahogany dining chair, scroll horizontal, *c.* 1850.

E6 A rosewood chair, the almost balloon-shaped back with carved and pierced double-scroll splats and the stuffed serpentine seat on moulded cabriole legs, *c.* 1850.

E9 A pair of Victorian walnut dining chairs on cabriole legs with shaped backs, seats in red plush.

E1 A Victorian rosewood chair, the pierced and scrolled hoop back above pierced and interlaced horizontal splats, on slender moulded cabriole legs.

E4 A Victorian oak and parcel-gilt dining chair in revived Jacobean style, with the monogram MH below a crest.

E7 A late Victorian oak-framed dining chair, with pierced rectangular back, carved and incised with interlocking geometric motifs.

Early 19th-Century Chairs
In 1827 the redecoration of Crockford's Club in London by Benjamin Dean Wyatt heralded the French revival movement in the decorative arts. Furniture at first designed for the feminine apartments of the house bred counterparts for every room in the style of nos 7, 9 and 10 opposite.

There remained however a constant demand for the more florid interpretations of the classically inspired chair, such as nos 2 and 3 opposite, drawings for which were published by George Smith in his *Cabinet-Maker's and Upholsterer's Guide* in 1828.

Basic furniture design changed little during the next 15 years, with the result that in many cases there is little stylistically to distinguish late Regency, William IV and early Victorian chairs.

E2 A Victorian mahogany-framed dining chair with balloon back, pierced splats, upholstered serpentine-fronted seat on cabriole legs.

E5 A mahogany dining chair, with tan leather padded back within scale moulded frame, seat on turned, fluted supports, mid 19th century.

E8 An ormolu-mounted marquetry chair, French style, in mahogany and satinwood banding, the sprays inlaid with musical trophies, *c.* 1880.

E10 A "Charles II" walnut dining chair, with padded back and stuffed seat above barley-twist supports, late 19th century.

E3 A Victorian rosewood chair, the waisted back with pierced waved crestings and horizontal bar.

E6 A walnut parlour chair of eclectic design, *c.* 1865.

E9 A Victorian mahogany dining chair with upholstered seat and back, on turned and reeded front legs.

E11 A William and Mary style walnut-framed side chair, the baluster legs joined by stretchers and terminating in braganza feet.

E 1 A beechwood dining chair in late-17th-century style, with scroll cresting above pierced splat, with turned legs.

E 2 A gilt-gesso side chair in the Queen Anne style, with arched moulded top rail and a solid vase-shaped splat.

E 3 A black and gilt Edwardian Regency-style drawing room chair.

E 4 An Edwardian dining chair in the classical manner, recalling the designs of 130 years before.

Hall chairs

E 5 A George II mahogany hall chair, gadrooned scalloped back painted with the crest of Elwes of Roxby.

E 6 A George II mahogany hall chair, *c.* 1740; with plain eared back over an upholstered seat on sturdy cabriole legs.

E 7 A George II mahogany hall chair, *c.* 1740.

E 8 A mahogany hall chair, *c.* 1740; the traditional back shape mimicked throughout the rest of the chair.

E 9 A mahogany hall chair, mid-18th century, on straight turned legs joined by turned cross stretchers and terminating in pad feet.

E 10 A late George II/early George III elm hall chair, solid vase splat with solid dished seat and arched trestle supports, *c.* 1760.

D 11 A late George II mahogany "Grotto" hall armchair, with pierced shell-shaped back centring a cartouche, *c.* 1756.

E 12 A mahogany hall chair with exaggeratedly vase-shaped back over waisted seat on trestle supports, *c.* 1800.

E1 A George III mahogany hall chair, panelled back with reeded upright and centred by a painted coat of arms within circular brass frame, on lobed and turned legs, *c.* 1800.

E4 A Regency mahogany hall chair, the waisted back with initial B in oval recess.

E5 A Regency oak hall chair, with shell-carved back, solid seat and panelled tapering legs, showing arms of Carew with Palk, *c.* 1815.

E8 A Victorian pine hall chair, *c.* 1850.

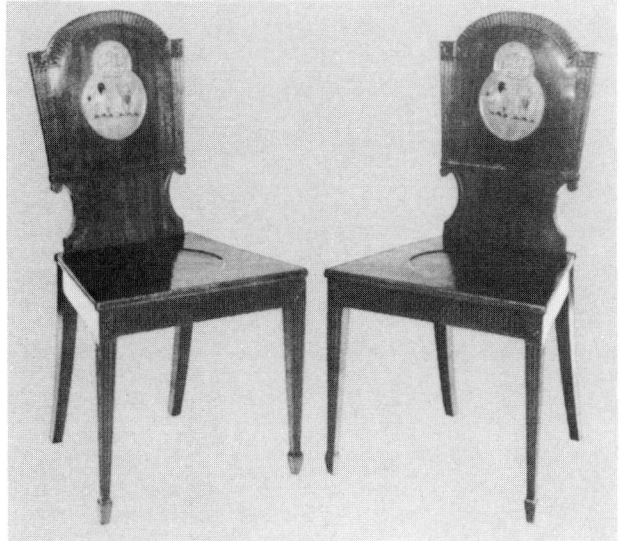

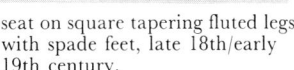

E2 A pair of George III mahogany hall chairs, each with tablet back with arched fluted top rail, fluted stiles and dished plank seat on square tapering fluted legs with spade feet, late 18th/early 19th century.

E6 A William IV mahogany hall chair with acanthus carved back on fluted turned front supports.

E9 A mahogany hall armchair, early George III style, scrolled scalloped solid back carved with acanthus, *c.* 1880.

E3 A pair of Regency mahogany wheelback hall chairs, each with pierced oval back, the crest crisply carved with lappets and radiating reeded and leaf-carved splats centring an oval satinwood panel, early 19th century.

E7 A walnut hall chair, *c.* 1850; with pierced and paper-scrolled cartouche back.

E10 An oak hall chair with waisted, scroll-carved back over shaped and moulded seat, late 19th century.

Library chairs/steps

D 1 A Regency mahogany rope-back combined library chair and steps, with overscroll arms and cane seat, on sabre legs, hinged seat rail, *c.* 1810.

E 2 A Regency mahogany library chair/steps, the chair with wide overhanging top rail, scrolled arms and sabre legs.

E 4 A Regency mahogany metamorphic library chair/steps, in the manner of Morgan and Sanders, with curved top rail, leaf-carved crossbar, scroll arms and caned seat, on sabre legs and hinged to form four leather-lined treads, *c.* 1820.

E 3 A Regency mahogany metamorphic library chair, in the manner of Morgan and Sanders, caned seat hinged and opening to form four leather-lined steps, *c.* 1810.

E 5 A Regency mahogany metamorphic library bergère, converting to library steps with four felt-lined treads, on sabre legs.

Porters' chairs

E 6 A rare oak lambing armchair, with high back and arched hood, plain arms on columnar supports with solid seat, turned legs joined by turned stretchers, *c.* 1700.

E 7 A Georgian country hall porter's chair in ash and elm, with high back and curved canopy.

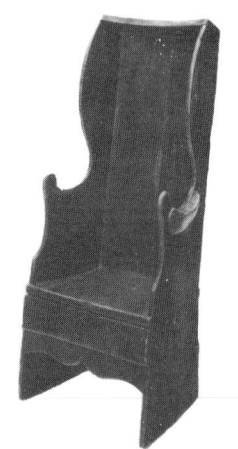

E 8 A lambing chair, partly in elm, the panel seat with drawer beneath, 55 by 24 in. (138 by 60 cm), 18th century.

E 9 A Georgian oak wing armchair with plain panel back and low panel seat, 40 in. (100 cm) high.

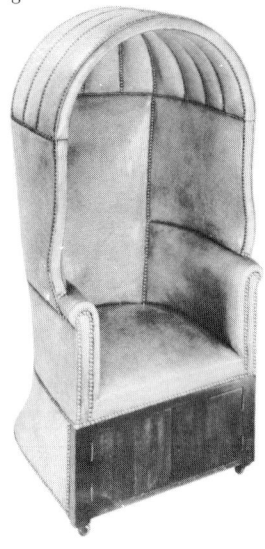

D 10 A late 18th-century hall porter's chair of fine quality and with no trace of the rustic, suggesting a commission for a grand house.

E 11 An oak lambing chair, panelled back and seat with side drawer underneath, 47 in. (117 cm) high.

E1 An oak provincial wing-back armchair, with high back and waved sides, moulded seat and conforming base, fitted with a single drawer.

E4 A pair of fine late 17th-century walnut side chairs, deeply carved front stretchers, barleysugar turned middle stretchers and back rails, on paw feet.

E7 A Queen Anne walnut chair, with upholstered back and seat, square-cut cabriole front and back legs joined by double H-stretchers, c. 1710.

E2 An English ash canopied armchair with arched back and bentwood canopy, and moulded rectangular seat, on casters, 19th century.

E5 A pair of Queen Anne walnut and beechwood side chairs, with padded backs and arched tops, scrolled bottom, scrolled aprons, on trumpet and baluster legs, c. 1700; 24 in. (60 cm) wide.

E8 A Queen Anne side chair, with arched and waisted back over a shaped seat on moulded legs.

Side chairs

E3 A Charles II Turkey-work upholstered beech back stool, 17th century; 35 in. high by 17 in. wide (89 by 45 cm).

E6 A pair of Queen Anne walnut chairs with tall rectangular backs over shaped seats on fine, scroll-carved, collared cabriole legs.

E9 A George I walnut chair on plain cabriole legs, slightly carved on the knees with scrolls and ending in club feet; covered in floral tapestry cloth.

E1 A George I walnut side chair, with arched, waisted back over a shaped seat on collared cabriole legs joined by turned stretchers.

E4 A pair of George II mahogany library chairs, the serpentine seats in nailed yellow ground needlework, finely carved cabriole legs, with cabochons at the knees flanked by scrolls and ending in matching feet.

D8 A Chippendale Gothic chair, 37 in. high by 22 in. wide (92 by 55 cm).

E2 A George II carved mahogany and upholstered chair, covered in brocade, c. 1755.

E5 A George II mahogany side chair, the waved top rail carved with scrolling foliage with cartouche-shaped upholstered back and seat, the moulded frieze centred by a clasp on cabriole legs headed by foliage on scrolled feet.

E6 A George II carved mahogany chair with stuffed back and seat, the cabriole legs carved with leaves and leafy brackets and ending in leaf-carved scroll feet, c. 1750.

E9 A George III mahogany library chair on foliate carved cabriole legs.

E10 A George III mahogany side chair with arched padded back, serpentine seat.

E3 A George II carved walnut single chair with stuffed back and seat covered in contemporary jardinière velvet.

E7 A pair of George III carved mahogany back stools, each with padded back with a serpentine crest above an over-upholstered seat, on cabriole legs with ball-and-claw feet, the rear legs also cabriole with pad feet, third quarter 18th century; 38 in. (95 cm) high.

E11 A George III mahogany chair, in the French taste, on moulded cabriole legs.

E1 A mid-Georgian beechwood side chair, padded back, upholstered seat covered in blue ground tapestry woven in reds and greens with parrots and sprays of tulips, on square legs joined by turned stretchers.

E2 A George III mahogany side or dining chair of the plainest design but of very pleasing proportions, with rectangular back over a square seat on square-section stretchered legs.

E3 A George III giltwood chair, attributed to Francis Hervé, with padded back and bowed seat, moulded frame carved with ribbon-tied bellflower cresting, stepped seat rail on fluted tapering legs.

E4 A George III mahogany chair with beaded cartouche-shaped back and serpentine seat rail, on square tapering legs, *c.* 1785.

E5 A George III mahogany chair with reeded borders to the back, the seat frame on turned and tapering legs.

E6 A mahogany chair, with concave scroll back applied with rosettes, padded back, seat with downcurved sides, *c.* 1840.

E7 A Victorian mahogany dining chair, attributed to Holland and Sons, with moulded border to the arched back on turned tapering legs upholstered in imitation red leather.

E8 A Victorian mahogany framed dining chair, upholstered in red dralon, with waisted oval back, serpentine fronted seat and on moulded cabriole legs.

E9 A Victorian walnut side chair with an exceptionally deep padded crest rail over an ornate pierced splat, with carved seat rail on cabriole legs and scroll feet displaying French influence.

Side Chairs
The side chair, particularly of the type illustrated in nos 1 to 7 opposite, made complete the seat furniture of the well appointed 18th-century house. At the height of its popularity it displayed lines that must be considered the best of the curvilinear period.

The side chair was used, as its name implies, against the walls of hall, gallery, salon, library and other rooms where being in attendance was to be expected though they were drawn forward as necessary.

The degree of quality is perceptible by the shape and carving to the legs – especially those at the back; the finest were of cabriole form, the lesser brethren being merely curved.

As a chair without arms but fully upholstered its use could be universal, and the type lent itself well to adaptation and modification during the hectic 19th century.

E10 A Victorian carved walnut balloon-back occasional chair, *c.* 1855.

E11 A Victorian mahogany lady's chair, cameo back on cabriole legs, floral tapestry upholstery.

E1 A rosewood side chair, with waisted back upholstered with petit-point and bead-work flowers and leaves, above a conforming sprung serpentine seat, on moulded cabriole legs, *c.* 1860.

E4 A Micmac quilled wood "gossip" chair, with geometric panels of quillwork on shaped seat, *c.* 1880; 37 in. (94 cm) high.

E7 A Victorian mahogany desk chair, with raised, flaring back and deeply dished solid seat, *c.* 1880.

E10 A comb-back Windsor elbow chair in elm, 18th century.

Swivel chairs

E2 A Victorian walnut nursing chair and similarly upholstered foot stool, the serpentine top on scrolling cabriole legs.

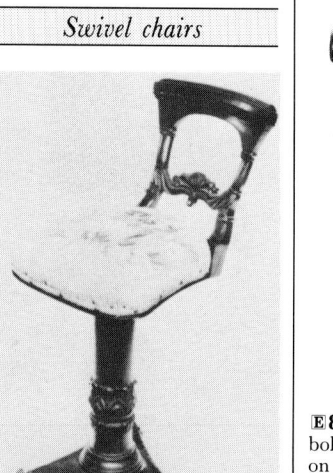

E5 A rosewood swivel chair, with moulded back, needleworked padded seat on a columnar stem, mid 19th century.

E8 A ship's mahogany chair, boldly scrolled, the seat revolving on a cast iron fluted column, 19th century.

E11 A yew-wood Windsor chair, 18th century.

Windsor chairs

E3 A Victorian mahogany armchair, with carved back, button-back upholstery, scroll arms, on French cabriole supports.

E6 A Victorian mahogany music chair, serpentine cresting rail, *c.* 1850.

E9 A mid-Georgian elm Windsor armchair, with waved top rail, railed back with pierced splat, shaped solid seat, cabriole legs and pad feet.

E12 A yew-wood Windsor armchair with back-swept arm supports and wheel-carved splat; 18th century.

E1 A yew-wood Windsor chair, with bow, spindle and splat back, 18th century.

E2 A yew-wood Windsor rocking chair, with elm seat, *c.* 1790.

E5 A yew-wood and elm Windsor chair, early 19th century.

E6 A Windsor chair, with part yew back, *c.* 1800; 35 in. (88 cm) high.

E3 Three yew-wood draught back Windsor armchairs, each with a triple carved splat, on relatively plain turned legs joined by crinoline stretchers.

E7 A yew-wood Windsor chair, with finely shaped pierced splat and crinoline stretcher, *c.* 1800.

E4 Three yew-wood Windsor armchairs with hoop backs centred by ornate splats, late 18th/early 19th century.

E8 A yew and elm-wood Windsor armchair, pierced splat back, crinoline stretcher rail, early 19th century.

E1 An elm and yew wood Windsor armchair of fine, sturdy construction, with a particularly ornate splat, early 19th century.

E2 An elm and fruitwood Windsor armchair, with tall dowelled back, shaped top rail, elegant solid splat, outcurved arms, shaped seat on turned legs, early 19th century.

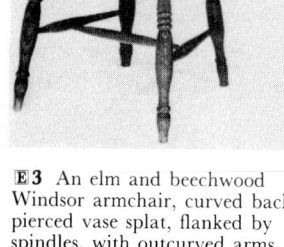

E3 An elm and beechwood Windsor armchair, curved back, pierced vase splat, flanked by spindles, with outcurved arms, solid seat, ring-turned legs with H-stretcher.

E4 A yew Windsor side chair, moulded hoop back above central pierced splat flanked by spindles, 19th century.

CHESTS
1640-1900

Chests divide into two main groups – those with lift tops and those fitted only with drawers – of which the latter became by far the more important. The single chest of drawers was fully evolved by the early 18th century, though chests-on-stands continued to be made for several decades thereafter. The tallboy or chest-on-chest was the final development in the evolution of chests.

Chests of drawers

E5 A Jacobean oak and walnut chest with three long panelled drawers.

E6 An oak chest, with dentilled frieze, 17th century; 49in. (123 cm) wide.

D7 A Cromwellian oak chest, in two sections, inlaid with ivory and mother-of-pearl, 44 in. (110 cm) wide.

E8 A Commonwealth oak chest, in two parts, with two long drawers above a pair of panelled doors, enclosing three long drawers *c.* 1660; 48 by 45 in. (122 by 120 cm).

E9 A Commonwealth oak chest in two parts, with four long graduated drawers, *c.* 1660; 35 in. high by 39 in. wide (89 by 99 cm).

D10 A Commonwealth oak and mother-of-pearl inlaid chest, with a deep long drawer and a pair of cupboard doors below, *c.* 1660; 37 in. high by 38 in. wide (94 by 98 cm).

E11 A walnut chest in two parts, with pearwood veneer and ebonized mouldings, mid 17th century; 44 in. by 45 in. (112 by 115 cm).

E12 A Charles II oak and walnut chest, with a panelled and fielded long drawer, with similar cupboard doors below, on plank feet, 45 in. (114 cm) wide.

E13 A Charles II brass-mounted walnut and fruitwood chest, the top dated 1678 and with the initials BTH, 52 in. (132 cm) wide.

E14 A Charles II oak chest, inlaid with engraved bone and mother-of-pearl, 48 in. by 48 in. (122 by 122 cm).

E1 A Charles II oak and fruitwood chest, on later turned feet, 44 in. (112 cm) wide.

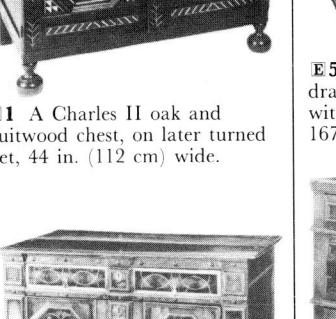

E2 A Charles II oak oyster-veneered walnut and yew-wood chest, with four various sized drawers, 38 in. (98 cm) wide.

E3 A Charles II ebonized oak chest of drawers, c. 1670; 36 by 38 in. (90 by 95 cm).

E4 A Charles II oak chest, with four long panelled and coffered drawers, 35 in. high, 40 in. wide (90 by 120 cm).

E5 A Charles II walnut chest of drawers, cushion fronted drawers with moulded decoration, 1660-1670; 38 by 40 in. (95 by 100 cm).

E6 A Charles II oak chest of four long drawers, with moulded plank top, c. 1670; 34 by 37 in. (86 by 94 cm).

E7 A Charles II oak chest of four long drawers of varying depths, with panelled sides, on stile feet c. 1680; 37 in. high by 38 in. wide (94 by 96 cm).

°8 A Charles II oak chest of drawers, the top edged with bobbin turned borders above four long drawers, on bun feet, mid 17th century; 34 in. (87 cm) wide.

E9 A chest of four drawers, with brass drop handles, on bun feet, c. 1680.

C10 A late Stuart walnut and marquetry chest of drawers, with two short and three graduated long drawers, all inlaid, late 17th century; 38 in. (97 cm) wide.

E11 A William and Mary walnut and marquetry chest, with veneered crossbanded top, c. 1690; 36 in. high by 39 in. wide (93 by 99 cm).

D12 A William and Mary walnut and marquetry chest, with inlaid top, crossbanded drawers, c. 1690; 35 in. high by 37 in. wide (90 by 95 cm).

E13 A William and Mary oak and inlaid straight front chest, with dentilled frieze above one large double drawer, with inlaid panels above two smaller inlaid drawers.

D14 A William and Mary burr elm chest, very finely figured and richly mounted, with moulded crossbanded top over two short drawers and three long, on sturdy bun feet.

Adapted Chests of Drawers
On the larger scale the adaptation of chests-on-chests should always be borne in mind. Originally large chests have also been reduced, in response to the early 20th century taste for smaller pieces.

On the smaller scale, handles and feet are obvious features to have suffered in the cause of fashion. In order to realize the proper appearance of a piece it is more desirable to attach good quality reproduction fittings than to retain out-of-period old fittings, however good.

For the greater part of the 18th century chests of drawers were constructed using primary and secondary timbers. While walnut, mahogany and satin-wood were the primary timbers, oak – secondary for the finest furniture – was used as the primary on much good, everyday furniture. It was however rarely used for surfaces that were to be veneered, and the discovery of a veneered drawer front made in oak instead of lime or pine might indicate later veneering.

D 1 A William and Mary walnut marquetry chest, with two short and three graduated long drawers, *c.* 1700; 35 in. by 38 in. (89 by 97 cm).

E 2 A William and Mary walnut chest, the figured quartered surface geometrically inlaid with boxwood stringing, *c.* 1700; 31 in. by 35 in. (77 by 87 cm).

D 3 A William and Mary oyster veneered walnut chest, the top inlaid with concentric roundels, 37 in. (95 cm) wide.

E 4 A William and Mary oyster veneered walnut chest, with two short and three long drawers, 37 in. (94 cm) wide.

D 5 A William and Mary oyster walnut veneered chest, with crossbanded and inlaid top, two short and two long drawers also veneered, *c.* 1695; 30 in. high by 38 in. wide (77 by 96 cm).

E 6 A William and Mary oyster veneered chest, with two short and three long drawers, the top, sides and drawer fronts veneered within boxwood bands and lines, 38 in. (95 cm) wide.

E 7 A Queen Anne walnut chest of drawers, with well-figured quarter-veneered top, crossbanded with chevron pattern, five graduated long drawers, similarly banded, early 18th century.

E 8 A small burr yew-wood chest of drawers, early 18th century; 32 in. (80 cm) wide.

E 9 A walnut inlaid chest, crossbanded, early 18th century; 35 in. by 36 in. (87 by 90 cm).

D 10 A Queen Anne walnut chest of drawers, sides with C-shaped gilt-bronze handles, early 18th century; 31 in. by 36 in. (79 by 91 cm).

C 11 A Queen Anne walnut dressing chest with slide, 32 in. high by 31 in. wide (80 by 78 cm).

E 12 A Queen Anne walnut chest, with crossbanded top, with an oak slide, 32 in. (81 cm) wide.

E 13 A Queen Anne stained walnut and yew-wood chest, with crossbanded top, 30 in. (78 cm) wide.

D 14 A Queen Anne walnut bachelor's chest of drawers, 30 in. (74 cm) wide.

E 15 A walnut and burr elm bachelor's chest, 59 in. (150 cm) wide.

D 16 A small walnut bachelor's chest, with unfolding top to reveal baize-covered fitted interior.

C 1 A yew-wood bachelor's chest, veneered on to oak, *c.* 1710; 23 in. (57 cm) wide.

E 5 A George I walnut chest, with an oak top, 36 in. (92 cm) wide.

D 9 A George I walnut chest, with crossbanded top and eight short drawers in two tiers, 29 in. high by 40 in. wide (74 by 103 cm).

D 10 A George I walnut bachelor's chest, with hinged top, *c.* 1725; 30 in. by 28 in. (77 by 71 cm).

D 2 A burr-walnut bachelor's chest, with folding top, early 18th century; 32 in. by 30 in. (83 by 76 cm).

D 6 A George I walnut and crossbanded bachelor's chest, *c.* 1720; 29 in. by 29 in. (75 by 75 cm).

C 11 A walnut bachelor's chest, crossbanded top inlaid with double herringbone, opening to reveal a baize cover with secret compartment, the front with folding gate legs, double panel doors and a central drawer with three small drawers below, flanked by six small drawers with brass handles, on short turned legs, early 18th century; 29 in. high by 34 in. wide (72 by 85 cm).

D 3 A George I walnut chest, with four graduated long drawers. *c.* 1720; 30 in. (76 cm) wide.

D 7 A George I walnut chest, with quarter-veneered, crossbanded top, *c.* 1720; 30 in. (76 cm) wide.

E 13 A George II walnut chest, *c.* 1703; 33 in. (84 cm) wide.

D 4 A George I walnut chest, on bracket feet, 37 in. (95 cm) wide.

D 8 A George I yew-wood chest, with a slide, *c.* 1720; 34 in. high by 34 in. wide (85 by 85 cm).

D 12 A George II chest, in figured walnut veneers of excellent fading and patina, the quartered herringbone inlaid crossbanded surface with moulded edge above a brushing slide and graduated drawers, *c.* 1740; 34 in. high by 33 in. wide (85 by 82 cm).

E 14 A George II mahogany chest of drawers, with brushing slide, *c.* 1740; 35 in. (89 cm) wide.

E1 A George II mahogany bachelor's chest, with folding top, 29 in. (75 cm) wide.

E5 A George II mahogany bachelor's chest, hinged top supported by lopers, *c.* 1750; 29 in. (73 cm) wide.

D9 A George III mahogany and crossbanded chest, *c.* 1770; 34 in. high by 37 in. wide (87 by 93 cm).

E13 A mahogany chest of drawers with crossbanded top, 18th century; 36 in. high by 34 in. wide (90 by 85 cm).

E2 A mid-Georgian padoukwood and olivewood chest, with crossbanded top, on ogee bracket feet.

E6 An unusual George II oak travelling chest of drawers, with iron loop handles, *c.* 1750; 36 in. (90 cm) wide.

D10 A George III mahogany chest of drawers with brushing slideover four graduated long drawers.

E14 A Georgian mahogany chest of drawers, with brushing slide, 32 in. high by 30 in. wide (83 by 76 cm).

E3 A George II mahogany chest with four graduated drawers and moulded top, *c.* 1750; 30 in. (76 cm) wide.

E7 A late George II/early George III chest of drawers, 54 in. high by 42 in. wide (135 by 105 cm).

E11 An early George III mahogany bachelor's chest, with fold-over top, *c.* 1755; 29 by 32 in. (73 by 80 cm).

E15 An early George III mahogany serpentine chest, the top drawer fitted with a slide, 46 in. (117 cm) wide.

E4 A mid-Georgian mahogany small chest of drawers, with brass escutcheons and handles, 31 in. (77 cm) wide.

D8 An early George III mahogany provincial bachelor's chest, *c.* 1760; 30 by 37 in. (75 by 92 cm).

E12 A George III small mahogany chest, on shaped bracket feet, *c.* 1760; 28 in. by 30 in. (71 by 75 cm).

E16 An early George III mahogany chest, with moulded rectangular top, on ogee bracket feet, 34 in. (85 cm) wide.

D 1 An early George III mahogany serpentine chest, 43 in. (107 cm) wide.

E 2 A George III mahogany serpentine chest, the eared top crossbanded with tulipwood, 39 in. (99 cm) wide.

D 3 A George III mahogany serpentine chest, with brushing slide between chamfered angles, 49 in. (122 cm) wide.

D 4 A George III mahogany chest of drawers, with moulded serpentine top, over three ranks of four graduated drawers, between corner colonnettes with blind fret, on bracket feet, 40 in. (101 cm) wide.

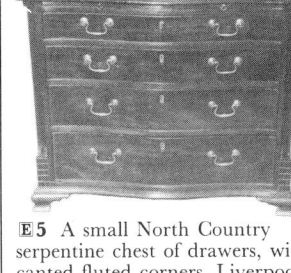

E 5 A small North Country serpentine chest of drawers, with canted fluted corners, Liverpool beech work, oak lined, c. 1770; 29 by 33 in. (73 by 83 cm).

D 6 A Chippendale mahogany chest of drawers, with serpentine front, 30 in. high by 36 in. wide (75 by 90 cm).

E 7 A George III mahogany serpentine chest, with moulded top and canted corners above blind gothic fret and shaped bracket feet, c. 1770; 43 in. (118 cm) wide.

D 8 A Chippendale period serpentine mahogany chest, finely carved, beautifully figured wood, original fire gilt handles, 35 in. high by 40 in. wide (88 by 100 cm).

D 9 A George III mahogany serpentine chest, with moulded rectangular top above a felt lined slide and four graduated long drawers, 40 in. (102 cm) wide.

D 10 A George III mahogany dressing chest, serpentine top crossbanded with satinwood and inlaid with fan spandrels, 45 in. (113 cm) wide.

E 11 An early George III mahogany serpentine chest, of four graduated long drawers, with shaped apron and outset feet, c. 1770; 44 in. (110 cm) wide.

D 12 An early George III mahogany serpentine dressing chest, the crossbanded top with moulded border, rococo angles cast with foliage, 41 in. high by 48 in. wide (103 by 120 cm) wide.

E 13 A George III mahogany serpentine chest, crossbanded with tulipwood and inlaid with chequered lines, 43 in. (108 cm) wide.

E 14 A George III mahogany serpentine chest, the border inlaid with simulated fluting and paterae, 39 in. (98 cm) wide.

D 15 A George III mahogany and crossbanded serpentine fronted chest, c. 1770; 31 by 33 in. (78 by 83 cm).

C 16 A George III satinwood-veneered serpentine-fronted chest, c. 1775; 33 in. high by 33 in. wide (83 by 83 cm).

D 1 A Hepplewhite commode, of finely figured and faded mahogany, with serpentine front, 46 in. (116 cm) wide.

D 2 A George III mahogany chest, bordered with boxwood lines, 33 in. high by 38 in. wide (83 by 96 cm).

E 3 A Georgian mahogany bow-front chest of drawers, the top with crossbanding and chequered inlay, 34 by 32 in. (84 by 80 cm).

E 4 A Georgian mahogany shaped-fronted chest, with crossbanded and inlaid top, 35 in. (87 cm) high.

E 5 A Georgian mahogany bow-front chest of drawers, with satinwood crossbanding, 36 by 34 in. (90 by 85 cm).

D 6 A Georgian satinwood bow-front chest, 42 by 46 in. (105 by 115 cm).

E 7 A George III mahogany bow-front chest, early 19th century; 39 in. high by 41 in. wide (100 by 104 cm).

E 8 A George III satinwood bow-fronted chest, with inlaid frieze, 42 in. (107 cm) wide.

E 9 A Regency mahogany chest of drawers, with reeded, pillar corners and palm leaf motif. 35 in. high by 36 in. wide (87 by 90 cm).

E 10 A bow-fronted mahogany chest of drawers, *c.* 1820; 41 in. high by 43 in. wide (102 by 107 cm).

E 11 An inlaid mahogany bow-front chest, with satinwood crossbanded top, early 19th century; 39 in. high by 42 in. wide (97 by 105 cm).

D 12 A serpentine fronted mahogany chest, of Georgian style, mid 19th century.

Chests-on-chests

C 13 A Queen Anne walnut tallboy chest of drawers, on stand.

B 14 A Queen Anne walnut tallboy, with arched moulded broken pediment, 85 in. high by 41 in. wide (217 by 105 cm).

D 15 A Queen Anne-style walnut chest-on-chest, early 19th century; 41 in. (105 cm) wide.

D 1 A Queen Anne walnut tallboy, with cavetto cornice, three short and three graduated drawers, base with drawers and brushing slide, 41 in. (105 cm) wide.

D 4 A George I walnut tallboy, with cavetto cornice, *c.* 1725; 40 in. (100 cm) wide.

D 7 A George I walnut tallboy, *c.* 1720; 71 in. high by 42 in. wide (180 by 106 cm).

D 10 A George I oak and walnut chest-on-chest, with feather-banding, *c.* 1700; 64 in. high by 40 in. wide (164 by 102 cm).

C 2 A George I walnut tallboy, the upper part with cavetto cornice, 77 in. high by 44 in. wide (195 by 111 cm).

D 5 A George I walnut tallboy, with concave cornice, 69 in. high by 42 in. wide (172 by 105 cm).

D 8 A George I walnut secretaire tallboy, with feather line inlay, 42 in. (105 cm) high.

E 11 A George I walnut chest-on-chest, the burr veneered drawers with mahogany banding, *c.* 1720; 68 by 40 in. (170 by 100 cm).

D 3 A George I walnut tallboy, top with three short and three long drawers, canted cornice and corners, the base with three long drawers.

D 6 A walnut secretaire tallboy, crossbanded and inlaid, 18th century; 75 by 44 in. (187 by 110 cm).

D 9 A George I double chest of drawers, of figured walnut, drawers oak lined, *c.* 1720; 72 in. high by 42 in. wide (180 by 105 cm).

D 12 A George I walnut tallboy, base with a brushing slide, *c.* 1720; 68 in. high by 41 in. wide (170 by 102 cm).

D 1 A George I walnut tallboy, with cavetto cornice and canted corners, the lower section on bracket feet, *c.* 1725; 40 in. (101 cm) wide.

D 2 A chest-on-chest in fine figured walnut, 72 in. high by 40 in. wide (182 by 101 cm).

D 3 A George II walnut chest-on-chest, with three crossbanded short over three long drawers, 71 in. (181 cm) high.

E 4 A George II walnut tallboy, with moulded cornice, *c.* 1745; 69 in. high by 39 in. wide (174 by 99 cm).

E 5 A George II walnut chest-on-chest, *c.* 1740; 69 in. high by 41 in. wide (174 by 103 cm).

E 6 A George II mahogany tallboy, with moulded cornice carved with bead-and-reel ornament, 48 in. (121 cm) wide.

D 7 A George III mahogany chest-on-chest, with broken scrolled cresting, pierced with fretwork on ogee bracket feet, 49 in. (123 cm) high.

A 8 A chest-on-chest, from a Philadelphian household, made of deep orangeish flame-grain mahogany.

E 9 A Georgian mahogany tallboy, the moulded cornice with dentil, bead and reel decoration, 80 in. (202 cm) high.

D 10 An early George III mahogany secretaire chest, the dentil cornice with blind fretwork, 49 in. (123 cm) wide.

E 11 A George III mahogany chest-on-chest, with a dentil cornice and fluted frieze, 70 in. high by 41 in. wide (176 by 103 cm).

C 12 A mahogany tallboy chest, of the Chippendale period with blind fret carving to the frieze and canted corners.

D1 A mahogany chest-on-chest, of fine colour and patination, *c.* 1765; 73 in. high by 43 in. wide (182 by 107 cm).

E2 A George III mahogany chest-on-chest with a dentil cornice, 72 in. high by 42 in. wide (180 by 105 cm).

B3 A Chippendale mahogany tallboy, 78 in. high by 44 in. wide (195 by 110 cm).

B4 A Chippendale double chest of drawers, in finely figured mahogany, the secretaire concealing a serpentine-shaped fitted interior, with cupboard and secret drawers, *c.* 1757; 88 in. high by 46 in. wide (220 by 115 cm).

D5 A Chippendale double chest of drawers, with secretaire, 75 in. high by 36 in. wide (188 by 90 cm).

D6 An early George III mahogany tallboy, with moulded dentilled cornice, the top with chamfered angles, carved with scrolled foliage clasps and trailing flowering foliage, the base on ogee bracket feet, 49 in. (123 cm) wide.

Chests-on-Chests
The quality and quantity of decoration to a chest-on-chest will be a good indication of its original cost and will still have a considerable bearing on its value today.

The lower order is a simple chest-on-chest of secondary wood or faced with mahogany but having painted softwood ends; the handles will be of the simplest form. Next is the mahogany throughout version with well shaped bracket feet and a good moulded cornice; the maker will often have fitted over-elaborate handles.

Of high quality is the version with canted corners to the top, either fluted or decorated with blind fret, surmounted by a carved, moulded cornice and possibly on ogee bracket feet. The very best examples have an architectural cornice of swan-neck or tympanum form, and any of the better versions may incorporate a brushing slide or a secretaire drawer.

E7 A George III mahogany tallboy, with stepped pediment, 76 in. high by 42 in. wide (190 by 105 cm).

E8 A George III figured mahogany tallboy, the top with dentil cornice and blind fret frieze, 46 in. (114 cm) wide.

E 1 A Chippendale mahogany chest-on-chest, base fitted with brushing slide, *c.* 1780; 73 in. high by 42 in. wide (184 by 105 cm).

D 2 A George III mahogany chest-on-chest, base with writing slide, late 18th century, 72 in. (182 cm) high.

E 3 A George III oak tallboy, with moulded cornice and crossbanded drawers, 40 in. (101 cm) wide.

D 4 A George III mahogany tallboy, with blind scrollwork frieze, *c.* 1780; 72 in. high by 42 in. wide (182 by 106 cm).

E 5 A George III figured mahogany tallboy chest, with brass handles, 73 by 45 in. (185 by 114 cm).

E 6 A Georgian mahogany bowfronted tallboy, with oval brass drop handles, 42 in. (106 cm) wide.

Chests-on-stands

D 7 A Nonsuch chest, with flowers and gardens in the arches, applewood inlaid with various woods.

D 8 A Charles II chest-on-stand, in walnut and oak, the front with geometric raised panels, on turned legs.

D 9 A Charles II chest-on-stand, on turned baluster legs, with waved stretchers, 36 in. (91 cm) wide.

E 10 A Charles II oak chest-on-stand, with four graduated panelled drawers, 37 in. (93 cm) wide.

D 11 A Charles II oak chest-on-stand, the stand with two drawers, 40 in. (101 cm) wide.

E 12 A William and Mary period tallboy, in oak, on cabriole legs with Spanish feet.

D 13 A William and Mary oak chest-on-stand, with elaborate cornice, with curved stretchers and turned legs, 71 by 43 in. (180 by 43 cm).

D 1 A William and Mary walnut chest, the stand with one central and two side drawers, with shaped apron above turned legs, joined by stretchers.

D 2 A William and Mary chest-on-stand, with quarter veneered, crossbanded top, with two short and three graduated drawers and one long drawer in the base, *c.* 1690; 50 in. high by 39 in. wide (127 by 99 cm).

D 3 A William and Mary chest-on-stand, veneered in walnut on oak, the base with one long drawer over an arched apron, turned baluster legs, shaped stretchers and ball feet, brass drop handles with shaped back plate; 57 in. high by 40 in. wide (144 by 101 cm).

B 4 A William and Mary high chest in burr-maple, top with cushion frieze below the cornice, base with drawers above shaped apron, with central arch, 1700–1725.

B 5 A William and Mary walnut chest-on-stand, the wood very finely figured, with well pronounced crossbanding, *c.* 1695; 65 in. high, 42 in. wide (165 by 107 cm).

E 6 A William and Mary walnut veneered chest-on-stand, the chest with everted cornice, above a stand with one drawer, on barley-twist legs joined by stretchers, 42 in. (106 cm) wide.

E 7 An oak chest-on-stand, drawers with bevelled fronts, stand with one drawer on turned baluster legs, ending in bun feet, *c.* 1690; 63 in. (160 cm) high.

E 8 A William and Mary oak chest-on-stand, the moulded top fitted with two short and two long panelled drawers, on turned baluster legs and waved stretchers, 32 in. (81 cm) wide.

E 9 A William and Mary oak chest-on-stand fitted with two short and four long panelled drawers (compare no. 8 above), with arched apron on turned baluster legs joined by curved stretchers, 36 in. (91 cm) wide.

C 10 A Queen Anne oyster veneered walnut chest-on-stand, the top bordered and inlaid with fruitwood roundels, the base with a drawer on spiral turned legs, 37 in. (93 cm) wide.

D 11 A Queen Anne walnut chest-on-stand of the classic pattern, with two short drawers over three long in the upper case, three drawers to the stand.

D 12 A Queen Anne chest-on-frame, walnut with inlay on drawer fronts, oak lined, *c.* 1720.

C 1 A Queen Anne walnut chest of drawers on stand, with good patina and marking, 71 in. high by 39 in. wide (180 by 98 cm).

E 4 A George I walnut chest-on-stand, the upper section with three short and three long drawers, the base with five short drawers and arched underframe, 66 in. high by 41 in. wide (165 by 102 cm).

E 7 A black japanned chest-on-stand, ornately decorated in gilt, the stand with arcaded frieze, with legs joined by waved stretchers, 59 by 40 in. (147 by 101 cm).

E 10 A mahogany chest-on-stand, with a dentil cornice and canted corners, the base with arched underframe and acanthus-carved cabriole legs, with claw-and-ball feet, 69 in. high by 42 in. wide (172 by 105 cm).

E 2 A very fine Queen Anne oak chest-on-stand, inlaid in walnut, with finely carved cabriole legs and ball-and-claw feet.

E 5 A George I chest-on-stand, from Derbyshire, with cabriole legs and castellated feet, 67 in. high by 42 in. wide (167 by 105 cm).

E 8 An inlaid walnut chest-on-stand, with swan-neck handles, 18th century; 44 in. (110 cm) wide.

Coffers

D 11 A Gothic oak chest, with plank top, the front carved with gothic tracery motifs, *c.* 1450.

D 12 A Mediaeval oak chest, carved with perpendicular tracery, 15th century; 22 in. high by 54 in. wide (55 by 135 cm).

D 3 A walnut and pollard oak chest-on-stand, with moulded cavetto cornice, early 18th century; 39 in. (99 cm) wide.

E 6 An early Georgian black and gold lacquer chest-on-stand, 39 in. (99 cm) wide.

E 9 A mid-Georgian oak chest-on-stand, with a series of drawers beneath an everted cornice, the stand with cabriole legs, 46 in. (118 cm) wide.

E 13 An oak chest, with plank top, the front and sides carved with linenfold panelling between the stiles, *c.* 1525.

E 1 A 6-plank oak chest, the front with interlaced foliage arches, *c.* 1550; 23 by 50 in. (58 by 125 cm).

E 2 A late Gothic oak boarded chest, the two-plank top with cleats, *c.* 1540; 26 in. high by 54 in. wide (67 by 138 cm).

D 3 An oak clamped-fronted chest, the front iron-mounted and the wide stiles iron-bound, 16th century.

E 4 A late Gothic oak boarded chest, the moulded front stiles curved on inner edge to form an arch, with iron hinges, early 16th century; 28 in. high by 53 in. wide (71 by 133 cm).

E 5 A rare oak coffer, with rectangular moulded fluted plank top, the front carved with geometric patterns between notched stiles, on solid plank feet, 16th century; 60 in. (151 cm) wide.

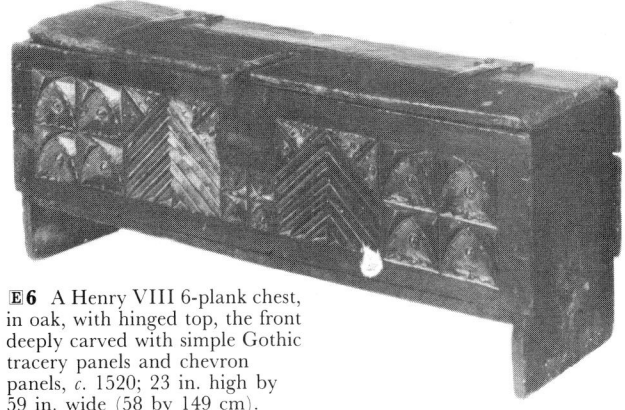

E 6 A Henry VIII 6-plank chest, in oak, with hinged top, the front deeply carved with simple Gothic tracery panels and chevron panels, *c.* 1520; 23 in. high by 59 in. wide (58 by 149 cm).

E 7 An oak chest, with hinged top, the front carved with stylized motifs, 16th century.

D 8 A late Gothic oak coffer, with hinged lid, the front carved with primitive geometric motifs and chevrons, with bracket feet.

E 9 An early type of English Gothic oak coffer, with elaborate front parchemin panels adorned with a Greek "I" motif and bunches of grapes and with linenfold ends.

D 10 A small Gothic oak coffer, with hinged lid and sides panelled in wainscot, the front with panels of geometric carving, *c.* 1500; 28 in. (70 cm) long.

E 11 A Gothic carved oak chest, hinged top panelled with wainscot, front with recessed panels between stiles, carved with serpents, 16th century.

E 12 A finely carved Gothic oak coffer, 28 in. high by 52 in. wide (70 by 130 cm).

D 13 A coffer of the time of Henry VII, in which some of the charters of the Borough of Portsmouth were kept.

D 14 A small Gothic coffer, 16th century; 12 in. high by 25 in. wide (30 by 62 cm).

D 15 A Gothic oak coffer, mid 16th century; finely carved with arcading, flowers and foliage.

D 16 A Gothic oak chest, with baluster ornament and old lock.

E 17 An oak chest of the Elizabethan period, 22 in. high by 43 in. long (55 by 107 cm).

BRITAIN/*COFFERS*

Coffers

It may seem unreasonable to expect something so old to be in immaculate condition, but coffers were made in large numbers and many survive in good order. They were valued pieces of furniture and were cared for accordingly.

There are three main points that can be used to determine value. One: whether the coffer be joined or of six-plank construction, the feet will be a continuation of the corner or end members; they may be worn, but should not have been cut off and replaced. A replacement has often been camouflaged by applying a moulding to the bottom edge.

Two: most coffers were decorated with carving, paint or inlay, but many were made plain and these have often suffered at the hands of an amateur carver of the last century,–but only experience can guide the judgment. Three: the metal mounts. From the late 16th century in particular these were often noticeably more sophisticated than the woodwork.

D 1 An oak chest, with plank top, front with decorative panels, between linenfold panels, 16th century

D 2 An early oak linenfold chest, 27 in. high by 45 in. wide (68 by 114 cm).

E 3 An Elizabethan miniature or child's oak chest, the top with a pair of panels inlaid with geometric design, c. 1600; 15 in. high by 20 in. wide (38 by 50 cm).

D 4 A joined oak chest, with carved Gothic tracery, 16th century; 74 in. (187 cm) wide.

D 5 A large oak coffer, with plain top, the quadripartite niched front with carved strapwork, with marquetry panels of flowering foliage, with birds issuing from urns, flanked by male caryatid figures, framed by chevron bands, late 16th/early 17th century; 117 in. (297 cm) wide.

D 6 An oak chest, with linenfold panels, front with four recessed panels, carved with heads in relief amongst elaborate scrolls, base with scrolling brackets, c. 1580.

D 7 A fine Elizabethan oak coffer, top and sides panelled, front with carved terms, dividing two arched panels, inlaid with flowers.

D 8 An oak inlaid coffer, sides panelled, front with pilasters topped by Ionic capitals, separated by arched panels, late 16th/early 17th century.

E 9 An oak coffer, on bun feet, front elaborately carved with central star motif, flanked by raised geometric panelling, early 17th century.

E 10 A carved oak chest, with plank top and panelled sides, and decorative frieze above panels, early 17th century.

E 11 An oak chest with panelled top, sides and front, the uprights with decorative carving, 17th century.

E 12 An Elizabethan oak chest, with three-panelled front, with moulded diamond bosses, c. 1600; 55 in. (139 cm) wide.

E 13 A Charles I oak coffer, with hinged lid, c. 1630; 17 in. high by 38 in. wide (43 by 96 cm).

E 14 A child's coffer, 17th century; of good colour with delicate scratch carving, in original condition.

E 15 An oak plank chest, with chip carved edges, the sides extending to form legs, early 17th century; 26 in. (66 cm) wide.

E 16 A Charles I oak boarded chest, carved with initials and date "1638", on block feet, c. 1635; 36 in. (91 cm) wide.

E 17 An oak six-plank chest, the sides continuing to form the arched feet, mid 17th century; 31 in. (78 cm) wide.

E 18 A Carolean period oak chest, finely carved decorated front with initials "W L 1671", 57 in. (144 cm) wide.

E1 An oak chest, with panelled carved front, mid 17th century; 28 in. by 50 in. (71 by 127 cm).

E2 A small oak chest, with two-panelled carved front, mid 17th century; 34 in. (86 cm) wide.

E3 An oak chest, with two arcaded panels, divided by stop-fluted uprights, on stile feet, early 17th century.

E4 An oak chest with panelled top, sides and front, the front with later initials and date, mid 17th century.

E5 An oak coffer, with a triple panelled front, with stylized scrolling decoration, 17th century; 46 in. (116 cm) wide.

D6 A Charles II coffer, with hinged panelled top and sides, the front carved with panels of stylized birds and animals amongst scrolls, 17th century.

E7 An oak chest, with panelled hinged top, the front and sides carved with flutes and vertical reeding, early 17th century; 25 in. high by 45 in. wide (63 by 119 cm).

E8 A James I oak and marquetry coffer, the hinged top with moulded fielded panels, carved with lozenges centring flowerheads, early 17th century; 56 in. (142 cm) wide.

E9 An oak chest, with carved front, second quarter 17th century; 25 by 47in. (64 by 120 cm).

E10 A James I oak chest, frieze carved with a geometric pattern, with blind fretwork, 58 in. (147 cm) wide.

E11 A James II oak blanket chest, the front carved with initials "M W", 39 in. (99 cm) wide, mid 17th century.

E12 An oak chest, the front carved with recessed arched panels, 17th century.

E13 A walnut coffer, with iron carrying handles, 17th century; 58 in. (147 cm) wide.

E14 A James I oak coffer, mid 17th century; 52 in. (132 cm) wide.

E1 A Charles I carved oak chest, with a key pattern frieze and triple panel front, *c.* 1630; 55 in. (138 cm) wide.

E2 An oak blanket chest, front inlaid in bone with geometric designs, base with a long drawer, *c.* 1700; 48 in. (121 cm) wide.

E3 A Queen Anne oak corn chest, with wainscot panel front and carved initials "DH" and "AH" and the date 1706; 42 by 89 in. (107 by 223 cm).

E4 A fine Queen Anne hall chest, in walnut banded with yew, the interior lined with cedar, 36 in. high by 48 in. wide (90 by 120 cm).

E5 A George I walnut coffer on stand, the crossbanded top with hinged lid with two locks, with brass carrying handles; 37 in. high by 48 in. wide (93 by 120 cm).

E6 A George I black and gold lacquer coffer on stand, 60 in. (151 cm) wide.

E7 A rare George II chinoiserie blanket chest, *c.* 1740; 35 in. high by 47 in. wide (89 by 119 cm).

E8 A George II walnut coffer on stand, with moulded crossbanded and quartered lid inlaid, 49 in. (123 cm) wide.

E9 A George II walnut coffer on stand, crossbanded and inlaid with herringbone bands, 51 in. (128 cm) wide.

E10 A mid-Georgian mahogany chest-on-stand, Irish, mid 18th century; 40 by 51 in. (102 by 128 cm).

D11 An unusual and exceptionally fine late Chippendale chest-on-stand.

D12 A fine Chippendale mahogany chest-on-stand, 42 in. high by 50 in. wide (105 by 125 cm).

E13 An oak dower chest, with two drawers in the base, *c.* 1740; 51 in. (127 cm) wide.

E14 An English lacquered coffer, mid 18th century; 36 by 43 in. (91 by 107 cm).

E15 An early pine chest, *c.* 1750; 46 in. (115 cm) wide.

E16 A domed pine coffer, with interior candle box, on bracket feet, early 19th century; 29 in. high by 43 in. wide (72 by 107 cm).

Military chests

E17 A campaign chest, with flat swan neck handles, ▪ 1800; 32 in. high by 28 in. wide (80 by 70 cm).

E18 A mahogany military chest in two parts, mid 19th century; 40 in. high by 36 in. wide (101 by 90 cm).

E19 A Victorian mahogany campaign chest, with brass-mounted corners, drawers with inset brass pulls, sides with brass handles, 42 in. (105 cm) wide.

E1 A small brass-mounted camphorwood campaign secretaire, in two parts, *c.* 1870; 39 in. high by 30 in. wide (99 by 75 cm).

E2 A Victorian camphorwood secretaire military chest, with foliage scroll-carved gallery, 42 in. (105 cm) wide.

Mule chests

E3 A George II period mule chest, in oak, with fretted back and hinged moulded lid above crossbanded drawers, with mainly original brasswork, on shaped ogee bracket feet, *c.* 1740; 38 in. high by 64 in. wide (95 by 160 cm).

E4 A mid-Georgian oak and mahogany crossbanded mule chest, with low back above a hinged lid, with two upper dummy drawers, 61 in. (152 cm) wide.

E5 A George III oak mule chest, with six dummy drawers and three real drawers, flanked by quadrant corners, late 18th century; 34 by 63 in. (86 by 158 cm).

E6 A George III oak mule chest, with four dummy drawers and two real drawers, on stump feet, mid 18th century; 33 in. high by 56 in. wide (84 by 140 cm).

E7 A George III Lancashire oak mule chest, with six false drawer fronts and three drawers below, with brass swan neck handles, 38 by 63 in. (95 by 158 cm).

E8 A late Georgian mahogany oak lined mule chest, standing on ogee bracket feet, *c.* 1780; 64 in. high by 63 in. wide (160 by 157 cm).

E9 An oak chest with drawers, the panelled front carved with figure motifs and lunettes, 37 by 51 in. (93 by 128 cm).

Secretaire chests

D10 A walnut secretaire chest, with crossbanded quartered top, with fitted secretaire drawer, on bracket feet.

E11 A George III mahogany serpentine secretaire chest, 40 in. high by 46 in. wide (101 by 115 cm).

E12 A George III mahogany dressing and secretaire chest, *c.* 1770; 32 in. high by 36 in. wide (80 by 91 cm).

D13 A William IV rosewood-banded burr-elm secretaire chest, 39 in. (99 cm) wide, second quarter 19th century.

Secretaire Chests

The secretaire drawer would appear to have developed during the late George II/early George III period. Ince & Mayhew's first mention of it is in their *Universal System*, 1759–63. As an alternative to the sloping fall of a bureau it offers a pull-out drawer, the front of which lets down and is supported by a quadrant at each end.

The secretaire drawer became a popular feature on chests made with and without cabinets and the interiors are invariably of the finest quality.

Some of the finest military chests are also equipped with secretaire drawers, nominally to increase their utility and save transporting a desk. It should not be thought however that every military chest was made for a campaign, as the style became so popular that it was widely adopted for furnishing the masculine apartments of the home.

C14 A George III satinwood and rosewood crossbanded secretaire chest, *c.* 1790; 58 in. high by 34 in. wide (145 by 85 cm).

E15 A late Georgian mahogany secretaire, of small proportions, 30 in. (75 cm) wide.

COMMODES
1720-1920

The commode in the sense of a chest of drawers in the French style became fashionable in England after the mid 18th century, but the expense of its creation limited it always to an elite market. For this reason it reflects changes in taste as accurately as any category of furniture. The commode in the sense of a night table became by contrast extremely common in the 19th century, its discreet name chiming happily with the Victorian tendency to prudery.

B1 A mahogany commode, supported on leafy consoles, mid 18th century.

A2 A George II mahogany commode, possibly the work of Benjamin Gooderson.

A3 A sweep-front commode, with elaborate mounts, in French style, *c.* 1735.

C4 A George II mahogany serpentine commode, with finely carved canted corners.

C5 A George II mahogany commode, with gilt metal decorations, *c.* 1745; 35 in. high by 55 in. wide (83 by 139 cm).

B6 A George II commode, with elaborately carved apron; 24 in. high by 30 in. wide (60 by 76 cm).

C7 A George III mahogany commode of serpentine form, the drawers with shaped fielded panels, *c.* 1760.

A8 A Chippendale mahogany commode of serpentine form, carved with volutes, *c.* 1765.

A9 A Chippendale mahogany commode of serpentine form, the sides with canted scrolls, *c.* 1765; 45 in. (123 cm) wide.

C10 A serpentine commode, with brushing slide, *c.* 1755; 33 in. high by 54 in. wide (83 by 137 cm).

A11 A serpentine mahogany commode, crossbanded in kingwood, mid 18th century.

A12 A veneered commode, of bombé form, with scroll feet and ormolu mounts, *c.* 1770; 34 in. high (85 cm).

A13 A marquetry commode, inlaid with birds and flowers, the corners mounted with ormolu, *c.* 1770.

B14 A lacquer serpentine commode, decorated in Chinese style, *c.* 1770; 30 in. high by 56 in. wide (76 by 142 cm).

A15 A mahogany commode with serpentine top, inlaid with floral marquetry, *c.* 1770.

C16 A George III marquetry commode, *c.* 1775; 32 in. high by 44 in. wide (81 by 111 cm).

D17 A George III mahogany serpentine commode, with a baize-lined slide; 35 in. wide (88 cm).

C18 A Hepplewhite satinwood serpentine commode, 34 in. high by 45 in. wide (86 by 114 cm).

A19 A Chippendale commode, veneered in harewood, inlaid and crossbanded, *c.* 1770–1775.

B1 A George III marquetry commode, 32 in. high by 48 in. wide (81 by 121 cm).

A2 A Hepplewhite period inlaid serpentine commode, with gilt metal mounts, *c.* 1775.

D3 A Sheraton period commode cabinet, *c.* 1790; 32 in. high by 44 in. wide (81 by 111 cm).

C4 A George III rosewood and satinwood dwarf cabinet, 36 in. (91 cm) wide.

C5 A Sheraton serpentine-shaped mahogany commode, with four doors, the drawers satinwood inlaid.

D6 A mahogany commode, with chamfered serpentine top, crossbanded with satinwood, three drawers in bowed centre, 60 in. (152 cm) wide.

B7 An inlaid Sheraton marquetry commode, with shaped serpentine front, 56 in. (137 cm) long.

B8 A serpentine commode, the top inlaid with geometric marquetry, the cupboard doors inlaid with swags, late 18th century.

E9 A George III mahogany commode, in the manner of Gillows, 28 in. (71 cm) wide.

E10 A George III painted satinwood commode, with decorated borders, late 18th century; 42 in. (106 cm) wide.

A11 A Sheraton satinwood bow-fronted commode, delicately decorated with painted floral sprays and groups of musical trophies, 35 in. high by 64 in. wide (88 by 162 cm).

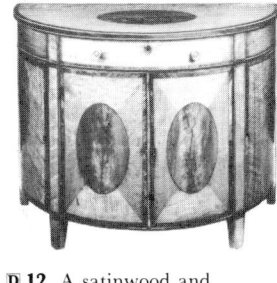

D12 A satinwood and mahogany commode, with semi-elliptical top, crossbanded with tulipwood, and inlaid with a well-figured oval, 42 in. (106 cm) wide.

E13 A George III painted D-shaped side cabinet, the doors and side panels decorated with flowers in ivory and rust, *c.* 1790; 36 in. (91 cm) high.

A14 A satinwood half-round commode, with four oval medallions, late 18th century.

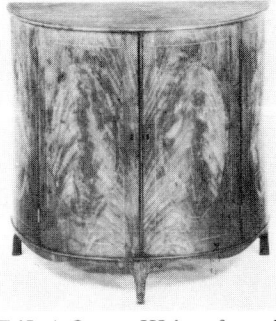

D15 A George III bow-fronted mahogany semi-circular side cabinet, *c.* 1780; 32 in. high by 36 in. wide (81 by 90 cm).

C16 A Hepplewhite commode, in plum-pudding mahogany, *c.* 1780; 34 in. high by 43 in. wide (83 by 109 cm).

C 1 A small Adam satinwood commode with kingwood borders, 29 in. high by 19 in. wide (72 by 47 cm).

C 2 A George III mahogany secretaire commode, with chamfered top, 51 in. (128 cm) wide.

C 3 A George III satinwood commode, the top inlaid, with central lunette, 42 in. (106 cm) wide.

E 4 A Regency mahogany commode, with reeded scroll terminals, c. 1815; 34 in. high by 49 in. wide (86 by 123 cm).

B 5 A Regency commode, in the manner of Louis le Gaigneur, the top inlaid with a foliage design, within a moulded border.

E 6 A George III-style plum-mottled mahogany and sycamore commode, c. 1910; 38 in. high by 37 in. wide (97 by 94 cm).

CUPBOARDS
1500-1920

Over the last four centuries the common meaning of "cupboard" has become so far removed from its origins that it is rare now for the word to be used in its original sense.

In the beginning "cupboard" described that board upon which cups and other utensils were set; early references describe shelves and dressers as cupboards. Today however a cupboard is unthinkable without doors, and the distinction between cupboard and cabinet is often uncertain.

Bedside cupboards

E 7 A rare small mahogany cupboard, with a swivelling envelope top and inset casters, c. 1755; 30 in. high by 22 in. wide (75 by 55 cm).

E 8 A mahogany cupboard with folding envelope top, 18th century.

E 9 A rare mahogany Georgian wine cupboard, with folding top, c. 1775; 44 in. high by 18 in. wide (110 by 45 cm).

E 10 A mahogany bedside cupboard, with waved top and fretwork frieze, 17 in. (43 cm) wide.

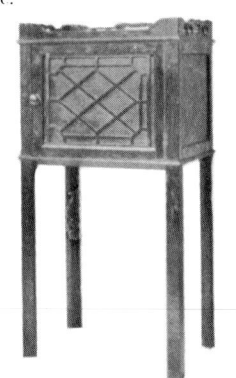

E 11 A Chippendale tray-top bedside cupboard.

E 12 An early George III mahogany bedside cupboard, with pierced gallery and carrying handle, c. 1760; 19 in. (48 cm) wide.

E 13 A Sheraton pedestal cupboard, with carrying handle, 35 in. high by 19 in. wide (87 by 48 cm).

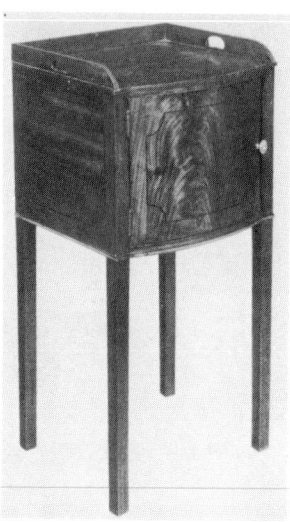

E 14 A George III mahogany bedside cupboard, with galleried top, early 19th century; 15 in. (38 cm) wide.

E 1 A George III mahogany bedside cupboard, with tray top enclosed by a tambour, the draw-out base with two false drawers, 21 in. (52 cm) wide.

E 4 A Regency stained mahogany bedside cupboard, attributed to Gillows, with panelled fall-flap and door, 24 in. (60 cm) wide.

E 2 A Regency tambour-fronted bedside cupboard, *c.* 1820; 18 in. (45 cm) wide.

E 5 A George III inlaid mahogany bedside cabinet, *c.* 1800; 30 in. high by 13 in. wide (75 by 33 cm).

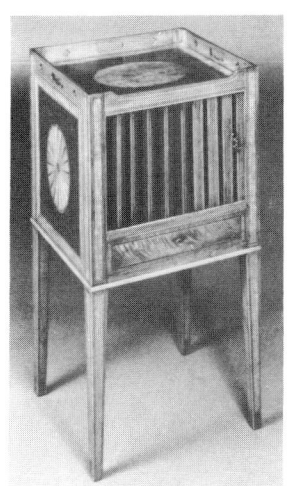

E 3 A George III mahogany and satinwood tambour-fronted bedside cupboard, 15 in. (38 cm) wide.

E 6 A William IV Gothic mahogany bedside cupboard, *c.* 1835; 31 in. high by 17 in. wide (78 by 43 cm).

Buffets

D 9 A fine Elizabethan oak buffet, in two sections, elaborately carved, the upper with recessed two-door cupboard, with inlaid foliate marquetry along the front.

D 7 A rare Stuart canted-front oak buffet, with applied ornament; 49 in. high by 48 in. wide (122 by 120 cm).

E 10 An oak buffet carved with arcading and lozenges, 17th century; 45 in. high by 64 in. wide (112 by 160 cm).

D 8 A finely carved oak buffet, in original condition, 17th century.

D 11 A James I three-tier oak buffet, with carved bulbous supports and canted shelves, *c.* 1610.

E1 A Jacobean oak buffet, consisting of three tiers, on turned front supports, 17th century.

E2 A cupboard of simple form, with a pair of doors, *c.* 1630; 43 in. high by 51 in. (109 by 129 cm).

Corner cupboards

C3 An oak corner cupboard, decorated with carved panels, late 15th century.

D4 A black and gilt lacquered corner cabinet, early 18th century; 79 in. (200 cm) high.

E5 A Queen Anne oyster-veneered walnut hanging corner cupboard, 48 in. high by 27 in. wide (121 by 68 cm).

E6 A George I black lacquer corner cupboard, of bowed form, decorated in gilt with chinoiserie scenes on a river, *c.* 1715; 36 in. (90 cm) high.

E7 A mahogany corner cupboard, with canted corners, the door with fielded panel and brass lock plate, 18th century.

E8 A George II bow-fronted japanned hanging corner cupboard, *c.* 1730; 36 in. high by 22 in. wide (91 by 55 cm).

E9 A George II mahogany corner cupboard, *c.* 1750; 46 in. high by 32 in. wide (116 by 81 cm).

E10 A George III mahogany bow-fronted hanging cupboard, with H-hinges and decorated lock plates.

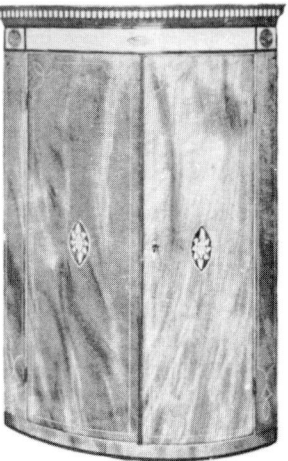

E11 A Sheraton mahogany circular-front corner cupboard, 42 in. high by 17 in. deep (106 by 43 cm).

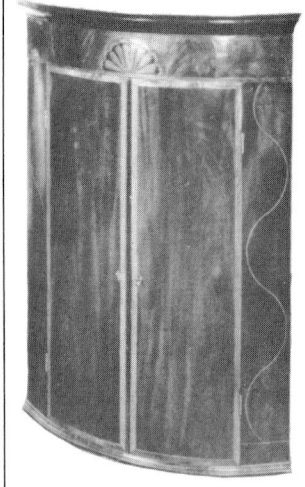

E12 An inlaid mahogany corner cupboard, with fan decorated frieze, early 19th century; 30 in. (76 cm) wide.

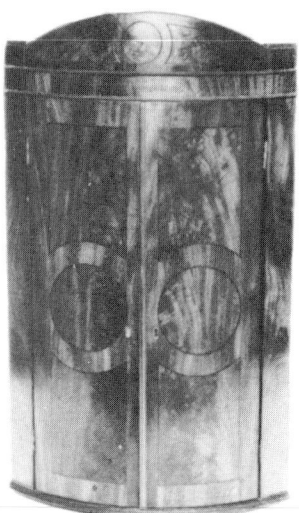

E13 A George III mahogany bow-front hanging wall cupboard, early 19th century; 46 in. by 31 in. (116 by 78 cm).

E1 A carved mahogany two-stage corner cupboard, with panelled doors, late 18th century; 88 in. high by 55 in. wide (223 by 139 cm).

E2 An Irish pine corner cupboard, with rope twist and cottonreel mouldings, 18th century; 72 in. high by 60 in. wide (213 by 152 cm).

E3 A Chippendale pine corner cupboard, with carved and gilded enrichments, 84 in. high by 48 in. wide (213 by 121 cm) on cornice.

E4 A mahogany full-height corner cupboard, late 18th century; 84 in. high by 41 in. wide (213 by 104 cm).

E5 A mahogany two-tier corner cabinet, 18th century; 43 in. (109 cm) wide.

E6 An elm standing corner cupboard, 18th century; 92 in. high by 60 in. wide (233 by 152 cm).

Court cupboards

D7 A late Gothic oak aumbry, the doors with carved and pierced roundels, and three drawers, *c.* 1660; 63 in. high by 58 in. wide (161 by 147 cm).

D8 An oak press, the front carved with three zones of recessed panels, decorated with geometric motifs, 16th century.

C9 An oak cupboard, of architectural form, divided by columns, flanked by carved panels, 16th century.

D10 A carved oak court cupboard, inlaid with sycamore and bog oak, late 16th century.

D11 A Scottish oak court cupboard, late 16th century; 64 in. high by 47 in. wide (162 by 119 cm).

E12 A carved oak court cupboard, early 17th century; 64 in. (162 cm) wide.

D13 An Elizabethan inlaid and carved oak court cupboard, with marquetry panels.

D14 An Elizabethan carved oak cupboard, 64 in. high by 48 in. wide (162 by 121 cm).

E1 A painted, carved West Country oak cupboard, the panels with ebonized mouldings, *c.* 1640; 78 in. high by 63 in. wide (200 by 160 cm).

E2 An oak court cupboard, with carved pine decoration, 17th century; 60 in. high by 60 in. wide (150 by 150 cm).

E3 An oak two-part cupboard, intricately carved, mid 17th century; 74 in. high by 63 in. wide (188 by 160 cm).

E4 An oak court cupboard, carved with foliage lozenges, the initials "LH" and the date 1694, with two panelled doors, basically 17th century.

E5 An extremely fine carved oak court cupboard of Charles II period, bearing the initials "HL" and the date 1661 carved in two places on the front; 70 in. high by 60 in. long (178 by 150 cm).

E6 An oak press cupboard, with elaborately carved front dated 1648, with strapwork to the frieze, 64 in. high by 60 in. wide (160 by 150 cm).

E7 A Charles II oak court cupboard, *c.* 1680; 72 in. high by 51 in. wide (183 by 128 cm).

E8 A Charles II oak Lancashire press cupboard, carved with leaves, berries and "Thomas Meller and Ellen Meller 1681", *c.* 1680; 75 in. high by 55 in. wide (190 by 140 cm).

E9 A cupboard with three drawers, with four carved panel doors with brass strap hinges, 17th century; 56 in. (140 cm).

E10 An oak court cupboard, the upper part with moulded overhanging cornice and bold turned pendant finials, early 18th century; 60 in. high by 57 in. wide (150 by 143 cm).

E11 A George II oak tridarn, the upper section with a moulded cornice on ringed pillars, over a projecting frieze hung with turned finials, and a pair of arched, fielded panel doors, *c.* 1740; 80 in. high by 52 in. wide (205 by 130 cm).

E12 An oak deudarn, with moulded cornice above a plain frieze, applied with bulbous ringed drops, the two cupboard doors flanking an arched panel, with three frieze drawers below, *c.* 1750; 69 in. high by 56 in. wide (175 by 141 cm).

Hanging cupboards

E1 An oak carved and panelled hanging wardrobe, *c.* 1600; 69 in. high by 51 in. wide (175 by 128 cm).

E2 A Charles I period oak wardrobe, with fine carving and iron hinges, 67 in. high by 72 in. wide (170 by 183 cm).

E3 A Charles II oak hanging cupboard, *c.* 1680; 69 in. high by 72 in. wide (175 by 183 cm).

E4 A carved oak clothes press or wardrobe, 17th century; 84 in. high by 75 in. wide (213 by 191 cm).

E5 A James I oak hanging cupboard, 69 in. high by 48 in. wide (175 by 120 cm).

D6 A Queen Anne walnut wardrobe, with finely figured front, *c.* 1710; 80 in. high by 60 in. wide (203 by 150 cm).

D7 A walnut wardrobe, with colour and patination, *c.* 1710; 81 in. high by 61 in. wide (205 by 153 cm).

E8 A George II oak cupboard, with moulded dentil cornice, *c.* 1750; 81 in. high by 73 in. wide (205 by 185 cm).

E9 A George III oak cupboard on chest, *c.* 1755; 85 in. high by 73 in. wide (215 by 185 cm).

C10 A Chippendale carved wardrobe, in mahogany, 67 in. high by 56 in. wide (168 by 140 cm).

E11 A fine oak hanging cupboard, 18th century.

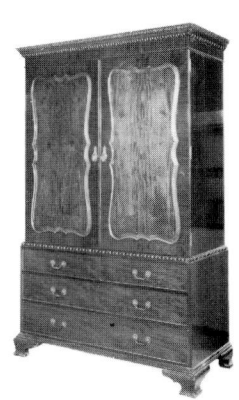

E12 A mahogany gentleman's wardrobe, with fielded panelled doors, 84 in. high by 54 in. wide (212 by 136 cm).

E13 An Adam gentleman's wardrobe, in mahogany, with two fielded doors in matching figured mahogany, the interior with shelves.

E14 A Chippendale bachelor's wardrobe with secretaire, in good condition, of mellow colour, 90 in. high by 55 in. wide (228 by 138 cm).

E15 A mahogany wardrobe of fine design, 18th century; 102 in. high by 55 in. wide (262 by 138 cm).

E1 A George III mahogany breakfront wardrobe, the cornice with broken pediment, the doors with fielded panels and a series of cupboards below, 97 in. high by 84 in. wide (246 by 213 cm).

E2 A George III mahogany hanging wardrobe, 87 in. high by 46 in. wide (220 by 116 cm).

E5 A mahogany and marquetry wardrobe, with one mirrored door, late 1890s; 85 in. by 52 in. (215 by 132 cm).

E8 An oak wardrobe, with planished copper hinges, by Liberty and Co., *c.* 1900; 78 in. high by 48 in. wide (199 by 124 cm).

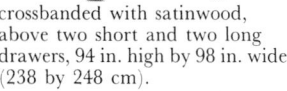

E3 An Irish mahogany breakfront wardrobe, with broken scrolled pediment with fretwork, fitted with two panelled doors crossbanded with satinwood, above two short and two long drawers, 94 in. high by 98 in. wide (238 by 248 cm).

E6 A pine wardrobe, with panelled doors and drawer to base, early 19th century; 78 in. high by 60 in. long (198 by 152 cm).

E9 An Edwardian mahogany wardrobe, by Edwards & Roberts, with swan neck frieze, two inlaid and crossbanded doors, and six short drawers below.

E4 A Regency mahogany breakfront wardrobe, inlaid with satinwood stringing, the centre panelled doors enclosing sliding trays, with drawers below on a plinth base, *c.* 1815; 84 in. high by 97 in. wide (213 by 246 cm).

E7 An oak wardrobe, bearing the printed label, "Liberty, London", *c.* 1899; 77 in. high by 35 in. wide (198 by 91 cm).

E10 An Edwardian mahogany inlaid fitted wardrobe, with centre oval panel door enclosing four slides, over two short and three long drawers, with a concealed cheval mirror, 71 in. (180 cm) wide.

Hutches

E 1 An Elizabethan period oak hutch, with panelled doors, 34 in. high by 51 in. wide (86 by 129 cm).

E 2 A Charles I oak food cupboard, with central pierced door; 41 in. high by 36 in. wide (104 by 91 cm).

E 3 A Charles I oak hutch, *c.* 1630; 32 in. high by 33 in. wide (81 by 84 cm).

E 4 An oak hutch, with notched carved frieze, with a single panelled cupboard door and double-arcaded apron with turned central finial, 17th century; 36 in. (91 cm) wide.

D 5 A Tudor period oak aumbry, with linenfold decoration and spandrels on all four sides, 39 in. high by 42 in. wide (99 by 106 cm).

D 6 An oak hutch, with plank top and panelled sides, the door carved with rosette motif between two slim tracery panels, 16th century.

E 7 A George II oak food cupboard, each door with 17 turned fruitwood spindles, enclosing a shelf, *c.* 1740; 32 in. high by 60 in. wide (81 by 152 cm).

E 8 An oak spice cupboard, inlaid with bone and mother-of-pearl, with enclosed drawers and secret space, 17th century; 36 in. high by 22 in. (91 by 56 cm).

E 9 An oak cupboard on stand, 17th century; 60 in. high by 38 in. wide (152 by 96 cm).

Livery cupboards

E 10 A small court cupboard, *c.* 1620; 43 in. high by 42 in. wide (109 by 106 cm).

E 11 A carved oak joined standing livery cupboard, 17th century; 48 in. high by 48 in. wide (121 by 121 cm).

E 12 A James I oak livery cupboard, *c.* 1610; 48 in. high by 48 in. wide (121 by 121 cm).

E 13 A carved oak buffet, the supports joined by a pot-board, late 17th century; 44 in. (111 cm) wide.

E 14 An oak court or livery cupboard, 17th century; 48 in. high by 49 in. (121 by 124 cm).

E 15 An oak livery cupboard, 50 in. high by 43 in. wide (127 by 109 cm).

D 16 A livery cupboard, with two tiers, in oak and fruitwood, elaborately carved and ornamented, early 17th century.

Press cupboards

E1 A Commonwealth oak clothes press, of wainscot panelled construction, with moulded frames and plain panels, *c.* 1650; 66 in. high by 72 in. wide (168 by 184 cm).

E2 A Welsh oak bacon cupboard, in two parts, *c.* 1680; 67 in. high by 48 in. wide (170 by 120 cm).

E3 A late Georgian Welsh oak two-part linen press, the upper part with two cupboard doors under a deep frieze with equivalent apron below, the lower part with nine variously sized drawers.

E4 A mid-Georgian oak and elm press, with a later ogee pediment, above a pair of fielded panelled doors, mid 18th century; 73 in. high by 55 in. wide (185 by 138 cm).

E5 A George III mahogany clothes press, with dentil cornice and blind fret frieze over fielded panelled doors, late 18th century; 82 in. high by 52 in. wide (209 by 133 cm).

E6 A George III mahogany linen press, with satinwood banding, and fitted, shelved interior, 81 in. high by 52 in. wide (205 by 130 cm).

E7 A Georgian mahogany linen press, with panelled and crossbanded doors, 78 in. high by 55 in. wide (198 by 138 cm).

E8 A Chippendale gentleman's wardrobe, in figured Spanish mahogany, 18th century; 79 in. (200 cm) high.

E9 A finely carved Chippendale wardrobe, in mahogany, 48 in. (120 cm) wide.

E10 An early George III mahogany clothes press, 50 in. (126 cm) wide.

E11 A Georgian mahogany breakfront wardrobe cupboard, 97 in. (245 cm) wide.

E1 A breakfront mahogany wardrobe of the Sheraton period, of fine colour, the upper part with two central panelled doors, with five sliding trays enclosed, above drawers of graduated depths, 75 in. high by 96 in. wide (190 by 243 cm).

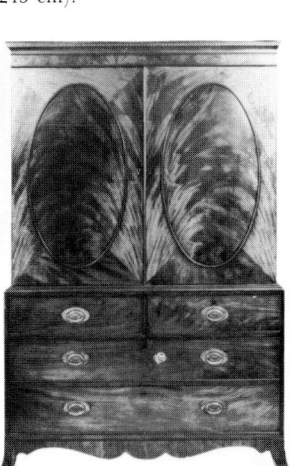

E2 A Georgian mahogany linen press, with dentil cornice, the cupboard doors with oval fielded panels, 49 in. (123 cm).

E3 An Irish press, constructed in two parts, with fielded panelled doors, *c.* 1790; 58 in. (146 cm) wide.

E4 A Regency mahogany linen press, inlaid with ebony lines, with panelled doors enclosing fitted sliding linen shelves, *c.* 1820; 87 in. high by 49 in. wide (220 by 123 cm).

E5 A William IV mahogany linen press, the cupboard doors with shaped rectangular panels, the drawers with brass ring handles, the feet carved with flutes, 85 in. high by 49 in. wide (213 by 127 cm).

E6 A mahogany linen press, inlaid with floral and other marquetry, mid 19th century; 48 in. (120 cm).

Wall cupboards

E7 A Charles II oak hanging cupboard or glass case, the top with applied dentil frieze, *c.* 1680; 28 in. high by 29 in. wide (71 by 74 cm).

E8 A small oak hanging cupboard, with a spindle front, with applied split baluster mouldings in fruitwood, mid 17th century.

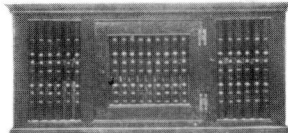

E9 An oak dole cupboard, the front with louvres of turned bobbins, late 17th century; 22 in. high by 48 in. wide (55 by 120 cm).

E10 An oak dole cupboard, with carved cornice, the cupboard with turned louvred doors, flanked by columns, 17th century.

E11 An early oak spice cupboard, with panelled door, 14 in. (35 cm) high.

E12 An oak hanging cupboard, the pediment carved with stylized scrolls, early 18th century; 50 in. (127 cm) wide.

E13 A miniature pine cupboard, with a fielded panel door, 18th century; 17 in. high by 16 in. wide (44 by 40 cm).

DAVENPORTS
1800-1850

The English davenport emerged as a fully fledged piece of furniture towards the end of the 18th century, but examples dated before 1800 are rare. The simple clean lines of early models are well shown in nos 1, 2 and 3 below.

Victorian davenports can be of excellent quality, with finely made moving parts, inlay, veneering and carving, but others were the object of every kind of fussy ornament, quite destroying the lines of the original design.

E1 A Regency rosewood davenport the sliding slope with brass gallery; 18 in. (45 cm) wide.

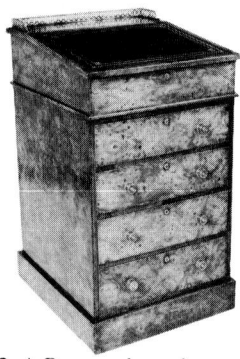

E2 A Regency burr-elm swivel-top davenport, *c.* 1815; 32 in. high by 18 in. wide (81 by 45 cm).

E3 A Regency mahogany davenport desk, the swivel top with leather inset writing slope.

E4 A Regency rosewood davenport, with ormolu galleried top and leather-lined flap, stamped W & C Wilkinson, 14 Ludgate Hill, 19562; 19 in. (48 cm) wide.

E5 A rosewood davenport with satinwood lined interior, with four drawers to side and pen drawer, early 19th century; 21 in. (53 cm).

E6 A rosewood davenport, with three-quarter gallery, each side with a brushing slide and four concealed drawers, *c.* 1830; 20 in. (50 cm) wide.

E7 A William IV rosewood veneered davenport, the interior with maple veneered drawers, and false drawers, with sliding superstructure, four drawers to one side, with Bramah locks; 20 in. (50 cm).

E8 A William IV rosewood davenport, the sliding upper part with a hinged writing surface, enclosing a fitted interior, *c.* 1830; 34 in. high by 19 in. wide (86 by 48 cm).

E9 A George III mahogany davenport, with sliding brass galleried top, above green leather inset writing surface, *c.* 1825; 32 in. high by 14 in. wide (81 by 37 cm).

E10 A William IV rosewood davenport, the sliding boxed top with a baluster gallery, with an inset leather-lined sloping flap above a hinged side pen compartment; 24 in. (60 cm).

E11 A William IV rosewood davenport, the upper writing section with hinged sloping front, above a series of four small drawers, on plinth base, *c.* 1835; 19 in. (48 cm) wide.

E12 A William IV mahogany davenport, with three-quarters brass galleried superstructure with mirrored back on scroll supports, *c.* 1835; 40 in. high by 24 in. (101 by 60 cm).

E1 A William IV rosewood davenport, with forward-sliding top, *c.* 1835; 58 in. high by 20 in. wide (86 by 30 cm).

E2 A rosewood veneered davenport, *c.* 1835; 36 in. high by 35 in. wide (91 by 89 cm).

E3 A rosewood davenport, 1830-1840; 35 in. by 19 in. (89 by 48 cm).

E4 A mahogany davenport, by Johnstone & Jeanes, *c.* 1840; 33 in. by 22 in. (83 by 55 cm).

E5 A walnut harlequin davenport, with jack-in-the-box drawers and pigeonholes, *c.* 1840; 33 in. high by 22 in. wide (88 by 55 cm).

E6 A rosewood veneered davenport, with a shelf on a pierced scrollwork support, a hinged leather-lined writing surface and fitted with a pen drawer, with a slide above a door enclosing three drawers, *c.* 1840; 41 in. high by 24 in. wide (104 by 60 cm).

E7 A Victorian walnut davenport, the sloping hinged leather-lined top with retractable pigeonholes, supported on turned legs, with a series of drawers in the side, with plinth base on extended feet.

E8 A Victorian burr-walnut davenport, the hinged rear stationery compartments with pierced brass gallery, the lined writing slope enclosing two small drawers, with scroll supports and pierced fret decoration, the side with a panel door enclosing four drawers, on bun feet and casters, *c.* 1850; 33 in. high by 22 in. wide (83 by 55 cm).

E9 A Victorian burr-walnut davenport desk, the rising superstructure activated by a concealed lever fitted with stationery compartments. The hinged front opening to reveal pull-out adjustable writing slope and two drawers, having four side drawers and carved column supports.

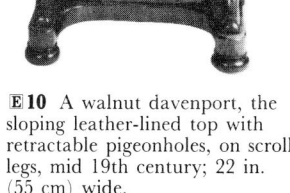

E10 A walnut davenport, the sloping leather-lined top with retractable pigeonholes, on scroll legs, mid 19th century; 22 in. (55 cm) wide.

E11 A figured walnut davenport, with hinged stationery compartment, *c.* 1850; 32 in. high by 21 in. wide (81 by 53 cm).

Davenports

The earliest English Davenports are of plain, box-like form, the upper section sliding or turning to provide knee space. The name Davenport appears to come from an entry in the records of the firm of Gillow, who made a small desk for a Captain Davenport to the specification that has become familiar under his name.

This early pattern remained popular until the 1820s when knee space was provided by reducing the drawer width and supporting the overhang on turned columns. As the century progressed the supports became elaborately curved as fashion demanded, and on some later models the top was cantilevered and supported on token brackets.

Superstructures were sometimes added, the best rising on counterbalance weights when a secret lever inside was depressed. Such novelty features denote quality and thus expense when made and have a considerable bearing on the price today.

E1 An early Victorian rosewood davenport, with writing slope and turned and tapered front supports.

E2 A rosewood davenport, fitted with inkwell and writing slope, mid 19th century; 35 in. high by 24 in. wide (87 by 60 cm).

E3 A Victorian rosewood davenport, the inset hinged writing slope revealing small drawers, *c*. 1850; 33 in. high by 23 in. wide (82 by 60 cm).

E4 A Victorian inlaid walnut davenport, on carved dolphin supports, with shaped front, lift-up stationery compartment, above four side drawers, 21 in. (52 cm).

E5 A rosewood davenport, the fall-front with inset writing surface enclosing a maple veneered fitted interior, on moulded scrolling front supports, the sides fitted with four real and four dummy drawers and a further drawer fitted for pens and ink, on claw casters, mid 19th century; 33 in. high by 21 in. wide (83 by 53 cm).

E6 A Victorian ebonized davenport, with piano top, pull-out writing slide, and raised stationery compartment with secret catch release.

E7 A Victorian walnut davenport, with a rising stationery compartment, the bowed front with two short drawers and writing slide, *c*. 1860; 23 in. (58 cm) wide.

E8 A Victorian burr-walnut davenport, with bowed front and four drawers to the side, with carved and scrolled front supports.

E9 A fine Victorian walnut davenport, with rising back section and a cylinder front enclosing a sliding writing compartment and drawers, 22 in. (56 cm).

E10 A Victorian walnut piano top davenport, the top with a wood gallery to the shaped hinged flap, the panelled front with floral and leaf carved cabriole supports, 22 in. (55 cm).

E11 A fine Victorian walnut piano front davenport, with pierced gallery, 22 in. (55 cm) wide.

E1 A burr-walnut harlequin davenport, with flap enclosing a pull-out writing surface, with pen scoops, *c.* 1860; 45 in. by 23 in. (113 by 58 cm).

E2 A pale walnut and satinwood-lined davenport, with pen tray at side, on spiral legs and bun feet.

E3 A burr-walnut harlequin davenport, with sprung superstructure enclosing fitted compartments for letters, above a flap enclosing two short drawers, a pull-out writing surface and compartments for pen and ink, *c.* 1870; 36 in. by 22 in. (90 by 66 cm).

E4 A Victorian walnut and tulipwood banded davenport, by Gillow, with three-quarter gilt-metal gallery above a writing slope, enclosing an arrangement of mock and true drawers, on lobed and fluted baluster columns, the pedestal fitted with a slide, hinged pen drawer and cupboard, stamped Gillow, 21 in. (52 cm) wide.

E5 A walnut davenport, in well figured wood and inlaid with small burr-wood medallions, *c.* 1860; 38 in. high by 21 in. wide (96 by 53 cm).

E6 A Victorian walnut davenport, of bombé form, with hinged leather-lined top, the side with a series of small drawers, supported on turned baluster legs.

E7 A walnut harlequin davenport, with rising stationery compartment working in conjunction with the writing slope, walnut lined, with pine carcase, *c.* 1860; 22 in. (57 cm) wide.

E8 An inlaid rosewood davenport, by Thomas Turner of Manchester, with hinged galleried stationery compartment, above sloped writing surface, the front inlaid, 22 in. (56 cm) wide.

E9 A late Victorian inlaid walnut davenport, the hinged leather-lined top with raised base, supported on a series of four drawers, the plinth base with extended feet.

E10 A late Victorian rosewood and floral painted cylinder top davenport, the interior with lined writing slide and two short drawers, *c.* 1880; 39 in. high by 18 in. wide (99 by 46 cm).

E11 A japanned davenport, with gallery enclosing a short drawer and four pigeonholes, *c.* 1900; 32 in. high by 27 in. wide (80 by 68 cm).

E12 An Edwardian oak davenport, with scrimshaw mounts, slant front over cupboard door, with the name of the ship on back: "Congaree"; *c.* 1900.

DESKS
1690-1910

It has long been the custom when categorizing writing furniture to disregard function. Fall-front bureaux, bonheurs du jour and writing tables are all by function desks but rarely bear the name, which is traditionally reserved for the kneehole, pedestal and Carlton House types and, habitually but with little good reason, for cylinder- and tambour-top desks which are but variants on the fall-front bureau pattern.

Carlton House desks

B1 A Carlton House writing desk in mahogany, 18th century; 48 in. high by 60 in. wide (121 by 152 cm).

D2 A Regency mahogany Carlton House desk, the upper section with brass gallery, with hinged leather-lined writing flap, surrounded by four drawers and flanked at the sides by two further small drawers, fitted with three drawers in the frieze, on turned tapering legs, 58 in. (147 cm) wide.

E3 A mahogany Carlton House desk, the U-shaped superstructure with cupboard doors, flap and small drawers crossbanded with satinwood framing the leather-lined writing surface, the frieze with three drawers on square tapering legs, 54 in. (137 cm) wide.

E4 A Regency mahogany tambour desk of Carlton House form, with three-quarter galleried top with two letter slots, the tambour centre enclosing a fitted interior, framed by eight cedar-lined drawers, 50 in. (127 cm) wide.

E5 A satinwood Carlton House desk, mid 19th century; 41 in. (106 cm) wide.

E6 A satinwood Carlton House writing desk, painted with flowers, late 19th century; 51 in. (129 cm) wide.

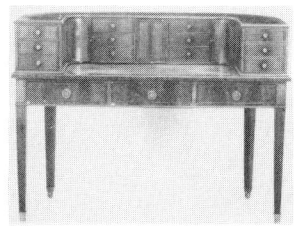

E7 A George III style mahogany and crossbanded Carlton House writing desk, *c.* 1910; 39 in. high by 53 in. (99 by 134 cm).

E8 An Edwardian writing desk of Carlton House design, veneered in mahogany, with satinwood crossbanding.

Cylinder desks

E9 A George III mahogany tambour writing desk, with three-quarters brass gallery and the tambour enclosing a slide with a leather-lined book rest, drawers and pigeonholes, with five drawers around an arched kneehole, on square tapering legs with casters, *c.* 1780; 36 in. (91 cm) wide.

E10 A George III mahogany cylinder desk, with tambour shutter, enclosing leather-lined easel, 52 in. (132 cm) wide.

E11 A mahogany partners' desk, with tambour shutter, enclosing pigeonholes and small drawers, 33 in. high by 48 in. wide (83 by 121 cm).

E12 A George III mahogany cylinder writing desk, the curved tambour front opening to reveal a fitted interior, on square chamfered legs.

E13 A mahogany writing desk, with tambour top enclosing a fitted interior and a leather-lined writing slide, late 18th century; 41 in. high by 36 in. wide (104 by 91 cm).

C 1 A Sheraton marquetry roll top desk, 18th century; 43 in. high by 33 in. wide (111 by 83 cm).

E 2 A George III mahogany tambour top writing desk, with small drawers and pigeonholes, and an adjustable baize-lined slope, 40 in. (101 cm).

E 3 A mahogany tambour fall writing table, in Sheraton taste, *c.* 1800; 38 in. high by 36 in. wide (96 by 91 cm).

E 4 A Regency rosewood lady's cylinder desk, with brass-galleried top, 45 in. high by 30 in. wide (114 by 76 cm).

E 5 A Regency mahogany tambour desk, with enclosed slide and fitted interior, drawers banded in satinwood, 36 in. (91 cm) wide.

E 6 A Victorian mahogany cylinder top pedestal desk, the fitted interior with pigeonholes and drawers, and sliding writing slope, 48 in. high by 59 in. wide (121 by 149 cm).

Kneehole desks

E 7 A William and Mary walnut marquetry desk, inlaid with entwined massed foliate scrolls in various shaped panels, the crossbanded top folding open to reveal a fitted writing compartment, with a fall-down front, with four drawers either side of the recessed kneehole with cupboard, the door inlaid in a geometric design, on bracket feet, 37 in. (93 cm).

E 8 A mahogany cylinder front pedestal writing desk, with pull-out writing surface, small drawers and pigeonholes, 19th century; 60 in. (152 cm) wide.

D 9 A William and Mary kneehole walnut desk, with finely quartered veneering, *c.* 1698.

D 10 A Queen Anne walnut kneehole desk, with fitted secretaire drawer, 30 in. (76 cm) wide.

D 11 A Queen Anne walnut kneehole writing table, with quarter veneered crossbanded top, 32 in. (82 cm) wide.

D 12 A Queen Anne walnut kneehole desk, with crossbanded rounded rectangular top, 30 in. (76 cm) wide.

D 13 A Queen Anne walnut kneehole desk, with quartered crossbanded top, 32 in. (81 cm) wide.

D 14 A Queen Anne walnut kneehole desk, with feather and crossbanded top, c. 1710; 30 in. high by 31 in. wide (77 by 80 cm).

D 1 A Queen Anne walnut kneehole desk, with crossbanded and quartered rectangular top, on bracket feet, 31 in. (78 cm) wide.

E 5 A George I walnut kneehole desk, with moulded top, and drawers with flanking brass-mounted fluted quadrant columns, *c.* 1720; 36 in. (91 cm) wide.

E 9 A George I walnut kneehole desk, the moulded top with quarter veneering, bounded by feather and crossbanding, 28 in. (69 cm) wide.

E 13 A George II mahogany kneehole desk, with brushing slide above a frieze drawer and fret carved shallow drawer, *c.* 1750; 33 in. high by 37 in. wide (84 by 93 cm).

E 2 A Queen Anne walnut and burr-walnut kneehole desk, with quartered crossbanded top, on bracket feet, 30 in. (75 cm) wide.

E 6 A George I walnut kneehole desk, with crossbanded rounded rectangular top and drawers flanking the central kneehole cupboard, on bracket feet, 35 in. (89 cm) wide.

D 10 A George II walnut kneehole desk, with fitted secretaire drawer and cupboard to kneehole, on bracket feet, 31 in. (77 cm).

E 14 A George II mahogany kneehole desk, with hinged top, *c.* 1740; 34 in. high by 40 in. wide (86 by 102 cm).

D 3 A George I walnut kneehole writing desk, *c.* 1720; 30 in. high by 32 in. wide (76 by 80 cm).

E 7 A George I walnut kneehole desk, with crossbanded top, and frieze drawer above a recess, on bracket feet, early 18th century; 33 in. (84 cm) wide.

E 11 A George II mahogany kneehole desk, with chamfered crossbanded rectangular top and seven drawers, 36 in. (91 cm) wide.

E 15 A mahogany kneehole desk or dressing table, with fine mellow colour, 18th century; 36 in. (91 cm) wide.

D 4 A George I walnut kneehole desk, with quarter veneered crossbanded top, early 18th century; 31 in. (78 cm) wide.

D 8 A George I walnut kneehole desk, the quartered top crossbanded and inlaid with herringbone, 35 in. (89 cm) wide.

E 12 A George II red walnut kneehole desk, with moulded rounded rectangular top and fitted secretaire drawer, on bracket feet, 33 in. (84 cm) wide.

E 16 A mahogany kneehole desk, of the Chippendale period, with sliding cupboard and on ogee feet, 30 in. high by 39 in. wide (75 by 99 cm).

D 1 A George II mahogany kneehole desk, with serpentine top, enclosing fitted interior and easel mirror, on ogee bracket feet, 44 in. (114 cm) wide.

E 2 A dark mahogany kneehole desk, of the Chippendale period, *c*. 1760; 36 in. (91 cm) wide.

E 3 An early Georgian mahogany kneehole desk, with frieze drawer, six small drawers, recess drawer and cupboard, on shaped ogee bracket feet, 33 in. (83 cm).

E 4 A George II mahogany kneehole desk, with moulded rounded rectangular top and eight various-sized drawers surrounding central kneehole cupboard, on bracket feet, 33 in. (83 cm) wide.

E 5 A Chippendale mahogany kneehole desk, of fine colour, with original brasses, 31 in. high by 30 in. wide (78 by 75 cm).

D 6 A carved mahogany serpentine kneehole dressing chest, of the Chippendale period, with a moulded edge and baize-lined brushing slide, 42 in. (110 cm).

E 7 A mahogany pedestal writing table, of the Chippendale period, 38 in. (96 cm) wide.

D 8 A George III mahogany kneehole desk, the drawers all with Gothic blind fret, labelled by William Shreeve, London, third quarter 18th century; 35 in. (88 cm) wide.

E 9 A George III mahogany kneehole desk, the central cupboard flanked by banks of three drawers, on shaped bracket feet, *c*. 1765; 32 in. high by 34 in. wide (80 by 85 cm).

E 10 A George III mahogany kneehole desk, with frieze drawer above a recessed cupboard, flanked by six short drawers, *c*. 1770; 32 in. high by 36 in. wide (82 by 91 cm).

D 11 A serpentine-fronted mahogany kneehole desk, 41 in. (104 cm) wide.

D 12 A Sheraton serpentine-front inlaid kneehole desk with well matched veneers, a writing slide over one long drawer with three concave drawers to each side, on splay feet; 34 in. high by 39 in. wide (85 by 99 cm).

D 13 A satinwood kneehole desk with gold tooled, green leather top, oak lined, *c*. 1790; 31 in. high by 46 in. wide (78 by 116 cm).

E 14 A late Georgian mahogany pedestal desk, the crossbanded top with ledge back, the cupboard doors inlaid with burr-walnut ovals, 48 in. (121 cm) wide.

E 15 A Victorian pollard oak-veneered kidney-shaped writing desk, the top with a tooled leather inset, three drawers to each pedestal, on plinth bases, 30 in. high by 54 in. wide (75 by 136 cm).

E 16 A Victorian mahogany pedestal desk, the fitted writing drawer with shaped fall front, and four drawers to each pedestal, with ebonized mouldings throughout, 56 in. (140 cm) wide.

Pedestal desks

B 1 A George III mahogany desk, of serpentine form, the two tiers of drawers with contemporary drop handles, supported on scroll feet.

E 2 A George II mahogany architect's pedestal desk, with cockbeaded mouldings and gilt-brass loop handles, the baize-lined top adjusting on double ratchets, 38 in. high by 49 in. wide (95 by 145 cm).

A 3 An early Chippendale pedestal writing desk, in finely figured mahogany, 72 in. (183 cm) wide.

E 4 A George III mahogany double-sided kneehole desk, with leather-lined top, the two pillars of four drawers with brass ring handles, c. 1780; 32 in. high by 49 in. wide (81 by 123 cm).

E 5 A Hepplewhite pedestal desk, in mahogany, with top lined in gilt tooled green leather, 54 in. (135 cm) wide.

D 6 A Chippendale kneehole desk, with two tiers of drawers, supported on bracket feet, 32 in. high by 50 in. long (81 by 125 cm).

E 7 An early George III kneehole desk, of serpentine form, with two tiers of drawers, the top lined with leather, the corners canted and reeded, 46 in. (117 cm) wide.

D 8 An early George III mahogany desk, with easel with ribbon-and-rosette border, 62 in. (157 cm) wide.

D 9 A George III mahogany partners' desk, with moulded rectangular leather-lined top, and nine drawers, 61 in. (153 cm) wide.

D 10 A George III mahogany kneehole desk, 50 in. (125 cm) wide.

D 11 A Georgian mahogany partners' desk, 77 in. (195 cm) wide.

B 12 A Hepplewhite satinwood partners' desk, inlaid on top edge, 29 in. high by 63 in. wide (73 by 159 cm).

D 13 A George III mahogany writing desk, by George Seddon, London, late 18th century; 55 in. (138 cm) wide.

C 14 A George III mahogany partners' desk, with a hinged easel, 33 in. high by 71 in. wide (83 by 180 cm).

C 15 A mahogany double-sided partners' desk, on four pedestals, late 18th century; 29 in. high by 54 in. wide (73 by 135 cm).

D 16 A George III mahogany partners' desk, with leather-lined moulded top, 67 in. (169 cm) wide.

D 17 A George III "plum-pudding" mahogany partners' desk, the top with moulded border, with moulded plinth base, 33 in. high by 65 in. wide (83 by 164 cm).

D 18 A George III mahogany partners' desk, with moulded rectangular leather-lined top, each cupboard door enclosing three oak drawers, stamped "IC", 66 in. (166 cm) wide.

E1 A Georgian mahogany partners' desk, crossbanded and line inlaid in ebony, 31 in. high by 56 in. wide (78 by 140 cm).

D2 A Georgian mahogany partners' desk, with moulded rectangular leather-lined top, nine drawers each side surrounding kneehole, 58 in. (146 cm) wide.

E3 A brass-mounted mahogany pedestal desk, in Empire style, the top with leather panel, 19th century; 30 in. high by 48 in. wide (75 by 145 cm).

E4 A late Georgian mahogany pedestal partners' desk, the front with two frieze drawers, 31 in. high by 56 in. wide (76 by 140 cm).

E5 A Regency mahogany kneehole secretaire writing desk, inlaid with ebony stringing, the writing drawer with line inset on ratchet support, *c.* 1810; 31 in. high by 42 in. wide (78 by 105 cm).

E6 A mahogany partners' pedestal desk, with cupboards enclosing drawers, original brasses and leather top, early 19th century; 71 in. (180 cm) wide.

C7 A late Regency mahogany library desk, with paw feet flanking pierced gilt-metal trellis-work panels, lined with yellow silk, on plinth base, 84 in. (212 cm).

D8 A Regency mahogany pedestal desk, bordered by ebony lines and roundels, flanked at either side by hinged flaps, 78 in. (198 cm) wide.

E9 An early Victorian walnut pedestal writing table, with rounded rectangular crossbanded top, the frieze with three drawers over two pedestals, each with cupboard door, on moulded base, 42 in. (107 cm) wide.

E10 A mahogany pedestal desk, the top with leather inset, mid 19th century; 53 in. (136 cm) wide.

D11 An early Victorian brass-bound mahogany partners' desk, 59 in. (149 cm) wide.

E12 A mid-Victorian mahogany partners' desk, 36 in. high by 60 in. wide (90 by 150 cm).

E13 A Victorian mahogany pedestal desk, the drawers with side-locking pilasters, the front with central false drawer, 48 in. (120 cm).

E14 A carved oak pedestal desk, mid 19th century; 34 in. high by 62 in. wide (85 by 156 cm).

E1 A Victorian mahogany architects' pedestal desk, the top opening on to gate-leg supports, a slide with a reading rest, 29 in. high by 48 in. wide (73 by 121 cm).

E2 A Victorian mahogany pedestal partners' desk, top inset with green leather panel, 19th century; 54 in. (137 cm) wide.

E3 A mahogany serpentine-fronted pedestal desk, with a three-quarter gallery and tooled leather top, *c.* 1870; 30 in. high by 81 in. wide (76 by 205 cm).

E4 An ebonized kneehole writing table, inlaid with fruitwood stringing, with gilt-metal mounts and inset leather top, *c.* 1870; 30 in. high by 48 in. wide (76 by 121 cm).

E5 A mahogany kneehole desk, labelled Wooton Desk Co., *c.* 1875; 32 in. high by 49 in. wide (78 by 124 cm).

E6 An oak partners' desk, *c.* 1880; 60 in. wide by 41 in. deep (152 by 104 cm).

E7 A walnut kneehole writing table, of inverted breakfront form, the frieze containing three drawers, *c.* 1870; 30 in. high by 49 in. wide (76 by 124 cm).

E8 A mahogany pedestal desk, crossbanded in satinwood, and inlaid with pierced gilt-metal galleries, stamped Edwards and Roberts, *c.* 1880; 48 in. wide (122 cm).

E9 A Chippendale-style carved mahogany pedestal desk, with gilt tooled green leather inset top, 53 in. (137 cm) wide.

E10 A satinwood pedestal desk, with six short drawers, crossbanded with rosewood, stamped Gillows, late 19th century; 64 in. (162 cm) wide.

E11 An early Victorian writing desk, the drawers with shaped fielded panels, supported on lion's paw feet.

E12 A mahogany kneehole desk, each pedestal with four graduated drawers, with one long drawer between, late 19th century; 52 in. (132 cm) wide.

E13 A 'George III' mahogany partners' desk, with a leather-lined rectangular top, *c.* 1900; 31 in. by 60 in. (78 by 152 cm).

E14 An inlaid satinwood-veneered pedestal desk, the top crossbanded with kingwood and an inset moulded brass border, *c.* 1910; 30 in. high by 60 in. long (76 by 152 cm).

E15 An Edwardian mahogany writing desk, crossbanded in satinwood and inlaid with boxwood lines, early 20th century; 30 in. by 48 in. (76 by 121 cm).

Writing desks

D 1 A mid-Georgian mahogany library desk, 72 in. (182 cm) wide.

D 2 An early George III mahogany double-sided writing desk, with five drawers each side, *c.* 1760; 31 in. high by 55 in. long (78 by 139 cm).

D 3 A George III mahogany kneehole writing table, the top lined with green leather, *c.* 1770; 40 in. (101 cm) wide.

E 4 A George III mahogany writing desk, with a small drop leaf on either side, *c.* 1790; 23 in. (58 cm) wide.

E 5 A George III mahogany table desk, fitted interior of drawers, pigeonholes and a cupboard, on square tapering legs, 18 in. (47 cm) wide.

E 6 A Georgian mahogany desk, with drawers around the kneehole, and oak-lined drawers, 19th century; 30 in. high by 38 in. wide (76 by 96 cm).

E 7 A William IV rosewood writing desk, with an adjustable bead and reel top above a drawer, and a woolwork fire screen, on trestle supports, *c.* 1830; 24 in. by 17 in. (60 by 43 cm).

E 8 A walnut coaching writing desk, with hinged open front, enclosing fitted interior, *c.* 1830; 44 in. high by 5 in. deep (111 by 12 cm).

E 9 A mahogany slope-top clerk's desk, by Gillow of Lancaster, with pen-and-ink compartment and slide to each end, *c.* 1835; 37 in. (93 cm) wide.

E 10 A mahogany folding desk, the top with folding writing slope and fitted pen compartment, above three drawers with cockbeaded edges and cedar linings, *c.* 1800; 35 in. high by 24 in. wide (88 by 60 cm).

E 11 A Victorian walnut writing desk, the top inset with leather, fitted with five drawers around the central kneehole, on turned legs and casters, with maker's plate of Ross & Co., Dublin, 46 in. (116 cm) wide.

E1 A late Victorian inlaid writing desk in the "Tous les Louis" style into which the various specific revivals of the early 19th century eventually merged. The overall conception is that of a bureau Mazarin of Louis XIV period, the style of ornament that of Louis XV and the legs Louis XVI.

E2 A late Victorian rosewood serpentine-fronted writing desk, by Shoolbred & Co., London, the superstructure with a mirrored recess, flanked by six short drawers; 42 in. high by 44 in. wide (105 by 110 cm).

E3 A Wootton's walnut desk, with raised back portion incised with lines, the front fitted with a lift-up frieze, late 19th century; 72 in. high by 43 in. wide (183 by 108 cm).

E4 A mahogany writing desk, with a serpentine front and superstructure with a pull-out fitted writing slide, flanked by four short serpentine drawers, late 1890s, 44 in. (111 cm) wide.

E5 A late Victorian mahogany and inlaid kneehole desk, by Shoolbred, with satinwood crossbanding and floral scroll arabesques.

E6 A satinwood and marquetry desk, with a kidney-shaped top, inlaid throughout with scrolling foliage and flowers, early 20th century; 29 in. high by 53 in. wide (73 by 133 cm).

DRESSERS
1680-1860

The term "dresser" is derived from the board on which food was dressed or set ready, with the secondary function of displaying plate. It is now generally accepted that the term describes a country sideboard, with or without the shelves above (the "rack") that would make it a high dresser.

Immediately below the serving board a dresser will have a row of drawers, below which it may be completely open or the legs may be joined at the bottom with stretchers which may then be filled in to form a pot board; as an alternative, the whole space may be taken up with a series of cupboards.

North country high dressers sometimes show the variant of a small cupboard at each end of the rack, and may in addition be crossbanded in mahogany.

Low dressers

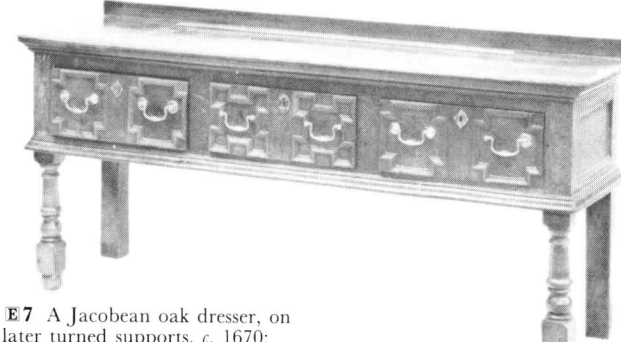

E7 A Jacobean oak dresser, on later turned supports, *c.* 1670; 70 in. (178 cm) wide.

E8 An oak low dresser, with moulded rectangular top and three geometrically panelled drawers, 17th century; 78 in. (198 cm) wide.

E9 A Charles II oak dresser base, with brass ring handles and escutcheons, with boarded top above a series of drawers, with shaped moulded panels, supported on turned baluster legs, late 17th century; 71 in. (181 cm).

E1 An oak dresser, with moulded rectangular top above three panelled frieze drawers, on baluster legs, joined by plain stretchers; 81 in. (206 cm).

E2 A Charles II oak dresser base, with three spiral-twist front legs, *c.* 1680; 34 in. high by 78 in. wide (85 by 198 cm).

E3 A low dresser, with moulded rectangular top, on turned legs and square stretchers, late 17th century/early 18th century; 84 in. (213 cm) wide.

E4 An oak dresser base, the three drawers with recessed panels, on turned barleysugar legs, with pot board base, late 17th century.

E5 An oak dresser base, with panelled drawers above a shaped apron, with square legs and solid base, 17th century.

E6 A George I oak dresser base with moulded top over four short frieze drawers and scalloped apron, on baluster-turned legs joined by a moulded undertier, on turned feet.

E7 A small oak low dresser, the drawers with moulded panels, early 18th century; 57 in. (143 cm) wide.

E8 An oak open low dresser, with front supports of baluster form, late 17th century; 33 in. high, 80 in. wide, (83 by 203 cm).

E1 An oak dresser, the back with a spice drawer, with four large drawers above shaped front, supported on turned legs, late 17th century.

E2 A William and Mary oak dresser, with six drawers flanking a cupboard, *c.* 1700; 34 in. high by 71 in. wide (86 by 180 cm).

E3 An oak dresser base, with panelled drawers and doors, late 17th century; 73 in. (185 cm) wide.

E5 A George I oak dresser base, with a moulded top above three deep drawers, on ringed baluster legs, ending in ball feet, *c.* 1720; 35 in. high by 81 in. wide (88 by 205 cm).

E6 An oak dresser, on elegant cabriole legs, with drawers relieved with mahogany crossbanding, 34 in. high by 78 in. long (86 by 198 cm).

E7 A George II oak dresser base, with central arch flanked by drawers with shaped aprons, on cabriole legs, 30 in. (76 cm) high.

E4 A George I oak and mahogany crossbanded dresser, with arcaded apron, *c.* 1740; 37 in. high by 76 in. wide (93 by 193 cm).

E8 An inlaid oak dresser, fitted with seven drawers with brass handles and escutcheons, centre cupboard fitted with two drawers, on bracket feet, 30 in. high by 81 in. wide (76 by 205 cm).

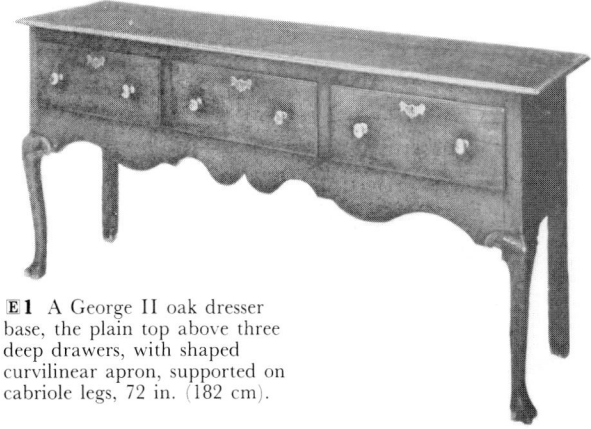

E1 A George II oak dresser base, the plain top above three deep drawers, with shaped curvilinear apron, supported on cabriole legs, 72 in. (182 cm).

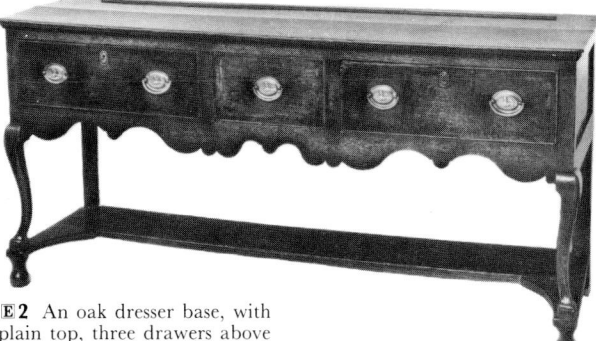

E2 An oak dresser base, with plain top, three drawers above shaped apron, on cabriole legs, first half 18th century.

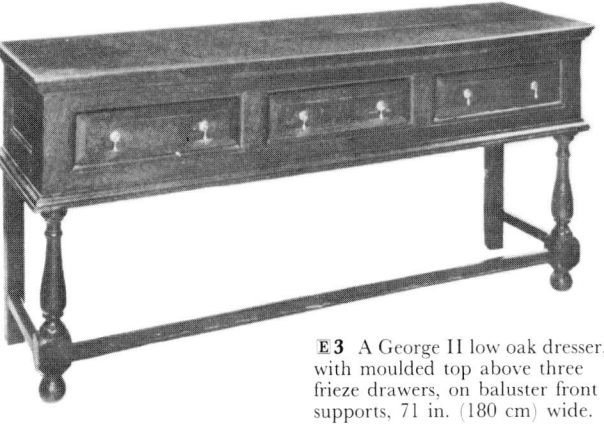

E3 A George II low oak dresser, with moulded top above three frieze drawers, on baluster front supports, 71 in. (180 cm) wide.

E4 A George II oak backless dresser, with cockbeaded drawers and pierced brass handles, *c.* 1730; 77 in. (195 cm) wide.

E5 A Georgian oak dresser base, with mahogany crossbanding, *c.* 1800; 35 in. high by 78 in. long (88 by 198 cm).

E6 A George II oak dresser, with three mahogany crossbanded drawers and shaped apron, *c.* 1750; 33 in. high by 69 in. wide (83 by 175 cm).

E7 A George II oak dresser, with five short spice drawers above three long drawers, *c.* 1750; 38 in. high by 78 in. wide (96 by 198 cm).

E8 A Georgian oak low dresser, corssbanded with walnut and outlined with ebonized and boxwood lines, 50 in. (127 cm) wide.

E1 A George II oak and mahogany dresser base, with three drawers above a shaped apron, supported on cabriole legs.

E2 An oak dresser, mid 18th century; 31 in. high by 78 in. wide (80 by 199 cm).

E3 A George II oak dresser, with moulded terminals, *c.* 1750; 34 in. high by 93 in. wide (86 by 236 cm).

E4 A Georgian oak and elm low dresser, with ogee-arched panelled and fielded cupboard doors, 76 in. (194 cm) wide.

E5 An oak dresser with moulded edges to the top, early 18th century; 38 in. high by 64 in. wide (95 by 160 cm).

E6 An oak dresser, with brass swan neck handles, 18th century; 54 in. (135 cm).

High dressers

E7 An oak dresser, with moulded dentil and pierced cornice, drawers with carved hearts, 17th century; 83 in. high by 75 in. wide (211 by 190 cm).

E 1 A George I oak dresser, the lower part with three drawers in the frieze, *c.* 1720; 81 in. high, 70 in. wide (206 by 178 cm).

E 2 A George I oak and elm dresser, with stylized carving, *c.* 1720; 86 in. high by 76 in. wide (218 by 193 cm).

E 3 A Montgomeryshire oak dresser, with good colour and patination, early 18th century; 96 in. (243 cm) wide.

E 4 A George III oak dresser, *c.* 1770; 84 in. high by 70 in. wide (214 by 178 cm).

E 5 An oak dresser, with baluster turned legs joined by a pot-board, *c.* 1730; 57 in. (143 cm) wide.

E 6 A George II oak dresser, the base with arched apron, *c.* 1750; 84 in. high by 55 in. wide (214 by 139 cm).

E 7 An oak dresser, with moulded cornice, 18th century; 59 in. (151 cm) wide.

E 8 A George II oak dresser, *c.* 1750; 82 in. high by 72 in. wide (208 by 183 cm).

E 9 An oak dresser, the open frieze with cupid bow fret motifs, with four drawers and three cupboards with panelled doors, the back with six spice drawers, brass knob handles, 18th century; 60 in. (150 cm).

E 10 A George II oak and elm dresser, with raised open shelved back above three frieze drawers and a pair of fielded panel doors, on shaped bracket feet, *c.* 1740; 79 in. high by 80 in. wide (210 by 203 cm).

E 1 A north Wales dresser, in oak, with upper section with cornice above shelves and spice drawers, above cupboards with ogee-panelled doors, on bracket feet, 18th century.

E 2 An oak Welsh dresser, carved with the letters A.M.O.W.B., early 18th century; 64 in. (163 cm) wide.

E 3 A Georgian oak dresser, the delft rack with moulded cornice, three shelves with fluted sides, the base with three drawers and shaped apron, 60 in. (150 cm) wide.

E 4 A George III Welsh dresser, the shelf top with ogee arch shaped frieze, with three mahogany crossbanded drawers, 77 in. (196 cm) wide.

E 5 A Georgian oak dresser, with moulded cornice and panelled frieze, 94 in. (238 cm) wide.

E 6 An oak dresser, the base with drawers and elaborately shaped apron, with pot shelf, first half 18th century.

E 7 A George III oak dresser, with moulded cornice above two shelves, mid to late 18th century; 66 in. (168 cm) wide.

E 8 An oak dresser, with spoon rack above the shelves and open rail below the drawers.

E 9 A Georgian oak high dresser, 81 in. high by 68 in. wide (205 by 172 cm).

E 10 A George III oak dresser, *c.* 1780; 84 in. high by 71 in. wide (213 by 180 cm).

E 11 An oak dresser, with matching pierced friezes and cupboards to back, on cabriole legs.

E 12 An old oak Welsh dresser, with shelves at back, 74 in. high by 84 in. wide (213 by 187 cm).

E 13 A George III oak dresser, the upper part with open shelves and a pair of panelled doors, *c.* 1780; 76 in. high by 78 in. wide (193 by 199 cm).

E 14 An oak dresser, with mahogany crossbanded borders, with delft rack fitted with two cupboards, with three drawers below, 18th century; 78 in. (198 cm).

E 15 An enclosed dresser, crossbanded in mahogany, with brass drop handles, 18th century; 85 in. (215 cm) wide.

E 1 An oak Welsh dresser, 18th century; 62 in. (157 cm) wide.

E 2 A George III inlaid oak dresser, with flat moulded cornice, on bracket feet, *c.* 1800; 61 in. (154 cm) wide.

E 3 A Georgian oak high dresser, 78 in. high by 71 in. wide (198 by 181 cm).

E 4 An oak cupboard dresser, 18th century; 80 in. high by 71 in. wide (203 by 180 cm).

E 5 A George III oak dresser, the rack with shaped frieze and fluted uprights, the lower part crossbanded in oak, with chevron stringing, 81 in. high by 83 in. wide (205 by 211 cm).

E 6 A George III mahogany dresser, the top of inverted breakfront outline, 77 in. by 86 in. (196 by 218 cm).

D 7 An Irish pewter cupboard, in walnut and oak, 18th century; 89 in. high by 77 in. wide (226 by 195 cm).

E 8 A George III oak and pine Welsh dresser, with three drawers in the frieze, 66 in. (167 cm) wide.

E 9 An oak clock/dresser and rack, with centre longcase clock, movement by Thos. Lister, Halifax, 18th century; dresser 86 in. (218 cm) wide.

E 10 An oak dresser, the rack with moulded cornice above pierced apron, with panelled sides, late 18th century; 82 in. high by 74 in. wide (208 by 187 cm).

E 11 A George III oak and mahogany dresser, 71 in. high by 48 in. wide (180 by 121 cm).

E 12 An oak dresser, of honey colour, with unusual drawer formation, 58 in. (147 cm) wide.

High Dressers
It is of the first importance that dresser base and rack should be original together, as the very nature of two-part furniture has meant that many pieces have become separated over the years.

Two parts liable to damage, which, if it is not severe can also be used as an indication of authenticity, are the legs and feet. The frequent washing of the stone floors on which most dressers stood will often have rotted the feet. The back legs, which were for the most part undecorated or of plain stile form, may have been spliced; they were often screwed to the wall, and even infrequent moves over 250 years may have required that they be sawn through to release the dresser.

E 13 A pine "chicken coop" dresser, *c.* 1850; 57 in. (144 cm) wide.

E 14 A Victorian pine open rack dresser, with glazed doors, 90 in. high by 66 in. wide (228 by 167 cm).

DUMB WAITERS
1740-1840

"A useful piece of furniture to serve in some respects the place of a waiter, whence it is so named," was Sheraton's description in 1803. Dumb waiters had existed in England since at least the 1720s to hold plates, desserts, wine and so on, permitting parties to continue after the servants had been dismissed.

The shallow-tray version is the best known, but in the late 1800s more capacious models rising from drum tables and cellarets were also made.

E3 A George III mahogany three-tier dumb waiter, with turned column and on tripod base.

E6 A George III mahogany two-tier dumb waiter, the top with brass gallery, with brass casters, *c.* 1800; 35 in. high by 23 in. diameter, (88 by 58 cm).

E9 A Regency three-tier dumb waiter, with tray supports of lacquered brass, the tripod base with pad feet.

E1 A three-tier dumb waiter, in mahogany, with turned column on tripod supports, with claw feet, *c.* 1740.

E4 A George III mahogany three-tier dumb waiter, with turned, writhen and fluted column, and on tripod supports.

E7 A Regency mahogany dumb waiter, with swivelling circular shelves, on turned supports, 25 in. (63 cm) diameter.

E10 A William IV mahogany collapsible dumb waiter, on triangular concave platform base, *c.* 1830; 21 in. (52 cm) diameter.

E2 An early George III mahogany three-tier dumb waiter, *c.* 1765; 43 in. high by 24 in. maximum diameter (108 by 61 cm).

E5 A George III mahogany dumb waiter, the two concentric trays with reeded edges, *c.* 1770; 35 in. (18 cm) high.

E8 A Regency mahogany dumb waiter, of three tiers, each with two flaps, on baluster column, 47 in. high by 22 in. diameter (121 by 55 cm).

E11 A collapsible oak dumb waiter, with gadrooned support, *c.* 1840; 43 in. (109 cm) open, 31 in. (80 cm) closed.

E1 A James I oak armchair, *c.* 1605. The plain back panel beneath a recessed frieze outlined with pellet carving; the arms are supported on fluted baluster supports, which are repeated in the legs.

E3 A Charles II carved and punch-decorated oak armchair, dated 1682.

Dates carved on any furniture, particularly that of the 17th century, should always be viewed with the knowledge that they were a popular addition during the middle and later part of the 19th century. The style and type of numerals and initials, if any, are important clues, and the surface of the carved parts must obviously be compatible with the plain, as is evidently the case here.

E5 A William and Mary period armchair, *c.* 1690, painted cream and grey and gilded.

The moulded arms are on flower-carved scroll supports. The swagged scroll legs are headed by masks and joined by a curved X-stretcher of flower-carved scrolls.

See R.W. Symonds, *Furniture-Making in 17th and 18th Century England*, 1929, figures 127 and 128.

D2 A James I panel back armchair, *c.* 1620. The arched toprail is carved with a fluted fan and the initials "IMK", above a panel inlaid with an interlaced lozenge in bog oak and holly.

The extremely fine quality of the carving and inclusion of geometric inlay make this an outstanding example.

E4 A William and Mary walnut armchair, *c.* 1690, the upholstered and fringed arms supported on deeply carved uprights, the inverted scroll legs joined with flamboyant curvilinear stretchers and similarly shaped cross member.

Chairs of this type have been referred to as "French", and much Continental influence is evident in the decoration.

E6 A William and Mary walnut armchair, *c.* 1690, the scrolled legs joined by a scrollwork front stretcher and a turned H-stretcher.

As an alternative to the upholstered arm, the moulded show wood arm gave a certain grace and elegance and a lighter appearance to chairs of this period. The exceptionally rich colour of the walnut of this chair — like that of no. 4, left — increases considerably its commercial desirability.

E 1 A Queen Anne walnut open armchair. A slightly later (*c.* 1720) chair of similar form is illustrated in R. Edwards and P. Maquoid, *The Dictionary of English Furniture*, revised edition 1954, volume I, at p.259.

D 3 One of a pair of George I armchairs, *c.* 1720, with painted and gilt decoration on a red japanned ground.

D 5 A George I tapestry-covered walnut armchair, *c.* 1720. See for comparison R.W. Symonds, *English Furniture from Charles II to George II*, 1929, figure 91.

C 2 *(above)* A fine Queen Anne walnut writing armchair.

Many types of chair dating from this period changed little in the 20 years spanning the reigns of Queen Anne and George I, and the description of them may use the name of the monarch to signify a style rather than an historical period.

D 4 *(right)* A George II walnut library armchair, *c.* 1740, covered in contemporary petit point.

The downcurved arm supports are carved with acanthus and flowerhead terminals, the legs with deep foliate carving on hairy paw feet. Compare figure 102 in R.W. Symonds, *English Furniture from Charles II to George II*, 1929.

D1 A George II walnut library armchair, *c.* 1740, covered with contemporary gros and petit point needlework.

Of fine sturdy proportions, this chair is of excellent quality: every surface is carved and the wood is of fine colour.

Certain decorative features of this chair make it an unusual example of a much sought after type. The ball-shaped foot is deeply carved to represent a leaf-capped scroll and the ankle is fluted beneath the cabochon on the knee. These decorative features are repeated on the arm supports, which at the junction of the upholstery and the show wood have a distinct collar, indicating that the arm shape has never been changed.

D3 A George II walnut side chair, *c.* 1745.

Comparative scarcity of armed versions of this chair led inevitably to side chairs having arms added during the late 19th and early 20th centuries. The width of the seat – always less on a side chair – is the thing to look at if suspicion arises.

D5 One from a set of four early George III mahogany side chairs, *c.* 1760.

This is an interesting piece showing design in transition. The chair is narrower and the seat less deep than was the norm in the broad, strong furniture of 20 years previously (compare no. 1, left), but it is still generously proportioned, with a high back. The cluster-column legs are unmistakably Chinese Chippendale, making the whole piece eclectic in the best mid-century tradition.

C2 One of a pair of late George II giltwood armchairs, *c.* 1740, with drop-in seat. The needlework, which is contemporary, depicts Venus and Vulcan and Europa and the Bull.

Throughout the century a certain taste for gilt furniture remained and so the shape and underlying style are still the important guides to dating.

E4 One of a pair of George III mahogany library armchairs, *c.* 1760.

The popularity of Thomas Chippendale's *Director* played a considerable part in the development of finely proportioned furniture which became fashionable without the elaborately carved and scrolling legs and stretchers of the rococo style. This transitional style gave birth to the bulk of what we recognize today as fine quality 18th-century English furniture.

E6 A George II mahogany side chair, *c.* 1760.

The rococo style here is still dominant, with the serpentine seat rails carved to appear encrusted below a matching shaped seat and back. However, both seat rails and legs are slimmer than in high-style rococo, giving a taller and more graceful appearance.

C1 One of a pair of George III mahogany library armchairs, *c.* 1760, attributed to Thomas Chippendale.

The pair are almost identical to a set of 14 armchairs that Chippendale supplied to the fifth Earl of Dumfries in 1759, en suite with a pair of sofas and card tables. Chippendale's description of those chairs on his invoice was as follows: "14 Mahogany Elbow chairs with stuffed Backs & Seats Cover'd & brass nailed the Elbows and fronts of the seats richly carv'd & scroll feet & castors."

B3 A pair of early George III mahogany open armchairs, *c.* 1760.

The carving is very fine, from the rosettes and foliage on the arm supports through the foliage, rockwork and lustrous cabochons on the knees to the crustacean scrolled feet.

The important feature of the carving to these chairs is undoubtedly the extended knee in almost acroterion form up into the upholstery over the seat rails. Any impression of heaviness is avoided by the use of a plain tapering back leg conforming with the front only in its carved foot.

D2 A George III gilded beech open armchair, *c.* 1772.

This chair is part of a large suite of seat furniture made for Edward Morant at 17 Park Lane, London. The suite included eight such armchairs, of which a pair are in the Metropolitan Museum, New York, five window seats – again, a pair is to be found in the Metropolitan – and a confidante, now also in the Metropolitan. The firm of Gordon and Tait were the most likely makers, though the evidence is wholly circumstantial.

D4 A pair of George III mahogany open armchairs in the manner of John Cobb, *c.* 1770, with lobed back rails and legs, acanthus clasps and scrolled arms and feet. The legs terminate in a scroll raised from the ground by a short turned foot, which Hepplewhite referred to as a French foot.

There are a number of variants on this successful design, which is traditionally associated with Cobb. A similar armchair is illustrated in M. Harris, *The English Chair*, at plate 70.

While curvilinear in style, this design is a totally different interpretation to that favoured in the earlier rococo period. There are few if any straight lines visible and the whole chair suggests fluid elegance.

D2 A George III mahogany armchair, *c.* 1785. The back displays a fusion of the then current French and classical styles, whereas the front legs are purely classical.

D3 A George III gilded beech open armchair, *c.* 1790, the gilding probably later.

This chair is the issue of a happy marriage between the styles influential in the later 18th century. Robert Adam's classicism contributed the bold anthemion splat, France the legs (compare no. 1, left) and yet the feel of the whole is broad, strong, confident mid-century Georgian.

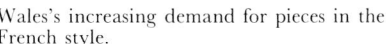

D1 A George III giltwood bergère in the Louis XVI style, by François Hervé, *c.* 1780.

Hervé was described as a "Cabriole Chairmaker" and listed in the *British Universal Directory*, 1790-1798, as being in Lower St John Street, Marylebone. He was employed by the Prince of Wales to supply chairs through the agency of Guillaume Gaubert.

The style of the chair shows a distinctively French interpretation of the classical revival, co-opting for further impact the use of spirally twisted ribbon borders and bows in conjunction with stiff-leaf foliage and classical motifs. The sumptuous gilding reflects the importance of the chair and the Prince of Wales's increasing demand for pieces in the French style.

E1 A George III cream-painted and gilt open armchair, *c.* 1795.

This is a wholly classical interpretation of a formal side chair, with a combination of carving and painting, the legs fluted and terminating in spade feet, the seat rails with husks between carved paterae. The double sweep of the unsupported arm forbids anything but the utmost elegance in use.

D3 A pair of late George III mahogany open armchairs, *c.* 1795, two from a set of 14.

The arcaded backs have panelled tapering splats carved with bellflowers under fluted squares, whereas the simple downcurved arms on baluster supports and the turned and collared legs are elegant renderings of the native tradition.

These chairs correspond closely to the design for parlour chairs which appears as plate 39 in Sheraton's *Cabinet-Maker's and Upholsterer's Drawing Book*, 1791-1794.

E2 A George III painted open armchair, *c.* 1795. It is one of a set of 12 – 11 of them bearing contemporary workmen's labels.

It would be difficult to find a better exemplar of neoclassical taste. The proportions of this chair are beginning to stray from the severe purity of the Adam-style chair immediately above: the arms have been lengthened and scrolled in the English tradition, and the architectural feeling is refined. The black and gold colouring, the drapery swags and the abundance of decoration are eminently early Empire.

E4 A pair of north country Windsor armchairs in yew and elmwood, from the second quarter of the 19th century. They are of fine colour, with agreeable pierced splats and double H-stretchers.

Compare R.W. Symonds, *Furniture-Making in 17th and 18th Century England*, figures 150 and 151, and see Victor Chinnery, *Oak Furniture, The British Tradition*, page 536, figure 4:302.

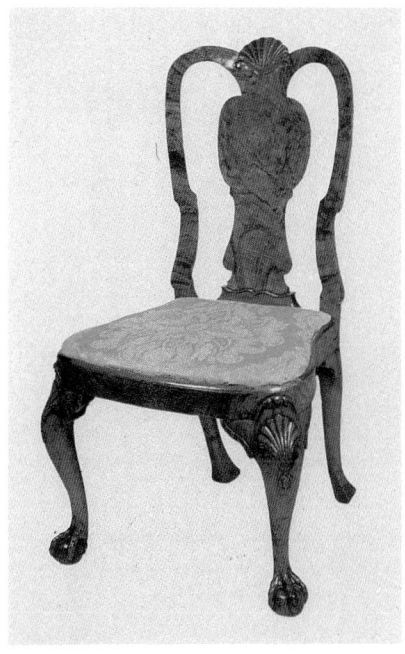

D1 A William and Mary period walnut armchair and one from a set of similar side or dining chairs, *c.* 1690.

These are two particularly fine examples of a type of late Stuart chair, the back of which contains panels of formal carving and pierced foliage instead of canework, giving a somewhat European appearance.

The curved X-stretchers, often with lobed knops, between moulded legs were an alternative to the carved and scrolled legs containing a deeply carved and pierced bowed front stretcher; see R. Edwards and P. Maquoid, *The Dictionary of English Furniture*, revised edition 1954, figures 63 and 64.

E3 A George I burr-walnut side chair, *c.* 1725.

Of simple, sturdy design, it relies for its effect on the excellent figuring of the wood and on deep carving to the crest rail, the knees and the feet.

D2 A pair of unusual Queen Anne walnut side chairs, early 18th century.

They have rectangular backs with yoke-shaped toprails carved with acanthus over a distinctive, narrow vase-shaped pierced splat between turned stiles; the over-stuffed seats on cabriole legs carved with acanthus and joined by turned stretchers.

E4 One from a set of 10 George I walnut dining chairs, formerly in the collection of the Dukes of Leeds at Hornby Castle.

The use of highly figured burr veneers on the backrail and splat supplies all the decoration necessary to complement the fine carving to the front seat rail and legs.

C 3 A mid-18th century carved mahogany dining chair from a set of nine comprising one armchair and eight side chairs, *c.* 1755.

This particular splat is one of the most popular patterns of the mid 18th century for good, rather than exceptional, mahogany chairs.

E 4 An early George III mahogany dining chair in the Chinese Chippendale style, *c.* 1765.

A number of similar chairs exist, all differing in detail but all bearing a distinct resemblance to Chippendale's designs, notably plate 27 in the 1762 third edition of his *Director*. The distinctive pagoda crest rail of the chair shown is especially close to Chippendale's design and is similar to those on a set of chairs at Normanton Hall which may have a Chippendale association.

C 1 An important George I walnut chair with gilt-metal and verre églomisé mounts, *c.* 1724; the arms are of Lord Scarsdale. A matching chair is illustrated in R. Edwards and P. Maquoid, *The Dictionary of English Furniture*, revised edition 1954, at figure 93.

C 2 A pair of George I walnut dining chairs, *c.* 1725, of very fine quality and rich colour.

The backs are raked and moulded, with paper scrolls. The splat is carved with strapwork, lobing and matching scrolls under a generous shell-shaped crest, a motif which is taken up on the knees, which are further carved with leafage and scrolls. The seat frame is fluted and the shoe-piece is carved with S-scrolls.

The backs of these chairs are related to a pair of walnut and parcel-gilt dining chairs formerly at Worsborough Hall, Barnsley, Yorkshire, and

now in the collection of the Colonial Williamsburg Foundation; the chairs shown here may well have been similarly decorated with gilt-gesso.

E 5 An early George III mahogany dining chair, the top rail carved with acanthus and rockwork over a formalized open knot splat on completely plain legs with block feet. The chair combines the classical (the legs) with rococo (the top rail) in the best 1760s manner.

E1 A George III mahogany side chair, early 1770s, attributed to Thomas Chippendale. It bears the contemporary ink inscription "Jos Worthen".

Severely classical in its detail, the chair's waved top rail centres a patera. Under fluted capitals the square tapering legs are panelled with carved rosette decoration on collared, moulded block feet.

E3 A George III mahogany chair, *c.* 1775. The circular back, the seat rails and the legs are all moulded and beaded, the splats fluted with central paterae.

This was an extremely popular style and may also be found painted and/or gilded throughout.

E5 A George III cream-painted and parcel-gilt side chair, *c.* 1800.

In fine Gothic style, this chair contrives to be both pretty and witty – pretty in its fine gilt decoration and witty in its eclectic use of ecclesiastical architectural features.

E2 A George III mahogany dining chair, *c.* 1775, one of a set of 10.

Both back and splats are of unusual shape, the fore-edges of the crest rail and stiles being carved with lobing, the fan-shaped splat with laurel and bellflowers, the lower serpentine splat pierced but not carved. In contrast to the imaginative profusion of the back, the legs are square, tapered and moulded on padded block feet.

E4 A George III mahogany dining chair, *c.* 1780, the shield back with flowers, foliage, entrelacs, a rosette and beading, on moulded tapering legs.

A similar chair is illustrated in R. Edwards and P. Macquoid, *The Dictionary of English Furniture*, revised edition 1954, volume I, figure 229.

E6 A mahogany dining chair in late George II style, *c.* 1900.

Although of solid worth, this chair should not pass for its model: while it reflects indisputable quality in the carving and pierced work to the back, and there is no scrimping on the timber used to create the well formed cabriole legs, it does not stand well.

C1 One of a pair of Queen Anne walnut stools, *c.* 1710, the cabriole legs carved with lambrequins, bellflowers and C-scrolls.

A3 *(above)* A George II mahogany settee, *c.* 1745; it is 85 in. (216 cm) long.
Made as part of a suite, this is undoubtedly a fine piece of furniture, for despite its size there is nothing ponderous about it. In common with most upholstered furniture of the early part of the century, there is no show wood to the top rail, but in contrast to earlier pieces the impression of spreading sturdiness has been foregone.
Another point of interest is that whereas this settee is undoubtedly Chippendale in style it precedes publication of the *Director* by approximately a decade, showing how much that work was a compilation of existing styles rather than an original essay setting trends for the third quarter of the 18th century.

C2 *(above)* An early 18th-century carved and gilt double stool, one of a pair; 24 in. high, 57 in. long (61 by 146 cm).
There was a marked increase in the popularity of formal columnar legs as an alternative to the deeply scrolled variety during the latter part of the 17th century and this style of panelled, tapering square-section leg can be seen to re-occur throughout the 18th.
The bellflower motif, which was one of the earlier panel-infills, surmounted by a crusty rosette became replaced, particularly after the 1760s, with more purely classical motifs, and the rosette became a more finely represented patera.

B4 *(right)* A fine George III giltwood settee, *c.* 1780, designed by Robert Adam; 51 in. (130 cm) wide. It was made as part of a suite comprising another similar settee, a larger sofa, a confidante and armchairs, for Sir Abraham Hume of Hill Street, London.
Adam's design, which differs only in that he showed four front legs rather than three as made, is dated 9th March 1780 and is in the Sir John Soane Museum.

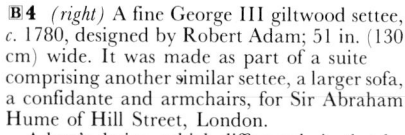

E 3 *(above)* A George II walnut wing armchair, *c.* 1745, a fine, high-backed example with out-scrolled arms and deep carving to the legs.

The proportions of such chairs could vary considerably – compare for example no. 4 below – but will always be generous. They may echo the high back of late 17th century and some Queen Anne furniture, as here, or the capacious breadth of George I seat furniture, as below.

D 1 *(above)* Part of a suite of giltwood drawing room furniture in the Louis XV style, made in England *c.* 1850.

Whereas in the second half of the 18th century French influence on English furniture had been strong but intermittent, in the 19th century there were wholesale adoptions and imitations, starting in the late 1820s and carrying on right through the century with revivals of earlier French styles, the more intricate of which became accessible through the combination of modern furniture-making machinery with the large supply of cheap skilled labour for tasks such as gilding.

C 2 *(left)* A painted rosewood-veneered chair from a dining suite by W.H. Windridge, *c.* 1890.

Of fine quality, this chair is an excellent example of Victorian re-interpretation of earlier styles with the addition of finely worked decoration that was wholly of the period. The back is Regency, the arms a stylish rendition of 18th-century classical revival models and the legs a pure form of the same. But the tulipwood basket weave inlay to the back and seat rails is *sui generis* and the painted panels, though in form an acknowledgement of Adam, owe their content and style to Greuze, not Rome.

E 4 A George II walnut wing armchair, *c.* 1750.

A fellow to no. 3 immediately above, this chair exhibits some of the standard variations. The back has the serpentine toprail that is more familiar than the flat-arched form above, and it is eared. The seat is bowed and the front seat rail moulded, as are the side rails, and only the front legs are of cabriole form.

D1 *(above)* A late Elizabethan carved and inlaid oak chest, *c.* 1600; 37 in. high by 52 in. wide (93 by 131 cm).

The top has six moulded panels and an elaborately moulded cornice over the fluted frieze, which is paralleled in the base. The split pillars are also fluted on prominent niched pedestals, emphasizing the architectural conception of the chest. The front and ends show small inlaid panels within egg-and-dart, lobed and moulded borders, and the repertoire of carved ornament is extended by the dentil border below.

D2 A George I walnut bachelor's chest, *c.* 1725; 29 in. high, 30 in. wide (74 by 76 cm), crossbanded, with two short drawers over three long and of fine light colour.

D4 A George I walnut secretaire tallboy, *c.* 1720; it stands 71 in. high and is 42 in. wide (180 by 107 cm).

The piece is unusual in having canted fluted corners to both parts, and is further embellished by an inlaid concave sunburst to the bottom drawer with conforming moulded base.

C3 A small George I period walnut chest of drawers, early 18th century, 30 in. (77 cm) wide, with crossbanded quarter-veneered top over a brushing slide and four graduated long drawers.

D5 A George III mahogany serpentine chest, with three graduated long drawers, *c.* 1770; 42 in. (107 cm) wide.

The serpentine form, taken with the rounded, panelled corners and the French-style cabriole legs all suggest a strong influence from the French commode.

D6 A George III mahogany commode, with serpentine front, *c.* 1765; 35 in. high by 43 in. wide (89 by 108 cm).

The interpretation of a Continental commode may be restrained, but this is far more commode than English chest of drawers – see the pronounced carved corners, the scrolled legs and the carved edges of the top.

C7 A George III marble-topped serpentine marquetry commode, in the manner of John Cobb, *c.* 1755; one of a pair, each 34 in. high and 46 in. wide (87 by 117 cm), one opening to drawers, the other to shelves.

Under a mottled rust and beige marble top the satinwood frieze is inlaid with trailing flowers. The front and sides are in quarter-banded kingwood with large satinwood ovals inlaid with ribbon-tied bunches of flowers.

C 1 *(above)* A George III satinwood, sycamore and marquetry commode, *c.* 1785; it is 35 in. high and 46 in. wide (91 by 117 cm). The top is inlaid with demi-paterae, radiating flutes, fan lunettes and foliate scrolls.

C 2 *(left)* A late George III mahogany semi-elliptical commode in the manner of Gillow of Lancaster, *c.* 1790; 36 in. high by 51 in. wide and 22 in. deep (90 by 130 by 56 cm). The centre door encloses a secretaire drawer.

This piece, one of a pair, depends entirely on the figuring of the wood – especially of the oval panels – for its effect.

A 4 *(above)* A George III satinwood and marquetry semi-elliptical commode, attributed to Ince & Mayhew, *c.* 1785; it stands 37 in. high, and is 43 in. wide (94 by 184 cm).

The elaborately inlaid top bears three painted ovals in conformity with those to the cupboard doors. The centre door opens to three mahogany drawers, the side doors reveal cupboards. There is an almost perfectly concealed drawer in the frieze. The ormolu borders and ram's head masks are as fine in their execution as the inlay.

C 5 *(above)* A carved mahogany serpentine commode, the top with a border carved with oval cartouches, scrolls and flowers over a brushing slide. The doors are panelled to resemble three long drawers and are centred by a large cartouche carved with flowers and leafage; the corners canted and carved on scroll feet. The silver-gilt handles are by Elkington, hallmarked 1930.

B 3 A George III painted and gilded commode, *c.* 1790; height 34 in., width 48 in. (86 by 122 cm).

The white marble top is painted with a fan lunette and a border of entwined ribbon and wheatears within a beaded ormolu border. The central panel shows a painting of Una and the lion, the two roundels on the cupboard doors contain paintings of Muses. The legs are later.

A similar painted commode is illustrated in M. Jourdain and F. Rose, *English Furniture, The Georgian Period (1750-1830)*, 1953, as figure 1112.

D1 A George III painted satinwood bonheur-du-jour, *c.* 1780; 49 in. high, 30 in. wide (134 by 77 cm).

The cupboard doors open to a mahogany-lined interior fitted with small drawers and pigeonholes. The stand has a hinged writing surface supported on discreet lopers, with a drawer at either side.

D3 A George III satinwood bonheur-du-jour, *c.* 1795; it stands 47 in. high and is 26 in. wide (119 by 66 cm). The drawer contains a leather-lined writing slide with pen and ink compartments.

The workmanship is very fine, making excellent use of the well figured wood. An unusual and agreeable feature is the inclusion of a Wedgwood plaque at the centre of the gallery, matching the back plates of the drawer pulls.

D5 A Regency ormolu-mounted and parcel-gilt rosewood bonheur-du-jour, attributed to John McLean, 1800-1810; it is 45 in. high and 32 in. wide (114 by 81 cm).

The piece exhibits a marked French influence, which is in keeping with McLean's advertisement that he specialized in "Elegant Parisian Furniture". His name appears in the list of cabinet-makers given by Sheraton in his *Cabinet Dictionary* of 1803, on page 292 of which is a design for a work table "taken from one executed by Mr McLean in Marylebone Street . . . who finishes these small articles in the neatest manner."

D2 A George III tulipwood-veneered bonheur-du-jour, *c.* 1790; it is 46 in. high and 30 in. wide (117 by 76 cm).

An elegant piece in the Sheraton style, this desk relies wholly on proportion – note the elongated, splayed tapering legs – and on colour, aided by a subtle display of veneering – not just the cupboard doors but the chevron banding to the drawer as well.

C4 A pair of Regency rosewood and satinwood bonheurs-du-jour; 56 in. high 37 in. wide (141 by 95 cm).

The bonheur-du-jour, in its original form, was enthusiastically taken up in England from French models in the 1770s. As the three previous examples show, it was varied with all the refinements of late 18th-century taste, but gradually grew larger and more complex, tending, as here, to assume the functions of display cabinet and dressing table as well as retaining its original purpose of ladies' writing desk, until its ancillary functions obliterated its early definition altogether.

C 1 *(left)* A late Regency mahogany partners'
desk, *c.* 1825, 75 in. (189 cm) wide.

This is a good example of late Regency
library furniture, in which the lavish eclectic
inventiveness of the earlier Regency was
foregone in favour of traditional woods –
chiefly mahogany and oak – unadorned except
for strong carving.

C 2 *(right)* A late George III satinwood
library desk, 56 in. (142 cm) wide.

The top is crossbanded with rosewood, inlaid
with ebonized and natural boxwood lines; the
sides, including the sides of the kneehole, are
inlaid with ovals. The side not shown has a
single long drawer panelled with false drawer
fronts over two oval-inlaid cupboard doors
opening to shelves.

Desks such as this may require some effort to
be properly appreciated: we are so familiar
with functional mahogany versions that
attempts to make them less sombre and more
fashionable can seem frivolous, as though
business were being taken into the boudoir. To
take this view however would be to ignore the
strength of the revolution in furniture design of
the late 18th century, and the then current
demand for pieces that were light and graceful.

D 3 *(left)* A George III mahogany kneehole
writing desk, *c.* 1810; 49 in. (133 cm) wide. The
handles, though sympathetic, are later.

This desk makes an interesting comparison
with no. 2 above. It is altogether smaller, and
owes its proportions more to the kneehole
dressing tables of the George II period than to
their weighty pedestal desk contemporaries.
Similarly, the painted decoration has the effect
of making the piece lighter and prettier without
seeking an association with the fragile-seeming
refinement of contemporary veneered
furniture. There is then no obvious attempt to
update a traditionally shaped desk but rather
an acknowledgement that familiar designs can
be refreshed with contemporary decoration.

C 1 A George I giltwood pier glass, *c.* 1720; one of a pair it measures 66 in. high by 37 in. wide (168 by 94 cm).

C 3 An early George II giltwood mirror, *c.* 1740; 68 in. (173 cm). In the vigour of its design it owes as much to late baroque as to contemporary rococo.

B 5 An early George III giltwood pier glass, *c.* 1760; 111 in. high, 63 in. wide (282 by 160 cm). Such ornate rococo frames have rarely survived intact; the degree of damage is therefore important in assessing their value.

C 2 A George II giltwood pier mirror of architectural form, *c.* 1730; 34 in. (86 cm) wide. Of good mellow colour, the frame has a broken pediment centring a cartouche over a lion's head in the frieze. Shell spandrels ornament the upper corners of the frame, a motif that is repeated in the shaped base.

D 4 A late George II giltwood chinoiserie mirror, *c.* 1755; 79 in. high, 44 in. wide (201 by 112 cm); a splendid example of mid-18th century chinoiserie.

C 6 An early George III giltwood mirror, *c.* 1760; height 65 in., width 43 in. (165 by 109 cm).
The vigorous C-scrolls and leaf-carving are in the best Chippendale manner. An interesting comparison is the frame of an overmantel supplied by Chippendale in 1759 for Dumfries House, illustrated as figure 301 in C. Gilbert, *Thomas Chippendale*, 1978.

GLOBES
1750-1880

The 18th-century fascination with science in all its forms, and particularly with the new data brought back from voyages of discovery, meant that no gentleman's library was complete without a terrestrial globe and possibly a celestial globe as well.

Globes should always be dated by their cabinet work, not by the projections they show, as it was the pactice to replace older projections with new ones as they became available.

E 1 A late George II library globe, by Benjamin Martin, on turned baluster support with tripod stand, dated 1757; 33 in. high by 23 in. diameter (89 by 58 cm).

E 2 A George III terrestrial table globe, dedicated to Sir Joseph Banks, President of the Royal Society, and incorporating Captain Cook's discoveries to the year 1799; 23 in. (58 cm) diameter.

D 3 A Cary's library globe on turned pillar, early 19th century; 47 in. high by 27 in. diameter (120 by 68 cm).

E 4 A celestial globe, by Newton, *c.* 1820; 14 in. (35 cm) high.

E 5 A Regency Cary's terrestrial globe, dated 1815; 35 in. (89 cm) high.

D 6 A Cary's terrestrial globe, dated 1815; 47 in. high by 32 in. wide (119 by 81 cm).

E 7 A pair of Regency globes, the terrestrial inscribed "manufactured by T.M. Bardin 16, Salisbury Square, London, wth corrections and additions to 1821", the celestial inscribed "made by T.M. Bardin", the terrestrial with a glazed compass; 36 in. (91 cm) high.

E 8 A George IV miniature table globe, signed "Lanes Improved Globe, London 1829", decorated in colours and mounted on three S-shaped legs, well carved as dolphins, early 19th century; 3 in. (7 cm) high.

E 9 A silver, gold, enamel, ivory, brass and bronze celestial globe, on a carved ivory shaft rising from a circular base, *c.* 1832; 23 in. (58 cm) high.

D 10 A Charles Smith & Sons globe, on a turned and carved rosewood stand, *c.* 1840; 44 in. high by 18 in. diameter (111 by 45 cm).

E 11 A Newton's library globe, bearing an engraved silver plaque, 40 in. high by 22 in. diameter (101 by 56 cm).

LOWBOYS
1700-1780

"Lowboy" has in recent years became generally acceptable on both sides of the Atlantic to describe a small table with drawers to an arched frieze, formerly known in England as a dressing table. The term has been adopted as the form plainly derives from the lower part of a chest-on-stand or tallboy. Lowboys are so much in demand that care should always be taken to ensure that the top is original and that a piece is not an altered tallboy base.

E 1 A Queen Anne lowboy, with chinoiserie black and gold laquer decoration, 1700-1720; 28 in. high by 29 in. wide (71 by 73 cm).

E 2 A Queen Anne walnut lowboy, feather and crossbanded, *c.* 1710; 28 in. high by 30 in. wide (71 by 76) cm.

E 3 A Queen Anne walnut lowboy, with two long drawers, 27 in. high by 28 in. wide (70 by 72 cm).

E 4 A Queen Anne walnut lowboy, with moulded crossbanded top, *c.* 1710; 27 in. high by 30 in. wide (70 by 76 cm).

E 5 A George I pollard elm lowboy, with walnut banding, *c.* 1720; 27 in. high by 33 in. wide (68 by 83 cm).

E 6 A Queen Anne walnut dressing table, on cabriole legs with pad feet, early 18th century.

E 7 A George I five-drawer lowboy, in walnut, 30 in. high by 36 in. wide (76 by 91 cm).

E 8 A George I crossbanded and herringbone inlaid walnut lowboy, with quartered top.

E 9 A George I walnut lowboy, the canted rectangular top and drawer fronts herringbone inlaid, the cabriole legs with club feet.

E 10 A George I oak lowboy with three drawers and carved arched apron, with cabriole legs to the front and square-section legs to the rear; early 18th century.

E 11 A well proportioned lowboy, with single drawer and scalloped frieze, *c.* 1720; 29 in. wide by 32 in. high (73 by 81 cm).

E 12 An early Georgian oak lowboy, with one long and two short drawers flanking arched carved apron, on cabriole legs, 29 in. high by 31 in. wide (73 by 78 cm).

E 13 A George I oak lowboy, fitted with three frieze drawers, on cabriole legs, *c.* 1730; 30 in. (76 cm) wide.

E 14 An oak lowboy, of deep golden colour with one long and two short drawers, and ornately carved apron, *c.* 1730; 27 in. high by 31 in. wide (68 by 78 cm).

E 15 A late George II mahogany dressing table, the frieze with shallow centre drawer flanked by deep drawers over scrolled apron, on carved cabriole legs, mid 18th century; 31 in. (78 cm) wide.

E 16 A Georgian oak lowboy, with single drawer, all line inlaid, on cabriole legs, 30 in. (76 cm) wide.

E 17 A Queen Anne-style oak lowboy with single drawer, 18th century; 31 by 20 in. (78 by 50 cm).

E 18 A George III oak lowboy with one long drawer over three short, on moulded legs.

E 19 A George II oak lowboy, with three drawers; 28 in. high by 30 in. wide (71 by 76 cm).

E 20 A George III mahogany dressing table, 28 in. high by 33 in. wide (73 by 85 cm).

D 21 A harewood inlaid enclosed dressing table, of good colour, *c.* 1780; 29 in. (73 cm) wide.

MIRRORS
1680-1900

Reflecting glass was a preserve of the wealthy few until the 1700s. Much of the advancement in its manufacture is attributed to the second Duke of Buckingham who, granted a patent in 1663, established a factory at Vauxhall that came to dominate English mirror-making and gave its name to the finest quality mirror plate.

Cheval glasses

E 1 A George III mahogany cheval glass, supported on turned uprights with finials, *c.* 1800; 69 in. high by 33 in. wide (175 by 83 cm).

E 2 An inlaid Sheraton mahogany cheval mirror, with arched feet and stretchers.

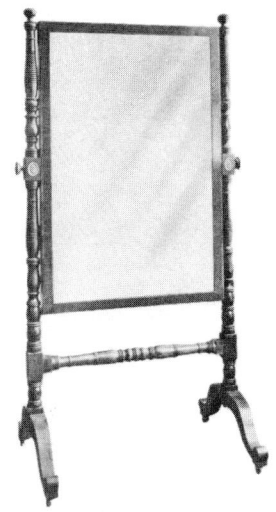

E 3 A mahogany cheval glass, overall size 70 in. high by 36 in. wide (177 by 91 cm).

E 4 A Regency mahogany cheval mirror, on square supports, 30 in. (76 cm) wide.

E 5 A Regency mahogany cheval mirror, with ring-turned frame, two candle branches and vase finials, 29 in. (73 cm) wide.

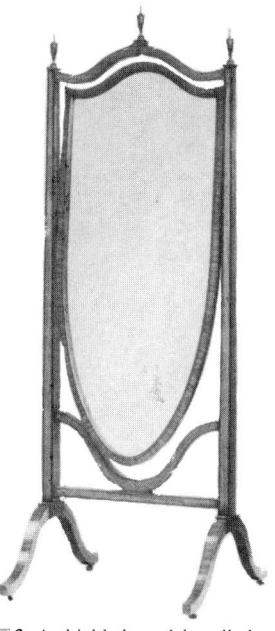

E 6 A shield-shaped bevelled plate cheval mirror, with three finials, on arched splayed feet, 73 in. high by 26 in. wide (185 by 66 cm).

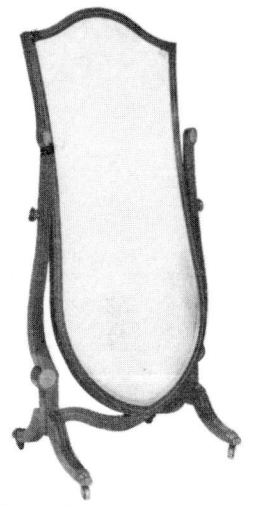

E 7 An Edwardian inlaid mahogany cheval mirror, with satinwood crossbandings, 62 in. (157 cm) high.

Overmantels

D 8 A Charles II giltwood overmantel with rectangular plate, on carved moulded frame; 51 in. by 54 in. (129 by 137 cm).

D 1 A Queen Anne carved gilt walnut mirror, with panel of fruit and flowers by de Heem; 56 in. by 47 in. (142 by 119 cm).

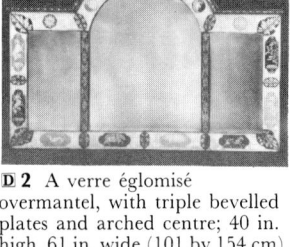

D 2 A verre églomisé overmantel, with triple bevelled plates and arched centre; 40 in. high, 61 in. wide (101 by 154 cm).

E 3 A Queen Anne walnut framed three-plate mirror, with carved and gilt enrichments; 38 in. high, 45 in. wide (96 by 114 cm).

E 6 A George II parcel-gilt red walnut wall mirror, *c.* 1735; 43 in. high by 33 in. wide (109 by 86 cm).

E 7 A George III walnut and gilt framed landscaped mirror, under an 18th-century North Italian school oil panel, *c.* 1770; 40 in. high, 58 in. wide (102 by 147 cm).

E 4 A Queen Anne gesso landscape three-plate mirror, with original bevelled plates, the formal

border decorated at each end with a stylized Vitruvian scroll, leaf-capped; 17 in. (43 cm) high.

E 5 A giltwood overmantel, with early Georgian triple plate, the outer panels cut with baskets

of flowers; 26 in. high by 59 in. wide (66 by 149 cm).

D 8 A Chippendale finely carved wood and gilt overmantel mirror, with three plates surrounded by rococo-style borders, the C-scrolls and decorations pierced in true asymetrical form; 22 in. high by 60 in. wide (55 by 152 cm).

D 9 A Chippendale finely carved and gilt overmantel mirror, with panelled glass borders; 57 in. high, 60 in. wide (144 by 152 cm).

E 10 A George II style giltwood overmantel, possibly *c.* 1840; 55 in. high by 70 in. wide (139 by 177 cm).

D 11 A Chinese Chippendale carved giltwood landscape mirror, *c.* 1760; 35 in. high by 66 in. wide (88 by 167 cm).

D 12 A fine Chippendale overmantel mirror, *c.* 1760, the three plates surmounted by classical arches flanked by scrolls

dripping waterfalls, with flowers and leaves to the sides; 58 in. (147 cm) wide.

Pier glasses

D 1 A William III period mirror, with red églomisé borders decorated in gold and silver, with frame and crest of églomisé panels in the Renaissance style, 1695–1700.

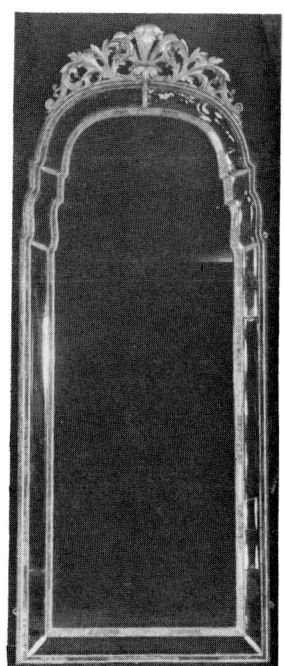

E 2 A William and Mary gesso looking glass, with bevelled and faceted border, surmounted by a cartouche of acanthus and scrolls; 87 in. high by 35 in. wide (220 by 88 cm).

E 3 A Queen Anne giltwood framed pier glass, with arched divided bevelled plate; 65 in. high, 29 in. wide (165 by 73 cm).

E 4 A Queen Anne giltwood pier glass, with carved frame; 55 in. high by 26 in. wide (139 by 66 cm).

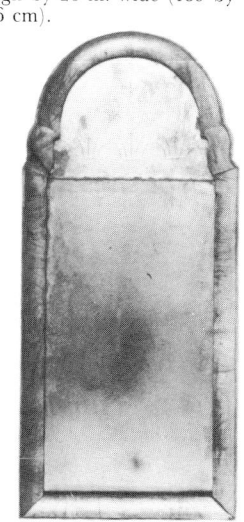

E 5 A Queen Anne walnut mirror, with engraved top section, 1710-1725; 37 in. high by 17 in. wide (93 by 43 cm).

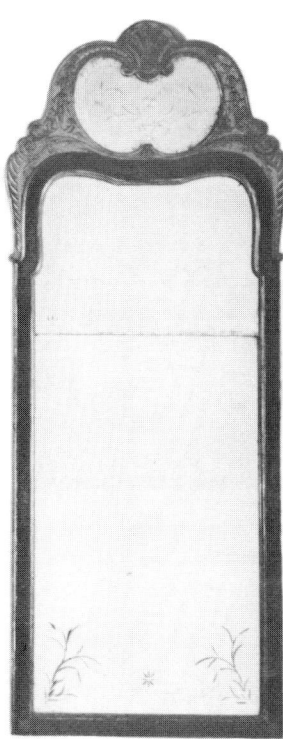

E 6 A Queen Anne gilt-gesso and black lacquer pier glass, with arched divided bevelled plate, in broad frame decorated with gilt flowers; 60 in. high by 23 in. wide (152 by 63 cm).

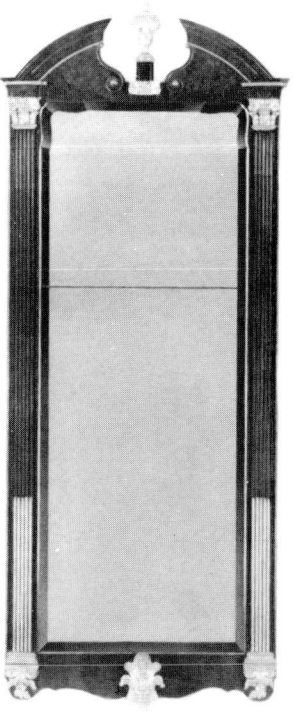

E 7 A George I walnut pier mirror, with gilt enrichments, *c*. 1720; 84 in. high by 34 in. wide (213 by 86 cm).

E 8 A George I gilt-gesso pier glass, with bevelled-plate in narrow frame, moulded with foliage; 49 in. high by 21 in. wide (117 by 53 cm).

C 9 A George I giltwood pier mirror, in the manner of John Belchier, *c*. 1725; 80 in. (120 cm) high.

C 10 A fine early Georgian gilt mirror, of architectural form, the sides carved with pendent husks, *c*. 1735; 50 in. (127 cm) high.

E 1 A George II giltwood pier glass, with an arched, slightly bevelled plate, in a gadrooned frame, with pierced and moulded cresting, second quarter 18th century; 62 in. high by 21 in. wide (158 by 54 cm).

E 2 A George II walnut and parcel-gilt pier glass, with arched plate divided by a band of fruiting and flowering foliage, the frame edged with egg-and-dart ornament, the scrolled base centred by an applied cabochon cartouche, 68 in. high by 31 in. wide (172 by 78 cm).

E 3 A George III Carton Pierre mirror, with shaped oval plate, in moulded and pierced frame, 59 in. high by 35 in. wide (149 by 89 cm).

D 4 A George III giltwood pier glass, attributed to Francis and John Booker of Dublin, *c.* 1765; 72 in. high by 46 in. wide (182 by 116 cm).

D 5 A George III giltwood pier glass, with bevelled plate in sectional mirrored borders, with a C-scrolled cartouche cresting, 98 in. high by 46 in. wide (249 by 117 cm).

E 6 A George III giltwood pier glass, *c.* 1760; 70 in. high by 34 in. wide (178 by 88 cm).

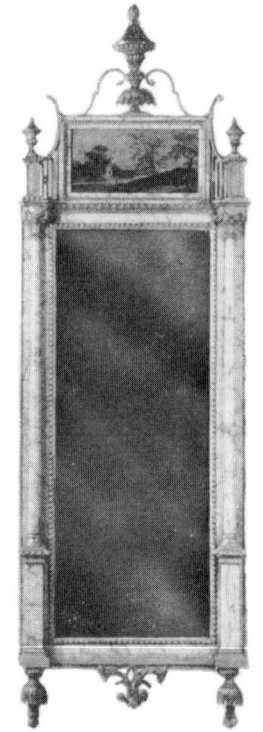

E 7 A George III pier glass in a marble and carved wood gilded frame incorporating a painted panel beneath the crest, *c.* 1785.

E 8 A Sheraton carved and gilded overmantel mirror, *c.* 1800; 41 in. by 33 in. (104 by 83 cm).

E 9 A Regency giltwood pier glass, with bevelled plate, 69 in. (175 cm) high.

E 10 A Regency giltwood pier glass, *c.* 1805; 46 in. high by 21 in. wide (116 by 53 cm).

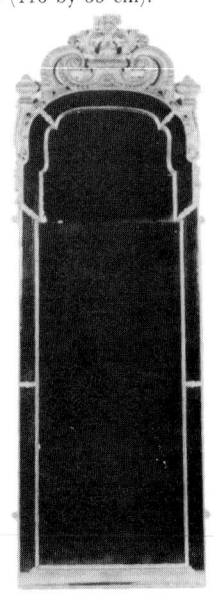

E 11 A George I style giltwood pier mirror, with arched divided plate, 79 in. (200 cm) high.

E1 A giltwood and gesso pier glass, in Chippendale style, late 19th century; 83 in. high by 24 in. wide (211 by 60 cm).

Dressing mirrors

E2 A Stuart embroidered frame mirror, *c.* 1660; 26 in. high by 20 in. wide (66 by 55 cm).

E3 An English silver repoussé work framed toilet mirror, *c.* 1660.

E4 An English repoussé silver frame for toilet mirror, showing London hallmark of 1683-1684.

E5 A Queen Anne verre églomisé mirror, 22 in. high by 19 in. wide (55 by 48 cm).

E6 A Queen Anne black japanned toilet mirror, *c.* 1700; 38 in. high by 21 in. wide (96 by 53 cm).

E7 A Queen Anne green and gold lacquer toilet mirror, 15 in. (38 cm) wide.

E8 A George I walnut and parcel-gilt toilet mirror, with arched bevelled plate, in foliate slip, 19 in. (48 cm) wide.

E9 A George II scarlet japanned toilet mirror, with serpantine-fronted base, *c.* 1740; 27 in. high by 20 in. wide (68 by 50 cm).

E10 An early Georgian walnut framed bevelled toilet mirror, with three drawers in box base, plate 19 in. high by 11 in. wide (48 by 27 cm).

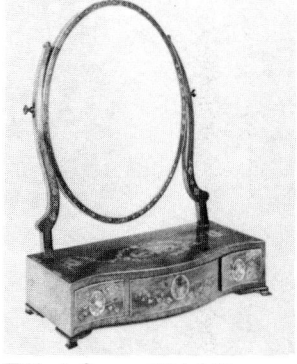

E11 A George III inlaid mahogany dressing glass, late 18th century; 26 in. (66 cm) high.

E12 A mahogany and boxwood strung serpentine-front dressing-table mirror, on bracket feet.

E13 A George III mahogany and satinwood inlaid oval framed toilet mirror, *c.* 1800; 16 in. (41 cm) wide.

E14 A George III mahogany shield-shaped cheval toilet mirror.

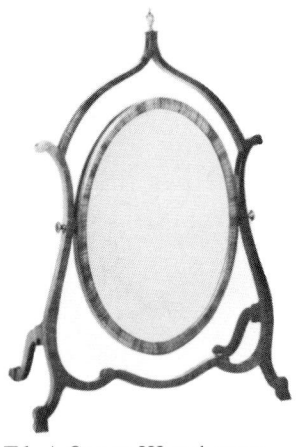

E1 A George III mahogany crossbanded "skeleton" toilet mirror, *c.* 1780; 28 in. high by 22 in. wide (71 by 56 cm).

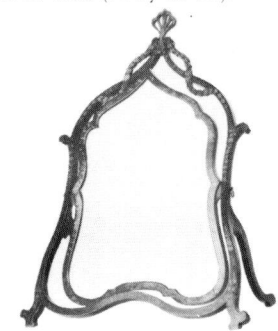

E2 A George III black japanned toilet mirror, the plate of inverted heart shape, *c.* 1770; 29 in. high by 22 in. wide (75 by 56 cm).

E3 A William IV mahogany dressing table mirror, the glass plate outlined with ebonized banding, *c.* 1830; 26 in. (66 cm) wide.

E4 A Victorian mahogany toilet mirror with three drawers, *c.* 1870; 29 in. (73 cm) wide.

E5 A satinwood and tulipwood cheval mirror, second quarter 19th century; 71 in. high by 39 in. wide (180 by 99 cm).

Wall mirrors

E6 A Charles II giltwood wall mirror, the bevelled plate enclosed by a hollow cushion carved frame, 54 in. high by 35 in. wide (137 by 89 cm).

E7 A Charles II black and gold lacquer mirror, with bevelled plate in convex frame, decorated in raised gilt; 62 in. high by 38 in. wide (157 by 98 cm).

E8 A William and Mary oyster veneered walnut mirror, with bevelled rectangular plate and moulded frame; 38 in. high by 32 in. wide (96 by 81 cm).

D9 A William and Mary walnut mirror, with fret cresting, with finely matched veneer to form geometrical designs; 56 in. high by 36 in. wide (142 by 91 cm).

E10 A William and Mary period marquetry mirror, on a ground-work of walnut veneer.

D11 A William III period mirror, with frame in marquetry and carved cresting, attributed to J.M. Botibol.

C12 A stained pine mirror, with bevelled plate, the border carved with overlapping laurel foliage, the shaped frame richly pierced and carved, late 17th century; 88 in. high by 65 in. wide (225 by 166 cm).

C13 A finely carved mirror frame, in the style of Grinling Gibbons, the densely filled border incorporating flowers, fruit, birds, military trophies and amorini supporting a crown, *c.* 1685.

E1 A Renaissance-style mirror of the baroque period, with the large scrolls characteristic of Italian workmanship.

A2 A carved limewood mirror frame, attributed to Grinling Gibbons, 17th century.

D3 A mirror, decorated with hammered and pierced silver scrollwork, the frame and mouldings in ebony, *c.* 1850.

E4 A Queen Anne walnut mirror, with two scrolled candle branches; 24 in. high by 18 in. wide (60 by 45 cm).

E5 A Georgian mirror, with arched divided plate, the upper part engraved, in narrow giltwood frame; 54 in. high by 24 in. wide (137 by 61 cm).

D6 An early Georgian giltgesso mirror; 54 in. high by 28 in. wide (137 by 71 cm).

E7 An early 18th century gesso silvered looking glass, *c.* 1730; 39 in. high by 22 in. wide (99 by 55 cm).

D8 A George I mirror, the bevelled plate within a leaf-carved parcel-gilt and walnut frame, *c.* 1720; 49 in. high by 25 in. wide (124 by 63 cm).

D9 A George II parcel-gilt and mahogany wall mirror, with swan-neck carved cresting.

E10 A George II parcel-gilt walnut mirror, second quarter 18th century; 57 in. (144 cm) high.

E11 A George II gilded gesso and carved looking glass, *c.* 1750; 52 in. (132 cm) high.

E12 A George II giltwood mirror, with ornately carved frame; 64 in. high by 33 in. wide (162 by 83 cm).

E13 A George II rococo giltwood wall mirror, *c.* 1750; 60 in. high by 35 in. wide (153 by 89 cm).

E1 A George II giltwood wall mirror, *c.* 1755; 46 in. high by 26 in. wide (117 by 67 cm).

E2 A George II carved giltwood wall mirror, 50 in. high by 37 in. wide (127 by 94 cm).

E3 A Chippendale carved wood and gilt mirror; 45 in. high, 26 in. wide (114 by 66 cm).

D4 A George II giltwood wall mirror, 70 in. high by 46 in. wide (177 by 116 cm).

D5 A Chippendale mirror, with deep carving, 66 in. high by 33 in. wide (167 by 83cm).

C7 A pair of carved Chippendale mirrors, in pine, painted grey; 79 in. high by 42 in. wide (200 by 106 cm).

C8 A Chippendale carved and gilt mirror, 87 in. high by 52 in. wide (220 by 132 cm).

E6 A carved wood and gilt mirror frame, with C-scrolls, flowerheads and formal column borders showing Florentine influence, mid 18th century; 42 in. high by 26 in. wide (106 by 66 cm).

C9 An early George III period carved wood and gilt mirror, with glass borders and stylized foliate frame.

E10 A fine carved wood and gilt mirror frame, in the rococo style.

C11 A Chinese Chippendale mirror, surmounted by a pagoda, with a waterfall, *c.* 1755.

D12 A George III giltwood mirror, 58 in. high by 29 in. wide (147 by 75 cm).

D 1 A small George III oval giltwood mirror, with pierced cartouche apron and larger cartouche cresting; 41 in. high, 23 in. wide (104 by 59 cm).

D 4 A Chippendale carved and giltwood mirror, with fine carving, *c.* 1760; 52 in. high by 36 in. wide (132 by 91 cm).

E 7 A George III giltwood mirror, the plate in narrow moulded border, the frame pierced and carved, 56 in. high by 29 in. wide (142 by 75 cm).

E 10 A Chippendale walnut veneer and parcel-gilt mirror, 1750–1780; 55 in. high by 27 in. wide (139 by 68 cm).

E 2 A carved wood and gilt mirror frame, formed as two stylized branches, joined at the base with a bow, *c.* 1760.

D 5 An elaborately carved wood and gilt mirror frame, the C-scrolls headed at the top corners with birds, flanking a central foliate crest, *c.* 1770; 50 in. high by 30 in. wide (127 by 76 cm).

E 8 An early George III carved giltwood looking glass, with shaped plate, *c.* 1760; 39 in. high by 27 in. wide (99 by 68 cm).

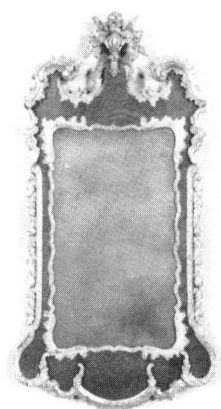

D 11 A Chippendale carved and gilt walnut veneer mirror, 1760–1790; 52 in. high by 28 in. wide (132 by 71 cm).

D 3 A Chippendale oval wall mirror, with fine carving and gilding, *c.* 1765; 52 in. high by 31 in. wide (132 by 78 cm).

C 6 An early George III period carved wood and gilt mirror, in the Chinese Chippendale manner, *c.* 1760.

D 9 A George III giltwood mirror, framed with colonettes, with acanthus cresting, *c.* 1765; 42 in. (107 cm) high.

E 12 A Chippendale mahogany and gilt mirror, 1750–1780; 29 in. high by 17 in. wide (73 by 43 cm).

D 1 A George III giltwood mirror, with oval plate; 54 in. high by 34 in. wide (138 by 88 cm).

E 2 A George III oval giltwood wall mirror, with wheatear cresting, *c.* 1775; 41 in. high, 17 in. wide (104 by 43 cm).

E 3 An Adam mirror, in pine frame, wax polished, with high-quality carving; 61 in. (154 cm) high (overall).

E 4 An Adam oval giltwood mirror with an urn crest, *c.* 1775; 36 in. high by 19 in. wide (91 by 48 cm).

E 5 A carved and gilt framed mirror, probably designed by Adam.

E 6 A George III giltwood mirror, with mirrored borders divided by a band of ribbon twist; 60 in. high by 43 in. wide (152 by 109 cm).

E 7 A painted carved wood mirror incorporating a barometer and a thermometer beneath the ribbon crest, 18th century; 59 in. (149 cm) high.

E 8 A Regency giltwood mirror, with ebonized slip and ball-encrusted frame, with an eagle cresting; 41 in. high by 25 in. wide (104 by 63 cm).

E 9 A Regency giltwood convex mirror, the frame with gadrooned edge, *c.* 1825; 66 in. (167 cm) high.

E 10 A Regency giltwood convex mirror, with candle branches; 37 in. by 28 in. (93 by 71 cm).

E 11 A Regency giltwood circular convex mirror, with ebonized slip surrounded by ropework; 25 in. (63 cm) in diameter.

E 12 A giltwood and gesso convex girandole, with tall eagle cresting, early 19th century.

E 13 A Regency giltwood mirror, with ebonized dragon cresting; 64 in. by 35 in. (162 by 88 cm).

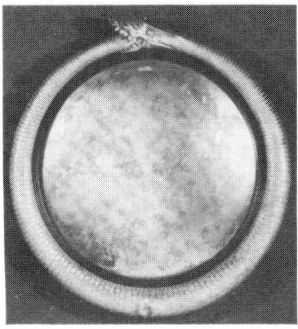

E1 A Regency convex mirror, with ebonized slip and scaly serpent frame, with serpent head cresting biting its tail; 27 in. by 26 in. (68 by 66 cm).

E2 A Regency giltwood mirror, with ebonized reed slip, ball-encrusted frame with shell base and displayed eagle cresting, framed by anthemion scrolls; 70 in. high by 43 in. wide (177 by 109 cm).

E3 A Regency giltwood bull's eye mirror, with moulded beaded border carved with leaf tips, surmounted by an ebonized eagle suspending a ball on fluted filial, early 19th century; 27 in. (69 cm) high.

E4 A Regency convex mirror, with moulded ebonized and parcel gilt frames, decorated with acanthus leaves; 48 in. high by 25 in. diameter (121 by 63 cm).

E5 A Regency ebonized and giltwood convex mirror, the moulded frame set with balls, with serpent candle-arms, *c.* 1805; 44 in. high by 33 in. wide (112 by 84 cm).

E6 A George IV giltwood mirror, with ebonized reeded inner border and outer border set with balls, with an eagle cresting, *c.* 1820; 29 in. (73 cm) high.

E7 A giltwood and plaster mirror, the divided plate with an elaborate waisted rococo frame of acanthus, C-scrolls and flowerheads, *c.* 1840; 52 in. high by 40 in. wide (132 by 101 cm).

E8 A carved giltwood and gesso girandole, in Régence style, mid 19th century; 50 in. high by 34 in. wide (127 by 86 cm).

E9 A "George II" parcel-gilt walnut mirror, with an arched cresting centred by an eagle, *c.* 1880; 47 in. high by 23 in. wide (120 by 58 cm).

Mirrors and Mirror-Making

In 1740 the tax on plate glass, repealed in 1699, was re-enacted. Mirror plate became very expensive again – the glass being worth more than the frame – and it is from this time that the superstition attached to breaking mirrors dates.

While convex mirrors from the mid-18th century are recorded, it was not until the 1790s that the large bull's eye contained within a deeply moulded and gilded frame surmounted by an eagle became the most popular wallpiece. So popular were they during this period however that they are the only kind of looking glass to be mentioned by Sheraton under the heading of "Mirror" in his *Cabinet Dictionary* of 1803.

E10 A "George II" giltwood pier mirror, with a bevelled glass, 19th century; 62 in. high by 38 in. wide (157 by 96 cm).

E11 A carved giltwood looking glass, with shell cresting; flanked by birds, 19th century; 72 in. (183 cm) high.

SCREENS
1750-1890

Examples of pole screens dating from before the early 18th century are rare, for while they had been known much earlier, it was only during the early 1700s that they were made in really large numbers to supply a sizeable increase in demand.

The publication of numerous designs for floral displays after the 1740s supplied the patterns for the needlework banners that still survive–and are valued accordingly–on mid-century examples.

E1 A Chippendale pole screen, with contemporary panel of petit point needlework.

E2 A Chippendale-style mahogany pole screen, inset with a tapestry panel; 58 in. (147 cm) high.

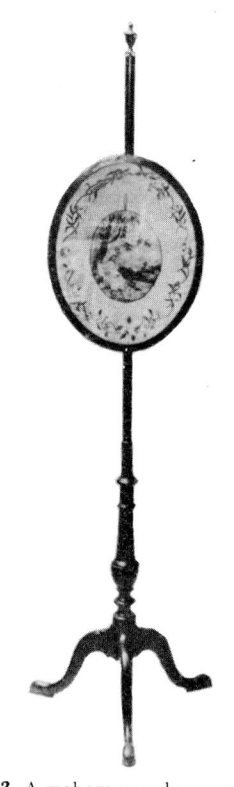

E3 A mahogany pole screen, of George III period, with finely turned finial.

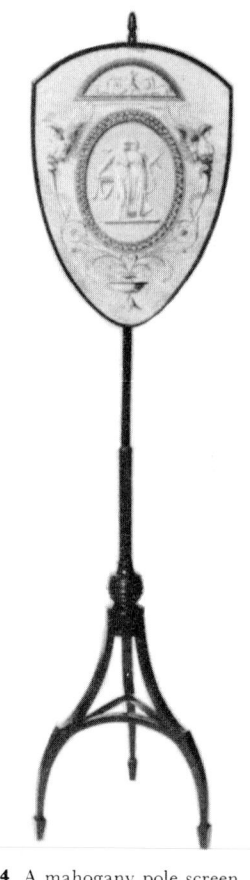

E4 A mahogany pole screen, with Adam design painted on silk, c. 1790; 55 in. (139 cm) high.

E5 A pole screen, with an oval cut scroll paper panel, centred by a silk picture of a young girl, contained by a japanned and parcel-gilt frame, on an adjustable mahogany stem and downswept supports, on ball feet, 18th century; 61 in. (156 cm) high.

E6 An early George III period mahogany folding screen, the lower part open below pierced fretwork panels, on finely turned legs, c. 1760; 45 in. (114 cm). This pattern was popular for occasional furniture.

E7 A late Regency rosewood pole screen, of banner form, c. 1830; 56 in. (142 cm) high.

E8 A rosewood firescreen, with a bright polychrome raised plush and wool worked panel, c. 1850; 44 in. high by 23 in. wide (112 by 59 cm).

E9 A Victorian giltwood firescreen, in the manner of A.W.N. Pugin, embroidered; 32 in. (81 cm) wide.

SETTEES & SOFAS
1750-1910

The 18th-century sofa and settee were natural evolutions from the settle. There were two main developments: the fully upholstered, sumptuous long seat with carved show wood frame; and the upholstered seat with open-work back and arms, designed as two or more joined chair backs.

The alteration or later construction of a chairback settee is usually disguised with carving applied at the joins.

D 3 A fine George II period mahogany show-wood frame settee, of double chair form, the back formed as a large cartouche over upholstered seat, with carved and scrolled rails and cabriole legs to the front and back, *c.* 1745; 55 in. (140 cm) wide.

E 4 A Chippendale period mahogany settee, of double chair form, the upswept back rail and pierced splats joined by a single central stile, the cabriole legs carved at the knee and foot below a stuff-over seat; 51 in. (129 cm) wide.

D 1 A George II padouk chairback settee, with waved toprail carved with acanthus, suspending bellflowers above three baluster-shaped splats carved with voluted acanthus, the drop-in seat on cabriole legs carved with lions' heads, scrolled acanthus and lions' paw feet, upholstered in cream herringbone wool, mid 18th century; 66 in. (167 cm) wide.

D 5 A Chippendale triple-back settee, the back, arms, frame, legs and underties all elaborately carved, with old needlework seat.

D 6 An early George III mahogany settee, with upholstered back in a triple serpentine moulded and carved frame with padded arms, the upholstered seat with triple serpentine carved seat rail, on carved cabriole legs, *c.* 1765; 93 in. (236 cm) wide.

D 2 An early Chippendale period settee, the show-wood walnut frame finely carved in the high-style rococo manner, *c.* 1745; 65 in. (167 cm) wide.

D 7 An early George III mahogany triple chairback settee, the chairbacks each with serpentine crest centring a ruffled shell, over a carved and pierced splat flanked by serpentine stiles, late 18th century; 38 in. high by 70 in. wide (96 by 177 cm).

D 1 A finely carved Chippendale double chairback settee, with moulded and carved toprail, with dished arms overhanging the ogee supports, carved with a scroll at the end, the severe front seat rail over square chamfered legs with curved corner brackets, *c.* 1760; 43 in. (109 cm) wide.

D 4 An early George III mahogany settee, of rare small size, the serpentine swept back continuing into the scrolling arms, the legs joined by a single H-stretcher; 49 in. (124 cm) wide.

D 2 A George III carved mahogany double chairback settee, with double serpentine crest over a pierced strapwork splat, the shaped arms with scrolled grips, on Marlborough legs with blind Gothic fretwork, *c.* 1780; 62 in. (157 cm) wide.

D 5 A fine open-arm settee, of double Gainsborough form, with legs and H-stretcher carved and pierced in the Chinese Gothic manner, on original leather casters, *c.* 1765; 36 in. high by 55 in. wide (91 by 139 cm).

D 3 An early George III mahogany double chairback settee, with scrolling toprail over two pierced, carved splats and scrolling arms, with upholstered seat and square tapering legs joined by stretchers, mid 18th century; 54 in. (137 cm) wide.

D 6 A fine scroll-end settee of large size, *c.* 1770; the four front legs moulded in serpentine section, the stretchers plain, with contemporary upholstery; it is 84 in. (213 cm) wide.

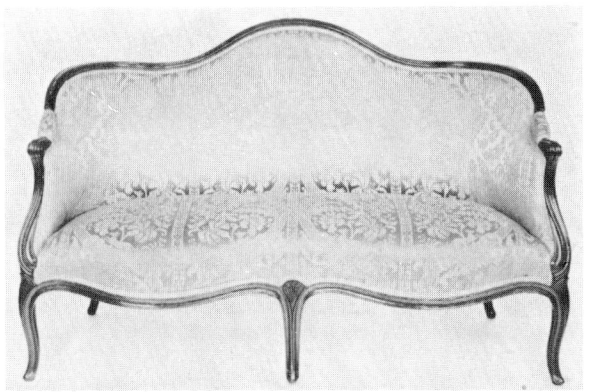

E1 A George III mahogany settee in the French manner, with curved arched padded back and upholstered serpentine seat in moulded frame, downcurved arms with C-scrolls, on cabriole legs headed by spreading flutes, late 18th century; 59 in. (147 cm) wide.

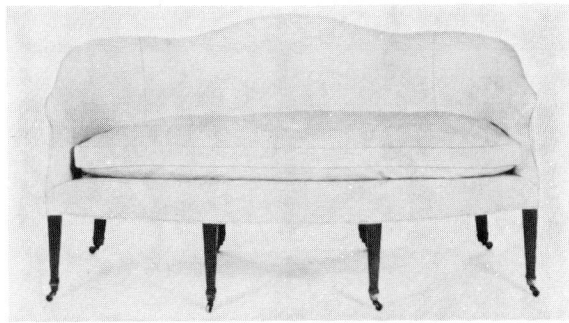

E2 A George III mahogany sofa, with arched U-shaped padded back and bowed upholstered seat, on square tapering legs, on block feet with casters, upholstered in yellow repp, late 18th century; 69 in. (175 cm) wide.

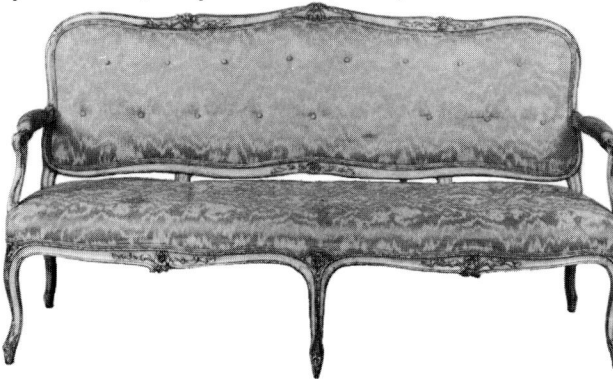

D3 A George III painted and parcel-gilt canapé, in the French manner, the moulded serpentine back carved with summer flowers, with moulded padded arms raised on cabriole legs, c. 1770; 78 in. (198 cm) wide.

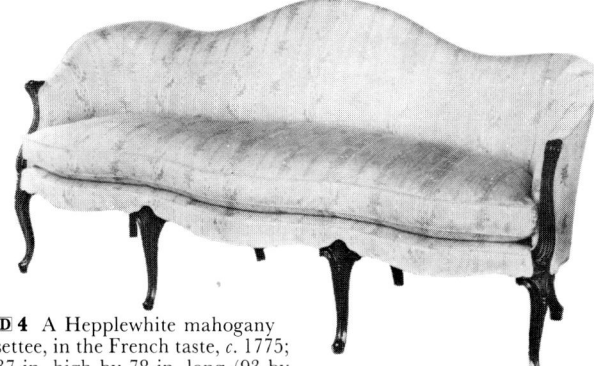

D4 A Hepplewhite mahogany settee, in the French taste, c. 1775; 37 in. high by 78 in. long (93 by 198 cm).

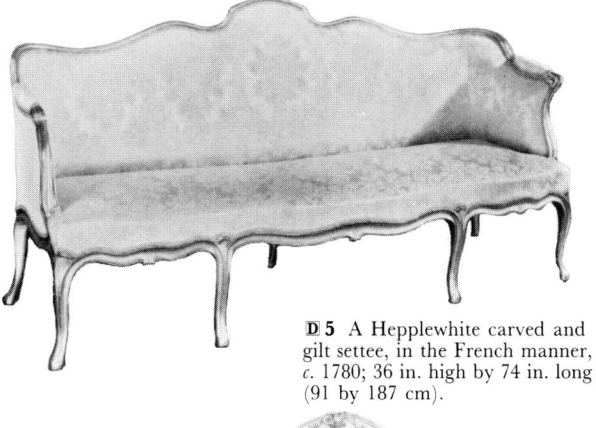

D5 A Hepplewhite carved and gilt settee, in the French manner, c. 1780; 36 in. high by 74 in. long (91 by 187 cm).

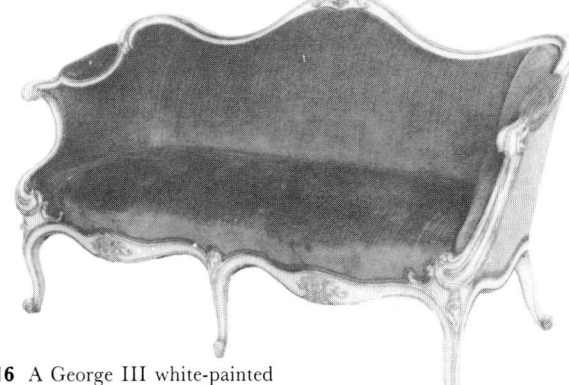

E6 A George III white-painted and gilded sofa; 69 in. (175 cm) wide.

E7 A George III cream and blue painted sofa, the bowed shaped back with fluted frame, the arms with husk carved supports, on square tapered legs, c. 1780; 60 in. (153 cm) wide.

E8 A Hepplewhite period eight-legged settee, in the French style, the curvilinear back upholstered and terminating with show-wood arm supports, on tapered legs.

E1 A George III mahogany humpback sofa, with detached scrolled foliate arm supports, and serpentine seat rail carved with entrelacs; 68 in. (172 cm) wide.

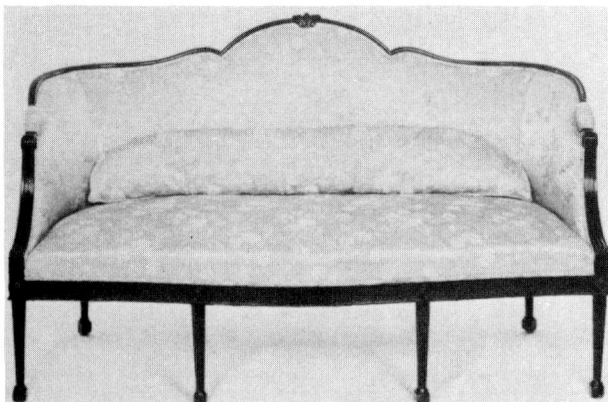

E2 An early George III mahogany sofa, with coved upholstered back in shaped moulded frame, with padded arms, late 18th century; 68 in. (173 cm) wide.

E3 An Adam carved gilt settee, covered in pale terra-cotta and green silk brocade; 37 in. high by 84 in. long (93 by 213 cm).

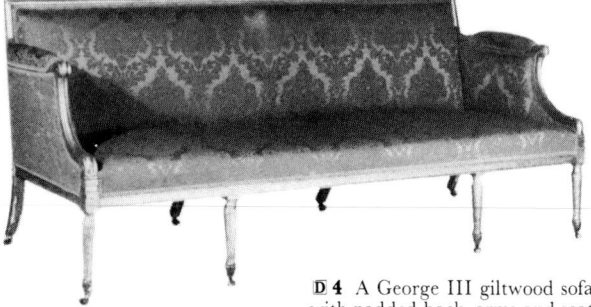

D4 A George III giltwood sofa, with padded back, arms and seat; 84 in. (213 cm) wide.

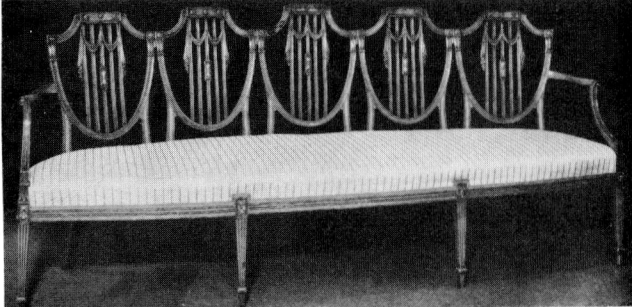

D5 A Sheraton-style carved and painted satinwood chairback settee, each back containing realistically executed drapery below entablatures, painted with classical scenes, 88 in. (224 cm) wide.

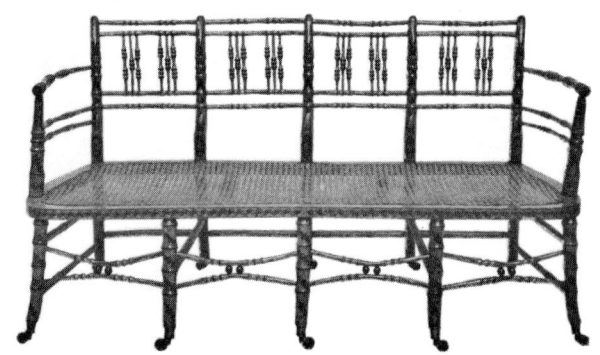

E6 A turned wood settee, with four connected chairbacks, carved seat and turned, tapered legs joined by double bow-and-ball stretchers, late 18th century; 62 in. (157 cm) wide. This settee is painted and decorated, in common with other furniture in this style.

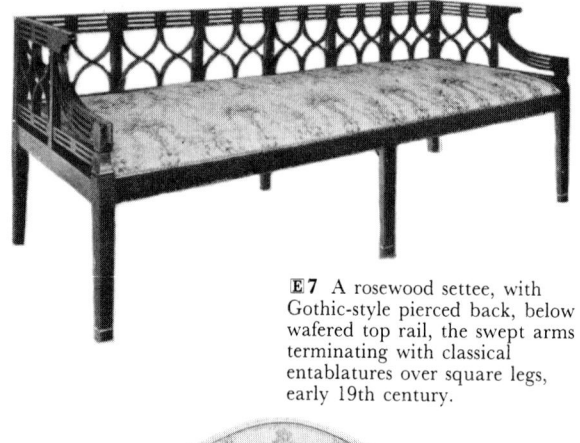

E7 A rosewood settee, with Gothic-style pierced back, below wafered top rail, the swept arms terminating with classical entablatures over square legs, early 19th century.

E8 An Adam sofa, with scroll ends and fluted tapering legs, carved with rosettes with painted green foliage and red lines on a white ground.

E1 A George III mahogany hall settee, with scrolled panelled back mounted with three copper ovals, painted with coat-of-arms and crests, solid panelled seat; 75 in. (190 cm) long.

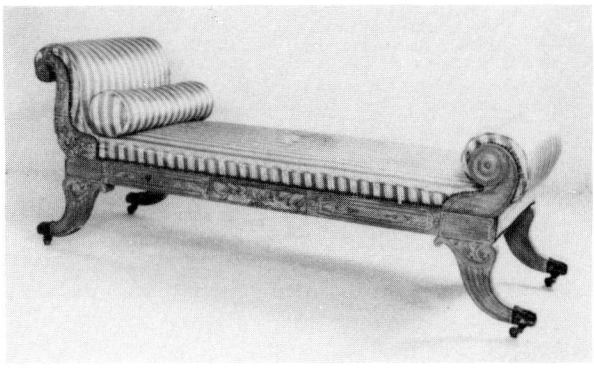

E5 A late Regency period rosewood framed chaise longue, in classical style, with curved legs further carved to represent cornucopiae, terminating in cast foliate casters, with upholstery in green and cream striped brocade.

E2 A Regency ebonized and gilded three-seat settee, in the manner of Thomas Sheraton, with shaped painted top rail; 77 in. (195 cm) wide.

E6 A mid-Regency period beech framed sofa, in the classical style, decorated with ebonized finish and gilded details, with short Grecian curved legs terminating in square-toe casters; 83 in. (211 cm) wide.

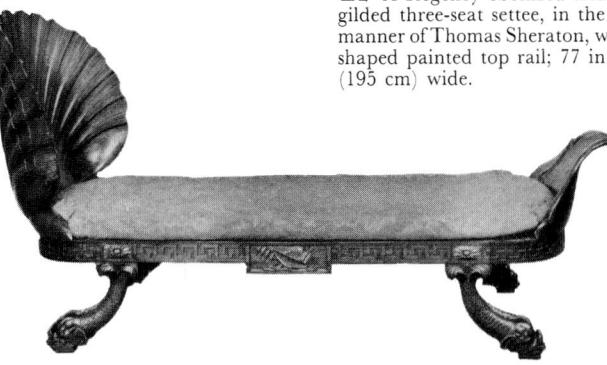

E3 A Regency period couch, in carved mahogany supported on dolphins, the carved plaques at the sides portraying a globe, anchor, boarding-pike and other objects of naval interest.

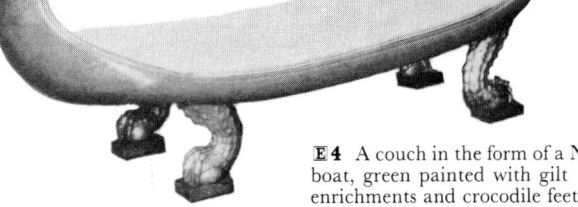

E4 A couch in the form of a Nile boat, green painted with gilt enrichments and crocodile feet, of Egyptian style, 1800-1810.

E7 A Regency cream painted simulated bamboo sofa, with ring-turned bar splats and conforming arm supports on slightly tapering legs, with raffia seat.

E1 A Regency painted beech caned settee, with outscrolled top rail set with four caned panels, and caned seat, early 19th century; 57 in. (144 cm) wide.

E2 A Regency mahogany sofa, with shaped padded back carved with scrolled acanthus, with upholstered seat, early 19th century; 80 in. (203 cm) wide.

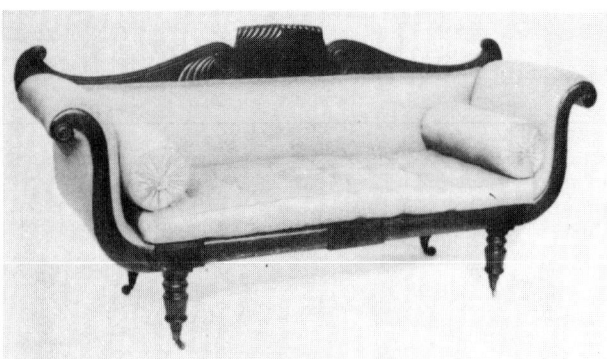

E3 A late Regency boat-shaped scroll end settee, with mahogany frame, the top rail extensively carved, on bulky turned legs; 78 in. (198 cm) wide.

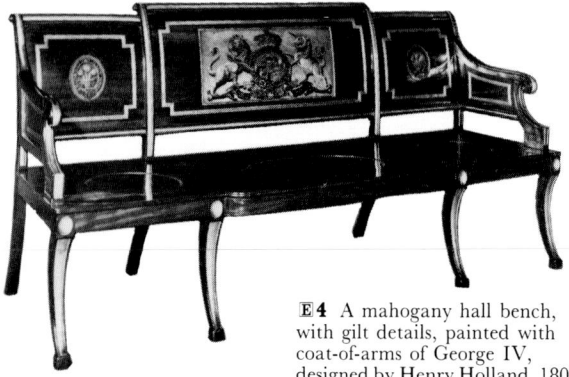

E4 A mahogany hall bench, with gilt details, painted with coat-of-arms of George IV, designed by Henry Holland, 1802.

E5 A Victorian carved walnut and button upholstered triple chairback serpentine-fronted settee, with carved top rails and padded arms, on cabriole legs with ceramic casters, *c.* 1850; 67 in. (170 cm) wide.

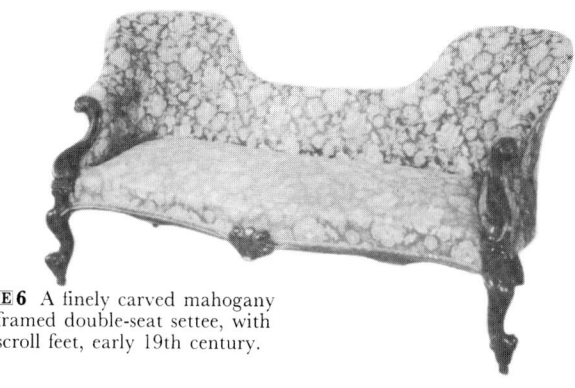

E6 A finely carved mahogany framed double-seat settee, with scroll feet, early 19th century.

E7 A Victorian settee, with carved walnut frame, the oval back and curved sides on leaf-carved squat cabriole legs; 74 in. (187 cm) wide.

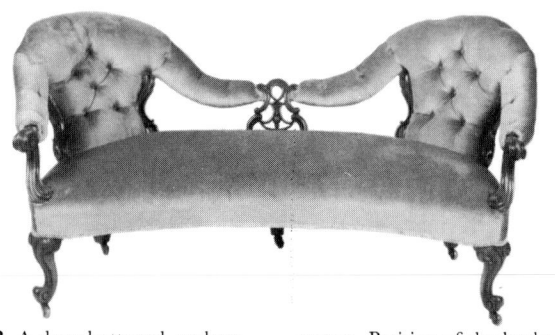

E8 A deep-buttoned, walnut show-wood double-back settee, with cabriole legs terminating in scrolls and brown porcelain casters. Position of the backs indicates its use as a conversation seat.

E1 A walnut chaise à méridienne, with green buttoned scroll back and end, plain padded seat on a serpentine rail and cabriole supports, third quarter 19th century; 70 in. (178 cm) wide.

E2 A walnut chaise longue, with moulded frame, the top rail centred by a leaf cartouche, raised on moulded cabriole legs, mid 19th century.

E3 A walnut double chairback settee, the shaped backs with moulded frames, centred by a circular upholstered panel, with upholstered seat, *c.* 1850; 69 in. (175cm) wide.

E4 A mahogany settee, with arched upholstered back, carved moulded frame, the upholstered seat with serpentine front, *c.* 1855; 77 in. (195 cm) long.

E5 A walnut settee, with central padded cartouche shaped back, flanked by ornate carving, with outscrolled arms, and sprung serpentine seat on carved cabriole legs, 1850s; 75 in. (190 cm) wide.

E6 A mid-Victorian walnut serpentine-front settee, with arched moulded frame, outscrolled arms and padded back, the upholstered seat on carved scroll legs.

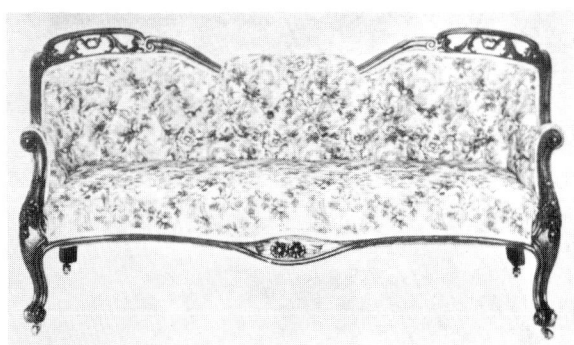

E7 A Victorian walnut framed settee, with buttoned back and moulded carved top rail, outscrolled arms, with serpentine front and upholstered seat; 62 in. (157 cm) wide.

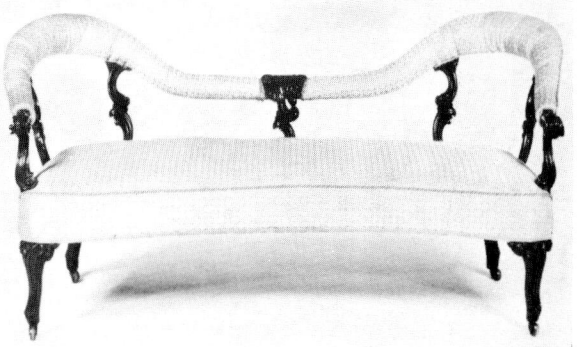

E8 A carved oak and walnut sofa, with padded top rail on carved supports, upholstered seat, on carved legs with casters, *c.* 1860; 64 in. (163 cm) long.

E1 A walnut chaise longue, one end with a waisted padded buttoned back flanked by pierced leaf-carved sides, the other with a padded buttoned overscrolled end, joined by a pierced and carved scrolling back, the sprung seat with serpentine front, on moulded cabriole legs, *c.* 1860; 70 in. (178 cm) wide.

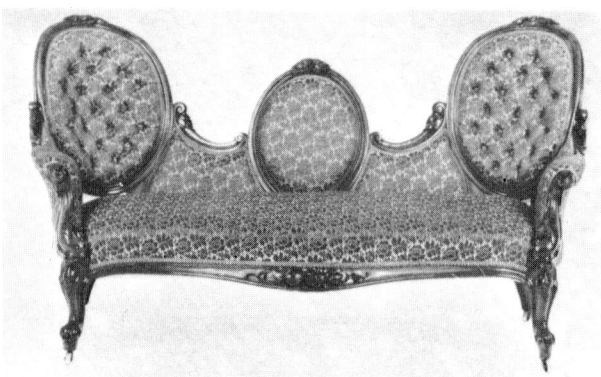

E2 A walnut show-wood frame triple-back settee, carved at the centres of the toprails and frieze to the seat with deeply undercut foliate ornaments, *c.* 1860; 70 in. (178 cm) wide.

E3 A Victorian mahogany show-wood frame settee, with cartouche-shaped back set well up from the seat, with serpentine front, on moulded cabriole supports, late 19th century; 52 in. (132 cm) wide.

E4 A walnut chaise longue, with arched carved moulded top rail and one end overscrolled, serpentine front, *c.* 1860.

E5 A rosewood sofa, in the rococo style, the padded back with shaped and scrolled cresting pierced and carved, the padded arms with foliate supports, *c.* 1840; 52 in. high by 89 in. wide (133 by 227 cm).

E6 A Victorian Chippendale mahogany settee, the triple chair back of ribbon back design, with carved arms and cabriole legs ending in claw-and-ball feet; 68 in. (172 cm) wide.

E7 *(right)* A mahogany framed George I-style settee, the high back framed with cresting rail of double serpentine form, with curved wings and curved open arms, upholstered in tapestry-style material, on cabriole legs, 19th century; 56 in. (142 cm) wide.

E8 A giltwood sofa, in the French Louis XVI style, stamped Gillow, with buttoned back surrounded by moulded carved frame, separate buttoned seat, padded arms, *c.* 1860; 64 in. (164 cm) long.

E9 An oak settee, by Thomas Tweedy, carved with Man Friday and Crusoe, padded back and arms, with upholstered seat and shaped seat rail, *c.* 1862; 91 in. (231 cm) wide.

E10 An Edwardian Art Nouveau mahogany settle, *c.* 1910; 56 in. (143 cm) wide.

E11 An Adam-style painted satinwood settee, with two elliptical panels, 19th century; 48 in. (121 cm) wide.

E12 A caned mahogany settee, the serpentine back and fluted top rail above a lower carved rail, with three oval wheel shaped splats set in cane, with double caned overscrolled arms, fluted serpentine seat rail, *c.* 1910; 82 in. (209 cm) wide.

SETTLES
1660-1860

The traditional settle with panelled back and either solid or rope-slung seat gave way in fashionable use to the more comfortable upholstered sofas and settees during the 18th century.

The settle in its customary form remained in use in taverns and cottages, but as a hall seat in large country houses its design altered as required to conform to the dictates of changing taste.

E1 A monks' bench or settle table, late 17th century. Most monks' benches are misnamed, dating from after the dissolution of the monasteries. More in use in farmhouses than convents.

E2 An oak settle, with carved and panelled back, and carved stretcher, late 17th century; 68 in. (172 cm) wide.

E3 An early oak settle, with panelled back and front, with three-section hinged seat; 78 in. (213 cm) wide.

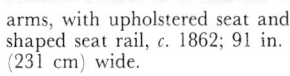

E4 *(left)* A finely carved oak settle, the panelled back with traditional lozenge and guilloche motifs, below a carved and moulded cornice, the solid seat with chip-carved front rail. Note the wear to the stretcher.

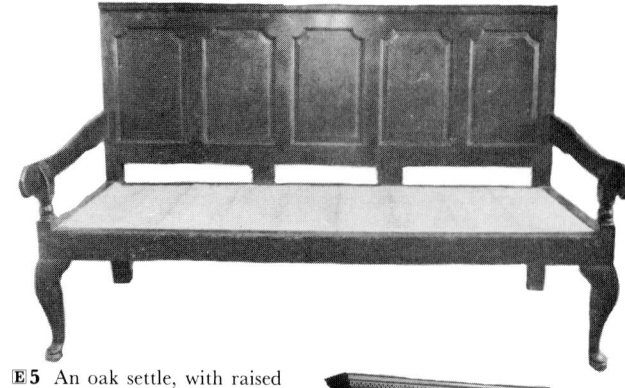

E5 An oak settle, with raised panelled back and shaped arms, on heavy cabriole legs, with pad feet, mid 18th century.

E1 An oak settle, with fine panelled back and contrasting simple joined seat and under-frame, late 17th century; 53 in. (134 cm) wide.

E2 An oak settle, with traditionally carved four-panel back, the open arms and wooden seat on turned front legs joined by stretchers, *c.* 1708.

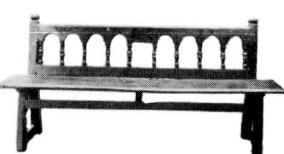

E3 An oak settle, the arcaded backrail supported on turned columns, over splay-form legs and central stretcher, early 18th century; 72 in. (182 cm).

E6 A mid-Georgian oak hall seat, the back with four fielded panels, with shaped arms on turned supports, over a strung seat; 73 in. (186 cm) wide.

E8 An oak bacon settle, with dentil pediment above cupboard with fielded panelled door, the armed seat above four drawers, the back and sides also in fielded panels, mid 18th century; 74 in. high by 37 in. wide (187 by 93 cm).

E4 A settle/bed, 71 in. (180 cm) wide, probably from the early 18th century, though simply made country pieces like this are difficult to date with precision.

E7 A George II settle, with fielded panels, *c.* 1750; 51 in. high by 75 in. wide (129 by 190 cm).

E9 An elm bacon settle, of curved shape, the back with a single cupboard below four short drawers, the solid seat with cupboard below, with shaped arms on turned supports, *c.* 1720. Settles combined with cupboards were popular in farmhouses; with ventilating holes to the upper panels, were used for food storage, hence the name "bacon settles".

SIDEBOARDS
1760-1890

The sideboard as we know it is a direct reflection of the new middle class prosperity of the later 18th century. Wealthy as the nouveau riche of the 1760s were, their houses were far smaller than those of the patricians they sought to emulate. The six-legged sideboard with a deep drawer at one end, a cupboard at the other and drawers between was the natural reduction of the serving table flanked by urn pedestals that graced the grandest dining rooms.

E1 A George III mahogany serpentine sideboard, with a drawer crossbanded with rosewood, flanked by cellaret drawers; 66 in. (167 cm) wide.

E2 A George III mahogany serpentine sideboard, with crossbanded top, inlaid with satinwood quadrant and oval fan medallions, *c.* 1775; 33 in. high by 53 in. wide (89 by 136 cm).

E4 A George III mahogany serpentine sideboard, with arched centre flanked by cellaret drawers, crossbanded with tulipwood and bordered with stained pollard-oak, on square tapering legs; 72 in. (183 cm) wide.

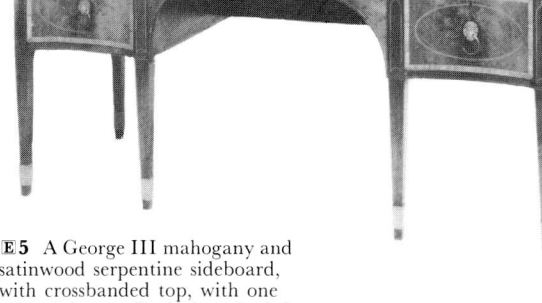

E5 A George III mahogany and satinwood serpentine sideboard, with crossbanded top, with one central drawer flanked to the left by two short drawers and to the right by a cellaret drawer; 76 in. (193 cm) wide.

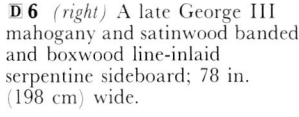

D6 *(right)* A late George III mahogany and satinwood banded and boxwood line-inlaid serpentine sideboard; 78 in. (198 cm) wide.

D8 A George III mahogany serpentine sideboard, of small size; 36 in. high by 60 in. wide (91 by 152 cm).

D9 A George III inlaid mahogany sideboard, with serpentine front and crossbanded and inlaid top, *c.* 1800; 52 in. (133 cm) wide.

E10 A serpentine sideboard; 67 in. wide, centre depth 29 in. (170 by 73 cm).

E11 A George III mahogany and inlaid serpentine sideboard, with crossbanded top, on square tapered legs; 73 in. (186 cm) wide.

E3 A George III mahogany sideboard, *c.* 1790; with inlaid splash-board, the conforming drawer to the bowed centre front flanked by deep drawers faced to simulate double drawers, all drawers crossbanded, on square-section tapering legs collared and with stringing; 72 in. (182 cm) wide.

E7 A George III mahogany sideboard, with bowed rectangular top, the conforming frieze with one long drawer flanked by two short satinwood crossbanded drawers, above a cupboard and a bottle drawer similarly veneered, on square tapering legs, late 18th century; 60 in. (154 cm) wide.

E1 A George III mahogany sideboard, with serpentine front and central drawer, *c.* 1780; 36 in. by 55 in. (92 by 140 cm).

D2 A Hepplewhite period sideboard, in finely figured mahogany, with serpentine front, crossbanded and inlaid, with central drawer, on square tapered legs; 72 in. (182 cm) wide.

D6 A Sheraton period mahogany bow-fronted sideboard, the top with rosewood crossband; 51 in. (129 cm) wide.

E9 A Sheraton period mahogany breakfront sideboard, with line inlay, the top banded in satinwood; 82 in. (208 cm) wide.

D3 A Sheraton sideboard, with highly figured veneers, accentuated with boxwood stringing and crossbanded inlays, the top with superstructure, with sliding panels in the front, surmounted by a brass rail, all on square tapered legs, *c.* 1800; 84 in. (213 cm) wide.

E7 A George III mahogany sideboard, crossbanded in tulipwood, with serpentine front, *c.* 1780; 74 in. (188 cm) wide.

E10 A George III mahogany serpentine sideboard, on square tapering legs; 37 in. high by 77 in. wide (93 by 195 cm).

E8 A George III mahogany serpentine-fronted sideboard, on square tapering legs; 38 in. high by 66 in. (96 by 167 cm).

E11 A mahogany sideboard, with serpentine front, the drawers crossbanded and with Sheffield plate handles, on square legs with block feet; 72 in. (182 cm) wide.

D4 A large mahogany sideboard, of serpentine shape, veneered with highly figured timber, contrasted with oval panels and fan marquetry of satinwood, the tapering legs, with collared feet, inlaid with pendent husks, 90 in. (228 cm) wide.

E12 A George III mahogany and kingwood crossbanded sideboard, of Sheraton design, decorated with fan medallions and boxwood stringing, *c.* 1800; 37 in. high by 70 in. wide (94 by 178 cm).

D5 A George III satinwood and mahogany sideboard, with crossbanded serpentine top, and two cellaret drawers; 78 in. (198 cm) wide.

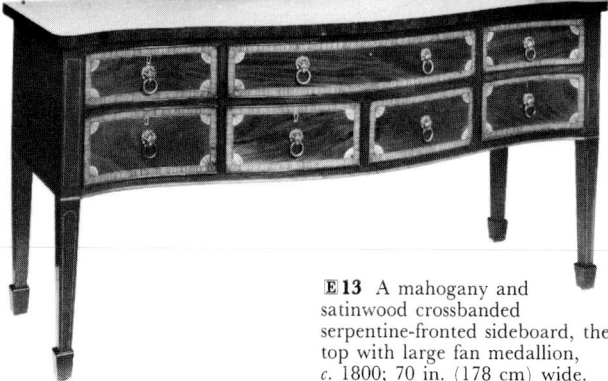

E13 A mahogany and satinwood crossbanded serpentine-fronted sideboard, the top with large fan medallion, *c.* 1800; 70 in. (178 cm) wide.

E1 A George III mahogany serpentine sideboard, c. 1785; 33 in. high by 42 in. wide (84 by 107 cm).

E2 A Georgian mahogany breakfront sideboard, the crossbanded top with ebony line inlay above a central drawer, flanked by a cellaret and two drawers; 34 in. high by 72 in. wide (86 by 183 cm).

E6 A Hepplewhite mahogany sideboard, with shaped serpentine front, c. 1785; 72 in. (182 cm) wide.

D7 A Hepplewhite period mahogany serpentine sideboard, with carved apron, on square legs with block feet; 71 in. (180 cm) wide.

Six-legged Sideboards
The most desirable type of six-legged sideboard dates from the 1770s and has square tapering legs supporting the main carcase of gently bow-fronted or serpentine form. In the machine age this model was supplanted by the turned leg variety, with breakfront, D-shape or bow-front carcase.

Early this century there was much demand for the earlier model and it was not unknown for turned legs to be replaced with square tapering. Also, early sideboards were generally of commodious depth–too much so for modern taste. As late as the 1950s it was still profitable to take a sideboard to pieces and reduce its depth–evidence of this is new joints to the backs of the drawers.

E3 A George III mahogany secretaire sideboard, with central fitted secretaire drawer, c. 1790; 36 in. high by 61 in. wide (91 by 155 cm).

D8 A George III mahogany serpentine sideboard, c. 1790; 32 in. by 42 in. (81 by 106 cm).

E11 A George III mahogany sideboard, with bowed front, late 18th century; 61 in. (155 cm) wide.

E12 A George III mahogany bow-front sideboard, inlaid with stringing, fitted with drawers and cupboards, 37 in. high by 72 in. wide (93 by 180 cm).

D4 A George III mahogany sideboard, the serpentine front with a flowerhead and scroll marquetry border, above a central bowed drawer, on square tapering legs with block feet, c. 1775; 36 in. high by 69 in. wide (92 by 176 cm).

D5 A George III mahogany serpentine sideboard, the crossbanded top inlaid with a rosewood line, fitted with a central drawer, 80 in. (203 cm) wide.

E9 A Sheraton mahogany bow-fronted sideboard, with fitted centre drawer, 18th century; 54 in. (137 cm) wide.

E10 A Sheraton design mahogany sideboard, having a brass gallery back, boxwood stringing, with two drawers and two side cupboards with revolving cellaret, on square tapering legs with spade feet; 96 in. (243 cm) wide.

E 1 A George III mahogany sweep-front sideboard, with kingwood crossbandings, boxwood and ebony stringing; 60 in. (152 cm) wide.

E 2 A Georgian mahogany bow-fronted sideboard, with crossbanded top and inlaid front; 60 in. (152 cm) wide.

E 3 A George III inlaid mahogany bow-front sideboard, crossbanded and inlaid, late 18th century; 55 in. (140 cm) wide.

E 4 A George III mahogany bow-front sideboard, late 18th century; 61 in. (155 cm) wide.

E 5 A George III mahogany sideboard, the bowed top inlaid; 54 in. (137 cm) wide.

E 6 A George III mahogany sideboard, with bowed top above a central frieze drawer, flanked by bottom drawers, late 18th century; 37 in. (94 cm) wide.

D 7 A George III mahogany small sideboard, with well figured bowed top crossbanded with rosewood; 47 in. (120 cm) wide.

E 8 A George III mahogany bow-front sideboard, the top crossbanded in satinwood, with central drawer flanked by cellaret drawers, 60 in. (152 cm).

E 9 A George III mahogany bow-fronted sideboard, crossbanded in kingwood, c. 1780; 36 in. high by 50 in. wide (92 by 128 cm).

E 10 A George II mahogany bow-front sideboard, fitted with a central cutler drawer; 65 in. (165 cm) wide.

E 11 A Sheraton mahogany bow-fronted sideboard, with central drawer above arched cupboard; 57 in. (144 cm) wide.

E 12 A George III mahogany bow-fronted sideboard, crossbanded in tulipwood, c. 1775; 54 in. wide, 26 in. deep (138 by 66 cm).

E 13 A George III mahogany bow-front sideboard, crossbanded in satinwood, c. 1790; 36 in. high by 60 in. wide (91 by 152 cm).

E 16 A Sheraton breakfront sideboard, of good deep colour, the drawer fronts with figured timber, on square tapered legs, c. 1790; 64 in. (163 cm) wide. The breakfront was a popular alternative at this time.

E 17 A mahogany straight-front sideboard, early 19th century. Small sideboards are extremely rare and may have been converted from dressing tables or reduced from larger pieces. A sideboard without the two centre legs might call for closer inspection.

E 14 A George III period sideboard, in mahogany veneers, with bow front and ebony inlay, c. 1800; 37 in. high by 75 in. wide (93 by 190 cm).

E 15 A George III mahogany sideboard, late 18th century; 47 in. (119 cm) wide.

E 18 A George III mahogany and inlaid serpentine-fronted sideboard, with curved sides and rounded back, the centre drawer flanked by end cupboards, on tapering diamond legs with spade feet; 36 in. high by 95 in. wide (91 by 241 cm).

D 1 A Sheraton mahogany bow-fronted sideboard, with brass rail incorporating candle holders; 84 in. (213 cm) wide.

E 2 A George III half-moon shaped sideboard, the apron with inlaid harewood spandrels; 39 in. high by 89 in. wide (99 by 226 cm).

E 3 A mahogany semi-elliptical sideboard, with small cupboards each end, two deep cellaret ·drawers, and one long drawer in the centre with tambour below, on square tapering legs, c. 1780; 38 in. high by 81 in. wide at back (96 by 205 cm).

D 4 A George III mahogany and tulipwood half-moon sideboard, crossbanded, with circular bands of tulipwood, and curved apron, on square tapering legs on spade feet; 72 in. (183 cm) wide.

E 5 A George III mahogany bow-fronted sideboard, crossbanded in rosewood, with arched apron, on square tapering legs with spade feet; 71 in. (180 cm) wide.

D 6 A George III mahogany sideboard, with semi-circular top; 66 in. (167 cm) wide.

E 7 A George III semi-circular sideboard, c. 1800; 37 in. high, 72 in. wide (94 by 183 cm).

E 8 A Georgian mahogany bow-front sideboard, with a brass rail back, fitted with three short drawers, two deep drawers, and three small cupboards with panel doors; 90 in. (229 cm) wide.

E 9 A George III period mahogany semi-circular sideboard, on tapering square legs, with spade feet; 37 in. high by 72 in. wide (92 by 183 cm). The brass rails at the back, supported on cast, turned columns, were meant to carry a curtain to prevent the wall covering being splashed during the serving of food.

E 10 A George III mahogany sideboard, of semi-circular shape, c. 1790; 36 in. high by 72 in. wide (91 by 182 cm).

E 11 A mahogany bow-front sideboard, 18th century; 37 in. high, 53 in. wide (93 by 134 cm).

E 12 A Sheraton period mahogany sideboard, c. 1790; 66 in. (167 cm) wide.

E 13 A George III mahogany and rosewood crossbanded sideboard, c. 1790; 92 in. (234 cm) wide.

E 14 A George III mahogany corner sideboard, with serpentine triangular top, and a drawer in the arched centre, flanked by cellaret drawers; 60 in. (152 cm) wide.

E1 A George III mahogany sideboard, with veneered serpentine top, on fluted tapering legs; 83 in. (211 cm) wide.

E2 A George III mahogany serpentine sideboard, with carved shaped apron, on fluted tapering legs; 67 in. (171 cm) wide.

E3 A George III mahogany sideboard, the fluted stiles carved with paterae and raised on turned fluted tapering legs, *c.* 1785; 35 in. high by 77 in. wide (88 by 195 cm).

E4 A George III mahogany serpentine sideboard, with chamfered top, 74 in. (189 cm) wide.

E5 A George III mahogany sideboard, with eared bow-fronted top and two drawers in the arched centre; 72 in. (183 cm) wide.

E6 A George III mahogany bow-front sideboard, crossbanded in satinwood, on fluted tapering legs; 78 in. (198 cm) wide.

E7 A George III mahogany sideboard, inlaid with boxwood lines and chequer bands, *c.* 1800; 38 in. high by 76 in. (97 by 193 cm).

C8 A mahogany pedestal sideboard, carved and inlaid, the pedestals surmounted by vases, *c.* 1795; 96 in. (244 cm) wide.

E1 A George III mahogany bow-front sideboard, on moulded sabre legs, 71 in. (180 cm) wide.

E3 A Georgian mahogany sideboard, *c.* 1840; 78 in. (198 cm) wide.

E2 A George III mahogany sideboard, of double breakfast form, *c.* 1805; 75 in. (191 cm) high.

E4 A George III mahogany pedestal sideboard, with bowed centre front, *c.* 1825; 50 in. (127 cm) wide.

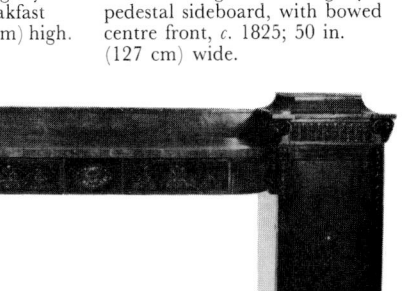

E5 A George III mahogany pedestal sideboard, with crossbanded top with quadrant corners, on fluted frieze, late 18th century; 111 in. (282 cm) wide.

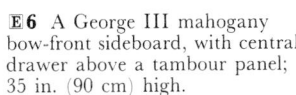

E6 A George III mahogany bow-front sideboard, with central drawer above a tambour panel; 35 in. (90 cm) high.

E7 A Regency mahogany sideboard, with central arched drawer and four flanking drawers; 50 in. (127 cm) wide.

E8 A Regency ormolu-mounted mahogany sideboard; 83 in. (210 cm) wide.

E9 A Regency mahogany serpentine-fronted sideboard, with satinwood crossbanding; 36 in. high, 63 in. wide (91 by 160 cm).

E10 A mahogany bow-fronted sideboard, banded in satinwood and tulipwood, early 19th century; 48 in. (121 cm) wide.

E11 A Regency mahogany sideboard, with semi-elliptical top, the arched centre with a drawer flanked by two drawers, with a cupboard on the left and a cellaret drawer and cupboard on the right, on strung square tapering legs; 87 in. (221 cm) wide.

E12 A Regency mahogany sideboard, inlaid with ebony line decoration, the recess with a pair of smaller cupboard doors enclosing a bottle rack, *c.* 1818; 31 in. high by 95 in. wide (78 by 241 cm).

E13 A mahogany sideboard, with brass rail with candle holders, cylinder fall front, on turned tapering legs, 96 in. (244 cm) long.

E1 An early 19th-century bow-fronted mahogany sideboard, the centre drawer flanked by a deep drawer and a cupboard.

E2 A Regency figured mahogany kneehole sideboard, *c.* 1810; 46 in. (118 cm) wide.

E3 A Regency mahogany double pedestal sideboard, *c.* 1830; 51 in. (129 cm) wide.

E4 A George IV mahogany three-lobed bow-front sideboard, with turned fluted legs and arched apron frieze.

E5 A William IV serving table, with bow centre front and concealed drawer under; 96 in. (243 cm) wide.

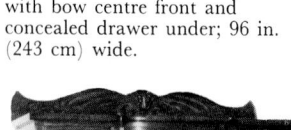

E6 A William IV mahogany sideboard; 44 in. high by 65 in. wide (111 by 165 cm).

E7 A Victorian mahogany pedestal sideboard, with shaped and carved back panel; 64 in. (162 cm) wide.

E8 A large oak and parquetry sideboard, the lower part with a geometrically inlaid top above three marble slides and drawers, and cupboard doors enclosing sliding shelves, all elaborately carved, *c.* 1850; 80 in. high by 85 in. wide (203 by 215 cm).

E9 *(above)* A Victorian sideboard with walnut panels and crossbanding, three oak-lined drawers, three cupboards, one with cellaret drawer, surmounted by an arched three-mirror overmantel with ebonized pillar supports; 107 in. high by 102 in. wide (271 by 259 cm).

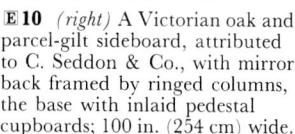

E10 *(right)* A Victorian oak and parcel-gilt sideboard, attributed to C. Seddon & Co., with mirror back framed by ringed columns, the base with inlaid pedestal cupboards; 100 in. (254 cm) wide.

E 11 A serpentine mahogany sideboard, with crossbanded top, a drawer above an arch, a fitted bottle drawer on the right and a cupboard on the left, with shaped sides, on six square and diamond-shaped legs with spade feet, *c.* 1890; 72 in. (183 cm) wide.

E 12 A painted satinwood and parcel-gilt sideboard, late 1800s; 37 in. (93 cm) high.

E 13 An Edwardian mahogany sideboard, in Sheraton style, with ivory panel inscribed J.S. Henry, London, EC; 72 in. (182 cm) wide.

E 15 An Edwardian mahogany mirror-backed sideboard, *c.* 1910; 73 in. (185 cm) wide.

E 14 A mahogany and satinwood sideboard, probably by William Morris & Co., *c.* 1900; 64 in. (160 cm) wide.

E 16 A mahogany sideboard, elaborately carved, *c.* 1910; 41 in. high by 48 in. wide (104 by 122 cm).

STANDS
1650-1910

During the last 20 years it has become generally accepted that "stand" may be used equally to describe small tables made as or in the style of cabinet stands (as no. 1), torchères, small occasional tables and, later, urn stands and jardinières. Each needs to be assessed according to all the rules of materials, construction and decoration applying to contemporary pieces.

E 1 A Charles II stand, with simulated portor marble top; 34 in. (86 cm) high.

E 2 A Charles II walnut side table, with inset verde antico marble top; 34 in. (86 cm) wide.

E 3 A pair of William and Mary walnut and oak torchères, with scrolled tripod stands; 37 in. high by 10 in. wide (93 by 22 cm).

E 4 A William and Mary occasional table in elm and oak, with octagonal top on barley-twist stem, *c.* 1690.

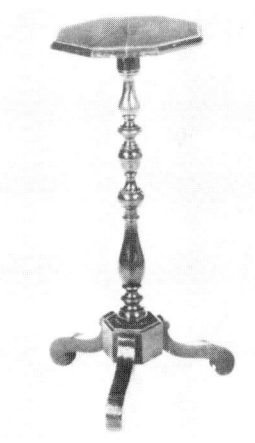

E 5 A William and Mary oak tripod stand, on a baluster stem with hexagonal base and three scroll legs, *c.* 1680; 32 in. high by 14 in. wide (81 by 35 cm).

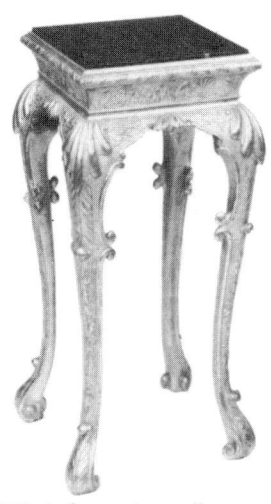

E 6 A Queen Anne gilt-gesso stand, with marble top; 28 in. high by 14 in. wide (72 by 35 cm).

C 1 A pair of carved and gilded term torchères, probably to a design by William Kent, early 18th century; 52 in. high by 11 in. diameter (132 by 27 cm).

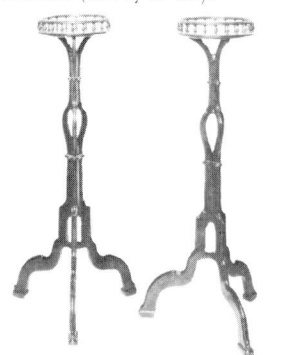

D 2 A pair of George II mahogany torchères, *c.* 1755; 40 in. high by 11 in. diameter (101 by 27 cm).

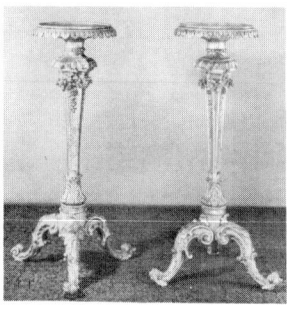

C 3 A pair of early Georgian carved and giltwood torchères; 43 in. (111 cm) high.

E 4 A George II mahogany kettle stand, on baluster shaft; 9 in. (24 cm) diameter.

E 5 An early George II mahogany tripod table, with circular pierced ormolu verde antico marble top, above a stop-fluted vase-shaped stem, on boldly carved downcurved tripod legs; 17 in. (43 cm) diameter.

D 6 A George II mahogany tripod stand, with dished circular top, on turned stem with acanthus-carved baluster at the base, *c.* 1750; 20 in. high by 14 in. diameter (50 by 35 cm).

D 7 A George II mahogany urn stand, the top with gadrooned edge and sliding tray beneath, and supported on four slender moulded cabriole legs, joined by scrolled cross-stretchers, *c.* 1750; 16 in. (40 cm) wide.

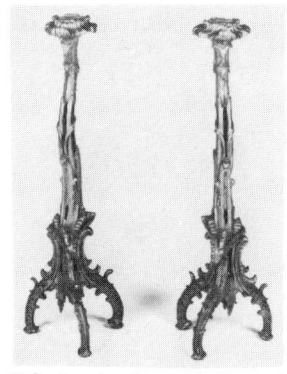

D 8 A pair of carved giltwood torchères, in the rococo style, mid 18th century. Similar designs were made by leading cabinet makers of the period.

E 9 An early George III mahogany stand, the circular recess with scalloped border, on C-scroll supports joined by an arched cross-stretcher, centred by platform shelf carved with cabochons, 23 in. (58 cm) high.

C 10 A mahogany tripod-base stand, the tray top with pierced border in the Chinese manner, over turned and reeded column entwined with tendrils, *c.* 1750.

E 11 A George III mahogany tripod music stand, with adjustable top and stem, late 18th century; 53 in. (135 cm) high.

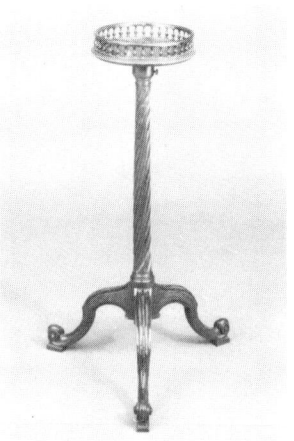

D 12 A George III mahogany torchère, with adjustable galleried top on spirally turned shaft; 33 in. high by 10 in. diameter (83 by 25 cm).

D 13 A three-tier stand, on four curvilinear supports, the centre columns and double C-scroll feet in rococo style, mid 18th century.

E 1 A Chippendale mahogany urn table, with fretted gallery and carved frieze, on cluster column legs and block feet, *c.* 1770.

E 4 A mid-Georgian brass plate stand, with turned supports on cabriole tripod base; 23 in. (58 cm) high.

E 7 A mid-Georgian mahogany reading stand, with revolving top and sloping flap each side, one enclosing fitted interior, on cabriole tripod base; 24 in. (62 cm) wide.

E 10 An oval urn stand, the top with wavy-edge border over serpentine-shape frieze and square taper legs, terminating in spade feet, late 18th century.

E 2 A George III painted torchère, with ribbon tied baluster stem, *c.* 1760; 51 in. (129 cm) high.

E 5 A Chippendale mahogany stand, 38 in. high by 14 in. diameter of tray (96 by 35 cm).

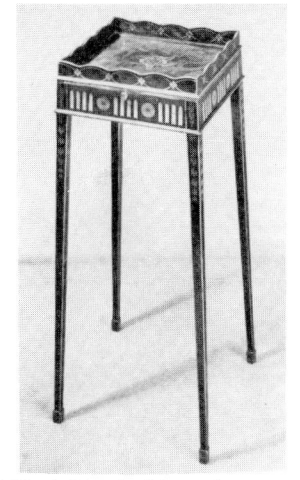

E 8 A Hepplewhite mahogany urn table, in the classical manner, the architectural decoration achieved by the application of marquetry to the frieze, the wavy-edged border and the top, *c.* 1780.

E 11 A George III mahogany urn stand, outlined with boxwood and ebony lines, the square top above a slide in the frieze, on slender tapering square legs; 25 in. high by 10 in. square top (63 by 25 cm).

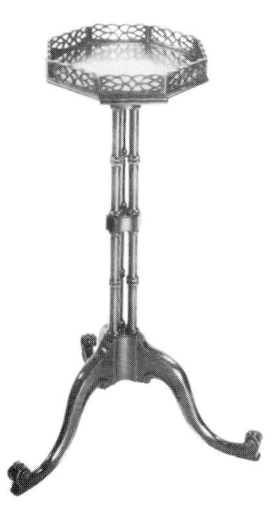

D 3 A Chippendale mahogany urn stand, on cluster column support; 29 in. (73 cm) high.

E 6 A George III white painted and gilded torchère, 33 in. (84 cm) high.

9 A George III oval mahogany and marquetry urn table, the galleried top with satinwood banding, *c.* 1780; 25 in. high by 14 in. wide (65 by 37 cm).

E 12 A George III mahogany octagonal urn stand, with concealed slide, on square tapering legs, with cross-stretchers.

D 1 A George III stainwood and marquetry tripod torchère, with dish-shaped triangular top, waved frieze inlaid with foliage sprays on moulded tapering in-curved supports, joined by a circular platform, with ormolu caryatids with finely chased feather head-dresses ending in various clasp sabots; 49 in. high by 18 in. wide (124 by 45 cm).

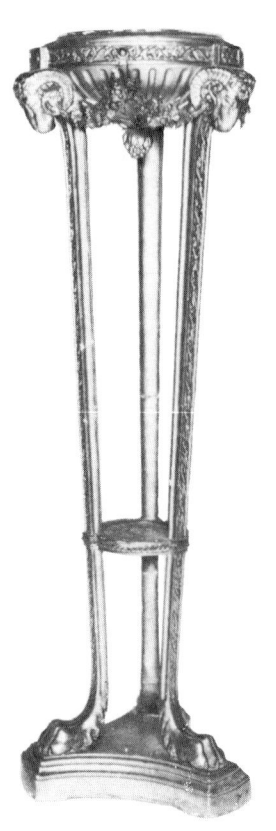

E 2 A George III giltwood torchère, with moulded circular top on three moulded supports, carved with foliage and mythical beasts' heads; 55 in. (139 cm) high.

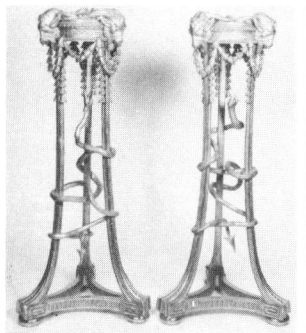

C 3 A pair of George III giltwood torchères, elaborately carved with a serpent entwined around the supports and mythical beasts' heads; 56 in. (142 cm) high.

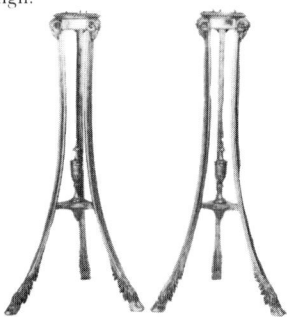

E 4 A pair of George III carved giltwood torchères, with circular top and splayed legs with "cloven hoof" feet, *c.* 1770; 55 in. (140 cm) high.

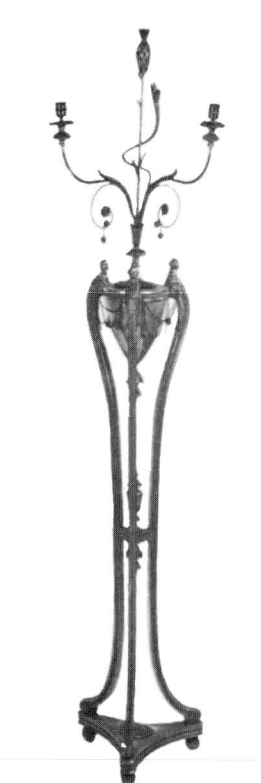

E 5 A George III giltwood torchère, in the Adam style, with foliate urn centre; 73 in. (185 cm) high.

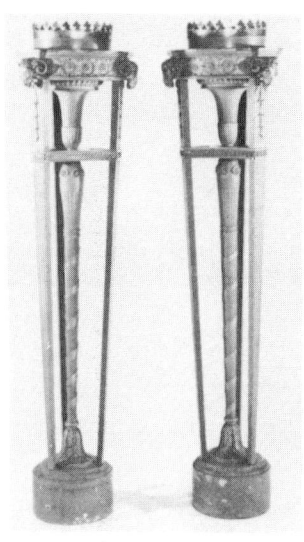

E 6 A pair of George III cream painted and gilded tripod torchères, with crown-carved top; 61 in. (154 cm) high.

E 7 A Regency rosewood music stand, with brass inlaid chamfered rectangular top on ring-turned shaft, with splayed tripartite base and bun feet; 16 in. (40 cm) wide.

E 8 A pair of Regency giltwood tripod stands, in the manner of Thomas Hope, with mahogany tops on lion-headed monopodia and circular bases; 32 in. high by 14 in. diameter (81 by 35 cm).

E 9 A George IV mahogany duet music stand, the twin folio racks with lyre-shaped splats and ratchet adjustments, *c.* 1825; 17 in. (44 cm) wide.

E 10 A William IV mahogany folio stand, in the manner of Holland & Son, with slatted sides and X-pattern ratchet action on trestle ends; 28 in. (71 cm) wide.

E 11 A William IV folio stand, with hinged sides, turned double supports at each end, with splayed feet joined by stretcher; 34 in. (86 cm) wide.

E1 A William IV mahogany cue stand, with turned and reeded columns, fitted with two drawers and bun feet.

E2 A William IV inlaid rosewood folding reading stand, in Regency style, early 19th century; 25 by 18 in. (63 by 45 cm).

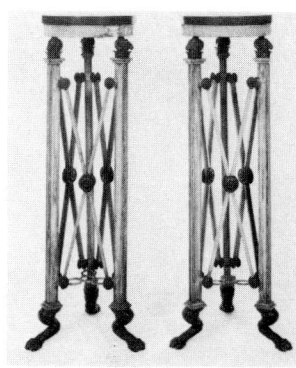

E3 A pair of Regency-style cream painted torchères, with circular black marble tops, on tripartite stems; 47 in. (119 cm) high.

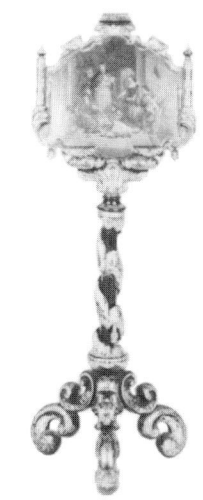

E4 A papier maché music or reading stand, with an adjustable brass ratchet, in gilt, with acanthus and painted with green foliage, *c.* 1840; 52 in. (132 cm) high.

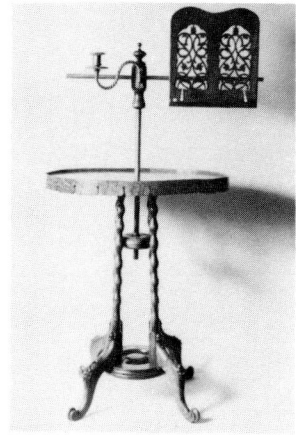

E5 A walnut reading stand/table, fully adjustable, with candle holder, *c.* 1860.

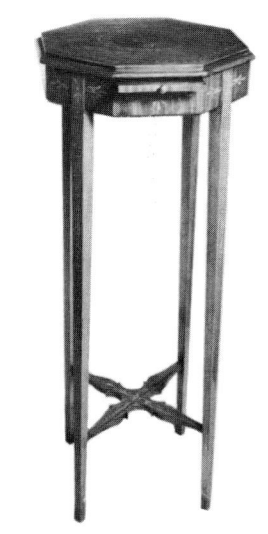

E6 A small mahogany samovar table, with painted portrait medallion, on square tapering legs, *c.* 1860; 29 in. (73 cm) high.

E7 A Coalbrookdale cast-iron hall stand, stamped indistinctly Coalbrookdale No.19, *c.* 1860; 77 in. (195 cm) high.

E8 A music or reading stand, with finely fretted rest supported on embossed brass fully adjustable stand, with candle holder, on clustered columns and swept paw feet, *c.* 1870; 53 in. (133 cm) high.

E9 A pair or walnut pedestals, the coffered moulded circular tops in foliate lunette borders above winged cabochoned friezes, 19th century; 46 in. (116 cm) high.

E10 A pair of parcel-gilt burr-walnut pedestals, of square tapering form with canted corners, the frieze with fretwork above drapery and a patera at each side, the corners with flower-hung corbels, *c.* 1910; 39 in. high by 14 in. square (99 by 35 cm).

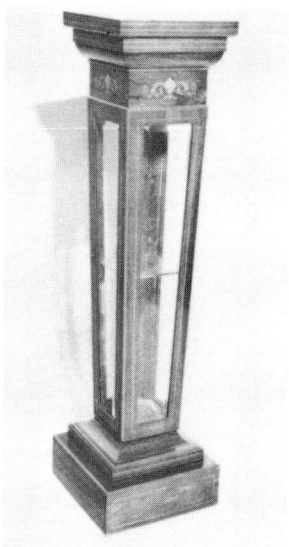

E11 A rosewood square tapering pedestal, inlaid with box and other coloured woods, fitted as a display cabinet with bevelled glazed panels and door; 46 in. (116 cm) high.

STOOLS
1550-1890

Early stools of plank or board construction, such as nos 1, 2 and 5 below, were slotted together and held by clout nails. During the second half of the 15th century joined furniture became available when the mortise and tenon joint, secured with willow pegs, was introduced from the Continent, though it did not become standard for another hundred years.

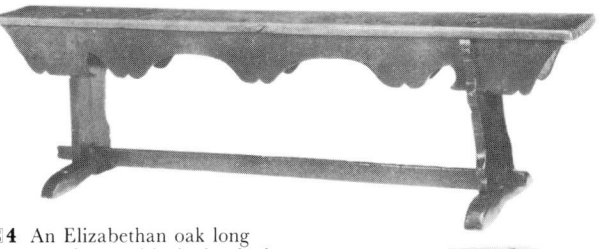

E4 An Elizabethan oak long bench or form, with single plank top, *c.* 1600; 19 in. high by 75 in. long (49 by 191 cm).

E1 A late Gothic oak boarded stool, with moulded top, and pierced frieze; 21 in. high by 19 in. long (53 by 48 cm).

E2 A late Gothic oak boarded stool, with moulded elm top, mid 16th century; 18 in. high, 22 in. long (45 by 56 cm).

E5 A James I elmwood boarded stool, the top with a moulding along the long sides and gouge carving at each end, *c.* 1620; 21 in. high, 22 in. wide (54 by 55 cm).

E6 A James I oak joint stool, the frieze carved with leafy lunettes, *c.* 1620; 19 in. high, 17 in. wide (50 by 45 cm).

E8 A James I oak joint stool, the frieze rail carved over baluster and carved legs, on original stretchers.

E9 A Charles I oak joint stool, the turned legs of double baluster form, *c.* 1630; 23 in. high by 17 in. long (58 by 44 cm).

E11 A Charles I oak low stool, with moulded square top, baluster shaped legs and plain stretchers, *c.* 1640; 14 in. high, 15 in. wide (37 by 40 cm).

E12 A Charles I oak joint stool-table, with oval drop-leaf top supported by lopers; 21 in. high, 30 in. wide (54 by 77 cm) open.

E13 An oak joint stool, with lunette-carved frieze on turned legs joined by square stretchers, 17th century; 18 in. (46 cm) wide.

E3 An Elizabethan oak joint stool, with moulded top and carved frieze, *c.* 1600; 20 in. high by 19 in. long (52 by 48 cm).

E7 A James I oak joint stool, the frieze with punched decoration, *c.* 1610; 21 in. high by 18 in. wide (54 by 46 cm).

E10 A Charles I oak joint stool, with moulded top, the frieze carved with leafy lunettes on all sides, on baluster shaped legs with plain stretchers, *c.* 1630; 23 in. high by 17 in. long (60 by 45 cm).

E14 An upholstered oak stool, on shaped legs joined by straight stretchers, 17th century; 22 in. (55 cm) high.

E1 An oak joint stool, with fluted frieze on turned baluster legs with square stretchers, 17th century; 17 in. (43 cm) wide.

E2 An oak stool-table, with oval top, over a frieze drawer, on splayed baluster legs, 17th century; 23 in. (58 cm) wide.

E3 An oak joint stool, with fluted frieze, 17th century; 22 in. (55 cm) high.

E4 A joint stool, on ring-turned baluster legs, 17th century; 18 in. (45 cm) wide.

E5 A Charles II oak joint stool, with ball-turned legs joined by plain stretchers, *c.* 1680; 21 in. high by 18 in. long (53 by 46 cm).

E6 An oak box stool, with hinged lid, with a carved frieze on baluster shaped legs, mid 17th century; 17 in. high, 17 in. wide (43 by 43 cm).

E7 A joint stool, with simple column turned ringed legs and detachable elm sliding top, mid 17th century; 20 in. high by 18 in. long (51 by 46 cm).

E8 A Charles II oak table-stool, with splayed baluster turned legs, joined by plain stretchers, with hinged drop-leaf detail.

E9 A Charles II oak stool, with stuffed seat and spiral twist legs, *c.* 1680; 16 in. high, 23 in. wide (42 by 58 cm).

E10 A folding stool, with stuffed seat and X-shaped supports.

E11 A walnut stool, with stuffed seat and waved cross-stretchers, *c.* 1690.

E12 A Stuart stool, decorated with silver and gilt, covered in silk velvet, with elaborately carved cross-stretchers.

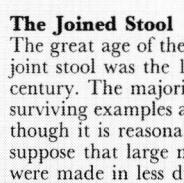

E13 A William and Mary walnut stool, on tapering turned legs joined by similar H-shaped stretchers, upholstered in bargello, late 17th century; 18 in. (45 cm) wide.

E14 A walnut seat or long stool, with squab seat over a pierced carved apron, on elaborately carved scroll legs, *c.* 1680.

The Joined Stool

The great age of the joined or joint stool was the 17th century. The majority of surviving examples are in oak, though it is reasonable to suppose that large numbers were made in less durable woods.

Most of the good oak stools that survive were not made as cottage furniture, simple though they may be. The stool was the standard form of seat in the very grandest houses, the few chairs being reserved for the most important people in the household. Period cottage stools would have been much more likely to be three-legged, a form that accommodates to uneven floors.

An authentic period joint stool will show the following features: the pegs securing the joints of the frame and those holding the top to the frame should stand proud owing to differential shrinkage of the timber; the feet should be original; when the stool is upturned the timber should display a certain crustiness to the undersides of the top and the stretchers; the long willow pegs should protrude or show signs of having been snapped off rather than cut neatly.

E 1 A Queen Anne walnut stool, with oval drop-in seat, on cabriole legs headed by shells and scrolls, joined by turned H-shaped stretcher and pad feet; 18 in. high by 21 in. wide (45 by 53 cm).

E 2 A Queen Anne walnut stool, with cabriole legs and pad feet joined by an H-stretcher, with upholstered seat; 22 in. (55 cm) wide.

E 3 A Queen Anne walnut stool, with needlework covered seat in petit point, with simple cabriole legs with plain brackets and square feet, *c*. 1710; 20 in. (50 cm) wide.

E 4 A Queen Anne walnut stool, with needlework drop-in seat, on cabriole legs carved with acanthus and pointed pad feet.

E 5 A walnut stool, covered in petit point needlework, with carved cabriole legs on pad feet, early 18th century; 16 in. diameter (40 cm).

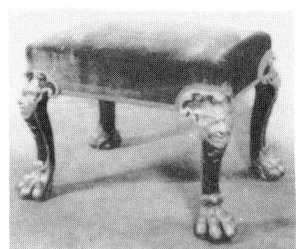

D 6 A William Kent walnut and parcel-gilt stool, carved with masks on the knees and paw feet, with upholstered seat, *c*. 1730; 16 in. by 23 in. (40 by 58 cm).

E 7 A George I walnut stool, with drop-in gros point needlework top, on cabriole legs with paw feet, *c*. 1725; 21 in. (53 cm) high.

E 8 A George I walnut stool, with drop-in needlework seat, on cabriole legs with claw-and-ball feet; 24 in. (60 cm) wide.

E 9 An early Chippendale period stool, with upholstered seat and carved cabriole legs, with claw feet.

E 10 A Chippendale stool, with upholstered tapestry seat, with carved frieze and carved cabriole legs, on claw-and-ball feet.

D 11 A Chippendale stool, with upholstered seat and carved cabriole legs, on claw-and-ball feet.

D 12 A Chippendale mahogany stool, with upholstered seat and finely carved cabriole legs terminating in paw feet.

D 13 A Chippendale mahogany stool, finely carved, with petit point needlework seat.

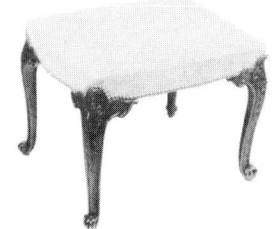

E 15 A George III mahogany stool, with shaped upholstered seat; 23 in. (58 cm) wide.

E 14 A walnut stool, with upholstered seat, finely carved frieze and cabriole legs.

E 16 A George III mahogany Royal stool, branded SR 1912, beneath a crown, *c*. 1760.

E1 A George III mahogany stool, with crimson velvet upholstered seat, on cabriole legs carved with acanthus and claw-and-ball feet; 24 in. (60 cm) wide.

E2 A Hepplewhite mahogany stool, with drop-in upholstered seat, on square tapering legs with H-stretcher.

E3 A Georgian library step stool, in faded mahogany, upholstered seat in leather opens; 45 in. (114 cm) high when open.

E4 A George III mahogany stool with padded seat, on chamfered square legs carved with blind fretwork; 24 in. (60 cm) wide.

E5 A George III mahogany stool, with upholstered seat, carved square legs with blind fretwork; 22 in. (56 cm) wide.

E6 A mahogany gout stool, with buttoned upholstered seat and back, on turned legs with casters, c. 1800; 19 in. (48 cm).

E7 A late Regency period stool, the four turned legs swept out at the toe, c. 1820. This type of stool was a popular model of the period, often with its original needlework seat.

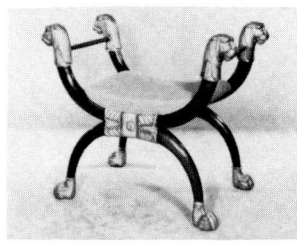

D8 A Regency parcel-gilt stool, designed by Thomas Hope, with upholstered seat, c. 1810. A similar stool is shown in Household Furniture and Interior Decoration, 1807.

E9 A walnut stool, with ornate carving, with upholstered seat, mid 19th century; 32 in. (80 cm) wide.

E10 A "rope" stool, in the manner of Fournier, with circular buttoned top, the seat rail carved as rope continuing into the legs, c. 1850; 15 in. (53 cm) high.

E11 A walnut piano stool, with padded buttoned seat, on extending carved turned stem with tripod legs, c. 1860; 22 in. (55 cm) high (down).

E12 A beadwork and giltwood stool, with circular moulded frame on bun supports, c. 1860; 10 in. (25 cm) diameter.

E13 A mid-Victorian velvet covered sarcophagus-shaped stool, with mahogany beadings, c. 1865; 20 in. (50 cm) wide.

E14 A Victorian joint stool, with open double twist supports and plain stretchers.

E15 An animal foot stool, with octagonal shaped top on cloven hoof feet, c. 1875

E16 A beech music stool, stained to simulate mahogany, on outward tapering square legs, with H-stretcher, c. 1910.

TABLES
1600-1910

Better than any other type of furniture, the table reflects the evolution of a stable society as the Middle Ages waned. In a period when noble households were frequently on the move and when furniture-making skills were sparse, the standard domestic table was of boards set on trestles, easily dismounted and moved. Thus pre-15th century tables are very rare unless of ecclesiastical provenance, to which considerations of mobility were less applicable.

Architects' tables

D 1 An early Georgian mahogany architect's table, with candle arms, drawer and flap.

D 2 A mid-Georgian mahogany architect's desk, *c.* 1750; 31 in. high by 39 in. (78 by 99 cm).

D 3 A Chippendale mahogany rising-top architect's table, with slide and fitted drawer.

D 4 An architect's table in finely figured mahogany, the top with a ratchet adjustment, the slide-out

E 5 A Georgian mahogany extending architect's table, with drop side flaps, *c.* 1780.

E 6 A Chippendale mahogany artist's table, with a centre fitted drawer, *c.* 1780; 31 in. high, 38 in. wide (78 by 96 cm).

E 7 A Georgian mahogany architect's table, the pull-out drawer with interior compartments; 36 in. (90 cm) high.

front revealing a well fitted dummy drawer, *c.* 1775; 31 in. high by 25 in. wide (77 by 62 cm).

E 8 A George II mahogany architect's table, the adjustable hinged top with a bookrest and Chinese fret flaps, with brass candle slides, *c.* 1760; 34 in. high, 32 in. wide (86 by 81 cm).

E 9 A George III mahogany architect's table, with easel top fitted with drawers, on fluted square legs; 36 in. (91 cm).

E 10 A mahogany drawing table, signed Gillow of Lancaster, fitted with drawers and a slide, on square tapering legs, *c.* 1790; 29 in. high by 24 in. wide (73 by 60 cm).

C 11 A George III rosewood and satinwood architect's table, the top inlaid and crossbanded with mahogany; 36 in. (91 cm) wide.

E 12 A George III artist's mahogany chest, with easel top and fitted with drawers and slides; 27 in. (68 cm).

E 13 A George IV mahogany architect's or draughtsman's combined table and cabinet.

E 14 A Regency mahogany architect's table, with fitted writing drawer and compartments; 42 in. (106 cm) wide.

E 1 A Regency burr-elm and faded oak architect's table, with hinged easel top and two candle slides, on trestle ends, early 19th century; 36 in. (91 cm) wide.

E 2 A Regency period mahogany draughtsman's table, with easel top and swivel candle shelves, the shaped square pedestal supports with rising mechanism; 39 in. (99 cm) wide.

E 3 A George IV oak architect's or writing table, with mahogany veneered double-hinged top crossbanded in rosewood, *c.* 1815; 28 in. high by 48 in. wide (71 by 121 cm).

E 4 A mahogany architect's pedestal desk, stamped Graygoose, 57 Great Queens Street, with adjustable leather-lined top and adjustable central writing slope, 19th century.

Breakfast tables

E 5 A Chippendale-style mahogany breakfast table, with a drawer, drop-leaf top, on square legs, with fine fretwork.

E 6 A Chippendale mahogany breakfast table, with shelf under, *c.* 1755; 26 in. high by 39 in. long (66 by 99 cm).

E 7 A George III mahogany octagonal tip-up breakfast table; 42 in. (106 cm) wide.

D 8 A Sheraton rosewood breakfast table, crossbanded in satinwood, with claw casters; 48 in. (121 cm) diameter.

E 9 A George III mahogany breakfast table, the top inlaid with rosewood banding; 50 in. (127 cm) diameter.

E 10 A George III mahogany breakfast table, crossbanded in satinwood, *c.* 1795; 28 in. high, 59 in. wide (71 by 149 cm).

E 11 A Georgian mahogany breakfast table, the top with segmental veneers and crossbanded; 61 in. by 47 in. (154 by 119 cm).

D 12 A George III plum-pudding mahogany breakfast table, the tip-up top crossbanded in satinwood; 52 in. (132 cm) wide.

E 13 A George III mahogany breakfast table, banded in satinwood and rosewood, *c.* 1800; 50 in. (127 cm) long.

E 14 A George III mahogany breakfast table; 28 in. high by 49 in. diameter (71 by 126 cm).

E 15 A George III rosewood breakfast table, with rounded crossbanded tip-up top; 44 in. (111 cm) wide.

E 16 A George III mahogany and crossbanded small drop-leaf breakfast table, with satinwood banding, *c.* 1800; 29 in. (74 cm) wide.

E 17 A George III rosewood breakfast table, with tip-up top inlaid with a boxwood line; 44 in. (111 cm) wide.

E 18 A George III mahogany breakfast table, the tip-up top with moulded edge; 39 in. high, 53 in. wide (99 by 134 cm).

E 19 A George III mahogany breakfast table, the crossbanded top with reeded edge, *c.* 1810; 56 in. (142 cm) wide.

Breakfast Tables

Moveable tables specifically made for intimate rather than communal meals have been noted since Tudor times. Until the middle of the 18th century they were small, often with drop or folding leaves. It is in fact that 17th-century invention, the tea table, that best continues the tradition, being small, moveable and designed for occasional refreshment.

The substantial breakfast table of the later 18th century reflects a major change in eating habits. No longer was breakfast served individually in private apartments but taken in company, albeit a restricted number.

The classic form of the breakfast table would seat up to eight people, preserving a trace of its forebear's function only in that it has a snap top that allowed it to be moved aside. It was oval or rectangular in form – the former being considered more desirable today – and was supported on a single columnar pedestal on three or four splayed legs terminating in castors. The most elegant design is that in which the legs sweep straight off the column, as in no. 3, right.

E3 A Regency rosewood breakfast table, with crossbanded tilt-top with rounded corners, on turned part-ebonized shaft support, on four splayed legs, with casters; 54 in. (137 cm) wide.

E4 A Regency mahogany breakfast table, with circular fiddleback top on massive turned shaft and reeded splayed quadripartite base; 66 in. (169 cm) diameter.

E5 A Regency mahogany oval tilt-top breakfast table, the top with a moulded edge supported on a collared turned shaft and four reeded splayed legs fitted with brass shoes and casters; 60 in. (151 cm) wide.

E1 A George III mahogany breakfast table, *c.* 1800; 29 in. high by 60 in. wide (74 by 153 cm).

E2 A Regency rosewood breakfast table, the top with broad crossbanded edge, *c.* 1810; 57 in. high by 44 in. wide (145 by 113 cm).

E6 A Regency mahogany breakfast table, the tip-up top inlaid with ebonized lines, 64 in. (163 cm) wide.

E7 A George III burr-elm octagonal breakfast table, with octagonal tilt-top crossbanded with ebony and centring a conforming central panel; 46 in. (115 cm) wide.

D8 A Regency mahogany breakfast table, in the manner of George Smith, having a moulded brass edge and beaded frieze; 46 in. (115 cm) wide.

E9 A Regency mahogany tilt-top pedestal table, the rectangular top with disc-mounted frieze, *c.* 1810; 63 in. (161 cm) wide.

E10 A Regency mahogany and crossbanded pedestal table, *c.* 1820; 47 in. high by 64 in. wide (120 by 163 cm).

E1 A Regency rosewood breakfast table, with brass-bordered frieze; 56 in. (142 cm) wide.

E10 A Rosewood veneered breakfast table, with moulded hinge top on an octagonal baluster and circular base with three scroll feet, *c.* 1840; 58 in. (148 cm) diameter.

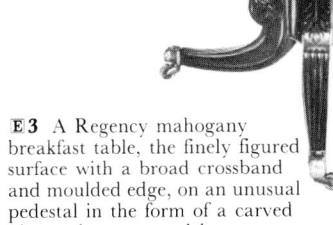

D2 A Regency tulipwood breakfast table, with snap-top crossbanded in satinwood; 47 in. high by 57 in. wide (116 by 149 cm).

E6 A late-Regency rosewood breakfast table, with well figured tip-up top and reel border, on plinth support; 57 in. (145 cm) wide.

E7 A George IV mahogany breakfast table, with tip-up top crossbanded and inlaid with brass, with brass feet and casters, *c.* 1825; 48 in. (120 cm) diameter.

E11 A burr-walnut breakfast table, with quarter-veneered tip-top on a fluted jewelled column, stamped John Taylor & Son Manufacturers, Edinburgh number 3443, *c.* 1850; 52 in. (132 cm) diameter.

E12 A walnut breakfast table, with lobed oval tip-top, *c.* 1850; 59 in. (150 cm) wide.

E3 A Regency mahogany breakfast table, the finely figured surface with a broad crossband and moulded edge, on an unusual pedestal in the form of a carved pineapple, supported by acanthus-carved and reeded swept legs, *c.* 1825; 28 in. high by 66 in. wide (75 by 165 cm).

E8 A George IV mahogany drop-leaf breakfast table, crossbanded in padoukwood, with a fitted drawer and a turned and ringed pillar on quadruple reeded splayed legs, *c.* 1825; 37 in. (95 cm) wide.

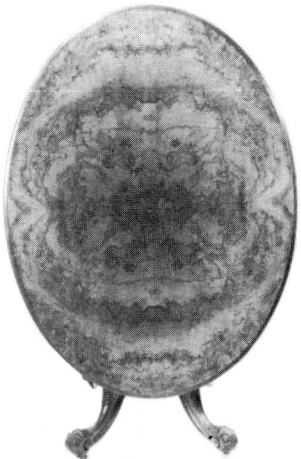

E4 A Regency rosewood breakfast table, with tip-up top crossbanded with pollard-yew and concave-sided quadripartite base; 56 in. (142 cm) wide.

E5 A George IV rosewood breakfast table, with gadroon edge frieze; 45 in. (112 cm) diameter.

E9 An early Victorian mahogany breakfast table, with a lancet moulded border, mid 19th century; 30 in. high by 54 in. diameter of top (76 by 135 cm).

E13 A Victorian burr-walnut breakfast table, with oval snap-top raised on carved column and quadruple base, *c.* 1860; 56 in. high by 45 in. wide (140 by 112 cm).

Centre tables

E 1 A James II walnut side or centre table, with quarter-veneered top; 28 in. high by 30 in. wide (74 by 77 cm).

E 2 A Charles II carved oak centre table; 31 in. high by 32 in. wide (77 by 80 cm).

E 3 A William and Mary centre table, with inlaid top; 52 in. (130 cm) wide.

E 4 An oak centre table, with oval top and plain frieze, 17th century; 43 in. (109 cm) wide.

D 5 A small walnut centre table, with oysterwood top; 27 in. (77 cm) wide.

D 6 A William and Mary marquetry centre table, with a finely inlaid top in a seaweed pattern in rosewood and walnut; 43 in. (110 cm) wide.

D 7 A William and Mary walnut centre table, with octagonal top, the well-shaped legs ornately carved, ending in claw feet; 55 in. (137 cm) wide.

E 8 A Queen Anne gilt-gesso centre table, in the manner of Moore and Gumley, with top carved with trailing acanthus and foliage divided by a bellflower at each corner; *c.* 1700; 39 in. (99 cm) wide.

E 9 A Queen Anne walnut centre table, with moulded crossbanded top, bordered with herringbone bands; 32 in. (81 cm) wide.

D 10 A walnut and parcel-gilt centre table, with moulded crossbanded top; 22 in. (86 cm) wide.

E 11 A giltwood centre table, with ornately carved frieze, 18th century; 38 in. (95 cm) wide.

E 12 A George II mahogany rectangular centre table, with curved legs ending in padded feet.

E 13 A giltwood centre table, with grey-veined white marble top, late 18th century; 48 in. (122 cm) wide.

E 14 A Regency centre table, with crossbanded tip-up top; 48 in. (122 cm) diameter.

D 15 A Regency circular rosewood and brass inlaid breakfast table, with a monopodium base, *c.* 1810; 49 in. (122 cm) wide.

E 16 A Regency calamanderwood centre table, with tip-up top on octagonal baluster shaft, the concave-sided triangular base on massive gilt-metal paw feet, issuing from winged scrolls; 52 in. (132 cm) diameter.

D 1 A Regency rosewood pedestal table, the tilt-top with satinwood inlaid bellflowers to the borders, *c.* 1815; 47 in. (121 cm) diameter.

D 2 A Regency rosewood and brass line inlaid pedestal table, the top with broad zebrawood crossbanding and reeded apron, *c.* 1810; 45 in. (116 cm) diameter.

D 3 A Regency brass-inlaid rosewood centre table, *c.* 1810; 51 in. (127 cm) diameter.

E 4 A Regency rosewood circular table, with crossbanded top, the frieze with beaded moulding, on graduated support, the curved legs ending with brass feet and casters.

D 5 A brass-inlaid rosewood and parcel-gilt centre table, the top inlaid with geometric pattern borders, the solid turned shaft carved with foliage; 76 in. (193 cm) wide.

D 6 A Regency satinwood and parcel-gilt centre table, with well-figured top crossbanded with rosewood and mahogany, inlaid with brass stars, the moulded frieze mounted with gilt-metal rope-twist above a parcel-gilt stem, early 19th century; 53 in. (134 cm) wide.

E 7 A Regency rosewood centre table, the tip-up top with ormolu border, the solid shaft well carved with foliage, on tripartite chamfered concave-sided base, on scrolled feet; 51 in. (130 cm) diameter.

E 8 A Regency brass-inlaid rosewood centre table, with circular top, hexagonal stem, concave-side base and gilt-metal feet, *c.* 1820; 48 in. (122 cm) diameter.

D 9 A circular table, in elm and burr-elm veneer, the top mounted with a gilt-brass tongue-and-dart ovolo bead, resting on three dolphins on waves, in carved and gilt wood, *c.* 1815.

D 10 A Regency amboyna centre table, the octagonal top edged with brass moulding, on a solid chamfered support with square well-decorated base; 42 in. high by 51 in. wide (105 by 127 cm).

E 11 A Regency rosewood centre table, with beaded top inset with Italian specimen marbles and a central roundel of two songbirds in a cherry tree, on a ring-turned baluster shaft and tripartite base; 29 in. (73 cm) wide.

E 1 A Regency rosewood centre table, with rounded scagliola verde antico top with broad ormolu border cast with stylized leaves; 26 in. (67 cm) wide.

E 2 A carved giltwood centre table, on melusine feet, early 18th century; 28 in. high by 27 in. wide (71 by 69 cm).

E 8 A mahogany and parcel-gilt centre table, Regency style, with segmentally-inlaid top with raised border and pagoda edge; 45 in. (116 cm) diameter.

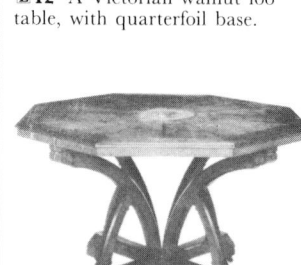

E 12 A Victorian walnut loo table, with quarterfoil base.

E 3 A William IV coromandel-veneered centre table, the hinged top with a broad crossbanding and inner ebony band inlaid with foliate scrollwork, and gadrooned ebonized outer border, *c.* 1830; 60 in. (154 cm) wide.

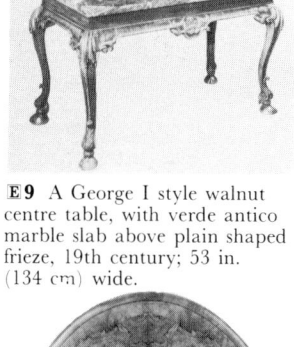

E 9 A George I style walnut centre table, with verde antico marble slab above plain shaped frieze, 19th century; 53 in. (134 cm) wide.

E 13 An oak centre table, *c.* 1850; 30 in. high by 49 in. wide (76 by 124 cm).

E 4 A marquetry centre table, inlaid with bands and sprays of flowers and butterflies on a walnut, rosewood and ebony ground, *c.* 1840; 39 in. (100 cm) wide.

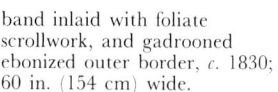

E 6 A Victorian loo table, with mahogany circular top inlaid with roses; 51 in. (127 cm) wide.

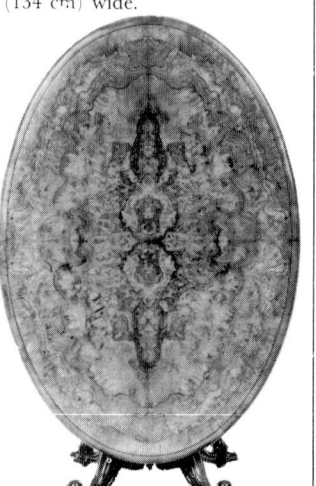

E 10 A walnut loo table, with a quarter-veneered tip-top, in well-figured wood above a serpentine apron, *c.* 1860; 29 in. high by 60 in. wide (74 by 152 cm).

E 14 A specimen marble centre table, *c.* 1860; 32 in. high by 35 in. wide 882 by 90 cm).

E 15 A Victorian walnut centre table; 29 in. high by 60 in. wide (72 by 150 cm).

E 5 A Victorian walnut loo table, with figured oval top on quadruple turned columns; 47 in. (117 cm) wide.

E 7 A Victorian burr-walnut serpentine loo table, with quarter-veneered tilt top, *c.* 1850; 58 in. (147 cm) wide.

E 11 A Victorian black lacquer papier mâché centre table, inlaid with mother-of-pearl; 52 in. (130 cm) wide.

E 16 A walnut centre table, in well-figured wood, with crossbanded top in tulipwood, *c.* 1860; 29 in. high by 56 in. wide (75 by 147 cm).

E17 A coromandel marquetry and bone-inlaid centre table, *c.* 1870; 28 in. high by 45 in. wide (73 by 114 cm).

E18 A rosewood centre table, *c.* 1880; 29 in. high by 35 in. wide (74 by 90 cm).

E19 A Chinese Chippendale design mahogany centre table; 32 in. (82 cm) wide.

E20 A Chinese Chippendale design mahogany centre table, *c.* 1880; 34 in. (86 cm) wide.

E21 A walnut and fruitwood rococo table; 29 in. high by 36 in. wide (75 by 92 cm).

Console & pier tables

D1 A George II gilt carved wood console table, with onyx top, the masks and legs picked out in dark green; 33 in. high by 50 in. wide (82 by 125 cm).

E2 A George II polished pine console table, with mottled green marble top, with moulded foliate frieze edged with bead-and-reel; 37 in. (95 cm) wide.

D3 A William Kent carved and gilt dolphin table; 56 in. (140 cm) wide.

E4 A walnut pier table, with moulded rounded white marble top, early 18th century; 24 in. (51 cm) wide.

E5 A George II mahogany console table, with eared top, the frieze carved with key-pattern; 33 in. high by 35 in. wide (85 by 89 cm).

E6 A giltwood pier table, of Kentian design, with pink spar top and moulded frieze, 18th century; 28 in. (72 cm) wide.

E7 A carved wood and gilt console table, with elaborately carved eagle base and shaped marble top, early 18th century; 37 in. high by 71 in. wide (92 by 177 cm).

E8 A giltwood console table, with serpentine carrara marble top, mid 18th century; 21 in. (55 cm) wide.

D9 A carved wood and gilded console table, with marble top, mid 18th century; 35 in. high by 43 in. wide (87 by 107 cm).

E10 A George III giltwood console table, with a black marble top, with segmental corners and conforming fluted frieze, late 18th century; 23 in. (55 cm) wide.

E11 A George III pine console table, with burr yew-wood top above a fluted frieze, *c.* 1770; 47 in. (117 cm) wide.

E 1 A George III painted satinwood pier table, 1780-1790; 50 in. (128 cm) wide.

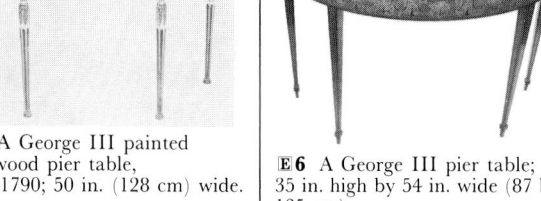

E 6 A George III pier table; 35 in. high by 54 in. wide (87 by 135 cm).

E 2 A George III giltwood pier table, the semi-elliptical satinwood top crossbanded with purpleheart, 74 in. (189 cm) wide.

E 7 A George III satinwood pier table, the top crossbanded with tulipwood, 46 in. (117 cm) wide.

E 3 A George III mahogany pier table, with top crossbanded in rosewood, 36 in. high by 58 in. wide (92 by 149 cm).

E 4 A George III giltwood pier table, with semi-elliptical top crossbanded with rosewood; 35 in. high by 48 in. wide (90 by 122 cm).

E 8 A George III console table, with rosewood veneered top, crossbanded in satinwood, *c.* 1800.

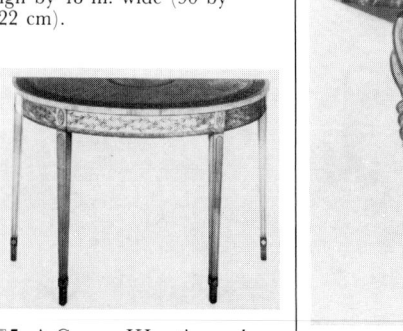

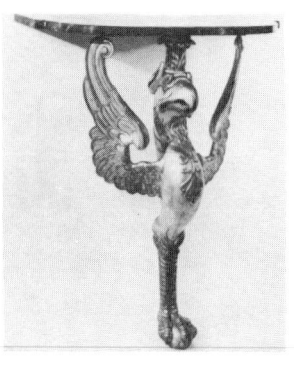

E 5 A George III satinwood console table, the top crossbanded with wide rosewood borders, late 18th century; 45 in. (114 cm) wide.

E 9 A giltwood console table, with bowed Portor marble top, *c.* 1820; 33 in. (85 cm) wide.

E 10 A Regency rosewood and parcel-gilt console table, in the manner of George Smith, with marble top, the frieze with applied moulding, supported by two well-carved griffins, on a simple plinth of inserted breakfront form; 58 in. (147 cm) wide.

E 11 A late Regency rosewood and parcel-gilt pier table, with grey speckled scagliola top, the tablet-centre frieze outlined with reel ornament, the panelled back lined with pleated silk on plinth base; 52 in. (132 cm) wide.

E 12 A William IV rosewood console table, with sienna marble top, early 19th century; 34 in. high by 42 in. wide (87 by 107 cm).

E 13 A William IV parcel-gilt pier table in mahogany with a marble top in the rococo manner, with scrolled foliate pierced frieze centring a cartouche, between massive scrolled legs with foliate ornament, on a mahogany plinth with gilt lobing, *c.* 1835; 61 in. (155 cm) wide.

D 14 A Victorian oak pier table, by Gillow of Lancaster, with green marble top; 72 in. (183 cm) wide.

E 15 A giltwood and gesso pier table, with a serpentine moulded green and red marble top, mid 19th century; 36 in. high by 62 in. wide (91 by 158 cm).

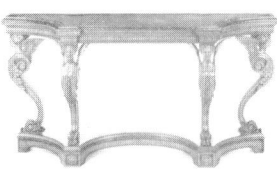

E 16 A Victorian satinwood and marquetry console table, with the label of Howard and Sons; 72 in. (180 cm) wide.

E 17 A carved giltwood pier table, with dark green top, mid 19th century; 32 in. high by 55 in. wide (82 by 141 cm).

E 18 An Adam-style mahogany pier table, 20th century; 36 in. high by 70 in. wide (92 by 188 cm).

Credence tables

E 1 A James I oak credence table, the hexagonal fold-over top supported by barrel turned legs, with ornately carved frieze of geometric form, on a plain plinth; 30 in. high by 47 in. wide (75 by 117 cm).

E 2 An oak table, with octagonal folding top supported on unusual turned legs of bulbous form, mid 17th century.

E 3 An oak credence or folding table, with hinged top, the moulded frieze with a drawer and broad canted corners, *c.* 1640; 31 in. high by 40 in. wide (78 by 103 cm).

E 4 An oak credence table, with folding top, supported by barrel turned legs, the frieze with ornate carving, 17th century; 60 in. (150 cm) wide.

E 5 A carved oak credence table, the ornately carved frieze above turned legs, 17th century.

E 6 A credence table, of panelled form, with a cupboard in the front, on turned legs joined by sturdy stretchers.

E 7 A Charles I oak folding table, the semi-circular top with iron butterfly hinges, *c.* 1630; 29 in. high by 31 in. wide (73 by 79 cm).

E 8 An oak credence table, with folding top, opening to reveal a frieze compartment, late 17th century; 39 in. (97 cm) wide.

Cricket tables

E 1 A Charles II oak cricket table, *c.* 1670; 27 in. high by 30 in. wide (70 by 76 cm).

E 2 An oak cricket table, with plank top and moulded frieze, late 17th century; 30 in. (76 cm) wide.

E 4 An elm and ash tripod cricket table, late 18th century; 21 in. (52 cm) wide.

E 5 An oak cricket table, *c.* 1780; 21 in. (52 cm) wide.

E 3 An oak cricket table, with plank top, mid 18th century; 27 in. (70 cm) wide.

E 6 An oak cricket table, *c.* 1820; 30 in. (75 cm) wide.

Dining tables

E 7 An oak dining table, with triple plank top, the frieze carved on one side with S-scrolls, 17th century; 61 in. (152 cm) wide.

E 8 An oak dining table, with plank top, late 17th century; 99 in. (252 cm) long.

D 9 A William and Mary oak dining table, the rectangular top with four hinged curved flaps, supported on iron bolts and opening to form an oval, *c.* 1695; 78 in. (198 cm) wide, open.

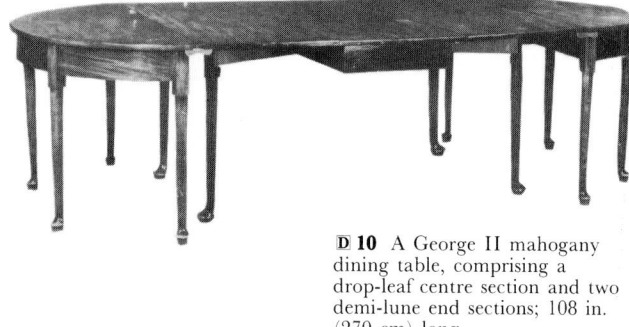

D 10 A George II mahogany dining table, comprising a drop-leaf centre section and two demi-lune end sections; 108 in. (270 cm) long.

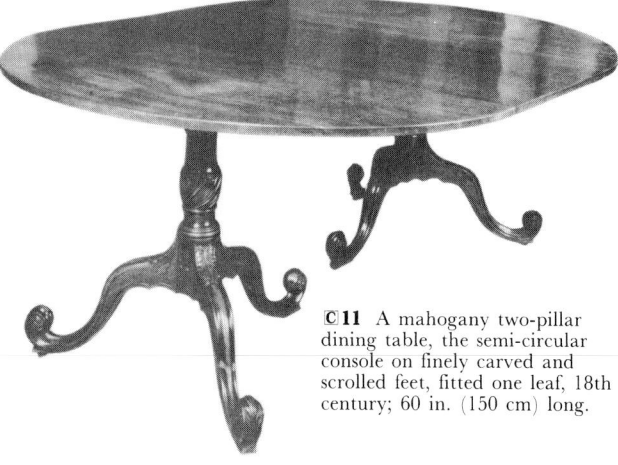

C 11 A mahogany two-pillar dining table, the semi-circular console on finely carved and scrolled feet, fitted one leaf, 18th century; 60 in. (150 cm) long.

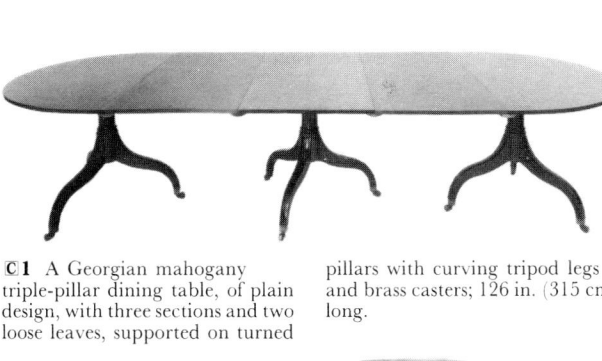

C1 A Georgian mahogany triple-pillar dining table, of plain design, with three sections and two loose leaves, supported on turned pillars with curving tripod legs and brass casters; 126 in. (315 cm) long.

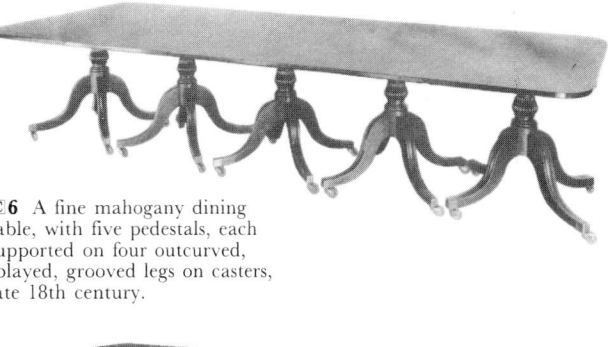

C6 A fine mahogany dining table, with five pedestals, each supported on four outcurved, splayed, grooved legs on casters, late 18th century.

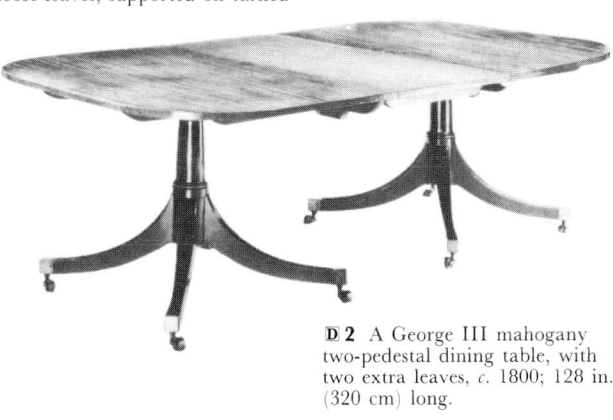

D2 A George III mahogany two-pedestal dining table, with two extra leaves, *c.* 1800; 128 in. (320 cm) long.

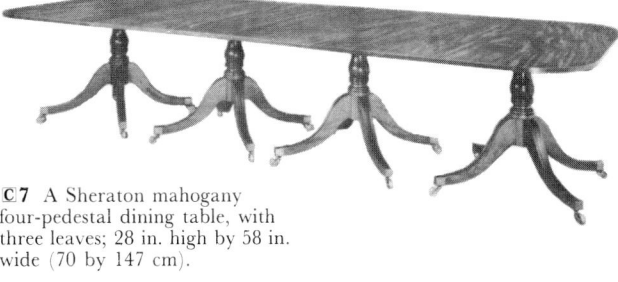

C7 A Sheraton mahogany four-pedestal dining table, with three leaves; 28 in. high by 58 in. wide (70 by 147 cm).

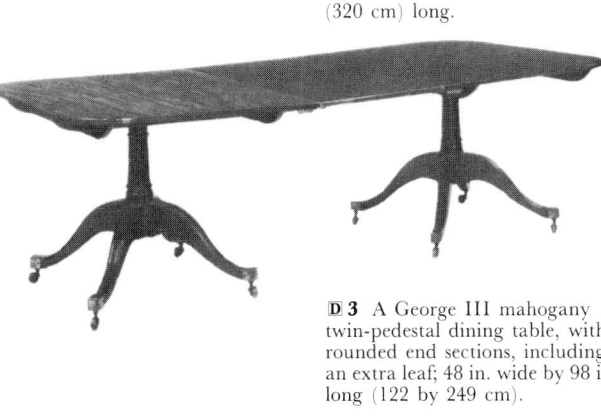

D3 A George III mahogany twin-pedestal dining table, with rounded end sections, including an extra leaf; 48 in. wide by 98 in. long (122 by 249 cm).

E8 A Regency mahogany two-pillar dining table, the rounded rectangular top with a reeded edge and on turned stems, each with four reeded hipped splayed legs, brass caps and casters; 28 in. high by 97 in. long (70 by 242 cm), includes two extra leaves.

C4 A George III mahogany three-pillar dining table, *c.* 1800; 27 in. high by 122 in. long (70 by 310 cm).

E9 A Regency extending mahogany dining table, the top with rounded ends and two leaves, on plain pillar with reeded sabre legs, *c.* 1800; 83 in. (211 cm) long.

C5 A late Georgian mahogany three-pedestal dining table, including an extra leaf; 66 in. (168 cm) wide.

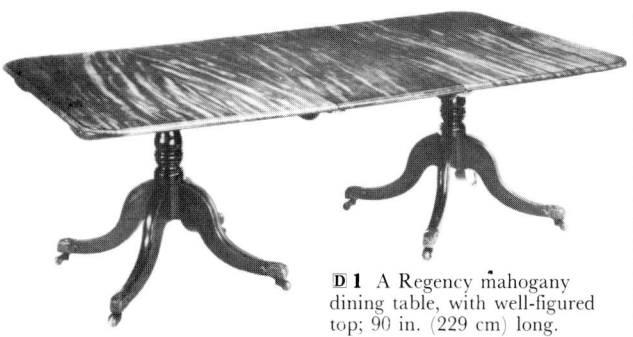

D 1 A Regency mahogany dining table, with well-figured top; 90 in. (229 cm) long.

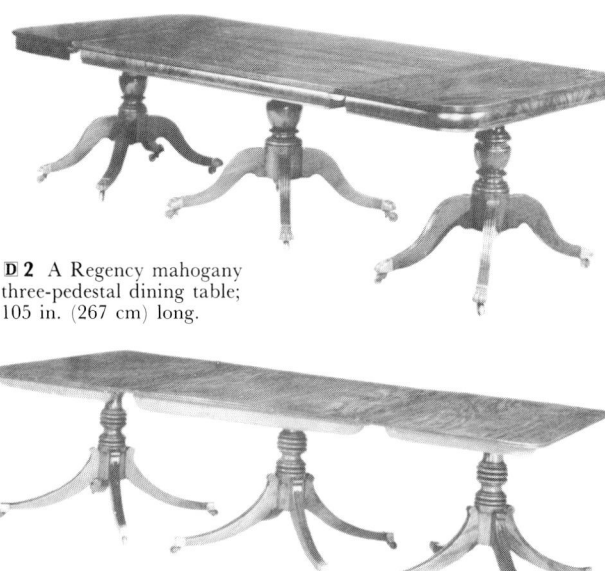

D 2 A Regency mahogany three-pedestal dining table; 105 in. (267 cm) long.

D 3 A George III mahogany three-pedestal dining table; 148 in. (376 cm) long.

E 4 A Regency mahogany dining table, with plain frieze, the centre section with turned column and splayed quadruple supports, brass paw feet and casters, 130 in. (325 cm) long.

E 6 A George III mahogany dining table, with semi-elliptical top and a single detached flap; 53 in. (136 cm) across.

E 7 A George III mahogany dining table; 28 in. high by 52 in. across (71 by 132 cm).

E 8 A mahogany "D" end dining table, early 19th century; 28 in. high by 104 in. long (70 by 260 cm).

E 9 A George III mahogany dining table, with figured folding surface above inlaid apron and simple square taper legs, *c.* 1800; 28 in. high by 112 in. long (70 by 280 cm).

E 5 A Georgian mahogany fall-flap dining table; 54 in. (135 cm) long.

E 10 A Georgian design mahogany "D" end dining table, with two-flap centre section, 19th century; 89 in. (247 cm) wide.

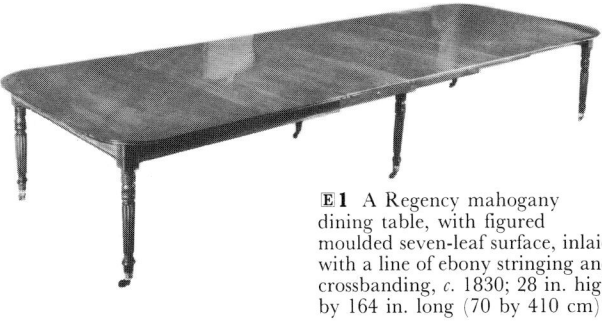

E1 A Regency mahogany dining table, with figured moulded seven-leaf surface, inlaid with a line of ebony stringing and crossbanding, *c.* 1830; 28 in. high by 164 in. long (70 by 410 cm).

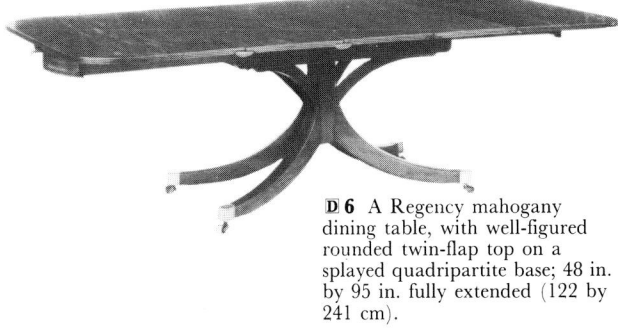

D6 A Regency mahogany dining table, with well-figured rounded twin-flap top on a splayed quadripartite base; 48 in. by 95 in. fully extended (122 by 241 cm).

E2 A William IV mahogany extending dining table, with a reeded border, the central section with double gate-leg supports, on 14 ringed and gadrooned tapering legs with brass casters; fully extended, *c.* 1830; 123 in. (313 cm) long.

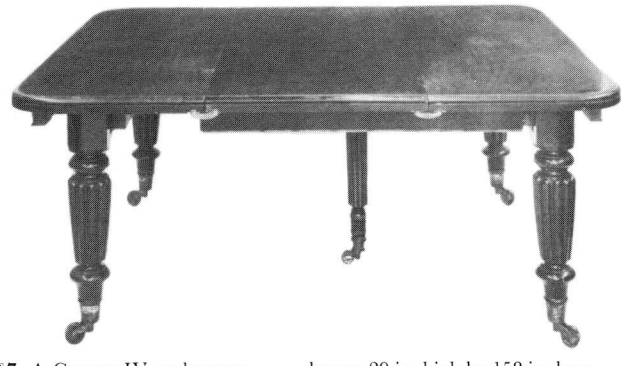

E7 A George IV mahogany dining table, with telescopic underframe, and five additional leaves; 29 in. high by 158 in. long, fully extended (72 by 395 cm).

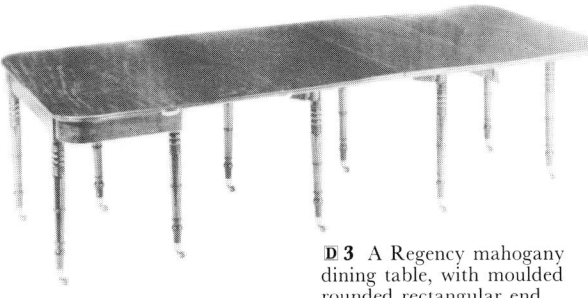

D3 A Regency mahogany dining table, with moulded rounded rectangular end sections and panelled frieze, on ring-turned tapering legs; 125 in. (338 cm) long.

E8 A William IV mahogany three-pillar dining table, with rectangular top on baluster and downswept fluted supports, on claw feet, early 19th century; 29 in. high by 110 in. long (74 by 279 cm).

E4 A Regency mahogany patent dining table, with rounded rectangular end sections, with panelled frieze on turned tapering ribbed legs, extending to fit three extra leaves; 45 in. by 110 in. fully extended (115 by 280 cm).

E5 A George IV mahogany extending dining table, the reeded top with a hinged end section, on eight turned reeded legs, *c.* 1825; 94 in. (240 cm) wide, open.

E9 A William IV mahogany dining table, the square top with a reeded border, on reeded tapering legs and brass casters, with three extra leaves; 28 in. by 122 in. fully extended (72 by 310 cm).

E 1 A mahogany pull-top extension dining table, *c.* 1830; 44 in. (111 cm) diameter.

E 2 An early Victorian mahogany mechanical circular extending table, circular when closed and oval when opened; 29 in. high by 55 in. closed diameter, 88 in. open diameter (73 by 139 cm).

D 3 An early Victorian expanding or capstan table, by Johnstone, Jupe & Co., London; 55 in. diameter closed, by 79 in. extended (140 by 203 cm).

D 4 An early Victorian Jupe's patent mahogany extending circular dining table, the segmented top in two diameters with six removable leaves, stamped "Jupe's Patent" on the central brass plate, on baluster stem, four-cornered base and paw feet; 54 in. diameter closed, 92 in. diameter open (137 by 235 cm).

D 5 A William IV mahogany extending dining table, by Robert Jupe; 55 in. (140 cm) diameter closed.

E 6 An early Victorian oak extending dining table, on a turned leaf-carved stem, four legs; 51 in. (129 cm) wide.

D 7 An early Victorian circular hinged dining table, *c.* 1840; 28 in. high by 61 in. diameter (71 by 156 cm).

E 8 A mahogany extending dining table, with rounded frieze carved with foliate scrolls, 19th century; 60 in. (153 cm) diameter.

E 9 An early Victorian extending dining table, on an octagonal column and quatrefoil platform, maximum extension 216 in. (548 cm).

E 10 A Victorian mahogany extending dining table, on turned legs with casters; 28 in. high by 92 in. long (71 by 234 cm).

E 11 A mahogany extending dining table, with D-shaped ends and three extra leaves, *c.* 1850; 28 in. high by 135 in. long (71 by 342 cm).

E 12 A mahogany dining table with five extra leaves, *c.* 1850; 28 in. by 128 in. (71 by 326 cm).

E 13 A circular mahogany extending dining table, raised on five square tapering supports, 19th century; 60 in. (152 cm) diameter closed.

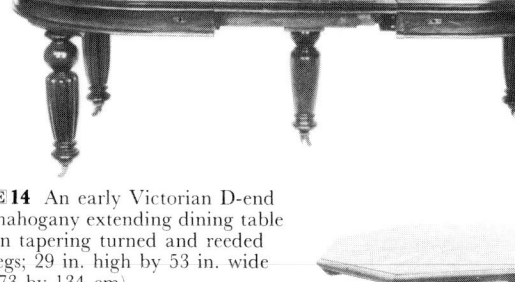

E 14 An early Victorian D-end mahogany extending dining table on tapering turned and reeded legs; 29 in. high by 53 in. wide (73 by 134 cm).

E 15 *(right)* An oak octagonal dining table, with inlaid top; 29 in. high by 60 in. wide (73 by 152 cm).

Display tables

E 1 A satinwood and mahogany display table, the frieze with a flowerhead trellis, on square tapering legs with casters, 1860s; 39 in. by 24 in. (99 by 61 cm).

E 2 A console display table, of architectural form, with Belge noir breakfront marble top, *c.* 1860; 36 in. by 46 in. (91 by 117 cm).

E 3 A late Victorian mahogany maple and satinwood crossbanded bijouterie table, *c.* 1900; 30 in. (77 cm) wide.

E 4 An Edwardian mahogany bijouterie display table, with blind fret carving, on cabriole legs with stretchers supporting a circular under-tier; 30 in. (76 cm) wide.

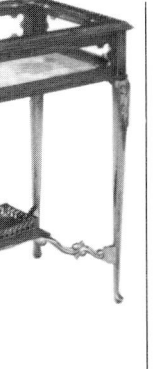

E 5 An Edwardian mahogany bijouterie table, on turned slender legs; 24 in. (60 cm) wide.

E 6 A mahogany heart-shaped display table, with bevelled glazed hinged top and gilt metal borders and mounts, on cabriole legs, late 19th century.

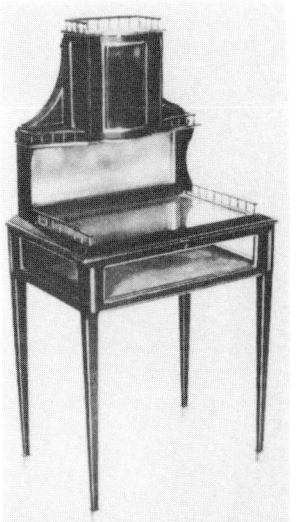

E 7 A mahogany display table, with glazed cupboard above an outside display surface, with brass galleries, on square tapering legs, *c.* 1900; 48 in. high by 24 in. (122 by 61 cm).

Draw-leaf tables

C 8 A walnut table, heavily carved with lions holding shields, and allegorical figures of Hope and Faith, *c.* 1600.

C 9 An Elizabethan oak withdraw table, with heavily carved bulbous legs and plain stretchers; 31 in. high by 59 in. long (78 by 149 cm).

C 10 An Elizabethan withdraw table, with inlaid floral frieze on carved bulbous legs; 33 in. high by 65 in. long (83 by 165 cm).

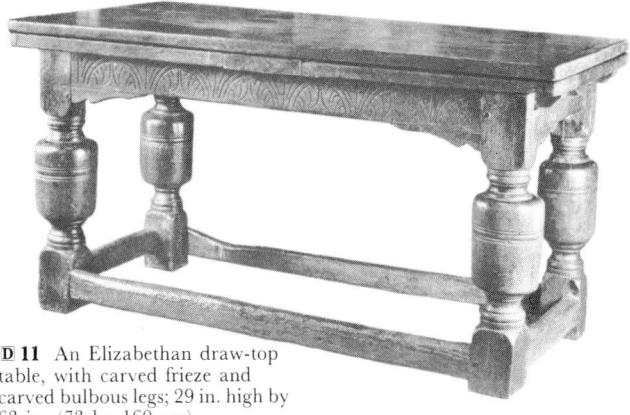

D 11 An Elizabethan draw-top table, with carved frieze and carved bulbous legs; 29 in. high by 63 in. (73 by 160 cm).

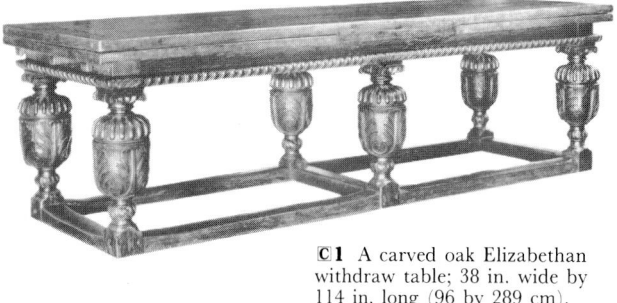

C 1 A carved oak Elizabethan withdraw table; 38 in. wide by 114 in. long (96 by 289 cm).

D 2 An Elizabethan oak draw-leaf table, with carved frieze, *c.* 1600; 52 in. long (closed) by 33 in. wide (132 by 83 cm).

E 3 An oak draw-leaf dining table, with banded top on fluted bulbous baluster legs, with plain stretchers, 17th century; 103 in. (261 cm) extended.

E 4 A William and Mary style walnut veneered draw-leaf table, the baluster legs joined by waved stretchers, *c.* 1920; 29 in. high by 132 in. long (73 by 335 cm).

Dressing tables

D 5 A satinwood dressing table, with inlaid panels of Chinese figures, musical instruments, other Chinese features, *c.* 1770.

D 6 A George III sycamore and rosewood dressing table; 25 in. (63 cm) wide, closed.

E 7 A George III inlaid mahogany dressing table; 41 in. (104 cm).

E 8 A George III satinwood dressing table; 37 in. (93 cm) wide.

E 9 A George III mahogany toilet table, with adjustable mirror, *c.* 1790; 33 in. high by 36 in. wide (83 by 91 cm).

E 10 A George III mahogany dressing table, with serpentine front, *c.* 1780; 33 in. high by 22 in. wide (81 by 55 cm).

E 11 A George III mahogany toilet table, with fitted interior; 26 in. (66 cm).

E 12 A George III satinwood dressing table, enclosing a fitted interior and mirror; 28 in. (71 cm) wide.

Dressing Tables
Cosmetics have been in use since at least the 14th century, but we do not know with any certainty the form dressing tables took before about 1660.

The earliest form to survive in quantity is what we now know as the lowboy, generally with three drawers, the centre one shallower to create a kneehole space. These tables were also used for writing and were made in considerable numbers until the middle of the 18th century, at which time the twin functions tended to divide, and cabinet-makers supplied more specialist designs of dressing table with complicated fitted interiors, and more functional writing tables with adjustable slopes.

The distinctive feature of the purpose-made dressing table was its in-built mirror – or more rarely pair of mirrors. Later in the century, responding to the taste for novelty, metamorphic furniture of exquisite craftsmanship became fashionable and the harlequin dressing table proved most popular.

E1 A George III mahogany and marquetry dressing table, the two side drawers pivoting, each containing adjustable mirrors and lidded compartments, on square tapering legs, *c.* 1780; 33 in. high by 46 in. wide (84 by 116 cm).

E5 A George III inlaid mahogany dressing table, with concealed sliding mirror screen and swinging writing drawers, on square tapering legs; 29 in. (73 cm) wide.

E2 A George III satinwood dressing table, with divided crossbanded top enclosing an easel mirror above two concave cupboard doors, on chamfered square legs joined by a cross stretcher; 27 in. (68 cm) wide.

E3 A George III satinwood, fruitwood and faded rosewood dressing table, with enclosed fitted interior; 23 in. (58 cm) wide.

E6 A George III mahogany dressing table, by Gillows, with bowed top and two hinged flaps; 54 in. (137 cm) wide.

E4 A Sheraton period mahogany and satinwood crossbanded dressing table, the two flap folding top enclosing a fitted interior with folding mirror and small compartments, pull-out brushing slide and single drawer below, on square tapered legs terminating in brass casters; 24 in. (60 cm) wide.

E7 A George III mahogany dressing table, the superstructure with small drawers and pigeonholes, double flap top, the interior with hinged flaps, the serpentine front shaped drawers with fine inlay, on turned legs with casters; 26 in. (66 cm) wide, closed.

E8 A Regency mahogany dressing table, with bowed rectangular top, four partially cedar lined drawers and a central drawer, on square tapering legs with spade feet; 44 in. (111 cm) wide.

E1 A Regency mahogany kneehole dressing table, with centre concave frieze drawer, *c.* 1810; 39 in. (100 cm) wide.

E2 A mahogany bow-front dressing table, with central drawer flanked by two deep drawers, with arched apron and turned legs, *c.* 1800; 37 in. (93 cm) wide.

E5 A Regency mahogany dressing table, attributed to Gillows, in the form of a sofa table, with hinged and folding top enclosing a divided interior; 36 in. (92 cm) wide.

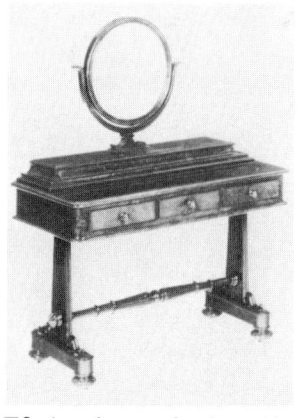

E8 A mahogany dressing table with a circular swing toilet glass on a moulded base, three drawers to the frieze, *c.* 1840; 57 in. high by 48 in. wide (144 by 121 cm).

E3 A Regency mahogany dressing table, attributed to Gillow of Lancaster, with concave central front drawer, flanked by four short drawers; 42 in. (107 cm) wide.

E6 A Regency birchwood and rosewood dressing table, with crossbanded top, two drawers and one false drawer, on square tapering legs; 46 in. (116 cm) wide.

E9 A pine dressing table, with gesso decoration, the central mirror flanked by two small drawers, the base with two drawers on shaped apron, on cabriole legs, 19th century; 68 in. high by 48 in. wide (172 by 121 cm).

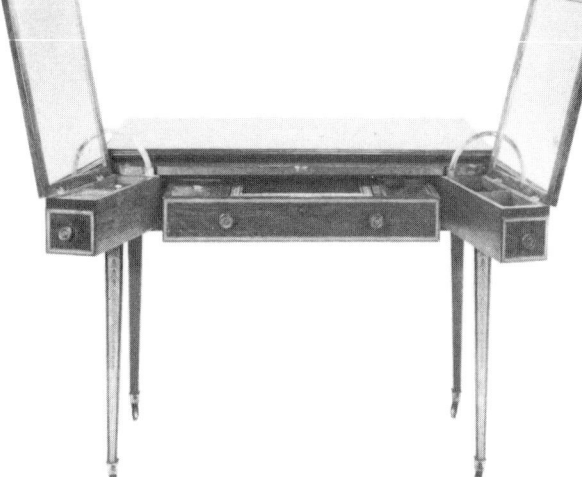

E4 A Regency mahogany Rudd's dressing table, with satinwood banded top, the frieze flanked by hinged drawers with easel mirrors, on square tapering legs, 42 in. (107 cm) wide.

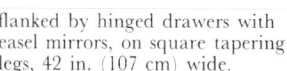

E7 A William IV mahogany dressing table, with lyre-shaped trestle supports and bun feet; 53 in. (134 cm) wide.

E10 A walnut dressing table, with oval mirror in carved moulded frame with an arrangement of small drawers, with serpentine-shaped base with kneehole, *c.* 1860; 65 in. high by 53 in. wide (165 by 134 cm).

E4 An Edwardian mahogany kidney-shaped kneehole dressing table, by Maple & Co., in the manner of Edwards & Roberts, with boxwood and harewood marquetry, *c.* 1910; 30 in. high by 54 in. wide (76 by 137 cm).

E6 An Edwardian mahogany inlaid dressing table, with shield-shaped swivel mirror; 47 in. (120 cm) wide.

E5 A mahogany shaped-front dressing table, with shield-shaped mirror over two long drawers, on square tapering legs, 20th century; 30 in. (76 cm) wide.

E7 A Sheraton-style mahogany toilet table, with oval-shaped mirror, the base serpentine-shaped, with two long drawers, on square tapering legs and spade feet, *c.* 1920; 36 in. (91 cm) wide.

E1 A painted satinwood dressing table, with embellished shield-shaped mirror, supported on cupboards, the doors with oval panels painted with classical figures, the table with one frieze drawer painted with flowers, supported on legs joined by curved stretcher, *c.* 1900.

E3 A satin walnut dressing table, by Maple & Co., the swing mirror in carved frame, mounted with seven drawers and a frieze drawer, on cabriole legs; 52 in. (132 cm) wide.

E2 A dressing table, veneered in thuyawood with tulipwood crossbanding, with ebonized mounts and porcelain plaques; 48 in. (121 cm).

D8 A Queen Anne walnut dressing table, with concave shaped central drawer flanked by four shaped drawers, on cabriole legs, with unusual shaped apron, 42 in. (106 cm) wide.

Drop-leaf tables

E1 A Queen Anne walnut oval drop-leaf gateleg dining table, with oval twin-flap top, on circular tapering legs headed by lappets and ending in pad feet, early 18th century; 67 in. (170 cm) wide, extended.

E7 A George II mahogany drop-leaf table, the oval top on leaf-carved cabriole legs ending in claw-and-ball feet, *c.* 1740; 28 in. (71 cm) high.

E2 A George I red walnut oval drop-leaf dining table, with circular tapering legs ending in pad feet.

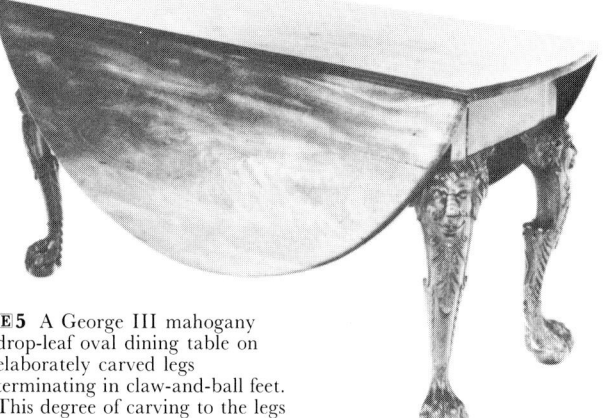

E5 A George III mahogany drop-leaf oval dining table on elaborately carved legs terminating in claw-and-ball feet. This degree of carving to the legs shows the ultimate in sophisticated ornament on what is basically a utility item, and for interest might be compared to its humble predecessor, the gateleg table. The table is 28 in. high by 71 in. diameter (72 by 180 cm).

E8 A mahogany oval twin-flapped dining table, on cabriole legs and pad feet, on casters; 48 in. by 54 in. (121 by 137 cm).

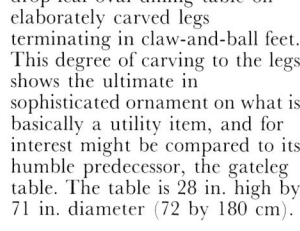

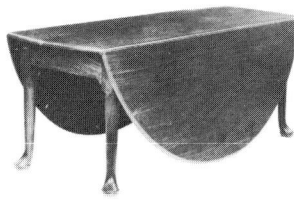

D3 A George III large mahogany oval drop-leaf table, with bold circular tapering legs ending in pad feet, *c.* 1740; 80 in. by 82 in. fully extended (203 by 208 cm).

E9 A Chippendale mahogany drop-leaf dining table, on shaped cabriole legs.

E6 A George II red walnut drop-leaf table, with plain oval top and four well-shaped cabriole legs on pointed pad feet, *c.* 1740; 57 in. (145 cm) wide, open. Versions of this table exist from the same period with straight legs descending directly from the underframe, and though elegant are less prized than the cabriole-legged versions.

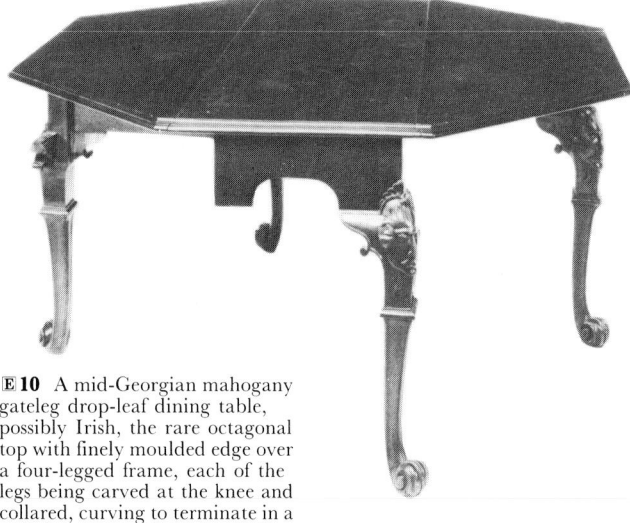

E4 A mahogany drop-leaf dining table, with carved cabriole legs ending in claw-and-ball feet on casters, *c.* 1730.

E10 A mid-Georgian mahogany gateleg drop-leaf dining table, possibly Irish, the rare octagonal top with finely moulded edge over a four-legged frame, each of the legs being carved at the knee and collared, curving to terminate in a well-defined scroll foot, *c.* 1745; 56 in. (142 cm) wide, open.

E1 A mahogany drop-leaf dining table, on slender shaped legs with pad feet, 18th century; 27 in. high by 48 in. diameter open (68 by 121 cm).

E2 A mahogany drop-leaf dining table, with plain top, on circular tapering legs with pad feet, mid 18th century; 43 in. (109 cm) wide.

E3 A George III yew-wood drop-leaf table, on square chamfered legs, *c.* 1770; 42 in. (107 cm) wide.

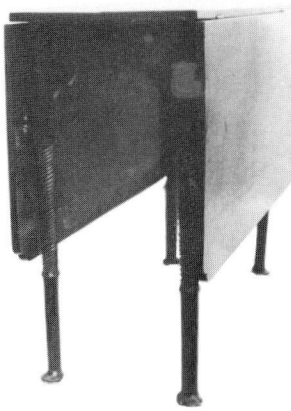

E4 A mahogany drop-leaf Sutherland table, with finely carved spiral-twist legs, ending in pad feet, 19th century; 54 in. by 37 in. extended (137 by 93 cm).

E5 A Regency rosewood Sutherland table, with rounded twin-flap top, on turned twin trestle ends joined by a stretcher, all on casters; 43 in. (109 cm) wide.

E6 A walnut Sutherland table, with a highly figured but machine-cut veneer to the top, with turning to the standard ends, above deeply scrolled and moulded legs with turned central pendant, mid 19th century; 36 in. high by 46 in. long, extended (91 by 116 cm).

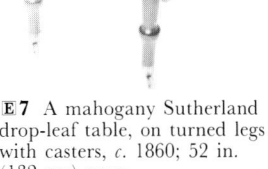

E7 A mahogany Sutherland drop-leaf table, on turned legs with casters, *c.* 1860; 52 in. (132 cm) open.

Drop-Leaf and Spider Tables

Drop-leaf tables of dining size fall into two main categories – those large enough to take up to 8 people, which were generally made in oval, round or octagonal form – and those intended to form the centre parts of 3-piece dining tables intended to seat up to 20. On the latter type the leaves were sometimes made detachable, the hinges being of strap form and bolting onto the underside of the top. The ends of such tables could be placed together without the centre part or they could stand against a wall to act as side or serving tables. The central parts have on occasion been separated from the ends and reduced in size.

During the mid-18th century the gateleg table, ancestor of the drop-leaf, was revived in finely turned and delicate form as the spider table. These were usually made in mahogany, but can be found in satinwood or even yew. 19th-century copies of spider tables abound, but are usually detectable by being much lighter in weight.

E8 A Victorian mahogany Sutherland table, on turned legs joined by a turned stretcher, on casters, *c.* 1880; 39 in. (99 cm) wide, open.

E9 A Victorian mahogany Sutherland table, on turned standard ends with central spindle stretcher, the deep leaves supported on hinged turned legs, enabling the top to fold to small size, terminating in casters, *c.* 1880; 49 in. (124 cm) long, extended.

Drum tables

D 1 A Sheraton satinwood and mahogany drum table, with revolving top, fitted with four drawers, on tapering sabre legs; 29 in. high, 26 in. diameter (73 by 66 cm).

E 2 A Sheraton mahogany drum table, crossbanded with rosewood, fitted with drawers, on turned support with splayed tripod base, *c.* 1780; 23 in. (58 cm) diameter.

E 3 A George III mahogany drum table, with inset leather top, the frieze with four drawers and four dummy drawers, with central turned support and splayed legs; 30 in. high by 42 in. diameter (76 by 106 cm).

D 4 A George III satinwood drum table, with revolving leather lined and crossbanded top, 25 in. (63 cm) diameter.

D 5 A George III mahogany drum table, with crossbanded and inlaid top, the frieze with four drawers and three false drawers on a segmental drawer, on partly ebonized ring-turned shaft, with splayed tripod base, also inlaid; 39 in. (99 cm) diameter.

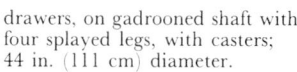

E 6 A Regency mahogany drum table, with cloth-lined top and four drawers divided by false drawers, on gadrooned shaft with four splayed legs, with casters; 44 in. (111 cm) diameter.

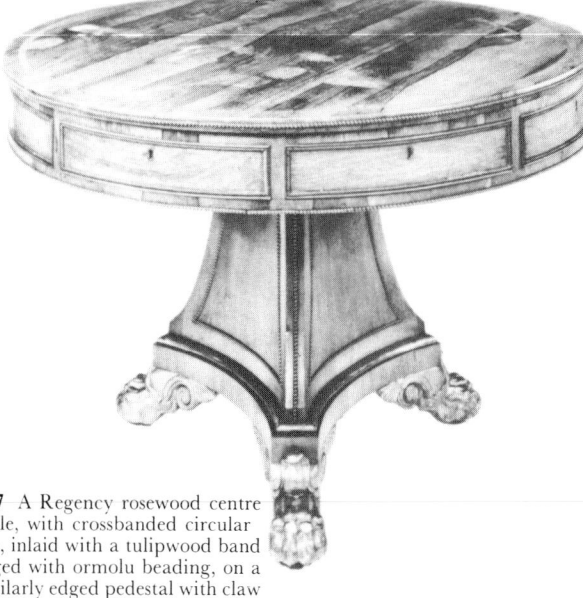

D 7 A Regency rosewood centre table, with crossbanded circular top, inlaid with a tulipwood band edged with ormolu beading, on a similarly edged pedestal with claw feet; 42 in. (106 cm) wide.

E 8 A George IV mahogany drum table, the top crossbanded with rosewood and pollard elm, with beaded border; 63 in. (160 cm) diameter.

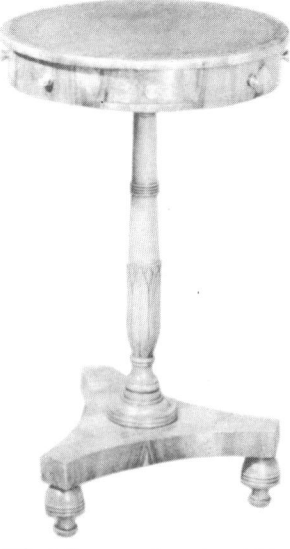

E 9 A Regency drum-top table, of yew-wood and walnut, with revolving top and four drawers; 18 in. (45 cm) diameter.

E 10 A William IV mahogany drum table, with carved base and scrolled feet, *c.* 1830; 39 in. (99 cm) diameter.

E 11 A rosewood drum table, the frieze with three triangular hinged drawers, *c.* 1910; 28 in. by 24 in. (71 by 60 cm).

D1 A Queen Anne burr walnut semi-elliptical games table, *c.* 1710; 28 in. high, 30 in. wide (71 by 77 cm). Of good colour and figuring throughout. One half of the top opens to a velvet-lined surface with walnut crossbanding, the other to a walnut surface crossbanded in oak. There is a small drawer with candle slide over to each side of the frieze.

E4 A George II mahogany card table, stamped "LC", *c.* 1750; 36 in. (91 cm) wide.

This is an extremely fine example of the turret-top design: the frieze rail is crossbanded in well figured veneer, cut and matched at the centre; the stylized foliate capping to the knees extends well down the legs and can be seen to protrude in high relief, and the original rosettes have survived.

E5 A Regency satinwood and rosewood swivel-top table, *c.* 1815; 29 in. high, 35 in. wide (74 by 89 cm).

The contrast in the colours of the timbers has become subdued with time to magnificent effect, but shows clearly the careful choice of well figured rosewood crossbanding and the highly stylized stringing in the neoclassical manner.

D2 A George I laburnum-veneered concertina-action card table, *c.* 1720; 34 in. (86 cm) wide. The veneering and colour are very fine, and the lightness of the piece is emphasized by the delicacy of the legs. There is a similar example in the Victoria and Albert Museum.

C3 A George II burr walnut concertina-action games table, *c.* 1740; 36 in. (90 cm) wide.

The carving is unusual and of exceptional quality, transforming a fine piece into a work of art.

E6 *(above)* A George III painted satinwood card table, *c.* 1790; 36 in. wide, 18 in. deep when folded (91 by 46 cm). Both back legs swing out to give even support and an elegant appearance.

This table exemplifies the finest of English furniture design in the late 18th-century classical style. The careful choice of finely figured satinwood veneers is further enhanced by the application of painted garlands, swags, festoons, husks, vases and other classical motifs.

The appearance of height and grace was given to such furniture by a perfectly proportioned top supported on carefully tapering legs, the outer edges of which are so arranged as to make the taper appear from the three inside edges.

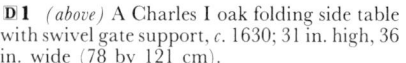

D 1 *(above)* A Charles I oak folding side table with swivel gate support, *c.* 1630; 31 in. high, 36 in. wide (78 by 121 cm).

This type of table is often referred to as a credence table (from the Italian *credenza*) as it may be used as a serving board.

This piece is a fine example of what one should look for in early oak furniture – fine quality carving, deep colour and a good state of preservation.

B 3 *(above)* A Charles II marquetry centre table, 30 in. high, 43 in. wide and 27 in. deep (77 by 108 by 69 cm). The marquetry is of walnut and stained ivory on an ebony ground.

This table is an important example of the marquetry cutter's craft – all the more so given its fine state of preservation, as marquetry is singularly prone to damage.

C 4 *(left)* A fine Regency rosewood, ormolu and bronze table, *c.* 1807; it stands 31 in. high and the top measures 25 by 19 in. (78; 64 by 48 cm).

The present top, which is not original, is of onyx, on a rosewood frieze ornamented with Roman theatrical masks, supported by patinated bronze gryphons joined by an ormolu H-stretcher.

The intensely antique appearance of this piece is typical of high-style Regency as propounded by such eminent arbiters of taste as Thomas Hope and George Smith, both of whom had produced books illustrating designs for furniture in this style before 1810.

B 2 *(above)* A William and Mary gilt-gesso centre table, late 17th century; 40 in. (101 cm) wide. The top is carved with rosettes, foliate scrolls and interlaced bands; its edge is spirally lobed.

The mellow colour of the gold and the bleeding through of the gesso are important indications of authenticity on a piece of this period.

C 5 *(right)* A Regency rosewood and parcel-gilt centre table, *c.* 1825; 53 in. wide by 29 in. deep (135 by 74 cm).

The top is inlaid with squares of various marbles and semi-precious stones, including malachite, lapis lazuli, jasper, alabaster and porphyry in a trellis grid, bordered with verde antico.

The fine proportions of the architectural columnar legs and moulded frieze to the top become unmistakeably late Regency when combined with the inswept platform base.

E1 *(right)* A Regency rosewood pedestal centre table, *c.* 1820; the diameter is 52 in. (132 cm).

The tilt top has a brass marquetry band and nulled edge, which is echoed on the concave edges of the plinth.

The inclusion of brass marquetry indicates a post-1815 date. This form of Boulle work was re-popularized by Louis le Gaigneur, who opened his factory in Edgware, London, in that year.

C2 *(below)* A George IV rosewood centre table attributed to Gillow of Lancaster; 30 in. high, 58 in. in diameter (75 by 148 cm).

The well figured top is inlaid with a brass marquetry border, the edge is richly carved with scallops. An almost identical table is shown in an undated Gillow room setting of *c.* 1825 in the Gillow archive.

The tendency away from antique and architecturally based decoration toward realistic and fleshy foliage began during the mid-1820s and set a pattern that would be much followed during the Victorian period.

D3 *(above)* A late Regency rosewood and specimen wood centre table, inlaid with an ivory plaque, *c.* 1825; 52 in. diameter (131 cm). The woods used include maple, satinwood, ebony and amaranth and the fine filleting of the top is echoed in the divided spandrels to the plinth.

While the stem is carved to represent a foliate cup in the latest fashion, the traditional lion's paw foot remains an important feature on this type of table until well into the middle of the 19th century.

D4 *(left)* A giltwood centre table, *c.* 1840; it stands 31 in. high and is 56 in. across (77 by 142 cm). The top is inset with a central marquetry panel of flowers and strapwork in Elizabethan revival style.

The design resembles the work of Philip Hardwick in the mid-1830s, and the combination of highly figured burr-veneers, marquetry and gilding is a definite indication of 19th-century manufacture.

B1 *(right)* A Queen Anne gilt-gesso side table, *c.* 1710; 37 in. (94 cm) wide. The top is decorated with carved foliate strapwork around a central cartouche of an eagle killing a serpent.

Furniture of this period should always show a totally compatible blend of formality of design with exuberance of decoration. Here the rectangular top of architectural proportions is on curvilinear but severe legs terminating in animal feet, the whole then lightened with bas relief carving, applied with gesso and gilded.

D2 *(above)* A George II giltwood console table, *c.* 1730; 30 in. high by 39 in. wide (75 by 99 cm). The verde antico top is a replacement.

Console tables of ponderous proportions incorporating animal motifs, shells, C-scrolls and foliage combined with strictly architectural features became popular in England after the 1720s, when William Kent began designing furniture in this style.

C3 *(right)* A George II parcel-gilt walnut side table, *c.* 1740; 67 in. (170 cm) wide.

The combination of highly figured veneers, high relief carving and gilding cannot be said to be representative of English furniture during the mid-18th century; such pieces show a definite Continental influence.

C4 *(right)* A George II mahogany pier table, with verde antico marble top, *c.* 1740; 34 in. high by 62 in. wide (86 by 156 cm).

This massively built table with exceptionally sturdy insweeping cabriole legs and rich deep carving is a prime example of the heaviness against which furniture designers such as Adam, Sheraton and Hepplewhite were to react later in the century; nothing could be further from the grace and elegance for which Adam called, but by the same token, nothing could demonstrate more clearly the massive confidence and fortune of mid-century England.

Similar designs for pier tables are recorded in William Jones's *The Gentlman or Builder's Companion*, 1739, and compare also P. Ward Jackson, *English Furniture Designs of the 18th Century*, 1958, figure 21.

B1 *(left)* A George II giltwood side table, *c.* 1745; 60 in. (153 cm) wide. The marble top is a replacement.

The front legs do not sweep smoothly down to the hairy-paw feet, but render the contours of an animal's leg in the best rococo manner; in contrast, the scrolling back legs end in block feet.

This table compares interestingly with the one at the foot of the facing page – note how relatively small differences in proportion make this example considerably lighter, an effect which is increased by the gilding.

B2 *(right)* A Chippendale carved wood and gilt side table with breche pernice marble top, *c.* 1755; 34 in. high by 55 in. wide (86 by 140 cm).

This is English rococo at its most flamboyant; gone now is the substantial frieze that would normally lend apparent support to the top in favour of lavish open carving that springs directly from the legs in an upward movement.

The term "Chippendale" in this context describes a period and a design rather than indicating manufacture in Chippendale's workshop. Most of the leading cabinet-makers of the day produced designs for furniture in this curvilinear style, but it has become standard practice to use Chippendale's name for them, largely as a result of the widespread popularity of his *Director*.

C3 *(left)* A George III marquetry console table in the manner of John Cobb, *c.* 1765; 31 in. high, 48 in. wide (79 by 122 cm).

The serpentine top has a moulded brass border and three shaped marquetry panels of flowers and fruit on harewood reserves within kingwood borders. The drawers are inlaid with swags of flowers and leaves also on a harewood ground within kingwood borders. The back support is later, as are the drawer-pulls.

C1 *(right)* A George III giltwood side table, *c.* 1785; 34 in. high, 58 in. wide (86 by 148 cm).

The rectangular white marble top is decorated in scagliola in the manner of Bossi, with alternating roundels of birds and rosettes, framed by entwined bellflowers.

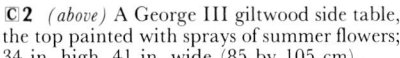

C2 *(above)* A George III giltwood side table, the top painted with sprays of summer flowers; 34 in. high, 41 in. wide (85 by 105 cm).

The refined neo-classicism of this table reflects the influence of French craftsmen working in England during the 1780s. In its general style it is similar to the pair of pier tables at Nostell Priory designed by Robert Adam in 1775.

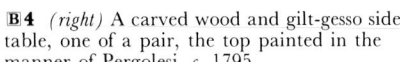

D3 *(above)* A George III harewood and marquetry pier table, *c.* 1785; 34 in. high by 43 in. wide (87 by 109 cm).

The top is crossbanded with rosewood and inlaid with a fan lunette within a broad satinwood border inlaid with green stained flower heads. The frieze is inlaid with flutes, the three-dimensional effect of which is achieved by scorching each inset piece in hot sand.

B4 *(right)* A carved wood and gilt-gesso side table, one of a pair, the top painted in the manner of Pergolesi, *c.* 1795.

There are several variations on this particular model, the prototype for which is believed to have been designed for Carlton House by Henry Holland.

C1 *(below)* A Regency rosewood library table, in the manner of Gillow of Lancaster, early 19th century. It stands 29 in. high and is 60 in. long (74 by 152 cm).

Late rather than early Regency is denoted in this piece by the nulled edges to the drawer fronts and frieze panels, the accentuated and deeply scrolling knees and the foliate motif to the gilt metal castors.

D2 *(left)* A late George III painted and rosewood side table, *c.* 1810: 34 in. high, 33 in. wide (86 by 85 cm). The top has a wide satinwood crossbanded border painted with flowers: the panelled frieze is divided by gilt lions' heads.

C3 *(above)* A George I walnut kneehole dressing table, *c.* 1725; 35 in. (88 cm) wide. The top is crossbanded, quarter-veneered and inlaid with chevron-pattern lines.

D4 *(above)* A George III faded mahogany rent table of the late 18th century; 47 in. (119 cm) in diameter.

The leather-lined revolving top has a well enclosed by a flap with 12 alphabetized drawers in the frieze. The base has two doors.

D5 *(left)* A Regency mahogany writing table, *c.* 1810; 29 in. high, 48 in. wide, 41 in. deep (74 by 122 by 104 cm).

The top is inlaid with scrolled ebonized lines, which are echoed on the legs. There is a frieze drawer on each side, one with a divided interior and another with a leather-lined flap.

E3 *(above)* A Regency brass-inlaid rosewood kidney-shaped table, *c.* 1810; 30 in. high, 35 in. wide (75 by 89 cm).

Note the lavish use of brass in the gallery, the inlay to the frieze, the collars, feet and in the cast ornament to the legs. The top may originally have been leather-lined.

D1 *(above)* A Regency rosewood writing table, attributed to Gillow of Lancaster, *c.* 1825; it stands 30 in. high and the top measures 63 by 30 in. (76 by 159 by 76 cm).

Both top and frieze have panels of brass marquetry, the lower edge of the frieze is lobed, as are the under edges of the scroll stretchers, and there is fine crisp carving on the legs, stretchers and centre rail.

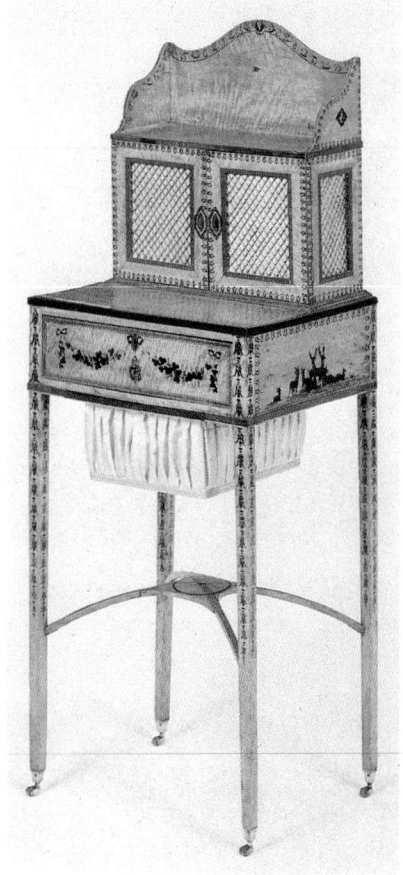

D4 An Edwardian painted satinwood Carlton House desk, *c.* 1905; 39 in. high, 54 in. wide (99 by 137 cm).

Whereas the lines and proportions of this piece are broadly true to early 19th-century patterns, the decoration, though finely executed, is more in imitation of 18th-century art than of classical originals.

D2 *(left)* A small painted satin-birch work table, *c.* 1800; 49 in. high, 18 in. wide (124 by 45 cm).

The cupboard doors with wire trellis open to six short drawers, the lower part has a fitted sewing drawer above the work bag. The whole is crossbanded in rosewood and palisander and painted, sometime later, with deer, husks and armorial devices.

B1 *(right)* A yew-wood gateleg dining table of the late 17th century. It stands 28 in high and the top measures 72 by 61 in. (71 cm; 183 by 156 cm).

This table has all the marks of good, solidly made country furniture, and could have been made several decades before or at any time up to the late 18th century if design is the only feature to go by. The stretchering is as plain as can be – compare the William and Mary table below – and the tradition of elaborate turning to the legs (maintained in the table shown at the foot of this page) is simplified to a pleasant collared baluster on each leg with a turned foot.

C2 *(left)* A William and Mary oval cedarwood gateleg table, *c.* 1690. It stands 29 in. high and the top measures 43 in. by 52 in. (73 cm; 110 by 132 cm).

Both the design of the stretchering and the colour are particularly fine, and the braganza or Spanish feet and the use of cedar nominate this an unusual example of the period.

Compare figure 82 in R.W. Symonds' *Furniture Making in 17th and 18th Century England.*

D3 *(right)* A William and Mary walnut two-part gateleg dining table, *c.* 1690; the top measures 50 in. by 65 in. (126 by 165 cm).

The veneered top has a broad crossbanding with a crossbanded moulded edge. Each part of the table has one broad flap, four ball-turned legs and double gateleg supports with turned feet.

C 1 *(above)* A late Elizabethan draw-leaf refectory table, *c.* 1600. It stands 32 in. high, is 36 in. wide, 115 in. long closed and 188 in. extended (82 cm high, 92 cm wide, 292 and 468 cm long).

The geometrical inlay of the frieze is echoed in the stretchers. The lower edge of the frieze is carved with egg and dart framing a central carving of foliate lobing; the legs are leaf-carved and lobed.

C 2 *(above)* A late Elizabethan oak draw-leaf refectory table, *c.* 1590. It stands 34 in. high and measures 84 in. long closed, 158 in. extended (85 by 121/400 cm).

The top is mitre-framed over a heavily lobed frieze on elaborately carved cup-and-cover legs.

D 3 *(above)* An Elizabethan oak refectory table, the rectangular two-plank top with cleated ends, formerly a draw-leaf table, *c.* 1600; 33 in. high by 99 in. long (85 by 250 cm).

It is not uncommon for early tables of this type to have been re-topped, particularly when the original was of extending form and may have been damaged in use. There is serious detriment to the value only when the top replacement has evidently been done at a much later date — post-1850, for example.

C 4 *(below)* A Charles I oak draw-leaf table, *c.* 1630; 33 in. high, 96 in. long when closed (82 by 224 cm).

The square legs are almost certainly not original. They may have been incorporated to make the piece look more like a side table, but the effect is marred by the use of existing timbers with prominent and redundant mortice holes.

C1 *(above)* A George III faded mahogany four-pedestal dining table, *c.* 1800; 54 in. wide by 176 in. long, fully extended (137 by 447 cm), with finely figured top.

C2 *(below)* A Regency mahogany dining table, attributed to Gillow of Lancaster, *c.* 1815; 60 in. wide, it is 143 in. long with all five leaves inserted (153 by 363 cm).

D3 *(above)* A Regency rosewood table, *c.* 1815; the top measures 69 by 57 in. (173 by 142 cm).

Both the top and the four-cornered base are inlaid with brass lines, those to the top having stylized foliate sprays at the corners. The pedestal and supporting scrolls have gilt-metal enrichments.

D4 *(above)* A mahogany extending dining table, *c.* 1840. It is 56 in. (142 cm) wide and extends to 192 in. (438 cm) when all eight leaves are in place.

Such tables show to their best advantage when extended to their full length; when closed up the combination of solid pedestal and finer legs in juxtaposition can appear incongruous.

B5 *(left)* A Victorian mahogany extending table, stamped Johnstone Jupe & Co, *c.* 1840; it is 66 in. in diameter when closed.

C1 A William and Mary walnut, elm, kingwood and olive wood parquetry side or dressing table, *c.* 1695; 30 in. (76 cm) wide. The oyster veneer top is inlaid with two concentric circles surrounded by quatrefoils and hearts.

C4 A Regency penwork sofa table, *c.* 1810; 28 in. high, the top measures 60 in. long when open by 23 in. (72 by 152 by 59 cm).

The top is decorated with Greek dancers and musicians flanking a central reclining figure in a vine-clad bower, a theme that is recalled in the vine-decorated lyre supports.

D2 A George III mahogany sofa table, with satinwood crossbanding, *c.* 1790; 29 in. high, 60 in. wide with the flaps up (74 by 152 cm).

The turned columns make this table remarkably elegant and the absence of a low cross-stretcher indicates a good early model.

D5 A Regency rosewood sofa table in the manner of Gillow of Lancaster, *c.* 1815; 28 in. high, 59 in. wide (71 by 150 cm).

A rather severe effect is achieved by the blank standard ends, solid platforms and scrolled legs, being lightened only with boxwood stringing and tapering inlay.

D3 A George III rosewood sofa table, *c.* 1800; 29 in. high, 60 in. wide with the flaps up (74 by 152 cm). The top is double crossbanded in satinwood, the drawers are banded and there is satinwood stringing to the legs.

B6 A Regency rosewood and amboyna sofa table with ormolu mounts, early 19th century; 45 in. (115 cm) wide. The lavishness of the mounting indicates an expensive piece when made; this is an outstanding example of English Regency in the Empire style.

C1 *(left)* A Regency rosewood sofa table in the manner of George Bullock; it stands 28 in. high and the top measures 63 by 25 in. (71 by 160 by 64 cm).

The top is crossbanded with satinwood and pollard oak, bordered with ebonized and boxwood lines. The frieze drawers are outlined in brass and the lower edge of the frieze is decorated with an ebony and brass border. Ebonized roundels are used to decorate the yoke stretcher.

Two grander tables with related inlay at Scone Castle, Perth, are attributed to Bullock, who is known to have designed some of the more ponderous examples of Regency furniture. He contributed greatly to the later Regency popularity of oak as a decorative wood.

D2 A George III oval mahogany Pembroke table, *c.* 1775; 40 in. (102 cm) across when open.

Emphatically in the French style, this table has a flame-figured top with narrow crossbanding and a single frieze drawer.

E3 A George III Pembroke table, late 18th century; 43 in. (80 cm) wide. The top is decorated with parquetry and inlay of yew and sabicu.

Sabicu is a Central American wood used after 1750, chiefly for veneers.

D4 A George III penwork-decorated Pembroke table in the French style, *c.* 1780; the top measures 30 by 36 in. (76 by 91 cm) with the flaps up.

The serpentine top has a central chinoiserie design of figures with a parasol and child within a broad floral border; the drawer-front also has a chinoiserie design surrounded by fruiting vines, which are carried down the slender cabriole legs.

C5 A George III satinwood Pembroke table in the French manner, *c.* 1785; it is 30 in. high and 37 in. wide when open (76 by 94 cm). The top with an oval central inlay is narrowly crossbanded.

C6 A George III satinwood harlequin Pembroke table to a design by Thomas Sheraton, *c.* 1795; it stands 29 in. high and is 31 in. deep (74 by 78 cm). The design is in the *Cabinet-Maker and Upholsterer's Drawing Book*, 1793, pages 417-430, plate 56. The crossbanding is of amaranth.

The interior has two rising cases of drawers, one with a long drawer fitted as a dressing table with a toilet glass, bottles and fitted compartments, the other with small drawers and pigeonholes. The harlequin mechanism is operated by the pull-out supports for the leaves.

Novelty mechanical furniture of this type was extremely popular during the second half of the 18th century and is generally referred to as metamorphic. Sheraton however used the name harlequin, explaining that it was "for no other reason but because in exhibitions of that sort there is generally a great deal of machinery introduced in the scenery".

C1 A fine George III mahogany tea table, *c.* 1760; 31 in. high, 34 in. wide and 23 in. deep (80 by 87 by 59 cm); with fretwork gallery, on cluster-column legs.

E2 A William and Mary cedarwood triangular table, *c.* 1690; 28 in. high, 27 in, across. The top has three flaps on spring supports. Compare Chinnery, *Oak Furniture: The British Tradition*, p.305.

C3 A George II brass-inlaid mahogany tilt-top supper table, 1740-1750, in the manner associated with Abraham Roentgen; 29 in. high, with a diameter of 24 in. (74 by 62 cm).

C4 A small late George II Cuban mahogany tripod table. *c.* 1755; it is 23 in. high and 12 in. wide (58 by 32 cm).

Small tables of this type have been so much in demand that many have been made up from a dish-top tray and the lower part of a pole screen. One indication of authenticity is the length of stem — a highly placed knop, as here, is inconsistent with a pole screen origin.

D5 A fine George II octagonal mahogany tripod table, the gallery pierced with Chinese fretwork, *c.* 1750; 30 in. high, 20 in. wide (76 by 52 cm).

This is an unusual form of tripod base and, like much authentic furniture of the Chippendale period, more than compensates for the quaintness of its design by its amusing character.

C6 A late George II mahogany tripod table, mid-18th century; 29 in. high with a diameter of 26 in. (74 by 67 cm).

The pierced gallery is inlaid with brass stringing, the baluster column leaf-carved on leaf- and flower-carved legs with claw-and-pad feet. The table is of fine quality throughout and can be considered the epitome of its type.

C7 A rare George III mahogany kettle stand, *c.* 1760; 23 in. (58 cm) high. The kettle and heater shown are contemporary with the stand.

B3 A fine George II ormolu-mounted mahogany oval wine cooler, *c.* 1755; 28 in. (71 cm) wide. The brass-bound body has goat mask and ring handles. A similar but more elaborately mounted version is illustrated in Edwards and Macquoid, *The Dictionary of English Furniture*, revised edition 1954, vol. III, page 373, figure 5.

C4 A George II brass-bound mahogany wine cooler, *c.* 1755; 21 in. (73 cm) wide. The oval body is tapered with a gadrooned edge, and the bands are decorated with bead and reel ornament. The handles are less flamboyant than those of no. 3 (left), but the knees are applied with bacchic masks. The cloven hoof feet conceal castors.

B1 An early George III library staircase with two flights and a half landing, *c.* 1775. It stands 122 in. high, is 50 in. wide and 68 in. deep (310 by 126 by 172 cm). The risers are pierced, the handrail moulded over turned banisters and fluted terminals.

E2 *(left)* A Broadwood barless grand piano in a mahogany Empire-style case, 1909; 90 in. (229 cm). It is numbered 50164 and may originally have been bought as a gift for Lily Langtry.

C5 A George II walnut clothes press, *c.* 1755; 65 in. high, 54 in. wide (165 by 137 cm).
Of fine colour, it has a simple moulded cornice over quarter-veneered doors vigorously carved with scrolls, acanthus and flowering branches, that open to four shelves. The *bombé* lower part is carved with lion's head masks to the angles suspending acanthus and bellflowers. Note the carving disguising the otherwise plain bracket feet.

D 1 A George II mahogany polescreen, *c.* 1755; 59 in. (150 cm) high. The petit point panel is set in a frame carved to show a combination of the rustic with the rococo. There is pierced carving to the pedestal and the pole is surmounted by an elaborate flowering finial.

C 3 A Chinese mirror painting of the early 18th century in an English frame of *c.* 1760; 50 in. high, 45 in. wide (127 by 113 cm).

The picture is a highly stylized view of Windsor Castle in an idealized landscape, with royalty and mythological figures in the foreground. The frame, elaborately scrolled and swagged and surmounted by military motifs, is exceptionally fine.

C 5 *(below)* A painted and gilded wardrobe by William Burges, dated 1879. It is 95 in. (240 cm) high and 51 in. (129 cm) wide.

An eclectic medievalist fantasy, this is characteristic Burges work. The front shows the domestic distractions of Socrates, Aristotle, Diogenes and Luther; the sides show St Paul and Virgil escaping the torments of matriarchy.

Burges was an eminent architect whose name is always associated with the 19th-century medievalist movement. Like his 18th-century predecessors, Burges was involved in designing the interiors of his houses and the style and decoration of the furniture to go in them. Among his best known commissions was the reconstruction of Cardiff Castle for the Marquess of Bute, and the best known artist to collaborate with him in the execution of his schemes was Edward Burne-Jones.

C 2 A Chinese mirror picture of the mid-18th century in an English frame of the period; 43 by 22 in. (110 by 56 cm).

One of a pair, it shows an exotic bird against a background of tree peony with a house behind. The frame has an exaggeratedly broken pediment with cartouches top and bottom and suggestions of rococo waterfalls.

E 4 A Regency revolving bookstand in mahogany, *c.* 1810; 34 in. (86 cm) wide. A similar example is illustrated in Jourdain, *Regency Furniture*, revised edition 1965, figure 197.

Games tables

D 1 A William and Mary card table, with fold-over top, on finely tuned legs, joined by stretchers.

C 2 A black and gold lacquer card table, of the William and Mary period, *c.* 1668.

D 3 A walnut and marquetry games table, late 17th century; 31 in. (77 cm) wide.

D 4 A walnut games table, with crossbanded folding top, late 17th century; 33 in. (84 cm) wide.

D 5 A Queen Anne walnut card table, the top with counter wells and candle recesses; 33 in. (84 cm) wide.

C 6 A Queen Anne walnut card table, with concertina action, fitted with drawer, *c.* 1710.

C 7 A harlequin Queen Anne table, with two flaps, japanned black and gold with chinoiserie decoration, *c.* 1710; 31 in. high by 32 in. wide (77 by 80 cm).

C 8 A Queen Anne laburnumwood card table, with recesses for counters and candle stands, with a concertina action and cylindrical legs.

D 9 A Queen Anne burr-walnut card table, with concertina action; 36 in. (90 cm) wide.

D 10 A Queen Anne walnut card table, fitted with a drawer; 28 in. high by 32 in. wide (70 by 80 cm).

D 11 A Queen Anne gilt-gesso card table, with lobed folding top incised and moulded on a punched ground; 30 in. high by 34 in. wide (76 by 86 cm).

D 12 A George I walnut, banded and herringbone inlaid card table, with concertina action, with lined folded top; 34 in. (85 cm) wide.

D 13 A George I walnut card table, with lobed crossbanded baize-lined top, fitted with centre well and candle wells; 35 in. (89 cm) wide.

E 14 A George I mahogany card table, with folding top revealing a playing surface, *c.* 1720; 25 in. high by 34 in. wide (62 by 85 cm).

D 15 A George I walnut card table, with shaped folding top, and a drawer in the undulating frieze, the legs carved with foliage and leaf motifs.

E 16 A George II concertina-action mahogany card table, with folding moulded top baize-lined, and Greek-key patterned frieze; 29 in. high by 36 in. wide (75 by 91 cm).

E1 A George II mahogany card table, the polished interior with candle stands and money wells, a drawer in the frieze, *c.* 1740; 28 in. high by 37 in. wide (72 by 94 cm).

E2 A George II mahogany triple-top card, tea and writing table, on pad feet, *c.* 1740; 28 in. high by 29 in. wide (70 by 72 cm).

E3 A George II mahogany card table, the projecting top and interior with candle stands and candle wells, with a frieze drawer, *c.* 1740; 33 in. (85 cm) wide.

E4 An early George II card table, the serpentine top opening to reveal guinea wells and candle stands; 33 in. (82 cm) wide.

E5 A George II red walnut card table, the top enclosing a baize-lined interior, above one frieze drawer; 35 in. (89 cm) wide.

E6 An early George II mahogany triple-flap games table, with square-eared recessed top, enclosing a marquetry games board in stained and light woods; 32 in. (81 cm) wide.

E7 A George II mahogany concertina-action card table, the top with rosette and ribbon-carved edge, candle stands and counter wells, *c.* 1740; 33 in. (85 cm) wide.

E8 A late George II mahogany card table, the serpentine baize-lined top with leaf-carved border; 29 in. high by 36 in. wide (74 by 90 cm).

E9 A George II mahogany card table, with moulded eared hinged top enclosing a baize-lined surface, with wells; 36 in. (90 cm) wide.

E10 A George II mahogany card table, the top with a cabochon moulding enclosing a baize-lined interior and opening on a concertina action, *c.* 1770; 36 in. (90 cm) wide.

E11 A George II mahogany card table, with eared baize-lined folding top with counter wells and candle recesses, plain frieze on cabriole legs carved with acanthus on claw-and-ball feet; 35 in. (89 cm) wide.

E12 A George II mahogany card table, with baize-lined folding top with ribbon-tied border, the plain frieze edged with narrow wave moulding, 34 in. (86 cm) wide.

E13 An early Georgian mahogany card table, the interior with counter wells, 38 in. (82 cm) wide.

E14 A George II mahogany card table, the top with projecting corners opening to reveal candle stands, the shaped frieze with a short drawer; 29 in. high by 35 in. wide (70 by 87 cm).

E15 A mahogany card table, with folding top, the frieze with a shallow drawer, on well-carved cabriole legs terminating in ball-and-claw feet.

E16 A Chippendale mahogany card table, with fold-over top, edged with "ribbon and rose" carving, the well-carved legs on scroll feet, *c.* 1750.

E 1 A Chippendale card table, the fold-over top with carved edge; 29 in. high by 36 in. wide (72 by 91 cm).

D 2 A Chippendale mahogany card table, with folding top above a serpentine frieze, with well-decorated straight legs.

E 3 A late George II mahogany serpentine-fronted card table, the top with egg-and-dart moulding, *c.* 1750; 35 in. (90 cm) wide.

E 4 A late George II mahogany card table, the serpentine baize-lined top with leaf-carved border, *c.* 1760; 29 in. high by 36 in. wide (74 by 90 cm).

E 5 A late George II mahogany card table, with serpentine baize-lined top raised on four leaf-carved cabriole legs, *c.* 1755; 29 in. high by 36 in. wide (74 by 90 cm).

E 6 A George II mahogany card or tea table, with hinged top edged with crisply carved flower-heads, the carved frieze with Chinese blind fretwork; 32 in. (82 cm) wide.

E 7 A Chippendale card table, with intricately decorated frieze on straight square legs, ending in block feet.

E 8 An early George II mahogany card table, with moulded top, plain frieze with concertina action; 36 in. (91 cm) wide.

E 9 An early George III mahogany card table, with moulded baize-lined folding top, plain frieze and cabriole legs headed by acanthus; 36 in. (90 cm) wide.

E 10 A George III card table, with well-figured baize-lined moulded serpentine top, the stepped feet headed by rosettes; 36 in. (90 cm) wide.

E 11 An early George III mahogany card table, the fold-over baize-lined top with one fitted drawer; 36 in. (90 cm) wide.

E 12 An early George III carved mahogany card table, the fold-over top with baize lining, the frieze with a drawer, *c.* 1760; 32 in. (81 cm) wide.

E 13 A mahogany card table, with concertina frame, rare inlaid border, 18th century, 36 in. wide by 18 in. deep (90 by 45 cm).

D 14 A Chippendale mahogany card table, with veneered top, baize-lined, the frieze carved and shaped in the manner of the Gothic revival of the 1770s.

E 15 An Adam walnut card table, with fold-over top, the frieze serpentine shaped, *c.* 1780; 29 in. high by 33 in. wide (72 by 80 cm).

E 16 A serpentine-shaped mahogany card table, the top edges carved, the lower edge of the apron similarly decorated, on chamfered legs with carved brackets, the outer corners of the legs also carved; 36 in. (90 cm) wide.

Games Tables

The fold-over top card or games table as we know it was not developed until towards the end of the 17th century. Prior to that time it had been the practice to spread a cloth over a centre or occasional table when it was required for a hand at cards. But the huge popularity of gaming after the Restoration in 1660 created a wide demand for purpose-made gambling tables.

Throughout the 18th century card tables with fold-over tops were made in pairs, one with a polished surface to act as a stowaway tea table, the other with a surface rebated to take a panel of petit point needlework; turret top tables were often fitted with counter as well as candle wells.

The finest opened with a concertina action; alternatively one or both back legs was hinged to swing out as a support for the fold-over top. In the early 19th century however a swivel top was introduced, based on an eccentric pivot; the top then opened and turned on a fixed base and was supported equally whether open or closed.

E 1 A George III mahogany serpentine card table, in the French style, with moulded top, the frieze with a rope moulding at the lower edge, *c.* 1770; 37 in. (94 cm) wide.

E 2 A George III mahogany serpentine card table, with concertina action, the frieze with gadrooned border, *c.* 1770; 29 in. high by 36 in. wide (74 by 90 cm).

D 3 A Hepplewhite mahogany card table, of semi-circular form, on cabriole legs, the whole well decorated.

E 4 A George III mahogany serpentine card table, with crossbanding in coromandelwood and raised on square tapering stop-fluted legs with shaped feet, headed by inlaid ovals, *c.* 1780; 36 in. (90 cm) wide.

E 5 A George III satinwood card table, with rounded top painted with a bat's-wing motif; 32 in. (82 cm) wide.

E 6 A George III satinwood card table, the serpentine top inlaid with a demi-lunette crossbanded with rosewood; 35 in. (90 cm) wide.

E 7 A George III marquetry card table, the top inlaid with a fan medallion, crossbanded with flowers and laurel divided by lilies, *c.* 1785; 38 in. (96 cm) wide.

E 8 A George III mahogany demi-lune card table, with crossbanded top inlaid with an urn, foliate scrolls and husk chains, above an inlaid frieze, late 19th century; 37 in. (92 cm) wide.

E 9 A George III mahogany card table, with semi-circular baize-lined folding top, crossbanded with rosewood and satinwood, on square tapering legs inlaid with lines; 36 in. (90 cm) wide.

E 10 A George III satinwood card table, with baize-lined top decorated with peacock feathers and summer flower swags; 41 in. (105 cm) wide.

D 11 A George III marquetry card table, *c.* 1770-1790; 37 in. (92 cm) wide.

E 12 A George III mahogany card table, with tulipwood crossbanded top; 42 in. (96 cm) wide.

D 13 A George III satinwood card table, with baize-lined top; 28 in. high by 40 in. wide (72 by 103 cm).

D 14 An Adam period satinwood card table, crossbanded with kingwood, *c.* 1775.

E 15 A George III mahogany and satinwood card table, crossbanded with rosewood; 45 in. (114 cm) wide.

E1 A George III mahogany and satinwood crossbanded card table, with fold-over top and inlaid frieze; 37 in. (92 cm) wide.

E5 A George III mahogany card table, the top crossbanded in purpleheart; 37 in. (91 cm) wide.

E9 A Sheraton period satinwood fold-over-top card table, the top crossbanded in rosewood, with frieze drawer, on square tapering legs; 36 in. (90 cm) wide.

E13 A Regency mahogany card table, with rounded rectangular baize-lined top, crossbanded in rosewood on spirally turned tapering legs, headed by rosettes; 36 in. (90 cm) wide.

E2 A Georgian mahogany card table, with chamfered baize-lined top, inlaid with geometric designs, the frieze centred by tablet; 36 in. (90 cm) wide.

E6 A George III mahogany card table, with baize-lined crossbanded breakfront top, on square tapering legs; 37 in. (91 cm) wide.

E10 A Sheraton figured satinwood card table, with satinwood veneers, the hinged folding crossbanded surface above ebony decorated apron, on slim turned legs, *c.* 1805; 28 in. high by 36 in. wide (70 by 90 cm).

E14 A Regency rosewood card table, with baize-lined top, the frieze mounted with gilt-metal rope twist borders on ebonized and parcel-gilt ring-turned splayed legs; 34 in. (86 cm) wide.

E3 A George III satinwood card table, with baize-lined top crossbanded with rosewood and painted; 36 in. (90 cm) wide.

E7 A George III satinwood card table, with rounded rectangular baize-lined top, crossbanded with rosewood, with a plain frieze, on square tapering legs; 37 in. (94 cm) wide.

E11 A mahogany "D" form card table, with folding top, decorated with boxwood stringing, on slim tapering legs ending in casters, 19th century.

E15 A Regency calamander and satinwood card table, with baize-lined top with scrolled satinwood banding, swivelling to reveal compartments; 36 in. (90 cm) wide.

E4 A George III satinwood card table, stamped Gillows, Lancaster, with rosewood crossbanded baize-lined hinged top, on square tapering legs edged with dark lines, early 19th century; 42 in. (106 cm) wide.

E8 A rosewood card table, with folding top, on square tapering legs, *c.* 1800; 29 in. high by 35 in. wide (72 by 85 cm).

E12 A Regency rosewood "D" shaped card table, with yew-wood banding, fold-over top with green baize lining, the panelled frieze with a brass moulding; 36 in. (90 cm) wide.

E16 A Regency mahogany card table, with well-figured baize-lined folding top, crossbanded with rosewood; 36 in. (90 cm) wide.

E1 A Regency card table, in kingwood with ormolu mounting, the fold-over top above finely decorated curved legs, ending in claw feet, on casters.

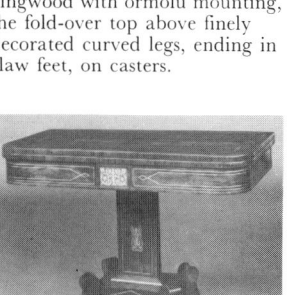

E2 A Regency card table, in brass-inlaid rosewood, with folding baize-lined top, the frieze inlaid with sylized scrolls, 36 in. (91 cm) wide.

E3 A Regency ormolu-mounted calamanderwood card table, the top inlaid with burr-maple bands and ormolu beading, on scrolled quardripartite base, 36 in. (91 cm) wide.

E4 A Regency rosewood and crossbanded card table, inlaid with boxwood, *c.* 1815; 36 in. (91 cm) wide.

E5 A Regency rosewood and cut brass inlaid card table, the crossbanded fold-over top with baize lining, the splayed feet ending in brass cappings and casters; 36 in. (91 cm) wide.

E6 A crossbanded and inlaid rosewood card table, with decorated frieze, *c.* 1810; 36 in. (91 cm) wide.

E7 Regency rosewood card table, with brass inlay, on turned support, the curved legs also inlaid.

E8 A Regency rosewood card table, the top with chamfered corners over a conforming frieze, on four curved supports over severe scroll legs joining at a concave plinth, *c.* 1820; 28 in. high by 36 in. wide (72 by 91 cm).

E9 A Regency mahogany card table, with rounded rectangular felt-lined top; 36 in. (91 cm) wide.

E10 A Regency rosewood and cut brass inlaid card table, with green baize lining, on scroll feet with casters; 36 in. (91 cm) wide.

E11 A Regency rosewood and brass-mounted games table, inlaid with cut brass stringing, with reversible top, *c.* 1810; 28 in. high by 25 in. wide (73 by 65 cm).

D12 A Regency amboyna card table, with baize-lined folding top; 36 in. (91 cm) wide.

E13 A Regency mahogany folding rectangular card table, 36 in. (91 cm) wide.

E14 A Regency ebonized games table, the rounded square penwork top well decorated with birds and trophies; 21 in. (53 cm) square.

E15 A Regency rosewood games table, the rectangular top with hinged D-shaped ends enclosing wells, the centre panel reversing to form a chessboard; 31 in. high by 55 in. wide (74 by 138 cm).

E16 A Regency mahogany games table, with D-ended galleried rounded rectangular sliding top, reversing to a chessboard, early 19th century; 30 in. (77 cm) wide.

E1 A William IV rosewood card table, with baize-lined, beaded rounded rectangular top, with scrolled paw feet; 37 in. (94 cm) wide.

E2 A William IV rosewood card table, with rectangular hinged top, edged with broad gadrooning and acanthus, enclosing a baize-lined playing surface, on incurved rectangular base with scroll feet carved with acanthus; 36 in. (92 cm) wide.

E3 A William IV mahogany folding card table, with elaborately carved frieze, the turned support on circular base, with well-defined feet; 36 in. (91 cm) wide.

E4 A mahogany fold-over card table, on tapering stem, with incurved quadripartite base, on bun feet, early 19th century; 36 in. (91 cm).

E5 A Victorian rosewood card table, the serpentine apron with the Prince of Wales feathers; 36 in. (91 cm) wide.

E6 A rare papier mâché chess table, the top with alternating ebonized and simulated malachite squares, on cabriole legs, 1840s; 25 in. (64 cm) wide.

E7 A chess table, in penwork and ivory-inlaid ebony, c. 1850; 29 in. high by 23 in. square (75 by 58 cm).

E8 A walnut and marquetry serpentine card table, with swivelling top, c. 1850; 36 in. (91 cm).

E9 A Victorian walnut and marquetry games table, the top inlaid with a chessboard, c. 1860; 39 in. (97 cm) wide.

E10 A mahogany envelope games table, the interior lined with a circular panel of needlework, executed in gros and petit point; 31 in. (81 cm) square, open.

E11 An ebonized and boulle serpentine-fronted card table, with ormolu mounts and claret baize lining, on cabriole legs ending in sabots, mid 19th century; 35 in. (89 cm) wide.

E12 A Victorian well-figured walnut serpentine card table, with fold-over top, on a baluster stem with ornately carved cabriole legs, on original casters, c. 1860; 30 in. high by 33 in. wide (76 by 85 cm).

E13 A Victorian rosewood card table, the fold-over swivel top above a compartment, with splay legs and scroll feet; 36 in. (91 cm) wide.

E14 A rosewood card table, the folding surface revealing a blue baize lining with leather tooled border, 19th century.

E15 A neo-classic-style marquetry card table, with rectangular brassbound folding top, with segmental corners, inlaid with a central panel of arabesques on mahogany crossbanded ground, with tulipwood flowerhead borders, late 19th century; 39 in. (100 cm) wide.

E16 A Victorian rosewood card table, attributed to Heal & Sons, with swivelling rectangular baize-lined folding top and plain frieze, on reeded baluster turned legs, joined by a deep pierced H-stretcher, late 19th century; 36 in. (91 cm) wide.

E1 A mahogany folding-top card table, *c.* 1900; 34 in. (85 cm).

E2 A late Victorian rosewood envelope card table, with frieze drawer and curved legs, on brass casters.

E3 A rosewood and marquetry envelope card table, *c.* 1900; 29 in. by 21 in. (75 by 54 cm).

E4 A rosewood card table, the top crossbanded, enclosing baize-lined interior, *c.* 1910; 30 in. by 36 in. (76 by 91 cm).

Gateleg tables

E5 A Charles II oak oval gateleg table, with flat baluster-shaped end supports, *c.* 1680; 24 in. long by 30 in. open (61 by 77 cm).

E6 A gateleg table, with pearwood top, lyre-shaped supports, mid 17th century; 29 in. (72 cm) wide.

E7 A rare table, on flat shaped, end supports, without any lathe-turned members, late 17th century.

E8 A Charles II oval oak gateleg table, the gates with simple waved uprights; 28 in. long by 36 in. open (72 by 92 cm).

E9 A Charles I oak gateleg table, with oval top and a pair of heavy baluster-shaped end supports, wtih a pair of simple rectangular "gate" supports, 40 in. long by 52 in. open (101 by 132 cm).

E12 A gateleg table, with oval fall-flap top, on turned baluster front legs and square back legs, 17th century.

E10 A Charles I oak large gateleg dining table, with oval twin flap above baluster-turned legs, joined by box stretchers, mid 17th century; 77 in. wide (197 cm) extended.

E11 A Charles II walnut gateleg large dining table, the oval top on turned double gatelegs, with box stretchers and square feet, 59 in. (150 cm) wide.

Large gateleg tables are always sought after and if in walnut, even more so. This example is quite plain and conventional, but still a very good looking piece. It also has the added advantage of Spanish feet.

E13 A large oval gateleg table, the simple baluster legs with splayed feet, 17th century; 70 in. by 60 in. (195 by 150 cm).

E1 A large William and Mary oak gateleg dining room table, with square lower sections and braganza feet, *c.* 1690; 60 in. (152 cm) long.

E7 A yew-wood gateleg table, with oval twin flap top with a drawer, on spirally-turned supports joined by moulded stretchers, 17th century; 57 in. wide, open (145 cm).

Gateleg Tables
The primary timbers for 17th-century gateleg tables were oak and walnut, though all convenient timbers were used in country versions. The best examples of large gatelegs from this period will have four gates rather than two, and may well have a small drawer at each end of the underframe. The construction is of joiner rather than of cabinet-maker class.

The tops of gateleg tables were necessarily made from several planks and it is common to find the tips – the outer edges of the leaves – replaced. The feet too, through standing on stone floors, have often suffered damage.

The rarity of large gateleg tables has been increased by the early 20th-century practice of reducing the tops for a market that demanded small examples. A cut-down table will show only a narrow overhang to frame and gates.

E2 A James II oak gateleg table, with oval twin flap top above baluster turned legs, 47 in. wide extended (117 cm).

E5 An oval yew-wood gateleg table, with turned legs, square section stretchers, and bun feet, late 17th century.
Yew wood furniture is greatly sought after and gateleg tables in this wood are quite rare.

E8 A large Charles II oak drop leaf dining table, 70 in. wide by 65 in. long (176 by 163 cm).

E3 A Charles II period rectangular top table, 37 in. wide by 29 in. open (92 by 73 cm).

E9 A solid yew-wood gateleg table, with oval twin-flap on bobbin-turned supports, 49 in. (125 cm) wide, open, 17th century.

E4 An oak gateleg table, with hinged rectangular top on spirally turned legs, late 17th century; 27 in. high by 47 in. extended (70 by 120 cm).

D6 A double gateleg oak table, with baluster turned legs and unusual carving on the gates and ends.
Large gateleg tables of this type are quite rare, mainly being made in the 17th and 18th century.

E10 A Charles II oak gateleg table, on ball-turned legs, with bobbin-turned crossbars, *c.* 1675; 29 in. high by 51 in. wide (74 by 129 cm).

E1 A Charles II oak rectangular double-action gateleg table, with a drawer, on turned baluster legs and square-section stretchers, *c.* 1680; 56 in. (144 cm) wide.

E2 A large Charles II oak gateleg table, the oval top on bobbin and baluster-turned legs, joined at the square section by bobbin stretchers, *c.* 1680; the top 55 in. by 66 in. open (139 by 169 cm).

E3 A red walnut gateleg table, with oval top, on eight baluster-turned legs, moulded stretchers and splay feet, late 17th/early 18th century; 28 in. high by 47 in. wide (72 by 119 cm).

E4 An elm gateleg table, with oval twin-flap top and end drawers, 17th century; 74 in. (185 cm) wide.

E5 An oak gateleg table, with oval top, shaped apron, turned legs and gates, joined by turned understretchers, late 17th century; 38 in. (95 cm) wide.

E6 An oak gateleg table, 18th century; 50 in. by 62 in. (127 by 157 cm) extended.

E7 A Charles II red walnut gateleg table, *c.* 1680; 41 in. (104 cm) wide.

E8 A walnut dining table, early 18th century; 52 in. by 79 in. (130 by 197 cm).

E1 A mahogany gateleg table, with triangular frame and flap, on baluster-turned legs and stretchers, *c.* 1710.

E2 A Chippendale mahogany tea table, with double gatelegs; 27 in. high by 35 in. long (77 by 87 cm).

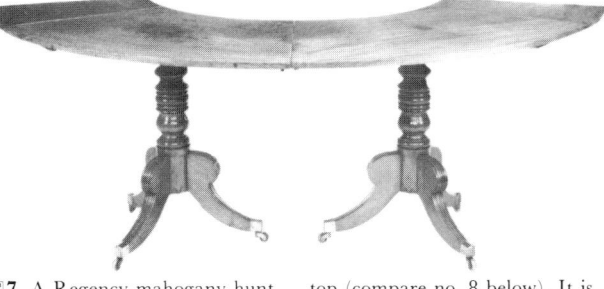

E7 A Regency mahogany hunt table in two parts, each on a turned column with four splayed feet, each part with a flap to the top (compare no. 8 below). It is 93 in. (236 cm) wide with the flaps down.

E3 A George III mahogany "spider leg" tea table, with spindle legs and stretchers, *c.* 1760; 31 in. (77 cm) wide, open.

E4 A mahogany gateleg spider table, with spindled columns, 19th century; 26 in. (65 cm).

Hunt tables

D5 A hunting table, in mellowed satinwood, crossbanded in rosewood, *c.* 1790; 86 in. long by 28 in. high (205 by 70 cm).

E8 A Regency mahogany drinking table, attributed to Gillow of Lancaster, the semi-circular reeded top with two flaps, detachable centre and brass railback, supporting a net below, the screw-off fluted legs with brass sockets; 65 in. (165 cm) wide.

D6 A complete mahogany wine table, with decanter compartments on tripod stand; 28 in. high by 53 in. wide (70 by 132 cm).

E9 A mahogany hunt table, of semi-circular form, with a pair of hinged flaps and detachable circular centre enclosing a brass rail and a net, on four circular tapering reeded legs with brass casters, *c.* 1840; 71 in. (182 cm) wide.

Library tables

D 1 A George III mahogany library table, with folding twin flaps; 30 in. high by 45 in. wide (77 by 114 cm).

D 2 A George III mahogany library table, with baize-lined top; 33 in. high by 109 in. wide (85 by 278 cm).

E 3 A mid-Georgian mahogany and parcel-gilt library table, with twin-flap top; 62 in. (157 cm) wide, open.

E 4 A George III mahogany extending library table, with cleated top divided in two panels, *c.* 1790; 27 in. high by 40 in. wide, closed (70 by 102 cm).

E 5 A George III bleached padouk and mahogany metamorphic table, with lifting top enclosing library steps above two false drawers, late 18th century; 48 in. (122 cm) wide.

E 6 A George III mahogany library steps table, with moulded rectangular top opening to form steps, on square tapering legs; 34 in. (86 cm) wide.

E 7 A George III mahogany draw-leaf library table, with well-figured top fitted at each end with an architect's drawer with baize-lined slide; 46 in. (117 cm) wide.

C 8 A Sheraton mahogany and satinwood oval library table, inlaid, with various shaped drawers, on square tapering legs ending in casters, 18th century; 72 in. long by 46 in. wide (182 by 116 cm).

D 9 A George III mahogany library table, with baize-lined top above a central frieze drawer, with baize-lined writing slide, *c.* 1790; 32 in. high by 56 in. wide (81 by 142 cm).

E 10 A Regency mahogany writing table, the leather-lined top with lobed angles, the frieze fitted with five drawers and a slide, with leather-lined easel, on reeded tapering legs; 60 in. (154 cm) wide.

E 11 A Regency mahogany writing table, the frieze with three shallow drawers, on turned tapering legs, ending in casters.

D 12 A Regency mahogany library table, with rounded rectangular twin-flap top and panelled cupboard door, enclosing folio shelves, flanked by ring-turned pilasters on splayed feet; 45 in. (116 cm) wide.

E1 A Regency mahogany library table, with rounded lectern above two frieze drawers, on square-section baluster end supports, on turned-stretcher; 29 in. (73 cm) high.

D2 A Regency mahogany library table, the top fitted with five rising flaps, all inset with green leather, *c.* 1780; 31 in. high by 66 in. long (79 by 168 cm).

D3 A George III mahogany library table, with revolving leather-lined top, fitted with small drawers, divided by cupboard doors with false drawer fronts; 45 in. (116 cm) diameter.

D4 A Regency mahogany library table, the circular top revolving, fitted with embossed hide above cockbeaded drawers and dummy drawers, mounted on a turned pedestal with swept reeded legs, *c.* 1820; 31 in. (78 cm) high.

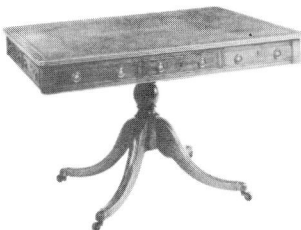

E5 A Regency mahogany library table, with leather-lined top, fitted with six drawers, on a turned pedestal; 46 in. (116 cm) wide.

E6 A Regency gilt-metal mounted rosewood library table, with burr-elm crossbanded top and eared crossbanded single flap, opposing two short frieze drawers, *c.* 1820; 51 in. (129 cm).

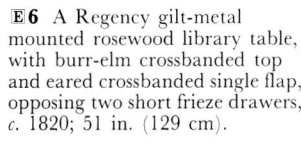

D7 A Regency centre library table, with adjustable easels at each end, on a turned pedestal with splayed feet and casters.

D8 A Regency mahogany library table, with circular leather-lined top above four frieze drawers, flanked by false drawers, on moulded and shaped solid shaft, quadripartite platform and paw feet; 59 in. (150 cm) wide.

E9 A Regency rosewood library table, on twin carved supports with stretcher, with two drawers and two dummy drawers.

E10 A Regency rosewood library table, with well-figured rounded top above a plain frieze, the shaped end standards with a turned stretcher; 29 in. high by 54 in. wide (74 by 138 cm).

D11 A Regency rosewood library table, with crossbanded top heavily inlaid with a leafy brass border, the frieze fitted with two small drawers with brass inlay, supported on turned pillars with ormolu mounts.

B12 A Regency mahogany library table, the top inset with gilt tooled leather, with four drawers at front and back, *c.* 1820; 29 in. high by 72 in. long (73 by 182 cm).

E13 A George IV mahogany library table, the circular top fitted with six drawers in the frieze, on S-scroll supports carved with foliage, on a turned central support; 72 in. (183 cm) diameter.

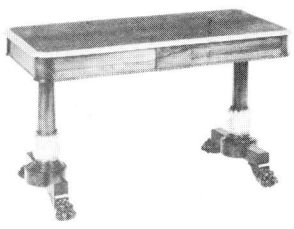

E1 A William IV rosewood library table, the top with leaf-carved moulded edge, the frieze with two bead-moulded drawers, *c.* 1835; 28 in. high by 52 in. wide (71 by 132 cm).

E2 A William IV rosewood library table, on pillar and platform support, with two drawers in the frieze; 28 in. high by 54 in. wide (71 by 137 cm).

E3 A mahogany sofa/library table, with drop leaves, with three drawers, 1815-1835; 44 in. (111 cm) wide.

E4 A William IV rosewood library table, on carved lion-paw feet, joined by carved and turned stretcher, *c.* 1835; 28 in. high by 59 in. wide (71 by 149 cm).

E5 A William IV rosewood library table, with a foliate carved frieze with two short drawers opposing two false drawers; 29 in. high by 48 in. wide (73 by 121 cm).

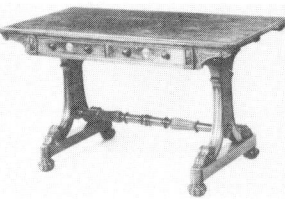

E6 A William IV rosewood library table, the carved frieze with two drawers and two dummy drawers, with scroll trestle end supports, joined by a pole stretcher, on gadrooned bun feet, *c.* 1830; 54 in. (137 cm) wide.

E7 A rosewood library table, by Holland & Sons, the leather-lined top with two frieze drawers, on fluted trestle supports joined by a pole stretcher, with Greek key feet carved in relief, stamped Holland & Sons, *c.* 1835; 48 in. (122 cm) wide.

E8 A William IV rosewood drum-top table, inset with leather and crossbanded with rosewood, with four real and four dummy drawers, *c.* 1835; 29 in. high by 47 in. diameter (74 by 119 cm).

E9 A Victorian oak octagonal library table, with leather-lined top and four drawers in the frieze, on arched supports; 47 in. (119 cm) diameter.

E10 A pollard oak and walnut library desk, the frieze fitted with drawers on either side, mid 19th century; 32 in. high by 48 in. wide (81 by 122 cm).

E11 A rosewood library table, with an inset top, with bowed ends, two frieze drawers and two dummy drawers, on baluster supports, *c.* 1850; 29 in. high by 57 in. (75 by 145 cm).

E12 A walnut library table, with serpentine top on lyre standards, mid 19th century; 29 in. by 52 in. (73 by 132 cm).

Occasional tables

E13 An oak monk's bench, the plank top on turned legs, above a coffer with lift-out lid, mid 17th century.

E14 An oak monk's table, with adjustable back hinged for use as a table, *c.* 1640.

E15 A Charles II fold over top table, with hinged fall-flap, on turned legs and square stretchers; 30 in. (76 cm) wide, open.

D 1 A vermilion and yellow lacquer table signed and dated John Hop, 1721, with gilt bronze capitals; 34 in. (87 cm) wide.

E 2 A Georgian mahogany occasional table, the top inlaid; 28 in. (71 cm) wide.

E 3 An early George III yew-wood occasional table, with waved frieze; 22 in. (55 cm) wide.

E 4 A George III coromandel and satinwood crossbanded oval occasional table, c. 1790; 36 in. (91 cm) wide.

E 5 A George III mahogany triangular table, with two tiers showing shaped friezes, c. 1755; 29 in. high by 23 in. wide (73 by 58 cm).

E 6 A George III inlaid mahogany occasional or lamp table, with inlaid top over and inlaid frieze drawer, on square legs, with plain stretcher; 22 in. (55 cm) wide.

E 7 A George III mahogany oval occasional table, with crossbanded top segmentally veneered, on square tapering legs joined by an X-stretcher with a bead-moulded edge and centred by an oval, c. 1800; 28 in. high by 20 in. wide (71 by 50 cm).

E 8 A George III rosewood lady's occasional table, the octagonal lifting surface crossbanded in holly and other woods, c. 1800; 28 in. high by 17 in. wide (71 by 43 cm).

E 9 A Regency mahogany occasional table, with bowed top, a shallow frieze drawer inlaid with boxwood lines; 27 in. (68 cm) wide.

E 10 A Regency rosewood occasional table, with crossbanded top, single frieze drawer with slide below, c. 1810; 29 in. high by 18 in. wide (74 by 46 cm).

E 11 A Regency rosewood occasional table, the shallow drawer with brass strapwork; 29 in. (73 cm) high.

E 12 A Georgian mahogany three-tier expanding serving table, with rounded shelves on trestle ends and bar feet; 46 in. high, extended, by 54 in. (117 by 137 cm).

E 13 A rosewood leaf lap table, the hinged top about a cylinder, on a column support, c. 1830; 30 in. by 34 in. (76 by 86 cm).

E 14 A William IV calamander occasional table, the top above a lotus-carved frieze, c. 1835; 31 in. by 31 in. (79 by 79 cm).

E1 A Gothic oak and parquetry occasional table, on central turned column, with four ornate outer columns, *c.* 1840; 28 in. by 26 in. (70 by 65 cm).

E2 An unusual rosewood two-tier table, each dished tier with a galleried top, on a turned stem and concave-sided base, mid 19th century; 30 in. high by 17 in. wide (76 by 43 cm).

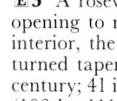

E3 A rosewood bagatelle table, opening to reveal a baize-lined interior, the stand with four turned tapering legs, mid 19th century; 41 in. high by 43 in. wide (106 by 111 cm).

E4 A papier mâché occasional table, with finely inlaid and painted top, mid 19th century; 29 in. (74 cm) high.

E5 A hardstone marquetry occasional table, probably Ashburton, *c.* 1850; 24 in. (61 cm) diameter.

E6 A mahogany and marquetry occasional table, *c.* 1890; 30 in. high by 18 in. wide (76 by 46 cm).

E7 A late Victorian inlaid satinwood occasional table, inlaid with ribbon-tied husk swags, urns and foliage; 29 in. (72 cm) high.

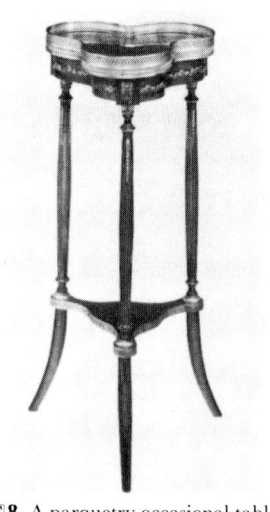

E8 A parquetry occasional table stamped 011919, late 19th century; 32 in. high by 14 in. wide (80 by 36 cm).

E9 A green onyx marble circular occasional table, on three columns, with gilt bronze paw feet, *c.* 1910; 25 in. high by 17 in. wide (63 by 43 cm).

E10 An Edwardian "Sheraton" painted satinwood occasional table, 28 in. (69 cm) wide.

E11 A "William and Mary" walnut and seaweed marquetry occasional table, inlaid with foliage, early 1900s, 27 in. by 32 in. (69 by 82 cm).

Pembroke tables

E12 A George III mahogany Pembroke table, with frieze drawer, *c.* 1765; 28 in. high by 24 in. wide (70 by 60 cm).

E13 A George III mahogany Pembroke table, with chamfered moulded legs and pierced brackets, *c.* 1765; 28 in. high by 23 in. wide (70 by 57 cm).

E1 A George III mahogany "butterfly" shape Pembroke table, 31 in. (79 cm).

E2 A George III mahogany Pembroke table, with two curved serpentine flaps.

E3 An early George III mahogany Pembroke table, with waved twin-flap top; 30 in. (71 cm) wide.

E4 A George III mahogany Pembroke table, the slender legs with X-stretcher, *c.* 1775; 27 in. (69 cm) wide.

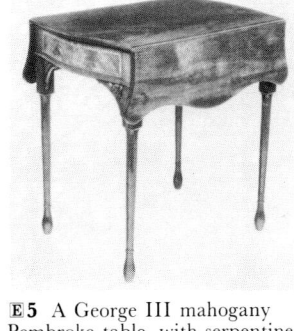

E5 A George III mahogany Pembroke table, with serpentine moulded top on frieze with crossbanded bowed drawer; 28 in. high by 36 in. wide, extended (72 by 91 cm).

E6 A mahogany Pembroke table, with legs and frieze decorated with fluting, the frieze containing a drawer, *c.* 1780.

E7 A Hepplewhite mahogany folding-leaf tea table, with original shaped stretcher, *c.* 1785; 27 in. high by 36 in. wide (67 by 91 cm).

E8 A George III mahogany Pembroke table, with serpentine twin-flap top, crossbanded with rosewood, the tapering legs headed by paterae; 38 in. (97 cm) wide.

E9 A George III mahogany Pembroke table, with oval twin-flap top, on square tapering legs; 35 in. (89 cm) wide.

E10 A Sheraton mahogany Pembroke table, the top with a broad satinwood band, the fitted drawer opposing a dummy drawer, also banded in satinwood.

E11 A George III mahogany Pembroke table, the folding surface inlaid and crossbanded with satinwood above cockbeaded drawers, the square tapering legs inlaid on two sides with classical urns and pendent husk decoration, on small brass feet, *c.* 1790; 28 in. high by 38 in. wide (70 by 95 cm).

E12 A George III satinwood Pembroke table, the top with rosewood crossbanding, edged in ebony stringing; 31 in. by 42 in. extended (79 by 107 cm).

D13 A George III oval Pembroke table, veneered in satinwood, mahogany and other exotic woods, fitted with a drawer opposing a dummy drawer, the square tapering supports having edge string lines, with brass terminals and casters; *c.* 1790.

E1 A George III satinwood Pembroke table, the top crossbanded with rosewood and inlaid with an amboyna; 37 in. (95 cm) wide, open.

E2 A George III satinwood Pembroke table, with oval double flap top, fitted with a drawer; 42 in. (106 cm) wide, open.

E3 A George III mahogany "harlequin" Pembroke writing table, *c.* 1780; 32 in. long by 43 in. wide, open (81 by 109 cm).

E4 A George III sycamore and satinwood Pembroke table, with moulded rectangular twin flap top; 37 in. (94 cm) wide.

E5 A George III burr yew-wood and satinwood Pembroke table, the top with a moulded edge crossbanded in tulipwood, 34 in. by 28 in. extended (85 by 71 cm).

E6 A George III mahogany and inlaid "harlequin" Pembroke table, the hinged top with a moulded edge and crossbanded in tulipwood, the frieze with dummy drawer; 30 in. by 42 in. (74 by 106 cm).

E7 A George III mahogany and satinwood Pembroke table, with rectangular twin flap top, the frieze panelled with false drawers; 34 in. (88 cm) wide, open.

E8 A George III mahogany Pembroke table, with serpentine twin flap top inlaid with parquetry above one long drawer; 41 in. (105 cm) wide.

E9 A Regency satinwood Pembroke table, with rounded rectangular top banded with rosewood, 39 in. (100 cm) wide, open.

E10 A mahogany Pembroke table, with a drawer, on square tapering legs, late 18th century.

E11 A George III small mahogany Pembroke table, *c.* 1790; 28 in. high by 40 in. wide, open (73 by 102 cm).

E12 A George III palisander crossbanded Pembroke table, with yew-wood banding and boxwood stringing, *c.* 1800; 32 in. (81 cm).

E13 A George III satinwood Pembroke table, painted at a later date with an oval of fruit, with a frieze drawer on tapering legs decorated with pendent bellflowers; 36 in. (93 cm) wide, open.

E14 A George III satinwood Pembroke table, the twin flap top bordered with a plumwood band, fitted with a drawer; 40 in. (103 cm) wide, open.

E15 A George III satinwood Pembroke table, the twin flap top framed by bands of tulipwood and painted with trailing flowers, the frieze with a drawer on tapering legs headed by partridgewood panels, 42 in. (86 cm) wide, open.

E16 A Regency mahogany Pembroke table, inlaid with ebonized stringing and fitted with a drawer, with tapering supports with reeded surmounts, *c.* 1810; 33 in. (84 cm) wide.

E17 A Regency mahogany Pembroke table, by Gillows; 36 in. (91 cm) wide, open.

E18 A George III mahogany Pembroke table, *c.* 1800; 28 in. high by 45 in. wide (70 by 112 cm).

E19 A small mahogany Pembroke table, *c.* 1800; 29 in. high by 25 in. wide, open (72 by 62 cm).

E20 A Regency mahogany Pembroke table, the top crossbanded in rosewood; 41 in. (104 cm) wide, open.

E21 A Regency mahogany Pembroke table, crossbanded with satinwood and rosewood; 42 in. (107 cm) wide, open.

Quartetto tables

E1 A set of George III rosewood quartetto tables, *c.* 1800; 19 in. (50 cm) wide.

E2 A set of mahogany quartetto tables, early 19th century; 21 in. by 15 in. maximum size (52 by 37 cm).

E3 A nest of Regency rosewood and satinwood quartetto tables, the largest 18 in. (46 cm) wide.

D4 A set of Regency satinwood and rosewood quartetto tables, the largest 23 in. (60 cm) wide.

E5 A set of four Victorian black lacquered and papier mâché occasional tables, the largest 25 in. (62 cm) wide.

E6 A nest of four Victorian papier mâché and ebonized tables, with shaped papier mâché tops, on turned frames with splayed feet; the largest 24 in. (60 cm) wide.

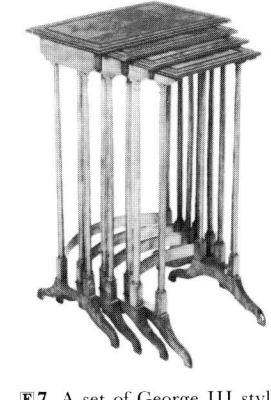

E7 A set of George III style satinwood quartetto tables, labelled Morant & Co., each with crossbanded top on colonnette standards; the largest 18 in. (46 cm) wide.

E8 A set of three George III style mahogany quartetto tables, the beaded rimmed rectangular tops on pierced and cusp end standards, the splayed downcurved legs with turned cross-stretchers, 19th century; the largest 21 in. (52 cm) wide.

E9 A nest of four satinwood side tables, each quarter-veneered and painted with swags of flowers, with turned spindle legs and curved single stretcher, *c.* 1900; the largest 28 in. by 20 in. (71 by 50 cm).

Reading tables

E1 A George III mahogany reading table, the rising moulded top with two candle stands, on an adjustable stem, the downcurved legs ending in pad feet and casters, mid 18th century; 31 in. (78 cm) wide.

E4 A mid-Georgian mahogany reading table, with easel top, on baluster stem and tripod cabriole base; 20 in. (51 cm) wide.

E7 A Regency mahogany kidney-shaped reading table, with double ratchet top and a drawer in the frieze, on square legs headed by paterae; 35 in. (89 cm) wide.

E8 A Regency mahogany reading table, on turned baluster support, with three-cornered incurved base; 23 in.(58 cm) wide.

E2 A tripod-base reading table, of adjustable height, the turned central column with spirally lobed vase, the rising top plain with a moulded edge, mid 18th century.

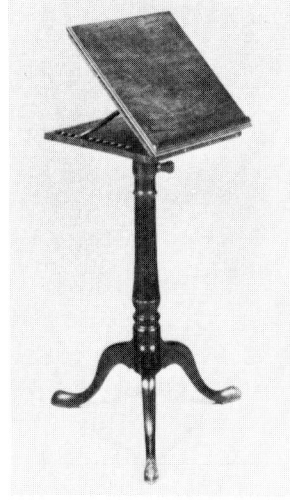

E5 A George III mahogany reading table, with square moulded, adjustable top above a ring-turned pedestal with wooden fitting, on slipper feet; 30 in. (75 cm) high.

E9 *(above)* A mahogany reading table, the rectangular top with two adjustable flaps and two adjustable candle stands, late 1830s; 33 by 42 in. (82 by 105 cm).

E3 A George II mahogany reading table, with adjustable top, on turned stem with brass fitting and tripod cabriole base; 24 in. (61 cm) wide.

E6 A mahogany adjustable reading table, on tripod base, *c*. 1790; 20 in. (50 cm) wide.

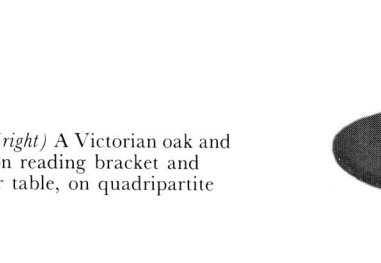

E10 *(right)* A Victorian oak and cast-iron reading bracket and circular table, on quadripartite base.

Refectory tables

C1 An Elizabethan table, extensively decorated with rails carved on both sides of the table; 128 in. (325 cm) wide.

D2 A refectory table, with quadruple plank top and foliate carved fluted frieze, carved at the angles with S-scrolls, on turned baluster legs with square stretchers, early 17th century; 114 in. (290 cm) wide.

E3 An early oak refectory dining table, the widely overhanging top surmounting a joined frame, comprising upper rails with lozenge decoration, with six turned legs and plain stretchers; 130 in. (330 cm) long.

E4 An early 17th-century oak refectory table with four-plank top over a carved frieze on baluster legs headed by capitals; 85 in. (216 cm) long. Some wear to the stretchers is to be expected, but too much, as here, is commercially advantageous.

E5 A fine carved oak table, with well-turned supports, joined by worn stretchers, 17th century; 67 in. (170 cm) wide.

E6 An oak refectory table, with quadruple plank top, on well-turned supports, joined by H-stretcher, 17th century; 110 in. (280 cm) wide.

E7 An oak refectory table, with ornately shaped end supports, joined by a single stretcher, 17th century; 76 in. (194 cm) wide.

E8 A William and Mary oak refectory table, with a single plank top, the frieze on all sides with gouge carving, the spiral-twist supports with scroll brackets; 78 in. (198 cm) wide.

E 1 A Queen Anne oak refectory table, the two plank top with mitred border, the frieze incised with date "1719"; 108 in. (274 cm) wide.

E 2 An oak draw-leaf refectory table, in the early 17th century style, on four heavily carved supports, joined by an H-stretcher, mid 19th century; 78 in. (198 cm) long.

E 3 A 17th century style refectory table, the frieze carved with rams and foliage, on carved baluster supports, *c.* 1900; 127 in. (323 cm) wide.

E 4 An oak refectory table, on six baluster supports, joined by stretchers; 31 in. high by 100 in. wide (79 by 254 cm).

Rent tables

D 5 A Chippendale rent table, on square cupboard base in figured mahogany, the revolving top with wedge-shape drawers, showing the letters of the alphabet, a central well for money; 30 in. high by 49 in. diameter (75 by 124 cm).

D 6 A George III mahogany rent table, with circular leather-lined top, the frieze with four drawers divided by narrow cupboard doors, with false drawer fronts, the square pedestal with a panelled cupboard door; 30 in. high by 49 in. diameter (76 by 124 cm).

D 7 A George III mahogany revolving rent table, the hexagonal top with central lidded well, with six drawers in the frieze, revolving on a cubincal cupboard base, applied with mouldings; 46 in. (106 cm) wide.

D 8 A George III style mahogany drum-top library table, the lower part fitted with a cupboard door, on cast bronze claw feet, late 19th century; 50 in. (127 cm) diameter.

Serving tables

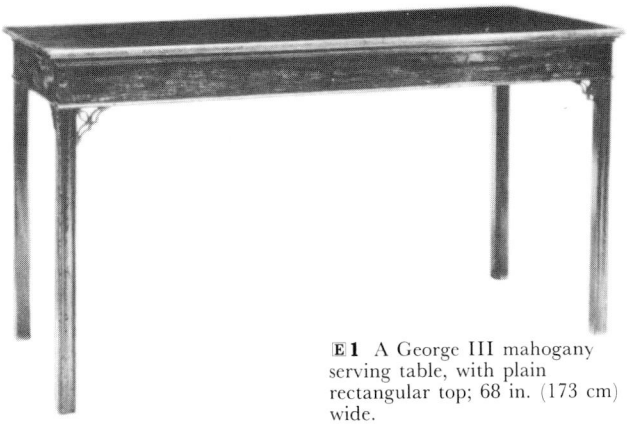

E1 A George III mahogany serving table, with plain rectangular top; 68 in. (173 cm) wide.

E2 A George III serving table, crossbanded with curved sides and semi-elliptical front, mid 18th century; 36 in. high by 100 in. wide (92 by 254 cm).

E3 A George III mahogany serving table, the top with splayed sides and concave centre, with dummy drawers in the front; 73 in. (105 cm) wide.

E4 A late George III mahogany serving table, the frieze crossbanded with rosewood, fitted with a tablet-centred drawer; 69 in. (175 cm) wide.

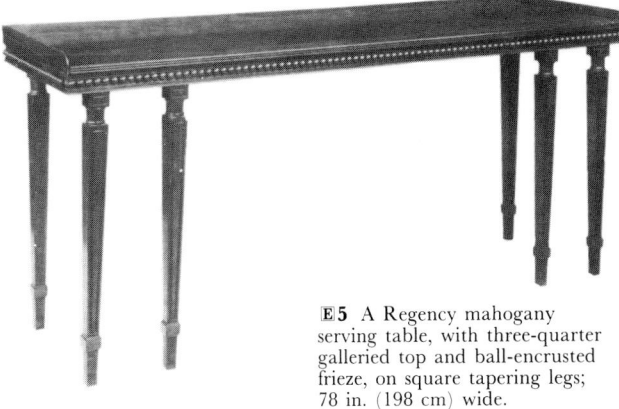

E5 A Regency mahogany serving table, with three-quarter galleried top and ball-encrusted frieze, on square tapering legs; 78 in. (198 cm) wide.

E6 A Regency mahogany breakfront serving table, fitted with a drawer; 108 in. (275 cm) wide.

E7 A mahogany serving table, with narrow bowed top, the fluted roundel frieze of curved shape, on square tapering legs ending in block feet; 81 in. (206 cm) wide.

E8 An oak Gothic revival livery table, with raised back centred by an armorial device, the moulded top on perpendicular cluster supports, mid 19th century; 48 in. (122 cm) high.

E9 A late Victorian pollard oak Gothic serving side table, the moulded top with a pierced cusp ledge back, above three frieze drawers; 72 in. (183 cm).

Side tables

E1 A Charles I oak side table, with two drawers, the whole elaborately carved, *c.* 1640; 28 in. high by 28 in. wide (71 by 71 cm).

E2 An oak side table, the plank top edged with overlapping scale pattern, with a frieze drawer carved with flowerheads, 17th century; 47 in. (120 cm) wide.

E3 An oak side table, with double plank top, fitted with a single drawer, on turned columnar legs, mid 17th century; 34 in. (86 cm) wide.

E4 An oak side table, with double plank top, on baluster front legs and square back legs, mid 17th century; 34 in. (86 cm) wide.

E5 A Charles II oak table, with a moulded plank top, the frieze with a drawer, raised on ball-turned legs and stretchers, *c.* 1680; 30 in. (76 cm) wide.

E6 A Charles II oak side table, with cleated two-plank top, the frieze with a two panelled drawer veneered in fruitwood, *c.* 1675; 28 in. high by 35 in. wide (72 by 90 cm).

E7 A Charles II walnut table, with a moulded cleated plank top, the frieze carved with guilloche, with a shallow drawer, *c.* 1680; 29 in. high by 36 in. wide (74 by 91 cm).

E8 A James II side table, with a rectangular top over a panelled frieze drawer, on baluster and acorn-turned supports, *c.* 1685; 30 in. high by 35 in. wide (77 by 89 cm).

D9 A William and Mary oyster-veneered walnut side table, the moulded top inlaid with boxwood roundels, on spirally turned legs, 31 in. (80 cm) wide.

E10 A William and Mary oyster-veneered walnut side table, the top inlaid and framed by boxwood lines and bordered with fruitwood, on turned feet; 31 in. (79 cm) wide.

E11 A lignum vitae side table, with moulded rectangular top inlaid with oyster roundels, on spirally turned legs, joined by well curved stretcher, 17th century; 35 in. (89 cm) wide.

E12 A walnut side table, with moulded top over a frieze drawer, the spirally turned tapering legs with ebonized collars joined by a waved cross-stretcher, late 17th century; 38 in. (97 cm) wide.

E13 A William and Mary period side table, in walnut veneers, the figured surface with crossed leaf inlay, *c.* 1690; 30 in. (75 cm) high.

E14 A William and Mary oyster and laburnum side table, inlaid with beechwood strapwork, *c.* 1695; 29 in. (73 cm) high.

E15 A William and Mary oak side table, with frieze drawer, on ornately turned legs, with unusual stretcher.

D16 A William and Mary side table, in well figured walnut, the quartered top crossbanded and inlaid with herringbone banding, above three small drawers, *c.* 1690; 30 in. (75 cm) high.

D 1 A William and Mary yew and burr-yew side table, with crossbanded moulded top inlaid with a compass-medallion, with three drawers in the arcaded frieze, on cup and baluster tapering legs; 30 in. (77 cm) wide.

E 2 A William and Mary oak and walnut side table, the two plank top with end cleats above a walnut veneered drawer, *c.* 1695; 28 in. high by 35 in. wide (70 by 90 cm).

E 3 A William and Mary walnut side table, fitted with a drawer with moulded facing, on inverted cup turned supports, with wavy X-stretcher, 40 in. (100 cm) wide.

E 4 A William and Mary yew and walnut table, the yew top with moulded edge, the walnut underframe with three yew-wood drawers, on five turned walnut legs, on bun feet, *c.* 1695; 28 in. high by 33 in. wide (71 by 84 cm).

E 5 A William and Mary oak side table, the two plank top above a single shallow drawer, on five turned supports, joined by curved stretchers.

E 6 A William and Mary burr-oak side table, on twist turned supports, the top crossbanded in fruitwood with herringbone inlay, 38 in. by 22 in. (95 by 55 cm).

E 7 An oak side table, with moulded rectangular top, the frieze with a coffered drawer, on baluster legs, joined by an H-stretcher, late 17th century; 31 in. (80 cm) wide.

E 8 A Queen Anne gilt-gesso side table, the shaped frieze with trellis pattern panels, 33 in. (84 cm) wide.

E 9 A Queen Anne walnut table, with three drawers in the triple-arched frieze, *c.* 1710; 25 in. high by 26 in. wide (64 by 66 cm).

E 10 A Queen Anne walnut side table, with crossbanded top, on cabriole legs with pointed feet, 30 in. (77 cm) wide.

E 11 A Queen Anne walnut side table, with frieze drawers above shaped apron, *c.* 1710, 30 in. (76 cm) wide.

E 12 A Queen Anne walnut lowboy or side table, with crossbanded top, *c.* 1710; 29 in. (74 cm) high.

Side Tables

The side table, particularly the type with one or more drawers to the frieze, emerged as a distinct article during the second half of the 17th century; designs followed closely those of contemporary stands for cabinets.

The earliest examples were made with turned legs joined by plain box stretchers – see. no. 3 opposite. Box stretchers were soon supplanted by turned versions (no. 5 opposite), and by the William and Mary period turned legs were joined by shaped, curving X-stretchers, as in no. 9 opposite. In the Queen Anne period both turning and stretchers disappeared in favour of cabriole legs.

It is an apparent contradiction that many side tables will have the back rail made of the same timber as the front and sides – in contrast to many of the fine pier tables of the 18th century, for example – and may also have a moulding worked to the bottom edge. These features indicate the real function of the table: to be pulled out and used as an occasional table rather than left permanently against the wall.

E 13 A Queen Anne walnut side table, the crossbanded quartered top with re-entrant corners, fitted with three drawers in the arcaded frieze, on cabriole legs, 28 in. (71 cm) wide.

E 14 A Queen Anne walnut side table, with crossbanded rectangular top, outlined with feather-banding, a drawer in the cavetto frieze, on cabriole legs and pad feet, 30 in. (75 cm) wide.

E 1 A George I walnut side table, with veneered, moulded and crossbanded top, three drawers above the shaped apron, on plain cabriole legs, *c.* 1720; 28 in. (70 cm) wide.

D 2 A George I carved giltwood and gesso side table, the moulded frieze carved with acanthus above a foliate carved apron, early 18th century; 58 in. (147 cm) wide.

D 3 A George I gilt-gesso side table, in the style of James Moore, *c.* 1720; 30 in. high by 43 in. wide (75 by 107 cm).

D 4 A George I walnut and marquetry side table, with well-decorated top and frieze, and curved apron on cabriole legs with claw feet; 28 in. high by 31 in. wide (70 by 78 cm).

E 5 An elm side table, with veneered and inlaid top, the frieze with one long drawer and curved apron, on cabriole legs, early 18th century.

E 6 A George II walnut side table, the quartered bookmatched crossbanded surface with moulded edge above single cockbeaded drawer, *c.* 1740; 28 in. high by 32 in. wide (70 by 80 cm).

E 7 A George II walnut side table, the shaped frieze centred by a lambrequin, on pointed pad feet; 35 in. (90 cm) wide.

D 8 An early George II walnut side table, with inset Sicilian jasper-veneered top, the frieze with ornately carved central mask, with carved carbriole legs on claw feet springing from a carved apron; 62 in. (160 cm) wide.

D 9 An early George II carved giltwood and gesso side table, with verde antico marble top, the moulded frieze carved with wreaths and roundels, centred by a wreath and shell, the legs carved with scales, *c.* 1740.

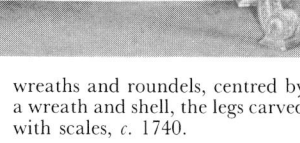

C 10 A small William Kent mahogany side table, ornately carved, 44 in. (110 cm) wide.

D 11 A William Kent carved and gilt eagle side table, with marble top.

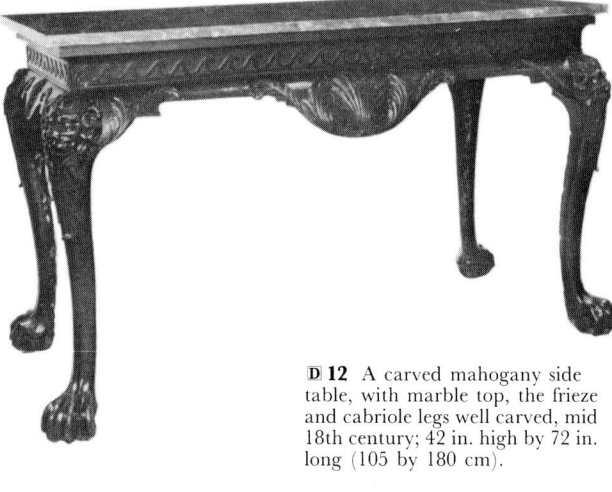

D 12 A carved mahogany side table, with marble top, the frieze and cabriole legs well carved, mid 18th century; 42 in. high by 72 in. long (105 by 180 cm).

D 13 A mahogany side table, with fleur-de-pêche marble top, a scroll carved frieze with heavily carved apron and cabriole legs, on claw-and-ball feet, *c.* 1740; 33 in. high by 78 in. wide (82 by 195 cm).

D 1 A George II period mahogany side table, with carved frieze and cabriole legs; 60 in. (150 cm) wide.

E 3 A George II giltwood side table, with portor marble top, the frieze with moulded border; 46 in. (118 cm) wide.

E 7 A Chippendale period carved mahogany side table, 34 in. high by 49 in. wide (85 by 124 cm).

C 10 A George II mahogany side table, of slanting asymmetric pierced outline; 33 in. high by 67 in. wide (84 by 170 cm).

C 2 A George II white-painted and gilded mahogany side table, with pink marble top, the frieze centred by Herculean masks; 67 in. (171 cm) wide.

D 4 A George II gilded pine side table, with green marble slab on fluted frieze, *c.* 1745; 51 in. (129 cm) wide.

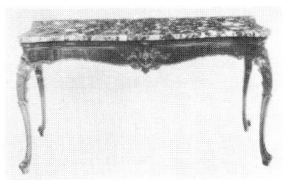

D 8 An early George III mahogany side table, with serpentine mottled marble top over cabriole legs, *c.* 1765; 72 in. (183 cm) wide.

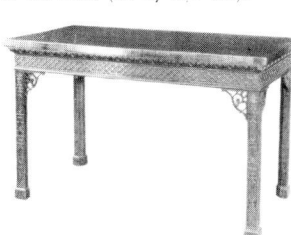

E 11 A George III mahogany side table, with blind fretwork frieze; 58 in. (148 cm) wide.

E 5 A George III mahogany side table, the top with ribbon-and-rosette border, above three long drawers with drop ring handles, the legs carved with blind fretwork and pierced angle brackets, 69 in. (176 cm) wide.

E 9 A George III mahogany side table, in the manner of John Cobb, with rectangular brecholito top; 71 in. (180 cm) wide.

E 12 A late George II mahogany silver table, with Gothic-pierced frieze, *c.* 1760; 29 in. high by 33 in. wide (74 by 84 cm).

D 6 A Chippendale mahogany side table, the frieze elaborately carved with floral scrolls, on ornate cabriole legs headed by masks and on paw feet; 60 in. long by 34 in. wide (152 by 75 cm).

E 13 A Hepplewhite mahogany serpentine side table, with shaped sides and fluted frieze; 33 in. (82 cm) high.

E 14 A Chippendale mahogany side table or serving table, 36 in. high by 66 in. wide (90 by 168 cm).

E 15 A George III mahogany side table, with moulded top and four short drawers; 37 in. (95 cm) wide.

E1 A George III mahogany side table, with well-figured serpentine top, inlaid with boxwood lines; 39 in. (99 cm) wide.

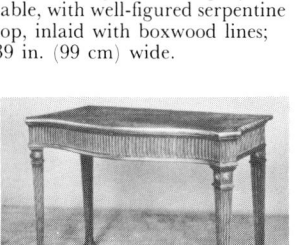

E2 An Adam mahogany side table, of serpentine form, on tapered fluted legs, 31 in. high by 46 in. wide (78 by 115 cm).

D3 A Hepplewhite carved mahogany semi-circular side table, the top crossbanded with lignum vitae, with an oval panel inlaid with flowers, *c.* 1780; 34 in. (85 cm) high.

E5 A George III mahogany silver table, with rectangular tray top, the frieze carved with geometric blind fretwork, on shaped square tapering legs; 36 in. (91 cm) wide.

D6 An Adam mahogany side table, the top with a surrounding gallery, a single drawer in the frieze, on fluted tapering legs, *c.* 1780; 63 in. (160 cm) wide.

D7 An Adam period satinwood side table, of small proportions, the top and frieze of D-shape with crossbanding, stringing and painted decoration, over square tapering legs collared at the ankle.

D9 A fine Adam carved giltwood side table, with shaped underframe, the satinwood top fitted with a gadrooned ormolu moulding, in rosewood, kingwood and boxwood, on slender cabriole legs, *c.* 1770; 33 in. high by 55 in. wide (82 by 140 cm).

C8 A George III satinwood and marquetry side table, in the French Hepplewhite style, the half-moon top inlaid with an anthemion, a flower spray and ribbon-tied swags, the frieze with beaded border, on cabriole legs; 43 in. (109 cm) wide.

C10 An Adam side table, with inlaid satinwood top, with demi-paterae and swag motifs, the frieze with carved flutes, on tapering reeded legs, the lower part in white and gilt gesso, *c.* 1790.

E4 An early George III mahogany serpentine side table, with moulded top, the frieze with three small drawers, on square tapering legs with block feet; 36 in. (91 cm) wide.

E 1 A George III satinwood-veneered D-shaped side table, crossbanded in kingwood, *c.* 1790; 32 in. high by 20 in. wide (81 by 51 cm).

D 2 A George III giltwood side table, in the Adam style, with specimen top inlaid with marble squares and semi-precious stone, and black, red and white marble border; 49 in. (125 cm) wide.

C 3 A Hepplewhite satinwood and harewood semi-circular side table, 48 in. (122 cm) wide.

E 4 A George III mahogany semi-circular side table, with "plum pudding" veneered top, *c.* 1780; 28 in. (72 cm) high.

D 5 A semi-circular side table, the top inlaid with marquetry of scrolls and feathers, the apron carved with paterae, the central oval enclosing putti, supported on tapering square-section legs, *c.* 1780.

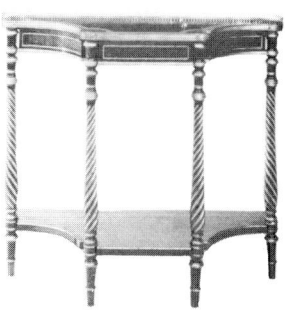

E 6 A Regency rosewood side table, the eared top with concave sides and slightly curved back, with Gothic-arcaded gilt-metal gallery, inlaid with a broad satinwood band, on spirally fluted legs; 40 in. (103 cm) wide.

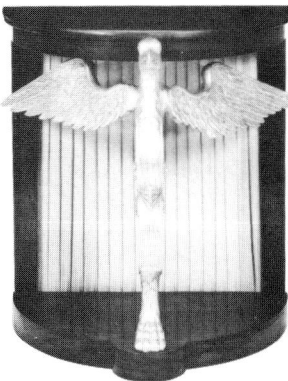

E 7 A George IV parcel-gilt rosewood side table, the D-shaped top, above pleated silk back, supported by an eagle, *c.* 1820; 36 in. high by 34 in. wide (91 by 87 cm).

E 8 A Regency mahogany side table, of bowed breakfront form, the top crossbanded and inlaid with ebony stringing, the frieze centred by a panelled drawer; 37 in. high by 98 in. wide (94 by 249 cm).

E 9 An early Victorian oak side table, with white marble top, the Tudor arched frieze centred by the Garter badge below the royal crown and VR monogram; 54 in. (139 cm) wide.

E 10 A papier mâché side table, the moulded-edge top painted with flowers and inset with insects, supported on outswept octagonal turrets, on downswept trestles, *c.* 1840; 28 in. (71 cm) high.

E 11 A Victorian black lacquer papier mâché side table, the moulded serpentine top inlaid with mother-of-pearl fruit and flower filled baskets, above baluster-shaped trestle ends, *c.* 1850; 25 in. (72 cm) wide.

E 12 A giltwood side table, with a serpentine marble top, with ornately scrolled frieze and legs, joined by a C-scroll stretcher, 19th century; 34 by 53 in. (88 by 136 cm).

Sofa tables

C 1 A George III satinwood sofa table, the rounded twin-flap top bordered with broad rosewood band, outlined with ebonized and boxwood lines, on solid trestle ends joined by an arched stretcher; 56 in. (142 cm) wide.

E 2 A George III mahogany sofa table, with rounded rectangular twin-flap top, crossbanded with satinwood, the frieze with two drawers on each side, on ring-turned supports, joined by a stretcher and splayed legs; 59 in. (150 cm) wide, open.

E 3 A George III faded rosewood sofa table, with rounded rectangular twin-flap top, crossbanded with rosewood, the frieze with two drawers on each side, the drawers with fine geometric inlay and original handles, with reeded splayed trestle ends, 66 in. (168 cm) wide, open.

E 4 A George III mahogany sofa table, crossbanded with rosewood; 63 in. (160 cm) wide, open.

E 5 A Georgian mahogany sofa table, the frieze with two drawers, *c.* 1800; 65 in. (165 cm) wide, open.

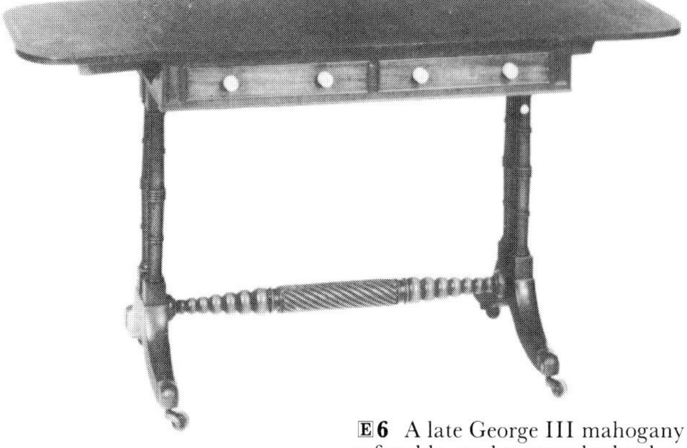

E 6 A late George III mahogany sofa table, on downward sabre legs with brass casters, *c.* 1805; 28 in. high by 56 in. wide (72 by 143 cm).

D 7 A Regency brass-mounted rosewood veneered sofa-table, attributed to John McLean, *c.* 1810; 61 in. (156 cm) wide, open.

D 8 A Regency mahogany sofa table, crossbanded with satinwood and inlaid with lines, on trestle ends, joined by a reeded pole stretcher; 59 in. (151 cm) wide, open.

E 9 A Regency mahogany sofa table, the plain top above a pair of frieze drawers, the trestle supports with reeded sabre legs, *c.* 1810; 65 in. (165 cm) wide.

E 1 A Regency rosewood sofa table, with rounded rectangular twin-flap top, inlaid with a satinwood line; 59 in. (150 cm) wide, open.

E 2 A Regency mahogany sofa table, with kingwood crossbanding and inlaid with boxwood lines; 28 in. high by 52 in. wide (70 by 132 cm).

E 3 A Regency rosewood and mahogany dwarf sofa table, the frieze with one drawer, early 19th century; 29 in. (75 cm) wide, open.

E 4 A Regency rosewood sofa table, inlaid with brass lines, with a frieze drawer, on brass casters; 42 in. (107 cm) wide.

D 5 A Regency mahogany sofa table, with rounded twin-flap top, bordered with a wide band of satinwood; 67 in. (170 cm) wide.

D 6 A Regency pollard oak sofa table, with rounded rectangular two-flap top, on spindle-filled trestle ends, the frieze edge with entrelac; 63 in. (160 cm) wide.

C 7 A Regency rosewood veneered sofa and games table, the top crossbanded in burr yew, the central panel sliding and reversing to form a chess and cribbage board, *c.* 1805; 59 in. (150 cm) wide, open.

E 8 A Regency mahogany sofa table, the reeded edge top above two frieze drawers; 45 in. (114 cm) wide, open.

D 9 A Regency rosewood games and sofa table, the sliding top with chess board and tooled leather backgammon surface; 28 in. (70 cm) high.

D 10 A Regency rosewood and ormolu mounted sofa and writing table, with concealed leather-lined easel; 70 in. (178 cm) wide, open.

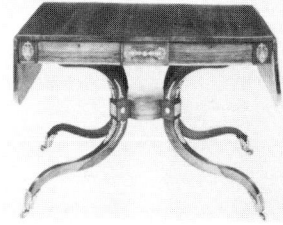

E 11 A Regency rosewood sofa table, the frieze with two drawers, on four incurving legs joined by shaped tablet, 58 in. (148 cm) wide, open.

D 12 A Regency amboyna sofa table, the top crossbanded with mulberry bordered with brass lines, on lyre support; 59 in. (151 cm) wide, open.

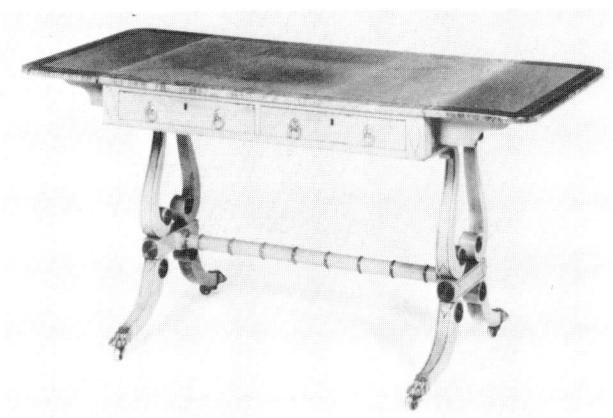

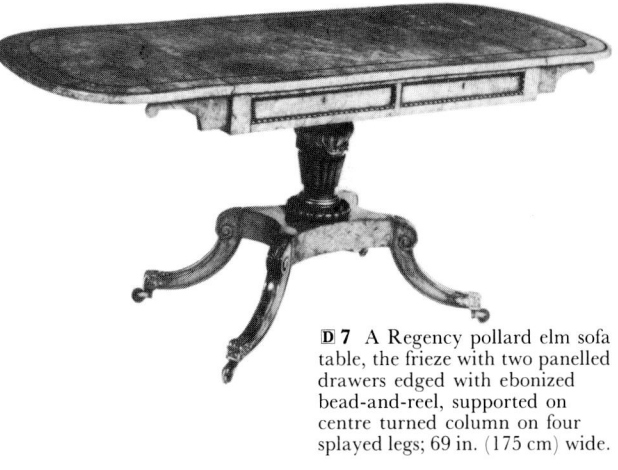

D 1 A Regency satinwood veneered sofa table, crossbanded in kingwood, with rounded corners, a pair of drawers with drop ring handles, having lyre supports with a ringed stretcher and sabre legs, *c.* 1810; 59 in. (159 cm) open.

D 7 A Regency pollard elm sofa table, the frieze with two panelled drawers edged with ebonized bead-and-reel, supported on centre turned column on four splayed legs; 69 in. (175 cm) wide.

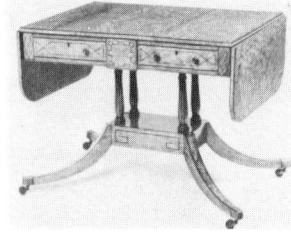

E 2 A Regency mahogany sofa table, with inlaid top on S-scroll supports and scroll mounted plinths; 57 in. (145 cm) extended.

E 3 A Regency satinwood sofa table, inlaid with ebonized stringing, *c.* 1810; 37 in. (94 cm) wide, when closed.

E 8 A Regency rosewood and cut brass inlaid sofa table, with one real and one dummy drawer, *c.* 1815; 36 in. (93 cm) wide.

E 9 A Regency rosewood and cut brass inlaid sofa table, *c.* 1810; 37 in. (94 cm) wide.

E 4 A Regency rosewood sofa table, with brass-inlaid two-flap top, supported on rectangular section columns with turned stretcher; 56 in. (142 cm) wide, open.

E 10 A Regency brass-inlaid rosewood sofa table, with rounded rectangular twin-flap top, the friezes with two drawers, on rectangular shaft; 56 in. (143 cm) wide, open.

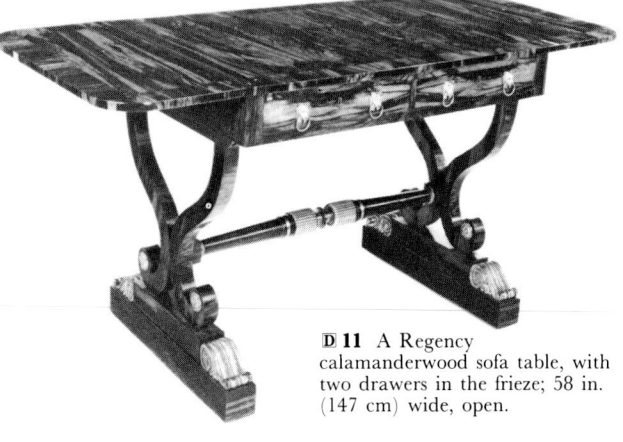

E 5 A Regency rosewood sofa table, with brass inlay and folding flaps; 56 in. (142 cm) long.

E 6 A Regency rosewood sofa table, with rounded rectangular twin-flap top, bordered with calamanderwood band, the frieze with two drawers, 48 in. (122 cm) wide, open.

D 11 A Regency calamanderwood sofa table, with two drawers in the frieze; 58 in. (147 cm) wide, open.

E1 A Regency rosewood sofa table, the top with a wide pollard oak banding, the frieze with two opposing dummy drawers on a tapering pedestal and concave platform stretcher, *c.* 1820; 59 in. (150 cm) open.

E2 A George IV rosewood sofa table, inlaid with brass lines, with hipped splayed legs, ending on brass caps and casters; 28 in. high by 59 in. wide (70 by 150 cm).

Tea tables

D7 A Queen Anne walnut and burr-walnut tea table, with concertina action; 29 in. high by 32 in. wide (74 by 81 cm).

E11 A mid-Georgian red walnut tea table, with fold-over top, the cabriole legs on hoof feet; 32 in. (82 cm) wide.

E3 A Regency mahogany and rosewood sofa table, the well-flared rounded rectangular twin-flap top with two frieze drawers, on ribbed trestle ends joined by a ring-turned splat with scroll feet, on brass casters; 62 in. (157 cm) wide.

E8 A George II mahogany tea table, the fold-over top above a plain frieze, on turned legs with pad feet, *c.* 1730; 29 in. (72 cm) diameter.

E12 A George II mahogany triple fold card and tea table, the top inset with counter wells and candle stands; 33 in. (84 cm) wide.

D4 A late Regency rosewood sofa table, with satinwood crossbanded well-figured twin-flap top, the frieze with two drawers, early 19th century; 56 in. (142 cm) wide, extended.

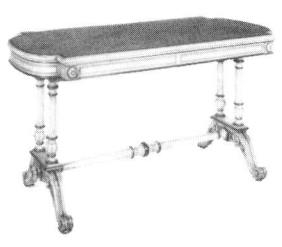

E5 An early Victorian burr-yew and ebony sofa table, with ebony-inlaid top, *c.* 1845; 29 in. high by 22 in. wide (73 by 54 cm).

E9 An early George II mahogany half round tea table, the flaps above a well-shaped frieze on plain turned legs; 30 in. (75 cm) wide.

E13 A George II mahogany tea table, the fold-over top above a frieze drawer, on plain turned legs and pad feet; 29 in. (72 cm) wide.

E6 An ormolu-mounted parcel-gilt and rosewood sofa table, with rounded rectangular twin-flap top and one frieze drawer, the four ring-turned supports on platform with scrolled feet; 54 in. (140 cm) wide, open.

E10 A mid-Georgian mahogany double fold-over tea and gaming table, with recessed counter trays and candle stands, on cabriole legs; 36 in. (90 cm) wide.

E14 A George II mahogany card or tea table, with triple flap top enclosing a baize-lined playing surface, mid 18th century; 30 in. (76 cm) wide.

E 1 A George III mahogany tea table with moulded folding top, the frieze carved with blind fretwork, and gadrooned border; 36 in. (91 cm) wide.

E 2 A George III serpentine mahogany tea or games table, carved with rosette and ribbon moulding, the pierced frieze with a drawer to the right, on square tapering legs, *c.* 1770; 36 in. (91 cm) wide.

E 3 A Chippendale carved mahogany tea table, with concertina action, pierced angle brackets and carved square legs with block feet; 30 in. high by 42 in. wide (76 by 106 cm).

E 4 A George III mahogany tea table, of serpentine outline, with small frieze drawer, on square legs moulded and carved with beading; 28 in. high by 35 in. wide (71 by 88 cm).

E 5 An Adam serpentine shaped folding tea table, on ebonized and gilt decorated base, with square tapering legs and block feet, *c.* 1780.

E 6 A George III mahogany tea table, with a demi-lune top and satinwood veneered frieze fitted with a drawer, on tapering legs and cup casters, third quarter 18th century; 30 in. by 40 in. (76 by 102 cm).

E 7 A George III mahogany tea table, with well-figured semi-elliptical folding top, plain frieze and moulded tapering legs centred by beading and headed by paterae; 39 in. (99 cm) wide.

E 8 A Sheraton figured mahogany tea table, with folding top of semi-circular shape, on turned tapering legs; 36 in. wide by 18 in. deep (92 by 46 cm).

E 9 A Georgian mahogany tea table, the folding top with rounded corners, on turned tapering supports; 33 in. (83 cm) wide.

E 10 A Regency tea table, with folding top, in figured and faded mahogany, with ormolu mounts, *c.* 1805; 29 in. high by 35 in. wide (73 by 88 cm).

E 11 A Regency mahogany tea table, bordered with ebonized lines, on twin lyre supports and scrolled splay legs; 36 in. (91 cm).

E 12 A Regency mahogany tea table, the folding top with rounded corners, with turned feet and brass casters; 28 in. high by 36 in. wide (71 by 91 cm).

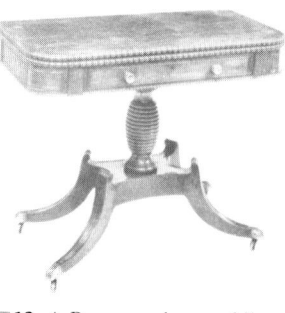

E 13 A Regency plum-pudding mahogany tea table, the fold-over top with bobbin border and frieze drawer, *c.* 1810; 39 in. (99 cm) wide.

E 14 A Regency mahogany folding tea table, with reeded column support and platform, with acanthus leaf carved splayed legs; 37 in. (93 cm) wide.

E 15 A Regency rosewood tea table, with fold-over top, on quadripartite support, the incurved platform on claw-and-ball feet.

E 16 A William IV mahogany tea table, raised on square pillar support with carved knops, on quatre-form base with scrolling feet; 36 in. (91 cm) wide.

E1 A Victorian rosewood tea table, on central pedestal and platform, raised on claw feet; 37 in. (93 cm).

E4 A rosewood tea or games table, the ogee frieze on slender downswept legs, *c.* 1840; 36 in. (91 cm) wide.

Tripod tables

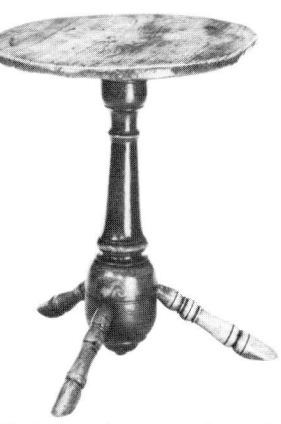

E8 A turner's table in elm, with circular top on turned pillar, with ball-shaped lower part and three turned fruitwood legs, *c.* 1700; 25 in. high by 23 in. diameter (63 by 58 cm).

E11 A scallop-top bird-cage tea table, with turned stem and tripod-shaped legs, *c.* 1750; 28 in. high by 28 in. diameter (71 by 71 cm).

E2 A Victorian rosewood fold-over tea table, with carved frieze; 36 in. (91 cm) wide.

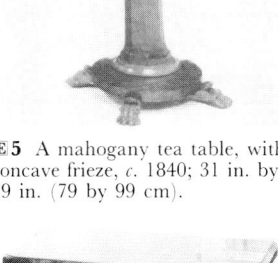

E5 A mahogany tea table, with concave frieze, *c.* 1840; 31 in. by 39 in. (79 by 99 cm).

E9 An oak tripod table, with tip-up top, on bird-cage support and turned stem, early 18th century; 22 in. diameter (55 cm).

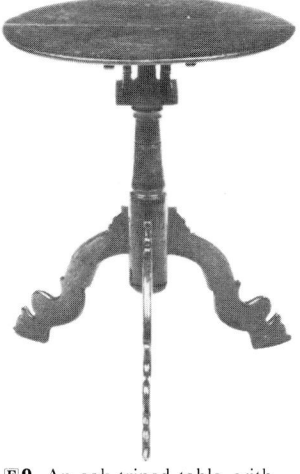

E12 A George II mahogany tripod table, with needlework top within a moulded edge and canted corners, with turned stem, *c.* 1750; 30 in. high by 32 in. wide (76 by 81 cm).

E3 An early Victorian rosewood serpentine tea table, the twin flap top resting on two pull out back cabriole legs with a well.

E6 A Victorian rosewood fold-over-top tea table, with carved frieze; 36 in. (91 cm) wide.

E7 A two-tier oval etagère, in satinwood and marquetry, by Edwards and Roberts, *c.* 1890.

E10 A George II mahogany tripod stand, with dished top and turned column; 21 in. high by 15 in. diameter (53 by 38 cm).

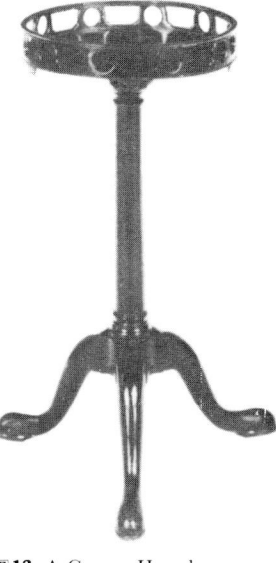

E13 A George II mahogany tripod table, the top with pierced moulded gallery, on a plain stand with cabriole legs and oval pad feet; 31 in. high by 16 in. diameter (78 by 40 cm).

Tripod Tables

The most elaborate and therefore desirable tops to tripod tables are those that are dished with a raised piecrust border; these were made from the 1740s onward.

Occasionally sections were spun from the top to indicate the table was made to hold several dishes – in this form it is known as a supper table – and the raised divisions were at times inlaid with brass in the manner of Roentgen.

Later in the century galleries were applied, being supported on turned pillars or on pierced fretwork in the Chinese or the Gothic manner. On such tables one would expect to find a base with similarly elaborate decoration.

The reverse however is not necessarily true. Many fine bases, elaborately carved, were made to support plain tops that in use would have been covered by a tablecloth. It is these tables that have been liable to "improvement" at a later date by dishing the top, leaving it too thin for comfort and compatibility.

E3 A George II mahogany tripod table, the hinged top with a moulded edge carved with scallop shells, on a baluster stem with cabriole legs, *c.* 1740; 31 in. high by 30 in. diameter (78 by 76 cm).

E6 A George II mahogany tripod table, with moulded serpentine top and baluster gallery on a "bird cage" support, the column with acanthus-carved downswept legs and pad feet, *c.* 1755; 25 in. (63 cm) wide.

E9 A George II mahogany tripod table, with gallery supported by turned spindles, on a bird-cage support; 26 in. high by 18 in. diameter (66 by 45 cm).

E4 A George II mahogany tripod table, with galleried edge, on carved baluster stem with cabriole legs, *c.* 1750; 28 in. high by 23 in. diameter (71 by 58 cm).

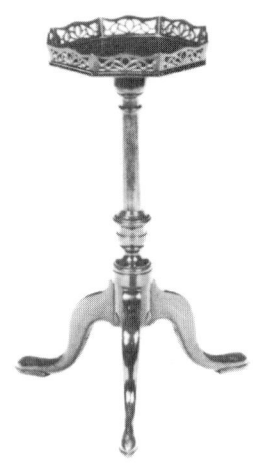

E7 A George III mahogany wine table, the octagonal shaped top with pierced gallery on a turned stem, the cabriole legs on pointed pad feet, *c.* 1755.

E10 A George II mahogany tripod table, with well-figured top, on bird-cage support and cabriole legs, with lion's-paw feet, mid 18th century; 31 in. (78 cm) diameter.

E1 A George II mahogany tripod table, *c.* 1740; 21 in. high by 12 in. diameter (54 by 30 cm).

E2 A mahogany tripod table, with plain edged top, on a bird-cage support with turned stem and cabriole legs, on pad feet, *c.* 1740; 21 in. (53 cm) diameter.

E5 A George II mahogany tripod table, the top with a "pie crust" edge, *c.* 1750; 28 in. high by 26 in. diameter (71 by 66 cm).

E8 A George II mahogany tripod table, with a moulded hinged top, the fluted stem richly carved, with cabriole legs heavily carved, the scrolled feet with casters, *c.* 1755; 29 in. (73 cm) wide.

E11 A mid-Georgian mahogany tripod table, the circular top on a turned shaft and foliate cabriole base with pointed pad feet; 21 in. (53 cm) wide.

D 1 A George III tilt-top tripod table, with lobed octagonal top with carved edge, revolving on a bird-cage support, on moulded cabriole legs, stamped under the base crowned W, third quarter 18th century; 25 in. (63 cm) wide.

E 2 A George III mahogany tripod table, *c*. 1760; 27 in. high by 26 in. wide (68 by 66 cm).

E 3 A mahogany octagonal top table, with carved edge, on a bird-cage support, with turned stem and cabriole legs ending in claw-and-ball feet, *c*. 1760; 33 in. (83 cm) wide.

D 4 A Chippendale carved tripod table, the tray top with galleried edge.

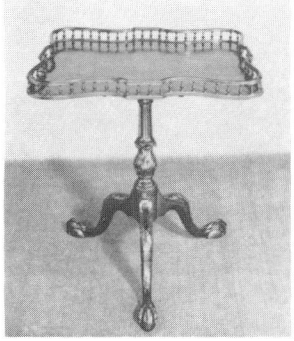

D 5 A Chippendale mahogany tip-up tripod table, with spindle gallery tray top, *c*. 1765.

E 6 A George III mahogany tripod table, 31 in. high by 22 in. wide (78 by 55 cm).

E 7 A Chippendale mahogany tripod table, the scalloped top supported by a bird cage, above a plain baluster turned stem, ending in plain cabriole legs with claw-and-ball feet, *c*. 1765; 27 in. high by 22 in. diameter (68 by 55 cm).

D 8 A Georgian mahogany tripod supper table, with lobed moulded circular top carved with eight recesses, on tripartite stem, with arched scrolled tripod base; 23 in. diameter (58 cm).

E 9 A Georgian walnut tripod table, the octagonal top with moulded gallery, on a baluster shaft with scrolled carved shaped legs; 26 in. (66 cm) wide.

D 10 A mahogany tripod table, with well-figured swivelling top and spindle gallery, on a turned and carved stem, with similarly carved cabriole legs, 30 in. (76 cm) wide.

D 11 A George III mahogany tripod table, the top with a brass-inlaid rim, with a carved baluster stem on carved legs with scrolled feet, *c*. 1765; 29 in, high by 26 in. diameter (73 by 66 cm).

E 12 A George III mahogany tripod table, with pie-crust edge, on a turned shaft with spirally fluted knops, the cabriole base carved with acanthus sprays on claw-and-ball feet; 23 in. high by 15 in. diameter (58 by 38 cm).

E 13 A George III mahogany tripod table, the rectangular tip-up top with waved gallery, on fluted shaft carved with foliage and flowerheads with gadrooned collar, on cabriole base and claw-and-ball feet; 26 in. (66 cm) wide.

E1 A George III mahogany tripod table, with tip-up top; 47 in. (119 cm) diameter.

E2 A George III mahogany tripod table, with an octagonal tip-up top on birdcage support; 26 in. (66 cm) high.

E3 A burr-walnut circular tip-up tripod table, mid/late 18th century.

E4 A George III carved mahogany "Manx" occasional table, the snap top with piecrust edge; 16 in. (42 cm).

E5 A mahogany tripod table, with a dish top, on turned stem with cabriole legs and pad feet, *c.* 1780; 28 in. high by 21 in. diameter (71 by 53 cm).

E6 A mahogany occasional table, with plain square top and moulded edge, on turned stem with plain cabriole legs ending in pointed pad feet, *c.* 1800; 23 in. (58 cm) square.

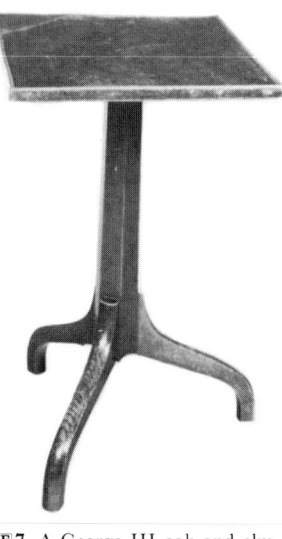

E7 A George III oak and elm tripod table, with rectangular elm top above a hexagonal pillar, on downcurving legs, early 19th century; 18 in. (45 cm) wide.

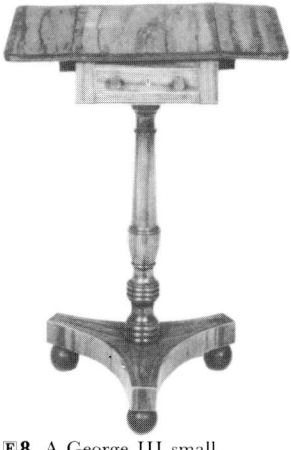

E8 A George III small satinwood tripod table, the rosewood crossbanded top with two flaps above the drawer, *c.* 1810; 33 in. (53 cm) wide, open.

E9 A mahogany pedestal table, the top with rounded corners, on a turned stem with downcurved legs, *c.* 1820; 16 in. (40 cm) wide.

E10 A Regency lacquered tripod table, with plain top on a birdcage support, with a turned carved stem, triangular base and lion's head feet; 30 in. (76 cm) high.

E11 A Regency rosewood lamp table, the top with brass border, *c.* 1815; 33 in. (53 cm) diameter.

E12 An elm two-tier tripod table, with turned stem and cabriole legs on pointed pad feet, early 19th century.

E13 A Regency stained beech wine table, the rectangular top with chamfered corners, the downcurved legs on brass ball feet, *c.* 1810; 18 in. (45 cm) wide.

E1 A Regency occasional table, in figured rosewood, with turned stem and downswept legs *c.* 1820; 28 in. high by 13 in. wide (71 by 33 cm).

E2 A mahogany tripod table, with scalloped top on a turned and carved stem, with cabriole legs on claw-and-ball feet, *c.* 1840; 14 in. (35 cm) diameter.

E3 A William IV rosewood pedestal table, with an Italian scagliola top, *c.* 1830; 31 in. high by 34 in. wide (78 by 86 cm).

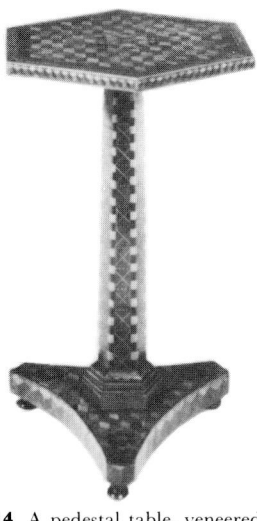

E4 A pedestal table, veneered with cube parquatry of walnut, rosewood, mahogany and other woods, *c.* 1835; 27 in. (68 cm) high.

E5 A Tunbridgeware octagonal table, with Berlin woolwork border, on a turned stem with carved cabriole legs and pad feet, *c.* 1875.

E6 A George III style brass inlaid mahogany tilt-top tripod table, in the style of Abraham Roentgen; 26 in. high by 20 in. diameter (66 by 50 cm).

Work tables

E7 A Sheraton rosewood work table, with lifting top, on square tapering legs with casters.

E8 A George III mahogany combined games and work table, of Sheraton design, inlaid with chevron stringing, on tapered square legs, *c.* 1790.

E9 A George III mahogany and kingwood banded work table, with a pleated-silk well, *c.* 1790; 30 in. high by 18 in. wide (76 by 45 cm).

E10 A George III harewood work table, the top inlaid with ribbon-pattern borders above a frieze drawer and rising back screen, on square tapering legs with casters joined by an X-shaped stretcher, late 18th century; 16 in. (40 cm) wide.

E11 A George III octagonal satinwood work table, the top centred by a print, the edge banded in stained holly and inlaid with star filled ribbon, *c.* 1795; 28 in. high by 15 in. wide (72 by 39 cm).

E12 A George III mahogany work table, the top inlaid with chequered lines, with lifting back screen above two drawers and a sliding basket frame, on square tapering legs with casters, late 18th century; 21 in. (53 cm) wide.

E1 A George III harewood work table, with domed hinged crossbanded lid, *c.* 1795; 36 in. high by 18 in. wide (91 by 46 cm).

E2 A George III satinwood work table, on turned tapering legs with casters.

E3 A George III satinwood needlework table, the oval top with lunette inlay; 29 in. high by 19 in. (73 by 48 cm).

E4 A George III satinwood and rosewood crossbanded work table, the top inlaid with geometric ebony and boxwood stringing, an inlaid frieze with drawer, on trestle supports, *c.* 1800; 28 in. high by 20 in. (71 by 50 cm).

E5 A George III satinwood work table, the top crossbanded with rosewood, fitted with a single flap, the other side with a concealed catch forming a door, on square tapering legs; 15 in. (38 cm) wide.

E6 A George III rosewood work table, the divided top with baize-lined interior, incorporating a small sunken panel concealing writing fitments, with a drawer in the frieze, *c.* 1800; 30 in. high by 22 in. wide (76 by 56 cm).

E7 A George III mahogany work table, inlaid with boxwood stringing, *c.* 1800; 28 in. (71 cm) high.

E8 A George III rosewood lady's writing and sewing table, early 19th century; 23 in. (58 cm) wide.

E9 A George III satinwood cheveret table, with galleried top and arched carrying handle; 16 in. (40 cm) wide.

E10 A Georgian mahogany work table, with two drawers; 20 in. (51 cm).

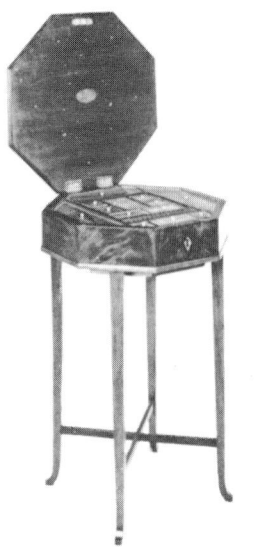

E11 A George III mahogany work table, with octagonal top enclosing yew and boxwood fittings, *c.* 1800; 30 in. high by 19 in. wide (77 by 48 cm).

E12 A George III mahogany and rosewood work table, with veneered top, *c.* 1800; 27 in. high by 16 in. (68 by 40 cm).

E1 A Regency mahogany and satinwood banded work table, fitted with a frieze drawer, the pillar with brass rail supports, *c.* 1810; 29 in. high by 22 in. wide (73 by 55 cm).

E2 A Regency satinwood and coromandel crossbanded work table, inlaid with ebony stringing, the drawer with compartments and lined slide, on turned ring supports with brass cappings, *c.* 1810; 30 in. high by 19 in. (76 by 49 cm).

E3 A Regency mahogany combined games and work table, the D-shaped ends with pierced brass galleries, the chessboard inset top with specimen veneers, with feather-banded border and brass stringing, the frieze with backgammon inset drawer above a deep drawer, *c.* 1815; 30 in. high by 34 in. wide (76 by 86 cm).

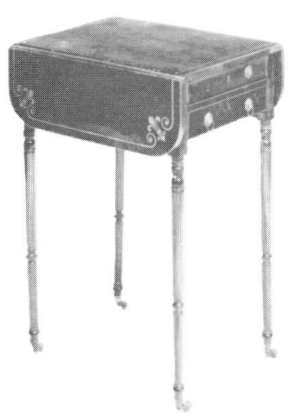

E4 A Regency rosewood and brass inlaid work table, the top inlaid with brass stringing, the frieze with opposing drawers, on turned tapering legs with brass casters, *c.* 1815; 29 in. high by 20 in. wide (73 by 50 cm).

E5 A Regency mahogany work table, inlaid with boxwood lines, the lid enclosing a fitted compartment; 18 in. (45 cm).

E6 A small Regency brass inlaid cheveret table, in the manner of John Maclean, with fine brasswork to the superstructure over four inlaid short drawers, three drawers to the frieze, on turned and collared legs; *c.* 1815.

E7 A Regency mahogany work table, with crossbanded rounded twin-flap top and two drawers, fitted with a slide, the upper drawer with baize-lined easel, the whole on splayed tapering legs; 38 in. (96 cm) wide, open.

E8 A Regency mahogany work table, with satinwood inlaid top and frieze drawer with divided lift-out interior, above a material-covered work basket, inlaid with ebonized and boxwood lines, on square tapering legs headed by gilt-metal rosettes; 17 in. (43 cm) wide.

E9 A Regency rosewood work table, in the style of McClean, the eared top bordered with a satinwood line with a single flap, with a divided drawer, a deep drawer inlaid with lozenges, a pen drawer and a slide, on splayed ring-turned and simulated rosewood and parcel-gilt "bamboo" supports, joined by concave sided platform; 24 in. (60 cm) wide.

E10 A Regency games/work table, in rosewood with brass inlay, fitted for backgammon, chess, silks and reels and with reading flap, the needlework bag in rose silk.

E11 A Regency rosewood work table, the top with rounded corners and inlaid with satinwood scrolls and spears to the corners, above a drawer and work basket, on lyre end supports; 20 in. (51 cm) wide.

E12 A Regency rosewood sewing table, the sarcophagus top centred with brass arabesques, lifting to reveal fitted interior, having brass ring handles, on lyre support and sabre legs with brass paw cappings.

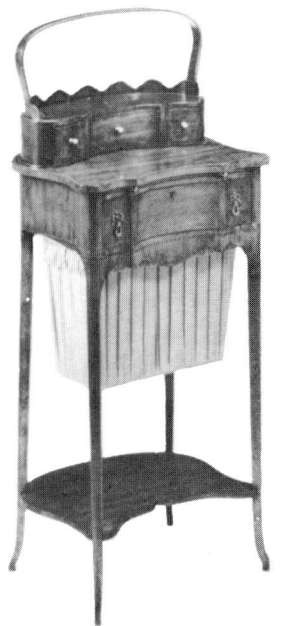

E1 A George III mahogany cheveret table, *c.* 1780; 42 in. high by 17 in. (107 by 44 cm).

E2 A Regency mahogany work table, the top with ebonized lines; 21 in. (53 cm) wide.

E3 A Regency rosewood work table, the top inset with a cream lacquered panel; 15 in. (38 cm) wide.

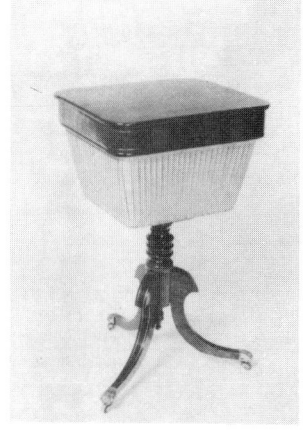

E4 A Regency rosewood work table, with pleated covering to basket, on pedestal with sabre legs, brass inlaid stringing to top and legs, with brass paw feet; 17 in. (44 cm).

E5 A Regency lady's work table, with fully fitted interior, and pleated silk covering to work basket, *c.* 1830; 31 in. (78 cm) high.

E6 A William IV grained rosewood work table, with two real opposing two dummy drawers, *c.* 1830; 17 in. by 15 in. (43 by 38 cm).

E7 A Regency rosewood and brass inlaid combined games, reading and work table, the top painted in gouache with a spray of flowers, above a shallow drawer inlaid for backgammon and with a slide inlaid for chess, above a fitted writing drawer with a work bag below, incorporating a fitted tray, inlaid throughout with brass stringing and foliage, *c.* 1815; 29 in. high by 27 in. wide (73 by 68 cm).

E8 A Regency rosewood work table, with a rounded rectangular drop-leaf top, a fitted drawer and a slide to the frieze, and on S-shaped supports with trestle feet joined by a stretcher; 30 in. high by 33 in. wide (76 by 83 cm).

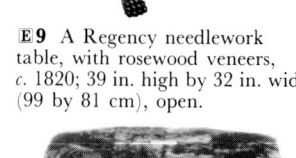

E9 A Regency needlework table, with rosewood veneers, *c.* 1820; 39 in. high by 32 in. wide (99 by 81 cm), open.

E10 A George IV octagonal tortoiseshell veneered work table, with fitted interior, *c.* 1830; 24 in. high by 12 in. wide (60 by 30 cm).

E1 A George IV rosewood work table, the hinged top revealing an inset, fitted with a frieze drawer, on trestle shaped supports with carved scroll decoration, *c.* 1825; 24 in. (60 cm) wide.

E2 A mahogany globe work table, in the manner of Morgan and Sanders, with hinged domed cover, early 19th century; 36 in. high by 17 in. diameter (91 by 43 cm).

D3 A burr-walnut and mahogany work table, of globe form, with hinged roll top enclosing a fitted interior, above a giltwood serpent, early 19th century; 38 in. (96 cm) high.

E4 A William IV rosewood combined games and work table, the reversible drop-leaf top revealing backgammon inlay, with two frieze drawers, the chamfered baluster pillar with a quatreform base and bun feet, on casters, *c.* 1835; 30 in. high by 22 in. wide (76 by 55 cm).

E5 A William IV carved rosewood and Tunbridgeware combined games and work table, *c.* 1835; 29 in. high by 24 in. wide (74 by 61 cm).

E7 A Victorian mahogany work and games table, with two-flap top inlaid as a chessboard, fitted with one drawer and a U-shaped work bag, on a short octagonal pedestal and concave sided base; 19 in. (48 cm).

E8 A burr-walnut games and work table, the interior for chess, backgammon and cribbage, with drawer and compartments above a work bag, *c.* 1850; 29 in. high by 24 in. wide (73 by 60 cm).

E6 A Victorian oak work table, by Holland & Sons, with baize-lined folding top crossbanded with pollard oak, above a concave frieze drawer and a material-lined work basket, on pierced trestle ends; 21 in. (54 cm) wide.

E9 A papier mâché work table, inlaid with mother-of-pearl and painted, the interior fitted with compartments and accessories, mid 17th century; 28 in. by 17 in. (71 by 43 cm).

E10 A Victorian papier mâché work table, decorated in gilt and mother-of-pearl on a black ground, enlcosing a compartment; 30 in. high by 19 in. wide (76 by 48 cm).

E11 A Victorian gilt papier mâché inlaid mother-of-pearl and reverse painted work table, with inscribed metal plaque "To Mrs. Garbett by the congregation of St. Georges, Birmingham, December 1851", 18 in. (45 cm) diameter.

E1 A Victorian walnut work table, with fitted interior, the octagonal-shaped top and tripod pedestal with carved cabriole legs, 1850-1860.

E2 A papier mâché work table, with lacquer and mother-of-pearl decoration, and fitted interior, *c.* 1860; 18 in. (45 cm) wide.

E3 An ebonized work table, the panelled frieze with an ash-lined drawer, *c.* 1870; 28 in. high by 26 in. (71 by 66 cm).

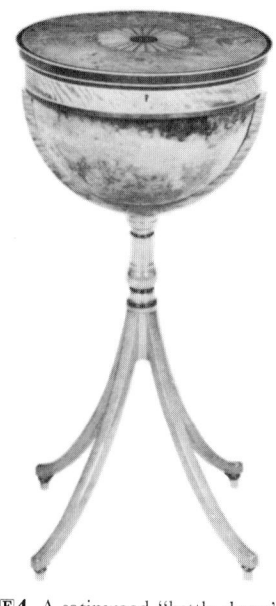

E4 A satinwood "kettle drum" work table, the hinged top inlaid with a giant patera, with velvet-covered drum-shaped bag, *c.* 1900; 29 in. high by 16 in. diameter (73 by 40 cm).

E5 An Edwardian period inlaid rosewood work table, with a swivel top, petal-shaped drawers which are concealed when closed.

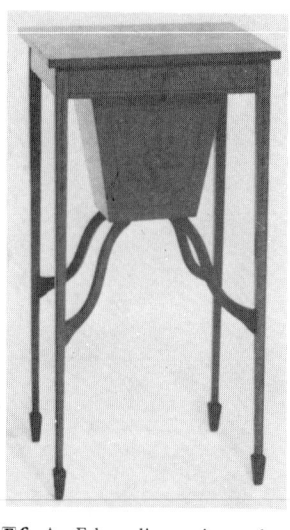

E6 An Edwardian satinwood work table, with a hinged top enclosing a fitted interior, early 20th century; 28 in. high by 15 in. wide.

D7 A late Stuart walnut double gate leg writing table, with locking folding top, late 17th century; 30 in. (78 cm) wide.

E8 A William and Mary oak double gate leg writing table, *c.* 1690; 29 in. high by 30 in. wide (73 by 76 cm).

E9 An oak folding-top writing table, on turned supports with gate leg action, 18th century; 32 in. (81 cm) wide.

D10 A George I burr-walnut card and writing table, 29 in. high by 18 in. wide (73 by 45 cm).

D11 A George I walnut writing table, with brass ring handles to real and dummy drawer fronts, on carved cabriole legs.

E12 A George II mahogany "jack-in-the-box" writing table, with small drawers and compartments, *c.* 1740.

D13 A padouk combination writing, card and tea table, *c.* 1735; 29 in. high by 30 in. wide (73 by 76 cm).

A1 A mahogany writing table, by William Kent, with gilt ornaments, ornately carved, with central kneehole.

B2 A Chippendale mahogany writing table, the upper part with two panelled arched doors, flanked by eight small drawers, the curving lower section with larger drawers, above an arched and shaped apron, 63 in. (160 cm) wide.

D3 A sabicu wood writing table, with pierced gallery and angles, with one long, flanked by two short, drawers, on square legs with block feet and casters, 18th century.

C4 A George II walnut writing table, with writing slide; 39 in. high by 40 in. wide (99 by 101 cm).

E5 A George III padoukwood writing table, the top crossbanded with satinwood, the frieze with a hinged flap enclosing ten various sized short drawers; 59 in. (149 cm) wide, open.

B6 A George III tulipwood and kingwood writing table, in Louis XV style, with serpentine leather-lined top with moulded ormolu borders and foliate angle plaques; 62 in. (157 cm) wide.

E7 A George III mahogany harlequin writing table; 39 in. high by 36 in. (99 by 92 cm).

E9 A George III oval mahogany lady's writing table, the top crossbanded in satinwood, and with arising firescreen back, *c.* 1785; 27 in. (68 cm) wide.

D8 A George III mahogany and satinwood draw-leaf writing table, with crossbanded top; 49 in. (125 cm) wide, open.

E10 A George III mahogany kidney-shaped writing table, the rosewood crossbanded leather inset writing surface above a mock and real drawer to either end; 38 in. (97 cm) wide.

E 1 A Hepplewhite mahogany writing table, with sliding screen at the back covered in silk; 30 in. high by 20 in. wide (76 by 50 cm).

D 2 A George III rosewood lady's writing table, to a design by Thomas Sheraton, *c.* 1785; 36 in. high by 30 in. wide (91 by 76 cm).

C 3 A George III mahogany writing table, in the French taste; 31 in. (78 cm) high.

D 4 A George III mahogany writing table, 59 in. (150 cm) wide.

E 5 A late George III mahogany writing table, with leather-lined top; 42 in. (107 cm) square.

D 6 A George III satinwood writing table, the top crossbanded with rosewood; 39 in. wide by 23 in. deep (100 by 58 cm).

E 7 A George III rosewood writing table, with inset leather top, early 19th century; 39 in. (99 cm) wide.

D 8 A Regency mahogany writing table, fitted with three frieze drawers each side; 60 in. (152 cm) wide.

E 9 A Regency mahogany writing table, fitted with five drawers, around centre kneehole; 53 in. (135 cm) wide.

E 10 A Regency mahogany kidney-shaped writing table, with galleried leather-lined top and three frieze drawers; 46 in. (116 cm) wide.

E 11 A lady's inlaid satinwood and lacewood grained writing table, with double hinged top incorporating a pull-up fire screen.

E 12 A Regency mahogany writing table, with bowed rectangular inset leather top above a conforming frieze with two short drawers opposing two false drawers, on reeded circular tapering legs, early 19th century; 62 in. (157 cm) wide.

E 13 A Regency mahogany writing table with rounded rectangular baize-lined top, the frieze with six drawers, inlaid with lines on ring-turned tapering legs; 52 in. (132 cm) wide.

E 14 A George III mahogany reading and writing table, *c.* 1800; 29 in. (73 cm) high.

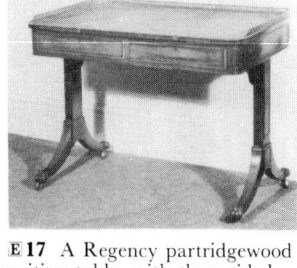

E 15 A Regency rosewood writing table with leather top, 28 in. high by 36 in. wide (71 by 91 cm).

C 16 A Regency rosewood writing table in the manner of John McLean, 48 in. (122 cm) wide.

E 17 A Regency partridgewood writing table, with three-sided gallery; 39 in. (99 cm).

E 18 A Regency rosewood writing table, with inset leather top; 43 in. (109 cm) wide.

D 1 A Regency mahogany writing table, with leather-lined U-shaped top; 91 in. wide by 58 in. deep (230 by 147 cm).

E 2 A Regency mahogany writing table, crossbanded with rosewood; 47 in. (120 cm) wide.

E 3 A Sheraton mahogany kidney-shaped table fitted with a centre drawer; 31 in. high by 41 in. wide (78 by 104 cm).

E 4 A Regency kidney-shaped writing table, *c.* 1810; 28 in. high by 51 in. deep (129 by 71 cm).

D 5 A Regency mahogany lady's combined writing and work table, *c.* 1810; 30 in. (76 cm) high.

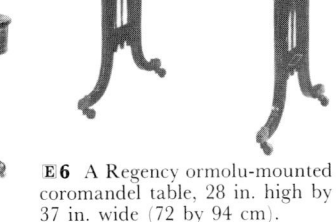

E 6 A Regency ormolu-mounted coromandel table, 28 in. high by 37 in. wide (72 by 94 cm).

E 7 A Regency ormolu-mounted rosewood writing table, early 19th century; 44 in. (112 cm) wide.

E 8 A Regency rosewood writing table, with hinged flap top; 23 in. (58 cm) wide.

E 9 A mahogany writing table with fitted drawer and undershelf, stamped Gillows of Lancaster, *c.* 1810.

E 10 A Regency mahogany writing table, rosewood crossbanded and boxwood line inlaid, with two drawers and two false drawers; 41 in. by 28 in. (104 by 71 cm).

E 11 A Regency pollard elm writing table, the top crossbanded with rosewood; 40 in. (101 cm) wide.

E 12 A George IV coromandelwood and simulated coromandelwood writing table, *c.* 1825; 29 in. high by 32 in. wide (74 by 81 cm).

E 13 A late Georgian small mahogany writing table, the top with a hinged panel rising to reveal pen and ink wells, with one frieze drawer; 29 in. (73 cm).

Writing Tables

Dressing tables, in lowboy form, had doubled as writing tables in the first half of the 18th century. Designers then produced specialized writing tables in quantity, small and delicate with pull-out writing slides, fitments for ink bottles and other writing necessaries, the fitted part sometimes with a rising action. Adjustable screens were also built into some models, to protect either the ankles or the face of the sitter from the heat of the fire.

Introduced in the curvilinear style of "French Hepplewhite" (see no. 1 on the facing page) delicate writing tables achieved wide popularity in the classically elegant form designed by Thomas Sheraton, as no. 2 opposite.

Throughout the 19th century the inventiveness of furniture-makers produced many combinations of function. Thus the writing table could be combined with the work table, as no. 5 below, or with the dressing table, harking back to the early 18th century when both purposes were satisfied by the same piece of furniture. Leather writing surfaces were also made to reverse to an inlaid chequer board.

E 14 A late Georgian mahogany kneehole writing table, inlaid with boxwood lines; 42 in. (106 cm) wide.

E 15 A small mahogany writing table, stamped Gillows, Lancaster, with a leather writing surface above a drawer, *c.* 1830; 28 in. (71 cm) high.

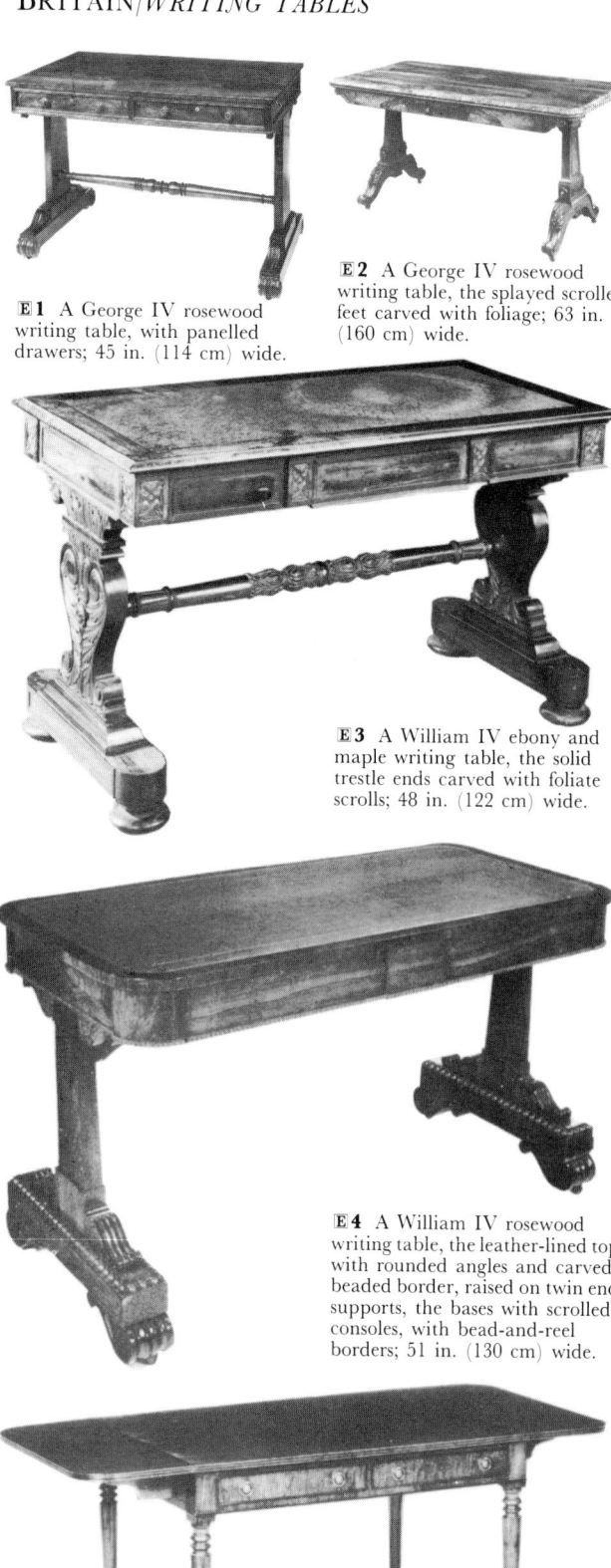

E1 A George IV rosewood writing table, with panelled drawers; 45 in. (114 cm) wide.

E2 A George IV rosewood writing table, the splayed scrolled feet carved with foliage; 63 in. (160 cm) wide.

E3 A William IV ebony and maple writing table, the solid trestle ends carved with foliate scrolls; 48 in. (122 cm) wide.

E4 A William IV rosewood writing table, the leather-lined top with rounded angles and carved beaded border, raised on twin end supports, the bases with scrolled consoles, with bead-and-reel borders; 51 in. (130 cm) wide.

E5 A mahogany writing table, stamped Gillows Lancaster, the top with unusual "fiddle" figuring, *c.* 1840; 62 in. (157 cm) wide, open.

E6 An unusual small William IV mahogany writing or reading table, with two tiny leaves, the top raises on an adjustable ratchet and this piece also contains a fire screen to protect the lady's face, *c.* 1830. When closed it measures 28 in. high by 14 in. by 12 in. (70 by 35 by 30 cm).

E7 A William IV rosewood partners' writing table, with leather-lined top; 80 in. (203 cm) wide.

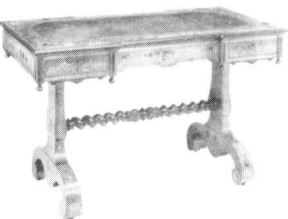

E8 A Victorian walnut writing table, inlaid with floral marquetry; 48 in. (122 cm) wide.

E9 An ebonized satinwood veneered writing table, in the manner of Holland, *c.* 1850; 42 in. (107 cm) wide.

E10 A George II-design games and writing table, consisting of a tea table, a card table with baize-lined wells and candle stands, and a section with drawers and pigeonholes, the cabriole legs carved at the knees, *c.* 1840; 30 in. wide (76 cm).

E 1 A Victorian walnut veneered writing table, stamped Maple & Co., *c.* 1850; 39 in. high (99 cm).

E 2 An ormolu-mounted tulipwood and marquetry writing table, *c.* 1850; 48 in. (123 cm) wide.

E 3 A walnut veneered bureau plat, by Edwards & Roberts, 19th century; 54 in. (132 cm) wide.

E 4 A Victorian walnut and marquetry bureau plat, by Edwards & Roberts; 45 in. (114 cm) wide.

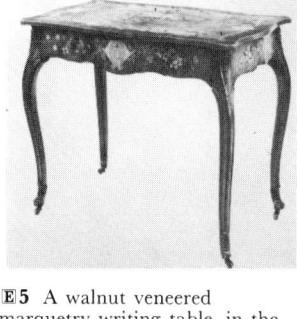

E 5 A walnut veneered marquetry writing table, in the French manner, with rococo floral inlay, the frieze drawer mahogany lined, early 19th century; 36 in. (91 cm) wide.

E 6 An Edwardian mahogany writing table, on panelled and fluted supports, the two drawers with brass handles, late 19th century; 40 in. (100 cm) wide.

E 7 An Edwardian mahogany lady's writing table, with inlaid decoration, the galleried top with drawers each side, the lower section with bowed central drawer.

E 8 A double-sided mahogany writing table, in George II style, *c.* 1900; 31 in. high by 56 in. wide (78 by 142 cm).

TEAPOYS
1790-1850

Teapoys, being tea caddies on stands ("poy" comes from the Spanish apoyo, support) were first made in the latter part of the 18th century.

A teapoy might have boxes for up to four teas, sometimes with the varieties' initials on the lids. In the centre there could be one or two glass bowls for blending or to hold sugar, and there might also be space for teaspoons and sugar nips.

E 9 A George III mahogany teapoy, with fitted interior, *c.* 1790; 24 in. (60 cm) high.

E 10 A Regency rosewood teapoy, on twisted column, on quadripartite base, *c.* 1810.

E 11 A Regency combined teapoy and cellaret, containing six cut glass bottles, *c.* 1810; 33 in. (84 cm) high.

E 12 A Regency mahogany and cut brass inlaid teapoy, the sarcophagus-shaped top with hinged lid, *c.* 1810; 31 in. (78 cm) high.

E 13 An unusual yew-wood teapoy with string inlay, the sarcophagus-shaped structure with hinged top, the interior with a pair of lidded canisters and the original blending bowls, *c.* 1810; 21 in. (52 cm) wide.

E 14 A Regency rosewood teapoy, the cover with satinwood marquetry, enclosing a fitted interior with four hinged caddies; 29 in. high by 17 in wide (72 by 42 cm).

E1 A late Regency rosewood pedestal teapoy, the hinged coffered rectangular lid enclosing four canisters and a pair of cut-glass mixing bowls; 18 in. (45 cm) wide.

E2 A Regency rosewood teapoy, on faceted tapering column and shaped platform base with scroll feet on casters.

E3 A Regency rosewood teapoy, of sarcophagus design, raised on a column tapering from a platform base with scroll feet.

E4 A William IV brass-inlaid rosewood teapoy, of sarcophagus design with beading and drop-ring handles, raised on a column tapering from the scrolled tripartite platform base.

E5 An early Victorian rosewood teapoy, raised on a polygonal baluster column and circular platform base, with four upturned feet on casters.

E6 An early Victorian teapoy of sarcophagus form, the top lifting to reveal two bowls and four caddies, on a baluster column and platform base.

WASHSTANDS 1740-1900

While there are records of side tables being designated as toilet stands from the 16th century, it was not until the mid-18th century that a piece of furniture designed exclusively for the purpose appeared in any quantity.

The most attractive were of tripod form, the top being a circular frame to hold a basin over a triangular box fitted with two drawers, with a platform below that was dished to hold the ewer.

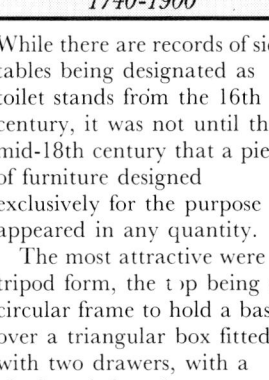

E7 A George II two-drawer mahogany wig stand, on three spindle shafts on a triangular base with three pad feet.

E8 An early George III mahogany basin stand, mid to late 18th century; 13 in. (34 cm) diameter.

E9 A mahogany washstand, rising of four square-section legs to a single central drawer with drop ring handle.

E10 A mahogany washstand, with fold-back top forming two trays, supported on four square-section legs, with a single central drawer with drop ring handle, mid 18th century; 30 in. (75 cm) wide.

E11 A Sheraton mahogany enclosed washstand, the top with two fold-back trays and a mirror, supported on four square-section legs with a cross-stretcher.

E1 A George III mahogany corner basin stand, with quadrant-shaped top shelf with scrolling apron, late 18th century; 26 in. (68 cm) wide.

E2 A mahogany corner washstand, with bow front and splayed legs, *c.* 1820; 32 in. (80 cm) high.

E3 An inlaid Sheraton mahogany corner washstand, with tambour front, raised on square supports with splayed legs and tripartite stretcher.

E4 A mid-Georgian mahogany Davenport type ship's washstand, with sloping front, on turned legs, with washbowl and stopper; 24 in. (60 cm) wide.

E5 A George III mahogany washing table, with brass washing bowl and four canisters with an adjustable concealed mirror, *c.* 1795; 36 in. high by 22 in. wide (91 by 56 cm).

E6 An inlaid mahogany bow-front corner washstand, the pierced top with splash back, centre open shelf with single frieze drawer flanked by dummy drawers, on square supports with splayed legs, early 19th century; 24 in. wide by 40 in. high (60 by 100 cm).

E7 A Victorian bentwood washstand, of unusual design, with swing toilet mirror; *c.* 1880.

E8 A George II-style mahogany washstand, the top enclosing a blue printed Wedgwood jug and basin, the centre section with two drawers, on downswept supports, late 19th/early 20th century; 11 in. diameter by 36 in. high (27 by 92 cm).

The English whatnot, a close relative if not a direct descendant of the French étagère, existed from at least 1800 – it appears in Gillow's cost book for that year, though its curious name is not recorded until later.

The form, being necessarily delicate, forgave nothing but the finest craftsmanship. Most early whatnots are in plain mahogany, but fine inlaid and ormolu-mounted Regency examples can be found.

E9 A late George III mahogany whatnot, with two shelves, *c.* 1805; 60 in. high by 19 in. wide (153 by 48 cm).

E10 A Sheraton mahogany four-tier whatnot, with drawer in the base; 18 in. wide by 54 in. high (45 by 137 cm).

E1 A late George III mahogany whatnot, with four plain rectangular tiers, interposed by ring-turned supports, on metal casters, early 19th century; 47 in. high by 20 in. wide (120 by 52 cm).

E3 A brass-inlaid Regency rosewood whatnot, or reading stand, with one frieze drawer with brass handles, an adjustable reading stand and original brass casters, *c.* 1810; 45 in. high by 18 in. wide (112 by 45 cm).

E5 A Regency rosewood whatnot, with four-quarter galleried shelves, with ormolu borders; 20 in. (50 cm) wide.

E6 A rosewood whatnot, the three tiers on turned supports, early 19th century; 31 in. (78 cm) high.

E8 A rosewood étagère or whatnot, with three open shelves and two frieze drawers, on turned and scrolled supports, with turned legs and brass casters, the top with three-quarter brass gallery, *c.* 1840; 46 in. by 24 in. (117 by 61 cm).

E2 A late George III mahogany whatnot with four rectangular tiers on turned supports terminating at the foot in a ball and at the top in a finial; the third tier down has a frieze drawer. The piece dates from the first years of the 19th century and is 48 in. high and 18 in. wide (120 by 45 cm).

E4 A Regency black and gold lacquer whatnot, with three plain rectangular tiers with floral lacquer decorations, the cupboard underneath with elaborate chinoiserie scenes, early 19th century; 47 in. high by 18 in. wide (120 by 46 cm).

E7 A William IV mahogany whatnot, the top with three-quarter balustrade, *c.* 1835; 40 in. (108 cm) high.

E9 An early Victorian mahogany whatnot or reading stand, the three tiers joined by turned spindle supports, with adjustable reading stand over, with one frieze drawer and bun feet, *c.* 1840; 47 in. high by 20 in. wide.

E1 A rosewood whatnot, with well turned supports, *c.* 1850; 31 in. (78 cm) high.

E2 A Victorian rosewood whatnot, with three tiers on twisted columns, fitted with a drawer; 19 in. (46 cm) wide.

E3 A Victorian satinwood and mahogany crossbanded canterbury whatnot, fitted with a drawer.

E4 A Victorian rosewood canterbury whatnot, with a drawer; 30 in. (75 cm) wide.

E5 A Victorian burr-walnut three-tier whatnot, on turned supports; 31 in. (78 cm) wide.

E6 A Victorian rosewood bow-fronted whatnot, with mirror back; 26 in. (65 cm) wide.

E7 A Victorian walnut inlaid corner whatnot, with serpentine-fronted tiers, on shaped turned supports; 56 in. (142 cm) high.

E8 A Victorian teak whatnot, with four graduated tiers with shaped edges, with turned supports, *c.* 1890; 45 in. (112 cm) high.

E9 A Victorian three-tier whatnot, with lacquered decoration; 33 in. by 20 in. (82 by 50 cm).

Whatnots

The whatnot, first referred to by that name in about 1800, is a natural development of the mid-18th-century tiered stand. The Regency version however is larger in every way, and was intended at first to hold folios or music for easy access.

The whatnot became widely popular during the Victorian period. As it moved from the library or music room to the parlour it changed function, now being used to display the increasing number of objects without which no Victorian home was complete; to this end mirror backs were introduced. The transformation was not total however, as many whatnots were made with canterbury or music folio bases.

The change in function of the whatnot was paralleled by a change in appearance. After T.B. Jordan produced his wood-carving machine in 1845 it was possible to produce elaborate, scrolled supports and pierced galleries in multiples for the mass market.

E10 An Edwardian ebonized whatnot, the three tiers with incurved sides, *c.* 1910; 33 in. (82 cm) wide.

E11 A "Georgian" gilt corner hanging whatnot, the whole embellished giltwood in foliate design; 60 in. (152 cm) high.

WINDOW SEATS
1775-1825

A window seat, strictly defined, is a backless bench made to fit a window bay. It will probably taper from back to front, the legs on the narrower side being left plain. In its classical form it will have four legs to the front and only two to the back.

The lines of this type of stool are so pleasing that the shape was repeated in dressing stools, duet stools and other occasional seat furniture.

D 1 An early George III mahogany window seat, covered in nailed brown moiré silk, the legs carved with blind fretwork, joined by plain, straight stretchers; 80 in. (203 cm) wide.

D 2 A Chippendale carved and gilt day bed, in original cover, on claw feet; 63 in. (160 cm) long.

E 3 A George III mahogany window seat, c. 1765; 20 in. high by 34 in. wide (56 by 86 cm).

E 4 A George III mahogany window seat, in the French style, c. 1775; 34 in. (86 cm) wide.

D 5 A George III gilded beech window seat, with outscrolled padded arms carved with guilloche and husks ending in rosettes, with swept seat-rails similarly carved, on slender moulded cabriole legs ending in scroll toes, upholstered in peach damask, c. 1772; 51 in. (130 cm) wide.

E 6 A Hepplewhite mahogany window seat, with outscrolled padded arms and upholstered seat, the curved seat-rail with central carved rosette, on cabriole legs; 48 in. (122 cm) wide.

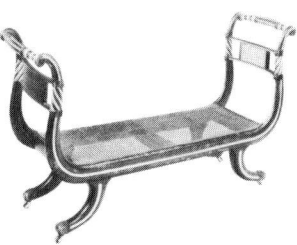

E 7 A George III giltwood window seat, with outscrolled padded arms, on upholstered seat with fluted seat-rail, on turned legs; 59 in. (150 cm) wide.

E 8 A Regency green-painted rosewood and parcel-gilt window seat, with outcurved sides, turned and reeded top rails and rectangular splats, with caned seat, early 19th century; 56 in. (142 cm) wide.

WINE COOLERS
1760-1830

Although in common use the terms are interchangeable, whereas all cellarets are wine coolers, not all wine coolers are cellarets. A cellaret should always have a lockable lid, making it a "little cellar".

The standard model is of coopered form, though the sarcophagus shape predominated in the Regency; fine classical urn-shaped coolers dating from the Adam period can still be found.

D 9 A Chippendale oval wine cooler, the cabriole legs with heavily carved knees, and ornate ball-and-claw feet.

D 10 A Chippendale mahogany wine cooler and stand, c. 1755; 52 in. high by 17 in. wide (132 by 42 cm).

E1 An early George III mahogany wine cooler, brass bound, the lead-lined interior with seven partitions; 20 in. (50 cm) wide.

E2 A mid-Georgian brass-bound mahogany oval bottle carrier, 15 in. (39 cm) wide.

E3 A George III mahogany hexagonal brass-bound cellaret, with carrying handles on the sides, *c.* 1765; 28 in. high by 18 in. wide (72 by 46 cm).

E4 A George III oval mahogany cellaret, the slightly tapering body with three brass bands, *c.* 1770; 28 in. high by 26 in. wide (71 by 66 cm).

E5 A George III mahogany and brass-bound wine cooler, 27 in. (68 cm) wide.

E6 A George III octagonal mahogany cellaret on stand, *c.* 1770; 27 in. high by 18 in. wide (68 by 45 cm).

E7 A George III mahogany cellaret, *c.* 1775; 25 in. high by 17 in. wide (64 by 44 cm).

E8 A George III mahogany wine cooler, lead lined, *c.* 1775; 25 in. (65 cm) high.

E9 A George III mahogany cellaret, 27 in. high by 21 in. wide (69 by 53 cm).

E10 A George III mahogany cellaret, *c.* 1780; 25 in. (62 cm) high.

E11 An Adam urn-shaped wine cooler on base, 18th century; 70 in. (178 cm) high.

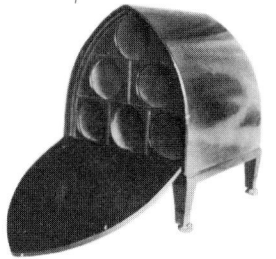

E12 A mahogany wine bin, with hinged front flap revealing six compartments, with four legs on casters, 18th century.

E13 An Adam mahogany cellaret, 26 in. high by 16 in. wide (65 by 40 cm).

E14 A Hepplewhite inlaid mahogany dome-shaped cellaret on stand, with carrying handles.

E15 A mahogany cellaret, with domed lid inlaid with a shell oval; 17 in. (43 cm) wide.

E1 A George III period mahogany cellaret, with rosewood crossbanded hinged cover; 18 in. (45 cm) wide.

E2 A late inlaid George III cellaret, with 12 partitions and brass carrying handles; 14 in. (36 cm) wide.

E3 A George III satinwood and mahogany cellaret, *c.* 1790; 20 in. (50 cm) high.

E4 A Sheraton wine cooler, of oval shape, on tapering legs with casters.

E5 A George III mahogany and brass-bound wine cooler, *c.* 1790; 18 in. (46 cm) wide.

E6 A George III crossbanded mahogany wine cooler; 19 in. (46 cm) wide.

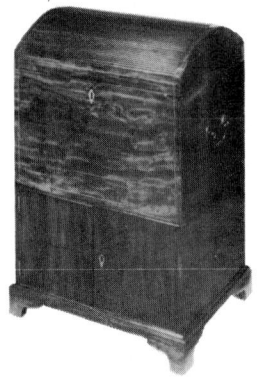

E7 A late Georgian mahogany cellaret, inlaid with boxwood lines; 21 in. (51 cm).

E8 A George III mahogany brass-bound wine cooler; 18 in. (47 cm) diameter.

E9 A Hepplewhite wine cooler, of faded mahogany, the top of octagonal form, the stand with four moulded legs with arched spandrels; 17 in. (45 cm).

E10 A George III brass-bound mahogany wine cooler on stand, of oval tapering form with two brass bands and two brass handles, lead liner, the whole on square tapering legs; 25 in. (64 cm) wide.

E11 A George III mahogany wine cooler, of oval form, crossbanded and inlaid with stringing, the sides with brass carrying handles and banding, *c.* 1790; 23 in. high by 21 in. wide (58 by 53 cm).

E12 A George III mahogany wine cooler, with brass carrying handles and bands, lead-lined interior; 27 in. (68 cm) high.

E13 A George III mahogany brass-bound wine cooler, *c.* 1790; 21 in. (52 cm) wide.

E14 A George III mahogany brass-bound wine cooler, 24 in. (61 cm) wide.

E15 A George III mahogany wine cooler on stand, 23 in. (58 cm) wide.

E1 A George III mahogany campana-shaped wine cooler, 26 in. (65 cm) diameter.

E2 A Sheraton mahogany wine cooler, inlaid with a marquetry panel, with an ivory escutcheon, on cast gilt-metal legs; 28 in. (69 cm).

E3 A mahogany wine cooler, with dummy drawers, with lion-mask handles, *c.* 1800; 21 in. (52 cm) high.

E4 A Regency mahogany and inlaid sarcophagus-shaped wine cooler, with moulded raised top, lion-mask ring-handles, a shallow drawer in the bottom, on carved bun feet; 31 in. (78 cm) wide.

E5 A Regency mahogany cellaret, with fitted interior, on a turned column with tripod support; 17 in. (43 cm).

E6 A late George III mahogany cellaret, holding 12 Dutch 18th-century blown-glass decanters; 21 in. (52 cm) wide.

E7 A George III mahogany cellaret, with a fitted interior, *c.* 1825; 25 in. high by 22 in. (63 by 54 cm).

E8 A Regency mahogany wine cooler, the coved chamfered lid with gadrooned border; 23 in. (58 cm) wide.

D9 A Regency mahogany wine cooler, in the manner of Gillows, with fluted oval lid and well-figured tapering body; 27 in. (68 cm) wide.

E10 A Regency mahogany cellaret, of sarcophagus form, 25 in. (63 cm) wide.

E11 A late Regency mahogany wine cooler, of sarcophagus shape, the tapering sides on four ball feet, outlined in ebony; 31 in. (79 cm).

E12 A George IV mahogany cellaret, the brass-bound body containing compartments, and removable ice container; 27 in. high by 24 in. wide (69 by 61 cm).

E13 A George IV mahogany cellaret, on lion-paw feet, *c.* 1820; 25 in. (65 cm) high.

E14 A William IV mahogany wine cooler, with ebony inlay, *c.* 1830; 16 in. (42 cm) high.

E15 A walnut cellaret, of sarcophagus form, the domed lid with bead-and-reel border, *c.* 1840; 33 in. (74 cm) wide.

D16 A George III mahogany wine cooler, in the manner of Adam, *c.* 1875; 29 in. high by 19 in. (72 by 48 cm).

E17 A carved mahogany wine cooler, in George III style, late 19th/early 20th century.

FRANCE

The route to France's eventual and undisputed glory in the arts of furniture-making lay through Florence and Flanders. The French were early dazzled by the wonders of the Italian Renaissance and imported both the style and the craftsmen. Then the tastes of Marie de Medici, regent during Louis XIII's minority, were as much for the arts of Flanders as for those of her native Florence.

Thus in the first half of the 17th century French craftsmen worked alongside the pick of those from Flanders and Italy. When the great workshops at the Gobelins were established to provide the furnishings for Versailles the tradition continued.

It is a truism that the building of Versailles impoverished the nation; but it is no less true that the decorative arts were as much enriched thereby. Le Brun, Bérain and then Boulle set unparalleled standards in the execution of majestic furniture for *Le Roi Soleil*. The guilds became very tightly regulated and highly specialized, with the *ébénistes* to the fore, and French craftsmanship was second to none.

THE ROCOCO

In his latter years Louis XIV retired into pious austerity with his devout mistress. The focus of French life was now Paris, not Versailles, and the market for fine furniture was as much the new bourgeoisie as the older aristocracy. But both classes were intent on pleasure, comfort and informality. The curvilinear style predominated and exuberance in decoration expressed the mood of the Régence.

When Louis XV came to the throne the rococo – that voluptuous, extravagant wholly original style – reached its apogee. Through the second and third quarters of the 18th century French styles were the most admired in Europe.

The reaction against rococo took the form of a conservative appeal to the taste of the Louis XIV period on the one hand, and an espousal of the new doctrine of neoclassicism on the other. Oeben and Riesener were the cabinet-making princes of the time, soon to be joined by Adam Weisweiler and George Jacob in the sumptuous classicism of Louis XVI.

The quality of French cabinet-making would never be the same again. Though fine furniture was to be made during the Directoire and Empire periods, the 19th century was to see from the beginning a degeneration of taste and, gradually, of workmanship too as machines first assisted, then replaced, artist-craftsmen.

BEDS 1815-1910

The four-poster bed fell from favour early in France. In the 17th century it was already rivalled by duchesse beds, with full-sized canopy supported on headposts only, and the lit à l'arge, with shorter tester. Under Louis XV the lit à la polonaise, set in an alcove, was highly fashionable.

Perhaps the most distinctive of French beds is the lit en bateau of the Empire period, a design that was pursued throughout the 19th century.

E5 A Louis XV-style carved giltwood bed, early 20th century; 64 in. (162 cm) wide.

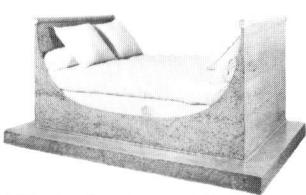

D1 An Empire period mahogany lit en bateau, with brass inlay; 48 in. high by 98 in. wide (120 by 248 cm).

D2 An Empire burr-elm lit en bateau, c. 1815; 48 in. high by 59 in. wide (102 by 50 cm).

E3 A French rosewood and kingwood double bed, 19th century; 58 in. wide by 76 in. long (147 by 193 cm).

E4 A Louis XVI-style grey-painted lit de repos, the head and end boards upholstered in pink satin, late 19th century; 78 in. (201 cm) long.

BIBLIOTHEQUES 1770-1910

The bookcase or bibliothèque developed differently in 18th-century France from the way it was evolving in England. While in the latter country bookcases, the library furniture in general, became almost exclusively architectural, in France freestanding bookcases were made in the curvilinear style through much of the century, remaining in harmony with the designs of smaller cabinets and similar display pieces.

D6 A Louis XV oak provincial bibliothèque, with narrow cornice above moulded rectangular cupboard door glazed with three shaped panels and flanked at the right and sides by similar glazed panels and enclosing shelves, mid to late 18th century; 72 in. (83 cm) high.

D 1 A Louis XV/XVI tulipwood bibliothèque, with rounded rectangular coffer top; 45 in. (114 cm) wide.

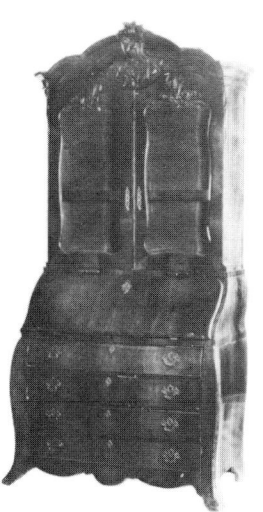

D 2 A Louis XV bureau-bibliothèque in palisander wood with finely carved cresting and concave sides, *c.* 1760; 48 in. (122 cm) wide.

D 3 An Empire mahogany bibliothèque, *c.* 1810; 94 in. high by 60 in. wide (235 by 150 cm).

E 4 A Louis XV-style pine display cabinet, early 19th century; 94 in. high by 54 in. wide (240 by 138 cm).

D 5 An ormolu-mounted bois satine bibliothèque, with shaped breccia marble top, inlaid with end-cut kingwood foliage, stamped G. Durand; 30 in. (78 cm) wide.

D 6 A Louis XVI-style ormolu-mounted kingwood and parquetry bibliothèque, late 19th century; 66 in. (163 cm) high.

E 7 A Louis XVI-style mahogany bibliothèque, with marble top and outset fluted corners with brass fillets, on toupie feet, 20th century; 58 in. high by 43 in. wide (147 by 109 cm).

BONHEURS DU JOUR
1775-1880

The bonheur du jour was an instant fashionable success when the design was first developed in the third quarter of the 18th century. The name is sometimes explained as a comment upon its rapid rise to popularity, but in truth its derivation must remain something of a mystery.

The form – of a small writing table surmounted by a cabinet – once established was the object of every stylistic variation.

D 8 A Louis XV/XVI kingwood and marquetry bonheur du jour, with crossbanded superstructure above an amaranth crossbanded top and frieze drawer enclosing an inset leather writing surface, third quarter 18th century; 27 in. (70 cm) wide.

D 9 A Louis XV/XVI Transitional kingwood bonheur du jour, attributed to Charles Topino, *c.* 1775; 37 in. high by 25 in. wide (95 by 62 cm).

D 10 A bonheur du jour, with marquetry, in box, kingwood and ebony on oak and pine, 1775-1780.

D 11 A Louis XVI tulipwood and marquetry bonheur du jour, with an inset-leather writing surface, late 18th century; 19 in. (49 cm) wide.

E 1 A Second Empire mahogany bonheur du jour, with a tambour roll-top working in conjunction with a frieze drawer, with gilt-bronze borders and stringing, *c.* 1855; 34 by 25 in. (86 by 63 cm).

E 2 A Directoire-style bonheur du jour, the rich mahogany veneers heightened by gilt-metal mounts in the form of mouldings, caps, sabots and a gallery, late 19th century. Period and revival examples were often fitted with marble tops.

E 3 A Louis XV-style rosewood and kingwood crossbanded ormolu-mounted bonheur du jour, with Sèvres-style porcelain mounts, *c.* 1860; 49 in. high by 28 in. wide (125 by 71 cm).

E 4 A Napoleon III boulle bonheur du jour, the lower section with velvet-lined writing slide above a shaped frieze drawer, with brass engraving on red tortoiseshell ground; 33 in. (83 cm) wide.

E 5 A Louis XV-style walnut and ormolu-mounted bonheur du jour, the frieze drawer inset with Sèvres-style porcelain plaque, crossbanded overall with kingwood and ormolu mounts and borders, 19th century; 39 in. high by 44 in. wide (99 by 108 cm).

E 6 A Louis XV-style serpentine bonheur du jour, in kingwood crossbanded walnut, the superstructure with fret carved galleried mirror back, having leather inset writing surface, the frieze with six Sèvres-style porcelain plaques, 19th century; 48 in. (122 cm) wide.

E 7 A Louis XV-style tulipwood and marquetry bonheur du jour, in the manner of Topino; 25 in. (64 cm) wide.

BUFFETS
1580-1910

The traditional two-tiered four-door buffet all but died out as a fashionable form of furniture in the 17th century. It became taller, then was fitted with a single pair of doors, thus resembling the armoire. Forms adapted more slowly in the provinces – see no. 12 below.

Low buffets were always made in the style of the time and evolved gradually into the familiar side cabinet.

E 8 An oak buffet, possibly Burgundian, 16th century; 71 in. (160 cm) wide.

E 9 A provincial buffet, with four carved panelled doors, with brass hinges and escutcheons, 18th century.

E 10 A Louis XV provincial walnut buffet, with a moulded top and rounded corners, the central open compartment containing a shelf, with two short drawers above two panelled cupboard doors, enclosing further shelves, the shaped apron with carved floral decoration, mid 18th century; 41 in. high by 69 in. wide (105 by 176 cm).

E 11 A provincial oak buffet, the frieze with two shallow drawers, above two panelled doors, shaped apron, 18th century; 49 in. (124 cm) wide.

E 12 A Louis XV provincial buffet, with serpentine moulded cornice, the frieze with a roundel of a basket of flowers flanked by fruiting grape, the doors with shaped fielded panels carved with flowers, the slightly projecting lower part with a pair of similar doors, with fluted oak corner posts, continuing into the scroll front feet, *c.* 1770; 94 in. high by 58 in. wide (239 by 146 cm).

E 13 A Normandy buffet, carved with flowers and scrolls, late 18th century; 55 in. (140 cm) wide.

E 14 A provincial walnut buffet, with two cupboards with panelled doors, above shaped apron, late 18th century.

E 15 A provincial oak buffet, early 19th century; 44 in. (110 cm) wide.

E 16 A provincial oak buffet, the panelled doors with pierced steel escutcheon plates, 19th century; 39 in. (100 cm) high.

BUREAUX
1690-1910

The slant-front bureau came late to France, where the early 17th-century writing table evolved into the bureau Mazarin and the secrétaire à abattant was always in style.

Cylinder-top desks existed from the Louis XIV era, complemented by the tambour-top – an invention attributed to Oeben – in the Transitional period. The slant-front desk was current under Louis XV, but as a refined piece for domestic rather than business use.

Bureaux à cylindre

D 1 A Transitional tulipwood bureau à cylindre, the solid cylinder inlaid with flower sprays, the top, sides and back with quartered veneers; 36 in. (91 cm) wide.

D 2 A Louis XVI marquetry bureau, the superstructure with fall-front book-shelves, above a desk with cylinder front, with writing slide and three drawers, on tapering legs, the whole piece decorated with marquetry panels depicting chinoiserie figures and ruins.

D 3 A Louis XVI tulipwood and purpleheart bureau à cylindre, with three drawers inside, 32 in. (80 cm) wide.

D 4 A Louis XVI mahogany and marquetry bureau à cylindre, stamped É-Avril, late 18th century; 45 in. (113 cm) wide.

E 5 A Louis XVI mahogany bureau à cylindre, with pull-out writing slides, c. 1790; 49 in. (125 cm) high.

E 6 A Louis-Philippe walnut kneehole roll-top desk, on cabriole legs with C-scrolled headings; 52 in. (127 cm).

D 7 A "Transitional" bureau à cylindre, with marble top over guilloche frieze, c. 1880; 41 by 29 in. (104 by 73 cm).

D 8 An ormolu-mounted amaranth and trellis parquetry bureau à cylindre, after J.H. Riesener, stamped Henry Dasson 1886; 44 in. (113 cm) wide.

D 9 An ormolu-mounted kingwood and tulipwood parquetry bureau à cylindre, of Louis XVI style; 52 in. (132 cm) wide.

E 10 A "Louis XVI" mahogany and vernis Martin bureau à cylindre, fitted interior, c. 1890; 35 in. (90 cm) wide.

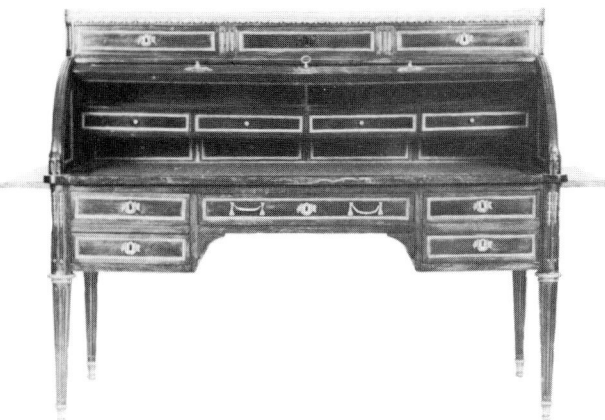

E 1 A Louis XVI-style mahogany ormolu-mounted bureau à cylindre, 19th century; 62 in. (158 cm) wide.

E 2 A French mahogany and brass-mounted writing desk, late 19th century; 35 in. (88 cm) wide.

D 5 A Louis XV-style kingwood crossbanded bureau à cylindre, c. 1900; 43 in. high by 37 in. wide (110 by 94 cm).

Bureaux de dame

C 6 A black lacquer secrétaire en pente, by Jacques Dubois, with chinoiserie-style decoration to flap, front and sides; 41 in. (102 cm) high.

D 3 A Louis XVI-style ormolu-mounted marquetry and parquetry mahogany bureau à cylindre, opening to shelves, drawers and a writing top, late 19th century.

E 4 A kingwood bureau à cylindre, attributed to F. Linke, c. 1900; 32 in. (80 cm) wide.

D 7 A Louis XV provincial kingwood parquetry secrétaire en pente, c. 1750; 37 in. high by 32 in. wide (94 by 81 cm).

D 8 A Louis XV tulipwood and marquetry bureau de dame, stamped N. Petit JME and EG twice; 22 in. (56 cm) wide.

D 9 A Louis XV secrétaire en pente, c. 1750; 37 in. high by 37 in. wide (94 by 94 cm).

E 10 A Louis XV small marquetry bureau, c. 1750; 36 in. high by 23 in. wide (92 by 60 cm).

D 11 A Louis XV kingwood secrétaire en pente, c. 1840; 34 in. (86 cm) wide.

E 12 A Louis XV tulipwood and marquetry miniature bureau de dame, enclosing a fitted interior; 21 in. (54 cm) wide.

C 13 A Louis XV tulipwood and marquetry bureau de dame, by Bernard van Risenburgh; 33 in. high by 23 in. wide (84 by 58 cm).

D 14 A Louis XV kingwood bureau en pente, stamped A. Criard, mid 18th century; 32 in. (81 cm) wide.

E 15 A Louis-Philippe parquetry bureau de dame, with fitted interior; 31 in. (79 cm) wide.

E 1 A Louis-Philippe ormolu and porcelain-mounted tulipwood bureau de dame, the fall-flap enclosing six shaped and tiered drawers and a well, on cabriole legs with pierced sabots; 34 in. (86 cm) wide.

D 2 A Louis-Philippe ormolu-mounted kingwood and parquetry bureau, the curved superstructure with six drawers inlaid with trellis pattern, the leather-lined serpentine writing surface with two drawers centred by a pierced plaque on cabriole legs; 49 in. (125 cm) wide.

E 3 An ebonized and ormolu-mounted bureau de dame, decorated with Sèvres-style plaques to the top and fall-flap, the fall revealing fitted interior, turned legs connected by a curved cross-stretcher, *c.* 1860; 37 in. high by 25 in. wide (94 by 64 cm).

E 4 A boulle bureau de dame, the outset lower part with a secrétaire frieze drawer with a sliding writing surface, *c.* 1860; 53 in. high by 33 in. wide (160 by 84 cm).

E 5 A bombé bureau de dame, in amboyna/thuya with kingwood quarter-banding, *c.* 1870; 36 in. high by 29 in. wide (91 by 74 cm).

E 6 A kingwood bureau de dame, the superstructure, fall-flap and frieze with marquetry floral trails, on slender cabriole legs with carved hips, 19th century.

E 7 A Louis XV style kingwood and ormolu-mounted bureau de dame, *c.* 1880; 46 in. high by 53 in. wide (117 by 135 cm).

E 8 A Louis XVI style mahogany kidney-shape veneered bureau de dame, heavily decorated with gilt mouldings; 59 in. (150 cm) wide.

E 9 A Louis XVI style mahogany and brass-mounted bureau, *c.* 1900; 40 in. high by 32 in. wide (102 by 82 cm).

E 10 An inlaid mahogany bureau de dame by Louis Majorelle; 50 in. high by 29 in. wide (125 by 72 cm).

Bureaux de Dame

The larger kind of desk that was so popular in most northern countries never really took hold in France, with the exception of the 17th-century bureau Mazarin. The probable reason for this is that the secrétaire à abattant was developed early as a substantial piece of furniture, obviating the need for the bureau cabinet.

Where French cabinet-makers excelled in the 18th century was in the production of an infinite variety of small desks or writing tables, collectively known as bureaux de dame, and in the production of elegant bureaux plats or library tables.

As fashionable pieces of delicate boudoir or salon furniture, bureaux de dame – either small slant-front desks on graceful cabriole legs or in the form of bonheurs du jour – lent themselves to the most exquisite marquetry, veneering and lacquer work. Alongside the slant-front or bureau en pente, which was the most popular Louis XV form, the cylinder desk remained current.

The inventiveness of cabinet-makers gave rise to pieces of writing furniture with more than one function. The table à la Bourgogne for example could be both dressing and writing table, with a writing slope to the centre and mirrors rising at the sides. Also known as à capucin, the table à la Bourgogne could take the form of a fold-over-top table with a rising superstructure or serre papiers.

E 11 An ormolu-mounted rosewood and mahogany writing desk, the superstructure with five and the frieze with three curved drawers, all inlaid with marquetry floral trails, above cabriole legs with carved swags to the hips, 20th century; 36 in. (90 cm) wide.

Bureaux Mazarins

D 1 A Louis XIV boulle bureau Mazarin, the top crossbanded with ebony and inlaid in première partie marquetry with Bérainesque designs, mounted with moulded and fluted ormolu border, fitted with seven drawers surrounding two further drawers in the recessed kneehole, on square tapering legs headed by ormolu collars and joined by interlaced stretchers; 33 in. high by 50 in. wide (85 by 127 cm).

C 2 A Régence bureau Mazarin, veneered in calamander, inlaid with floral marquetry, with a panel of tooled hide, the whole ormolu mounted, 67 in. by 34 in. (170 by 86 cm).

C 4 A Louis XIV boulle bureau Mazarin, the leather-lined top with foliate ormolu border and espagnolette mask angle clasps, inlaid with Bérainesque designs, fitted with five bowed drawers surrounding the central kneehole similarly inlaid in première and contre partie marquetry, on scrolled supports joined by waved cross-stretchers, branded D below a coronet and with paper label similar, inscribed in ink 1886, stamped Edwards & Roberts; 32 in. high by 64 in. wide (81 by 163 cm).

D 3 An ebony burr-walnut and marquetry bureau Mazarin, the raised superstructure with eight short drawers and central cupboard, the table base inlaid with panels of flower sprays, the square tapering legs headed by bronze capitals; 45 in. (114 cm) wide.

C 5 A Louis XVI-style kingwood bureau Mazarin, the top surface and lower drawers quarter-veneered, the upper drawers chevron-veneered, on square moulded legs.

C1 A Louis XV kingwood and marquetry bas d'armoire, with bowed and moulded top over two full-length doors each inlaid with an elongated spray of flowers; 58 in. (147 cm) high.

A2 A Régence kingwood bas d'armoire, with moulded breccia marble top, the doors inlaid à quartre faces, with mounts of gilt metal; 56 in. high by 45 in. wide (143 by 115 cm).

B3 An early Louis XV kingwood and tulipwood armoire of fine workmanship; 82 in. (208 cm) high. The coats of arms inlaid to the inverted cornice are of a later date.

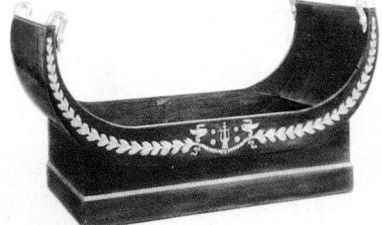

E4 An Empire mahogany and parcel-gilt lit en bateau, the curved head and foot with swan-neck finials, 42 in. wide by 81 in. long (107 by 206 cm).

B5 *(above)* A Louis XIV giltwood lit de repos, late 17th century; 72 in. (183 cm) long. The pierced scrolling back is centrally carved with the cipher of Louis XIV.

D6 *(left)* A Louis XVI grey-painted lit à la polonaise, the oval canopy with fringed floral silk damask pelmet, the interior lined with pleated grey silk, 56 in. wide by 84 in. long (144 by 213 cm).

A1 A transitional tulipwood bureau à cylindre, by J.F. Oeben, *c.* 1765; 48 in. high by 55 in. wide (123 by 141 cm).

C2 A Louis XV bonheur du jour, the frieze containing a drawer with a reading support, veneered with floral marquetry within bois satiné borders, the platform tray also inlaid; 43 in. high by 26 in. wide (107 by 63 cm).

C5 *(above)* A Louis XVI kingwood and parquetry ormolu-mounted bureau à cylindre, by Fidelis Schey, with three-quarter gallery and Carrara marble top; late 18th century. It stands 44 in. high and is 41 in. wide (112 by 102 cm).

D 6 *(below)* A Louis XVI tulipwood and parquetry bureau en pupitre, with nine small drawers behind the tambour shutters, the front, sides and back inlaid with panels of sycamore parquetry; 52 in. high by 30 in. wide (133 by 77 cm).

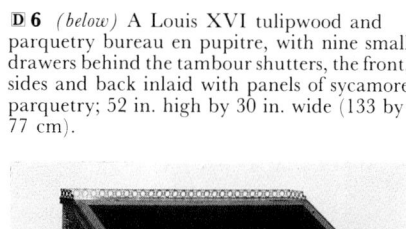

B3 *(above)* A Louis XV ormolu-mounted black lacquer secrétaire en pente, stamped I. Dubois JME; *c.* 1750; 36 in. high by 40 in. wide (91 by 100 cm).

C4 *(right)* A Louis XVI ormolu-mounted bois satiné bonheur du jour, stamped C.C. Saunier, with marble top, *c.* 1780; 40in. (100 cm) high.

B1 *(left)* A Louis XIV Boulle marquetry bureau Mazarin, fitted with a kingwood veneered interior with a fall front and fitted with four drawers, the kneehole with two drawers, flanked by two further drawers, late 17th century; 30 in. high by 42 in. wide (78 by 105 cm).

B2 *(above)* A Louis XIV Boulle bureau Mazarin of the late 17th century with two ranks of convex drawers flanking the concave kneehole, on scroll legs over elaborate wavy X-stretchers; 34 in. high by 59 in. wide (85 by 148 cm).

C3 *(above)* A Louis XIV writing table in Boulle marquetry, the frieze with a drawer and two slides, grotesque gilt-metal masks applied to the corners, on cabriole legs mounted with gilt-metal paw feet; early 17th century; 35 in. (88 cm) wide.

B4 *(above)* A Régence ormolu-mounted and ebonized bureau plat on cabriole legs with foliate scroll sabots, second quarter of the 18th century; 68 in. wide by 32 in. deep (172 by 80 cm).

B5 *(left)* A Louis XV kingwood writing table, with shaped leather-lined top sliding to reveal a fitted drawer with two hinged writing flaps, the frieze inlaid, mounted with ormolu plaques; 28 in. high by 33 in. wide (72 by 83 cm).

C6 An early Louis XVI marquetry writing table, stamped RVLC JME, the top with two hinged brassbound panels concealing wells, *c.* 1775; 28 in. high, 38 in. wide (60 by 91 cm).

A 1 A pair of fine and rare Louis XV ormolu-mounted marquetry ecoignures, stamped I.P. Latz and with the "EU" inventory mark of the Château d'Eu, mid 18th century. They are 37 in. (91 cm) high.

D 4 *(right)* A Louis XVI mahogany veneered folio cabinet with gilt-bronze foliate decorations, six drawers to the upper part, three each side to the lower; 53 in. high by 30 in. wide (135 by 74 cm).

C 2 *(above)* A Louis XV ormolu-mounted marquetry folio cabinet, the sloping superstructure with reading support and a small drawer at each side, the cabinet with two adjustable shelves, with tulipwood veneer inside kingwood borders; mid 18th century. It is 47 in. high and 41 in. wide (115 by 110 cm).

B 3 *(right)* A Louis XVI ormolu-mounted, ebonized and Boulle marquetry meuble d'appui, attributed to Étienne Levasseur, late 18th century.

C1 *(above)* A Louis XV ormolu-mounted marquetry cartonnier or folio cabinet, the sides inlaid with floral marquetry within kingwood borders, the ormolu mounts with the crowned C mark, the drawers fronted in gilt-tooled red leather, mid 18th century.

B2 *(right)* A Louis XVI meuble d'appui, with black marble top over a slightly coved breakfront frieze mounted with acanthus, the false drawer fronts below inlaid with scrolling foliage and central wreaths, the side panels mounted with stock figures of Winter and Ceres, framed by broad engraved pewter borders; 38 in. (97 cm) high.

D3 A Louis XIV small coffer with slightly domed lid covered with morocco leather tooled in gilt with the arms of Le Grand Condé, with fleur-de-lys angle clasps and gilt-brass bands; 21 in. wide, 7 in. high (54 by 19 cm).

B4 A kingwood and tulipwood gilt-bronze mounted parquetry regulator, stamped "BY" for Alfred Beurdeley, Paris, late 19th century.

The domed top is surmounted by a winged figure of death, with lobing and a large applied foliate ornament beneath the clock face. The main body of the case is applied with two classical busts arising out of leafage above the hatched and crossbanded gilt-mounted door, the scroll feet mounted with more foliate ornament, on a plinth with inswept sides and chamfered corners. The piece stands 107 in. (272 cm) high.

C1 *(left)* A pair of Louis XIV carved giltwood armchairs, the rectangular stuffed backs and seats covered in contempory turkey-work woven with baskets of flowers, scrolls and trailing flowers and foliage mainly in red and blue, the downcurved arms carved with acanthus on scroll supports, the leaf-carved scroll legs joined by a front stretcher carved with husks and foliage, the wavy H-stretcher carved with flowers; *c.* 1680.

C2 *(right)* Two from a set of six Louis XIV giltwood fauteuils, with arched rectangular backs, S-scrolled arms and rectangular upholstered seats, on moulded scroll legs joined by moulded waved stretchers, on scroll feet; late 17th or early 18th century.

These chairs, of considerable charm, show admirably the evolution of designs from the 17th century into the 18th. Their curves – notably the arched top rail, but also the lines of arms and legs – are considerably more pronounced than those of the chairs in no. 1 above. And their proportions – slimmer, lighter, more refined – point the way to the mid-century style exemplified in no. 3 below.

D3 *(left)* Two from a set of six Louis XV beechwood fauteuils of the mid-18th century, with the stamp of Claude-François Drouilly, who was admitted maître in 1748.

The cartouche-shaped caned back and U-shaped caned seat are in a moulded frame carved with wave-pattern and leaves, the crest centrally carved with a wave-pattern cartouche flanked by acanthus. The cabriole legs are headed by cabochons and acanthus and terminate in foliate scroll feet.

D 1 *(right)* A Louis XV blue-painted fauteuil, with cartouche-shaped padded back, padded arms on S-shaped supports and serpentine cushion seat in moulded frame, the crest crisply carved with central flowerhead, the seat-rail similarly carved, on cabriole legs, upholstered in gold cut velvet; mid 18th century.

C 2 *(above)* A Louis XV giltwood fauteuil, by J.-B. Lebas, with detachable cartouche-shaped padded back, upholstered arm-rests and serpentine drop-in seat, with waved seat-rail centred by trefoil cabochon cartouche, the moulded legs similarly headed; third quarter of the 18th century.

B 4 *(above)* A Louis XV beechwood bergère by J.-B. Boulard, the arched curved padded back and cushioned seat covered with polychrome floral gros point needlework, in green and red on ivory ground, the moulded frame carved with foliage and cabochon and rocaille cresting, on cabriole legs headed by shells. Third quarter of the 18th century.

C 5 *(left)* A Louis XV beechwood bergère, with arched padded back, padded arms and deeply upholstered and serpentine cushion seat, on cabriole legs with scrolled feet, upholstered in crimson silk damask, stamped J. Avisse; third quarter of the 18th century.

D 3 *(left)* A late Louis XV giltwood chaise, by Louis Delanois, upholstered in contemporary floral silk damask, the frame sumptuously carved.

Louis Delanois, admitted maître in 1761, appears to have been an official craftsman of Madame du Barry, supplying furniture for Versailles.

D 6 A Louis XV walnut canapé, with raked detachable padded back, held in place at the back by iron bands, serpentine cushion seat covered in moiré silk, the top rail crisply carved with flowerheads, on foliate legs, 50 in. high by 105 in. wide (127 by 267 cm).

C1 *(right and below right)* Two chairs and a canapé from a suite of Louis XV giltwood seat furniture by Jean-Jacques Pothier, third quarter of the 18th century. The composition of the suite as made is not known.

The canapé has an incurved padded back and serpentine cushion seat in a moulded frame, the top rail finely carved at the centre with ribbon-tied leaves and long C-scrolls; the seat rail is similarly carved on cabriole legs headed by bellflowers and terminating in scroll feet.

The fauteuils have cartouche-shaped padded backs and serpentine drop-in seats; their frames are carved similarly to that of the canapé.

The suite makes a fine impression, being of high quality workmanship and lavish decoration at the peak of the curvilinear style. The full-blown rotundity of this kind of mid-century furniture makes one appreciate however the drama of the aesthetic revolution effected by the classically inspired designers of the last quarter of the century.

D2 *(below)* A Louis Philippe giltwood canapé à oreilles, with arched and waved back and scrolled seat frame, carved with foliage and cabochons, on scrolled legs, upholstered in early 19th-century Aubusson tapestry, woven with flower sprays and strapwork enriched with silver thread on a brown ground, *c.* 1830; 142 in. (361 cm) wide.

A1 *(right)* A late Louis XIV ormolu-mounted Boulle commode with moulded marble top over two drawers on paw feet, the whole sumptuously mounted with foliate, scroll, flower and mask motifs, *c.* 1710.

The piece bears the stamp of Etienne Levasseur (maître in 1767) indicating refurbishment in the later 18th century. It stands 37 in. high and is 50 in. wide (89 by 125 cm).

C2 *(below)* A Louis XV ormolu-mounted serpentine-front kingwood parquetry commode, with a red Languedoc marble top over two short drawers and one long, *c.* 1735; 35 in. (89 cm) high.

B3 *(above)* A Louis XV ormolu-mounted parquetry commode, in bois satiné parquetry and with brêche d'Alep marble top over two short and one long drawer, *c.* 1740; 35 in. high, 67 in. wide (88 by 170 cm).

B4 *(above)* A Louis XV tulipwood and marquetry petite commode with the stamp of Denis Genty, third quarter of the 18th century; 38 in. (97 cm) wide. Of serpentine form under a shaped marble top, the two drawer fronts are inlaid with summer flowers and exotic birds in stained and engraved wood; the sides similar.

A5 *(above)* A Louis XV ormolu-mounted parquetry commode, attributed to Charles Cressent, *c.* 1740, with two drawers in the serpentine front and a shallow cupboard at each side, under a bleu turquin marble top; 35 in. high, 58 in. wide (87 by 147 cm).

B6 *(left)* A Louis XIV ebony and Boulle commode, the rounded top inlaid in contre partie marquetry, with Bérainesque designs, fitted with two short and three bowed long drawers, mounted with foliate ormolu handles, espagnolette, mask and trophy plaques, on hoof feet; 34 in. high by 49 in. wide (85 by 119 cm).

D 1 *(above)* A rare transitional Louis XV/Louis XVI painted commode, from Tours, *c.* 1760; 34 in. high, 42 in. wide (85 by 105 cm).

A 2 An early neoclassical vernis martin, bois satiné and ormolu-mounted commode, *c.* 1770; 57 in. (146 cm) wide.

The front has three hinged panels, all mounted with ormolu leaf-tip borders, the flanking panels being rectangular, the central one conforming in shape to the apron; the painting is after Monnoyer.

The design of this commode is attributed to Boullée and it appears to have been made for his principal patron, the connoisseur Nicolas Beaujon.

B 3 A Louis XV tulipwood, amaranth and floral marquetry bombé commode, by A. Delorme. It is 58 in. wide by 35 in. high (147 by 89 cm).

The breccia marble top is of serpentine form over two drawers inlaid with trailing flowering foliage and perched birds framed by cartouches of sinuous outline with foliate decoration. The handles echo the clasps to the angles and the pierced sabots.

Similar trailing foliage inlay appears on a commode illustrated in Nicolay, *L'Art et la Manière des Maîtres Ebénistes Français au XVIIIe Siècle*, 1956, p.139.

A 4 A Louis XVI ormolu-mounted marquetry commode, stamped J.F. Leleu, with inset bleu turquin marble top, *c.* 1775; 36 in. (88 cm) high.

C 5 *(above)* A Louis XV black lacquer petite commode, stamped F. Rubestuck, the bombé front decorated with figures in the Chinese style, the sides similar, mid 18th century; 39 in. (99 cm) wide.

A 6 *(left)* A Louis XV/XVI ormolu-mounted tulipwood and marquetry commode, stamped N.P. Severin, inlaid with architectural scenes and a garden vista, in stained and engraved woods, mother-of-pearl and engraved bone, third quarter of the 18th century; 48 in. (122 cm) wide.

D 1 *(above)* A kingwood and marquetry dressing table, the top inlaid within an crossbanded border, one lock signed P. Sormani, Paris, *c.* 1900; 58 by 46 in. (147 by 115 cm).

Sormani moved his business in 1867 to the Rue Charlot, where his widow continued it and then his son, until 1934. The firm made reproductions of Louis XV and Louis XVI furniture in the main, but there are also considerable numbers of pieces not following either style exactly. Sormani exhibited on various occasions between 1849 and 1878.

C 2 *(below)* An Empire ormolu-mounted thuyawood and mahogany dressing table, made for the Château de St Cloud and attributed to Jacob Desmalter, with inset white marble top, spring-operated drawer at each end of the frieze, *c.* 1805. It is 56 in. high and 50 in. wide (142 by 127 cm).

A similar dressing table was supplied by Jacob Desmalter in 1805 to the Empress Josephine for use in the Tuileries; it is now in the Musée des Arts Decoratifs, Paris, and is illustrated in Grandjean, *Empire Furniture* at figure 21.

C 3 *(above)* A Louis XV tulipwood and marquetry table de toilette, stamped L. Boudin JME.

The serpentine rectangular divided hinged top conceals a central dressing glass flanked by covered wells, one of which is fitted; the front has four drawers and a writing slide. The whole is inlaid with panels of flowers in stained and engraved woods on sycamore grounds, those to the top with interlaced banded borders, and sides within shaped line borders. Dating from the mid 18th century it is 35 in. (87 cm) wide.

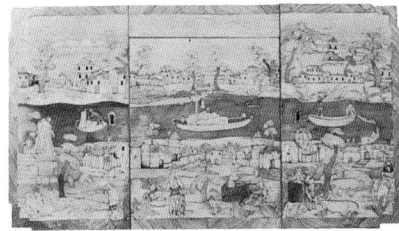

B 4 *(left and above)* A Louis XVI tulipwood, sycamore and marquetry poudreuse, ormolu-mounted, of the late 18th century. It is 35 in. (89 cm) wide.

The top opens to a central hinged dressing glass with a lidded well, inlaid with urns and books, to either side. The frieze is entrelac-mounted and contains a velvet-lined writing slide over three drawers. The sides and back are similarly mounted and inlaid.

The top (detail above) shows a detailed scene in stained and engraved woods of a village situated on both banks of a river. An improbably large piece of classical statuary surveys a pastoral scene of cattle in the fields and figures carrying out various agricultural tasks. Three boats appear on the river, one to each panel. The workmanship is of high quality and the design has a quaint charm deriving from its whimsical disregard for proportion and perspective, in utter contrast to no. 6 on the facing page. The drawers and sides are inlaid with scenes of cottages and trees.

D 1 A fine French Renaissance oak lectern, with moulded triangular shaped top above three stop-fluted Ionic pilasters dividing two panels carved in high relief, one with a figure inscribed S. Gregoire, the other with a figure inscribed S. Maria, each standing beneath a panelled architrave, 16th century; 45 in. (113 cm) high.

D 2 A large Empire bronze and ormolu-mounted thuyawood psyche or cheval glass, *c.* 1810; 80 in. (203 cm) high. The piece displays a diverse repertory of ornament, including rosettes, leafage, conch, classical female figures and boars' heads.

C 3 An early Louis XV giltwood pier glass, with arched and waved divided plate in a moulded slip, carved with alternating cabochons and rosettes; the scrolled mirrored surround is overlaid with flowering tendrils and foliate C-scrolls, centred at the base with a relief bust of Diana and at the crest with an amatory motif of billing doves, bow and quiver; 94 by 57 in. (239 by 145 cm).

C 4 A Louis XV painted and gilded six-leaf screen, the frames carved on both sides with flowerhead crestings, shell angles and trailing flower-sprays on a green ground, inset with paintings in the style of Watteau of Chinese figures, the reverse with birds, trees and Chinese buildings, each leaf 54 by 26 in. (137 by 65 cm).

C1 *(above)* A matched pair of Louis XV/XVI tulipwood and kingwood secrétaires, with rectangular brown and grey veined marble tops, the fall-fronts panelled with false drawers, fitted interiors, chamfered corners and berried laurel wreath handles; 45 in. high by 20 in. wide (114 by 49 cm).

C2 *(below)* A Louis XV secrétaire à abattant, with rosewood marquetry, with a tambour front and doors below decorated with rural scenes in the Chinese taste, with a marble brèche d'Alep top; 45 in. high, 27 in. wide, 14 in. deep (113 by 67 by 36 cm).

C3 A Louis XVI tulipwood and marquetry secrétaire à abattant, the drop front inlaid with a table laden with musical instruments beneath swagged draperies on a chequerboard floor, 37 in. (93 cm) wide.

C4 An unusual Empire ormolu-mounted thuyawood secrétaire, stamped IACOB, with a Spanish brocatelle marble top, the mirror-panelled front revealing a fitted writing interior, *c.* 1820; 59 in. 150 cm) high.

B5 A Louis XV/XVI tulipwood, kingwood and sycamore marquetry small secrétaire à abattant, with rectangular breccia marble top, the drop front inlaid with a basket of flowers in stained and engraved woods, the cupboard doors and sides inlaid with flowerheads and sprays; 50 in. high by 27 in. wide (127 by 69 cm).

C1 *(left)* A Louis XVI ebonized secrétaire à abattant, with pewter and brass marquetry, fleur-de-lys decoration on the drawer, the fall front concealing pigeonholes and four drawers in palisander with a cupboard drawer below, richly decorated with gilt bronze. The piece bears the stamp of Philippe-Claude Montigny and it is 55 in. high by 34 in. wide (141 by 85 cm).

A2 *(below)* A Louis XVI ebonized mounted and inlaid brass, pewter and mother of pearl secrétaire à abattant. The eared rectangular top is of verde antico over a frieze drawer, the drop-front below is decorated with an inlaid figure of Poseidon enthroned, with dolphins, putti, peacocks and seahorses, and opens to a fitted interior decorated with inlay and ormolu. The cupboard doors below are inlaid with fruit-filled urns and open to a long drawer.

The piece was made in the late 18th century but embellished later with German marquetry panels of the late 17th and early 18th centuries and with 18th-century ormolu mounts. It is 41 in. (104 cm) wide.

D3 A pair of Louis XVI ormolu and porphyry guéridons on serpent supports decorated with bullrushes; 32 in. high and 18 in. diameter (79 by 45 cm).

C4 A pair of Louis XVI giltwood torchères, with moulded circular tops and raised borders edged with lambrequins; 53 in. (136 cm) high.

B5 A Louis XVI porcelain-mounted thuyawood table ambulante, attributed to Adam Weisweiler, the glass covered top inset with a Sèvres plaque painted by Fontaine; 30 in. (76 cm) high.

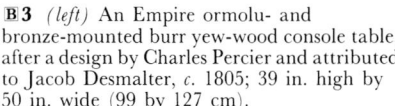

B 3 *(left)* An Empire ormolu- and bronze-mounted burr yew-wood console table, after a design by Charles Percier and attributed to Jacob Desmalter, *c.* 1805; 39 in. high by 50 in. wide (99 by 127 cm).

D 4 *(above)* A Louis XV giltwood console table, with moulded and bowed grey marble top and pierced frieze, the supports carved with foliage and berries; 37 in. (92 cm) wide.

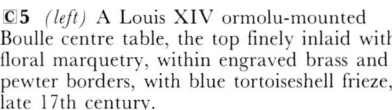

C 5 *(left)* A Louis XIV ormolu-mounted Boulle centre table, the top finely inlaid with floral marquetry, within engraved brass and pewter borders, with blue tortoiseshell frieze, late 17th century.

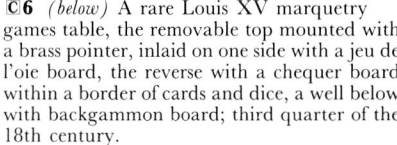

C 6 *(below)* A rare Louis XV marquetry games table, the removable top mounted with a brass pointer, inlaid on one side with a jeu de l'oie board, the reverse with a chequer board within a border of cards and dice, a well below with backgammon board; third quarter of the 18th century.

D 1 *(above)* A Régence giltwood centre table, with moulded grey, black and white marble top, the frieze incised with trellis-pattern and outlined with foliate scrolls, on moulded scroll legs headed by satyr masks with plumed headbands, on paw feet; 28 in. high by 27 in. wide (70 by 66 cm).

B 2 *(above)* A Louis XVI gilt bronze centre table in the classical manner, attributed to Gouthière, with a Spanish marble top; 34 in. high by 46 in. wide (85 by 115 cm).

C1 A Louis XV tulipwood, amaranth and floral marquetry table, the kidney shaped top with a raised border and inlaid with a musical trophy, framed by scroll borders enclosing foliage inlaid in green-stained and natural woods; the concave front is fitted with a tambour shutter mounted with false book spines that opens to a fitted writing drawer with an easel, two short drawers, one long and a secret drawer; 30 in. high by 22 in. wide (75 by 56 cm).

B3 A Louis XVI ormolu- and porcelain-mounted writing table *c.* 1786; stamped C.C. SAUNIER, and made for the Château de Bellevue, the porcelain top painted with sprays of flowers, the frieze containing a drawer fitted with a slide and silver ink pot, sander and box; 29 in. high by 18 in. wide (71 by 45 cm).

C5 A Louis XV amaranth, tulipwood and marquetry writing table with ormolu-bordered top inlaid with sprays of flowering foliage framed by interlaced scrolls, enclosing a divided interior, the frieze fitted with a leather-lined slide and a drawer on the right; 27 in. high by 17 in. wide (69 by 42 cm).

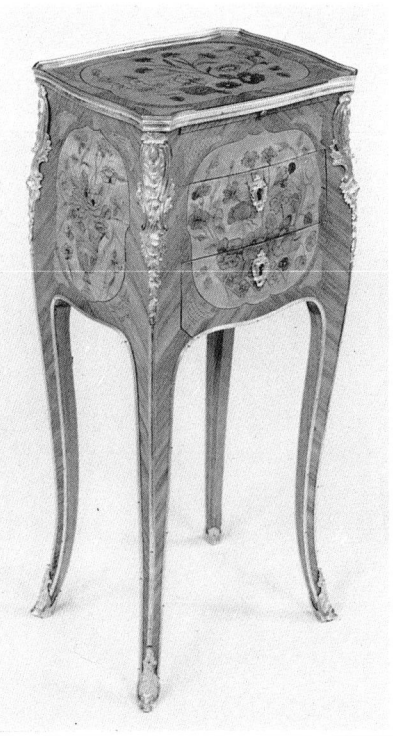

C6 A rare Louis XV ormolu-mounted marquetry table à la Bourgogne of the mid 18th century, the top with a hinged front section opening to reveal lidded wells, the back rising to form a cabinet superstructure fitted with drawers. It stands 28 in. (70 cm) high with an almost identical width. Of fine quality, this table has been attributed to Oeben.

An identical model is illustrated in Charles Packer, *Paris Furniture by the Master Ebénistes* at figure 61.

C2 A Louis XVI bois clair and parquetry table en chiffonnière, the top galleried with a leather inset over a drawer, the cupboard door inlaid with trellis-and-rosette enclosing three satinwood drawers, late 18th century.

C4 A Louis XV tulipwood and marquetry writing table, the serpentine ormolu-banded top inlaid with summer flowers over a slide and two drawers, mid 18th century; 13 in. (32 cm) wide.

Bureaux plats

D 1 A Régence ormolu-mounted kingwood bureau plat, with gilt-incised inset-leather top, the frieze with three drawers opposing sham drawers, *c.* 1720; 58 in. (149 cm) wide.

D 2 A Régence bureau plat, in black lacquered wood, the frieze with three drawers; 32 in. high by 70 in. wide (79 by 179 cm).

C 3 A Louis XV kingwood and marquetry bureau plat, with two end drawers; 40 in. (101 cm) wide.

D 5 A Louis XV kingwood bureau plat, with leather-lined top and ormolu handles and angles, on cabriole legs ending in sabots; 45 in. (114 cm) wide.

D 4 A Louis XV satinwood bureau plat, mid 18th century, 30 in. high by 58 in. wide (76 by 147 cm).

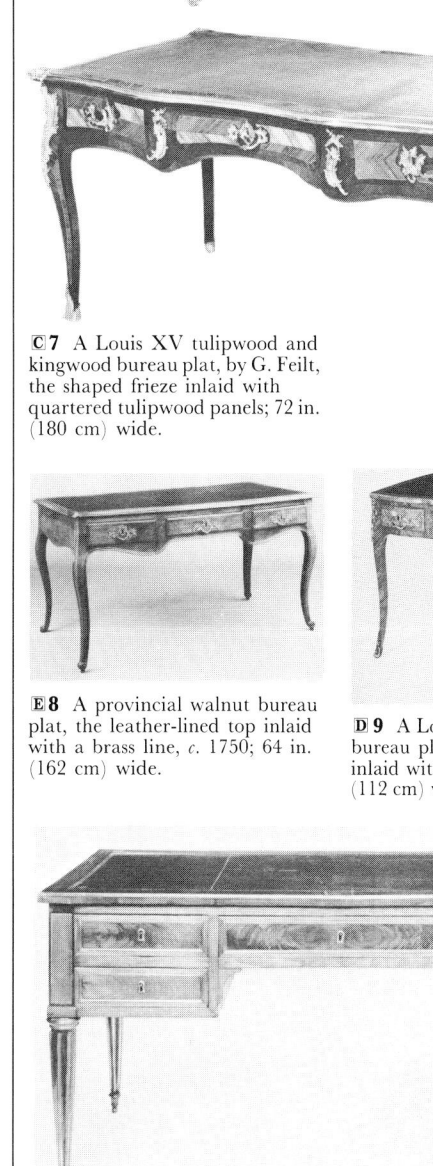

D 6 A Louis XV kingwood bureau plat, the frieze fitted with three drawers inlaid with shaped tulipwood panels, with cabriole legs on sabots; 58 in. (147 cm) wide.

C 7 A Louis XV tulipwood and kingwood bureau plat, by G. Feilt, the shaped frieze inlaid with quartered tulipwood panels; 72 in. (180 cm) wide.

E 8 A provincial walnut bureau plat, the leather-lined top inlaid with a brass line, *c.* 1750; 64 in. (162 cm) wide.

D 9 A Louis XV kingwood small bureau plat, with three drawers inlaid with chevron bands; 44 in. (112 cm) wide.

D 10 A Louis XVI mahogany bureau plat, with gilt-metal moulded inset-leather top above five fielded panelled drawers with gilt-metal borders opposing sham drawers, late 18th century; 58 in. (147 cm) wide.

D 1 A Louis XVI speckled mahogany bureau plat, in the style of J. H. Riesener, with rectangular leather-lined top, the panelled frieze with three drawers, on square tapering fluted legs mounted with chandelles; 42 in. (108 cm) wide.

D 2 A Louis XV-style kingwood bureau plat, with the stamp G. Durand, with ormolu moulded inset-leather top, above three shaped quarter-veneered frieze drawers, mid 19th century; 44 in. (112 cm) wide.

E 3 A Louis XV-style burr-walnut and floral marquetry serpentined bureau plat, with inset top and two frieze drawers, on square, tapering cabriole legs, late 19th century; 50 in. (128 cm) wide.

D 4 A Louis XV-style kingwood and ormolu-mounted bureau plat, crossbanded and veneered à quatre faces, the rectangular top of recessed broken out line inset with a panel of green tooled leather, the frieze with three short drawers and dummy drawers to the reverse, 19th century; 73 in. by 41 in. (185 by 103 cm) overall.

D 5 An ormolu-mounted boulle bureau plat of Régence design, the leather-lined serpentine top with broad border, the frieze fitted with a drawer in the recessed centre, flanked by two drawers and framed by curved plaques headed by bearded masks, 19th century; 58 in. (149 cm) wide.

E 6 A Louis XV-style kingwood and parquetry bureau plat and cartonnier, inlaid with a diamond trellis, the writing surface with a parquetry border, early 20th century; 47 in. high by 69 in. long (119 by 175 cm).

CABINETS
1645-1900

French patrons of the 17th century shared the Europe-wide passion for magnificently decorated cabinets. Early examples were made by foreign craftsmen, sometimes working in France. Oriental lacquer cabinets were also in vogue, especially after the foundation of the Compagnie des Indes in 1664.

"Cabinet" has a special association in France however, always bringing to mind the display case or vitrine so popular in the 19th century.

E 1 A Renaissance carved walnut cabinet, with moulded cornice above acanthus-carved frieze, above two panelled cupboard doors carved with grotesques, late 16th century.

C 2 A Louis XIII/Louis XIV marquetry cabinet, inlaid with copper, pewter and tortoiseshell, attributed to Jean Macé de Blois; 86 in. high by 57 in. wide (220 by 145 cm).

D 3 A carved walnut cabinet, both upper and lower parts with moulded panel doors flanked by Ionic columns, the lower part fitted with cushion frieze drawers, *c.* 1580; 47 in. (118 cm) wide.

D 4 A Louis XV kingwood cabinet, with oval marquetry reserves, and bearing the partially obliterated signature of Jean François Hache; 40 in. high by 36 in. wide (100 by 90 cm).

D 5 A Louis XVI ormolu-mounted mahogany writing cabinet, in the style of Martin Carlin; 50 in. high by 30 in. wide (127 by 75 cm).

C 6 A Louis XVI gilt bronze-mounted mahogany side cabinet, *c.* 1785; 35 in. high by 72 in. wide (89 by 184 cm).

E 7 A Louis XV provincial carved walnut side cabinet, *c.* 1770; 50 in. high by 53 in. wide (127 by 136 cm).

D 8 A Louis XVI period meuble d'entre deux, in sycamore and amaranth wood marquetry, stamped by J. H. Riesener.

D 9 A Louis XVI mahogany side cabinet, with mottled grey marble top, *c.* 1785; 42 in. high by 33 in. wide (107 by 85 cm).

D 10 A Directoire mahogany cabinet, *c.* 1800; 63 in. high by 24 in. wide (160 by 60 cm).

D 11 An Empire mahogany meuble d'appui, *c.* 1815; 36 in. high by 52 in. wide (92 by 132 cm).

E 12 An Empire rosewood side cabinet, with griotte marble top, *c.* 1815; 36 in. high by 41 in. wide (91 by 105 cm).

E1 A Louis-Philippe ormolu-mounted figured walnut credenza; 39 in. high by 50 in. wide (98 by 126 cm).

E2 A kingwood meuble d'appui, with white carrara marble top, *c.* 1840; 45 in. high by 51 in. wide (114 by 129 cm).

E3 A Louis XVI style hard-stone mounted ebonized cabinet, *c.* 1860; 66 in. high by 54 in. wide (167 by 138 cm).

E4 An ebony and ormolu-mounted cabinet, *c.* 1860; 50 in. high by 42 in. wide (128 by 108 cm).

E5 An ebonized and boulle cabinet, 19th century; 49 in. high by 36 in. wide (124 by 90 cm).

E6 A Napoleon III tulipwood veneered meuble d'appui, *c.* 1870; 49 in. high by 61 in. wide (126 by 130 cm).

E7 A Napoleon III ebony veneered ormolu-mounted cabinet, 19th century; 50 in. (126 cm) wide.

E8 A Louis XVI style kingwood and porcelain mounted side cabinet, the whole heavily carved, with five porcelain miniatures set into the frieze, the cupboard doors decorated with porcelain cartouches of rustic scenes.

E9 A Louis XVI style amboyna and mahogany cabinet, 19th century; 31 in. (77 cm) wide.

E10 A French bijouterie cabinet, *c.* 1880; 42 in. high by 23 in. wide (107 by 58 cm).

E11 A Louis XVI style kingwood, satinwood, burr-walnut and parquetry cabinet, *c.* 1880; 46 in. (115 cm) long.

Corner cabinets

C12 A Régence ormolu-mounted amaranth corner cabinet, with ormolu-moulded C-shaped cornice above panelled cupboard door inlaid with brass banding, early 18th century; 83 in. high by 25 in. wide (210 by 64 cm).

C13 A Louis XVI black lacquer encoignure, with moulded serpentine brecchia marble top, mid 18th century; 27 in. (69 cm) wide.

E 1 A Louis XV ormolu-mounted kingwood and tulipwood encoignure, with moulded shaped Sicilian jaspar top above a single cupboard door inlaid with a circular fan, the angles mounted with foliate clasps; 26 in. (66 cm) wide.

D 4 A Louis XVI encoignure en étagères, the marble top edged with a brass gallery above a moulded cornice, with single frieze drawer over three spindle legs, with an open lower marble shelf with brass gallery, late 18th century; 34 in. high by 28 in. wide (85 by 70 cm).

E 5 A serpentine boulle encoignure, with a white carrara marble top, above a cupboard door, the whole inlaid with cut-brass foliage on a tortoiseshell ground, *c.* 1860; 42 in. high by 28 in. wide (108 by 71 cm).

D 9 A Louis XVI style ormolu-mounted and marquetry mahogany encoignure, in the manner of Riesener, with a triangular marble top above a frieze centring an ormolu cartouche, the door inlaid in stained hardwood and sycamore, *c.* 1880; 40 in. (100 cm) high.

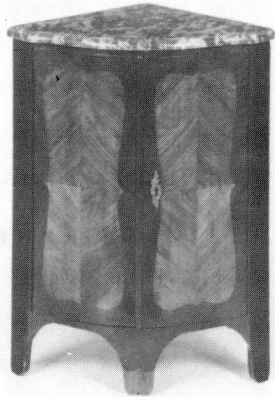

E 2 A Louis XV tulipwood veneered encoignure, with a moulded grey and rust mottled marble top, the serpentine front with a pair of doors, *c.* 1750; 33 in. high by 26 in. wide (84 by 66 cm).

E 6 A pair of Louis XV style kingwood encoignures, the marble tops over a shaped door inlaid with end-cut marquetry flowers on a quarter-veneered ground within gilt-bronze scroll mounts, with concave sides on short

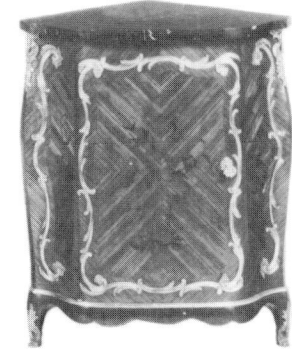

cabriole legs and gilt-bronze sabots, one with the original black- and yellow-veined marble, the other with replaced Belgian marble, *c.* 1880; 30 in. (76 cm) wide.

D 10 A Louis XV style ormolu-mounted marquetry, tulipwood and rosewood encoignure, in the manner of Jacques Dubois, with serpentine marble top; 33 in. (82 cm) high.

C 3 A Transitional encoignure by P. Roussel with marble top, the cupboard door inlaid in engraved and green-stained woods; 26 in. (66 cm) wide.

D 7 A mahogany and marquetry encoignure, with a moulded white carrara marble top, above a drawer and a bow-fronted cupboard, *c.* 1880; 41 in. high by 31 in. wide (104 by 79 cm).

E 8 A Louis XVI style ormolu-mounted tulipwood, satinwood and parquetry encoignure, the galleried top inlaid with octagonal flowerhead medallions above two cupboard doors, *c.* 1880; 40 in. (100 cm) high.

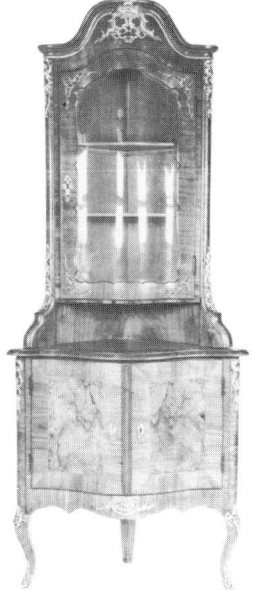

E 11 A Louis XV style ormolu-mounted and walnut corner cabinet, the serpentine glazed cabinet door over lower section with two cupboard doors, raised on cabriole legs; 36 in. (90 cm) long.

CHAIRS
1680-1900

French chairs of the 17th century resemble closely those made in all neighbouring countries – the high back, scrolling, carved arms, legs and stretchers are equally typical of Dutch, English and Spanish work.

From an early date the accent was on upholstery for fine chairs, but there was also a fairly constant demand for cane; this kind of work saw a massive revival at the end of the 19th century and the beginning of the 20th.

Armchairs

E 1 A Louis XIV walnut armchair, with upholstered back and seat, on turned ornate legs, joined by fluted stretcher, late 17th century.

E 2 A Louis XIV walnut framed armchair, with arched upholstered tall back and stuffed seat, *c.* 1670.

E 3 A walnut open armchair, with high arched back, scroll arms on bobbin-and-reel turned supports, joined by conforming stretchers, late 17th century.

D 4 A Louis XIV walnut fauteuil, with arched rectangular back, the S-shaped arms on similarly shaped supports, on S-scrolled legs, early 18th century.

E 5 An oak fauteuil, carved with leafy scrolls, possibly Liège, covered with Régence tapestry, fauteuil *c.* 1720.

D 6 A pair of Régence beechwood fauteuils, each with arched rectangular padded back, padded arms on S-shaped supports carved with acanthus, the serpentine cushion seat-rail carved with a pierced central foliate cartouche flanked by trailing leaves, on cabriole legs with cloven feet, early 18th century.

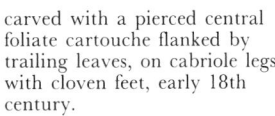

D 7 A Régence period carved walnut armchair, the leather back and seat with embossed decoration, the whole closely studded, the legs ornately carved, ending in hoof feet, joined by curved crossed stretcher.

E 9 A Régence caned beechwood fauteuil, the serpentine-topped back carved with foliate scrollwork and a cabochon, with outcurved arms, caned seat and cabriole legs headed by shells, *c.* 1720.

D 8 A Régence polished beechwood fauteuil, with waved padded back and serpentine upholstered seat, the scrolled arm-supports carved with shells, the waved seat-rail carved with trellis panels.

E 10 A Régence walnut fauteuil à la reine, the arched upholstered back with moulded arms carved with overlapping C-scrolls and leaves, with moulded serpentine seat-rail, *c.* 1725.

E 1 A Régence walnut fauteuil à la reine, the arched back with straight upholstered arms, the serpentine shell-carved seat-rail on cabriole legs with scroll toes, *c*. 1730.

D 4 An early Louis XV walnut fauteuil, with cartouche-shaped upholstered back with nailed borders, the seat-rail carved with flower heads and foliage.

D 7 A Louis XV varnished walnut fauteuil, with cartouche-shaped padded back and serpentine upholstered seat, moulded frame edged with acanthus scrolls, tapering cabriole legs similarly carved.

D 10 A Louis XV grey-painted fauteuil, stamped M. Delaporte, with cartouche-shaped slightly curved padded back, with scroll feet, mid 18th century.

E 2 A Louis XV painted and parcel-gilt armchair, the moulded frame carved with rococo scrolls, foliage and cartouches, with stuffed back, padded arms and stuffed seat, *c*. 1740.

D 5 A Louis XV beechwood fauteuil, stamped J. B. Tilliard, mid 18th century.

E 8 A Louis XV giltwood fauteuil, with cartouche-shaped padded back and serpentine upholstered seat, in moulded frame with flower head crestings, on cabriole legs.

D 11 A Louis XV giltwood fauteuil, with cartouche-shaped padded back and serpentine upholstered seat in panelled frame, the arched crest with well-carved C-scrolls and acanthus centring flowerheads, mid 18th century.

D 3 An early Louis XV walnut fauteuil, the cartouche-shaped padded back and seat upholstered in contemporary gros and petit point needlework.

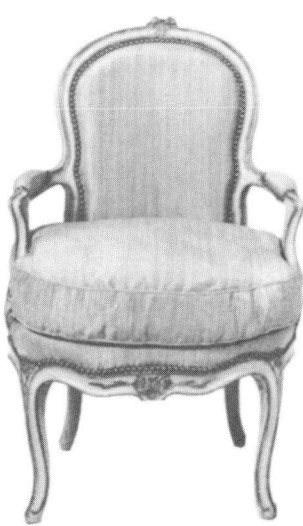

E 6 A Louis XV cream and blue painted fauteuil, with cartouche-shaped padded back, seat-rail carved with twin flowerheads, upholstered in blue silk, mid 18th century.

E 9 A Louis XV provincial walnut fauteuil, possibly Lyons, of small size, padded-cartouche back headed by trailing flowers and leaves with padded outcurved arms, *c*. 1750.

E 12 A Louis XV period carved fauteuil, with padded back, frame with moulding of flowers and foliage, the serpentine seat-rail above cabriole legs carved at the knees, ending in pointed shaped feet.

D 1 A Louis XV beechwood fauteuil, with cartouche-shaped padded back and serpentine upholstered seat in moulded frame, covered in red and white silk brocade, mid 18th century.

E 2 A Louis XV beechwood fauteuil, with cartouche-shaped caned back and serpentine caned seat, the moulded frame with flowerhead cresting and centre to the seat-rail.

D 3 A Louis XV beechwood fauteuil, with serpentine drop-in seat in moulded frame, upholstered in yellow brocade, mid 18th century.

D 4 A Louis XV giltwood fauteuil, stamped N. Heurtaut, with cartouche-shaped back and serpentine upholstered seat, covered in Aubusson tapestry, woven with Fontaine fables, in flower and scroll borders, the top rail covered with flower sprays, with moulded frame and seat-rail similarly carved, on scrolled legs.

E 5 A Louis XV beechwood fauteuil à canne, with cartouche-shaped caned back and serpentine caned seat in moulded frame, the crest and seat-rail carved with flowerheads, on cabriole legs headed by carved flowerheads, mid 18th century.

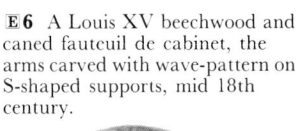

E 6 A Louis XV beechwood and caned fauteuil de cabinet, the arms carved with wave-pattern on S-shaped supports, mid 18th century.

E 7 A Louis XV beechwood fauteuil de bureau, with arched caned back and serpentine caned seat, mid 18th century.

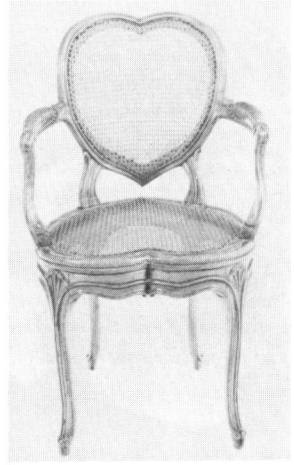

D 8 A Louis XV beechwood fauteuil à canne, with heart-shaped cane back and seat in moulded frame, the leather-upholstered padded arms on S-shaped supports carved with long S-scrolls, on slightly cabriole legs, mid 18th century.

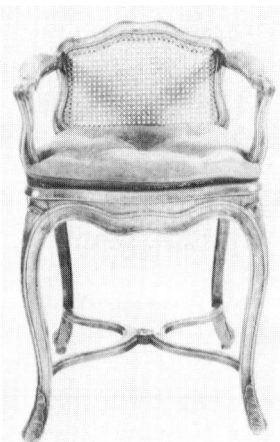

E 9 A Louis XV beechwood fauteuil à canne, with low cartouche-shaped caned back and serpentine caned seat in moulded frame, mid 18th century.

D 10 A Louis XV painted fauteuil, stamped Dargagny, with moulded cartouche-shaped caned back, the cresting carved with flowers, c. 1760.

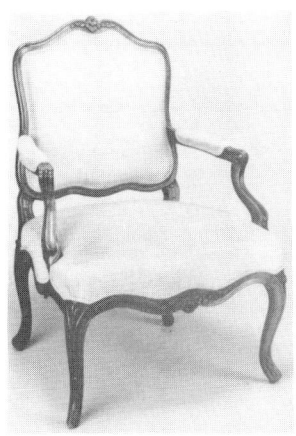

E1 A Louis XV walnut fauteuil à la reine, with moulded cartouche-shaped back, padded arms and cabriole legs ending in foliate toes, *c.* 1760.

D4 A Louis XV/XVI giltwood fauteuil, stamped L. M. Pluvinet, with padded back and serpentine upholstered seat in moulded frame, carved with beading and leaf tips, the padded arms on S-shaped supports.

D7 A Louis XVI walnut fauteuil, stamped P. E. Langlois JME, with oval padded back and bowed upholstered seat in moulded frame, with fluted tapering legs.

D8 A Louis XVI grey-painted fauteuil, with oval padded back and serpentine upholstered seat, in beaded and moulded frame with flowerhead and foliage cresting.

E2 A late Louis XV carved walnut fauteuil, stamped I. Pothier, the moulded frame carved with ribbons and husks, with stuffed back and padded arms, *c.* 1775.

C5 A Louis XVI carved giltwood fauteuil, stamped J. B. Fromageau JME, with oval padded back in moulded frame carved with beading, covered in pink-ground silk damask, *c.* 1780.

C9 Two Louis XVI beechwood fauteuils, stamped J. B. Sene, with oval padded backs and serpentine seats in moulded frames, crisply carved with

ribbon-twist and with tied berried foliage crestings, one chair without arms, the other with padded arms on carved and moulded supports, on tapering fluted legs.

E3 A provincial chair, with moulded cartouche-shaped back, padded arms and cabriole legs, late 18th century.

E6 A Louis XVI painted fauteuil, stamped Tilliard, with an oval ribbon-tied padded back, padded arms on downcurved leaf-carved supports, the bowed seat on fluted tapering legs, *c.* 1780.

D10 A pair of Louis XVI giltwood fauteuils, with padded backs in square beaded and channelled frames, with finials at the top corners, with padded arms on channelled outcurved supports

with finials, the seat-rail beaded and with rosettes carved at the squared-off corners, on tapering fluted legs, upholstered in pale blue silk damask, *c.* 1780.

D 1 A fine Louis XVI fauteuil, in grey lacquered wood, the arms and back finely carved, made by Jean-Baptiste-Claude Sené who became a maître in 1769.

E 4 A Louis XVI walnut fauteuil, with tapering curved rectangular padded back, the arm-supports with acanthus leaves, on tapering fluted legs headed by paterae.

D 7 A pair of Louis XVI walnut stained fauteuils, each with arched rectangular padded back and bowed upholstered seat in moulded frame carved with

leaf-tips, rope-twist and acanthus, on circular tapering fluted legs, upholstered in gold silk damask, late 18th century.

E 2 A rare Louis XVI beechwood fauteuil à transformation, with a moulded frame and a tongue-shaped reclining back, with padded arms and a bowed seat-rail, on tapering fluted legs, *c.* 1775.

D 5 A fine Louis XVI grey-painted fauteuil, à la Reine, with arched rectangular padded backs and bowed seats, covered in pink silk damask, the downcurved arm-supports carved with acanthus, the channelled seat-rails carved with scrolling vines.

C 8 A pair of fine Louis XVI green-painted fauteuils, each with arched rectangular padded back and U-shaped drop in seat in moulded and fluted frame, the well-carved crest-rail and arms

carved with tied laurel flanked by twin finials, the padded arms on supports carved with acanthus, upholstered in cream satin, late 18th century.

E 3 A Louis XVI caned mahogany fauteuil, stamped J.B.B.Demay, the tall moulded back with incurved top corners, raised on circular tapering fluted legs, *c.* 1785.

E 6 A Louis XVI cream-painted and parcel-gilt fauteuil, with rectangular padded back and bowed upholstered seat in moulded well-carved frame, late 18th century.

E 9 A Louis XVI mahogany and caned revolving fauteuil de cabinet, with incurved caned and padded back and circular caned seat, late 18th century.

E 10 A Louis XVI beechwood fauteuil de bureau, with arched padded back and serpentine upholstered seat, the circular fluted tapering legs headed by paterae.

E1 A Louis XV walnut and beechwood desk armchair, with moulded frame, upholstered back and seat, and cabriole legs ending in scroll feet, mid 18th century.

E4 A Louis XVI beechwood fauteuil de cabinet, stamped A.P. Dupain JME, upholstered in brown leather, *c.* 1780.

E7 A Directoire walnut fauteuil, the rectangular upholstered back with a panelled crest-rail carved with a wreath of laurel leaves, *c.* 1795.

E10 An Empire fruitwood fauteuil, the rectangular padded back with downcurved reeded arms, the bow front upholstered seat on sabre legs headed by stylized lotus leaves, *c.* 1810.

E2 A Louis XV carved walnut and beechwood fauteuil de bureau, the arched caned back continuing round to form the arms, mid 18th century.

E5 An important French Directoire mahogany X-frame writing chair, attributed to H. Jacob, with very finely carved detail; 47 in. high by 26 in. wide (120 by 65 cm).

D8 A fine Consulate mahogany armchair by Jacob Frères, made for the Tuileries Palace, with stuffed overscrolled back, stuffed bow-fronted seat, early 19th century.

E11 An Empire mahogany armchair, with ormolu mounts, and curving arms.

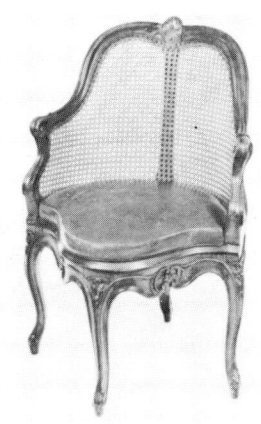

E3 A Louis XV beechwood fauteuil de bureau with arched caned back and serpentine upholstered seat, upholstered in tan leather, mid 18th century.

E6 A Directoire cream-painted fauteuil, with overscrolled square tapering back, sprung seat, padded arms with baluster supports and turned tapering legs, *c.* 1795.

E9 An Empire ormolu-mounted mahogany and parcel-gilt fauteuil, upholstered in blue velvet, *c.* 1810.

E12 A French Empire mahogany elbow chair, with curved arms formed as dolphin heads, upholstered in red silk.

D1 An Empire mahogany armchair, with curved top rail and curved arms supported on S-scrolls, *c.* 1825.

E3 A Louis XVI style giltwood fauteuil, late 19th century.

E2 A Louis XV style giltwood armchair, with a padded, waisted back surmounted by a C-scroll finial, *c.* 1880.

E4 A Louis XVI style giltwood fauteuil, with ribbon-carved back and fluted frame, *c.* 1900; 71 in. (180 cm) wide.

E5 A pair of giltwood and polychrome Gothic revival armchairs, the tall arched backs centred by a crocketted finial

above an ogee arched padded back, the support carved with a male and female head above lancet arches, *c.* 1900.

Bergères

E6 A Louis XIV walnut wing armchair, with rectangular back, shaped wings and padded arms on waved supports, the stuffed seat on similar legs joined by waved H-stretchers, *c.* 1680.

E7 A Louis XV walnut bergère, stamped Blanchard, with arched rectangular padded back and serpentine cushion seat in moulded frame, the padded arms on S-shaped voluted supports on cabriole legs with scroll feet, upholstered in floral moire silk, mid 18th century.

E8 A Louis XV period bergère, with a flat back in a natural wood frame, carved with a ripe pomegranate and shell motif, the seat-rail carved with a central flowerhead, on short, carved, cabriole legs, upholstered in blue silk.

E9 A Louis XV beechwood bergère, with arched, curved padded back and sides and a serpentine cushion seat in a moulded frame, upholstered in floral silk brocade, *c.* 1750.

E10 A Louis XV grey-painted bergère, with curved arched rectangular padded back and serpentine cushion seat in moulded frame, the crest and seat-rail similarly carved with twin flowerheads and trailing leaves, on cabriole legs, upholstered in peach velvet, mid 18th century.

E11 A Louis XV beechwood bergère, with curved arched padded back in moulded frame, the crest- and seat-rail crisply carved with a central flowerhead suspending leaves.

E1 A Louis XV grey-painted bergère, stamped J. Delaunay, with arched rounded back and curved arms in moulded frame with flowerhead cresting and seat-rail, the serpentine upholstered seat on cabriole legs.

E4 A Louis XV walnut bergère, the crest and seat-rail similarly carved with twin flowerheads, upholstered in green velvet, mid 18th century.

E7 A Louis XV walnut bergère à oreilles, with arched padded back and serpentine cushion seat, in moulded frame, the crest carved with flowerheads, mid 18th century.

D10 A Louis XV beechwood bergère, covered in brown velvet, the cushion above curved seat-rail, on cabriole legs.

E2 A Louis XV beechwood marquise, with arched rounded and padded back carved with a paired flowerhead cresting, shaped arm-supports and serpentine upholstered seat on moulded scrolled legs, covered in silk floral damask.

E5 A Louis XV beechwood bergère, covered in gold floral brocade in moulded frame with flowerhead cresting and seat-rail, on cabriole legs.

D8 A Louis XV giltwood bergère, with arched and rounded padded back and serpentine upholstered seat, the moulded frame carved with flowerhead cresting, the seat-rail with foliage sprays, on moulded cabriole legs.

E11 A rare Louis XV period carved wood and white painted marquise, bearing the signature I. Gourdin, third quarter of the 18th century; 31 in. high by 33 in. wide (78 by 82 cm).

E3 A Louis XV giltwood bergère, with curved padded back and serpentine upholstered seat in moulded frame, the seat with a loose cushion, over cabriole legs, mid 18th century.

E6 A Louis XV walnut bergère à oreilles, with arched scrolled top rail with foliate cresting, with arm supports carved with cabochons and foliage.

E9 A Louis XV beechwood bergère, stamped I. Gourdin, with moulded flower-carved frame, stuffed back and arms, loose cushion seat and cabriole legs, *c.* 1760.

E12 A Louis XVI giltwood bergère à la reine, the rectangular padded back carved with flowerheads above padded acanthus-carved arms and matching scrolling supports, the seat-rail similarly carved with flowerheads, upholstered in 18th-century Gobelins tapestry.

E 1 A Louis XVI parcel-gilt and grey-painted bergère, with arched incurved rectangular padded back and bowed cushion seat in moulded frame, the arms carved with long leaves, late 18th century.

E 4 A Louis XVI grey-painted bergère, stamped F. C. Menant, with arched incurved padded back, padded arms and sides, upholstered in crimson silk, with serpentine cushion seat in moulded frame, late 18th century.

E 7 A late Empire mahogany and parcel-gilt armchair, the scrolling bowed back, seat and armpads upholstered in stamped dralon, with rams-head terminals, on paw feet with stiff leaf headings.

E 10 An Empire walnut bergère, with rectangular concave back, down-scrolling arms carved with leaves at the base, the bow-front seat on sabre legs, c. 1810.

D 2 A Louis XVI giltwood chair, stamped Othon, covered in pale blue silk damask, c. 1780.

E 5 A Louis XVI provincial walnut bergère, with arched incurved padded back and bowed cushion seat in moulded frame, carved with stop-fluting, upholstered in yellow striped silk, late 18th century.

E 8 An Empire period mahogany causeuse or conversation chair. The distinctive feature of these English-inspired pieces is the way that the crest rail continues on one side, but drops to a padded arm on the other.

E 11 A carved walnut bergère, the curved top rail with carved decorative finials, with upholstered back and seat, the downcurving arms also upholstered, on cabriole legs ending on hoof feet, c. 1840; 39 in. (100 cm) high.

E 3 A Louis XVI painted bergère, with moulded grey-painted frame and scrolled hand rests on turned, fluted legs, c. 1780.

D 6 An Empire burr elm bergère, stamped Jacob D. R. Meslée, with arched incurved padded back and drop-in upholstered seat, upholstered in yellow striped silk, early 19th century.

D 9 An Empire period mahogany tub chair, the arm rests fronted by carved terms over paterae, on bulbous turned, collared legs, first quarter of the 19th century; 33 in. high, 18 in. wide (82 by 45 cm).

E 12 A beechwood bergère, in Louis XVI style, the shaped back carved with acanthus leaves and with floral cresting, upholstered in tapestry, 19th century.

E1 A "Louis XV" walnut and beechwood fauteuil, with upholstered back and sides, padded arms and sprung seat, contained in a moulded leaf-carved frame with cabriole legs, late 19th century.

E2 A salon armchair, with floral carved back, scroll hand grips on carved cabriole supports, 19th century.

E6 A Louis XV style beech framed bergère, with foliate and flower carved crest, late 19th century.

E9 A walnut dining chair, with serpentine-topped nailed stamped velvet back and seat, on turned legs and stretchers, late 17th century.

E3 A "Duchesse" suite, consisting of two bergères and a tabouret, the bergères with upholstered backs and sides, in moulded giltwood frames, the arm-rests on shallow S-shaped supports, the seat-rail regularly carved over slightly cabriole legs swagged at the hips, the tabouret similarly carved, with well-formed crests to the serpentine seat-rail, 19th century.

E7 An Empire revival gilt-bronze-mounted, leather-covered bergère, with a stuffed arched back, with bowed seat-rails and hairy paw feet, *c.* 1900.

E10 An oak nun's chair, on turned front legs, and plain back legs, joined by H-stretcher, *c.* 1700.

Side chairs

E4 A Louis XVI style giltwood bergère, with turned legs and floral upholstery, *c.* 1860.

E5 A "Louis XVI" armchair, the padded back and wings above stuffed squab seat, on stop fluted, turned, tapering legs, last quarter of the 19th century.

E8 A Louis XIII walnut dining chair, with raked rectangular padded back and upholstered seat, covered in olive-green velvet, on tapering octagonal legs joined by moulded waved X-pattern stretchers.

E11 A Louis XV white-painted voyeuse, with rectangular slightly incurved padded back and cushion seat, in moulded frame, mid-18th century.

E 1 A Louis XV chair, in natural wood, moulded and carved with shells and foliage, covered in fawn leather.

E 4 A Louis XV beechwood chaise, stamped C. Sene, with arched caned back and bowed caned seat in moulded frame, on crested cabriole legs.

D 7 A Louis XVI period mahogany chair, stamped Georges Jacob, with openwork back with slender columns and decorative motif.

E 10 A Louis XVI grey-painted voyeuse, with upholstered top rail, padded back and U-shaped padded seat in moulded fluted frame, on circular tapering stop-fluted legs, covered in floral silk brocade, c. 1780.

D 2 A Louis XV giltwood chauffeuse, with padded back and seat in moulded frame, the crest and seat-rails well carved, mid 18th century.

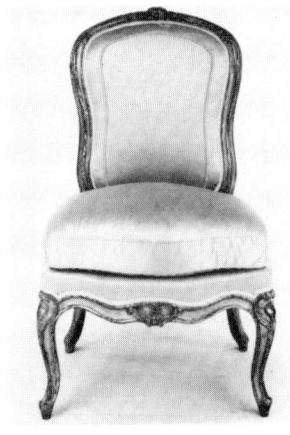

D 5 A Louis XV giltwood chair, stamped I. Gourdin, in moulded frame, the cresting carved with a heart-shaped cabochon framed by scrolls and foliage.

E 8 A late Louis XVI grey-painted chaise, the arched back with pierced lyre splat and reeded uprights headed by cone finials.

D 11 A Louis XVI white-painted chaise à l'anglaise, with an open arched back with a central lyre-shaped splat, late 18th century.

E 3 A Louis XV period chair, stamped Bovo, in natural moulded wood with a cabriolet back, covered in green damask.

E 6 A Louis XV grey-painted chaise, stamped C. Avisse, in a moulded frame, with crest and seat-rail carved with central flowerhead with foliage trails, c. 1750.

E 9 A Louis XVI cream-painted chaise à l'anglaise, with rectangular fluted back with panelled lyre, c. 1780.

E 12 A Louis XVI blue-painted and parcel-gilt chaise à l'anglaise, upholstered in contemporary needlework, c. 1780.

E 1 A Louis XVI grey-painted chaise, with moulded frame, on circular tapering stop-fluted legs, *c.* 1780.

E 4 A Louis XVI side chair, with ribbon-carved frames, carved seat-rails and fluted turned legs, *c.* 1780.

E 5 An Empire mahogany ormolu-mounted curricle chair, with shaped top rail and solid splat, and with sabre legs.

French 18th-Century Chairs
The unique quality of French seat furniture in the Régence and Louis XV periods was its overwhelming emphasis on decorative effect. The principal element in this was the use of rich fabrics for upholstery, the secondary features being carving, gilding and painting.

Opulent comfort was the characteristic of Régence interiors and rooms were crowded with deeply cushioned chairs. Fashion demanded a change of colours with the seasons, but prudent economy achieved this by the use of loose covers. Furniture makers took note of this trend and sometimes produced pieces with detachable backs for ease of re-covering.

The emphasis on the work of the tapissier should not be allowed to belittle the craft of the maker however. Just as the lavish ormolu mounts applied to, say, commodes were intended to add glory to his work, so the upholsterer's flamboyant art was intended as a compliment to, rather than a distraction from, his skill.

D 2 A Louis XVI mahogany chaise à l'anglaise, with moulded back pierced with X-shaped lattice work, *c.* 1780.

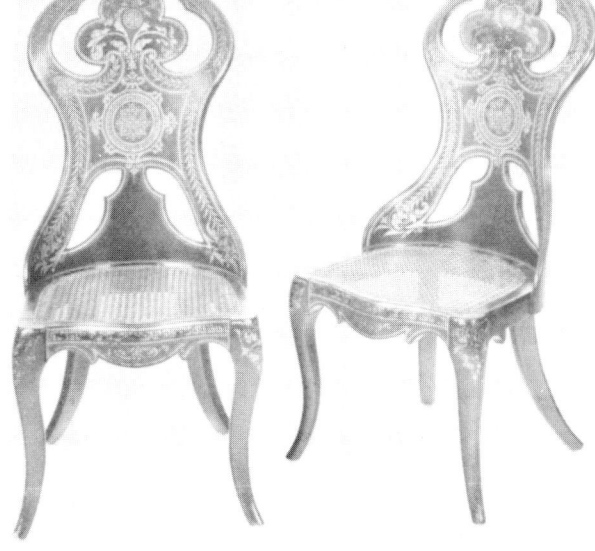

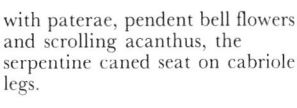

E 6 A pair of Louis Philippe black lacquer papier mâché chaises, each with spooned hooped back gilt and decorated in colours with paterae, pendent bell flowers and scrolling acanthus, the serpentine caned seat on cabriole legs.

E 9 An Empire-style mahogany dining chair, with a solid top rail, *c.* 1900.

E 3 A Louis XVI grey-painted chaise, with moulded and carved frame.

E 7 A beechwood salon chaise, stained to resemble rosewood, *c.* 1840.

E 8 A Louis XVI style painted and parcel-gilt chaise, the seat-rail with elaborate finials over fluted, garlanded uprights, 19th century.

D 10 A Louis XV style upholstered side chair, with oval medallion back with moulded frame, *c.* 1900.

COFFERS
1470-1550

The most splendid examples of the French coffer are equally in the native Gothic and in the imported Renaissance styles; the quality of their ornament may be said to have laid the foundation for French carvers' reputation.

The idea of the rude coffer was however inconsistent with the quasi-imperial grandeur of the Louis XIV style; the form continued in the provinces but disappeared from the fashionable repertoire, giving way to the commode.

D 4 An oak coffer with rectangular panelled hinged lid, applied with wrought-iron lock-plate, early 16th century; 54 in. (138 cm) wide.

E 5 A small carved oak coffret, with two plank top, the front with two panels carved with "Romayne" roundels of a bearded and moustachioed man, and a woman, each shown half-length, the sides with plain roundels, on a moulded base, *c.* 1530; 18 in. high by 27 in. wide (46 by 69 cm).

D 1 A Gothic chest with original lock; the Renaissance detail is blended with the Gothic style, *c.* 1470.

D 6 A Renaissance coffer, of large proportions, extensively carved, late 15th/early 16th century. This is a good example of the continental furniture of this period.

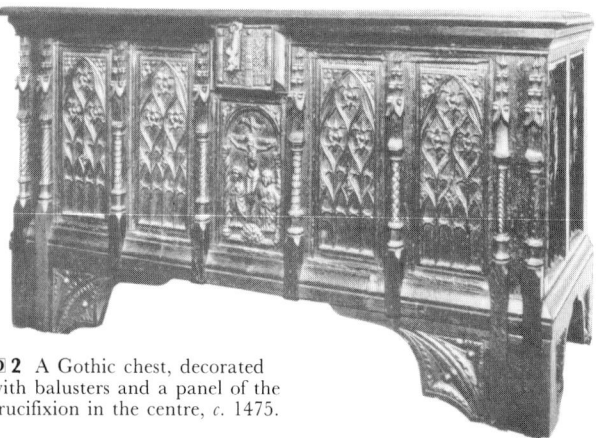

D 2 A Gothic chest, decorated with balusters and a panel of the crucifixion in the centre, *c.* 1475.

E 7 A marriage chest, the panelled front carved with the head of Christ and male and female heads in roundels, 16th century; 48 in. (112 cm).

E 8 An oak coffer, with original ironwork, 16th century; 18 in. high by 28 in. (45 by 80 cm).

D 3 A large oak coffer, with five finely carved arcaded panels, dating from about 1480.

E 9 An Henri II carved walnut coffer, mid 16th century; 29 in. high by 60 in. long (75 by 152 cm).

COMMODES
1710-1910

The term commode was not used, it seems, before 1708, though Boulle had produced three-tier versions rather earlier. In about 1715 he designed a lighter, two-tier version, a pattern that Cressent adapted and raised to a new height of splendour.

Breakfront commodes of more severe form were made under Louis XVI, but not after about 1780, at which time demi-lune and corner commodes or encoignures were being added to the ébénistes' repertoire.

D 1 A rare late Louis XIV green japanned commode, the bowed front painted and with gilt-bronze handles, early 18th century; 42 in. (98 cm) wide.

D 2 A Régence provincial walnut commode, the drawers mounted with bronze; 32 in. high by 50 in. wide (82 by 127 cm).

D 3 An early Louis XV palissander commode, by N. Marchand, with well-chased foliate handles, lock-plates and Indian mask angles, on scrolled feet, c. 1736.

D 4 An early Louis XV kingwood and tulipwood commode, with moulded breccia marble top, with clasps on bracket feet.

D 5 An early Louis XV kingwood commode, stamped F.C. of arc-en-arbalette outline; 33 in. (85 cm) high.

E 6 An early Louis XV kingwood and tulipwood bombé commode, with serpentine breccia marble top.

C 7 A Louis XV period lacquered commode, attributed to A. R. Gaudreau; 34 in. by 46 in. wide (88 by 117 cm).

D 8 A Louis XV tulipwood, purpleheart and marquetry commode, with moulded serpentine rectangular breccia marble top, the panels inlaid with summer flowers, mid 18th century.

D 9 A Louis XV ormolu-mounted kingwood and marquetry commode, with moulded serpentine liver, grey and white marble top, the angles mounted with pierced C-scrolls and wave-pattern extending to foliate scroll sabots, mid 18th century.

C 10 A Louis XV kingwood and floral marquetry bombé commode, with serpentine portor marble top; 44 in. (112 cm) wide.

D 11 A Louis XV kingwood parquetry commode, indistinctly stamped with a mottled pink and grey marble top, c. 1750; 34 in. (87 cm).

C 12 A rosewood marquetry commode with marble top, ornately carved with flowers and foliage, the curved legs ending in pointed feet, c. 1720; 32 in. high by 37 in. wide (77 by 93 cm).

D 13 A Louis XV ormolu-mounted kingwood commode, with moulded serpentine rectangular marble top, the splayed legs with foliate scroll and cabochon mounts, mid 18th century.

C 14 A Louis XV ormolu-mounted kingwood and floral marquetry tulipwood commode, mounted with floral and foliate scrolling escutcheons and animals.

D 15 A Louis XV ormolu-mounted tulipwood and marquetry commode, with moulded serpentine marble top, above bombé body with three short over two long drawers, on splayed feet with pierced sabots, mid 18th century; 56 in. (142 cm) wide.

D 16 A Louis XV ormolu-mounted rosewood bombé commode, by L. Villedieu, with waved moulded rouge marble top above three long drawers; 38 in. (96 cm) wide.

C 1 A Louis XV marquetry commode, by P. Roussel, fitted with three short and two long drawers, inlaid with flower sprays on shaped panels in kingwood borders, with scrolls reaching to foliate feet.

D 2 A Louis XV kingwood commode with moulded serpentine breccia marble top above two short and a long bombé drawer, quarter-veneered and crossbanded on splayed legs, mid 18th century.

D 3 A Louis XV kingwood bombé commode, with serpentine moulded grey and white veined marble top, the two drawers with foliate ormolu handles, lock-plates and angles, *c.* 1728.

D 4 A Louis XV kingwood commode, with moulded serpentine rectangular fossilized liver and tan marble top, the drawer is mounted with ormolu rocaille C-scroll handles and lock-plates on splayed legs.

D 5 A Louis XV gilt-bronze mounted kingwood parquetry commode, stamped P. Roussel, mid 18th century; 34 in. high by 45 in. wide (87 by 114 cm).

C 6 A Louis XV tulipwood and marquetry commode, with moulded lobed serpentine liver and grey mottled marble top, stamped P.G. Turcot, mid 18th century.

D 7 A Louis XV satinwood and tulipwood parquetry commode, by I. P. Latz, mid 18th century; 33 in. high by 38 in. wide (85 by 95 cm).

D 8 A Louis XV rosewood serpentine commode, by L. Delaitre, 24 in. by 49 in. wide (87 by 126 cm).

D 9 A Louis XV provincial carved walnut commode, of serpentine form with moulded top, shaped sides and two drawers, the top, front and sides all panelled, *c.* 1750; 35 in. high by 49 in. wide (89 by 124 cm).

E 10 A provincial oak commode, of serpentine form, the three drawers with elaborate handles, above shaped apron, mid 18th century.

E 11 A provincial chestnut and fruitwood commode, the gentle serpentine front fitted with two short and two long drawers, raised on bi-cusped feet, Breton, mid 18th century.

E 12 A Louis XV provincial mahogany commode, with a mottled brown marble top above panelled drawers, *c.* 1750; 33 in. by 50 in. wide (84 by 127 cm).

D 13 A Louis XV provincial walnut commode, with moulded serpentine rectangular top above two long drawers, carved with wave pattern, mid 18th century; 47 in. (119 cm).

D 14 A provincial chestnut bombé commode, the serpentine front with two short and two long drawers with shaped moulded panels, cast bronze rococo handles, mid 18th century; 50 in. (124 cm) wide.

E 15 A provincial walnut commode with later moulded serpentine top, mid 18th century; 45 in. (115 cm) wide.

E 16 A Louis XV provincial walnut commode, with serpentine moulded top above two drawers in the conforming front, mid 18th century; 54 in. (137 cm) wide.

D 1 A Louis XV/XVI walnut and marquetry commode, with rounded rectangular grey and brown mottled marble top, above two long drawers veneered with shaped rectangular panels; 42 in. (107 cm) wide.

D 2 A Transitional kingwood commode, with moulded breakfront fleur de pêche marble top, above two long and three short drawers; 52 in. (133 cm) wide.

C 3 A Transitional parquetry commode, by F.A. Reizell, with moulded breakfront mottled black and white marble top, with three short drawers above two long drawers with neoclassical ormolu handles, 51 in. (130 cm) wide.

C 4 A Louis XV/XVI tulipwood and parquetry commode, with moulded bowed rectangular breccia marble top, above two long drawers on cabriole legs with cloven sabots; 44 in. (110 cm) wide.

D 5 A Transitional kingwood and parquetry commode, stamped Roussel, with moulded breakfront mottled black marble top; 38 in. (97 cm) wide.

C 6 An important Transitional commode, with breakfront moulded carrara marble top, above lion-paw feet; 44 in. by 46 in. (112 by 119 cm).

D 7 A Louis XVI kingwood and marquetry commode, with moulded breakfront breccholito marble top, fitted with two drawers, above square tapering legs; 32 in. (82 cm) wide.

E 8 A Louis XV/XVI Transitional marquetry breakfront commode, with a brèche d'alep marble top, inlaid with marquetry panels, c. 1775; 50 in. (127 cm) wide.

D 9 A Louis XVI tulipwood and marquetry commode, with rounded rectangular breccia marble top, above three short drawers, late 18th century; 44 in. (112 cm) wide.

E 10 A Louis XVI mahogany commode, with moulded breakfront mottled grey marble top and two long drawers framed with ormolu stiff-leaf borders and panelled sides; 45 in. (115 cm) wide.

E 11 A Louis XVI tulipwood and mahogany crossbanded rectangular commode, of slight broken outline, and applied with gilt-metal mounts; 32 in. (79 cm) wide.

C 12 A Louis XVI lacquer commode, with two drawers flanked by two pairs of ormolu pilasters headed by chiselled lion masks, c. 1780; 52 in. (132 cm) wide.

C 13 A Louis XVI lacquer commode "à portes", of small size, signed C. Topino; 34 in. high by 46 in. (75 by 115 cm).

D 14 A Louis XVI mahogany and kingwood commode, with three-quarter galleried semi-circular white marble top; 37 in. (95 cm) wide.

D 15 A Louis XVI ormolu-mounted tulipwood and amaranth demi-lune commode, with eared mottled grey and white moulded marble top; 32 in. (82 cm) wide.

D 16 A semi-circular commode, the marquetry in a variety of woods with kingwood and mahogany surrounds, and figures with the undraped parts in ivory, c. 1780.

E 1 A Louis XVI tulipwood commode, with white marble top, fitted with three drawers flanked by two cupboard doors enclosing shelves, on turned tapering feet; 43 in. (110 cm) wide.

E 2 A Louis XVI mahogany commode, by Bernard van Risenburgh, stamped BVRB JME, with lobed carrara marble top, and ormolu-mounted frieze above two long drawers; 46 in. (118 cm) wide.

E 3 A Louis XVI mahogany commode, with grey and white marble top above three fielded panelled graduated drawers carved with flutes and flanked by fluted angles, late 18th century; 37 in. (96 cm) wide.

E 4 A Louis XVI period rosewood and satinwood marquetry commode, stamped Bircklé, the top drawer-front falling to reveal fitted interior; 36 in. (89 cm) high.

E 5 A Louis XVI mahogany commode, with grey and white marble top above three short fielded panelled drawers over two long drawers, late 18th century; 51 in. (131 cm) wide.

E 6 A provincial oak commode, with two short lozenge-shaped panelled drawers with elaborate drop handles over two matching long drawers, with panelled sides and curved apron, late 18th century.

E 7 A provincial elm commode, with three drawers with drop handles and escutcheons, the rounded fluted terminals with fluted apron and feet, c. 1780; 32 in. high by 46 in. wide (81 by 118 cm).

E 8 A Directoire period mahogany veneered commode, with white marble top above four rows of drawers flanked by fluted gilt angles, the central frieze drawer with writing flap, the drawer panels edged with bronze beading, on short, turned, tapered legs with casters; 38 in. high by 57 in. wide (94 by 145 cm).

E 9 An Empire ormolu-mounted mahogany commode, with black and white marble top, the frieze mounted with putti and foliage plaques, above two cupboard doors each carved with a horn motif, 51 in. (129 cm) wide.

E 10 An Empire mahogany commode, branded AP, with black fossil top fitted with an overhanging frieze drawer, above four long drawers; 51 in. (130 cm) wide.

E 11 An Empire ormolu-mounted mahogany commode, with black fossil marble top above overhanging frieze drawer and three long drawers between turned detached angles; 51 in. (131 cm) wide.

E 12 A Louis-Philippe kingwood commode, by Liebmann Frères, with white carrara marble top, above four graduated long drawers on a plinth, c. 1840; 34 in. high by 40 in. wide (87 by 103 cm).

E 13 A provincial kingwood commode chest, with a concealed drawer to the top, above three long drawers, with decorative drop gilt handles, on bun feet; 42 in. high by 53 in. wide (105 by 135 cm).

D 14 A Louis-Philippe tulipwood, rosewood, kingwood and parquetry commode, with fitted slide doors enclosing arcaded compartments with shelves and two drawers to base, c. 1850; 37 in. high by 39 in. wide (94 by 99 cm).

D 15 A Louis-Philippe maplewood commode, stencilled "Maison Le Marchand H. Lemoine, Rue de Tournelles à Paris Ebéniste..."; 51 in. (130 cm) wide.

E 16 A mahogany commode, with marble top above three long drawers with brass drop handles and escutcheons, flanked by fluted angles, 19th century.

E1 A Louis XV-style kingwood commode, with a serpentine marble top above three long drawers, *c.* 1880; 36 in. high by 50 in. wide (99 by 127 cm).

E2 A Louis XVI-style marquetry commode, with simulated marble top, the front containing three drawers flanked by cupboards, *c.* 1880; 33 in. high by 34 in. wide (84 by 88 cm).

E3 A Louis XV/Louis XVI Transitional-style kingwood and parquetry commode, *c.* 1880-1900; 32 in. high by 44 in. wide (81 by 112 cm).

E4 A Louis XV-style kingwood marquetry commode, the serpentine marble top above two drawers veneered sans traverse, *c.* 1910; 37 in. (95 cm) wide.

Petites commodes

D5 A Louis XV ormolu-mounted kingwood parquetry small commode, with marble top, *c.* 1735; 33 in. high by 23 in. wide (84 by 59 cm).

D6 A Louis XV kingwood small commode, stamped Migeon JME, *c.* 1745; 34 in. high by 23 in. wide (86 by 59 cm).

E7 A Louis XV kingwood and parquetry small commode, with moulded serpentine marble top over two crossbanded drawers between ormolu-mounted angles, *c.* 1750; 20 in. (52 cm) wide.

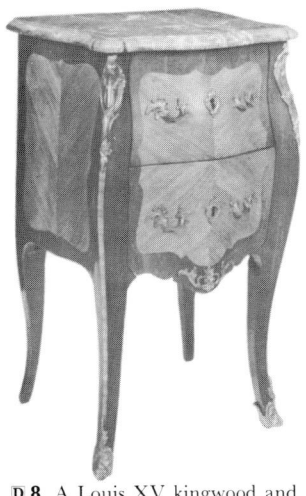

D8 A Louis XV kingwood and marquetry small commode, signed J Schmitz JME, with moulded serpentine marble top over a bombé front with two drawers, mid 18th century; 21 in. (53 cm) wide.

D9 A Louis XV tulipwood and marquetry small commode, stamped Tvartfils, three times, with moulded serpentine marble top over a bombé front with two crossbanded quarter-veneered drawers, mid 18th century; 25 in. (63 cm) wide.

D10 A Louis XV kingwood and marquetry small commode, stamped J B Fromageau JME, with moulded serpentine marble top above two conforming drawers, mid 18th century; 30 in. wide (76 cm).

D11 A Louis XV kingwood and ormolu-mounted small commode, stamped J Birckle, with marble top over bombé front with three conforming drawers; 32 in. (80 cm) high.

E12 A Transitional tulipwood and purpleheart small commode, stamped J P Letellier JME, with moulded black fossil marble top over three drawers with ormolu roundel handles, with foliate angles; 21 in. (54 cm) wide.

D13 A Louis XVI kingwood and marquetry small commode, with a marble top above a drawer and a cupboard door; 23 in. (58 cm) wide.

E 1 A Louis XVI marquetry mahogany D-shaped petite commode, the white marble top over two drawers with flowers flanked by fluted stiles on turned fluted legs, *c.* 1780; 32 in. (80 cm) wide.

E 2 A Louis XVI satinwood small commode, with chamfered mottled grey and white marble top, the angles mounted with neoclassical ormolu plaques, 17 in. (45 cm) wide.

E 3 A Louis XVI amaranth and marquetry petite commode, with moulded rectangular grey and white marble top, late 18th century; 25 in. (65 cm).

E 4 A rosewood and marquetry bombé petite commode, with rouge marble serpentine moulded top above two drawers on slender cabriole supports, mid 19th century; 32 in. (81 cm) wide.

E 5 A Louis XV style mahogany and ormolu-mounted petite commode, the serpentine moulded and eared rectangular marble top above two drawers, raised on cabriole legs; 24 in. (60 cm) long.

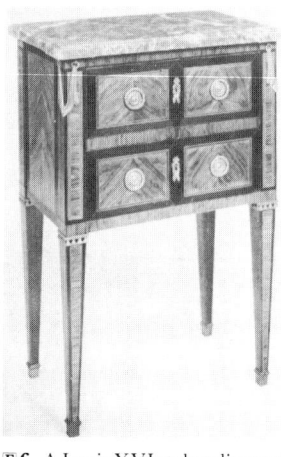

E 6 A Louis XVI style tulipwood and marquetry petite commode, with moulded rectangular liver and grey marble top, above two drawers inlaid with rectangular tulipwood panels within green-stained and purpleheart borders, above square tapering legs with sabots; 22 in. (58 cm) wide.

E 7 A rosewood veneered petite commode, with brèche-violette moulded serpentine marble top, *c.* 1900; 33 in. high by 22 in. wide (84 by 56 cm).

Cartonniers & semainiers

D 8 A Louis XV tulipwood semainier, the black and white marble top above seven drawers, 20 in. (53 cm) wide.

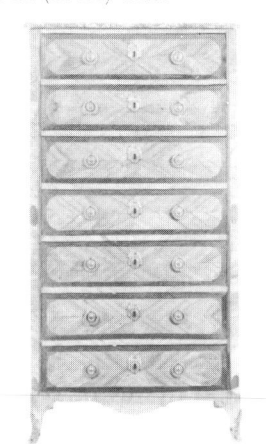

D 9 A Louis XV/XVI tulipwood and purpleheart semainier, grey and white marble top, mid 18th century; 31 in. (79 cm) wide.

D 10 A Louis XV/XVI tulipwood and marquetry cartonnier, grey and white marble top, mid 18th century; 33 in. (84 cm) wide.

D 11 A Transitional tulipwood cartonnier, stamped N. Petit, with later clock signed Masson à Paris; 38 in. (96 cm) wide.

D 12 A Louis XVI semainier, stamped J. B. Vassou JME, *c.* 1775; 60 in. (155 cm) high.

D 13 A Louis XVI mahogany semainier, with moulded eared rectangular grey and white marble top, on circular tapering legs, late 18th century; 36 in. (92 cm) wide.

D 14 A mahogany cartonnier, with brass panelled frieze and sides, stencilled "Janiaud Paris"; 36 in. (915 cm) wide.

E 15 A crossbanded kingwood Louis XV-style chest with original pulls and escutcheons, c. 1870; 37 in. (925 cm) high.

CUPBOARDS
1600-1900

The armoire – the classic tall French cupboard – evolved from the two-tier cupboard or buffet of the Gothic period – see no. 1 below. Made in all later periods, it has always given scope for both cabinet-maker and carver to display their skills in reflection of contemporary taste. The apogee of the form is the Louis XV period design – see no. 8.

Provincial examples of any period can however be of two-tier construction, either quite obviously, or in retaining a vestigial row of drawers to the base.

D 1 A late Gothic oak cupboard, with moulded rectangular cornice above a central fielded panel carved with wave-pattern and foliate scrolls and flanked by two fielded cupboard doors carved with linen-fold; 56 in. (142 cm) wide.

E 2 A carved walnut armoire, with canted ends and drawers to base, with concave top, c. 1725; 61 in. by 56 in. (155 by 143 cm). This type of armoire sometimes had a marble top.

E 3 An early Louis XV provincial walnut armoire, with lion-paw feet, early 18th century; 84 in. high by 77 in. (213 by 196 cm) wide.

E 4 A carved oak armoire, with brass escutcheons and hinges; 62 in. (157 cm) high.

E 5 A Louis XV Normandy oak armoire, with carved frieze, with panelled doors above a shaped apron; 62 in. (156 cm) wide.

E 6 A provincial oak armoire, with fitted shelves and drawers, original engraved brass escutcheons, 18th century; 62 in. (155 cm) high.

D 7 A provincial chestnut armoire with arched moulded cornice, with waved base, 18th century; 93 in. high by 58 in. wide (236 by 58 cm).

E 8 A Louis XV provincial walnut armoire, with two arched fielded panelled cupboard doors, on S-scrolled legs; 105 in. (267 cm) high.

E 1 A provincial oak armoire, the top with an arched and moulded pediment, 18th century; 92 in. high by 45 in. wide (234 by 113 cm).

E 2 A Louis XV kingwood parquetry small armoire, with galleried Brescia marble top, inlaid with an ogee trellis enclosing flowerheads, c. 1760; 54 in. by 39 in. (138 by 99 cm).

E 3 A provincial oak armoire, late 18th century; 52 in. (132 cm) wide.

E 4 A provincial chestnut armoire, the waved apron on squat cabriole legs, late 18th century; 54 in. (137 cm).

E 5 A tulipwood and marquetry petite armoire of transitional style; 26 in. (66 cm) wide.

E 6 A Louis XV-style wardrobe, signed Linke, of banded kingwood with fine ormolu mounts, 19th century.

DISPLAY CABINETS 1750-1920

Both the side cabinet and the fully glazed vitrine or display cabinet were immensely popular in 19th-century France. The finest examples were made as display pieces in themselves.

Vitrines in the curvilinear style owed as much to the glass-maker as to the cabinet-maker, requiring the utmost skill in making panels of convex and ogee-form glass to allow the design to run unbroken by a straight line.

E 7 A Louis XV kingwood vitrine, with two glazed doors; 44 in. (114 cm) wide.

E 8 A Louis XV small vitrine with marble top, mid 18th century; 48 in. (122 cm) high.

E 9 A mahogany Charles X display sideboard with beige marble top, with frieze drawer; 53 in. (134 cm) wide.

D 10 A Louis XIV-style ebonized and ormolu-mounted dwarf bookcase, with moulded rectangular verde antico marble top, mid 19th century; 52 in. (133 cm) wide.

E 11 A boulle side cabinet, the top inlaid after Jean Berain, with gilt-bronze mounts, 19th century; 48 in. high by 43 in. wide (122 by 109 cm).

E 12 A fine bijouterie cabinet, parquetry-veneered in rosewood with box and ebony outline panels, 19th century; 58 in. high by 22 in. wide (178 by 55 cm).

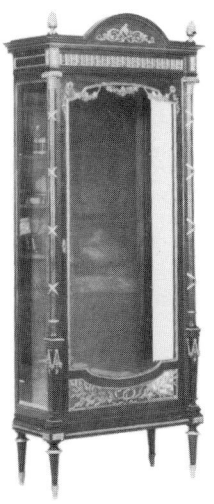

E 1 A gilt-bronze-mounted mahogany display cabinet, in Louis XVI style, lavishly mounted with flowers and ribbon mounts, c. 1880; 81 in. high by 30 in. (206 by 78 cm).

E 2 An Empire revival mahogany and ormolu-mounted marble-top vitrine, with mirror back, on claw-ball feet, c. 1800; 57 in. (145 cm) high.

E 3 A kingwood and ormolu-mounted breakfront vitrine, with velvet-lined interior, c. 1880; 63 in. (161 cm) high.

E 4 A Louis XV-style mahogany and kingwood dwarf vitrine, ormolu mounted and inlaid; 42 in. (105 cm) wide.

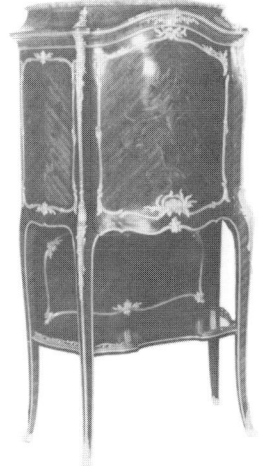

E 5 A Louis XV-style ormolu-mounted kingwood and marquetry vitrine with liver and grey marble top; 61 in. (155 cm) high.

E 6 A satinwood and ormolu-mounted display cabinet-on-stand, late 19th century; 34 in. (84 cm) high.

E 7 A Louis XVI-style ormolu-mounted mahogany corner vitrine, with carved marble top, late 19th century; 57 in. (145 cm) high.

E 8 A Louis XVI-style ormolu-mounted mahogany vitrine, with rectangular galleried top, late 19th century; 29 in. (70 cm) high.

E 9 A Louis XVI-style ormolu-mounted mahogany vitrine, attributed to F. Linke, late 19th century; 70 in. (178 cm) high.

E 10 A brass-mounted mahogany bijouterie display cabinet, with shaped galleried marble top, with glazed door, on tapered fluted legs.

E 11 A Louis XVI-style kingwood, marquetry and parquetry vitrine, with chased ormolu mounts, 63 in. high by 46 in. wide (160 by 115 cm).

E 12 A Louis XV-style mahogany display cabinet, glazed panels to the top and sides; 24 in. (60 cm) wide.

E1 A walnut and ormolu-mounted vitrine, with glazed serpentine front and sides above four painted scenes, *c.* 1880; 47 in. (120 cm) wide.

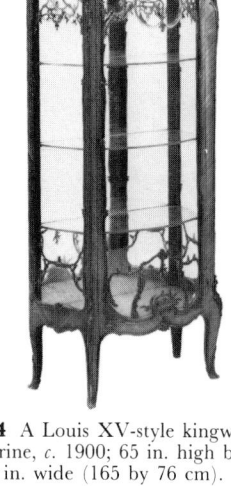

E2 A Louis XV-style ormolu-mounted and giltwood vernis Martin vitrine, with hour-glass shape glazed case, *c.* 1880; 31 in. (78 cm) long.

E3 A Louis XV-style kingwood and ormolu-mounted bow-fronted vitrine, *c.* 1900; 78 in. high by 41 in. wide (198 by 104 cm).

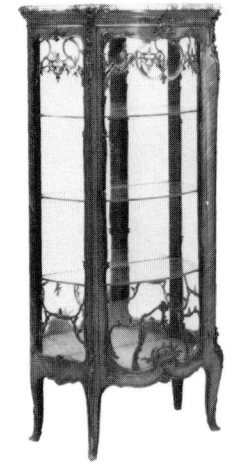

E4 A Louis XV-style kingwood vitrine, *c.* 1900; 65 in. high by 30 in. wide (165 by 76 cm).

E5 A Louis XVI-style mahogany vitrine, *c.* 1900; 54 in. high by 29 in. wide (138 by 73 cm).

E6 An Art Nouveau fruitwood and maple vitrine, in the style of Louis Majorelle; 26 in. (65 cm) wide.

DRESSERS
1750-1800

The dresser or vaisselier, by definition a modest, domestic piece of furniture, was affected only slowly by the great currents of stylistic and decorative change. It is therefore the case that the Louis XV-style panelling to a dresser's cupboard doors can be equally typical of 18th and 19th-century pieces, and of dressers made in Provence and in Brittany.

The local variety in detail is however immense, as is the range of timbers employed.

E7 A Louis XV carved oak dresser, with three drawers and two doors in the base, *c.* 1760; 83 in. high by 69 in. wide (208 by 173 cm).

E8 A provincial oak dresser, the cabinet top over two doors inset with embossed brass panels, 18th century; 47 in. (120 cm) high.

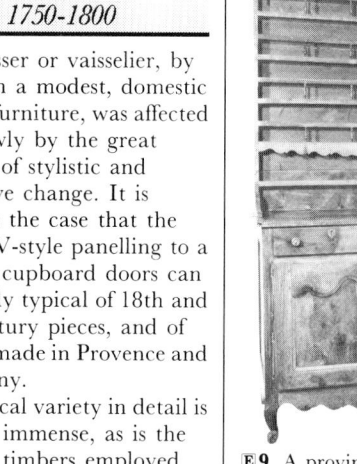

E9 A provincial cherrywood dresser, with a raised shelved back with a canopy and front rails, the base fitted with two drawers above panelled cupboard doors, 18th century.

E10 A provincial oak dresser, with a raised shelved back with a canopy and front rails, 18th century; 50 in. (127 cm) wide.

E11 A provincial chestnut dresser, with shelves to back with canopy and front rails, 18th century; 62 in. (157 cm) high.

ETAGERES
1760-1890

The étagère evolved in moderate stages from the small, pretty occasional tables of the later 18th century. A second tier was added either by setting a platform below or by placing a complete second table on top.

In the neoclassical period étagères became narrower and more contained, extending to three or more tiers, often on turned supports beneath a marble top. Gilt-metal mounts were applied to the frieze on fine examples.

E 1 A Louis XV kingwood étagère, *c.* 1770; 28 in. high by 34 in. wide (71 by 87 cm).

E 2 An Empire ormolu-mounted mahogany étagère, 21 in. (53 cm) wide.

E 3 A marble and ormolu-mounted fruitwood étagère, by Alfred Beurdeley; 54 in. high by 24 in. wide (137 by 60 cm).

E 4 A rosewood étagère, with gilt-metal gallery to the top and flambeau finials, late 19th century; 16 in. (40 cm) wide.

MIRRORS
1700-1870

Despite Samuel Pepys' claim that the English were the masters of mirror-making, that accolade must be accorded to the craftsmen of Italy. When it came to incorporating mirrors into decorative schemes however, the French led the field.

The resplendent Galerie des Glaces at Versailles must have been highly influential in this regard, setting a model to be imitated on a necessarily humbler scale in many a provincial château.

E 5 A Louis XIV giltwood looking glass, the frame with gesso strapwork and leafy clasps, *c.* 1700; 79 in. high by 43 in. wide (201 by 110 cm).

D 6 A Régence giltwood mirror, with arched plate in conforming mirrored and carved borders, early 18th century; 80 in. (204 cm) high.

D 7 A Régence giltwood pier glass, the plate bordered with foliate strapwork, the mirrored surround with cartouche and strapwork angles, 65 in. high by 32 in. wide (165 by 82 cm).

D 8 A Régence white-painted pier mirror, early 18th century; 73 in. (187 cm) high.

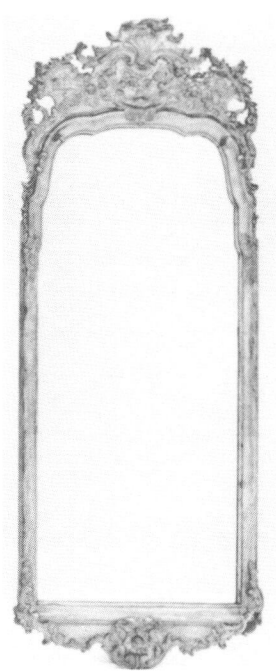

E 9 A Louis XV carved gesso and wood pier glass, with a bevelled plate, *c.* 1740; 65 in. high by 25 in. wide (165 by 64 cm).

E 10 A Louis XV giltwood overmantel glass, with mirrored border surrounded with carving, *c.* 1750; 76 in. high by 60 in. wide (193 by 153 cm).

D 11 A Louis XV giltwood pier mirror, with divided arched rectangular plate, mid 18th century; 67 in. (171 cm) high.

Dating mirrors
Nearly every style of mirror frame from the 17th century onwards was reproduced during the 19th century, necessarily including those of a highly delicate nature, prone to damage. Such damage and subsequent restoration may be a better guide to the age of the frame than the glass it contains, for the presence of an 18th-century plate does not automatically indicate a contemporary frame.

The presence of verre églomisé panels can also be helpful in dating. The process was known in antiquity, favoured by Italian craftsmen of the Renaissance and never altogether disappeared. It was made hugely popular however by Jean-Baptiste Glomy, a Parisian designer and framer who used the method extensively for framing prints. He died in 1786, by which time the process already bore his name.

D 1 A Louis XV giltwood mirror, with arched rectangular plate in lobed borders, mid 18th century; 70 in. (177 cm) high.

E 2 An Empire mahogany cheval mirror, mounted with gilt-brass winged griffons; 79 in. (200 cm) high.

C 3 An important ormolu-mounted marquetry, bronze, marble and tulipwood Psyche mirror, the arched cornice set with an elaborate pierced ormolu spray of chrysanthemums above a frieze inlaid in stained sycamore and maple with flowers and scrolls flanked by chrysanthemum-petal finials at the angles, the arched mirror within a citronnier frame, veneered with wisteria clusters and set with ormolu flower sprays, the green marble urn modelled as a brûle-parfum beneath a bronze cherub, the seated Belle Epoque maiden adjusting her hair-pin with the ormolu mirror in her raised left hand, dated 1900; 104 in. high by 66 in. wide (253 by 168 cm).

E 4 An ivory veneered dressing table mirror, of rectangular form with central drawer, swivel-mounted mirror and paw feet, the body elaborately incised with foliate arabesques and applied oak leaves surround portrait medallions of the Dauphin and Mary Stuart, the mirror frame applied with similar oak leaves and satyr masks, 19th century; 26 in. (68 cm) high.

SCREENS 1755-1890

The 18th century firescreen had three functions: to decorate the fireplace during summer, to display needlework or tapestry panels worked by the ladies of the household, and to prevent the heat of the fire melting the wax and white lead makeup worn at the time.

The 19th century firescreen shared the first two functions but not the third: by then its use was to protect unadorned faces from acquiring an unbecoming flush.

E 5 A Louis XV carved giltwood firescreen, the moulded cartouche frame carved with flowers, leaves and scrolls, with similarly carved trestle feet, c. 1755; 36 in. high by 23 in. wide (90 by 60 cm).

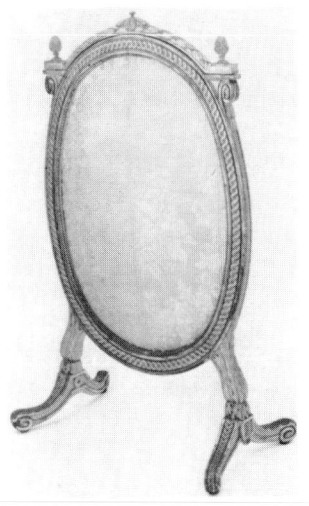

E 6 A Louis XVI period oval mirror, with giltwood decoration interlaced with pearls, the finials shaped as fir cones, with leaf-carved splayed feet.

E 1 A Louis XVI giltwood six-fold screen, each part carved along the edge with berried laurel leaves, *c.* 1780; each part 51 in. high by 25 in. wide (130 by 65 cm).

E 4 A Louis XIV needlework panel and Louis XIV-style walnut firescreen; 41 in. (105 cm) high.

SECRÉTAIRES
1750–1870

The classic secrétaire à abattant was a perfect vehicle for the display of the arts of furniture-making. The interior provided numerous possibilities for displaying ingenuity and the fall front could be veneered and inlaid with marquetry, painted, lacquered in the Oriental style or made to receive authentic Oriental panels. In the Empire period the decorative success of such pieces depended above all on the skill of the ormolu maker.

D 9 A Louis XV/XVI kingwood and marquetry petite secrétaire à abattant, with moulded serpentine grey and white marble top above a frieze drawer, mid 18th-century; 26 in. (66 cm) wide.

E 2 An Empire ormolu-mounted mahogany firescreen, decorated on both sides and with a rising panel, *c.* 1810; 46 in. high by 28 in. wide (115 by 70 cm).

E 5 A giltwood cheval firescreen, of Régence design, with pierced scrolled foliate cresting; 32 in. (81 cm) wide.

C 7 A fall-front secrétaire à abattant, by René Dubois, mid 18th century.

E 10 A Louis XV/XVI mahogany secrétaire à abattant, with two rectangular cupboard doors enclosing shelves, mid 18th century; 40 in. (95 cm) wide.

E 3 A "Louis XV" giltwood four-fold screen, the rococo frames asymmetrically carved with C-scrolls and acanthus, late 19th century; each fold 73 in. by 34 in. (186 by 87 cm).

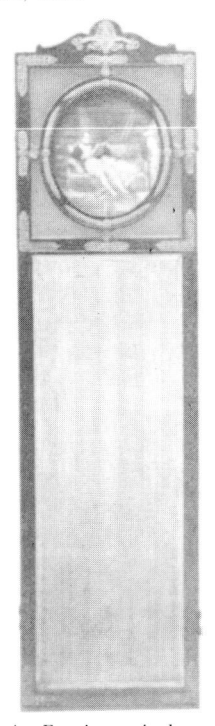

E 6 An Empire revival mahogany three-fold screen, *c.* 1890; each fold 63 in. by 18 in. (159 by 46 cm).

D 8 A Louis XV/XVI tulipwood and amaranth secrétaire à abattant, with marble top, mid 18th-century; 31 in. (80 cm) wide.

D 11 A Louis XV tulipwood-veneered secrétaire à abattant with a moulded mottled green and rose-coloured marble top, *c.* 1770; 52 in. (132 cm) high.

C1 A Louis XVI small marquetry secrétaire à abattant, by RVLC; 47 in. high by 21 in. wide (120 by 54 cm).

D2 A Louis XVI kingwood and palissander secrétaire à abattant, stamped N. Grevenich JME; 32 in. (81 cm) wide.

C3 A Louis XVI black lacquer secrétaire à abattant, late 18th century; 49 in. (101 cm) wide.

D4 A Louis XVI palissander secrétaire à abattant, stamped A.L. Gilbert, the panelled fall-front enclosing a fitted interior; 38 in. (97 cm) wide.

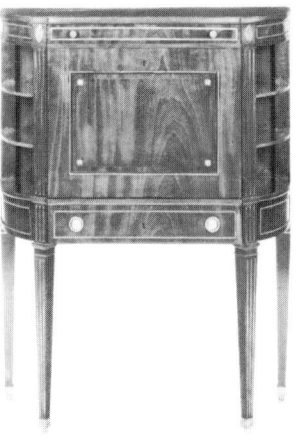

E5 A small brass-mounted mahogany secrétaire, in the manner of David Roentgen, c. 1780; 49 in. high by 38 in. wide (125 by 96 cm).

D6 A Louis XVI satinwood secrétaire cabinet, signed G. Dester, JME.; 53 in. high by 31 in. wide (135 by 78 cm).

C7 A Louis XVI ormolu-mounted secrétaire, stamped Nicholas Petit; 53 in. high by 29 in. wide (135 by 74 cm).

C8 A late Louis XVI citronnier secrétaire à abattant in the style of Adam Weisweiler; 48 in. high by 28 in. wide (122 by 71 cm).

D9 A Louis XVI mahogany cabinet, stamped twice J. Pafrat, the back with a secret door; 33 in. (86 cm) wide.

D10 A Louis XVI mahogany secrétaire à abattant, with marble top, above a frieze drawer; 55 in. high by 42 in. wide (140 by 105 cm).

D11 A Directoire ormolu-mounted secrétaire, in the style of Jacob Desmalta, with marble top above a frieze with ornate centrepiece, flanked by fluted angles surmounted by helmeted heads.

E12 An Empire ormolu-mounted secrétaire à abattant, with a long frieze drawer above panelled drop-front with fitted interior; 39 in. (99 cm) wide.

E 1 An Empire mahogany secrétaire à abattant, 51 in. (130 cm) high.

C 2 A Louis XVIII black lacquer ormolu-mounted secrétaire à abattant, 55 in. (140 cm) high.

E 3 A flame mahogany veneered secrétaire à abattant, *c.* 1820; 31 in. (78 cm) high.

D 4 A Charles X amboyna and ormolu-mounted secrétaire à abattant, with grey marble top above outcurved frieze, the front flap falling to reveal a fitted, mirrored interior with six small drawers, over a pair of cupboard doors with elaborate escutcheons, the whole on a rectangular plinth with beading to the top front edge.

E 5 A Louis-Philippe kingwood veneered small secrétaire à abattant, with a marble top to a flared frieze above a shallow serpentine front and sides, having gilt brass mounts, the fall front secrétaire with a fitted interior with four small drawers, cast brass handles, and four shaped drawers; 26 in. (65 cm) wide.

E 6 A tulipwood and trellis parquetry ormolu-mounted secrétaire à abattant, with marble top over a moulded frieze drawer, the pair of small panelled doors with pleated fabric, with fall front to a fitted interior, *c.* 1850; 56 in. high by 34 in. wide (142 by 56 cm).

E 7 A marquetry secrétaire à abattant, with galleried top, ornate fall flap and three drawers, 19th century.

E 8 A Louis XVI style tulipwood, kingwood and amaranth secrétaire à abattant, 19th century; 32 in. (81 cm) wide.

E 9 A Louis XVI style kingwood and tulipwood secrétaire, 19th century; 25 in. (63 cm) wide.

SETTEES & SOFAS
1690-1890

French settees of the 17th century have much in common with their contemporaries in the rest of Europe, but in the Régence and Louis XV periods their designs became emphatically French. The demand of the fashionable public for a wide variety of comfortable seat furniture seemed nearly insatiable and upholsterers' skills were at their peak as makers explored the possibilities of the new rococo style.

E3 A Louis XV settee with carved walnut frame, padded seat and back with open arms, covered in petit point needlework, above shaped apron with cabriole legs, straight legs at back, the whole piece studded.

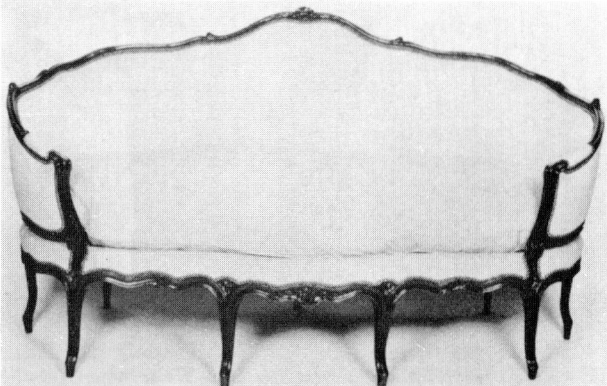

D4 A Louis XV beechwood canapé, with arched curved padded back and serpentine cushion-seat in moulded frame, the crest carved with a flowerhead flanked by trailing leaves and long foliate S-scrolls, the seat-rail similarly carved, on cabriole legs headed by flowerheads, upholstered in cream silk damask, mid 18th century; 83 in. (211 cm) wide.

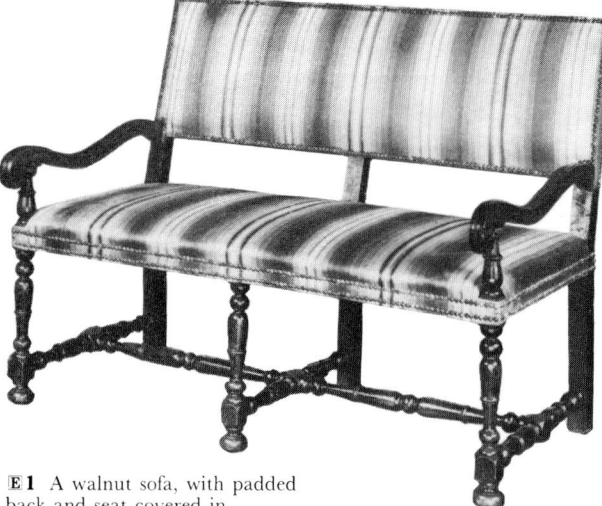

E1 A walnut sofa, with padded back and seat covered in 18th-century French Amberlene, curved scrolled arms, ornately turned legs and straight back legs all joined by stretchers, 17th century; 48 in. (119 cm) long.

D5 A Louis XV period canapé, with moulded wood frame, carved with flowers, with curved back and padded seat, small padded arm-rests, above elaborately carved apron, the whole piece extensively studded, on eight fluted cabriole legs; 64 in. (160 cm) long.

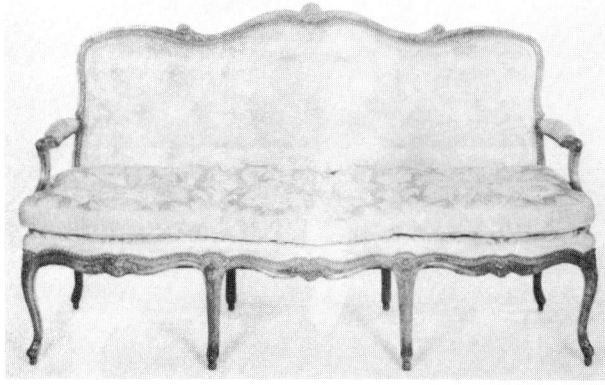

E2 An early Louis XV walnut canapé, stamped Heurtaud, with arched padded back and serpentine cushion-seat in moulded frame, on cabriole legs headed by flowerheads and with foliate feet, upholstered in yellow silk damask, mid 18th century; 68 in. (173 cm) wide.

E6 A Louis XV walnut canapé, with incurved padded arched back and serpentine cushion-seat in moulded frame, the crest carved with flowerheads and trailing leaves, on cabriole legs headed by flowerheads and scroll feet, upholstered in pale blue silk damask, mid 18th century.

D 1 A Louis XV grey-painted canapé à corbeille, with curved arched padded back and serpentine cushion seat in moulded frame, the crest centrally carved, the upholstered arms with voluted S-shaped supports, on cabriole legs, mid 18th century; 63 in. (161 cm) wide.

E 4 A Louis XVI blue and grey painted canapé with arched curved padded back and bowed seat covered in petit point needlework, in moulded frame on fluted tapering legs, headed by roundels; 72 in. (183 cm) wide.

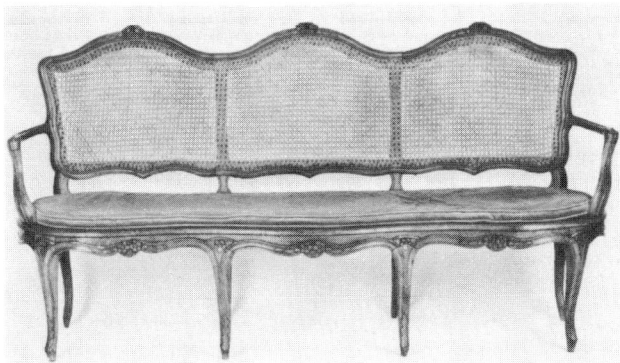

E 2 A Louis XVI walnut three-seat canapé, with curved canework back and seat, with open arms, the serpentine apron and back-rail carved with flowers, with blue velour cushion, on eight fluted cabriole legs; 65 in. (187 cm) wide.

E 5 A Louis XVI green-painted canapé à corbeille, stamped N. 9. Foliot, with curved padded back and cushion seat in moulded frame, on circular tapering stop-fluted legs, headed by paterae, upholstered in floral silk, late 18th century; 83 in. (207 cm) wide.

D 3 A Louis XVI giltwood settee, stamped Lelarge, with serpentine padded back and slightly bowed cushion seat in moulded beaded frame carved with leaf-tips, the crest crisply carved with forget-me-nots and rose leafs, the outcurved padded arms continuing to short stop-fluted circular tapering legs; 63 in. (160 cm) wide.

E 6 A Louis XVI grey-painted canapé à corbeille, with curved slightly arched padded back and bowed cushion seat in moulded fluted frame, the crest carved with bowed ribbon, on circular tapering stop-fluted legs headed by paterae, upholstered in yellow silk damask, late 18th century; 80 in. (203 cm) wide.

D 1 A Louis XVI giltwood canapé, with arched rectangular padded back and bowed cushion seat, in moulded and beaded frame, the crest carved with rope twist, the outscrolled upholstered arms with fluted columnar supports, carved with acanthus and headed by paterae, upholstered in yellow flame stitch; 75 in. (190 cm) wide.

C 4 A Louis XVI giltwood canapé, the frame by Louis-Charles Carpentier, the Beauvais tapestry covering depicting the "Quatre Parties du Monde", after designs by Eisen and L'Enfant; 74 in. (188 cm) wide.

E 2 A Louis XVI white painted canapé, stamped A.L. Meunier, with arched padded back and bowed cushion seat, in moulded and fluted frame carved with acanthus, on tapering legs headed by paterae, upholstered in pale blue silk; 53 in. (135 cm) wide.

E 5 A Louis XVI giltwood canapé, with rectangular padded back and bowed cushion seat, in moulded fluted frame, the top rail flanked by finials and crisply carved with guilloche centring rosettes, rope-twist and beading, the tapering legs headed by paterae, upholstered in pale blue velvet; 44 in. (110 cm) wide.

D 3 A Louis XVI white and blue painted marquise, stamped M. Jullien, the moulded frame carved with acanthus, upholstered in peach silk damask, *c.* 1775; 35 in. (90 cm) wide.

E 6 A "Louis XV" walnut canapé, with a moulded top rail centred by flowers, above a padded back and sprung serpentine seat, with tapestry covers of garden scenes, on moulded cabriole legs, *c.* 1860; 60 in. (154 cm) wide.

E1 A "Louis XVI" giltwood settee, the padded back with leaf-carved top rail, with turned finials, similarly carved padded sides with leaf-carved terminals, the sprung seat on twist-turned legs, *c.* 1880.

E2 A "Louis XV" parcel-gilt walnut canapé, the moulded frame extensively carved with leaves, the padded back, seat and sides covered in widely striped material, late 19th century; 53 in. (134 cm) wide.

Daybeds

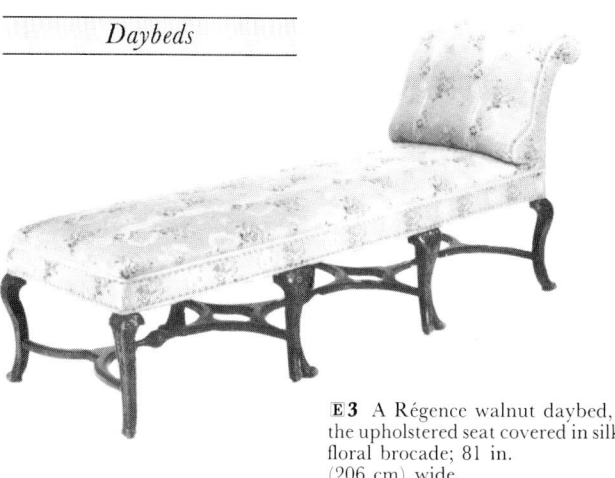

E3 A Régence walnut daybed, the upholstered seat covered in silk floral brocade; 81 in. (206 cm) wide.

E4 An early Louis XV daybed, the painted and parcel-gilt frame with shell and leaf carving, on cabriole legs and scrolled feet, *c.* 1725.

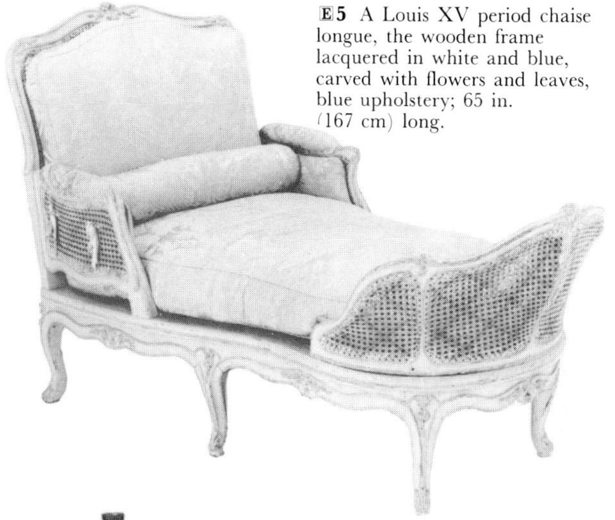

E5 A Louis XV period chaise longue, the wooden frame lacquered in white and blue, carved with flowers and leaves, blue upholstery; 65 in. (167 cm) long.

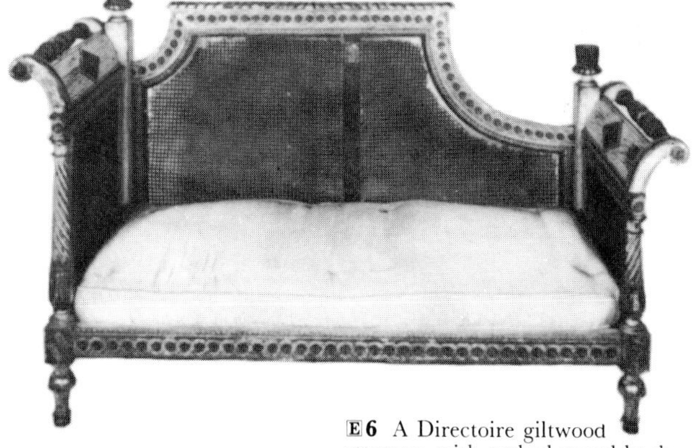

E6 A Directoire giltwood ottoman, with arched caned back and padded seat; 68 in. (172 cm) long.

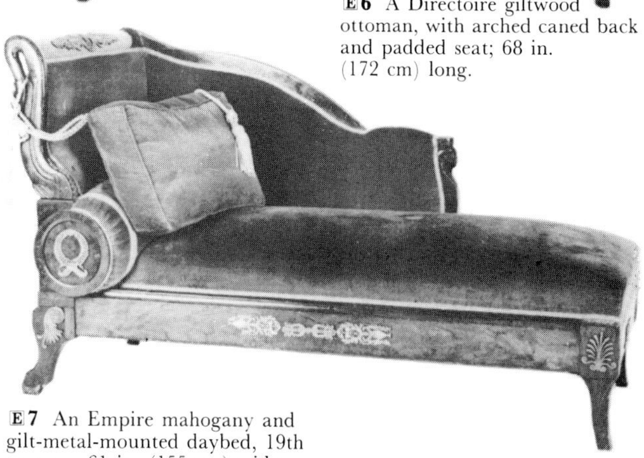

E7 An Empire mahogany and gilt-metal-mounted daybed, 19th century; 61 in. (155 cm) wide.

STANDS
1700-1880

Considerable and unjustified confusion arises from the number of names given to stands that could equally be small tables. To say that one should be called a torchère because it holds a candelabrum one day but a table ambulante the next because it does not is to insist too precisely on terms.

One kind of stand that is distinctively French however is the guéridon, made to support a light and named after the celebrated Moorish galley slave, Guéridon.

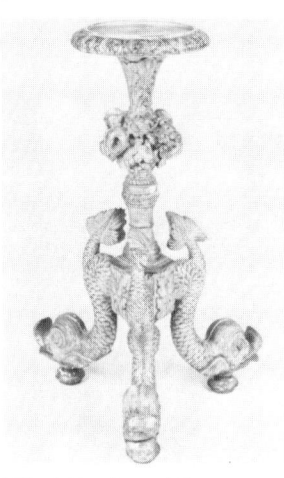

E1 A Continental Baroque giltwood torchère, with moulded top on a stem carved with acanthus emerging from a flower-filled basket above three dolphin supports, late 17th/early 18th century; 39 in. (101 cm) high.

E2 A Louis XVI grey and cream-painted jardinière, with lead-lined container, densely carved, on square tapering support carved with foliage, on splayed, quadripartite square legs, 20 in. (51 cm) wide.

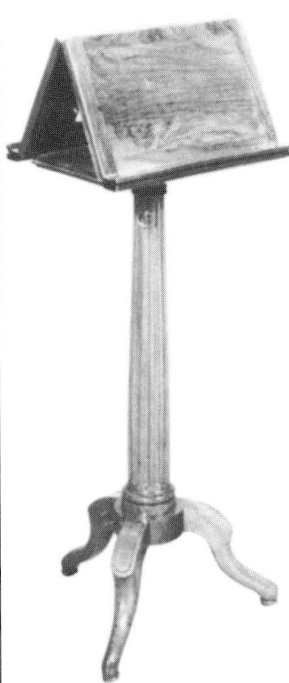

E3 A Louis XVI mahogany double music stand, stamped Levasseur JME, with a sliding double rectangular lectern, on circular fluted swelling columnar stem, springing from circular plinth supported on three curved legs, late 18th century; 15 in. (38 cm) wide.

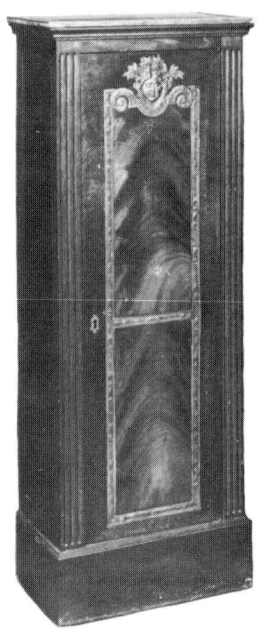

E4 A Louis XVI mahogany pedestal cabinet, the rectangular top crossbanded with satinwood, with a single fill-length ormolu-panelled cupboard door headed by a female mask between fluted angles, on a plinth base; 48 in. high by 18 in. wide (123 by 47 cm).

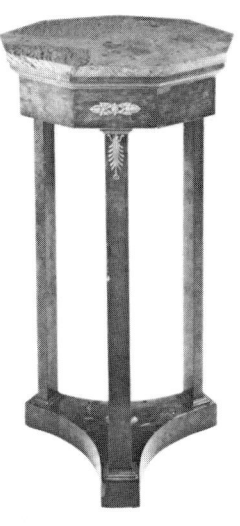

E5 An Empire mahogany jardinière stand, with marble top concealing a circular zinc liner; 19 in. (49 cm) wide.

E6 An Empire ormolu-mounted mahogany jardinière, the plant holder above three square legs on a concave triangular stretcher with central urn; 37 in. (92 cm) high.

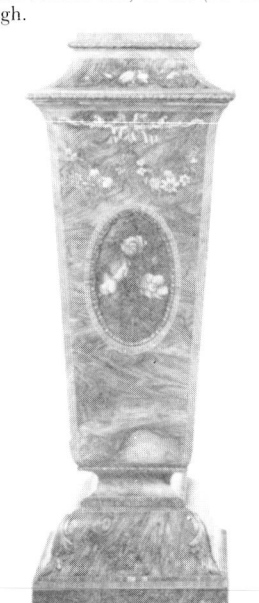

C7 A Napolean III walnut and marquetry plinth, the body inlaid with festoons and a roundel of flowers, c. 1850; 52 in. (133 cm) high.

E8 An ormolu-mounted ebony and boulle pedestal, with rectangular top above a moulded frieze, the inlaid tapering body supported on a plinth with arched base and ornate ormolu moulding to the corners; 56 in. (132 cm) high.

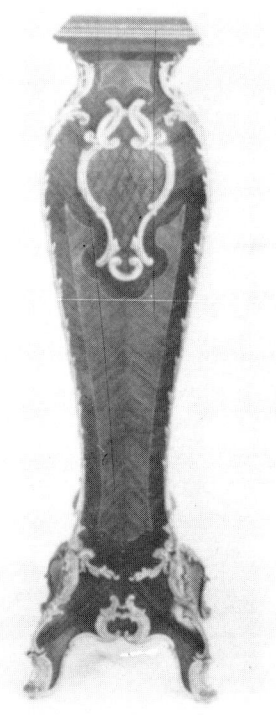

E9 A Louis XV style kingwood and tulipwood pedestal plant stand, of bombé outline, with inset breccia marble coffered top on a term graduating column with splayed downcurved legs; 49 in. (124 cm) high.

STOOLS
1770-1870

The stool or tabouret has come down in the world. In the royal court of France, even in the 17th century, chairs were reserved for monarchs and princes, and the right to sit on a stool was a privilege granted as a favour, for it meant sitting in the princely presence.

Even when chairs had become universal the stool did not go out of style, being useful if no longer honorific, and highly decorative when carved, gilded and upholstered.

E1 A stool, with a two-plank walnut top, with moulded edge and chamfered underside, *c.* 1670; 26 in. high by 25 in. wide (37 by 32 cm).

E2 A Louis XIV giltwood stool, on S-scroll legs joined by cross-stretchers, *c.* 1680; 24 in. (61 cm) wide.

E3 A Régence giltwood tabouret, the seat-rails and legs well-carved, *c.* 1730; 23 in. (59 cm) wide.

D4 A Régence grey-painted banquette, the moulded frame with crisply carved frieze on cabriole legs with hooved feet, early 18th century; 44 in. (113 cm) wide.

E5 A Louis XV giltwood tabouret, attributed to Jean-Baptiste Tilliard, *c.* 1750; 28 in. (72 cm) wide.

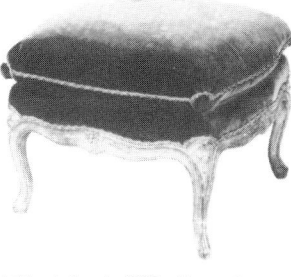

E6 A Louis XV giltwood tabouret, with carved seat-rail on cabriole legs, *c.* 1750; 23 in. (58 cm) wide.

E7 A Louis XV giltwood tabouret, with crisply carved seat-rail on cabriole legs, mid 18th century.

E8 A Louis XV beechwood tabouret, with moulded frame carved with cartouche at centre, on cabriole legs with acanthus at knee, on scroll feet, late 18th century; 21 in. (54 cm) wide.

E9 A Directoire amboyna and purpleheart tabouret, with conforming X-shaped frame, the arms carved with swans' heads, *c.* 1780; 26 in. (66 cm) wide.

E10 An Empire green-painted and parcel-gilt tabouret, stamped Lebrun, with upholstered seat on X-shaped fielded supports carved with a central rosette flanked by stiff-leaves, on gadrooned feet, early 19th century; 28 in. (71 cm) wide.

Tabourets and Banquettes

It is only the fine details of turning and stretchering that distinguish the joined stools of each country in the 16th and 17th centuries, but the carved scrolling legs and stretchers of no. 2 below show the beginnings of a uniquely French style that was to be highly influential in adjacent countries.

The 18th century saw a lightness peculiar to France, an effect underpinned by the durable elegance of the Régence period — the work of such masters as Pierre Le Pautre and Claude Audran, maintained later by such figures as Nicolas Pineau and A.J. Meissonnier.

Towards the end of this period of individuality, the forms of seat furniture blended once more as the fashion for the neoclassical in all its forms became universal; thus stools such as nos 9, 10 or 12 might have been made in Italy or England as well as in France.

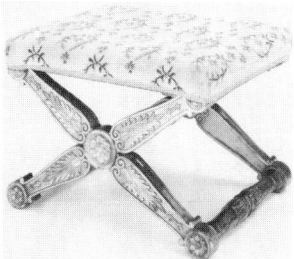

D11 An Empire period stool, in carved and gilt wood, with palmette decoration.

E12 A Charles X mahogany X-framed stool, on curved frames with ring-turned stretchers; 19 in. (50 cm) wide.

E13 A carved giltwood stool, with a fluted frieze and spirally fluted legs, 19th century; 20 in. (52 cm) diameter.

TABLES
1650-1900

While provincial tables were made to suit a variety of uses, in the sophisticated centres 18th-century cabinet-makers were called on to produce an enormous variety of small, exquisitely made tables, each theoretically ascribed to a specific purpose; there were even distinctions among kinds of work table.

Nothing could be more distinctively French than these fine pieces, and few objects could better demonstrate the complexity of the etiquette governing the everyday life of the beau monde.

Centre tables

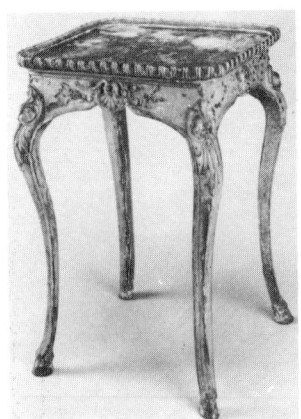

E1 An early Louis XV painted and carved centre table, the square dished top with rounded corners, and gadrooned border, the serpentine frieze ornately carved, raised on cabriole legs, *c.* 1735; 20 in. (50 cm) wide.

E2 A Louis XV centre table, with hinged leather inset opening to reveal a simple veneered interior, with panelled frieze, the exterior now lacquered with rococo gilt-bronze mounts, on cabriole legs, mid 18th century; 30 in. (76 cm) wide.

E3 A late Louis XVI mahogany centre table, with inset marble top and panelled frieze; 31 in. (80 cm) wide.

E4 An Empire mahogany centre table, with grey marble top, above a triangular base, *c.* 1800; 38 in. (95 cm) wide.

E5 An Empire bronze and ormolu centre table, with portor marble top, 34 in. (88 cm) wide.

E6 An Empire brass and bronze mounted centre table, *c.* 1810; 28 in. high by 30 in. wide (71 by 76 cm).

E7 A mahogany Charles X centre table, with brass-inlaid top, 45 in. (114 cm) wide.

E8 A Napoleon III burr yew-wood marquetry centre table; 27 in. high by 42 in. wide (67 by 105 cm).

D9 A Napoleon III ormolu-mounted and porcelain centre table, the top with a plaque depicting Louis XVI; 31 in. high by 29 in. wide (77 by 72 cm).

E10 A Louis XVI ormolu mahogany and marble centre table; 32 in. high by 47 in. wide (81 by 120 cm).

E11 A boulle centre table, inset with brass, red tortoiseshell and silver, *c.* 1870; 28 in. high by 28 in. wide by 18 in. deep (70 by 70 by 45 cm).

D12 A Louis XVI style ormolu and mahogany centre table, in the style of Weisweiler, with inset leather top, conforming frieze with fielded panelled drawer, late 19th century; 31 in. (78 cm) wide.

Console tables

D 1 A Louis XIV giltwood side table, with mottled green and white marble top; 32 in. high by 41 in. wide (82 by 106 cm).

E 2 A Louis XIV carved giltwood side table, with red marble top, *c.* 1700; 31 in. high by 49 in. wide (79 by 123 cm).

D 3 A Régence giltwood console table, with marble top, early 18th century; 37 in. (94 cm) wide.

D 4 A Régence oak console, with a serpentine marble top, early 18th century; 45 in. (115 cm) wide.

D 5 A Régence period console table, with red Languedoc marble top; 35 in. high by 69 in. wide (88 by 177 cm).

D 6 An early Louis XV giltwood console table, with serpentine breccia marble top, early 18th century; 43 in. (110 cm) wide.

E 7 A Louis XV carved giltwood console table, with marble top, *c.* 1735; 34 in. high by 53 in. wide (87 by 135 cm).

E 8 A Louis XV giltwood console table, with serpentine marble top, mid 18th century; 37 in. (95 cm) wide.

E 9 A Louis XV giltwood console table, with serpentine marble top, mid 18th century; 28 in. (72 cm) wide.

E 10 A Louis XV giltwood console table, with liver and grey marble top, mid 18th century; 48 in. (120 cm) wide.

E 11 A Louis XV giltwood console table, with grey and white marble top; 43 in. (110 cm) wide.

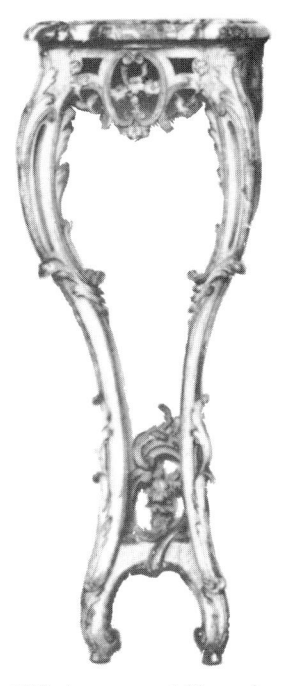

E 12 A cream and blue painted petite console table, with Sicilian jasper top, mid 18th century; 32 in. (81 cm) high.

E 13 A Louis XV giltwood petite console table, with breccia marble top, mid 18th century; 12 in. (32 cm) wide.

D 14 A Louis XV giltwood side table, with moulded serpentine mottled green marble top, the frieze centred by twin C-scrolls, on in-scrolled legs joined by shaped stretchers; 48 in. (123 cm) wide.

D 15 A Louis XVI mahogany console desserte table with white marble top, the frieze containing a drawer flanked by curved swing drawers, *c.* 1780; 35 in. (89 cm) high.

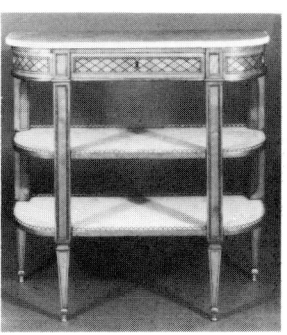

D 16 A Louis XVI bois citronnier and parquetry console desserte table; 39 in. high by 41 in. wide (99 by 105 cm).

E 17 A Louis XVI brass-inlaid mahogany console desserte table, with mottled grey marble top, with three-quarter gallery above a frieze drawer fitted with lion's-head pulls, on ebonized flute columns joined by a shelf, *c.* 1785; 38 in. (95 cm) wide.

D 1 A Louis XVI giltwood pier table, with moulded brèche violette marble top, the fluted tapering legs joined by a beaded stretcher, *c.* 1775; 56 in. (143 cm) wide.

E 3 A Louis XVI grey-painted console table, with carrara marble top; 35 in. (88 cm) wide.

E 2 A Louis XVI ormolu-mounted mahogany console table, with incurved canted sides, the galleried top of wine and ochre marble, *c.* 1780; 34 in. high by 22 in. wide (80 by 57 cm).

E 4 A Louis XVI mahogany console table, in the style of Saunier, with a white marble top, *c.* 1780; 35 in. (89 cm) high.

E 5 A Directoire tulipwood console table, stamped J. Stockel, with three-quarter galleried eared bowed breccia marble top, above a conforming frieze with one long and two short drawers, the tapering legs joined by galleried undertier, with circular ormolu sabots; 53 in. (34 cm) wide.

E 6 An Empire mahogany and ormolu-mounted console table, with chafered rectangular top, the frieze mounted with ormolu relief showing three frolicking putti with classical urns; 35 in. (89 cm) wide.

E 8 An Empire mahogany work table, the lid enclosing fitted interior above writing drawer and slide; 20 in. (52 cm) wide.

E 7 An Empire parcel-ebonized and mahogany pier console table, the marble top above chimera-carved supports before a mirror, on shaped plinth, *c.* 1825; 37 in. (95 cm) wide.

E 9 A Grohe mahogany console table, with grey-veined marble top, above a single frieze drawer centred by a ribbon-tied leaf-cast mount, with mirror back, *c.* 1870; 35 in. (90 cm) high.

Dining tables

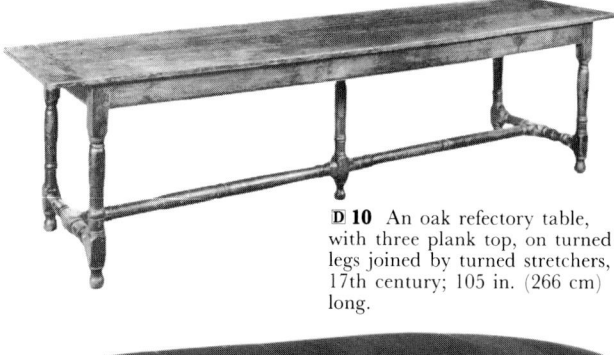

D 10 An oak refectory table, with three plank top, on turned legs joined by turned stretchers, 17th century; 105 in. (266 cm) long.

E 11 A Louis XVI mahogany extension dining table, with oval twin-flap top on square tapering chamfered legs, with casters; 29 in. high by 55 in. wide (74 by 141 cm).

E1 A Louis XVI mahogany extending dining table, forming a semi-circular side table when closed; 42 in. (105 cm) wide.

E2 A Louis XVI mahogany extension dining table, with oval twin-flap top; 86 in. (218 cm) wide, extended.

E3 A Napoleon III ebonized pedestal dining table, the inlaid segmented foliate brass circular tilt top with gilt metal borders, on turned bulbous column; 51 in. (130 cm) diameter.

Display tables

E4 A display table, with various woods, the shaped top with brass gallery, ornately decorated with flowers, *c.* 1840.

E5 An Empire-style ormolu-mounted mahogany specimen table, with velvet-lined interior, the frieze and tapering legs with classical leaf and mask mounts, *c.* 1880; 21 in. (53 cm) diameter.

E6 A Louis XV-style ormolu-mounted and giltwood vitrine table, the serpentine glazed top above the conforming case with a hinged door, on cabriole legs ending in sabots; 21 in. (52 cm) long.

E7 An ebonized brass mounted curio cabinet, with frieze drawer, the cabriole legs ending in tiny hoof feet; 29 in. (72 cm) high.

E8 An Empire revival mahogany and brass mounted bijouterie table, *c.* 1890; 30 in. (76 cm) high.

E9 A mahogany and floral marquetry bijouterie table, with hinged top, over velvet lining, *c.* 1900; 25 in. (63 cm) high.

Dressing tables

E10 A Louis XV provincial fruitwood dressing table, the triple-flap top with a mirror; 41 in. (105 cm) wide.

D11 A Louis XV kingwood and marquetry dressing table, the centre hinged flap backed by a mirror; 36 in. (91 cm) wide.

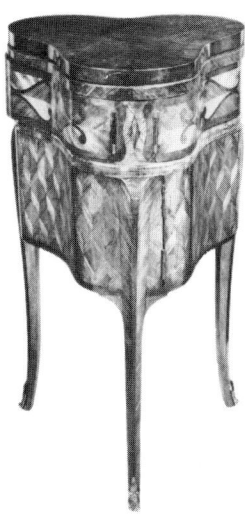

D12 A Louis XV kingwood dressing table, of heart-shaped outline, the hinged top with a mirror; 29 in. (74 cm) high.

D13 A Louis XV kingwood tulipwood and marquetry dressing table, by B. Durand, with mirror slide; 35 in. (89 cm) wide.

E14 A Louis XV marquetry dressing table, the hinged mirror flanked by two wells.

E15 A Louis XV provincial dressing table, the top with central sliding mirror.

E1 A Louis XVI mahogany table de toilette, with mirror-backed hinged top and marble-lined fitted interior; 31 in. high by 38 in. wide (79 by 98 cm).

E2 An Empire ormolu-mounted burr-maple washstand, with carrara marble top; 32 in. (82 cm) wide.

Games tables

D3 A Louis XV kingwood and marquetry card table, with swivelling, hinged top, *c.* 1750; 27 in. (69 cm) wide.

D4 A Louis XV kingwood and tulipwood tric-trac table, stamped I C Saunier JME twice, *c.* 1750; 45 in. (116 cm) wide.

D5 A Louis XV amaranth tric-trac table, stamped Lardin JME, with reversible baize- and leather-lined top enclosing an ebony-lined backgammon well, the shaped frieze with two drawers each side; 48 in. (123 cm) wide.

E6 A Louis XV kingwood and parquetry table, with cube-pattern inlay to top and frieze; 28 in. (71 cm) wide.

E7 A Louis XVI mahogany tric-trac table, stamped D L Ancellet, late 18th century; 44 in. (113 cm) wide.

E8 A Louis XVI brass-mounted mahogany card table, with pull-out top, *c.* 1780; 28 in. high by 34 in. wide (72 by 80 cm).

E9 A Louis XVI brass-mounted mahogany games table, with double-hinged semi-circular top, and panelled frieze, *c.* 1785; 43 in. (109 cm) wide.

E10 A boulle card table, the top swivelling and opening to reveal a baize-lined interior, with moulded cabriole legs, *c.* 1860; 39 in. (101 cm) wide.

E11 A boulle serpentine card table, the top opening to reveal a playing surface, *c.* 1870; 31 in. high by 37 in. wide (78 by 92 cm).

Guéridons

E12 A Louis XVI mahogany guéridon, the grey marble top with pierced gallery, the frieze with two drawers and two velvet-lined slides; 23 in. (60 cm) diameter.

E13 A Louis XVI period guéridon, the two tiers in grey marble with pierced gilt galleries, supported on legs decorated with amaranth and satinwood marquetry; 28 in. high by 29 in. diameter (70 by 73 cm).

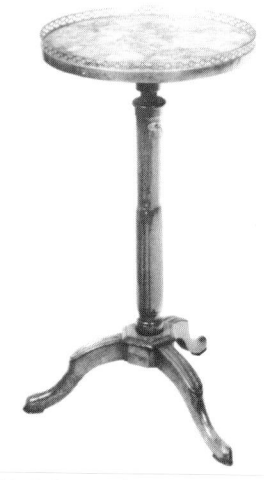

E14 A Louis XVI mahogany and adjustable guéridon, with galleried marble top and adjustable fluted stem, *c.* 1775; 16 in. (40 cm).

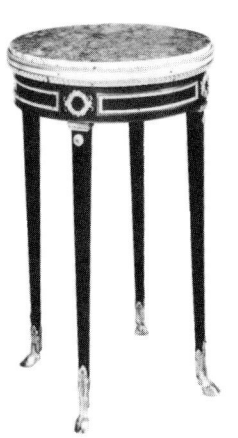

D 1 A Louis XVI ormolu-mounted ebony guéridon, with marble top above fielded panelled frieze, *c.* 1775; 30 in. high by 19 in. diameter (78 by 49 cm).

D 2 A Louis XVI ormolu guéridon, with marble top on ormolu tripartite lion monopodia straddling an undertier, above an urn flambeau, on casters, *c.* 1780; 28 in. (73 cm) wide.

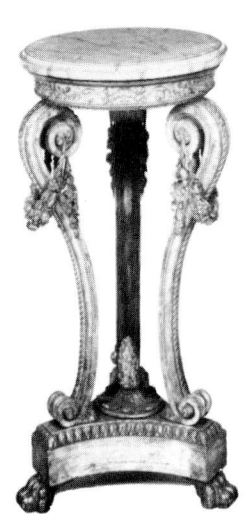

D 3 A Louis XVI giltwood guéridon, with inset-marble top and panelled frieze, on S-scrolled legs, on triangular plinth with paw feet, late 18th century; 34 in. (86 cm) high.

E 4 A Louis XVI satinwood guéridon, the brass-bound top crossbanded with amaranth, 30 in. (76 cm) wide.

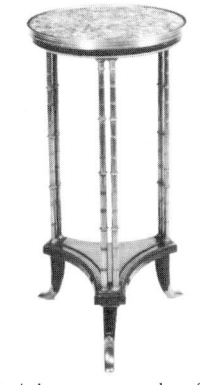

D 5 A brass-mounted guéridon, in the style of Adam Weisweiler, 19th century; 29 in. high by 26 in. diameter (72 by 65 cm).

E 6 A Louis XVI style gilt-metal guéridon, the marble top with pierced gallery over steel frieze, supported on tripartite legs centring a stem; 27 in. (68 cm) diameter.

E 7 A Directoire-style patinated bronze and ormolu guéridon, with marble top above engine-turned frieze, on tripartite ringed legs; 23 in. (59 cm) diameter.

D 8 A Louis XV porcelain-mounted parquetry table à café, attributed to R.V.L.C., 27 in. high by 12 in. wide at the top (69 by 31 cm).

D 9 A Louis XV kingwood parquetry table à ouvrage, stamped IP Latz and AF, with a hinged top quarter-veneered, enclosing four wells, the frieze with a fitted side drawer, on cabriole legs; 17 in. (43 cm) wide.

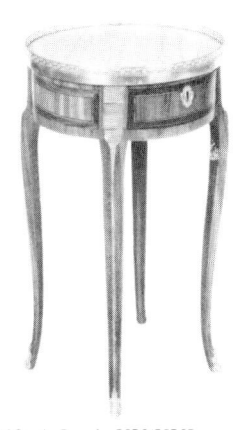

E 10 A Louis XV/XVI tulipwood and marquetry table ambulante, with marble top over a conforming frieze with a short crossbanded drawer; 16 in. (42 cm) diameter.

E 11 A Louis XVI mahogany petite bouillotte table, late 18th century; 23 in. (59 cm) diameter.

E 12 A Louis XV-style ormolu-mounted kingwood and tulipwood table ambulante, late 19th century; 22 in. (55 cm) diameter.

E 13 A Louis XV-style kingwood and ormolu-mounted occasional table, *c.* 1900; 33 in. (54 cm) diameter.

E 14 A marquetry table, signed Gallé; 29 in. (72 cm) high.

Work tables

D 1 A Louis XV black lacquer table en chiffonière, with breccia marble top, mid 18th century; 16 in. (40 cm) wide.

E 2 A Louis XV kingwood table en chiffonière, the back with rectangular sliding silk screen, mid 18th century; 16 in. (42 cm) wide.

D 3 A Louis XV tulipwood and marquetry table en chiffonière, stamped H. Hanson, with liver, beige and brown marble top, mid 18th century; 20 in. (51 cm) wide.

D 4 A Louis XV marquetry table en chiffonière, inlaid with sprays of flowers on a stained pearwood ground, *c.* 1760; 17 in. (44 cm) wide.

E 5 A Louis XV tulipwood table à rognon, with kidney-shaped top, above arched feet; 32 in. (81 cm) wide.

E 6 A Louis XV mahogany table en chiffonière, *c.* 1770; 27 in. (69 cm) high.

C 7 A Louis XV amaranth and marquetry table en chiffonière, 15 in. (38 cm) wide.

D 8 A late Louis XV chiffonière, in mahogany, with ormolu mounts, signed J.L. Michaut; 67 in. high by 22 in. wide (170 by 33 cm).

D 9 A Louis XV/Louis XVI Transitional parquetry table en chiffonière, with three drawers, *c.* 1775; 30 in. high by 18 in. wide (75 by 45 cm).

D 10 A Louis XVI kingwood table en chiffonière, stamped C. Topino, with white marble top, *c.* 1770; 29 in. high by 15 in. wide (75 by 38 cm).

E 11 A Louis XVI kingwood table en chiffonière, with galleried oval white marble top, 18 in. (47 cm) wide.

E 12 An ormolu-mounted mahogany vide-poche table, in Louis XVI style, mid 19th century; 30 in. high by 29 in. wide (75 by 74 cm).

D 13 An ormolu-mounted mahogany tricoteuse, of Louis XVI style, with fluted tapering legs joined by looped stretchers; 26 in. (66 cm) wide.

E 14 A marquetry and parquetry tricoteuse, in late Louis XVI style, 19th century; 30 in. (76 cm) long.

Writing tables

E 1 An early Louis XV rosewood writing table, the rectangular top inlaid with a central lozenge framed by chevron-pattern borders mounted with a matted ormolu frame; 26 in. high by 27 in. wide (67 by 70 cm).

D 2 A Louis XV black and gold lacquer writing table, with serpentine ormolu-edged leather-lined top and shaped frieze; 33 in. (84 cm) wide.

D 3 A Louis XV tulipwood writing table, the frieze with a side drawer, on cabriole legs headed by ormolu foliate C-scroll cartouches; 32 in. (82 cm) wide.

D 4 A Louis XV satinwood writing table, the frieze drawer with a red leather lined writing slide, *c.* 1750; 29 in. high by 32 in. wide (85 by 80 cm).

D 5 A Louis XV period rosewood veneered writing table, the fringe with drawer and slide; 28 in. high by 26 in. (72 by 73 cm).

D 6 A fine Louis XV kingwood and marquetry writing table, by J. Schmitz; 28 in. (73 cm) high.

D 7 A Louis XV/XVI tulipwood and marquetry writing table, mid 18th century; 26 in. (66 cm) wide.

D 8 A Transitional writing table, by Roger van der Cruse, with chamfered top; 18 in. (47 cm) wide.

E 9 A Louis XVI parquetry writing table, with galleried brown and grey mottled marble top; 15 in. (35 cm) wide.

D 10 A Louis XVI period writing table in rosewood, stamped S. Rebour; 30 in. high by 28 in. wide (73 by 70 cm).

D 11 A Louis XVI period writing table, with three frieze drawers, stamped J.H.Riesener; 31 in. (77 cm) high.

D 12 A Louis XVI tulipwood and parquetry writing table, late 18th century; 20 in. (51 cm) wide.

D 13 A Louis XVI tulipwood and parquetry writing table, stamped G.Cordie, late 18th century; 32 in. (81 cm) wide.

E 14 An Empire ebony writing table, with an inset leather top, *c.* 1820; 28 in. high by 38 in. wide (72 by 98 cm).

E 15 A satinwood writing table, the brass galleried top inlaid with strapwork, 19th century; 23 in. (59 cm) wide.

E 16 A Louis XV style-kingwood and marquetry writing table, the conforming frieze with a shaped rectangular drawer, 19th century; 24 in. (63 cm) wide.

GERMANY & AUSTRIA

The Italian Renaissance style reached Germany during the early 16th century but did not lead to the introduction of new types of furniture. Its decorative influence varied from region to region, although some national characteristics gradually emerged, such as the "facade" or architectural cabinet.

The customers for fine furniture in the 17th century were the prosperous merchants of the Hansa towns in the north and the numerous princes of the centre and south. In the north, where solid worth was valued more than ostentation, furniture forms changed slowly, but between the princely courts there was much rivalry to set a tone, and new styles were eagerly adopted from Italy and France.

During this time Augsburg established itself as a centre for the creative arts, producing extraordinary silver furniture in the baroque taste. The baroque was to dominate German furniture design until well into the 18th century, when the many enlightened rulers of German states turned enthusiastically to France and rococo.

FREDERICAN ROCOCO

Frederick the Great's palace of Sanssouci is perhaps the high point of German rococo. The name itself expresses the essential light-heartedness of the style and betrays the power of French influence in the arts.

A lavish use of marquetry exemplifies the most flamboyant German furniture from the late 18th century, running to such excesses that the pendulum was bound to swing the other way. Throughout Europe neoclassicism was to bite hard at overdone rococo and nowhere was it better interpreted than in the restrained Rhineland commodes and cabinet furniture. The new Empire style too was adopted with rapidity; fine work was produced by Raab at Würzburg and Roentgen at Berlin.

The 19th century witnessed the dominance of design for the middle classes, with the good-looking and practical Biedermeier style exemplifying the best of German furniture. The first wholly indigenous style, it lasted in its pure form only from 1815 to 1830, but its guiding principles of clean lines and fitness for purpose were to come to the fore again at the end of the century, when the founders of the Modern Movement reacted against mass-produced imitations of hand-made work.

BUFFETS 1580–1880

German buffets from the earliest times display an unmistakeable crispness to the execution of their architectural lines.

The deeply overhanging mouldings, whether to the cornice or to the serving board, over entablatures, pilasters and arcades are almost always of the highest quality and show a degree of fineness not found on contemporary furniture from other parts of Europe.

D 1 A south German walnut, ash and oak buffet, the central section with arched panelled back, late 16th century; 79 in. (200 cm) wide.

E 2 A south German inlaid oak buffet, 17th century; 40 in. high by 72 in. wide (101 by 180 cm).

E 3 A south German oak and fruitwood veneer buffet, 66 in. high, 51 in. wide, 23 in. deep (166 by 128 by 59 cm).

E 4 A German oak buffet, with two frieze drawers above ornately carved cupboard doors, mid 17th century; 56 in. high, 73 in. wide (140 by 182 cm).

E 5 A German oak dresser, with moulded and carved cornice and shelf above two carved panelled doors, on block feet, 18th century; 74 in. (185 cm) high.

E 6 A German oak sideboard, with plain top and three panelled doors, 18th century; 84 in. (221 cm) high.

E 7 A north German walnut and marquetry buffet, 53 in. (130 cm) wide.

E 8 A German walnut sideboard, ornately carved, with a marble top above four drawers with brass pulls and four carved panelled cupboard doors, 19th century; 84 in. (211 cm) high.

BUREAUX
1720-1860

German bureaux, which were made in a unique variety of forms, share the general characteristic of being imposing without necessarily being bulky.

Deeply serpentine chests are found surmounted by relatively small slant-front desks; substantial fall-fronts with cabinets of drawers over are supported on open stands.

Equally various are the forms of decoration – parquetry, marquetry and inlays of all kinds were used to the full.

D 1 A south German bureau cabinet, the top with arched cresting and stepped porcelain stands, the front enclosing a writing interior above three long drawers, 18th century; 91 in. high, 49 in. wide (227 by 124 cm)

E 2 A south German elm and walnut veneered bureau-on-chest, c. 1720; 37 in. high 38 in. wide (94 by 98 cm).

D 3 A south German walnut parquetry bureau cabinet, c. 1720; 85 in. high, 50 in. wide (216 by 128 cm).

E 4 A south German marquetry bureau, raised on scroll feet, early 18th century; 46 in. (114 cm) wide.

D 5 A German baroque walnut slant-front cabinet, c. 1725; 66 in. high, 46 in. wide (165 by 115 cm).

D 6 A German baroque walnut bureau cabinet, c. 1730; 70 in. high by 50 in. wide (175 by 125 cm).

E 7 A German baroque walnut inlaid bureau, c. 1730; 45 in. high by 49 in. wide (112 by 114 cm).

E 8 A south German rococo fruitwood and parquetry slant-front desk, the lid enclosing five drawers, c. 1740; 42 in. high by 50 in. wide (105 by 125 cm).

D 9 A south German walnut and parquetry bureau cabinet, c. 1740; 67 in. high by 46 in. wide (202 by 117 cm).

E 10 A south German walnut bureau cabinet-on-stand, the bureau section with moulded fall-front enclosing a fitted interior, the later oak stand with hipped cabriole legs, c. 1740; 41 in. high by 28 in. wide (106 by 71 cm).

E 11 A south German rococo walnut bureau, the crest containing a single concave drawer, above a central cupboard, a large conforming drawer above the drop-front bureau, flanked by two small drawers, 18th century; 79 in. high by 84 in. wide (197 by 210 cm).

E 12 A south German walnut serpentine-fronted bureau, with crossbandings and stringings, the fall front with fitted interior of drawers and lockers, 18th century; 41 in. (102 cm).

C1 A German softwood bureau, with cabinet on top, with various veneers and mother-of-pearl inlay, the sloping top opening to reveal pigeonholes and drawers, 18th century; 90 in. (230 cm) high.

E2 An Austrian Louis XV walnut veneered bureau, the flap enclosing four drawers and a pigeonhole, 18th century; 43 in. (108 cm) wide.

E3 A south German walnut bureau cabinet, veneered with panels of figured walnut, outlined with ebony, boxwood and oak, *c.* 1750; 83 in. (211 cm) high.

D4 A south German walnut and burr-walnut bureau cabinet, with arched moulded cornice above two shaped and fielded cupboard doors, the base with solid cylinder front enclosing ten various-shaped drawers, mid 18th century; 49 in. (124 cm) wide.

E5 A German Louis XV walnut veneered bombé bureau, the sloping top revealing drawers and pigeonholes inlaid in bone and ivory with hunting scenes, the bombé sides inlaid with hearts, 18th century; 42 in. (105 cm) wide.

E6 A south German walnut bureau, with boxwood inlay and angle crossbanding, enclosing a simple interior of small drawers with original brass handles, with a pull-out slide above three serpentine shaped drawers, and on small cabriole legs, 18th century; 45 in. (112 cm) wide.

D7 A south German walnut bureau cabinet, with double domed moulded cornice, over two cupboard doors inlaid in fruitwood, mid 18th century; 77 in. high by 43 in. wide (196 by 109 cm).

B8 A German walnut veneered and crossbanded brass-mounted bureau cabinet, the central arched door enclosing shelves, 18th century; 85 in. (218 cm) high.

C9 A German walnut veneered, crossbanded and fruitwood parquetry inlaid bureau cabinet, 18th century; 81 in. (205 cm).

E10 A German pine bureau cabinet, the panelled flap enclosing a fitted interior, 97 in. (246 cm) high; *c.* 1750.

C11 A south German walnut bureau cabinet, the base enclosing an oak fitted interior, mid 18th century; 90 in. (113 cm) high.

E12 A south German walnut bureau cabinet, the sloping front enclosing a fitted interior, mid 18th century; 80 in. (203 cm) high;

E 1 A south German walnut, crossbanded and parquetry bureau cabinet, 18th century; 45 in. (113 cm) wide.

A 2 A south German walnut and parquetry bureau cabinet, c. 1760; 112 in. high by 55 in. wide (285 by 140 cm) wide.

D 3 A German neoclassical mahogany cylinder bureau, late 18th century; 45 in. (114 cm).

E 4 A south German walnut and inlaid bureau cabinet, c. 1800; 73 in. high by 54 in. wide (185 by 138 cm).

D 5 A Biedermeier mahogany cylinder cabinet, c. 1820; 83 in. high by 44 in. wide (211 by 110 cm).

E 6 A German provincial oak bureau, of architectural form, early 19th century; 75 in. (190 cm) high.

E 7 A German mahogany cyclinder bureau, enclosing drawers, shelves and a baize-lined slide, with satinwood inlay, c. 1820; 50 in. high by 56 in. wide (128 by 142 cm).

E 8 A Biedermeier walnut roll-top bureau, the upper section with central fall front panel crested by scrolling foliage and an eagle, opening to fitted interior, the cylinder desk with drawers, doors and a leather-lined slide, c. 1835; 78 in. high by 58 in. wide (198 by 147 cm).

E 9 A German serpentine bombé marquetry bureau de dame, the flap inlaid with a lion, the interior inlaid with foliage, books and scrolls signed Louis, inset with six serpentine short drawers, late 19th century; 39 in. high by 24 in. wide (99 by 62 cm).

German Inlay Work

The large bureau cabinet with its multiplicity of surfaces is an ideal vehicle to show off the skills of the marquetry layer; all the more so if, like the great German cabinets it has a profusion of convex, concave and serpentine lines.

Among the greatest exponents of this art were the Spindler brothers who incorporated mother of pearl, silver and ivory into the pieces they created for Frederick the Great at Potsdam and Berlin.

The two Roentgens, Abraham and his son David, established an even finer reputation, and are recognized as probably the finest German cabinet-makers on record. It was the younger Roentgen whose delicate execution of marquetry designs was to influence craftsmen of the next 50 years.

The skill of unrecorded makers — as guild regulations required, very few German pieces are signed — who created almost unbelievably fine work should not go unsung. Nos 6 and 8 on page 513 and no. 9 on the facing page for example show marquetry and parquetry of exceptional quality.

E 10 A German parcel gilt and walnut writing table, c. 1880; 48 in. high by 44 in. wide (122 by 112 cm).

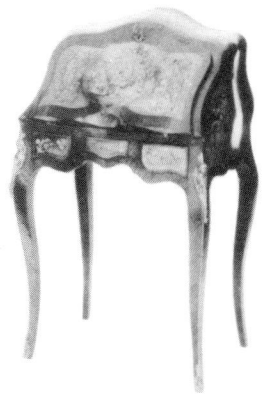

E 11 A German kingwood and marquetry bureau de dame, of bombé form, inlaid with armorial strapwork, late 19th century.

CABINETS
1600-1900

German cabinets are of two main types – those on stands and those on chest or cupboard bases. While both types were functional, at least in origin, the finest examples were created as display pieces in their own right.

Imported as well as native panels and paintings were incorporated into the doors and drawer fronts of such pieces. Traditionally the most elaborately conceived and finely executed cabinets were made in Augsburg and Nuremberg.

E3 An Ulm marquetry cabinet, the rectangular hinged lid enclosing a well, above a pair of cupboard doors enclosing a cupboard and five small drawers, the interior inlaid with various architectural perspective ruin-landscapes, *c.* 1600; 36 in. high by 19 in. (91 by 48 cm) wide.

C1 A fine and rare late Renaissance German cabinet, the upper part with an overhanging cresting supported by carved figure corbels, with a splayed cupboard at the centre and well-carved figures of the Virgin and Child standing in niches, *c.* 1600; 72 in. (183 cm) high.

E4 A South German walnut cabinet, the cupboard doors opening to reveal a number of small drawers with pictorial inlay of buildings, the stand with straight square legs, 17th century; 27 in. (66 cm) wide.

E2 A German walnut cabinet, the moulded cornice with a sliding frieze enclosing three secret drawers, a cupboard opening to reveal 20 painted and gilded drawers, the plinth base with pad feet, probably Cologne, 17th century; 69 in. high by 41 in. (179 by 119 cm) wide.

E5 A South German ebonized wood and ivory jewel cabinet, with hinged doors opening to reveal eight short drawers over a long drawer, decorated with trophies, scrollwork and grotesques, with iron hinges, handles, drawer-pulls and lock, mid 17th century; 14 in. (36 cm) long.

E6 A German ebony veneered table cabinet, the fall front with central brass panel engraved with a lady in medallion surrounded by birds and scrolling foliage, 17th century; 18 in. high by 24 in. wide (48 by 60 cm).

E7 A rare Swiss pewter inlaid walnut cabinet, with three small drawers and turned legs on bun feet, *c.* 1670; 62 in. high by 47 in. wide (159 by 120 cm).

D8 A German ebony and boulle cabinet-on-stand of breakfront form with panelled back, second half of the 17th century; 74 in. high, 72 in. wide (188 by 183 cm).

E 1 A fine German walnut coin cabinet, in two stages, each with a fall front, the upper with four, the lower with eight fitted drawers set with engraved horn panels, the front and sides set with ebony panels, *c.* 1700; 20 in. high by 13 in. wide (50 by 33 cm).

D 4 A German stained burr-elm cabinet-on-stand, the central cupboard enclosing a cupboard and drawers, early 18th century; 62 in. (133 cm) wide.

D 5 A rare German red-japanned hanging cupboard, *c.* 1750; 54 in. high by 33 in. wide (137 by 80 cm).

D 9 A German walnut veneered two-tier cabinet, both sections with brass carrying handles, 18th century; 84 in. (217 cm) high.

E 2 A German walnut and crossbanded cabinet-on-chest, the arched pediment with raised top, the pair of panelled doors enclosing a lined interior with shelves and an arrangement of small drawers, above shaped bracket feet, *c.* 1700; 82 in. high by 45 in. wide (208 by 115 cm).

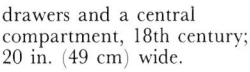

E 6 A south German walnut and satinwood table cabinet, having a rising top, the doors enclosing six drawers and a central compartment, 18th century; 20 in. (49 cm) wide.

E 10 A German walnut veneered breakfront cabinet, with four short drawers above curved shaped alcove, with heavy barley-twist turned legs united by stretchers, 18th century; 54 in. (135 cm) wide.

E 3 A German walnut veneered table cabinet, with doors and sides crossbanded and inlaid in ebony with strapwork, maple veneered interior, early 18th century; 23 in. high by 20 in. wide (60 by 50 cm).

D 7 A south German rococo walnut cabinet, with moulded broken arch pediment, mid 18th century.

C 8 An important south German writing cabinet, the serpentine superstructure with a drawer in the arched and carved cresting, the serpentine-fronted cupboard door inlaid with a coat-of-arms above a medallion showing a monastery, flanked by carved pilasters, mid 18th century; 78 in. high by 56 in. wide (196 by 142 cm).

E 11 A south German miniature walnut cabinet, with a bowed door inlaid with a pair of figures under an arch, mid 18th century; 28 in. high by 22 in. wide (71 by 57 cm).

E 1 A German neoclassical walnut bookcase, the glazed doors enclosing adjustable shelves, *c.* 1780; 82 in. high by 46 in. wide (240 by 115 cm).

E 2 An Austrian walnut cabinet-on-chest, with floral and scrollwork marquetry, the chest with three long drawers, *c.* 1780; 74 in. high by 45 in. wide (188 by 112 cm).

D 3 A North German neoclassic mahogany library cabinet, the eight glazed cupboard doors enclosing shelves, the lower part with marble top, *c.* 1820; 95 in. wide (242 cm).

E 4 A German figured mahogany collector's cabinet, of secrétaire form, with fall front, *c.* 1820; 53 in. high by 37 in. wide (136 by 94 cm).

E 5 A Biedermeier fruitwood cabinet, the glazed cupboard door with wheel-shaped mullion, early 19th century; 64 in. high by 40 in. wide (163 by 103 cm).

E 6 A Biedermeier maple vitrine, with glazed red doors over a base with concave drawer, *c.* 1825; 64 in. high by 47 in. wide.

E 7 A German ebonized and marquetry cabinet, inlaid with ivory, and decorated with hunting scenes, early 19th century; 60 in. (152 cm) wide.

E 8 An Austrian sculptural walnut bookcase, by Mich. Orley of Vienna, the upper frieze high relief carved over three glazed doors to shelves, *c.* 1860; 120 in. high by 80 in. wide (305 by 203 cm).

E 9 A German tortoiseshell and ebony-mounted cabinet, the four doors bearing fielded tortoiseshell, ivory and ebony panels, mid 19th century; 32 in. (81 cm) wide.

E 10 A German baroque-style ormolu and porcelain-mounted walnut and tulipwood cabinet-on-stand, 19th century; 75 in. (190 cm) high.

E 11 A German walnut display cabinet with gilt-bronze mounts, *c.* 1880; 62 in. high by 25 in. wide (158 by 64 cm).

E 12 A German kingwood parquetry side cabinet, the top veneered with a basketweave pattern, *c.* 1900; 39 in. high by 48 in. wide (99 by 123 cm).

COFFERS & CHESTS
1530-1780

Substantial numbers of early German coffers have survived, partly because chests of this kind were made in large numbers, being essential furniture in every home that had linen or valuables to store, and partly because of the exceptionally sturdy construction of the traditional form.

The tradition of making marriage chests to contain dowries perpetuated the coffer well after this kind of furniture had fallen from fashionable favour.

D 1 A Westphalian iron-bound oak coffer, the hinged lid, sides and front with iron strapwork with rosettes, 16th century; 37 in. high by 77 in. wide (94 by 196 cm).

E 2 A German oak muniments chest, carved with a scene of Jesus turning the money-lenders out of the Temple, 16th century; 71 in. (180 cm) wide.

E 3 A German ironbound walnut chest, with hinged lid, late 16th century; 46 in. long (115 cm).

E 4 A Tyrolean painted pine coffer, the frieze panels painted with city landscapes, c. 1620; 32 in. high by 56 in. wide (81 by 143 cm).

E 5 A German painted iron strong box, with hinged strapwork lid, 17th century; 34 in. (88 cm) wide.

E 6 A Nuremberg iron chest, the interior with a small fitted chest with a false escutcheon, mid 17th century; 28 in. high by 41 in. wide (71 by 104 cm).

E 7 A South German or Swiss pine painted coffer, the top with two inset panels with a raised lozenge, mid 17th century; 56 in. (132 cm) wide.

E 8 A South German walnut bridal chest, with fitted interior, 17th century; 41 in. (103 cm) wide.

E 9 A German baroque inlaid and parcel-ebonized oak coffer, with hinged plank top, 17th century; 62 in. (157 cm) wide.

E 10 A German oak two-handled iron-banded strong box on later stand, the box c. 1700; 24 in. (59 cm) wide.

E 11 A Nuremberg iron casket, with hinged lid above ogee sides, c. 1720; 23 in. high by 33 in. wide (60 by 84 cm).

E 12 A North German painted chest on a stand, dated 1722; 38 in. high by 67 in. wide (97 by 170 cm).

E 13 A South German walnut and marquetry coffer, early 18th century; 45 in. (115 cm) wide.

E 14 A South German walnut and marquetry coffer, early 18th century; 26 in. (66 cm) wide.

E 15 A German walnut and inlaid domed-top coffer, 18th century; 44 in. (110 cm) wide.

E 16 A South German walnut and parquetry domed-top coffer, 18th century; 48 in. (119 cm) wide.

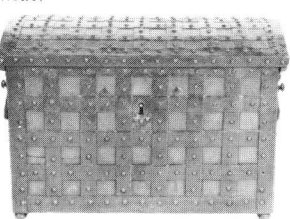

E 17 A German oak and iron-banded strong-box, with domed lid and carrying handles, 18th century; 25 in. (62 cm) wide.

E 18 A North German laburnum and mahogany coffer on walnut stand, mid 18th century; 53 in. (134 cm) wide.

E 19 A German scarlet and gold lacquer trunk, the sides with carrying handles, 18th century; 45 in. (114 cm) wide.

COMMODES
1680-1880

The German commode ranges from the rectangular and functional of early 18th-century Saxony to the flamboyant, bordering on grotesque, examples of mid-century Potsdam and Berlin.

The latter bear witness to the overriding influence of Paris, but distorted by the Germans' own inventiveness. Utility and even proportion were sacrificed in the name of novelty: for supreme examples of high-style rococo one has to look no further.

E1 An Austrian walnut and marquetry chest, of four drawers, late 17th century; 57 in. (145 cm) wide.

D2 A German Régence walnut and rosewood commode, the chamfered rectangular top inlaid with a Maltese cross within geometric circles, 44 in. (114 cm) wide.

E3 A south German rococo walnut and marquetry commode, with moulded serpentine rectangular crossbanded top, early 18th century; 44 in. (112 cm) wide.

E4 A German baroque walnut commode, the rectangular moulded top above three drawers, raised on bun feet, *c.* 1720; 52 in. (132 cm) wide.

E5 An Austrian walnut chest of drawers, with four panelled crossbanded drawers, early 18th century; 26 in. (65 cm) wide.

D6 An unusual German baroque walnut and boulle chest of drawers, with serpentine moulded top, *c.* 1730; 38 in. high by 45 in. wide (95 by 112 cm).

D7 A German gilt-bronze mounted walnut-veneered commode, with two short and two long drawers, *c.* 1740; 35 in. high by 55 in. wide (90 by 140 cm).

E8 A German walnut and elmwood parquetry chest, the low superstructure containing a drawer, the lower part with a double serpentine front containing three long drawers, *c.* 1740; 40 in. high by 46 in. wide (103 by 118 cm).

E9 A German rococo walnut chest of drawers, with moulded rectangular crossbanded top over three crossbanded drawers, raised on short cabriole legs, *c.* 1740; 46 in. (112 cm) wide.

E10 A German serpentine walnut commode, with a broad crossbanding and moulded top, the drawers outlined with simple ebony strapwork, *c.* 1740; 32 in. high by 48 in. wide (80 by 123 cm).

D11 A south German walnut fruitwood and parquetry commode, the shaped top inlaid with a spray of flowers, mid 18th century; 51 in. (131 cm) wide.

E12 A south German walnut commode, with shaped front, the top inlaid star design within three crossbands, 18th century.

E13 A south German baroque walnut and marquetry miniature commode, with serpentine rectangular top above four conforming crossbanded drawers, mid 18th century; 12 in. wide (30 cm).

E14 A German miniature softwood commode, veneered with various woods, the top with rounded front angles and an inlaid panel, the sides with similar panel, 18th century; 20 in. (48 cm) wide.

E15 A south German walnut serpentine chest, inlaid with geometric designs, mid 18th century; 47 in. (121 cm) wide.

D 1 A south German walnut commode, with crossbanded serpentine top inlaid with interlaced strapwork, with panels of stained burr-maple, mid 18th century; 33 in. high by 48 in. wide (85 by 123 cm).

C 2 A rare Bavarian rococo kingwood commode, with a serpentine-fronted russet marble top, above carved apron and cabriole legs, mid 18th century; 48 in. (122 cm) wide.

D 3 A German rococo parcel-gilt walnut commode, with moulded serpentine top above bombé front, mid 18th century; 51 in. (130 cm) wide.

E 4 A Swiss walnut serpentine chest, with crossbanded top, inlaid with arabesque marquetry, with three long drawers, on turned feet, mid 18th century; 35 in. (90 cm) wide.

E 5 A rosewood commode, with grey marble top over two small and two large drawers, 18th century; 32 in. high by 44 in. wide (84 by 112 cm).

E 6 A south German chestnut commode, of bombé outline, fitted with three long drawers with shaped panels, above scroll feet, 18th century; 34 in. high by 53 in. wide (85 by 135 cm).

D 7 A German walnut miniature commode, with C-scroll cresting, the secretaire on top, the shaped central section enclosing two small drawers, 18th century; 30 in. (76 cm) high.

E 8 An Austrian palisander and walnut veneered commode, stamped C.T.S., with inlaid escutcheons, second half of the 18th century; 38 in. high by 49 in. wide (93 by 123 cm).

E 9 A south German walnut veneered commode, 18th century; 34 in. high by 46 in. wide (87 by 114 cm).

E 10 A south German walnut crossbanded and parquetry commode, of arc-en-arbelette outline, inlaid with boxwood lines and ogee shaped geometric panels, 18th century; 48 in. (122 cm) wide.

E 11 A north German Transitional tulipwood and kingwood commode, with moulded breakfront tapering liver and grey marble top, above cabriole legs, late 18th century; 53 in. (135 cm) wide.

E 12 A south German walnut commode, with two drawers, on fluted and moulded square tapering supports, late 18th century; 32 in. high by 29 in. wide (81 by 75 cm).

E 13 A Louis XVI end-cut root elm and fruitwood parquetry petite commode, with grey and white marble top, *c.* 1780-1790; 32 in. (82 cm) wide.

E 14 A south German olivewood commode, the broadly crossbanded top above two drawers; 40 in. (40 cm) wide.

E 15 A German neoclassical walnut commode, the rectangular top over a projected drawer, *c.* 1800; 39 in. (100 cm) wide.

E 16 A Biedermeier maple chest of drawers, with stepped rounded rectangular top, early 19th century.

D 1 A Biedermeier fruitwood chest, the projecting frieze with drawer, *c.* 1825; 53 in. (135 cm) high.

E 2 A Biedermeier fruitwood and ebonized commode, the frieze drawer over two bowed drawers, on ebonized plinth, *c.* 1830; 49 in. (124 cm) wide.

E 3 A Biedermeier walnut commode, with crossbanded top, drawers similarly veneered, *c.* 1830; 52 in. (132 cm) wide.

E 4 A German rococo-style walnut and marquetry miniature commode, 19th century; 13 in. high, 14 in. wide (33 by 35 cm).

CUPBOARDS
1650-1870

The massive mid-17th century German cupboard was usually placed in the vestibule of the bourgeois house, being too large for the living room.

The balanced architectural appearance is sometimes countered by an over-wide cornice, the disproportion thus created being emphasized by the addition of bun feet.

The carving on mid-18th century Kleiderschränke in the Liège style often shows exceptional sensitivity.

E 5 A German walnut, pine and fruitwood hall cupbard, mid 17th century; 73 in. (186 cm).

E 6 A north German oak and parquetry cupboard, with drawer, on flat bun feet, 17th century; 73 in. (185 cm) high.

E 7 A Danzig ebonized and walnut armoire, *c.* 1670; 92 in. (235 cm) high.

E 8 A walnut armoire, with five drawers, 17th century; 91 in. high by 84 in. wide (232 by 215 cm).

E 9 A north German walnut armoire, carved overall; 79 in. high by 75 in. wide (201 by 192 cm).

E 10 A north German oak cupboard, with four doors divided by drawers; 78 in. (198 cm) high.

E 11 A baroque cupboard, decorated in parcel ebony, early 18th century; 82 in. high by 73 in. wide (208 by 185 cm).

D 12 A south German baroque walnut and burr-elm armoire, *c.* 1720; 83 in. high by 72 in. wide (211 by 183 cm).

E 13 A baroque walnut and parquetry armoire, inlaid with interlaced lozenge pattern, early 18th century.

E 14 A Mainz walnut armoire, early 18th century; 86 in. high by 85 in. wide (220 by 218 cm).

D 15 A south German baroque walnut armoire, probably Frankfurt or Bayern, early 18th century; 68 in. (172 cm) wide.

D 1 A Bavarian marquetry armoire, mid 18th century; 96 in. high by 66 in. wide (244 by 188 cm).

E 2 A rococo walnut and marquetry miniature cupboard, mid 18th century; 14 in. (35 cm) high.

E 3 A walnut cupboard, the base with a single drawer, mid 18th century; 86 in. (220 cm) wide.

D 4 An oak armoire, with two arched panelled cupboard doors, mid 18th century; 75 in. (190 cm) wide.

D 5 A south German baroque fruitwood and marquetry armoire, the two cupboard doors veneered with four fielded panels, mid 18th century; 57 in. (145 cm) wide.

E 6 A miniature cupboard, veneered in fruitwood and walnut, the concave top with marquetry panels, the sides veneered with geometric panels, the door oyster veneering, *c.* 1800; 88 in. (225 cm) high.

E 7 A provincial painted softwood cupboard, from Salzburg, richly carved with rosettes and garlands, on bun feet, the key dated "1797"; 75 in. high by 69 in. wide (190 by 175 cm).

E 8 A walnut cupboard, the cornice with canted corners, the two doors with shaped recessed panels, on turned bun feet, late 18th or early 19th century; 78 in. (200 cm) high.

E 9 A German or Austrian painted armoire, the concave cornice painted with the name "Anna Katharina Studle" and dated 1833, the door with two panels depicting a girl and a couple, the sides painted with vases of flowers, the base with a drawer; 73 in. high by 53 in. wide (155 by 135 cm).

E 10 A provincial painted softwood cupboard, the inserted cornice and base with canted corners, the doors with four recessed panels, on turned bun feet, 19th century; 70 in. (178 cm) high.

Schränke

While earlier forms of the Schrank may deter the collector on grounds of size and availability, those that date from the 19th century are much more accessible.

Provincial examples were made in all sizes with a great variety of surface decoration, the most popular being those in softwoods painted with sprays of flowers and other pastoral motifs. More sophisticated are the Biedermeier pieces, the austere lines of which are relieved by the use of highly figured veneers.

The quality of all these cupboards is usually very adequate. German cabinet-making in the mid 19th century was reckoned the best in Europe. In the third quarter of the century more than 12,000 German furniture-makers were employed in Paris, a city that had long prided itself on the skills of its native workmen.

E 11 A north German oak armoire, on bun feet, 19th century; 64 in. (183 cm) wide.

E 12 A mahogany armoire with carved crest above a pair of curved doors; 106 in. high by 72 in. wide (269 by 183 cm).

MIRRORS
1680-1840

The mirror frame is not a form to which German craftsmen made a substantial contribution. Those shown here display only minor points of design that could, at a casual glance, be determined as German. Thus nos 3 and 4 are Dutch in style, 5 and 6 Italian or English and 7 is Italian whimsy copied.

It is only in no. 10 that one can apprehend the Teutonic manner; here there is no compromise between the architectural principles and the rococo decoration.

E1 A German repoussé gilt-metal wall light, the backplate with a shaped mirror panel in a decorated frame, second half of 17th century; 24 in. high by 16 in. wide (61 by 41 cm).

E2 A south German (or Austrian) painted and parcel-gilt looking glass, the cresting with a small oval plate, the central plate set in a border of smaller plates engraved with stags, flowers and leaves, with an outer carved frame, *c.* 1680; 62 in. high by 42 in. wide (158 by 107 cm).

E3 A German engraved and painted glass looking glass, *c.* 1720; 20 in. high by 13 in. wide (50 by 34 cm).

E4 A north German rococo scarlet lacquer pier mirror; 52 in. high by 20 in. wide (130 by 50 cm).

E5 A German carved giltwood looking glass, surmounted by a Chinese bust, *c.* 1730; 72 in. (183 cm) high.

E6 A German painted looking glass with a scrolled cresting, the sides garlanded with C-scrolls and acanthus, *c.* 1740; 75 in. high, 65 in. wide (190 by 104 cm).

E7 A German wall bracket, 18th century; 27 in. high by 22 in. wide (67 by 55 cm).

E8 A German giltwood girandole, mid 18th century; 34 in. high by 18 in. wide (86 by 46 cm).

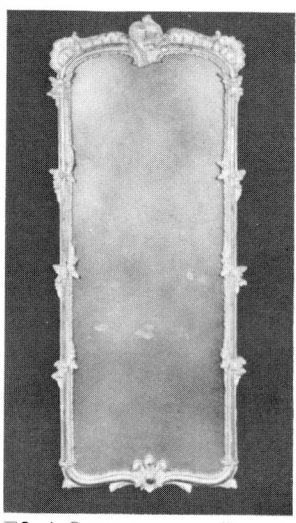

E9 A German rococo giltwood pier mirror, in moulded narrow giltwood frame, mid 18th century; 57 in. (145 cm) high.

E10 A German rococo painted and parcel-gilt mirror, *c.* 1750; 43 in. (107 cm) high.

E11 A German giltwood wall mirror, the oval plate surrounded by a deeply carved acanthus wreath with putti to the four quarters, *c.* 1840; 57 in. high by 44 in. wide (145 by 112 cm).

SEAT FURNITURE
1690-1850

In seating more than any other kind of German furniture the English influence is manifest. From the late 17th through to the early 19th centuries the English prototype is clear. No. 1 below shows the model of a typical Charles II style, no. 2 that of Queen Anne.

Hepplewhite's influence shows through in no. 5, but strongest in resemblance are chairs of the early 19th century – no. 9 below and no. 2 overleaf, so like the designs of George Smith.

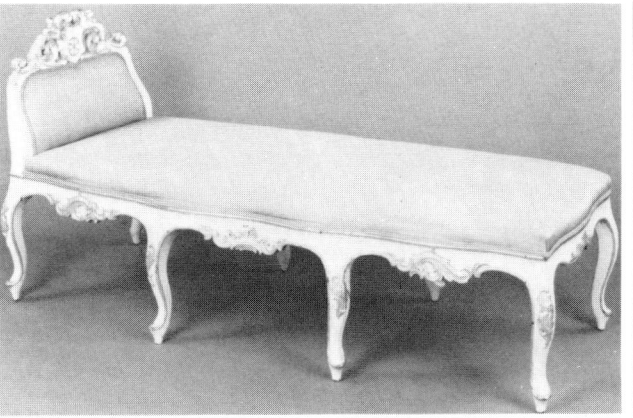

E3 A German rococo parcel-gilt and white-painted chaise longue, with arched pierced upholstered back, the crest carved with foliate scrolls and a central wheel, *c.* 1730; 72 in. (183 cm).

E4 A German neoclassical caned parcel-gilt mahogany settee, the four-chair-back with pierced Gothic crest-rails above Corinthian columns, with downcurved arms, caned seat and square tapering legs joined by stretchers, *c.* 1790; 71 in. (182 cm) wide.

E8 A German mahogany and cut-brass inlaid chair, the rectangular splat with brass-inlaid monogram of initials "C" and "D", the seat covered in blue velvet, on baluster-turned legs, *c.* 1820.

D1 A German baroque walnut armchair, the arms, supports and legs well carved, *c.* 1690.

E6 A south German rococo blue-painted and parcel-gilt tabouret, mid 18th century; 20 in. (51 cm) wide.

E9 A Biedermeier inlaid maple chair, the rectangular concave crest-rail above two bird heads scrolling to form a reeded crossbar, on square tapering legs, *c.* 1820.

E2 A north German rococo painted and parcel-gilt side chair, early 18th century.

E5 A north German neoclassical mahogany dining chair, with coved tablet top rail over interlaced palmette back, with downcurving reeded arms on turned reeded stumps, with square upholstered seat on turned reeded legs, early 19th century.

E7 An Austrian Biedermeier parcel-ebonized birch and fruitwood side chair, *c.* 1815.

E10 A Biedermeier fruitwood chair, with turned crest-rail above two reeded serpentine crossbars, on square cabriole legs, *c.* 1820.

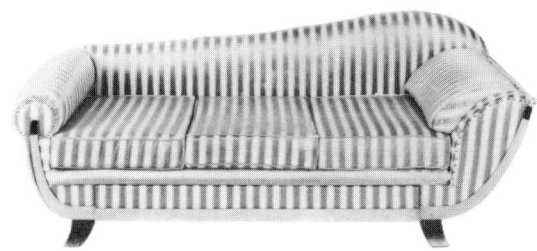

E 1 A Biedermeier fruitwood canapé, *c.* 1825; 83 in. (207 cm) wide.

E 3 A Biedermeier birch chair, the tapering top rail above two S-shaped sticks, flanking an ebonized splat, the slip seat on square tapering legs, *c.* 1836.

E 2 A Biedermeier dining chair, the shaped back with carved splat, on turned legs.

D 4 A Biedermeier canapé, the back with three medallions, the top rail extensively carved, *c.* 1840; 78 in. (195 cm) wide.

C 5 A Beidermeier fauteuil, in thuyawood, with sabre back legs, *c.* 1840.

E 6 A Nillius walnut armchair, the waisted button-upholstered back with a moulded frame, carved top rail, *c.* 1850.

SECRETAIRES
1780-1870

It was not until the 19th century that the secretaire gained equal popularity with the bureau. In an age when letter writing was a major social activity, secretaires became necessary signs of cultivated affluence.

The Biedermeier style lent itself admirably to the form. The front when closed displayed fine mouldings and a panel of highly figured veneer, and when open an interior of architectural rectitude.

D 7 A German neoclassical walnut and fruitwood secretaire bookcase, *c.* 1780; 77 in. high by 33 in. wide (192 by 82 cm).

E 8 A German mahogany and parcel-gilt secretaire, *c.* 1825; 66 in. (166 cm) high.

E 9 A north German mahogany secretaire, *c.* 1830; 89 in. (226 cm) high.

D 10 A south German Biedermeier secretaire, early 19th century; 79 in. (220 cm) high.

D 11 A Biedermeier secretaire, 78 in. high by 37 in. wide (195 by 92 cm).

E 12 A German mahogany secretaire, mid 19th century; 40 in. high by 42 in. wide (150 by 105 cm).

D 13 A north German Biedermeier mahogany secretaire, mid 19th century; 80 in. (204 cm) high.

E 14 A Biedermeier mahogany secretaire, 60 in. high by 42 in. wide (150 by 105 cm).

TABLES
1700-1880

German tables, like those of most other countries, fall into two categories: those made to support a relatively plain functional top and those made to display the decorative skill of the maker – and incidentally the prosperity of the owner.

Among the revivals of the 19th century there was a vogue for the recreation of the finest marquetry work of the 16th and 17th centruries and some highly desirable table tops were made in this manner.

Centre tables

D 1 A German boulle centre table, early 18th century; 29 in. (74 cm) wide.

D 2 A south German walnut marquetry centre table, mid 18th century; 30 in. (77 cm) high.

E 3 A German walnut table, 18th century; 32 in. high by 42 in. wide (79 by 105 cm).

E 4 A German inlaid walnut table, late 18th century; 29 in. high by 38 in. wide (71 by 96 cm).

E 5 A German neoclassical brass-mounted mahogany table, *c.* 1790; 26 in. (65 cm) wide.

E 6 A Biedermeier cherrywood centre table, with quartered mirror-figured top and a single drawer; 40 in. (105 cm).

E 7 A Biedermeier fruitwood and elm breakfast table, the round top with a deep frieze raised on a hexagonal support, *c.* 1830; 46 in. (112 cm) wide.

Games tables

E 8 A south German chess table, mid 16th century; 30 in. high by 24 in. wide (75 by 60 cm).

E 9 A German rococo bois clair, tulipwood and parquetry concertina-action card table, mid 18th century; 34 in. (88 cm) wide.

D 10 A German neoclassical tulipwood and kingwood parquetry games table, with crossbanded hinged top, the walls and panels inlaid with flowering branches on square tapering legs, late 18th century; 35 in. (90 cm) wide.

E1 A German walnut games table, 18th century; 32 in. high by 30 in. wide (80 by 74 cm).

Side tables

E2 A German baroque red-japanned and parcel-gilt side table, with shaped oval top, early 18th century; 48 in. (122 cm) wide.

E3 A carved walnut console table, with grey marble top, mid 18th century; 32 in. high by 40 in. wide (81 by 100 cm).

C4 A German rococo grey-painted and parcel-gilt console table, with grey and pale green marble top; 46 in. (117 cm) wide.

D 5 A Biedermeier console table, of thuyawood, with a mirror back, *c.* 1840; 38 in. high by 64 in. wide (93 by 170 cm).

Work tables

E6 A Biedermeier fruitwood work table, the rectangular top with chamfered corners, the concave front with a drawer, raised on a hexagonal support, *c.* 1825; 23 in. (60 cm) wide.

E7 A Biedermeier walnut work table, on an ogee plinth base, *c.* 1830; 19 in. (45 cm) wide.

E8 A German mahogany work table, the fitted interior with a sliding veneered workbox, 1840s; 29 in. high by 19 in. wide (75 by 48 cm).

E9 A German parquetry and palisander wood veneered work table, with hinged shaped top, 19th century; 28 in. (72 cm) high.

E10 A German walnut work table, of globe form, the domed cover swivelling to reveal a fitted interior; 21 in. (50 cm) wide.

Writing tables

E11 A German baroque walnut inlaid writing table, the rectangular moulded top with interlacing bands, *c.* 1700; 32 in. (80 cm) wide.

E12 A Swiss baroque walnut inlaid writing table, *c.* 1700; 40 in. (100 cm) wide.

E13 A German neoclassical walnut writing table, *c.* 1780; 22 in. (55 cm) wide.

E14 An Austrian Biedermeier writing and drawing table, *c.* 1820; 26 in. (66 cm) wide.

C15 A German mahogany and parquetry writing table, with rectangular hinged stepped top, *c.* 1800; 37 in. (94 cm) wide.

A3 *(above)* A pietra dura cabinet on stand, by Bernhard Ludwig of Vienna, applied with silvered metal and brass repousse swags of ribbon-tied flowers, above ten double panelled doors, the sides inset with semi-precious stones, *c.* 1880; 135 in. high by 94 in. wide (344 by 241 cm).

C1 *(above)* A Continental neoclassical ormolu-mounted mahogany and marquetry double bureau à cylindre on stand, probably Austrian. It has an ormolu-moulded top with three short patera-inlaid drawers, above a fielded roll front, centrally inlaid, enclosing a sliding inset leather panel with ratchet and opposing a similarly inlaid roll front above two opposing inlaid drop fronts, one enclosing an arcaded interior flanked by white colonettes and light short ormolu-moulded panelled drawers, the other enclosing a cupboard, the sides each with two ebonized niches enclosing carved and gilt deities; early 19th century; 57 in. high by 32 in. wide (144 by 82 cm).

B2 *(right)* A Viennese parcel-gilt mahogany secretaire of inverted tear-shape form, *c.* 1825; the semicircular pedimented top outlined with an egg-and-dart moulding, enclosing a pull-out fall-fronted door faced with a gadrooned half sunburst, above a frieze drawer and a panelled flap enclosing an assortment of drawers, surrounding a temple interior with a mirror shelf, enclosing secret drawers; two drawers below, on massive lion paw feet, resting on a low mahogany stand with drawer, and splayed bracket feet, 67 in. high by 42 in. wide (171 by 109 cm).

C4 An 18th-century Austrian commode of quasi-reverse serpentine form in white and gold lacquered wood, the shaped top with outswept corners painted to imitate marble; 39 in. high, 65 in. wide (100 by 166 cm).

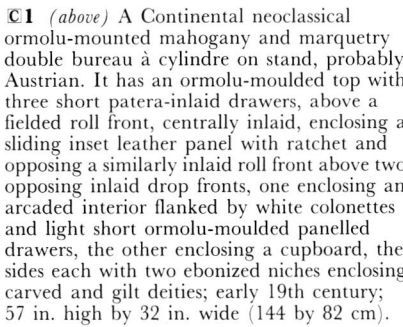

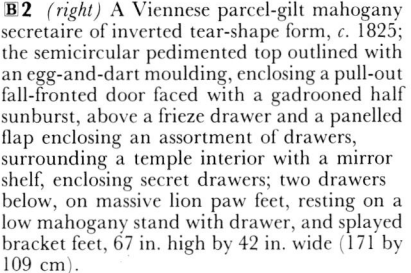

B5 A walnut and marquetry table of Austrian or East European origin, the top inlaid in stained and engraved woods, stone and ivory, on square tapering legs, last quarter of the 18th century; 37 in. (93 cm) wide.

D 1 *(above)* A German oak buffet, with moulded carved cornice above a florally carved frieze, set with cherub heads and lion masks, with a pair of fielded panelled cupboard doors, applied with scrolling terms, *c.* 1650; 74 in. high by 64 in. wide (190 by 163 cm).

E 2 *(right)* A Cologne marquetry buffet, with coved cornice containing a drawer faced with elaborate marquetry, the doors with arched panels and the plinth with strapwork marquetry, late 16th century; 43 in. high by 50 in. wide (107 by 128 cm).

D 3 *(above)* A German baroque walnut and amboyna armoire, with moulded breakfront corners above a pair of panelled doors, flanked and separated by freestanding twist-turned columns, with Corinthian capitals, the interior with shelves raised on brackets, with bun feet, *c.* 1700; 80 in. high by 70 in. wide (203 by 178 cm).

C 4 *(right)* A South German (probably Bavarian) baroque walnut and marquetry armoire, with moulded eared cornice above twin rectangular cupboard doors veneered with well-figured burr-walnut in conforming strapwork banded borders, with crossbanded panels centring scrolled cartouches, inlaid with pewter lines, mounted with engraved brass lock-plates, early 18th century; 68 in. (172 cm) wide.

B3 A marquetry cylinder bureau cabinet, North German or Baltic, in walnut and other woods, the breakfront superstructure with inlaid arched door with flanking gilt-brass rounded columns and tambour cupboards, the centre section with a cylinder inlaid with a view, possibly St Petersburg, opening with a slide, the sides inlaid, the lower part with two drawers veneered sans travers with two panels of ladies with flowers, with fluted base moulding and the sides inlaid with urns, *c.* 1780; 72 in. high by 49 in. wide (183 by 123 cm).

B1 A German scarlet lacquer bureau bookcase, with moulded arched cornice above conforming fielded panelled cupboard, with elaborate chinoiseries, *c.* 1720; 91 in. high, 41 in. wide (230 by 103 cm).

D2 A German or Bohemian painted bureau-cabinet, the whole inset with engraved mirror-glass panels within moulded gilt frames, *c.* 1730; 82 in. high by 35 in. wide (209 by 88 cm).

B4 A South German pewter-inlaid walnut bombé bureau, the fall front inlaid with central cartouche, with three drawers similarly decorated with Boulle-type inlay around elaborate escutcheons, the canted corners ending with scroll feet, mid 18th century; 39 in. high by 32 in. wide (97 by 80 cm).

C5 A German marquetry bureau in the French style, *c.* 1760. The top is inlaid with a musical trophy flanked by flowers with a guilloche border; the cylinder front inlaid with an oval chinoiserie scene, flanked by swags of flowers and leaves and opening in conjunction with a writing-surface inset with a tooled leather panel flanked by floral marquetry panels, with a central cupboard inlaid with a musical trophy flanked by pigeonholes and drawers inlaid with striped mouldings; the bombé serpentine lower part with three short and two long drawers inlaid with swags of flowers and leaves, on cabriole legs, the sides inlaid with oval panels of urns of flowers; 45 in. high by 47 in. wide (113 by 118 cm).

B 3 A North German walnut and parcel-gilt cabinet-on-chest, the arched and scrolled cornice pierced and carved, above a mirror panelled door enclosing shelves and two small drawers, the serpentine base with three long drawers divided by giltwood borders, the angles with scrolls and foliage on moulded base, with pierced lower border and short scrolled feet, Schleswig-Holstein, mid 18th century; 103 in. high by 42 in. wide (261 by 106 cm).

A 1 *(above)* A Biedermeier ormolu-mounted and parcel ebonized inlaid walnut secrétaire à abattant, Austrian, of lyre-shaped form, with well carved moulded cornice above four ebonized colonettes, the two central colonettes centring five ormolu strings and flanked by double-arched linenfold panels, over an inlaid drop-front enclosing a fitted interior, the entire drop-front and two lower drawers surrounded by inlaid borders, over two ebonized horn-shaped vessels headed by ormolu capitals, on moulded breakfront plinth, 1815-1820; 105 in. high by 37 in. wide (268 by 94 cm).

D 2 *(left)* An Augsburg marquetry cabinet, with hinged flap depicting an architectural perspective view of arcaded ruins overgrown with foliage, the sides similarly panelled, the top inlaid, the interior with an arrangement of twelve drawers and two cupboards, late 16th/early 17th century; 20 in. high by 36 in. wide (51 by 91 cm).

D 4 *(above)* An Augsburg ebony cabinet with simple panelled exterior, the interior cupboard and drawers faced with ivory and tortoiseshell and with silk collage pictures, the central cupboard enclosing a perspective architectural interior with secret drawers, mid 17th century; 37 in. (93 cm) wide.

C3 *(above)* A silver Renaissance revival throne chair, German, possibly Hanau, *c.* 1880. The padded back rail is flanked by cherub heads above large acanthus ornaments, the frame decorated with leafage and scrolls with large lion-mask bosses at the junctions, on massive claw-and-ball feet.

C1 *(above)* A south German painted and giltwood open armchair, the padded back with bow shaped top and padded seat, upholstered in white-ground crimson cut velvet, the scrolled arm supports carved with strapwork and foliage, the shaped seat rail on cabriole legs carved with foliage and scrolled feet, joined by waved X-shaped stretcher, *c.* 1730; 41 in. high by 27 in. wide (105 by 70 cm).

A4 A German ormolu-mounted kingwood parquetry commode reputedly made for the Elector of Saxony, with a brêche d'Alep marble top, the two top drawers centred by a narrow drawer with two long drawers below, the mounts with the crowned C mark, mid 18th century; 40 in. high by 67 in. wide (101 by 170 cm).

C2 *(left)* A German neoclassical giltwood side chair, with oval padded back and serpentine cushion seat, in moulded frame crisply carved with beaded guilloche enclosing stars, the pierced arched crest carved with gadrooning and bell-flowers, the panelled back carved with stars, volutes and lappets, the seat rail centrally carved with a sunburst, on tapering panelled octagonal legs carved with coin-pattern, headed by star paterae and Ionic capitals and ending in beaded cuffs, probably Bavarian, 1770-1780.

E5 A south German walnut and marquetry centre table in late 17th century style with shaped and inlaid moulded top, the angles with masks, the shaped frieze with a drawer, on spirally turned ebonized legs joined by an elaborately scrolled and pierced stretcher; 29 in. high by 47 in. wide (73 by 119 cm).

E1 *(below)* A pair of Krieger kingwood tall pedestals, with purple and white marble inset tops, the corners with lion masks, tapering to substantial acanthus-topped paw feet, *c.* 1880; 66 in. (166 cm) high.

D2 *(above, right)* A giltwood looking glass, South German or Austrian, with ribbon-tied pierced acanthus and C-scroll cresting and rococo apron, *c.* 1750; 51 in. high by 26 in. wide (128 by 65 cm).

D4 *(above)* An ormolu-mounted marquetry work table, the top sliding to reveal a well, with a spring-operated drawer at one side and a galleried stretcher, probably German, *c.* 1755; 25 in. high by 21 in. wide (62 by 52 cm).

D5 *(above)* A gilt-bronze-mounted kingwood and tulipwood bureau plat, the serpentine top inlaid with a leather panel and moulded gilt-bronze border, the frieze with three drawers on each side, on cabriole legs with modelled leaf-cast rococo gilt-bronze mounts, German, *c.* 1890; 32 in. high by 83 in. wide (81 by 211 cm).

C6 *(left)* A German neoclassical marquetry writing table, with ormolu-moulded rounded rectangular crossbanded top, mechanically raising inset-leather easel within wide borders inlaid with scrolled banding, the frieze with a short slide over an ormolu-moulded rectangular panel, elaborately inlaid, and a short drawer fitted with wells and two inkpots between ormolu rosettes, on square tapering legs with ormolu block sabots, late 18th century; 25 in. (64 cm) wide.

D3 *(above)* A palisander corner cabinet in two parts, with framed panels and gilt metal mounts, the upper part with glazed door and dragon-wing door hinges, German, early 18th century; 80 in. (202 cm) high.

D 1 An Italian walnut bureau with serpentine front, the drawers embellished with inlay panels, with canted corners on scrolled bracket feet, first half of the 18th century; 48 in. high by 58 in. wide (120 by 145 cm).

D 2 A Piedmontese walnut bureau of serpentine form, the fall front inlaid with a marquetry vase of flowers flanked by scrolls inlaid in palisander, the three long drawers similarly inlaid with palisander scrolls, second half of the 18th century; 44 in. high, 47 in. wide (110 by 118 cm).

C 3 *(left)* A North Italian rococo walnut and marquetry bureau bookcase, with moulded broken-arch ebonized cornice centring a moulded ebonized finial, carved with wave-pattern and S-scrolls, above two widely crossbanded cupboard doors, veneered with well-figured burr-walnut with shaped mirror plates, the lower part with a panelled slope-front enclosing a fitted interior over three long drawers, on voluted C-scroll feet, mid 18th century; 96 in. (244 cm) high.

A 4 *(above)* A Venetian lacquered bureau cabinet, with an arched cornice surmounted by four giltwood figures emblematic of the Seasons and a Papal cartouche, with a pair of arched mirror-glazed doors, enclosing an interior fitted with cupboards and doors, with a pair of candle-slides below, the lower part with sloping front enclosing an interior with drawers and pigeonholes, with four more drawers in the serpentine lower part, on scroll feet, the whole elaborately decorated on a red flower and strapwork ground, *c.* 1740; 103 in. high by 45 in. wide (261 by 114 cm).

E3 A Genoese walnut cabinet, the upper part with a mask- and swag-carved frieze drawer over an arrangement of cupboards and drawers flanked by grotesque figures and masks; the lower part with two panelled, fielded cupboard doors flanked by carved terms, masks and drapery; made *c.* 1600, and at one time fitted with a fall front.

C1 An Italian ebony marquetry writing cabinet signed by G.B. Gatti, Rome, 1855, exhibited at the Paris Exhibition the same year.

The doors show fine marquetry flower vases within ivory borders and open to a rosewood fitted interior over a sliding writing surface, a single drawer under, on carved scroll trestle supports; all surfaces richly inlaid. The cabinet is 52 in. (132 cm) high.

C4 *(above)* A Florentine ebony, boxwood and pietra dura cabinet in the Renaissance style by Ferri e Bartolozzi, with panelled frieze mounted with two carved drawers, above two cupboard doors, each inset with pietra dura panels, enclosing four drawers carved with mythical beasts and divided by Raphaelesque pilasters, late 19th century; 34 in. (86 cm) wide.

A5 *(left)* An Italian late Baroque parcel-gilt and ebonized cabinet-on-stand, the cabinet with moulded eared cornice applied with carved and gilt beading, ribbon-twist and leaf-tips above a central glazed cupboard door; the gilt stand with central apron carved with a winged mythical beast, on scrolled legs above a moulded plinth on paw feet, probably Rome, *c.* 1700; 87 in. high by 95 in. wide (220 by 241 cm).

A2 A Roman ebony, mother-of-pearl and ivory exhibition cabinet-on-stand, by G.B. Gatti (compare no. 1 above), set with semi-precious stones, the stand with long drawer and trestle supports joined by a turned, inlaid stretcher; 35 in. (89 cm) wide.

E 1 A Piedmontese painted and parcel-gilt armchair, with oval padded back and carved cresting, with padded arms, over serpentine stuffed seat on cabriole legs, the back and seat in the original painted silk, *c.* 1770.

D 4 An Italian painted and gilt armchair, together with a side chair from the same set, both with shaped splats decorated with a cartouche beneath a coronet within scrolled uprights, the armchair with outset padded arms with scroll handles and shaped supports, the webbed seat on cabriole legs and pad feet, *c.* 1740.

C 2 A Roman walnut and parcel gilt commode, the moulded top with slightly projecting corners, the lambrequin-carved frieze above three long drawers, 37 in. high by 48 in. wide, early 18th century; (93 by 127 cm).

D 3 A Sicilian three-drawer commode, the drawers reserved with panels of lacquered flowers, 18th century; 41 in. high by 48 in. wide (105 by 120 cm).

D 5 A pair of Italian polychrome painted chairs of the late 18th century, bizarre examples of late rococo and hybrid ornament in a classical age.

The Oriental parasol crest is flanked by gryphons stemming from crossed-over cornucopiae that have foliate terminals supporting pendent bellflowers, creating a swan-like effect. The arboreal splat contains a secondary design of tiered hearts.

The classical panelled seat rails with paterae to the corners are subdued by comparison with the back, but eclectic whimsy reasserts itself in the exaggeratedly splayed, leaf-decorated legs.

C1 An Italian walnut bureau cabinet, the upper part with moulded serpentine top inset with a cartouche borne by putti, surmounted by a coronet, and a pair of arched panelled doors inlaid with flowers enclosing pigeonholes and a well, with three drawers in the serpentine front, inlaid with rococo scrollwork borders throughout, mid 18th century; 88 in. high by 38 in. wide (226 by 97 cm).

C2 A Lombard bureau cabinet in walnut dated 1777. The scrolled broken pediment shows a cartouche with a winged putto bearing a pennant, over mirror-glazed doors, the plates shaped top and bottom, within inlaid borders, the canted corners similarly inlaid. Below the doors are two shallow short drawers.

The fall-front is inlaid with musical motifs over one shallow shaped drawer, a dummy bead (the piece is in two parts, not three) and three long drawers; 278 in. (109 cm) high.

B3 An 18th-century Venetian walnut bureau cabinet of particularly elaborate form, probably after simpler Dutch models, the concave sides having cupboards to the lower case and a short drawer in the upper; 98 in. high, 63 in. wide (250 by 160 cm).

D5 A Genoese painted bombé commode of double serpentine form, the moulded top painted to resemble peach and beige marble, the sides and two drawers delicately painted, mid 18th century; 55 in. (142 cm) wide.

A4 A Venetian painted and gilt bombé commode of the mid-18th century in the Régence style, on cabriole legs. This is a relatively restrained interpretation, there being a tendency in 18th-century Venice to exaggerate bombé forms (though note the sinuous sides), but the embellishment of painted flowers is delightfully typical of Venetian work. The commode is 54 in. (137 cm) wide.

C6 An Italian rococo walnut and parquetry commode, decorated with cartouches of radiating panels in a chevron-pattern ground, with rockwork fittings, on cloven feet; mid 18th century; 44 in. (111 cm) wide.

D 1 *(above)* A Neopolitan bombé commode, inlaid with ebony and contrasting woods, mid 18th century; 39 in. high by 57 in. wide (100 by 145 cm).

D 4 *(above)* An Italian Renaissance walnut centre table, the solid rectangular top on four re-entrant columnar legs, each with moulded and turned capitals over cabriole shapes decorated with Vitruvian scrolls and a drape, terminating in a well defined paw foot, resting on a moulded pedestal base, joined by rectangular section stretchers; 16th century; 56 in. (142 cm) wide.

D 2 *(above)* An Italian Renaissance painted pedestal with moulded rectangular top, the dentilled frieze decorated in scarlet and cream with foliate scrolls and strapwork on splayed baluster-shaped trestle-ends, similarly decorated, and joined by a vase-turned stretcher, Florentine, 16th century; 48 in. (121 cm) high.

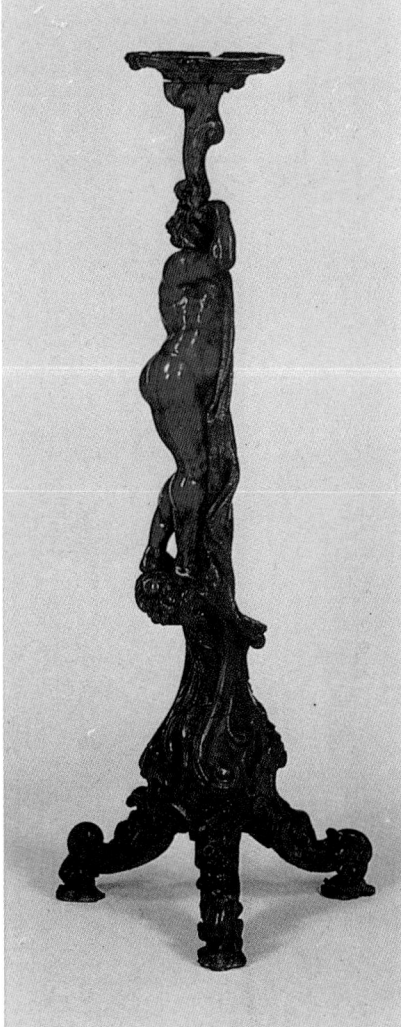

B 5 A pair of 18th-century Venetian painted and silvered blackamoor torchères, each with standing Nubian figure stem, carrying a tole foliate spray ending in twisting branches and nozzles, on chamfered square bases edged with moulded gilded borders on white marbled plinths and scrolled feet, 108 in. (271 cm) high.

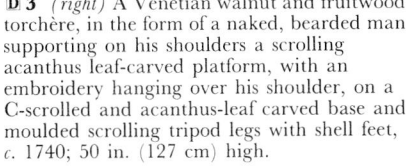

D 3 *(right)* A Venetian walnut and fruitwood torchère, in the form of a naked, bearded man supporting on his shoulders a scrolling acanthus leaf-carved platform, with an embroidery hanging over his shoulder, on a C-scrolled and acanthus-leaf carved base and moulded scrolling tripod legs with shell feet, *c.* 1740; 50 in. (127 cm) high.

C1 A Tuscan walnut table, the rectangular top with three square-cut stop-fluted trestle supports, each with outset feet boldly carved with acanthus, *c.* 1550; 84 in. high by 36 in. wide (213 by 91 cm).

C2 *(above)* An Italian late Renaissance walnut, ivory and mother-of-pearl marquetry centre table, the top inlaid with a sun and two coats of arms, early 17th century; 50 in. wide by 24 in. deep (127 by 60 cm).

C3 *(right)* A Venetian lacquered and gilded games table, with detachable top of lobed oval outline, painted with birds and flowers, with shaped frieze containing two drawers on bold cabriole legs painted and mounted, mid 18th century; 33 in. high by 40 in. wide (83 by 101 cm).

C4 *(left)* An early 18th-century Roman rosewood writing table, the quartered serpentine top with outswept corners edged with ebonized banding and inlaid with *angelino* leaves and stringing, with two raised, shaped corners each containing two drawers. The frieze contains three drawers over finely double-scrolled legs inlaid with foliate motifs and joined by a wavy X-stretcher which is chevron-pattern veneered, inlaid and carved at the sides, on inverted scroll feet.

D5 *(below)* A Venetian walnut side table in well figured wood, the serpentine top with wide crossbanding and outset corners inlaid with a monkey amongst foliage and strapwork, the frieze with acanthus and C-scrolls on four flowery carved cabriole legs, mid 18th century; 33 in. high by 56 in. wide (83 by 142 cm).

E1 *(above)* A Florentine Renaissance gilt-gesso and ebonized coffer, with moulded fielded hinged top, the fielded front with a rectangular panel of gilt-gesso carved with fleur-de-lys in a wide border decorated in black and gilt with foliate scrolls and applied winged cherub masks, interrupted by fleur-de-lys, with similar sides, 15th century; 47 in. (119 cm) wide.

C2 *(right)* A Venetian engraved glass and giltwood girandole, the shaped plate decorated with a figure of a hunter standing on a pedestal, within a flower-engraved border, the scallop cresting supported by female figures, *c.* 1740; 51 in. high by 31 in. wide (130 by 79 cm).

C4 *(above)* An 18th-century two-part Piedmont corner cupboard. The upper part consists of two shaped cupboard doors under a scrolling ebonized and gilt pediment surmounted by a substantial gilt plume. The doors are inlaid in a chequerboard pattern within Greek key borders within a futher border and crossbanding, over a scalloped apron, on bracket feet.

The lower part consists of a triangular bow-front chest with an inlaid and crossbanded top over three long drawers with key pattern inlay, between chevron reserves.

D3 *(above)* An Italian Renaissance walnut cassone, the rectangular lid above a bombé case with a fluted frieze and carved with a cartouche flanked by putti and scrolling foliage, on paw feet and plinth base; 16th century; 32 in. high, 58 in. wide (81 by 147 cm).

A5 *(above* and *right)* An Italian ebony and marquetry centre table, possibly Florentine, with serpentine tulipwood crossbanded top, intricately inlaid with a central oval panel enclosing a ewer, bowl and two cups and saucers within a border of birds and leafage, the serpentine frieze similarly inlaid, on triangular tapering legs, the angles inlaid with striped panels and mother-of-pearl; third quarter of the 18th century; 36 in. high by 59 in. wide (91 by 149 cm).

C 1 *(above)* A Flemish ebony-veneered and needlework cabinet *c.* 1670, the hinged lid with a needlework panel, the moulded panelled doors opening to reveal a fitted interior with needlework panels to the doors and drawers, the sides with iron loop carrying handles, 17 in. high by 19 in. wide (43 by 49 cm).

D 2 *(below)* A Flemish red tortoiseshell cabinet with gilt-metal mounts *c.* 1660, with a deep drawer above a pair of panelled cupboard doors opening to a tesselated mirrored interior surrounded by small drawers, with a drawer below, each of the drawers fielded and inlaid with ivory and ebony stringing; 53 in. (135 cm) wide.

D 3 *(above)* A Dutch palisander, ebony and floral marquetry veneered oak "William and Mary" cupboard, the upper section having two doors each inlaid with a vase of flowers on a table, the friezes above and below being of floral marquetry matching that to the stand, which has a single drawer to the front, over tapering square legs, joined by a shaped X-stretcher, on small bun feet; *c.* 1700; 80 in. (205 cm) high.

C 4 *(right)* A coromandel lacquer chest on Flemish giltwood stand, late 17th century. The cabinet is constructed from a contemporary Chinese screen, the door faces carved with figures on a verandah, and the interiors decorated with a courtyard scene. The ten drawers are faced with twelve panels ornamented with rabbits, stags, dragons, flowers and insects in colours on a black lacquer ground, with engraved gilt-foliate mounts. The giltwood stand with pierced apron on cabriole legs is carved with sea creatures; 68 in. high by 45 in. wide (173 by 114 cm).

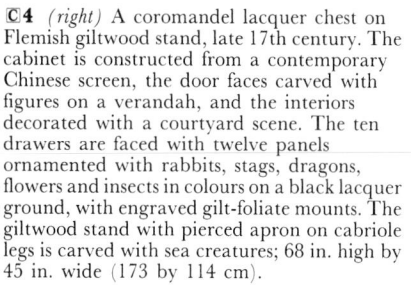

C4 A Dutch neoclassical mahogany bureau bookcase in three sections, with two mirrored cupboard doors, the slope front enclosing a fitted interior, the bombé base with three graduated drawers, late 18th century; 56 in. (143 cm) wide.

D1 *(above)* A mid-18th century Dutch marquetry press, the upper part with an arched moulded cornice centred by carved scrollwork above a pair of doors faced with carved scrollwork and enclosing shelves and drawers, the bombé lower part with two short and two long drawers, all inlaid with floral marquetry on a walnut ground, raised on claw-and-ball feet, 97 in. high by 67 in. wide (246 by 170 cm).

E2 *(above)* A Liègeois burr-elm writing desk, veneered in well figured wood, with divided hinged top enclosing a fitted interior, on ebonized bun feet, *c*. 1690; 31 in. high by 43 in. wide (79 by 111 cm).

E3 *(left)* A Dutch marquetry bureau, the top with a fitted interior above four graduated drawers. all inlaid with flowers, leaves and birds on a walnut ground, *c*. 1750; 43 in. high by 55 in. wide (111 by 140 cm).

D5 A Liègeois parcel-gilt bureau cabinet, inlaid with strapwork bandings, with mirrored doors enclosing a fitted interior, the lower part with sloping front and fitted interior, with an inverted breakfront base, *c*. 1740; 98 in. high by 42 in. wide (249 by 107 cm).

E4 *(above)* A Dutch cut-glass mirror in an ebony- and floral marquetry-veneered softwood cushion frame, the marquetry panels depicting fleur-de-lys motifs in the corners, with birds, flowers and acanthus scrolls to the sides, top and bottom; early 18th century; 43 in. high, 37 in. wide (110 by 95 cm).

D1 *(above)* An Antwerp boulle writing table, the top hinged at the centre and opening in conjunction with the frieze drawer to reveal a fitted writing interior, lined in floral marquetry, the front with seven drawers and a cupboard, the exterior inlaid, mainly in pewter, within red tortoiseshell strapwork borders, on an ebonized ground, late 17th century; 35 in. high by 39 in. wide (89 by 100 cm).

C2 *(above)* A commode with cartouche-shaped central panel inlaid with a basket of tulips, roses and other flowers on a quartered kingwood ground flanked by figured panels, the cupboard doors at the sides similarly inlaid, with rococo scrolling handles, angles and lock-plates, probably Northern Low Countries, mid 18th century; 63 in. (160 cm) wide.

D3 *(right)* An Antwerp centre table, the top inset with a panel of tortoiseshell inlaid with pewter stringing and within walnut crossbanding, the tortoiseshell veneered stepped frieze raised on columnar legs with tortoiseshell inlaid with pewter lines, above a collar of ebony inlaid with simulated hardstone, late 17th century; 32 in. high by 38 in. wide (81 by 98 cm).

D5 *(above)* A Dutch palisander, ebony and floral marquetry veneered oak "William and Mary" side table, the top with a panel depicting a bouquet of flowers bound with ribbons and surrounded by loose blossom branches, butterflies and birds, the floral marquetry frieze with a single drawer to the front, on tapering square floral marquetry and palisander legs with shaped floral marquetry X-stretcher and stud feet, early 18th century; 39 in. (101 cm) wide.

ITALY

The reputation that Italian designers enjoy today is but a shadow of the admiration they were accorded in the 16th and 17th centuries. Italian craftsmen were then supreme, executing the most opulent furniture for Europe's most sophisticated patrons: the elite of other nations had to confess themselves provincial in their understanding.

For all the magnificence of Italian Renaissance furniture, even the grandest *palazzo* was sparsely furnished in the 16th century. The one item of furniture that was widespread was the *cassone* or coffer, immediately distinguishable from its northern counterparts by its frequently classical outlines, and distanced even further by its carving, the application of painted panels of the very highest quality and, later, by intarsia panels too.

THE SUPREMACY OF ARTISTRY

The development of *pietra dura* work, especially in Milan under the Medici late in the century, set the seal upon Italian craftsmanship. Tables and cabinets were inset with *pietre dure* of such refined artistry that nothing could match it until the display pieces of the mid to late 19th century, by which time scagliola had assumed dominance.

In 17th-century Italy as in the rest of Europe the variety of furniture made increased considerably. Massive, richly carved tables, a profusion of chairs, fine credenzas instead of crude sideboards, wardrobes, chests of drawers, bookcases, console tables were all made for the wealthy in the Mannerist style and then the Baroque, outstripping in lavishness anything that other countries could show.

France, intimately open to Italian influence since the marriage of Henry IV to Catherine de Medici in 1600, absorbed Italian decorative styles with great rapidity, whereas the northern countries delayed a full-blooded adoption of Italian models until the early 18th century and such designers as William Kent.

As Italian design became fixed in the glories of the Baroque, France, England, the Low Countries and Germany took up the challenge; by the early 18th century their craftsmanship was superior and Rococo — a spirit that Italy would absorb later — was the dominant style of Europe.

The genius of Italian design was played out, and in the later 18th century, as in the 19th, Italy imported and localized the great European movements, retaining a characteristic brilliance in decoration, but lacking a commanding originality in design.

BEDS
1680-1760

Still the finest beds to come out of Italy are the massive, lavishly carved products of the Renaissance. 17th-century taste turned to more refined lines, but carved ornament remained opulent — see no. 2.

French styles dominated Italian furniture in the 18th century and the beds of the two countries can be barely distinguishable in this period.

E 1 A Piedmontese upholstered matrimonial bed, mid 18th century; 75 in. long by 63 in. wide (190 by 160 cm).

E 2 An Italian carved limewood bedhead, *c.* 1680; 56 in. high by 55 in. wide (142 by 140 cm).

E 3 A walnut four-poster bedstead, 17th century; 108 in. high by 70 in. wide (274 by 178 cm).

E 4 A Venetian rococo arte povera and giltwood cradle, mid 18th century; 34 in. high by 46 in. wide (85 by 115 cm).

BUREAUX
1730-1880

The fall-front bureau is not a design native to Italy but was imported from Holland, England and France.

One feature that is distinctively Continental and interpreted with subtlety on the Italian bureau is the supporting recess immediately below the fall. On other examples the fall is supported when open by the extended shaped front to the drawers – see no. 6 below.

D 5 A north Italian inlaid walnut bureau, the flap enclosing a fitted interior over two short drawers and two long drawers, *c.* 1730; 40 in. high by 44 in. wide (102 by 115 cm).

D 6 An inlaid walnut bureau, the flap enclosing drawers over a shaped front with drawers, *c.* 1730; 45 in. high by 45 in. wide (114 by 114 cm).

E 1 A walnut bureau cabinet, enclosing an interior of four drawers, mid 18th century; 52 in. (129 cm) wide.

D 2 A Lombard rococo walnut and marquetry bureau bookcase, mid 18th century; 96 in. (244 cm) high.

C 3 A walnut and giltwood bookcase/bureau, of serpentine outline; 60 in. (150 cm) high.

C 4 A rococo burr-walnut bureau, with crossbanded top and serpentine fall-front, mid 18th century; 43 in. (109 cm) wide.

D 5 A Trentino walnut veneered bureau, 46 in. high by 50 in. wide (114 by 127 cm).

D 6 A Venetian walnut bureau, mid 18th century; 46 in. high by 50 in. wide (117 by 127 cm).

D 7 A rococo walnut bureau bookcase, mid 18th century; 94 in. (222 cm) high.

D 8 A bureau bookcase, with sloping front enclosing drawers, mid 18th century; 92 in. high by 36 in. wide (205 by 90 cm).

E 9 A rococo green-japanned bureau cabinet, mid 18th century; 38 in. (96 cm) wide.

E 10 A walnut veneered bureau cabinet, c. 1760; 94 in. high by 43 in. wide (239 by 109 cm).

E 11 A walnut bureau, crossbanded with stained wood, c. 1760; 40 in. (102 cm) wide.

E 12 A walnut and olivewood bureau, the sloping front enclosing three drawers, on carved ebonized legs; 43 in. (108 cm) wide.

E 13 A fruitwood bureau, with crossbanded sloping flap enclosing a fitted interior, above two serpentine drawers; 40 in. (102 cm) wide.

E 14 A walnut bureau, with rosewood veneer, early 18th century; 43 in. high by 59 in. wide (108 by 148 cm).

E1 A walnut and marquetry bureau, the sloping front enclosing a well and shallow drawers, 18th century; 69 in. (172 cm) wide.

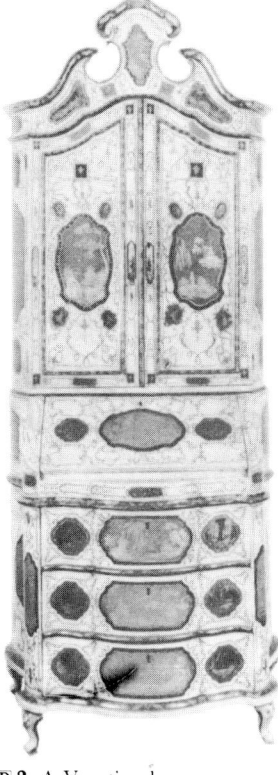

D2 A Venetian bureau bookcase, the vermilion reserves decorated with gilt chinoiseries en camaieu, 18th century; 84 in. high by 33 in. wide (210 by 82 cm).

E3 A walnut and floral marquetry bureau, inlaid with flowering foliage, enclosing pigeonholes and drawers, 18th century; 44 in. (113 cm) wide.

D4 A carved walnut and crossbanded bureau cabinet, inlaid with lines, candle slides, flanked by Ionic pilasters, the lower part having a sloping fall with a foliate cartouche enclosing six short drawers, secret drawers and compartments, probably Veronese, 18th century; 89 in. (221 cm) high.

E5 A Venetian cream lacquered small bureau cabinet, the doors decorated with chinoiserie landscapes enclosing a green lacquered interior, the bombé base with sloping flap enclosing a fitted interior, 18th century; 22 in. (57 cm) wide.

E6 A Venetian walnut bureau, late 18th century; 40 in. high by 46 in. wide (100 by 115 cm).

D7 A neoclassical walnut and marquetry bureau, late 18th century; 43 in. (111 cm) wide.

D8 A rococo-style burr-walnut bureau bookcase, on a moulded plinth; 55 in. (140 cm) wide.

E9 A marquetry bureau, inlaid with brass, ivory and mother-of-pearl, c. 1880; 31 in. (78 cm) wide.

CABINETS
1500-1900

The carved and inlaid cabinets of the Italian Renaissance are one of the glories of European furniture. Made to extremely high standards, they were sought by collectors all over the Continent. Their makers were given every encouragement to emigrate and work for patrons abroad.

The Renaissance revival cabinets of the 19th century were also spectacular works of art, as outstanding in their craftsmanship as their 16th-century models.

D10 A Tuscan intarsia walnut credenza, the top with a border inlaid with a continuous swastika motif, c. 1500; 39 in. high by 62 in. wide (99 by 159 cm).

E11 A Renaissance walnut credenza, with breakfront cornice above dentilled carving, with eight fielded panelled doors, 16th century; 85 in. (212 cm) wide.

E12 A walnut Armadio cabinet, with hinged moulded top and stepped dentilled cornice, 16th century; 36 in. (93 cm) wide.

E1 An Italian Renaissance walnut credenza, with moulded rectangular top above two fielded panelled frieze drawers, 16th century; 69 in. (176 cm) wide.

E2 An Italian Renaissance walnut credenza, with a drawer above a door carved with a cartouche, the sides with stop-fluted columns, late 16th century; 34 in. (85 cm) wide.

E3 A Bolognese Renaissance walnut cabinet, the upper part with a moulded top, above three arches, late 16th century; 72 in. high by 49 in. wide (183 by 150 cm).

E4 An Italian walnut side cabinet, with moulded rectangular top, cavetto cornice, early 17th century; 51 in. (131 cm) wide.

D5 A walnut cabinet, the upper part with overhanging cornice, the moulded frieze carved with cherub masks, above two deeply panelled cupboard doors, the base with carved doors and drawers, c. 1650; 109 in. (277 cm) high.

E6 A 17th-century walnut cabinet, the overhanging top above a deep carved frieze, with two panelled cupboard doors between carved stiles – the sides are panelled to conform – on a cushion base with handsome paw feet. It stands 34 in. (82 cm) high and is 38 in. (95 cm) wide.

E8 An Italian scarlet tortoiseshell and ebony cabinet, on a later stand, applied with ripple mouldings and bordered with simulated scagliola foliate scrollwork, heightened in mother-of-pearl, surmounted by a hinged cavetto frieze compartment and fitted with ten drawers about a central architectural cupboard, with a broken pediment with gilt-metal figures and columns, 17th century; 42 in. (104 cm) wide.

E9 A north Italian ebony table cabinet, the centre with an architectural niche inset, with a bronze figure of Adam, flanked by further architectural niches containing bronze figures of classical ladies, 17th century; 40 in. (100 cm) wide.

E7 A north Italian cabinet, in walnut with ivory inlay, the drawers featuring animal scenes, 17th century; 21 in. high by 41 in. wide (52 by 102 cm).

D10 A rare Italian red tortoiseshell cabinet, with 12 drawers and a pair of cupboards, mid 17th century; 60 in. high by 42 in. wide (150 by 102 cm).

D1 An Italian late Renaissance walnut bookcase, with a secret drawer in the sides, 17th century; 105 in. high by 111 in. wide (266 by 282 cm).

E2 A fine Italian ivory, ebony and rosewood table cabinet, the top inlaid with a plaque and a geometric design above a pair of cupboard doors, inlaid with panels depicting Delphica, Europa, Libica and Frigia, enclosing a finely fitted interior of nine various-sized drawers, 17th century; 13 in. (35 cm) wide.

E3 A Genoese rosewood veneered teak and bone inlaid cabinet, with an arrangement of 20 drawers inlaid with stylized floral motifs, containing secret drawers, early 18th century; 47 in. high by 36 in. wide (119 by 92 cm).

E4 A Florentine ebony cabinet, the doors opening to reveal an interior consisting of a central pediment flanked by eight drawers, with rock crystal columns, c. 1700.

E5 A tortoiseshell, rosewood and mother-of-pearl table cabinet, late 17th century; 32 in. (81 cm) wide.

E6 A Sicilian painted and parcel-gilt side cabinet, the top decorated to look like verde antico marble, the doors centred by a shaped mirror panel, with shaped leaf-carved apron, mid 18th century; 35 in. high by 38 in. wide (89 by 97 cm).

E7 An Italian walnut table cabinet, c. 1770; 18 in. high by 38 in. wide (45 by 92 cm).

E8 An Italian neoclassical inlaid walnut side cabinet, the rectangular top above two doors, on square tapering legs, c. 1780; 22 in. (55 cm) wide.

E9 An Italian walnut Renaissance-style cabinet, c. 1900; 33 in. (84 cm) wide.

E 1 A rosewood and tortoiseshell cabinet, consisting of 22 drawers with ivory handles, the drawers surrounded by beaded moulding, the faces inset with tortoiseshell, above an acanthus moulding to the base, 19th century.

CASSONI & COFFERS
1550-1880

Cassoni of the finest kind – superbly carved and sometimes inlaid with painted panels – have survived in considerable numbers. This is partly because they were frequently, though not always, made in pairs as marriage chests, and partly because the quality of their decoration was so high that subsequent generations have treasured them as works of art, even when the fashion of the period was for furniture of an altogether different kind.

Early in the 16th century cassoni set with painted panels within a classical framework were favoured, the paintings being chiefly of classical military heroes or of religious subjects. Intarsia panels were a popular alternative to paint and the whole might be gilded.

The Renaissance was the great period of the cassone, but the form continued to be made even into the 19th century. Examples from this period, generally decorated with gilded stucco rather than carved wood, are both attractive and accessible.

E 2 An engraved ivory inlaid ebony display cabinet, decorated throughout and composed of a pair of glazed doors and fielded lower doors, mid 19th century; 90 in. by 58 in. (225 by 145 cm).

E 4 A Renaissance-style walnut credenza, with moulded polygonal hinged top banded with inlaid cube-pattern, the similarly inlaid dentilled frieze above two fielded cupboard doors bordered with ribbon-twist, on cube-pattern inlaid moulded plinth, 36 in. (91 cm) wide.

E 6 A Tuscan parcel-gilt walnut cassone, the carved panelled lid with moulded edge, 16th century; 122 in. high by 53 in. wide (135 by 56 cm).

E 7 A walnut cassone, with plain hinged lid above extensively carved front panels, 16th century; 69 in. (172 cm) wide.

E 3 A Milanese ivory-inlaid ebony-veneered and ebonized cabinet, the front inlaid throughout with finely cut scrollwork and allegorical figures, late 17th century; 76 in. high by 50 in. wide (193 by 128 cm).

E 5 A Florentine Pietra Dura and ebony cabinet-on-stand, the centre with Medici arms flanked by standing gilt-metal figures; 93 in. high by 51 in. wide (237 by 127 cm).

E 8 A walnut cassone, the breakfront top with carved edge above a central panel depicting Neptune, raised on shell-carved plinth; 27 in. high by 75 in. wide (70 by 190 cm).

E1 A Tuscan walnut cassone, the front carved with a central armorial cartouche, with lunette-carved base, mid 16th century; 19 in. high by 42 in. wide (48 by 108 cm).

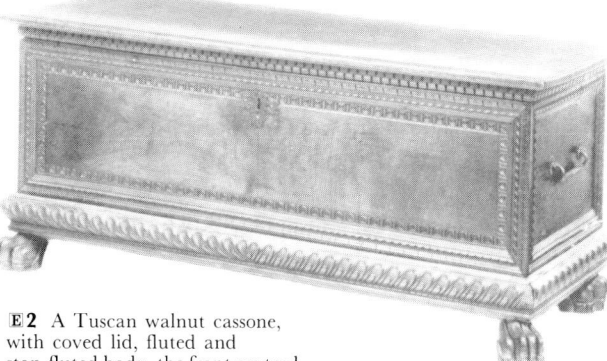

E2 A Tuscan walnut cassone, with coved lid, fluted and stop-fluted body, the front centred by an armorial cartouche within a wreath with a gadrooned base, mid 16th century; 69 in. (175 cm) wide.

E3 A Renaissance walnut cassone, the lid above a large panel with a centrally carved coat-of-arms, flanked by lions and female figures, terminating in scrolling acanthus leaves, the corners with terms, the base on double paw feet, 16th century; 69 in. (172 cm) wide.

E4 A Renaissance giltwood cassone, the domed lid with four quatrefoils centring shield-shaped coat-of-arms above trellised fleur-de-lys, the bombé-front and sides with continuous foliage and centred by another coat-of-arms, the corners with angels, 16th century; 29 in. high by 62 in. wide (72 by 55 cm).

E5 A walnut cassone, the stepped lid inlaid with the motto Dolenti Animo Nil Oportet Credere, above front and side panels inlaid with winged putti with floral swags and urns, on parquetry base, 16th century; 81 in. (203 cm) wide.

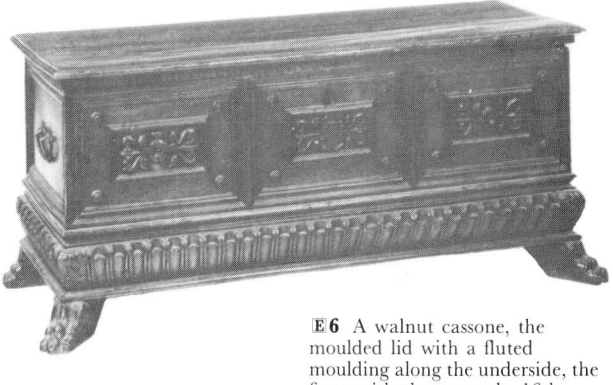

E6 A walnut cassone, the moulded lid with a fluted moulding along the underside, the front with three panels, 16th century; 27 in. high by 62 in. wide (69 by 158 cm).

E7 A Renaissance painted soft-wood cassone, with panelled lid above a pierced frieze above a quadripartite panel front with heraldic emblems, on bracket feet; 71 in. (177 cm) wide.

E8 A painted and gilded cassone, the lid painted with arabesques in black, 16th century; 27 in. high by 63 in. wide (68 by 160 cm).

E1 A Renaissance walnut and parcel-gilt cassone, the sides with C-shaped iron handles, on paw feet, late 16th century; 68 in. (174 cm) wide.

E2 A walnut cassone, the frieze with small chip-carved divisions above three pairs of arches, *c.* 1600; 27 in. high by 57 in. wide (68 by 145 cm).

E3 A tortoiseshell coffer, with domed lid and brass carrying handles, the carved front with central escutcheon, on similar stand with frieze drawer, six legs and inlaid stretchers, *c.* 1600; 38 in. (95 cm) wide.

E4 A small walnut coffer, the front and side panels well carved, the interior fitted with hinged covered box and iron lock, with two iron side handles, early 17th century; 29 in. (73 cm) long.

E5 A walnut cassone, with coffered lid, the front with central carved coat-of-arms, between mask angles, with lion feet, 17th century; 75 in. (190 cm) long.

E6 A painted cassone, with domed lid made from two planks, with three roundels to front panel, 17th century; 33 in. high by 64 in. wide (83 by 160 cm).

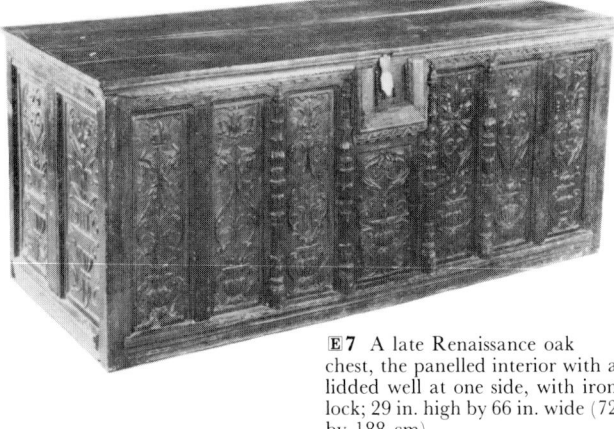

E7 A late Renaissance oak chest, the panelled interior with a lidded well at one side, with iron lock; 29 in. high by 66 in. wide (72 by 188 cm).

E8 A fruitwood chest, the inside of the plain cover etched with eagles in cartouche, trees, birds and a central cartouche, the front with two etched panels with scrolling branches, surrounded by animals within scrolling branches, on block feet, 18th century; 60 in. (153 cm) wide.

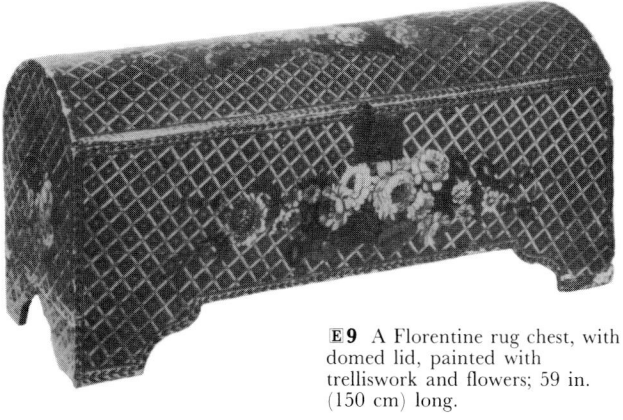

E9 A Florentine rug chest, with domed lid, painted with trelliswork and flowers; 59 in. (150 cm) long.

E10 A Renaissance-style walnut cassone, the hinged top with moulded carved edge above three panels carved in high relief, the sides with lifting handles, on paw feet and moulded plinth; 71 in. (182 cm) wide.

E11 A Florentine carved walnut cassone-on-stand, of inverted breakfast form, with a pair of cupboards each carved with a grotesque mask, on conforming plinth, c. 1880; 54 in. high by 95 in. wide (137 by 211 cm).

E12 A Renaissance-style walnut cassone, with coffered top carved with flutes and egg-and-dart, 64 in. (163 cm) wide.

CHAIRS
1490-1890

Regional variations apart, the basic forms of most Italian chairs from the Renaissance onward are in line with their contemporaries in other European countries. An exception must be made for the magnificent, sculptural chairs of the 17th century however, and there were two forms of chair specific to Italy. These were the sgabello or hall chair (properly called sedia da ingresso), a form copied by English chairmakers, and the Savonarola or X-frame chair.

Armchairs

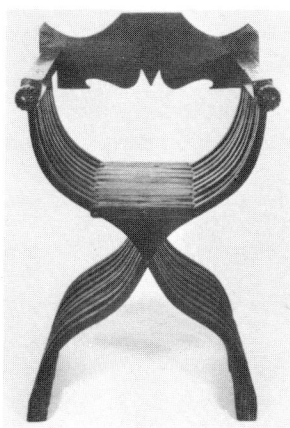

E1 A Tuscan Renaissance walnut Savonarola armchair, with waved hinged back and intersecting pierced S-curved bar supports joined by a bar seat, late 15th century.

E2 A Renaissance armchair, the rectangular back with acanthus-carved giltwood finials, the moulded flat arms with giltwood brackets, raised on square legs joined by stretchers, upholstered in 17th century tapestry.

E3 A Tuscan Renaissance walnut armchair, with two gilt finials of scrolling foliage, late 16th century.

E4 A Renaissance oak Savonarola folding chair, 16th century.

E5 An iron and brass chair of X-framed construction, with brass finials, 16th century.

E6 A Tuscan walnut armchair, with panelled box seat with a cupboard door, late 16th century.

E1 A Tuscan walnut and intarsia armchair, the top rail inlaid with a band of stars, above a panel inlaid with a geometric lozenge, the panelled lower part with a door, late 16th century.

E2 A Tuscany walnut "Savonarola" armchair, the shaped panel back centred by an armorial cartouche, the slatted folding frame chip-carved, on paw-carved feet, *c.* 1600.

E3 A walnut armchair, the padded back headed by gilt leaf-scrolled finials, with flat scroll arms, the plain square supports and front legs joined by pierced front and back stretchers, early 17th century.

E4 A baroque walnut chair, the upholstered back with giltwood plume finials, the moulded scroll arms on baluster supports, the upholstered seat on turned legs joined by turned stretchers, upholstered in floral red velvet, early 17th century.

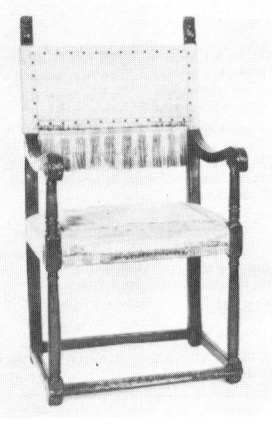
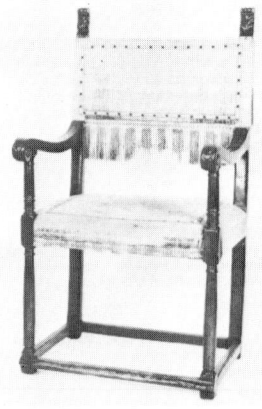

E6 Two walnut armchairs, the backs with acanthus-shaped grips, the plain backs and seats upholstered in worn velvet, with curved, carved armrests, the turned legs joined by plain stretchers, 17th century.

E7 A Venetian walnut armchair, the stuffed back supported by caryatids, the stuffed arms ending in scroll supports, with elaborately scrolled legs joined by a carved stretcher, *c.* 1680.

E5 A baroque walnut armchair, upholstered in green velvet with a 16th century metallic thread-embroidered velvet panel and fringe, mid 17th century.

D8 A giltwood throne, the arched back surmounted by a foliate and strapwork cresting centred by a cartouche supported by cherubs playing string instruments, late 17th century.

E9 A walnut armchair, with stuffed seat and back, with a fringe, the flat armrests above shaped supports, late 17th century.

E10 A Venetian walnut armchair, with stuffed spade-shaped back, the scrolling arms headed by leaves, the stuffed seat on bead-moulded scroll front legs, late 17th century.

D11 A Venetian baroque painted armchair, the carved scrolling arms, legs and stretchers decorated in the manner of Oriental lacquer, with mother-of-pearl inlay, *c.* 1700; 52 in. (132 cm) high.

D 1 An armchair, attributed to Andrea Brustalon, the back and seat covered in Spanish gilt leather, the arms as tree trunks entwined with leaves at the upper end of which lie blackamoor children, the whole on tree-trunk feet, early 18th century.

E 2 A Venetian giltwood throne, with stuffed cartouche-shaped back surmounted by coat-of-arms and carved with scrolls, fruit and flowers, with serpentine fronted drop-in seat and carved cabriole legs with shaped stretchers, early 18th century.

D 3 A Venetian giltwood armchair, with a stuffed cartouche-shaped back, scroll arms and shaped stuffed drop-in seat, early 18th century.

E 4 A rococo gilt-metal and iron sgabello di piuma, with rectangular cushion seat in X-shaped iron frame, the arms mounted with gilt-metal wave-pattern and C-scrolls engraved with crosses above crowned lions, upholstered in crimson velvet, early 18th century.

E 5 A Venetian rococo painted armchair, the oval moulded upholstered back centred by a scrolling cartouche, with padded scroll arms, painted with flowers on a cream ground with gilt highlighting, *c.* 1740.

E 6 A north Italian rococo giltwood armchair, with curved cartouche-shaped padded back and serpentine seat, in broad moulded frame with profile medallion cresting and seat rail, on cabriole legs, upholstered in green silk, mid 18th century.

E 7 A giltwood armchair, with upholstered rectangular back and seat, the scrolling arms with upholstered pads, the apron carved with scrolls, over carved rococo detail cabriole legs, mid 18th century.

E 8 A rococo walnut armchair, with cartouche-shaped padded back and rectangular upholstered seat, the seat rail centrally carved with a shell, on cabriole legs with pad feet, upholstered in yellow silk damask, mid 18th century.

E 9 A rococo walnut armchair, with moulded cartouche-shaped back carved with two summer flowers, with moulded arms carved with flowers at the scrolling ends, on cabriole legs, *c.* 1750.

Armchairs of the 18th Century
The inspiration for the Italian 18th-century open armchair is distinctly curvilinear, and thus of French origin. The style was however freely interpreted – see, for example no. 10 below, where the open back and deeply scrolling seat frame are typical of 1760s design. One earlier Italian design was carried through however – the sgabello di piuma, or X-frame stool with arms, made of steel and often having gilt-metal mounts – see no. 4 on this page.

The curvilinear style lasted rather longer in Italy than in France or England. Despite the excitement of designers in the rest of Europe over the rediscovery of Italian antiquity and the neoclassical designs that resulted, the new style was slow to take hold at its source.

One difficulty regularly encountered with Italian seat furniture of the 19th century is that revived styles of the 18th century were reproduced with perfect fidelity, making it hard to tell them apart.

E 10 A north Italian rococo walnut armchair, upholstered in yellow silk brocade, mid 18th century.

D 11 A carved and gilded armchair, the top rail centred with a mask of Apollo, and sprays of flowers, 18th century.

D 1 A Venetian painted armchair, with tall cartouche-shaped back and painted with sprays of summer flowers on an ivory ground, with downcurved arms on inswept scrolled supports, mid 18th century.

E 4 A silvered chair, the seat and back carved in the shape of a shell, supported on splayed legs, the arms in the form of dolphins, late 17th century.

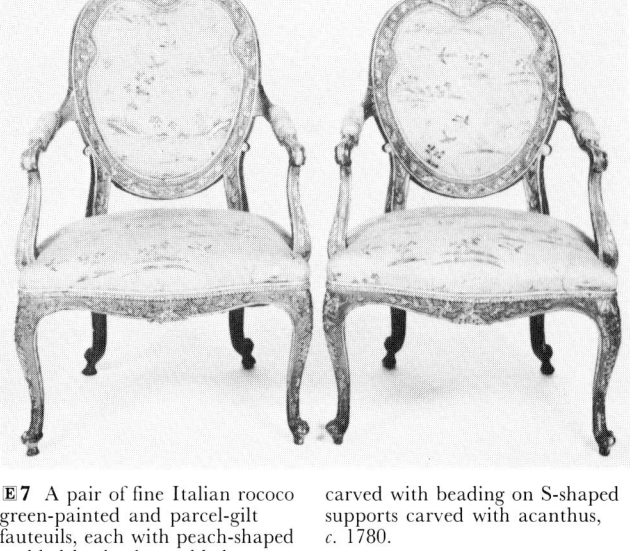

E 7 A pair of fine Italian rococo green-painted and parcel-gilt fauteuils, each with peach-shaped padded back, the padded arms carved with beading on S-shaped supports carved with acanthus, c. 1780.

E 2 An armchair, with a high stuffed back and upholstered seat, supported on carved scrolling legs joined by H-stretcher, late 17th century.

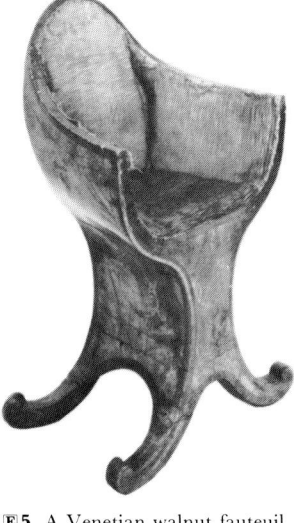

E 5 A Venetian walnut fauteuil de gondole, lined in blue ribbed cloth, the back centred by an inlaid chariot, crossbanded throughout, 18th century.

E 8 An Italian neoclassical painted and parcel-gilt fauteuil, with upholstered drop-in seats, c. 1780.

E 9 A Venetian cherrywood armchair, the top above tapering splat, the scrolling arms above incurved supports on tapering legs, late 18th century.

D 3 A Venetian armchair, attributed to Andrea Brustolon, with ornately carved arms and supports formed as figures of negroes, with yellow upholstery, 18th century.

E 6 A north Italian giltwood armchair, the guilloche-carved frame with arched padded back, with moulded outcurved arms, c. 1780.

E 10 A pair of north Italian neoclassical giltwood fauteuils, each with arched tapering curved rectangular padded back, upholstered in crimson silk damask, late 18th century.

E1 An Italian neoclassical cream and grey-painted fauteuil, with oval padded back and bowed upholstered seat, the cresting carved with pierced acorn wreaths, late 18th century.

E2 An Italian neoclassical walnut fauteuil, the slightly arched crest-rail above lyre-shaped splats, c. 1780.

E6 A pair of giltwood armchairs, the rectangular backs with oval stuffed panels, the scrolling arms on turned supports, the seats also stuffed, c. 1790.

E3 A pair of Italian neoclassical white-painted and parcel-gilt fauteuils, each with curved penalled rectangular top rail carved with acanthus and pendent bellflowers over a U-shaped padded splat, upholstered in white silk brocade, late 18th century.

D7 A pair of fine Italian neoclassical green-painted and parcel-gilt fauteuils, each with arched rectangular padded back and slightly bowed upholstered seat, the crest applied with laurel flanking a rosette, the fluted and reeded padded arms suspending from roundels carved with stiff leaves, on circular tapering fluted legs, c. 1800.

E4 An Italian cream-painted and parcel-gilt fauteuil, with tapering padded back and bowed seat, upholstered in plum coloured linen, the moulded frame on fluted tapering legs headed by rosettes, late 18th century.

E5 An Italian neoclassical green and white-painted armchair, with rectangular padded back and seat in moulded frame, upholstered in green silk, late 18th century; 44 in. (113 cm) wide.

E8 A pair of Italian neoclassical fruitwood and parcel-gilt seat furniture, each with curved rectangular top rail carved at the sides with parcel-gilt masks, upholstered in green silk, early 19th century; 65 in. (165 cm) wide.

E1 A neoclassical fruitwood and parcel-gilt fauteuil, with curved rectangular top rail, carved at the sides with parcel-gilt flowerheads and foliate scrolls and dropped upholstered seat in green silk, early 19th century.

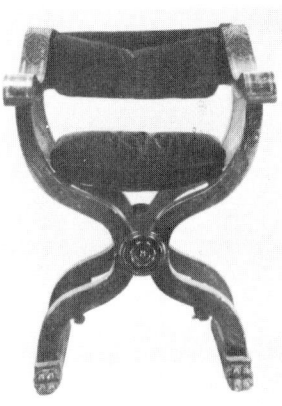

E2 A Savonarola walnut armchair, of double "X" shape, the downcurved arms carved with acanthus leaves and stylized banding, newly upholstered in red velvet fitted cushions, mid 19th century.

E3 An ivory-inlaid walnut court chair, in Mannerist style, the tall back with two panels of sporting putti in inlaid ivory, the straight arms and back strut bearing wide banding, mid 19th century; 53 in. (135 cm) high.

E4 A carved walnut Gothic revival armchair, the deep U-shaped back carved and pierced with Gothic tracery and leaves, the leafy cresting flanked by a pair of crouching lions each holding a shield, third quarter of the 19th century.

E5 An ivory-inlaid olivewood folding armchair, the tall back inlaid in the Renaissance style with scrolling flowers and figures, the downswept arms with folding "X" frame supports similarly inlaid, probably Milan, *c.* 1875.

E6 A Renaissance-style ivory-inlaid walnut and ebonized open armchair, with arched back inlaid with a flower filled urn, a musician and foliate scrolls.

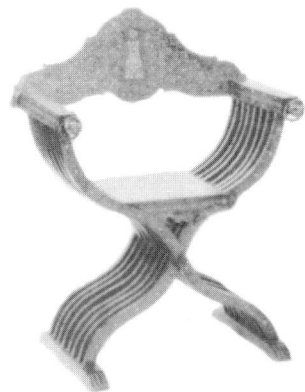

E7 A walnut Savonarola armchair, inlaid with bone foliate arabesques and parquetry chequered bands, with paw bar feet, late 19th century.

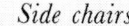

Side chairs

E8 A Renaissance walnut side chair, upholstered in velvet, 16th century.

E9 A Tuscan walnut chair, with leafy corbel finials, with carved panels of entwined branches, late 16th century.

E10 A Renaissance walnut sgabello chair, with rectangular seat with a loose cushion, first half of 17th century.

E11 A north Italian carved walnut chair inlaid with a geometric roundel, mid 17th century.

E12 A Lombardy walnut dining chair, late 17th century.

E1 An Italian walnut dining chair, with rectangular padded back and upholstered seat, on bobbin-turned legs, 17th century.

E2 An Italian walnut side chair, with padded back and seat upholstered in burgundy velvet, on shaped claw feet, joined by pierced scrolling foliate rails and H-shaped stretchers, 17th century.

E3 An Italian rococo green-painted and parcel-gilt side chair, 1710-1720.

E4 An Italian black-painted side chair, with arched tapering rectangular back with baluster-shaped splat and upholstered seat, the back upholstered in green velvet, early 18th century.

E5 A north Italian bone-inlaid walnut side chair, the serpentine top rail and vase-shaped splats inlaid with floral decoration and the figures of Orpheus, Mercury and Vesta flanked by turned supports surmounted by finials, early 18th century.

E6 A Venetian rococo cream-painted petite chaise, with upholstered seat in floral brocade, mid 18th century.

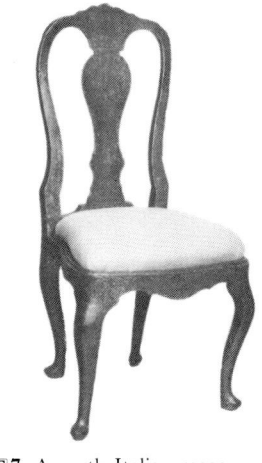

E7 A north Italian rococo green-painted side chair, with shaped drop-in seat, above pad feet, mid 18th century.

E8 A north Italian rococo green-painted and parcel-gilt chaise à canne, with cartouche-shaped carved back and serpentine carved seat in moulded frame, mid 18th century.

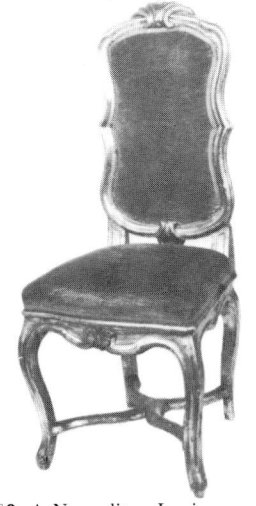

E9 A Neapolitan Louis XV-style chair, with gilded frame, second half of the 18th century.

E10 A neoclassical walnut chair, the drop-in seat in moulded bow-front rail, raised on fluted tapering legs with foliate toes, *c.* 1780.

E11 A neoclassical walnut chair, with moulded oval back and seat rail, on turned tapering legs, *c.* 1780.

E12 A Louis XVI-style grey-painted and parcel-gilt chaise, with peach-shaped padded back, late 18th century.

E1 A pair of north Italian neoclassical grey-painted and parcel-gilt side chairs, with moulded frame, the crest carved with ribbon-ties, on fluted tapering legs, upholstered in buff cotton, late 18th century.

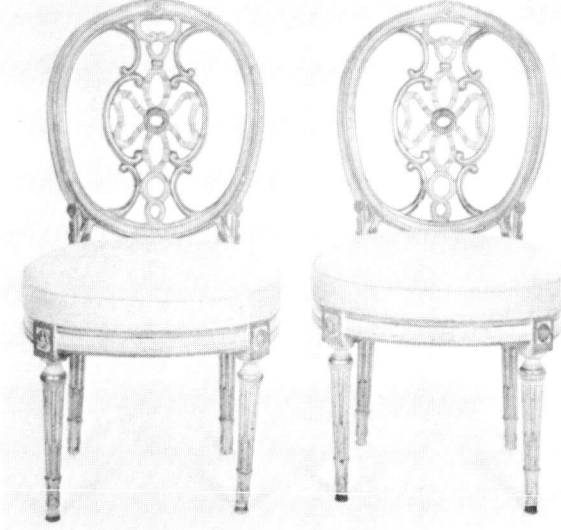

E2 A pair of neoclassical cream-painted and parcel-gilt side chairs, each with oval carved back pierced with ribbon-ties, the oval seats on tapering fluted legs, upholstered in yellow silk, late 18th century.

E3 Two Venetian side chairs with matching settee, the chairs and chair-back settee with central vase splats, with floral marquetry, late 18th century.

E4 A Venetian Louis XVI-style side chair, with carved back pierced with lozenges and rosettes, with deep carved seat rail, *c.* 1800.

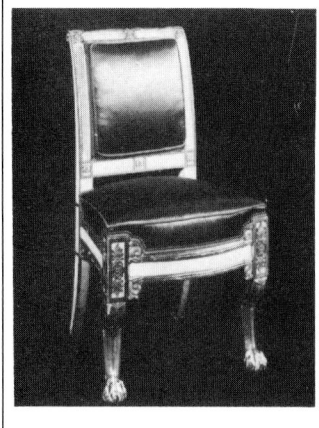

E5 A neoclassical white-painted and parcel-gilt side chair, the back carved with applied roundels in a moulded frame, the legs carved as animals' legs, *c.* 1815.

E6 A rococo-style giltwood side chair, with moulded and carved crested back, the padded back and seat covered in azure silk, 19th century.

COMMODES
1580-1900

The earliest Italian commodes are of fine Renaissance proportions, an indigenous design that would be imitated in France and influential in the Low Countries. In the later 17th century the block front appears.

With the assimilation of the curvilinear style, Italian commodes became almost indistinguishable from French in design, until the mid 18th century when the Louis XV style was adopted without any pretence at restraint.

E7 A Genoese walnut commode, with four long drawers with male bust handles, *c.* 1580; 29 in. (72 cm) wide.

E8 A Lombard baroque walnut commode, with four well-carved long drawers, late 16th/early 17th century; 59 in. (150 cm) wide.

E9 A baroque walnut chest of drawers, the moulded top over four drawers with raised panels, *c.* 1650; 41 in. high by 59 in. wide (102 by 150 cm).

E 1 A north Italian walnut commode, with well-carved frieze above four drawers, 17th century; 42 in. high by 61 in. wide (105 by 155 cm).

E 2 A Lombard walnut and marquetry secretaire commode, of inverted angled serpentine form, the top drawer fitted as a secretaire, with ebonized mouldings, late 17th century; 39 in. high by 56 in. wide (99 by 143 cm).

E 3 A baroque inlaid walnut chest of drawers, with moulded crossbanded top above drawers in the serpentine front, on bracket feet, late 17th century; 28 in. (70 cm) wide.

E 4 A Lombard bone-inlaid ebonized secretaire commode, with hinged divided top above three long drawers, the top one with a fall front, c. 1700; 34 in. high by 54 in. wide (86 by 138 cm).

E 5 A north Italian walnut and cedarwood small commode, inlaid with bone, of inverted angled serpentine form, c. 1720; 34 in. high by 27 in. wide (86 by 69 cm).

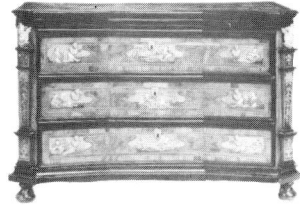

E 6 A north Italian large walnut and marquetry commode, decorated with bone and boxwood inlay, c. 1720; 40 in. high by 62 in. wide (102 by 158 cm).

E 7 An 18th-century Lombard inlaid walnut chest of drawers, the four fielded panelled drawers inlaid with floral and animal motifs; 42 in. high by 55 in. wide (105 by 140 cm).

E 8 A baroque walnut and marquetry small chest of drawers, on S-shaped bracket feet, early 18th century; 23 in. (58 cm) wide.

E 9 A south Italian walnut and seaweed marquetry commode, the drawers inlaid with shaped panels of interlaced scrolls, early 18th century; 55 in. (140 cm) wide.

E 10 A north Italian walnut breakfront commode, the four drawers with brass handles, c. 1750; 42 in. high by 61 in. wide (105 by 155 cm).

E 11 A Lombard ebonized chest of drawers, with secretaire top above four shaped inlaid drawers, 17th century; 44 in. high by 63 in. wide (110 by 160 cm).

E 12 A walnut parquetry inverted breakfront chest of drawers, c. 1720; 39 in. high by 75 in. wide (99 by 192 cm).

D 13 A walnut and marquetry chest of drawers, early 18th century; 44 in. high by 79 in. wide (112 by 202 cm).

E 14 A Piedmontese commode, with three drawers, 18th century; 40 in. high by 57 inb. wide (100 by 145 cm).

E 15 A rococo ormolu-mounted walnut commode, mid 18th century; 34 in. (85 cm).

E 16 A bombé small commode, c. 1750; 32 in. high by 21 in. wide (83 by 55 cm).

E 17 A north Italian rococo walnut and marquetry commode, c. 1750; 25 in. (65 cm) wide.

E1 A north Italian rococo cream-japanned petite commode, the bombé base decorated in colour sans traverse with figures of exotic birds and chinoiserie figures, possibly Venice, *c.* 1750; 34 in. (86 cm) wide.

D2 A rosewood commode, with serpentine quartered and crossbanded top, mid 18th century; 53 in. (143 cm) wide.

D3 A north Italian rococo kingwood and marquetry commode, with pink and grey marble top, above two short and four long quarter-veneered drawers, mid 18th century; 44 in. (112 cm) wide.

E4 A north Italian rococo tulipwood and parquetry commode, the moulded top above three crossbanded long drawers inlaid with cube pattern, between bombé angles, mid 18th century; 62 in. (157 cm) wide.

E5 A Sicilian commode, the three drawers and sides painted with panels of flowers on white reserves, mid 18th century; 40 in. (102 cm) high.

D6 A Venetian painted commode, decorated with fruit and flowers, the mouldings in blue, green and sepia; mid 18th century.

C7 A Venetian rococo green-japanned bombé commode, with verde antico marble top, mid 18th century; 55 in. (140 cm) wide.

D8 A Venetian commode, painted with sprays of polychrome flowers on grey-green ground, *c.* 1750; 33 in. (83 cm) high.

D9 A serpentine-fronted commode, with two drawers, 18th century; 35 in. high by 54 in. wide (87 by 138 cm).

E10 A Venetian painted commode, of bombé form, with two drawers painted with sprays of flowers, supported on short cabriole legs, mid 18th century.

E11 A bombé commode, in crossbanded and quarter-veneered kingwood, the mottled grey marble top with gallery, *c.* 1750; 32 in. (83 cm) high.

E12 A kingwood commode, with fine ormolu mounts, of bombé shape with cabriole legs, 18th century; 36 in. high by 53 in. wide (90 by 135 cm).

E13 A walnut and marquetry inlaid serpentine-front chest, the ivory inlay depicting hunting scenes, 18th century; 56 in. (142 cm) wide.

E14 A north Italian commode, parquetry veneered in mahogany and oak, on chevron-veneered legs, the corners of bombé form, 30 in. high by 34 in. wide (77 by 86 cm).

E15 A walnut serpentine commode, with crossbanded top, the three long drawers with scroll handles, on moulded cabriole feet, 18th century; 48 in. (123 cm) wide.

E16 A Venetian rococo cream-painted and parcel-gilt commode, the serpentine moulded top above two long drawers, raised on cabriole legs, 18th century; 42 in. (105 cm) wide.

E17 A rococo walnut commode, the rectangular moulded top over two long crossbanded and quarter-veneered drawers above a serpentine apron, raised on cabriole legs, *c.* 1760; 49 in. (124 cm) wide.

D 1 A kingwood and parquetry veneered commode, the three drawers with brass handles and pierced backplates, *c.* 1770; 39 in. (100 cm) high.

E 2 A north Italian rosewood commode, the marble top above two long drawers inlaid with scrolls, above shaped apron, *c.* 1770; 33 in. high by 40 in. wide (84 by 102 cm).

E 3 A rococo inlaid walnut and olivewood commode, the serpentine moulded top with a rosette above three crossbanded drawers, on tapering legs, *c.* 1770; 24 in. (60 cm) wide.

E 4 A north Italian walnut commode, the panels of hunting scenes in walnut and ivory, *c.* 1850; 37 in. (94 cm) high.

E 5 A Milanese walnut commode, with quarter-veneers and satinwood inlay, *c.* 1780; 34 in. (85 cm) high.

E 6 A Milanese walnut-veneered marquetry commode, the top inlaid with flowerheads, *c.* 1780; 34 in. (88 cm) high.

E 7 A Milanese parquetry commode, in quarter-veneered kingwood, with inset marble top, *c.* 1780; 38 in. (98 cm) high.

E 8 A north Italian neoclassical marquetry and parquetry commode, *c.* 1780; 53 in. (135 cm) wide.

D 9 A north Italian walnut parquetry commode, the top inlaid with rosewood and boxwood, *c.* 1785; 34 in. (88 cm) high, Milan or Turin.

E 10 A north Italian parquetry breakfront commode, in well-figured quarter-veneered walnut, *c.* 1790; 32 in. (81 cm) high.

C 11 A Milanese marquetry commode, with frieze drawer, *c.* 1790; 34 in. (86 cm) high.

E 12 A north Italian walnut commode, chequered crossbanding, *c.* 1790; 37 in. (95 cm) high.

E 13 A north Italian parquetry commode, with pink marble top, lower drawers with Greek key motif, *c.* 1790; 36 in. (93 cm) high.

D 14 A Milanese marquetry commode, by Giuseppe Maggiolini, with inlaid drawer, *c.* 1797; 32 in. (80 cm) wide.

D 15 A north Italian neoclassical walnut and parquetry commode, late 18th century; 49 in. (124 cm) wide.

E 16 A rosewood commode, the quarter-veneered top centred by flowers and floral sprays within geometric border, *c.* 1790; 35 in. (89 cm) high.

E 17 A north Italian neoclassical brass-inlaid rosewood commode, late 18th century; 45 in. (73 cm) wide.

E 18 A neoclassical provincial fruitwood commode, late 18th century; 50 in. (127 cm) wide.

E 19 A fruitwood and parquetry commode, with red and white marble top, late 18th century; 40 in. (103 cm) wide.

E 1 A neoclassical walnut and marquetry small commode, with rectangular top inlaid with ebonized lines above two drawers, late 18th century; 22 in. (54 cm) wide.

D 2 A neoclassical kingwood and parquetry small commode, with moulded breccia marble top, late 18th century; 34 in. (84 cm) wide.

E 3 A north Italian rosewood and fruitwood commode, in the style of Maggiolini, late 18th century; 48 in. (112 cm) wide.

E 4 A north Italian walnut commode, with barber's-pole banding throughout, late 18th century; 43 in. (110 cm) wide.

D 5 A Milanese rosewood and marquetry commode, the top centred by a patera above a frieze drawer, formed of two panels inlaid with swags, late 18th century; 35 in. high by 49 in. wide (89 by 124 cm).

E 6 A north Italian marquetry commode, in the Maggiolini style, inlaid with foliage, the frieze with a long drawer above two drawers, late 18th century; 48 in. (123 cm) wide.

E 7 A rosewood and marquetry commode, in the Maggiolini style with verde antico marble top, frieze drawer inlaid with grottesche, late 18th century; 49 in. (124 cm) wide.

D 8 A walnut tulipwood and marquetry commode, with eared crossbanded semi-elliptical top, inlaid with imbricated bands fitted with three drawers sans traverse inlaid with a swagged urn on a figured ground, late 18th century; 33 in. high by 54 in. wide (85 by 137 cm).

D 9 A commode, in walnut and fruitwood, the frieze inlaid with a series of portrait medallions and baskets of flowers, late 18th century; 47 in. (122 cm) wide.

D 10 A Milanese marquetry straight-front commode, with crossbanded and inlaid decoration; 48 in. (122 cm) wide.

E 11 A north Italian neoclassical marquetry commode, with rectangular liver, grey and white marble top, late 18th century; 52 in. (132 cm) wide.

E 12 A north Italian miniature parquetry commode, in kingwood within purpleheart banding, the top with green-stained Greek key border, late 18th century; 11 in. high by 15 in. wide (28 by 37 cm).

E 13 A Piedmontese commode, in walnut veneer, late 18th century; 38 in. high by 46 in. wide (94 by 120 cm).

C 14 A neoclassical walnut, burr-elm and parquetry commode, late 18th century; 59 in. (150 cm) wide.

E 15 A north Italian neoclassical rosewood and marquetry commode, late 18th century; 50 in. (127 cm) wide.

D 16 A neoclassical salmon and green-painted commode, late 18th century; 45 in. (115 cm) wide.

E 17 A walnut chest, with crossbanded top, late 18th century; 51 in. (131 cm) wide.

D 1 A Milanese kingwood, walnut and marquetry commode, late 18th century; 35 in. high by 48 in. wide (90 by 122 cm).

E 2 A Venetian painted bombé cupboard, with marble top; 24 in. high by 14 in. wide (60 by 35 cm).

E 3 A small walnut, marquetry commode, third quarter of the 19th century; 33 in. high by 31 in. wide (84 by 79 cm).

E 4 A rosewood and marquetry bombé commode, the canted corners continuing to slightly outswept legs; 35 in. (89 cm) wide.

E 5 A Venetian painted commode, of serpentine form with two drawers raised on outswept legs with cloven hoof feet, on a pale green ground; 35 in. high by 53 in. wide (90 by 135 cm).

E 6 A Venetian cream and blue painted serpentine chest, the waxed top decorated with raised scrolling foliage flowerheads and mythical beasts above three long drawers on cabriole legs; 34 in. (86 cm) wide.

E 7 A Venetian painted commode, of exaggerated baroque form, with a simulated verdeantico marble top, the whole painted with flowers and chinoiserie on a yellow ground with powder-blue base, c. 1900; 37 in. high by 30 in. wide (95 by 76 cm).

E 8 A satinwood marquetry chest of drawers, with a rectangular marble top, with two small drawers flanking a central drawer above two long drawers, geometrically banded throughout, on square tapering legs, c. 1900; 36 in. high by 49 in. wide (91 by 126 cm).

CUPBOARDS
1750-1800

The imagination and skill of Italian craftsmen are both reflected in the variety and decoration of their cupboards. Advanced methods of glass-making enabled vitrines to be produced in serpentine and bombé forms with a freedom of line not always found north of the Alps until later. Also, no shape that could be rendered useful was prohibited – for example the well disguised cupboard, no. 13 below.

E 9 A Venetian painted vitrine, with serpentine-fronted shelves, mid 18th century; 80 in. high by 40 in. wide (205 by 101 cm).

D 10 A tulipwood corner cabinet, c. 1750; 84 in. high by 40 in. wide (241 by 102 cm).

E 11 A rococo vernis Martin hanging corner cupboard, c. 1750; 39 in. (99 cm) high.

E 12 A walnut and marquetry encoignure, c. 1770; 26 in. (67 cm) wide.

E 13 A Venetian painted wood cyllindrical cupboard, 32 in. (79 cm) high.

DESKS
1710-1920

The rising middle class of the late 17th century expanded the demand for finely made writing furniture. Lacking a strong native tradition in this area, Italian cabinet-makers drew their inspiration largely from French models, favouring Louis XIV styles for pedestal and cylinder desks and adapting the form to Transitional and Louis XVI styles.

Similarly, the writing table or scrivania was modelled on the French bureau plat.

E1 A north Italian walnut kneehole desk with three frieze drawers and a leather-lined slide above two cupboards, early 18th century; 59 in. (150 cm) wide.

E2 A neoclassical fruitwood and parquetry cylinder desk, the rectangular surface above the roll-top surface, 18th century; 43 in. (110 cm) wide.

D3 An Italian ivory-inlaid cylinder bureau, the cylinder enclosing an elaborately fitted interior, inlaid with a figure of a Grecian warrior, c. 1800; 47 in. (121 cm) high.

E4 A north Italian neoclassical walnut and parquetry bureau plat, with rectangular inset-leather top; 56 in. (143 cm) wide.

E5 A walnut and floral marquetry kneehole writing desk, 50 in. (124 cm) wide.

MIRRORS
1670-1790

The purpose of palatial furniture has always been as much to make a *bella figura* as to suit the convenience of the palace's occupants. In no type of furniture is this principle better displayed than in the grandiloquent rococo mirror frames of the 18th century.

Italian mirror frames of the 19th century are generally provenanced as Florentine, but their style and tradition date to the 17th century and emanate from a much wider area.

E6 A carved and gilded mirror frame, of rectangular form, with domed top, the elaborate carving of foliate decoration and acanthus leaf scrolls, 17th century; 55 in. (140 cm) high.

E7 A north Italian late baroque giltwood mirror, with arched rectangular plate in conforming fluted glass, 17th century; 90 in. (230 cm) high.

E8 A rococo giltwood wall mirror, early 18th century; 74 in. high by 39 in. wide (185 by 95 cm).

E9 A Venetian carved giltwood looking glass, early 18th century; 46 in. (117 cm) high.

E10 A north Italian green-japanned toilet glass, the lower part with a fitted interior above a drawer containing compartments and boxes, the whole decorated in gilt, early 18th century.

E11 A rococo giltwood mirror, with rectangular plate in conforming moulded borders carved with C-scrolls, flowerheads and gadrooning, early 18th century; 55 in. (140 cm) high.

E12 A north Italian rococo giltwood mirror, with cartouche-shaped mirror plate in conforming bellflower, early 18th century; 51 in. (130 cm) high.

E1 A Florentine giltwood mirror, ornately carved with bold scrollwork forming the cresting apron and sides, early 18th century; 58 in. high by 46 in. wide (147 by 117 cm).

E4 A Venetian giltwood mirror, the two plates enclosed by a scrollwork and flowers, *c.* 1740; 59 in. high by 40 in. wide (150 by 103 cm).

D7 A giltwood looking glass, mid 18th century; 86 in. high by 60 in. wide (220 by 153 cm).

E10 A rococo giltwood mirror, mid 18th century; 67 in. (172 cm) high.

E2 A Venetian engraved glass and gilt-bronze looking glass, the bevelled plate within canted etched border glasses, outlined in bead-moulding, *c.* 1720; 52 in. high by 29 in. wide (132 by 74 cm).

E5 A rococo giltwood mirror, the crest surmounted by a foliate and plumed cartouche, the frame carved with foliate S- and C-scrolls, second quarter of the 18th century; 34 in. (87 cm) high.

C8 A Venetian rococo giltwood mirror, with arched divided plate in shaped and engraved mirror borders, mid 18th century; 111 in. (282 cm) high.

E11 A giltwood mirror, *c.* 1775; 26 in. high by 14 in. wide (66 by 36 cm).

E3 A large Roman giltwood frame, the deeply moulded oporture enclosing a mirror plate, *c.* 1730; 76 in. high by 66 in. wide (194 by 168 cm).

E6 A rococo giltwood mirror, with rectangular plate in conforming moulded and mirror borders carved with wave pattern, scrolled acanthus, plumes and flowerheads, mid 18th century; 68 in. (172 cm) high.

E9 A rococo giltwood mirror, the pierced arched crest carved with wave-pattern, mid 18th century; 68 in. (173 cm) high.

E12 A neoclassical giltwood pier mirror, late 18th century; 69 in. (173 cm) high.

E1 A north Italian neoclassical giltwood pier mirror, late 18th century; 68 in. (172 cm) high.

E2 A giltwood pier mirror, the plate between tapering slightly canted angles, *c.* 1780; 68 in. (172 cm) high.

D3 A green, cream-painted and parcel-gilt mirror, late 18th/early 19th century; 60 in. (152 cm) high.

E4 A baroque giltwood mirror, the plate in conforming border carved with plumes and acanthus, the pierced crest carved with large scrolling acanthus, the sides with acanthus and bellflowers, *c.* 1740; 67 in. (170 cm) high.

D5 A Venetian rococo engraved glass mirror, with bevelled arched plate within conforming mirrored borders engraved with foliage branches and beading, the crest similarly engraved, *c.* 1745; 77 in. (194 cm) high.

D6 A Venetian rococo engraved and blue glass mirror, the bevelled plate within conforming foliate-engraved and chip-carved mirrored borders; 84 in. high by 53 in. wide (212 by 135 cm).

SETTEES & SOFAS
1750-1820

It has to be admitted that Italian settees of the 18th century are rarely fine, in part through lack of attention to the lines of their French models, but also through the quality of their craftsmanship. Too often Italian makers sought to stretch settees to lengths which the design simply could not accommodate.

The arrival of the Empire style, fostered particularly by the new Bonapartist rulers, brought a welcome return of discipline to furniture design.

E7 A Venetian rococo painted two-chair-back canapé, the cartouch-shaped back with interlacing strapwork and carved with leaf-tips, with scrolling arms and moulded caned seats, raised on cabriole legs with cabochons at the knees, mid 18th century; 44 in. (110 cm) wide.

E8 A Louis XV white-painted and gilded canapé, with serpentine moulded back and seat rails, 57 in. (145 cm) wide.

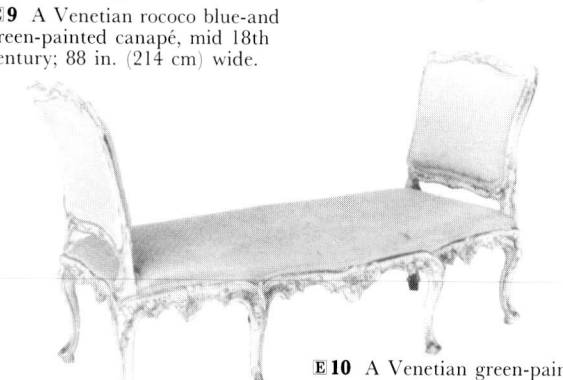

E9 A Venetian rococo blue-and green-painted canapé, mid 18th century; 88 in. (214 cm) wide.

E10 A Venetian green-painted and gilded banquette, 63 in. (161 cm) wide.

E1 A Piedmontese small canapé, the overscroll back and oval seat covered in ivory-ground gros point needlework, late 18th century; 49 in. (124 cm) wide.

E2 An Empire giltwood sofa, the back curved at the head and sloping to a rectangular end, the frame carved with a chain of berried laurel leaves, and headed by a dolphin above a panel of crossed arrows, the stuffed back and loose-cushioned seat above a panelled frieze set with flowerhead bosses and raised on circular tapering legs with winged brackets; 82 in. (208 cm) wide.

E3 A neoclassical fruitwood and parcel-gilt canapé, with curved rectangular top rail carved at the sides with parcel-gilt flowerheads and foliate scrolls, the outcurved arms with ormolu rosettes, on square outcurved tapering legs with ebonized cloven feet, early 19th century; 66 in. (168 cm) wide.

STANDS
1700-1900

The blackamoor is so popular that it has become almost synonymous with Italian stands of the post-Renaissance period. But the collector should be aware that Italian craftsmen remain well able to create the subtleties of shape and surface treatment that give age and character to the modern reproduction.

This same caveat should be borne in mind when assessing bible stands and bookrests: considerable experience is necessary to evaluate them.

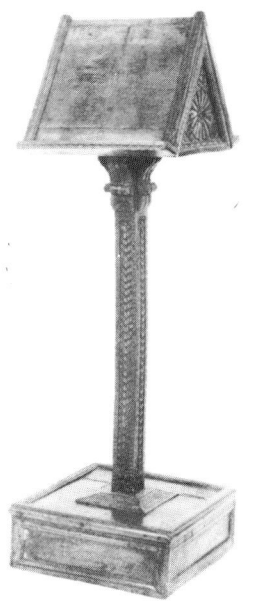

E4 A Renaissance walnut lectern, the sides carved with flowerheads, on a square support with chip carving, *c.* 1550; 65 in. (165 cm) high.

E5 A Tuscan painted and parcel-gilt lectern, the X-framed support turned and fluted, late 16th/early 17th century; 60 in. (153 cm) high.

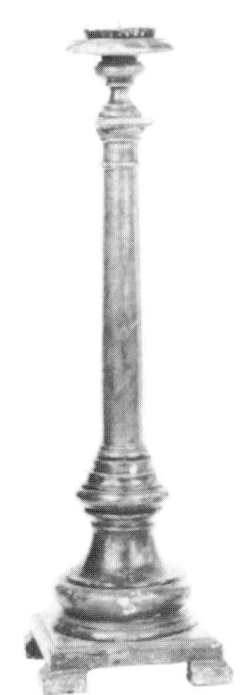

E6 A silverwood candlestand, with a circular moulded top on a turned stem with turned and square moulded base and shaped bracket feet, 17th century; 63 in. (160 cm) high.

E7 A Venetian blackamoor torchère, the turbaned figure holding a shaped breche-violette marble tray carved with tassels, and wearing a green and cream doublet and red breeches, early 18th century; 55 in. (140 cm) high.

569

E 1 A Venetian ebonized and gilded figural torchère, early 18th century; 45 in. (112 cm) high.

E 2 A giltwood and ebonized blackamoor torchère, *c.* 1740; 63 in. (160 cm) high.

D 3 A carved pine blackamoor torchère, with ivory teeth and mother-of-pearl eyes, *c.* 1725; 59 in. (150 cm) high.

E 4 A Venetian rococo polychromed figural torchère, decorated in colour, on a circular pedestal with scrolled acanthus feet, mid 18th century; 53 in. (135 cm) high.

E 5 A Milanese neoclassical green-painted and parcel-gilt small plant stand, with inset grey and pink marble top in conforming borders, on well-carved S-shaped legs, *c.* 1780; 23 in. (58 cm) wide.

E 6 A Venetian painted blackamoor stand, the figure in polychrome feather skirt, 18th/19th century; 44 in. high by 26 in. wide (112 by 66 cm).

E 7 A neoclassical ebony, mahogany and parcel-gilt torchère, with carrara marble top on fluted Corinthian columns, *c.* 1820; 54 in. (137 cm) high.

E 8 A Venetian painted figure of a monkey footman, smiling, and wearing an elaborate footman's costume but with chains around his wrists, on octagonal marble plinth, 19th century; 54 in. (137 cm) high.

E 9 A carved and polychromed Nubian torchère, the figure supporting a chased gilt bowl, on a simulated marble pedestal; 57 in. (140 cm) high.

D 10 A Venetian rococo ebonized and giltwood blackamoor, supporting a socle on the turbanned head; 45 in. (113 cm) high.

TABLES
1620-1880

It is almost a paradox that in Italy, where superb carving was the rule, tables should be admired more for their pietra dura or scagliola tops than for their supports. Magnificent examples of Renaissance and Mannerist carved tables do of course exist, but such was the skill of Italian craftsmen in working marble that one has to feel that table supports, however fine, were at times created because a top of outstanding quality had already been conceived.

Centre tables

E 11 A Venetian polychromed and parcel-gilt blackamoor torchère, in the form of a gondolier atop his gondola; 39 in. (87 cm) high.

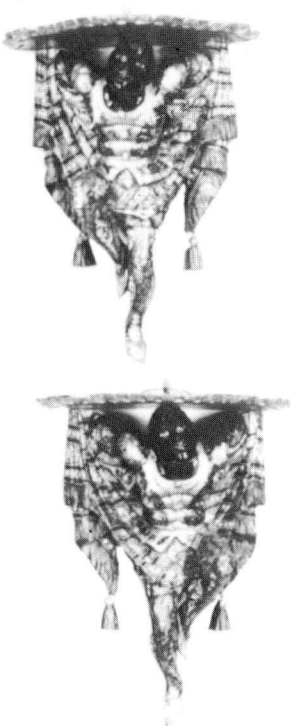

E 12 A pair of rococo-style parcel-gilt and polychromed wall brackets, with serpentine simulated verde antico marble shelves above a crouching blackamoor; 23 in. (59 cm) high.

E 1 A walnut octagonal centre table, on square frame, c. 1620; 52 in. (132 cm) diameter.

E 2 A rectangular walnut table, with multi-baluster legs, 17th century; 46 in. (116 cm) wide.

D 3 A marble-topped table, late 17th century; 44 in. (110 cm) wide.

E 4 A Venetian walnut veneered centre table, c. 1740.

D 5 A scagliola and marble inlay table, the top with simulated pictures depicting views, arranged around a central marble medallion, supported on an octagonal column, with three scroll feet embellished with ormolu detail, 18th century; 28 in. high by 42 in. diameter (70 by 105 cm).

E 6 A Milanese marquetry centre table, attributed to Ignazio Revelli, in quarter-veneered rosewood, c. 1780; 29 in. high by 36 in. wide (75 by 93 cm).

E 7 A north Italian neoclassical walnut, tulipwood and marquetry table, with moulded crossbanded top, the central panel and the frieze inlaid with foliate scrolls, on square tapering fluted legs ending in cuffs applied with roundels, late 18th century; 30 in. high by 31 in. wide (78 by 80 cm).

D 8 A neoclassical scagliola marble table top, decorated in colours with a central eared rectangular panel en grisaille depicting a frieze of a classical procession on a black ground with putti within wide pale-blue and brown scroll-carved borders, late 18th century; 26 in. wide by 55 in. long (65 by 1450 cm).

Pietra Dura and Scagliola

The decoration of fine furniture and especially of table tops with inlay of semi-precious stones and rare marbles – pietra dura – is an ancient art form in Italy.

The cost of pietra dura was always very high however and much effort went into the creation of a similar effect using cheaper material. Success came with the revival of scagliola early in the 17th century by Guido del Conte.

In pietra dura the stone is cut using its natural grain to enhance pictorial effects. Scagliola however is a composition of chips of smaller stones blended into a paste with plaster, glue and lime.

Scagliola was improved in mid-18th century Florence by an Irish friar, Henry Hugford, Abbot of Vallombrosa. His achievement was to create scenes of such definition and quality that the marble paste appeared to have been applied as paint.

A similar but still secret process was invented by Bossi, who used it notably in executing the architectural designs of Robert Adam in Ireland between 1785 and 1798.

E3 A mosaic table top, decorated with a still-life of flowers in a basket within a key-patterned border, the acanthus-decorated apron above turned and fluted tapering legs, *c.* 1845; 30 in. high by 30 in. wide (77 by 76 cm).

E4 A marble table top, the stylized petal top centred by a circular malachite panel and formed of expanding diamond-shaped hardstone and marble panels, contained within illusionistic banding, first half of the 19th century; 49 in. (123 cm) wide.

E1 A giltwood centre table, with massive black-bordered verde antico marble top, *c.* 1830; 53 in. (115 cm) wide.

D2 A fine scagliola table top, with a distant landscape in the manner of Zuccarelli, with a country inn and commedia dell'arte and rustic figures dancing framed by scrolling acanthus foliage centred by a coat-of-arms, the angles with crests framed by verde antico, *c.* 1830; 53 in. high by 36 in. wide (136 by 91 cm).

E5 A Milanese ivory-inlaid table, the rectangular top with three octagonal panels inlaid with deity in arabesque foliage surrounds and panelled border inlaid with trophies, *c.* 1800; 51 in. (130 cm) wide.

E6 A walnut centre table of J.-A. de Cerceau, the rectangular top with a mask and leaf carved border, *c.* 1870; 35 in. high by 55 in. wide (89 by 140 cm).

E7 A Renaissance oak rectangular table, the frieze carved with putto heads, flower vases and scrolling branches, 19th century; 65 in. (166 cm) wide.

E8 A specimen table, the rectangular top inset with 119 specimen marbles and semi-precious stones, above concave triform bases, 19th century; 21 in. high by 36 in. wide (55 by 90 cm).

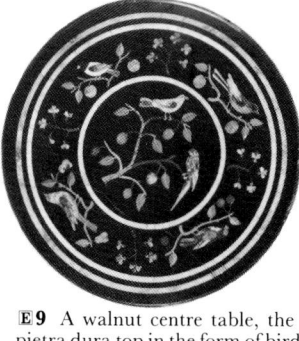

E9 A walnut centre table, the pietra dura top in the form of birds amongst flowering branches, above carved legs, 19th century; 27 in. wide (75 cm).

E10 An ivory-inlaid ebony and rosewood centre table, the rectangular top with a central ivory plaque depicting Fame in her chariot; 41 in. (104 cm) wide.

E11 A Tuscan walnut table of traditional form, with a thick, plain octagonal top over a deep moulded frieze underhanging moulded apron on four flat leaf-carved S-scroll legs terminating in lion paw feet. It is 32 in. high by 48 in. wide (83 by 122 cm).

Dining tables

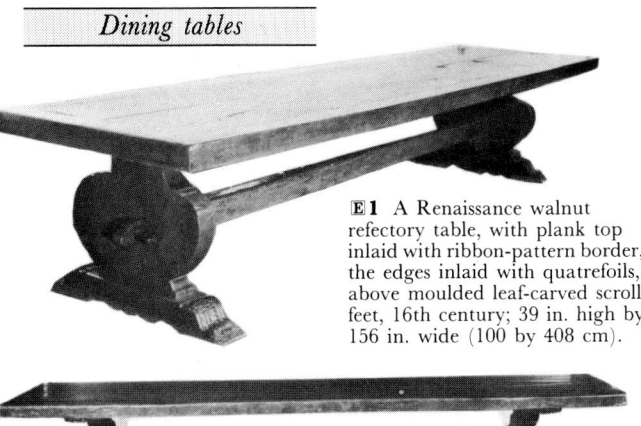

E1 A Renaissance walnut refectory table, with plank top inlaid with ribbon-pattern border, the edges inlaid with quatrefoils, above moulded leaf-carved scroll feet, 16th century; 39 in. high by 156 in. wide (100 by 408 cm).

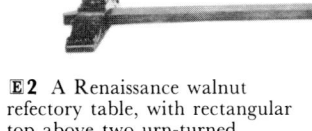

E2 A Renaissance walnut refectory table, with rectangular top above two urn-turned trestle-ends, on voluted feet carved with scrolled acanthus joined by box-stretchers; 102 in. (259 cm) wide.

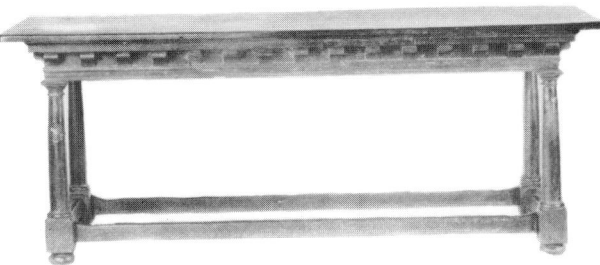

E3 A Renaissance walnut refectory table, the rectangular solid top above a moulded frieze applied with brackets and raised on columnar supports on bun feet, first half of the 17th century; 91 in. (232 cm) wide.

D4 A withdrawing table, 17th century; extending to 181 in. (456 cm).

E5 A Florentine painted and gilded refectory table, 19th century; 83 in. (212 cm) wide.

E6 An Italian Renaissance style draw-leaf dining table, the rectangular top above four stop-fluted columns, c. 1920; 84 in. (213 cm) wide.

Display tables

E7 A walnut and parquetry oval occasional table, late 18th century; 23 in. (57 cm) wide.

E8 A black lime-stone centre table, inlaid with specimen marbles and semi-precious stones, mid 19th century; 30 in. (77 cm) wide.

E9 A Florentine mosaic marble top table, worked with doves and views of Rome, on an English walnut stand, c. 1860; 30 in. high by 19 in. wide (77 by 48 cm).

E10 A parquetry and marquetry centre table, with drum top, above a tripod base, 19th century; 30 in. high by 29 in. wide (75 by 74 cm).

E11 An ivory-inlaid and mounted ebony guéridon, 19th century; 33 in. (80 cm) wide.

E12 A polychromed wood figural occasional table, 19th century; 28 in. (70 cm) high.

E13 A neoclassical style bronze a pietra dura guéridon, the circular surface inset with lapis, 28 in. (70 cm) wide.

E1 A Renaissance-style oak small table, with moulded D-shaped polygonal top, above six circular legs; 18 in. (46 cm) wide.

E2 A Regency-style giltwood occasional table, 22 in. (56 cm) wide.

Games tables

D3 A card table, richly inlaid with coloured woods, late 18th century.

E4 A games table, the shaped frieze containing a drawer, *c.* 1780; 34 in. (85 cm) wide.

E5 A north Italian marquetry card table, with cut corners, crossbanded in tulipwood, early 19th century; 40 in. (96 cm) wide.

Side tables

E6 A giltwood side table, late 17th century; 57 in. (145 cm) wide.

E7 A walnut side table with two drawers, *c.* 1600; 34 in. high by 54 in. wide (85 by 137 cm).

E8 A Roman parcel-gilt side table, with moulded simulated marble top, late 17th/early 18th century; 32 in. high by 55 in. wide (82 by 140 cm).

E9 A Roman giltwood pedestal table, with serpentine grey marble top, early 18th century; 37 in. high by 21 in. wide (93 by 55 cm).

E10 A rococo giltwood console table, with moulded serpentine top, polychromed to simulate verde antico marble, early 18th century; 51 in. (130 cm) wide.

D11 A Roman carved giltwood side table, with porphyry top, the scroll legs and stretchers carved with flowers and leaves, *c.* 1740; 36 in. high by 54 in. wide (93 by 137 cm).

E12 A Piedmontese kingwood-veneered side table, with a quarter-veneered quarter banded top, a drawer in the shaped frieze, on solid cabriole legs, *c.* 1760; 32 in. high by 40 in. wide (85 by 103 cm).

E13 A carved giltwood console table, with white marble top, 18th century; 43 in. (108 cm) wide.

E14 A giltwood small console table, with a shaped verde antico marble top, mid 18th century; 56 in. (142 cm) wide.

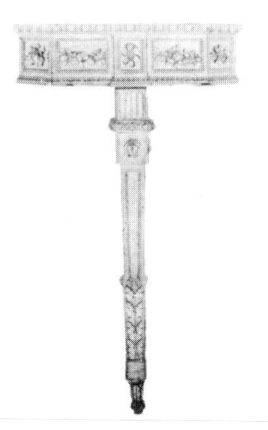

E15 A console table, giltwood carved with garlands of flowers, on a square support with a marble top; 42 in. high by 18 in. wide (104 by 47 cm).

E 1 A carved giltwood console table, of arc-en-arbalète outline, surmounted by a breccia marble top, 42 in. wide, (105 cm), 18th century.

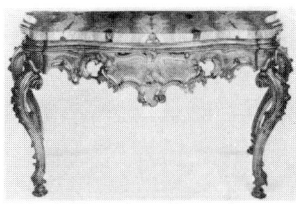

D 2 A Venetian giltwood serpentine console table, with striated onyx-veneered inset top, mid 18th century; 37 in. high by 76 in. wide (94 by 194 cm).

E 3 A north Italian rococo giltwood console table, with moulded serpentine grey and marble top, c. 1750; 47 in. (117 cm) wide.

E 4 A rococo giltwood and silvered console table, with simulated onyx top, mid 18th century; 53 in. (134 cm) wide.

E 5 A neoclassical green-painted and parcel-gilt console table, late 18th century; 44 in. (112 cm) wide.

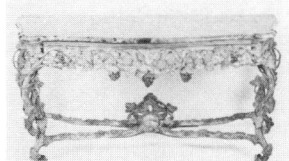

E 6 A carved and giltwood console table, 18th century; 77 in. (195 cm) wide.

E 7 A north Italian rococo walnut console table, mid 18th century; 53 in. (134 cm) wide.

E 8 A north Italian giltwood side table, with breccia marble top, mid 18th century; 43 in. (109 cm) wide.

E 9 A north Italian polychrome painted and gilded side table, mid 18th century; 37 in. (94 cm) wide.

E 10 A neoclassical ormolu-mounted mahogany console, with green marble top above twin caryatid feet, c. 1800; 53 in. (135 cm) wide.

E 11 A neoclassical giltwood console table, early 19th century; 46 in. (117 cm) wide.

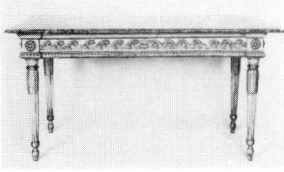

E 12 A Louis XVI style cream, gold and green-painted walnut table, early 19th century; 60 in. (152 cm) wide.

E 13 A neoclassical mahogany black-painted and parcel-gilt pier table, early 19th century; 42 in. (107 cm) wide.

E 14 A large giltwood console table, the shaped black marble top over well-carved legs, mid 19th century; 75 in. (191 cm) wide.

E 15 A Florentine giltwood side table, the inset wooden top simulated as yellow marble, above profusely carved legs and stretchers, mid 19th century; 62 in. (156 cm) wide.

Writing tables

E 16 A Tuscan walnut table, with frieze drawer, mid 16th century; 30 in. high by 36 in. wide (77 by 91 cm).

D 17 A north Italian inlaid walnut writing table, mid 17th century; 36 in. high by 49 in. wide (92 by 125 cm).

E 18 A north Italian neoclassical-style writing table, c. 1750; 41 in. (104 cm) wide.

E 19 A walnut veneered bureau plat, c. 1850; 31 in. high by 62 in. wide (79 by 159 cm).

E 20 A Renaissance-style walnut writing table, the frieze fitted with drawers; 34 in. (86 cm) wide.

THE LOW COUNTRIES

Holland and her neighbours were the most avid exponents of the Italian Renaissance style of furniture-making in Northern Europe and, from the 17th century, maintained a high standard of inventiveness and construction in the liveliest of styles. Indeed, it is the Dutch who are generally acknowledged as having developed the method of framing and joining furniture incorporating "wagenshot" or wainscot panelling and of devising the extending draw-leaf table. To complicate the issue, migrant Dutch craftsmen, highly skilled in marquetry cutting, moved to northern Italy and southern Germany to fuse their methods with the others' designs. While often made of massive bulbous parts, Dutch furniture is always ready to amuse, with a most useful and agreeable countenance.

MATERIALS FROM THE EAST

Through their vast trade with the East, the Dutch introduced novel materials such as cane and lacquer, which were avariciously imported as their potential became realized. As well as panels of lacquer, complete chests or "lacred tronks" were brought over to be placed on custom-made, highly ornate, occidental stands of gilt or silvered finish, while yet more sophisticated methods of construction were needed to house and display the increasingly popular Chinese and Japanese porcelains.

During Japan's 200 years of isolation from the 17th to the 19th centuries, Holland remained the West's only official channel of communication, and it is due to her policy of unbroken intertrade that the rest of Europe was able to share in the fruits of Dutch entrepreneurship.

It is unfortunate that the furniture which most often comes to mind in connection with Holland is that of the late 18th and 19th centuries' middle quality, bearing both contemporary and more often later decoration of crude inlay, erroneously referred to as Dutch marquetry. While the finest examples have character and charm, the later decorated pieces lack both fun and finesse. So widespread however was the demand for such furniture, particularly in the late 19th century, and so ample was the supply, that it is difficult to remember that it represents only part of Holland's contribution to the history of world furniture.

BUREAUX 1710-1900

The form of Dutch bureaux is finely various, and a very good indication of the facility with which Dutch craftsmen adapted to new styles. Very fine flat-fronted bureaux were made, but serpentine and bombé forms proved irresistible.

The decoration of bureaux relied heavily on marquetry, the complexity of which at times did little to complement the design. Lacquer work was also popular during the general surge of the first European chinoiserie.

D 1 A Dutch baroque walnut bureau, with rectangular top, above rectangular crossbanded well-figured slope front, early 18th century; 34 in. (85 cm) wide.

D 2 A Dutch baroque walnut and marquetry bureau, early 18th century; 34 in. high by 36 in. wide (86 by 96 cm).

E 3 A Dutch mahogany veneered waved "Louis XV" bureau, 18th century; 47 in. (117 cm) wide.

E 4 A Dutch colonial hardwood bureau, with ornate pierced brass hinges and mounts, 18th century; 29 in. (70 cm) wide.

E 5 A Dutch marquetry fall-front bureau, the block serpentine front with various designs, c. 1740.

E 6 A Dutch walnut and marquetry bureau, 18th century; 45 in. high by 36 in. wide (112 by 90 cm).

E 7 A rococo black-japanned writing box on stand, mid 18th century; 25 in. (64 cm) wide.

E 1 A Dutch marquetry bureau, the shaped sloping front enclosing a fitted interior, the ogee-shaped lower part with three graduated long drawers and a shaped apron, mid 18th century.

E 2 A Dutch walnut bureau, of bombé outline, inlaid with marquetry depicting flower baskets, 18th century; 47 in. (122 cm) wide.

E 3 A Dutch walnut bombé bureau, mid 18th century; 39 in. (107 cm) wide.

E 4 A Dutch marquetry bureau, inlaid overall in later marquetry, 18th century; 43 in. high by 38 in. wide (109 by 97 cm).

E 5 A Dutch mahogany bombé cylinder bureau, mid 18th century; 42 in. (90 cm) wide.

D 6 A Dutch Colonial padoukwood miniature bureau, *c.* 1760; 23 in. (58 cm) high.

E 7 A Dutch walnut and marquetry bureau, the flap enclosing a fitted interior with a well, *c.* 1760; 43 in. high by 42 in. wide (109 by 108 cm).

D 8 A walnut and marquetry bureau, of bombé form, the scrolled sloping front enclosing a fitted interior, *c.* 1755; 53 in. (135 cm) wide.

E 9 A Dutch marquetry and mahogany bureau, inlaid with vase, bird and floral motifs, *c.* 1760; 41 in. high by 35 in. wide (104 by 89 cm).

E 10 A Dutch walnut and marquetry bombé bureau, possibly the base of a bureau cabinet; 47 in. (121 cm) wide.

E 11 A Dutch walnut and floral marquetry bombé bureau, with shaped fielded flap enclosing a fitted interior including a well; 45 in. (114 cm) wide.

E 12 A Dutch mahogany and floral marquetry bombé bureau, decorated with vases of flowers, 18th century; 41 in. (102 cm). wide.

E 13 A Dutch mahogany and marquetry bureau, in two sections, inlaid extensively with vases, tulips and parrots, 18th century; 44 in. (112 cm) wide.

E 14 A Dutch bureau, with a sloping fall front above four graduating drawers on carved feet, *c.* 1770.

E 1 A Dutch mahogany and marquetry bureau, the serpentine fall enclosing a stepped and shaped interior of drawers and pigeonholes, *c.* 1770; 55 in. (140 cm) wide overall.

E 2 A Dutch marquetry bureau, the cylinder front concealing a pull-out writing surface and a fitted interior, *c.* 1770; 45 in. high by 45 in. wide (115 by 115 cm).

E 3 A Dutch mahogany and marquetry cylinder bureau, the writing slide opening in conjunction with the cylinder, *c.* 1770; 43 in. high by 43 in. wide (109 by 110 cm).

E 4 A Dutch walnut and marquetry bureau, with inlaid flap concealing a well-fitted interior, *c.* 1770; 43 in. high by 49 in. wide (110 by 125 cm).

E 5 A Dutch East Indies solid padouk bureau, third quarter 18th century; 38 in. high by 40 in. wide (96 by 102 cm).

E 6 A Dutch mahogany bombé cylinder desk, the fall flap disclosing a well-shaped fitted interior, with original brasses, *c.* 1770; 45 in. high by 45 in. wide (112 by 112 cm).

E 7 A Dutch mahogany cylinder bureau in two parts, *c.* 1775; 44 in. high by 48 in. wide (113 by 122 cm).

E 8 A Dutch mahogany bombé-fronted cylinder bureau, with a fitted interior, *c.* 1780; 49 in. high by 38 in. wide (124 by 95 cm).

E 9 A Dutch walnut bureau of bombé outlines, late 18th century; 45 in. (112 cm) high.

E 10 A Dutch mahogany cylinder bureau, with leather-lined writing surface, *c.* 1780; 44 in. high by 43 in. wide (113 by 109 cm).

E 11 A Dutch walnut and parquetry cylinder bureau, *c.* 1785; 43 in. high by 41 in. wide (110 by 103 cm).

E 12 A Dutch mahogany-veneered Louis XVI bureau, with a well-fitted interior, late 18th century; 42 in. (105 cm) wide.

E 13 A walnut and floral marquetry bombé bureau, the drawers with neoclassical brass handles, late 18th century; 48 in. (122 cm) wide.

E 14 A Dutch marquetry and walnut cylinder top bureau, the writing slide working in conjunction with the cylinder front, late 18th century; 56 in. (143 cm) wide.

E 15 A Dutch marquetry cylinder bureau, inlaid with walnut panels, swags, a roundel and a classical urn, *c.* 1800; 46 in. high by 40 in. wide (115 by 100 cm).

E 16 A Dutch mahogany cylinder bureau, with fitted interior, *c.* 1800; 42 in. high by 45 in. wide (107 by 115 cm).

E 1 A Dutch walnut and floral marquetry bureau, with brass furniture, early 19th century; 44 in. (110 cm) wide.

E 2 A Dutch satinwood bureau, 19th century; 41 in. high by 37 in. wide (102 by 92 cm).

E 3 A Dutch oak bureau in Louis XVI style, 19th century; 38 in. (96 cm) wide.

E 4 A Dutch marquetry bureau-on-stand, with shaped fitted interior, 19th century; 37 in. (94 cm) wide.

E 5 A Dutch marquetry lady's writing bureau, profusely inlaid, the ogee-shaped fall revealing a stepped and fitted interior above a drawer and a waved apron, *c*. 1860; 37 in. high by 33 in. wide (94 by 84 cm).

E 6 A mahogany cylinder bureau, with two shallow drawers surmounted by a carved pediment with central crest, above an interior fitted with three pigeonholes, three shallow drawers and a writing surface, the apron fitted with two drawers, 19th century; 40 in. (100 cm) wide.

E 7 A walnut bureau, in well-figured wood, the flap enclosing a serpentine interior including drawers, pigeonholes and a well, the frieze with two loper drawers, the whole raised on paw feet, *c*. 1900; 41 in. high by 40 in. wide (105 by 101 cm).

BUREAU CABINETS
1700–1850

The overall proportions of the Dutch bureau cabinet remained remarkably similar from the 17th century on. In this respect, though not in some details, they are very like contemporary English pieces.

It is the timber used that identifies the difference. Oak was always the preferred wood in Holland on which to lay veneers and marquetry. A bureau cabinet with veneer on oak will therefore be of Dutch origin or a provincial English piece later veneered.

D 8 A Dutch burr-elm and maple "mulberry" bureau bookcase, with two sections, both sections with fitted interiors, the front and sides ornately inlaid, *c*. 1700; 48 in. (123 cm) wide.

D 9 An Anglo-Dutch walnut and marquetry bureau bookcase, the double domed upper section with arched glazed doors above candle slides, the inlaid fall enclosing a stepped interior, *c*. 1700; 43 in. (108 cm) wide.

C 10 A Dutch walnut bureau bookcase, with well-fitted interior, early 18th century; 54 in. (137 cm) wide.

D 11 A Dutch walnut and floral marquetry bureau cabinet, *c*. 1750; 93 in. high by 50 in. wide (127 by 238 cm).

D 12 A Dutch walnut bureau cabinet, both sections with well-fitted interiors, *c*. 1750; 47 in. (120 cm) wide.

D 1 A Dutch walnut and floral marquetry bureau cabinet, the sloping flap with a fitted interior including a well; 93 in. high by 67 in. wide (236 by 160 cm).

D 4 A Dutch marquetry bureau bookcase, the bombé base with graduated long drawers.

C 7 A Dutch bureau cabinet, the small pediment above an oval mirror, mid 18th century.

D 10 A Dutch mahogany and floral marquetry bureau cabinet, the dentilled pediment with a central urn; 44 in. (113 cm) wide.

E 2 A Dutch miniature walnut and marquetry bureau cabinet, inlaid with vases of flowers and floral sprays, the lower panel enclosing long drawers; 37 in. high by 21 in. wide (92 by 52 cm).

D 5 A Dutch walnut bureau cabinet, with a fitted interior, *c.* 1750; 100 in. high by 55 in. wide (256 by 140 cm).

D 8 A Dutch mahogany and marquetry bookcase, *c.* 1760; 84 in. high by 33 in. wide (214 by 85 cm).

D 11 A Dutch mahogany cylinder bureau bookcase, in Louis XVI style, *c.* 1800; 80 in. (203 cm) high.

D 3 A Dutch walnut and floral marquetry bureau cabinet, the mirror glazed cupboard doors enclosing shelves and drawers; 99 in. (252 cm) high.

D 6 A Dutch bureau cabinet, the burr-wood veneered doors enclosing shelves and drawers, *c.* 1750; 87 in. (221 cm) high.

D 9 A Dutch mahogany bureau cabinet, the domed cornice with carved profile portrait, *c.* 1770; 96 in. (244 cm) high.

E 12 A Dutch marquetry bureau cabinet, modern; 101 in. high by 51 in. wide (269 by 131 cm).

CABINETS
1680-1910

The *cabinet* occupied a special place in the domestic life of 17th- and 18th-century Holland. Although they were utilitarian pieces fitted with drawers, shelves and sometimes a writing drawer, their special status in the home meant that cabinet-makers exhibited their finest talents in ornamenting the exteriors.

Even after glass-fronted display forms of the cabinet were introduced, the type with superbly decorated blind doors remained current.

E 1 A walnut and marquetry cabinet-on-chest, with two crossbanded cupboard doors over an arrangement of 14 variously sized drawers, on carved feet.

The piece was originally made in the late 17th century, but the floral marquetry dates from the 19th. Many such quite early pieces were later inlaid in this manner.

D 2 A Dutch mahogany and floral marquetry armoire, the arched moulded cornice with stands for vases; 90 in. high by 60 in. wide (229 by 159 cm).

E 3 A Dutch oak kabinet, the arched cornice with carved cresting, 18th century; 79 in. high (202 cm).

D 4 A Dutch walnut veneered Louis XV kabinet, the upper section with shelves and drawers, 18th century; 93 in. (238 cm) high.

E 5 A Dutch walnut and floral marquetry armoire, 93 in. high by 66 in. wide (236 by 175 cm).

D 6 A Dutch carved and burr-walnut serpentine-fronted armoire, *c.* 1760; 92 in. high by 70 in. wide (234 by 178 cm).

E 7 A Dutch mahogany armoire, with two serpentine-topped panelled doors, above two short and two long drawers, on bold claw-and-ball feet, *c,* 1750; 91 in. high by 51 in. wide (233 by 129 cm).

D 8 A Dutch rococo mahogany cabinet-on-chest, with moulded arched pediment above two panelled doors, the bombé lower section with three graduated long drawers, on splayed legs, mid 18th century; 68 in. (170 cm) wide.

D 9 A Dutch walnut and marquetry armoire, the bombé base with three long drawers with neoclassical gilt metal handles, 64 in. (160 cm) wide.

D 10 A Dutch floral marquetry armoire, the bombé base fitted with three long drawers, on claw-and-ball feet, 18th century; 69 in. (175 cm) wide.

D 11 A Dutch walnut marquetry armoire, with floral inlay throughout, the shaped top above two ornately panelled doors, over two short and two long drawers in the bombé base, 18th century.

E 12 A Dutch walnut and marquetry veneered armoire, with carved shaped pediment, 18th century; 95 in. high by 68 in. wide (242 by 172 cm).

D 1 A Dutch carved and burr-walnut serpentine fronted armoire, with ebonized floral scroll motifs, the interior with shelves and shallow drawers, the lower part of bombé form, *c.* 1760; 92 in. high by 70 in. wide (234 by 178 cm).

E 2 A Dutch mahogany veneered kabinet, shaped moulded cornice with carved cresting, the doors with a shaped panel and three long waved drawers below, on claw feet; 106 in. (268 cm) high.

E 3 A Dutch carved mahogany bow-front armoire, ecorated with floral scroll, wave and flame motifs, the domed cornice above a pair of cartouche-shaped panelled doors enclosing sliding trays, *c.* 1760; 110 in. high by 98 in. wide (280 by 250 cm).

E 4 A Dutch mahogany wardrobe, with shaped domed pediment, carved with male masks, ribbons and leaves, enclosed by a pair of panel doors, on claw-and-ball feet with leaf-carved apron; 65 in. (165 cm) wide.

E 5 A Dutch mahogany armoire, with moulded serpentine cornice, centred by a ribbon-tied floral appliqué, *c.* 1770; 89 in. high by 49 in. wide (226 by 150 cm).

E 6 A Dutch walnut armoire, cupboard doors inlaid with well-figured panels framed by ivory scrolls, the bombé base with three short and three long drawers; 101 in. high by 68 in. wide (250 by 173 cm).

D 7 A Dutch burr-walnut armoire, the upper part with arched moulded cavetto cornice and foliate cresting, above a pair of shaped panelled cupboard doors, the base fitted with a later secretaire drawer, flanked by two short drawers; 73 in. (186 cm) wide.

E 8 A Dutch mahogany armoire, the moulded cornice carved with acanthus scrolls and flowers above a pair of carved panelled doors, the bombé lower part with three graduated drawers, and hairy paw and pad feet, *c.* 1770; 102 in. high by 76 in. wide (259 by 193 cm).

E 9 A Dutch mahogany armoire, the moulded serpentine cornice centred by a porcelain stand carved with ribbon laurel wreaths and an oval portrait medallion, the pair of panel doors headed by ribbon-tied swagged urns and and flanked by a pair of fluted pilasters, *c.* 1770; 94 in. high by 69 in. wide (239 by 175 cm).

E 10 A Dutch marquetry cabinet-on-chest, decorated with floral vase, architectural motifs, and portraits on a mahogany ground, *c.* 1770; 91 in. high by 69 in. wide (232 by 167 cm).

E 11 A Dutch oak and marquetry press, the panelled doors enclosing shelves and drawers, *c.* 1780; 90 in. high by 67 in. wide (290 by 170 cm).

E 12 A Dutch burr-walnut and floral marquetry armoire, with arched moulded cornice, above a pair of cupboard doors inlaid with baskets of flowers above two short and two graduated long drawers on bun feet; 92 in. high by 68 in. wide (173 by 234 cm).

E1 A Dutch carved mahogany press cupboard, the arched pediment with acanthus carving, on square tapered feet, *c.* 1780; 102 in. high by 68 in. wide (260 by 173 cm).

E4 A Dutch Louis XV mahogany veneered bombé-fronted kabinet, the shaped moulded cornice with carved cresting and protrait medallion, the lower section with three long drawers, late 18th century; 96 in. (243 cm) ·high.

E7 A Dutch Louis XVI mahogany veneered kabinet, the top with openwork gallery and carved cresting to the centre, the lower section with three long drawers, early 19th century; 94 in. (241 cm) high.

E10 An oak armoire, the half-round pedimented top with applied carved medallion, surrounded by C-and acanthus scrolls, the two doors of the upper section with applied carved flowerheads and foliage, flanked by ebonized columns, 19th century; 104 in. (263 cm) high.

E2 A Dutch padoukwood armoire, with ornate panelled doors above three graduated long drawers, late 18th century; 76 in. (193 cm) wide.

E5 A Dutch oak armoire, the arched cornice faced with an appliqué of leaves and harvest trophies, above a pair of panelled doors flanked by ebonized split columns; 103 in. high by 75 in. wide (261 by 190 cm).

E8 A Dutch Louis XVI mahogany kabinet, the lattice work pierced gallery centring upon a foliage-decorated urn, above two panelled doors, 19th century; 93 in. (238 cm) high.

E11 A Dutch oak kabinet, plain moulded cornice with three gold-painted ball finials, the lower section with three long drawers flanked by fluted angles, 19th century; 94 in. (240 cm) high.

E3 A Dutch marquetry cabinet, decorated with satinwood medallions, floral baskets and chevron banding, below are three long graduated drawers, *c.* 1790.

E6 A Dutch Louis XVI mahogany kabinet, the broken moulded pediment centring upon a swag-decorated urn, upper section with panelled doors, the base fitted with three long drawers, 18th/19th century; 75 in. (190 cm) wide.

E9 A Dutchy Louis XVI mahogany kabinet, the S-scroll pierced cornice centring a swagged tablet above two panelled doors carved with rosettes, 19th century; 63 in. (160 cm) high.

E12 A Dutch mahogany kabinet, with a turned crest, with two small and two large drawers of bombé form, 19th century.

Cabinets-on-stands

E1 A Flemish ebonized table cabinet, with a dentil cornice above a long frieze drawer and three architectural pedimented drawers flanked by spiralling columns and an arrangement of eight small drawers on a solid moulded plinth base, each drawer set with an engraved bone panel, *c.* 1650; 28 in. high by 60 in. wide (52 by 72 cm).

E2 A Flemish painted table cabinet, with an arrangement of ten drawers surrounding a cupboard with a mirrored interior, all except one drawer painted with mythological scenes, within ebonized wave mouldings and tortoiseshell surround, mid 17th century; 22 in. high by 33 in. wide (56 by 84 cm).

E3 An Hispano-Flemish ebonized cabinet, with an architectural arrangement of seven short and one long drawers round a cupboard, veneered with engraved ivory flowers on a red tortoiseshell ground, on a George III black-japanned stand with pierced brackets and square legs, mid 17th century; 30 in. high by 26 in. wide (77 by 66 cm).

D4 A Flemish ebony and tortoiseshell cabinet-on-stand, the cupboard doors enclosing twelve drawers surrounding the central cupboard door, each drawer inset with a panel of Italian silk and silver thread embroidery of flowers, 17th century; 44 in. (112 cm) wide.

D5 A Flemish walnut cabinet-on-stand, the moulded top with an ormolu bead and leaf border, the cabinet with a central cupboard inset with a portrait of Charles I and enclosing four drawers, surrounded by twelve drawers each with a portrait miniature within a brass frame, the whole of the front covered in gilt-brass scrollwork, the giltwood stand heavily carved, *c.* 1670; 82 in. high overall by 44 in. wide (208 by 112 cm).

E 1 An Antwerp ebony and tortoiseshell cabinet-on-stand, the top with a hinged lid enclosing a compartment, above two cupboard doors which reveal eight small drawers, *c.* 1675; 53 in. high by 40 in. wide (134 by 110 cm).

D 2 A Flemish ebony and scarlet tortoiseshell cabinet, 17th century; 55 in. (139 cm) high.

E 3 A Flemish rosewood and tortoiseshell cabinet-on-stand, *c.* 1680; 50 in. high by 36 in. wide (131 by 91 cm).

E 4 A Flemish ormolu-mounted tortoiseshell, rosewood and ebony cabinet-on-stand, *c.* 1680; 50 in. (128 cm) wide.

E 5 A Flemish carved oak cabinet-on-stand, the door flanked by a pair of fluted pilasters with Ionic capitals, *c.* 1680; 61 in. high by 29 in. wide (156 by 75 cm).

E 6 A Dutch marquetry cabinet-on-stand, the top with a cushion frieze above cupboard doors with a fitted interior, *c.* 1910; 57 in. high by 28 in. wide (145 by 71 cm).

Display cabinets

E 7 A Dutch walnut display cabinet, the base with four short drawers above supports with scroll stretchers, *c.* 1690; 88 in. high by 67 in. wide (224 by 170 cm).

E 8 A Dutch oak display cabinet-on-stand, with glazed doors enclosing shelves, the stand with a pair of serpentine-fronted drawers, early 18th century; 84 in. high by 62 in. wide (214 by 159 cm).

E 9 A Dutch parcel ebony and satin hardwood vitrine, the chamfered cornice above a pair of arched glazed cupboard doors, the supports joined by waved stretchers, *c.* 1720; 57 in. (145 cm) wide.

E 10 A Dutch walnut veneered display cabinet-on-stand, 18th century; 92 in. (228 cm) high.

E 11 A Dutch walnut and oak floral marquetry bookcase, 101 in. (256 cm) high.

E 12 A Dutch walnut display cabinet, 93 in. high by 78 in. wide (236 by 198 cm).

E 13 A display cabinet, with arched cornice with central crest over two glazed doors, 18th century; 85 in. high by 84 in. wide (217 by 215 cm).

E1 A Dutch walnut display cabinet, mid 18th century; 102 in. high by 62 in. wide (259 by 188 cm).

E2 A Dutch walnut small corner display cupboard, mid 18th century; 73 in. high by 34 in. wide (185 by 86 cm).

E3 A Dutch marquetry and walnut shaped cabinet, 18th century; 60 in. (152 cm) high.

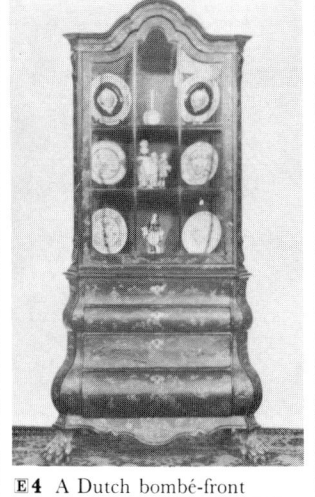

E4 A Dutch bombé-front lacquered display cabinet; 42 in. (105 cm) high.

E5 A Dutch marquetry and walnut display cabinet-on-chest, *c*. 1770; 66 in. high by 35 in. wide (198 by 89 cm).

D6 A Dutch neoclassical mahogany display cabinet, *c*. 1790; 104 in. high by 75 in. wide (263 by 190 cm).

E7 A Dutch satinwood and kingwood banded display cabinet, with chequered frieze and chamfered corners, the glazed door enclosing a velvet lined and shelved interior, *c*. 1790; 60 in. (152 cm) high.

E8 A Dutch marquetry corner display cabinet, in two parts, decorated with satinwood floral motifs, the domed cornice above a pair of glazed doors enclosing shaped shelves, *c*. 1800; 93 in. high by 44 in. wide (236 by 112 cm).

E9 A Dutch miniature softwood floral marquetry and walnut veneered display cabinet, two shaped doors, each with a shaped glass panel, 18th/19th century; 37 in. (92 cm) high.

D10 A Dutch walnut veneered waved display cabinet, in Louis XV style, the single door and sides with glass panels, the lower section with three long drawers, early 19th century; 100 in. (253 cm) high.

E11 A Dutch walnut display cabinet, on a stand fitted with two short and one long crossbanded drawer, on faceted tapering legs with serpentine stretchers and stud feet, early 19th century; 71 in. (212 cm) high.

E1 A Dutch marquetry display cabinet-on-chest, decorated with butterflies, birds and floral motifs, on a walnut ground, 19th century; 82 in. (210 cm) high.

E2 A green-painted and parcel gilt-oak display cabinet-on-stand, early 19th century; 86 in. high by 75 in. wide (218 by 191 cm).

E3 A Dutch marquetry cabinet, 19th century; 90 in. high by 72 in. wide (229 by 183 cm).

E4 A Dutch oak waved display cabinet, in Louis XV style, arched moulded cornice with carved cresting, the two doors and sides with glass panels, 19th century; 82 in. (209 cm) high.

D5 A Dutch waved walnut veneered display cabinet, the arched moulded cornice with variously carved crestings, the sides each with three simulated drawers, 19th century; 101 in. (256 cm) high.

E6 A Dutch walnut display cabinet, enclosing two shelves in yellow silk, the bombé base with one long and two short drawers on hairy-paw and ball feet, 19th century; 81 in. (206 cm) wide.

E7 A Dutch oak and softwood display cabinet, the arched moulded cornice with carved foliate scroll cresting, the two doors and sides with glass panels, 19th century; 83 in. (210 cm) high.

E8 A Dutch walnut and marquetry cabinet, 19th century; 102 in. high by 78 in wide (258 by 198 cm).

E9 A Dutch walnut-veneered display cabinet, with an arched moulded cornice, 19th century; 82 in. high by 45 in. wide (208 by 112 cm).

Dutch Display Cabinets
The classic, instantly recognizable Dutch display cabinet of the 18th century is wide, with two doors and glazed ends that return at an angle. The glazing bars are business-like, of rectangular form, in contrast to the deeply scrolling cornice and tops to the doors and the curvilinear base containing a number of drawers. The feet are either of curved bracket or carved animal foot design, and the whole may be decorated with foliate inlay.

During the second half of the 18th century the rage for things French was such that imported pieces were preferred to domestically made furniture, albeit to French patterns. So bad did the situation become from the cabinet-makers' point of view that in 1771 the Amsterdam Guild succeeded in having all furniture imports prohibited.

One consequence of this act of protectionism was that the traditional cabinet continued to be made in the customary way (and would be through the 19th and into the 20th centuries). The design did not evolve under foreign influence. This can make it very difficult to date such a cabinet by either style or method of construction.

E10 A Dutch mahogany and marquetry corner display cabinet, with glazed door enclosing shelves, 19th century; 77 in. high by 32 in. wide (197 by 91 cm).

E1 A Dutch marquetry cabinet, with frieze drawer, with bird, insect and flower motifs, mid 19th century; 39 in. (97 cm) wide.

E2 A Dutch mahogany and marquetry corner cabinet, with bowed lower section, 19th century; 32 in. (80 cm) wide.

E3 A miniature Dutch marquetry display cabinet, late 19th century; 28 in. (71 cm) high.

E4 A Dutch walnut display cabinet, 1900s; 91 in. high by 55 in. wide (231 by 140 cm).

Side cabinets

E5 A Dutch mahogany and marquetry side cabinet, with fitted door above a tambour shutter, late 18th century; 30 in. (75 cm) wide.

E8 A Dutch satinwood and marquetry side cabinet, with two drawers above octagonal panelled doors, late 18th century; 37 in. (94 cm) wide.

E6 A Dutch kettle warmer, satinwood ground within a partridgewood banding, the interior with brass liner, *c.* 1795; 21 in. high by 11 in. wide (55 by 28 cm).

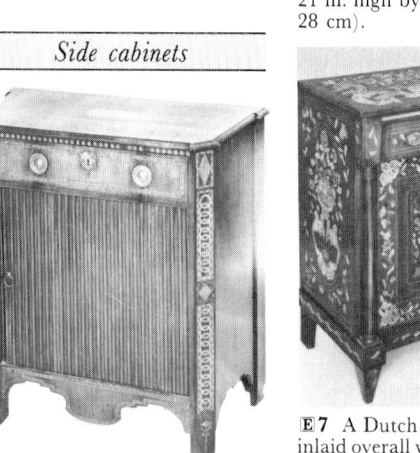

E7 A Dutch marquetry cabinet, inlaid overall with vases of flowers, rococo scrolls, birds and insects; 39 in. (99 cm) wide.

E9 A Dutch satinwood cabinet, the chamfered base with a cupboard and three drawers, framed by ebony mouldings; 29 in. (75 cm) wide.

E10 A Dutch mahogany veneered klapbuffet, in Empire syle, the hinged top with folding shelves, 19th century; 48 in. (120 cm) high.

E11 A Dutch walnut and inlay corner cabinet, 19th century; 36 in. (91 cm) high.

E12 A Dutch walnut and marquetry corner cabinet, inlaid throughout; 35 in. high by 32 in. wide (89 by 80 cm).

CHAIRS
1650-1870

Chairs from the Low Countries were the fashion leaders of Europe in the 17th century. The majority of the examples shown below were copied unreservedly on the Continent and particularly in England, where Charles II's return from exile furthered the English acknowledgement of superior Netherlands design.

It was not really until the beginning of the 18th century that regional differences became strongly apparent – see nos 10 and 11 for example.

Armchairs

E1 A Flemish walnut chair, the padded back and seat covered with petit point, the front legs, stretchers and arms formed of twist-turning, early 17th century.

E2 A Dutch armchair, with ornate carving throughout, the caned back and padded seat on barley-twist supports, *c.* 1675.

E3 A Dutch armchair, the back and seat on spiral twist supports, joined by a stretcher with an eagle motif, *c.* 1675.

E4 A Flemish walnut armchair, the high rectangular padded back with serpentine top rail, the stuffed seat on ring-turned legs joined by baluster stretchers, *c.* 1680.

E5 A Flemish walnut open armchair, covered in contemporary gros and petit point needlework, with finely scrolling arms and similar H-stretcher, 17th century.

E6 A Flemish ebonized open armchair, with rectangular padded back and cushion seat covered in floral crewelwork, the pierced front stretcher carved with flowers, 17th century.

E7 A Flemish walnut armchair, the padded back and seat upholstered in damask, on slender cup-and-ball turned legs, joined by a scrolled X-stretcher, 17th century.

E8 A Dutch walnut corner elbow chair, the slip-in seat covered in leather-cloth, *c.* 1680.

E9 A Flemish walnut armchair, late 17th century, the back and seat with early 18th century wool petit point.

E10 A Flemish walnut chair, the cartouche-shaped back and padded seat with gimp fringe and brass-headed nails, with shepherd's crook arms, deep shaped skirt, 18th century.

E11 A Dutch walnut and marquetry armchair, with serpentine drop-in seat, on cabriole legs and claw-and-ball feet, late 18th century.

E1 A Dutch elmwood armchair with beading to the whole frame, the open oval back with pierced oval splat, the arms with outcurved supports, *c.* 1780.

E4 A Dutch marquetry dining chair, second half of the 19th century.

E7 A Dutch open armchair, in the style of Daniel Marot, with a heavily carved pierced cresting and splat, 19th century.

E10 A Flemish caned walnut chair, with back supports, legs and stretchers in barley twist, late 17th century.

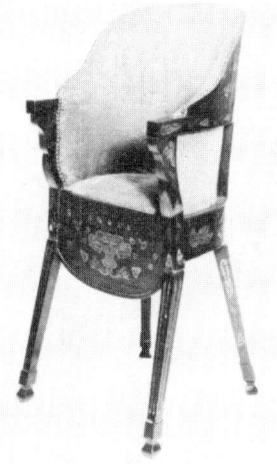

E2 A Dutch mahogany and marquetry child's high chair, with padded back, sides and seat above a deep apron, on splayed square tapering legs, *c.* 1790.

E5 A beechwood, walnut and marquetry armchair, inlaid throughout with figures and scrolling foliage, *c.* 1870.

E8 A Dutch walnut and marquetry double chair-back settee, with shaped splats, 19th century; 41 in. (102 cm) wide.

Side chairs

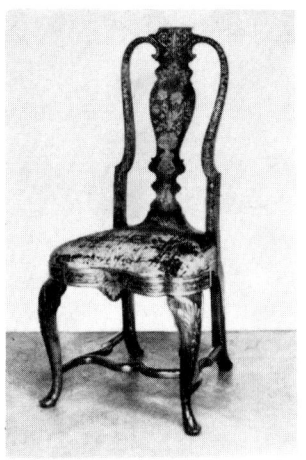

E11 A Queen Anne period Dutch inlaid chair, the curved backrail with solid vase-shaped splat, with serpentine seat-rail.

E3 A Dutch barber's chair, the mahogany frame with swan-neck handgrips, early 19th century; 38 in. (99 cm) high.

E6 An armchair, with ornate frame to the padded back and seat, 19th century.

E9 A Flemish baroque walnut dining chair, with twist-turned legs and stretchers, mid 17th century.

E12 A Dutch walnut and marquetry side chair, the motifs highlighted in mother-of-pearl and ivory, early 18th century.

E1 An Anglo-Dutch walnut chair, the lift-out seat over waved apron, early 18th century.

E2 A Dutch walnut and marquetry dining chair, 18th century.

E3 A Dutch marquetry chair, with ornate crest over a solid shaped splat, *c.* 1730.

E4 A pair of Dutch walnut and marquetry chairs, with waved back frame and solid vase-shaped splats above padded seats, 18th century.

E5 A Dutch rococo walnut side chair, with padded back and drop-in seat in horseshoe shaped seat-rail, second quarter 18th century.

E6 A Dutch beechwood dining chair, with pierced splat, the legs headed by paterae, on H-stretcher, *c.* 1790.

E7 A Dutch walnut side chair, the circular back filled with a boxwood inlaid splat, early 19th century.

E8 A Dutch elm and floral marquetry dining chair, early 19th century.

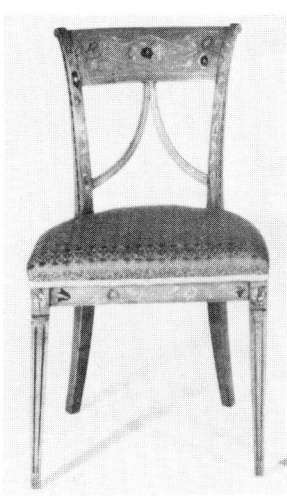

E9 A Dutch elm and floral marquetry dining chair, with curved tapering toprail and splayed splat.

CHESTS OF DRAWERS
1690-1880

There are two distinct views on the evolution of the 17th-century chest of drawers. One is that it evolved from the lift-top blanket box or coffer with one or two drawers to the base. An intermediary stage of this development is the mule chest, being neither one thing nor the other.

The alternative view – and the more likely, looking at no. 10 – is that the chest of drawers is a natural result of removing the doors from a multi-drawer cabinet.

E10 A Flemish kingwood veneered and seaweed marquetry chest-on-stand, *c.* 1690; 39 in. high by 40 in. wide (99 by 102 cm).

E11 A walnut veneered Dutch chest, early 18th century; 31 in. high by 32 in. wide (80 by 81 cm).

E12 A Dutch chest, with serpentine-shaped top above four conforming drawers, second half 18th century.

E1 A Dutch mahogany chest, with shaped crossbanded top above a baize-lined slide, *c.* 1755; 30 in. high by 36 in. wide (76 by 91 cm).

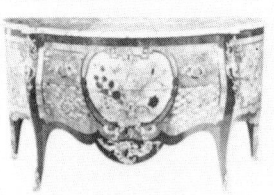

C2 A marquetry bombé commode, in Louis XV taste, probably northern Low Countries, mid 18th century; 63 in. (160 cm) wide.

E3 A Dutch serpentine burr-wood chest, 18th century; 44 in. (111 cm) wide.

E4 A Dutch Colonial walnut commode, with crossbanded serpentine top, 18th century; 48 in. (123 cm) wide.

E5 A Dutch walnut serpentine-front chest of drawers, with marquetry inlay and crossbanding, 18th century; 37 in. (92 cm) high.

E6 A Louis XV provincial walnut commode, with serpentine top, the bombé case with panelled drawers, possibly Low Countries, mid 18th century; 45 in. (116 cm) wide.

E7 A Dutch marquetry chest, veneered in walnut, the front with four shaped drawers veneered in burr-walnut and inlaid floral scrolls, mid 18th century; 40 in. (100 cm) overall.

E8 A Dutch walnut and marquetry chest, the top inlaid with flowers, birds and an urn, *c.* 1750; 32 in. high by 35 in. wide (82 by 90 cm).

E9 A Dutch mahogany and floral marquetry bombé chest, with neoclassical gilt-metal handles and lockplates; 36 in. (93 cm) wide.

E10 A Dutch marquetry chest, inlaid with floral urns, birds and scrolls, the top with shaped front and sides, the bombé front with four drawers, on carved claw-and-ball feet, 18th century; 34 in. (85 cm) overall.

E11 A Dutch walnut and floral marquetry bombé chest, with eared serpentine top, the angles carved with foliage, on paw feet; 42 in. (109 cm) wide.

E12 A Dutch marquetry bombé commode, the outset canted corners on hairy paw and ball feet, mid 18th century; 33 in. (84 cm) high.

E13 A Dutch ironwood commode, of bombé form, *c.* 1770; 39 in. (99 cm) wide.

E14 A Dutch mahogany and marquetry commode, with gilt-brass handles and keyhole plates, late 18th century; 52 in. (132 cm) wide.

E15 A Dutch walnut and marquetry chest, of bombé form, the serpentine top elaborately inlaid with a vase of flowers, scrollwork and further flowers to the angles; 39 in. (98 cm) wide.

E16 A Dutch walnut and oak bombé chest, the drawers with ornate handles and lockplates, 18th century; 33 in. high by 33 in. wide (82 by 82 cm).

E17 A Dutch parquetry commode, of breakfront form, the grey mottled marble top above parquetry-veneered drawers and dummy drawer rosewood-veneered, late 18th century; 35 in. high by 34 in. wide (90 by 86 cm).

E1 A Dutch red walnut bombé chest, with shaped top, the four long drawers and angles on large hairy paw feet, late 18th century; 43 in. (109 cm) overall.

E2 A Dutch mahogany bombé commode, with neoclassical gilt-metal handles, lockplates and cameo medallion angles, late 18th century; 41 in. (105 cm) wide.

E3 A Dutch marquetry commode, the flaring serpentine frame with four graduated drawers, raised on animal paw feet, late 18th century; 36 in. (92 cm) long.

E4 A Dutch marquetry chest of drawers, the top inlaid with a vase of flowers, above dentil moulding, with canted inlaid corners, *c.* 1790; 36 in. high by 35 in. wide (91 by 89 cm).

E5 A Dutch mahogany commode, of slightly breakfront form, fitted with three long drawers inlaid with bead stringing and roundels to the corners, on short outswept feet, *c.* 1800; 35 in. (89 cm) wide.

E6 A Dutch marquetry chest of drawers, the shaped top quarter-veneered in walnut with a central diamond-shaped panel, with four short and two long drawers, late 18th/early 19th century; 34 in. (87 cm) wide.

E7 A Dutch mahogany chest, inlaid with foliate marquetry and boxwood geometric lines, the coffered top with a frieze drawer above five long drawers, on turned bun feet, early 19th century; 40 in. (100 cm) high.

E8 A Dutch marquetry chest, the six drawers with brass ring handles, on turned feet, early 19th century; 40 in. (100 cm) wide.

E9 A Dutch marquetry and mahogany tall chest, inlaid with satinwood floral sprays, *c.* 1835; 60 in. high by 40 in. wide (152 by 100 cm).

E10 A Dutch marquetry chest, the shallow frieze drawer above three graduated long drawers, the recessed angles above block feet, *c.* 1840; 39 in. high by 37 in. wide (98 by 93 cm).

Dutch Chests

The predominant style of the 18th-century Dutch chest of drawers was that in which the drawer fronts and front corners were deeply curved, usually wider at the base, and terminating in scrolled bracket or carved animal feet. The shape was often multi-curved but chests were also made of single ogee form, as in no. 8 opposite.

In the 19th century a chest form developed that was taller than it was wide. It ran concurrently with the French semainier and the English Wellington chest, but was generally larger than either.

The chest, in common with all Dutch cabinet furniture, was subject to elaborate decoration, both contemporary and later. So popular is the style that even the later, inferior quality inlay is much in demand. Commercially however it is important to be able to recognize the finer, earlier work.

Inlay should be cut so that there is a perfect fit between the wood inlaid and that cut out to receive it.

E11 A Dutch marquetry chest, decorated in satinwood with floral displays, *c.* 1840; 36 in. high by 40 in. wide (92 by 100 cm).

E12 A Dutch marquetry commode, with three long drawers, *c.* 1880; 31 by 36 in. (78 by 91 cm).

593

COFFERS & CHESTS
1620-1860

Early Netherlandish coffers follow the ark form common to Gothic Europe and developed into the panelled coffers of joined construction. Both panels and framework were commonly treated with carving.

Colonial period coffers of exotic woods such as padouk show a distinctly Oriental influence in their metal mounts. The same source added lacquer to carving, leather and paint for decoration.

E5 A Dutch marquetry and ebonized coffer, inlaid with birds and floral cornucopia, late 17th century; 18 in. high by 26 in. wide (47 by 66 cm).

E1 A Flemish oak coffer, early 17th century; 22 in. high by 43 in. wide (55 by 110 cm).

E2 A Flemish brass and leather covered coffer, 17th century; 55 in. (140 cm) wide.

E3 A Dutch Colonial padoukwood chest, 17th century; 55 in. (140 cm) wide.

E4 A Flemish oak coffer, 17th century; 61 in. (154 cm) wide.

E6 A Dutch oak chest, with coffered lid, the lower section with initials and date, "ano 1765 IHV", 18th century; 61 in. (155 cm) wide.

E7 A Dutch East Indies chest, with hinged lid, profusely mounted with brass; 32 in. (80 cm) wide.

E8 A Dutch East Indies brass-mounted rosewood blanket chest, the moulded rectangular top decorated with pierced spandrels and geometrically-patterned nails, mid 18th century; 52 in. (132 cm) wide.

E9 A Dutch Colonial palisander-veneered and brass-bound chest, 18th century; 22 in. (54 cm) wide.

E10 A Dutch oak chest, with coffered lid, 19th century; 40 in. (101 cm) wide.

COMMODES
1775-1880

The Dutch commode developed elaborate concave and convex shapes to the front and sides in the early part of the 18th century. Later models were entirely French in inspiration and the bombé shape found great favour.

Commodes in the classical style have their own distinct charm and when placed on the tall curvilinear legs of the late 18th century can be almost animalesque – see the coltish no. 4 opposite.

E11 A Dutch Transitional mahogany and marquetry commode, with grey marble top, *c.* 1775; 50 in. (127 cm) wide.

E12 A Dutch neoclassical elm and mahogany breakfront commode, the rectangular crossbanded top above a dentil frieze and three crossbanded drawers, with ormolu pulls and escutcheons, *c.* 1775; 47 in. (122 cm) wide.

E13 A Dutch satinwood serving commode, the rising top crossbanded with figured mahogany, ebony and boxwood on a satinwood background, 18th century; 42 in. (102 cm) wide.

E 1 A Dutch mahogany commode, late 18th century; 54 in. (137 cm) wide.

E 2 A Dutch fruitwood and parquetry commode, late 18th century; 32 in. (81 cm) wide.

E 3 A Dutch mahogany buffet, *c.* 1790; 35 in. high by 37 in. wide (90 by 94 cm).

E 4 A Dutch marquetry commode, in Transitional style, *c.* 1880; 37 in. high by 32 in. wide (94 by 83 cm).

CUPBOARDS
1450–1860

The skill of the joiner cannot be better displayed than in the beeldenkasts and keefkasts of the 17th century. An imperfect joint would not have stood the stress of these heavy pieces and the movement inherent in such a fault would long ago have loosened carving applied as camouflage.

The addition of bun feet gives an endearingly human quality to these otherwise intensely formal pieces.

D 5 A Flemish Gothic cupboard with alabaster Madonna and Child in a nave, outstanding carving, 15th century.

E 6 A Flemish linenfold cupboard, with three doors, *c.* 1500; 40 in. high by 55 in. wide (100 by 140 cm).

E 7 A Flemish armoire, carved with religious figures, 16th/17th century; 80 in. high by 72 in. wide (203 by 183 cm).

D 8 A Flemish inlaid oak press cupboard, the upper part with simple inlay in ash and bog oak, the sides with fielded diamond and rectangular panels, *c.* 1620; 64 in. high by 51 in. wide (162 by 129 cm).

E 9 A Dutch baroque oak armoire, with moulded cornice, above a deep frieze elaborately carved with scrolling foliage and flowers, issued from a central basket above two panelled doors carved with foliage and birds, *c.* 1640; 82 in. high by 66 in. wide (215 by 168 cm).

E 10 A Flemish oak and ebony press cupboard, with fielded panel construction and projecting mouldings, *c.* 1680; 78 in. high by 63 in. wide (200 by 160 cm).

E 11 A Flemish oak armoire, with ebony panels, *c.* 1650; 70 in. high by 68 in. wide (179 by 174 cm).

E 12 A provincial Dutch oak and ebonized armoire, the gadrooned frieze flanked by lion masks above two panelled cupboard doors, 17th century; 30 in. (70 cm) wide.

E 13 A Flemish rosewood armoire, mid 17th century; 77 in. (195 cm) high.

E 14 A Flemish ebony and kingwood-veneered armoire, late 17th century; 73 in. high by 75 in. wide (185 by 190 cm).

D 1 A small Dutch oak beeldenkast, the four doors with carved panels between fluted pilasters, 17th century; 57 in. (145 cm) wide.

D 2 A Dutch oak four-door cupboard, the carved and scrolled frieze above carved doors, 17th century; 78 in. (199 cm) high.

E 3 A Dutch oak beeldenkast cupboard, the lower part with shallow frieze drawers, 17th century; 83 in. high by 65 in. wide (211 by 165 cm).

E 4 A Dutch oak cupboard, raised on heavy bun feet, 17th century; 77 in. high by 65 in. wide (196 by 165 cm).

D 5 A Dutch oak four-door cupboard, the upper section with a moulded cornice above a well-carved frieze flanked by three portrait heads, the two doors flanked by three allogorical figures, the doors of the lower section flanked by fluted and carved half round pilasters, 17th century; 70 in. (178 cm) high.

D 6 A Dutch oak keeftkast, the moulded and waved oversailing cornice above two panelled doors each with a partly ebonized arch, opening to reveal two openwork small doors, the panelled doors flanked by three fluted half-columns, 17th century; 73 in. (186 cm) high.

E 7 A Dutch carved oak cupboard, with scale pattern pediment, 17th century; 78 in. high by 66 in. wide (198 by 168 cm).

E 8 A Dutch ebony rosewood and oak cupboard, 17th century; 70 in. (178 cm) wide.

D 9 A Dutch oak partly palisander and ebony veneered kussenkast, 17th century; 84 in. (214 cm) high.

E 10 A Flemish oak cupboard, mid 17th century; 64 in. high by 61 in. wide (164 by 153 cm).

E1 A Flemish oak cupboard, with ebony and geometric moulded facings, carved lion masks to upper cupboard, two drawers and cupoards below on acanthus carved block feet, 17th century; 68 in. high by 69 in. wide (172 by 175 cm).

D2 A Flemish oak kast, with blind fretwork moulded cornice, the deeply carved upper cupboard doors above two concealed drawers, the lower section with two drawers in base, 17th century; 89 in. high by 76 in. wide (227 by 193 cm).

E3 A Flemish side cabinet, each section with a pair of panelled cupboard doors, the apron with a drawer, mid 17th century; 82 in. high by 44 in. wide (178 by 112 cm).

E4 A Flemish carved oak cupbaord, with gadrooned cornice faced by three masks above a pair of panelled doors with carved strapwork panels between fluted pilasters, with two drawers below, mid 17th century; 82 in. high by 60 in. wide (210 by 152 cm).

E5 A Flemish oak and ebony cupboard, each section with a pair of panelled cupboard doors between fluted pilasters, with a drawer in the base, *c.* 1650; 72 in. high by 55 in. wide (182 by 125 cm).

E6 A Flemish oak cupboard, the cornice with lion masks and acanthus brackets, the base fitted with two drawers, 17th century; 98 in. (249 cm) high.

E7 A Dutch oak cupboard on stand, the front covered with foliate scrolls,; 81 in. high by 35 in. wide (206 by 90 cm).

E8 A Flemish walnut armoire, with oversailing cornice above a pair of panelled doors, on massive bun feet, early 18th century; 73 in. (185 cm) wide.

D9 An oak cupboard, late 17th/early 18th century; 80 in. high by 79 in. wide (204 by 200 cm).

E10 A Dutch rosewood and marquetry armoire, *c.* 1700; 80 in. high by 73 in. wide (203 by 185 cm).

E11 A Flemish armoire, constructed of fruitwood, 18th century; 78 in. high by 68 in. wide (198 by 172 cm).

D12 A Dutch provincial oak four-door cupboard, inscribed "Anno 1744 FH", 18th century; 81 in. (205 cm) high.

E13 A Dutch oak kussenkast, the doors with palisander-veneered panels, 18th century; 84 in. (213 cm) high.

E14 A Dutch oak toogkast, with well-carved frieze above a pair of arched panelled doors, 18th/19th century; 81 in. (205 cm) high.

E 1 A Flemish chestnut armoire, with pierced brass escutcheons and cylinder hinges; 97 in. high by 59 in. wide (247 by 150 cm).

E 2 A Dutch mahogany serpentine corner cupboard, late 18th century; 66 in. (168 cm) wide.

E 3 A Dutch oak rankenkast, with carved vines and flowers, 17th century; 84 in. (214 cm) high.

E 4 A Dutch oak cupboard, in Renaissance style; 90 in. (229 cm) high.

E 5 A Dutch marquetry cupboard, inlaid and engraved with courtship scenes, *c.* 1830; 93 in. high by 66 in. wide (236 by 169 cm).

E 6 A Dutch oak, palisander and ebony-veneered kussenkast, with carving of fruits and flowers, 19th century; 69 in. (175 cm) high.

D 7 A Dutch oak ebonized and rosewood kussenkast, on heavy stud feet, 19th century; 90 in. (230 cm) high.

E 8 A Flemish cupboard, with 17th-century-style carving, 19th century; 78 in. (196 cm) high.

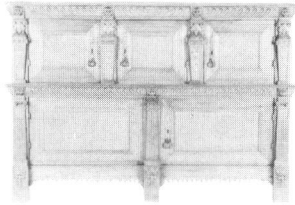

E 9 A Flemish oak cupboard, in 17th-century style; 71 in. (181 cm) wide.

D 10 A Dutch cupboard, with heavily moulded cornice above carved frieze, with two small above two larger panelled doors, 17th century.

E 11 A Flemish walnut and marquetry cabinet à deux corps, with a broken pediment above a pair of doors with two pairs of glazed lights, framed with inlaid roundels, cherubs and classical figures, flanked by fluted Corinthian columns, having two frieze drawers above panelled cupboard doors applied with bosses, on bun feet, mid 19th century; 54 in. (137 cm) wide.

E 12 A Flemish oak court cupboard, with carved panels depicting scenes with Madonna and Child, dated 1641, 19th century; with 17th-century panels; 61 in. (155 cm) wide.

MIRRORS
1680-1850

The production of extravagant frames to set highly prized mirror plates often required the involvement of more than one kind of craftsman, and the high arched cresting of early examples presented an excellent opportunity for expensive decoration. As well as the frame maker, marquetry cutter and inlay worker, gold-, silver- and coppersmiths might also be employed to create pierced, chased or repoussé work in the arabesque style.

E1 A Flemish ebonized mirror, the frame with foliate repoussé copper panels, 17th century; 65 in. (165 cm) high.

E2 A Flemish walnut mirror, with rectangular bevelled plate, 17th century; 15 in. by 17 in. (38 by 45 cm).

E3 A Dutch marquetry mirror frame, in the baroque style; 17th century.

E4 A Flemish ebonized mirror, with canted mirror frame, *c.* 1725; 46 in. high by 28 in. wide (117 by 72 cm).

E5 A Dutch marquetry toilet mirror, the sloping front with flowers and birds, 18th century.

E6 A Dutch mahogany and marquetry cheval dressing mirror, *c.* 1850; 82 in. high by 49 in. wide (208 by 124 cm).

SCREENS
1700-1900

The profound influence of the Far East on Dutch culture is as explicit in screens made in the Netherlands as it is in their chinaware.

The earliest examples of screens made in the Low Countries are more often than not imitations of Chinese lacquer work. Authentic Oriental screens were of course imported, but their quality was so much admired that they were quite commonly cut up and adapted to panel cabinets and chests. They were even, despite the delicacy of the material, set into table tops, their dark grounds foiled with harewood or satinwood, later in the 18th century.

In that same century French influence was as strong on screens as it was on other Dutch furniture types, until in the 19th-century the variety of styles of screens was so wide as to defy description. The materials were equally diverse – embossed leather, painted panels, fine machine-cut marquetry, plain glass and exotic hardwoods were all used in infinite combination.

E7 A Dutch painted and gilded leather screen, with six leaves, in imitation Coromandel lacquer with Chinese scenes, with a palace, a man on a donkey and dancers, in a setting of peonies and trailing flowers, 18th century; each leaf 84 in. high by 21 in. wide (213 by 55 cm).

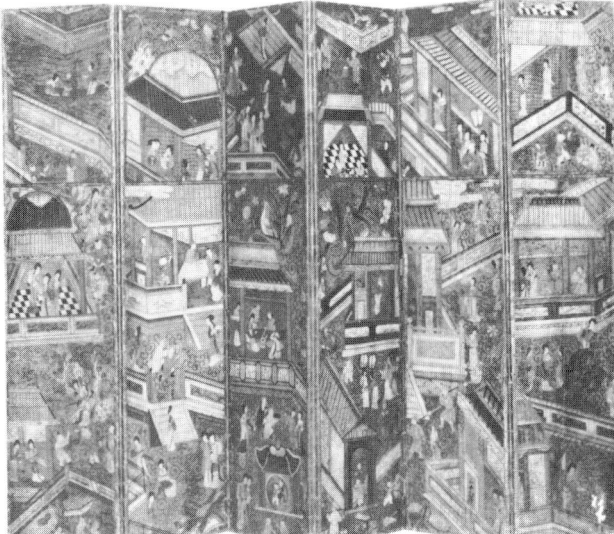

E8 A Dutch painted polychrome leather screen, with six leaves, decorated in imitation of Chinese Coromandel lacquer, the 18th-century panels backed on to canvas; each leaf 93 in. high by 21 in. wide (236 by 55 cm).

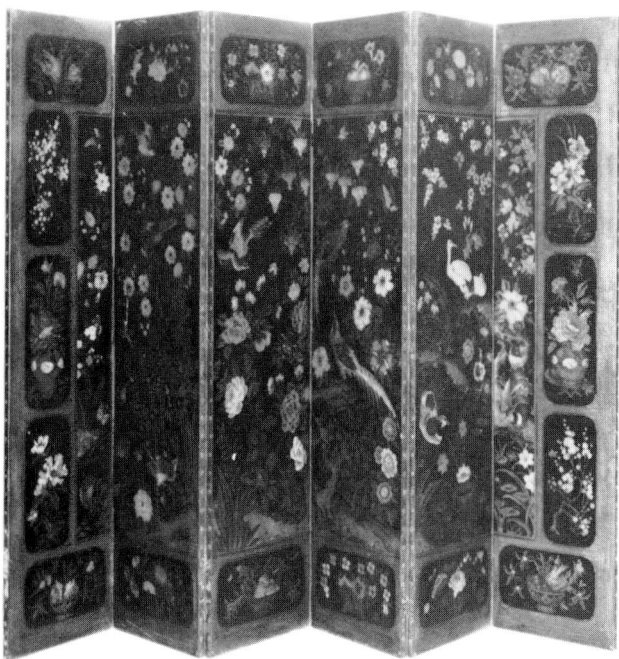

D 1 A Dutch painted and gilded six-leaf screen, painted in fresh colours and exotic birds, among flowering foliage including peonies, prunus and waterlilies framed by stamped gilt borders, interrupted by panels of flowering foliage and vases of fruit, and flowers; each leaf 84 in. high by 20 in. wide (213 by 51 cm).

E 2 A Dutch polychrome painted four-leaf screen, the reverse painted with panels of flowering foliage on a black ground; 68 in. (173 cm) high.

SECRETAIRES
1690-1900

The type of secretaire most popular in the Low Countries – apart from the inclusion of a secretaire drawer in a cabinet – was the fall-front or secrétaire à abattant.

Its most successful period was the last 40 years of the 18th century and the first half of the 19th. Following French models Dutch secretaires bore successively the marks of neoclassical, Directoire and Empire decoration. Those incorporating Japanese lacquer panels are greatly in demand.

E 3 A Dutch mother-of-pearl inlaid polychrome lacquer secretaire-on-stand, enclosing a fitted interior, late 17th century; 49 in. (124 cm) wide.

D 4 A Dutch burr-walnut secretaire cabinet, with black and gold japanned interior and two further bevelled mirrors above a fall flap above a pair of cupboard doors; 53 in. (134 cm) wide.

D 5 A Continental rococo oak double secretary-cabinet, *c.* 1750; 99 in. high by 56 in. wide (125 by 144 cm).

D 6 A Dutch neoclassical satinwood and marquetry secrétaire à abattant, last quarter of 18th century; 40 in. (102 cm) wide.

E 7 A Dutch satinwood secrétaire à abattant, late 18th century; 40 in. (100 cm) wide.

D1 A Dutch Louis XVI secretaire, veneered with various woods, the top with raised gallery, 18th/19th century; 57 in. (145 cm) high.

E4 A Dutch mahogany veneered secretaire in Louis XVI style, 19th century; 57 in. (145 cm) high.

E7 A Dutch satinwood marquetry and lacquer secrétaire à abattant, *c.* 1900; 62 in. high by 33 in. wide (158 by 84 cm).

D2 A Dutch neoclassical tulipwood, rosewood and marquetry secretaire à abattant, with chamfered rectangular tulipwood-banded rosewood top, *c.* 1800; 36 in. (93 cm) wide.

E5 A Dutch ormolu-mounted mahogany and marquetry secrétaire à abattant, with eared rectangular marble top above one long drawer, above tapering feet inlaid with flowers and butterflies, early 19th century; 38 in. (98 cm) wide.

E3 A Dutch mahogany secrétaire à abattant, with enclosing shelves, *c.* 1800; 49 in. high by 38 in. wide (150 by 96 cm).

E6 A Dutch marquetry and mahogany secrétaire à abattant, with a stepped and fitted interior; below are a pair of doors on turned feet, *c.* 1820; 61 in. high by 42 in. wide (156 by 110 cm).

TABLES 1660-1900

The archetypal early Dutch table was the ingenious draw-leaf. The often outrageous proportions of their bulbous legs gave these tables a light-hearted character that copies usually fail to capture.

Later table styles were common to most of Europe, but large, lavish console tables were little made in Holland. The reason is simple – palatial furniture found only a small market – the call was mainly for bourgeois pieces.

Centre tables

E8 A Flemish rosewood and boulle centre table, 17th century; 41 in. (104 cm) wide.

E9 A Flemish ivory-inlaid kingwood-veneered centre table, late 17th century; 29 in. high by 49 in. wide (74 by 125 cm).

E10 A Flemish parquetry side table, in oyster-veneered walnut and inlaid in ivory, 17th century; 33 in. high by 46 in. wide (80 by 112 cm).

E11 An Anglo-Dutch red walnut centre table, the lobed moulded top with a hinged flap enclosing a divided interior, mid 18th century; 32 in. (81 cm) wide.

E12 A Dutch oval mahogany centre table, the chequer galleried top inlaid with an oval shell patera, the whole inlaid with chequer stringing, late 18th century; 40 in. (101 cm) wide.

E13 A Dutch marquetry inlaid centre table, with complementary frieze fitted one drawer, set on four square tapered legs, terminating in brass bun feet, late 18th century; 30 in. high by 38 in. wide (75 by 96 cm).

E1 A Dutch tulipwood and marquetry table, the top inlaid with oyster veneers, late 18th century; 37 in. (95 cm) wide.

E2 A Dutch satinwood table, quarter-veneered, *c.* 1795; 32 in. high by 30 in. diameter (71 by 68 cm).

E3 A Dutch mahogany and marquetry centre table, *c.* 1820; 30 in. high by 40 in. diameter (75 by 100 cm).

E4 A Dutch neoclassical fustic and marquetry work table, *c.* 1820; 29 in. high by 28 in. diameter (75 by 71 cm).

E5 A walnut centre display table, with lobed serpentine top, *c.* 1850; 50 in. (127 cm) wide.

E6 A Dutch walnut and veneered side table, *c.* 1850; 30 in. high by 44 in. wide (75 by 113 cm).

E7 A kingwood and marquetry centre table, 1880–1900; 39 in. (99 cm) wide.

Dressing tables

E8 A Dutch marquetry poudreuse, *c.* 1790; 30 in. (76 cm) high.

E9 A Dutch walnut and beechwood kneehole poudreuse, late 18th century.

E10 A Dutch walnut and marquetry enclosed dressing table, late 18th century; 36 in. (90 cm) wide.

E11 A Dutch marquetry dressing chest, with small rectangular swing mirror on stand above a four-drawered chest, the whole profusely inlaid with flower and foliage trails.

Games tables

E12 A Dutch mahogany and marquetry card table, the serpentine top inlaid with floral marquetry, birds, insects and an urn, above a conforming frieze, supported on slender inlaid cabriole legs, *c.* 1750; 28 in. high by 36 in. wide (71 by 90 cm).

E13 A Dutch rococo marquetry games table, the top with candlestands at the corners, raised on cabriole legs; 31 in. (78 cm) wide.

E14 A Dutch walnut games table, with lobed rectangular top above a conforming frieze, the frieze drawer with ornate escutcheon and handles, on slender cabriole legs, *c.* 1750; 29 in. (72 cm) wide.

E15 A Dutch mahogany card table, with rectangular fold-over top, 1750–1780; 30 in. high by 35 in. wide (77 by 90 cm).

E16 A Dutch walnut and floral marquetry card table, the lobed top above a conforming frieze with a drawer, *c.* 1770.

E1 A Dutch neoclassical mahogany and marquetry games table, the top opening to baize-lined panel, *c.* 1790.

E2 A Dutch "Louis XVI" mahogany veneered demi-lune games table, early 19th century; 30 in. (74 cm) wide.

E3 A Dutch neoclassical walnut and marquetry games table; 30 in. high by 34 in. wide (75 by 85 cm).

E4 A Dutch card table, inlaid with foliate marquetry, 19th century; 31 in. (77 cm) wide.

E5 A Dutch marquetry serpentine card table, 19th century; 31 in. (77 cm) high.

E6 A marquetry games table, inlaid on mahogany, with a lobed top above a frieze drawer, 19th century; 29 in. (74 cm) wide.

E7 A Dutch East Indies satinwood card table with crossbanded top, *c.* 1830; 41 in. (106 cm) wide.

Refectory (draw-leaf) tables

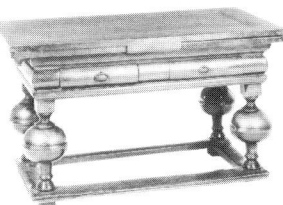

E8 A Flemish oak draw-leaf table, the bombé frieze with two drawers above bulbous baluster legs joined by flat stretchers, mid 17th century; 31 in. (77 cm) high.

E9 A Flemish oak draw-leaf table, with cleated top and four baluster legs, *c.* 1650; 31 in. high by 48 in. wide, closed (79 by 122 cm).

E10 A Flemish oak draw-leaf table, the cleated top over a plain frieze, mid 17th century; 28 in. high by 80 in. wide, extended (71 by 203 cm).

E11 A Flemish oak draw-leaf table, the panelled frieze on massive baluster legs headed by foliate brackets and joined by square stretchers, 17th century; 30 in. high by 90 in. wide extended (77 by 130 cm).

E12 A Dutch oak draw-leaf table, partly inlaid with ebony bands, the pronounced baluster legs with X-shaped stretcher, on ball feet, 17th century; 78 in. (168 cm) wide, extended.

E13 A Flemish oak draw-leaf table, with moulded frieze, 17th century; 50 in. (127 cm) wide.

E1 A Flemish oak draw-leaf refectory table, 17th century; 29 in. by 49 in. (74 by 124 cm) extending to 83 in. (211 cm).

D2 A Dutch oak side table, with rectangular plank top, and fluted frieze on pierced tapering square supports, 17th century; 93 in. (237 cm) wide.

E3 A Dutch oak refectory table, the plank top with pegged bearers, raised on a base of four baluster-turned legs, united by moulded stretchers, 17th century; 108 in. (275 cm) wide.

E4 A Dutch oak centre table, applied with C-scrolls, the rectangular top with a long frieze drawer, on bulbous turned column supports, 17th century style; 63 in. (160 cm) wide.

Side tables

E5 A Dutch oak folding table, 17th century; 38 in. (98 cm) wide, open.

E7 A Dutch oak folding table, late 17th century; 29 in. high by 38 in. wide (74 by 97 cm).

E6 A Dutch walnut and marquetry rectangular side table, late 17th century; 37 in. (95 cm) wide.

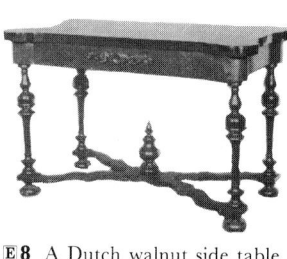

E8 A Dutch walnut side table, on turned legs, joined by waved stretchers, late 17th century; 54 in. (137 cm) wide.

E9 A Dutch walnut and seaweed marquetry side table, in the William and Mary taste, the rectangular top radially veneered with a symmetrical design composed of oyster veneers and panels of foliate scroll stems, having a moulded acacia border and containing a similarly inlaid frieze drawer, 18th century; 34 in. (85 cm) wide.

E10 A Dutch walnut, rosewood and floral marquetry side table, with elaborately waved, moulded and carved top, early 18th century; 29 in. (79 cm) wide.

E1 A Dutch marquetry side table, with moulded serpentine top, frieze drawer and short drawer in the shaped apron, mid 18th century; 28 in. (71 cm) wide.

E2 A Dutch marquetry side table, with serpentine front containing one long and one short drawer, mid 18th century; 28 in. (72 cm) high.

E5 A Dutch Pembroke table, in satinwood, the inlay with leafy branches on a rosewood ground, with a drawer in the frieze, late 18th century; 28 in. high by 35 in. wide (72 by 89 cm).

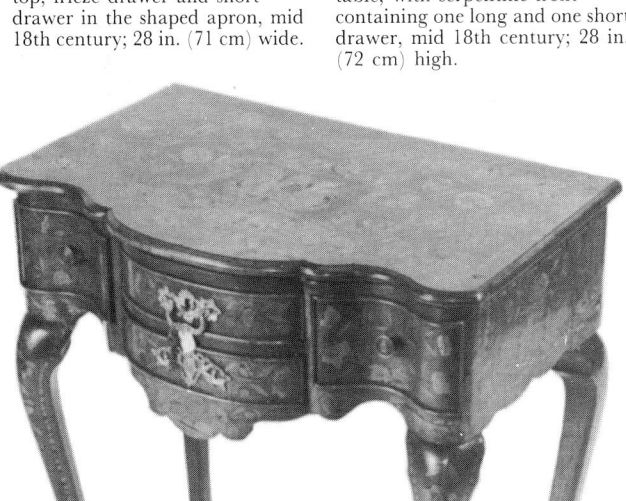

E3 A Dutch marquetry lowboy, with serpentine shaped front and four drawers, ornate handles and lockplates, with shaped apron, on cabriole legs, 18th century; 29 in. (74 cm) high.

E6 A Dutch "Louis XV" satinwood veneered side table, with shaped top, the front with a drawer with delicate handles, above a serpentine apron, on cabriole legs, 18th century; 32 in. (80 cm) wide.

E7 A Dutch marquetry table, with two rectangular flaps above a waved apron, the four cylinder supports joined by turned stretchers, inlaid overall with shell, floral and leaf designs on a mahogany ground, 19th century; 25 in. high by 43 in. wide (63 by 109 cm).

E4 A Dutch satinwood silver table inlaid with rosewood, of fine proportions; with a moulded top over a plain frieze on a very elaborately carved and pierced apron, the ornament of leaves,

scrolls and a flowerhead surmounted by a plume, on cabriole legs with paw feet. It dates from the late 18th century and is 32 in. (81 cm) long by 24 in. (61 cm) wide.

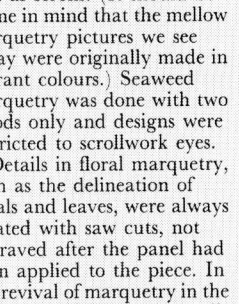

E8 A Dutch satinwood heart-shaped display table, *c.* 1890; 29 in. high by 22 in. wide (74 by 56 cm).

E9 A Dutch walnut lowboy, in early 18th century style, the shaped top above two short drawers flanked by two convex drawers in the rounded corners, late 19th/early 20th century; 30 in. (76 cm) high.

ORIENTAL FURNITURE

It is only within the last century – a blink in the timespan of Oriental history – that the West has distinguished between the arts of China, Japan and still more recently, Korea. Superficial similarities tended to hide the deep cultural differences.

THE CHINESE INTERIOR

The Chinese house contained furniture both plentiful and various in type. As early as the T'ang Dynasty (618 – 906 A.D.) chairs, tables and stools were customary. Cabinets became established as important articles and the bed, too, was a prestigious piece. This often went several stages further than its Western four-poster counterpart, being made like a portable room, with drawers and cupboards in the framework and space within for a table and chairs as well as the bed. In the guest room the long "bridge" table or kew tai still takes a place of honour.

Construction was highly sophisticated by means of fine mortice and tenon joints without pegs or dowels and very little glue. Decoration included lacquering – both as beautification and as proctection against insect attack – inlays of ivory, horn, mother of pearl and the inclusion of finely figured marble, tai-lee-sek, or the more ordinary variety, wan-sek. Furniture of the finest hardwoods was preferred plain and polished, bearing only the subtlest of carving.

THE FURNITURE OF JAPAN

By comparison, the Japanese interior contains next to no furniture and it may well be this employment of the void in decoration that so intrigued European "Japanaesthetes". Leaders of the Arts and Crafts movement found an immediate affinity with the Japanese simplicity of form and the aura of tranquility it created.

It is in the lacquer-decorated cabinets, arm rests, sword and kimono racks and the huge variety of boxes and screens that the collector will find an authentic aspect of Japanese culture, rather than the 19th-century bamboo furniture, much of which was copied from the Chinese and aimed at the Western market. There may also be a tier of shelves which, with the small low table (o-zen) and the simple cupboard or chest of drawers, will complete the inventory, except for the ubiquitous screen – the multi-leaved byobu or the single-leaf tsuitate.

CABINETS 1550-1920

The cabinet was among the most important pieces of furniture in the Chinese home. In its lacquered form it caught the imagination of the West in the mid-17th century. Many were imported and even more were made in imitation.

Plain hardwood cabinets did not achieve a similar popularity until the later 19th century, when they were siezed on by the forerunners of the Modern Movement for their simplicity and perfection of proportion.

D 1 A fine huanghuali seal box, the carving with interlocking scrolls of archaistic dragons, 1500-1600; 15 in. (38 cm) high.

C 2 A rare Ming camphorwood cabinet with hatbox, 17th century; 114 in. (291 cm) high.

C 3 A fine rare inlaid huanghuali cupboard, late 17th century; 62 in. (157 cm) high.

D 4 A small huanghuali cabinet, with recessed panel sides and pegged panel doors, 17th century; 39 in. (100 cm) high.

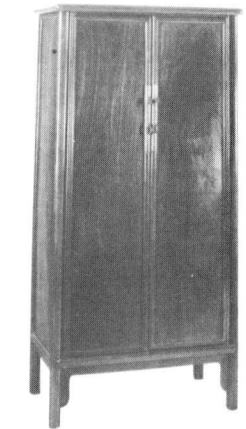

D 5 A fine large hongmu cabinet, of subtly splayed form and dark well-figured wood, 17th century; 73 in. (187 cm) high.

E 6 A huanghuali seal chest, the hinged deep cover locking two small doors over one long and four small drawers, 17th century; 12 in. (30 cm) high.

D 7 A Chinese red lacquer cabinet, Canton, the front gilt with Chinese landscapes, early 19th century; 71 in. (180 cm) high.

E 1 A small Chinese export lacquer table cabinet of the late 18th or early 19th century. The trade in such export wares continued vigorously alongside European manufacture of lacquer work, not least as they became relatively cheaper during the 18th century. Authentic Oriental lacquered pieces were always valued for the superior quality of their decoration.

D 2 An unusual gilt lacquered apothecary chest, the doors opening outwards above a row of three shallow drawers, the interior with a revolving octagonal drum of 80 small drawers, the black lacquered surface painted in gilt with quatrefoils of confronted dragons, early 19th century; 35 in. (90 cm) high.

E 3 A rare black and silver lacquered chest, with two hinged doors enclosing ten drawers, decorated in gilt and colours with flying birds, early 19th century; 36 in. (90 cm) high.

D 4 A Chinese ebonized enclosed cabinet, ornamented with pierced brass medallions, 44 in. (110 cm) high.

E 5 A Japanese lacquer cabinet, inset with 25 cloisonné enamel panels, 19th century; 36 in. (90 cm) high.

E 6 A Chinese lacquer shrine, the two doors with carved gilt panels, the interior also gilt and carved, Guangxu; 45 in. (112 cm) high.

E 7 A Korean cabinet in two parts, with two cupboards and four small drawers, 19th century; 47 in. (117 cm) high.

E 8 A Japanese walnut and cherrywood display cabinet, the 14 panels decorated with applied bone, ivory and mother of pearl, on blue lacquer ground, 19th century; 92 in. (234 cm) high.

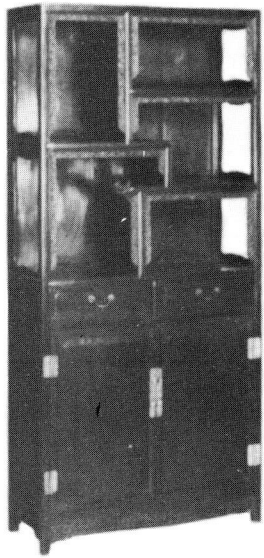

E 9 A dark hardwood display cabinet, the staggered shelves carved with floral flanges, set above two drop-handle drawers, 19th century; 74 in. (188 cm) high.

E 10 A hongmu cabinet, the pair of forward opening doors carved in relief with dragons pursuing flaming pearls, 19th century; 57 in. (145 cm) high.

D 1 A Chinese gilt black-lacquered cabinet, the doors gilt decorated with A Thousand Antiques, 19th century; 73 in. (186 cm) high.

B 2 A fine Japanese lacquer cabinet, decorated in gold, silver, red and black, with fitted interior, Meiji period; 65 in. (166 cm) high.

D 3 An inlaid gilt-lacquered carved wood display cabinet and stand, Meiji; 87 in. (221 cm) high.

E 4 A Chinese hardwood cabinet, the cupboard doors mounted with ivory and mother-of-pearl; 36 in. (91 cm) wide.

E 5 A Japanese carved wooden display cabinet, with shelves and compartments, and shibyama panels; 54 in. (137 cm) high.

D 6 A Chinese hardwood, rosewood and mother-of-pearl inlaid cabinet on stand, 19th century; 35 in. (88 cm) wide.

E 7 A carved hardwood display cabinet, with cloisonné enamel panels, late 19th century; 67 in. (171 cm) high.

E 8 A Chinese carved padoukwood display cabinet, with ornate floral decoration, *c.* 1880; 80 in. (203 cm) high.

E 9 A Chinese hardwood display cabinet on stand, carved overall with dragons, kylins and foliage, late 19th/early 20th century; 72 in. (183 cm) high.

E 10 A Chinese pierced and carved hardwood display cabinet, the hinged doors carved with prunus surrounded by basketweave borders; 81 in. (206 cm) high.

D 11 A Chinese shrine, veneered in exotic woods, the fitted interior with a gilded carved wood altar, decorated with dragons, late 19th century; 73 in. high by 43 in. wide (185 by 108 cm).

D1 A gilt-lacquered altar cabinet, the altar with two narrow compartments, late 19th century; 69 in. (176 cm) high.

E2 A hardstone inlaid hardwood miniature collector's cabinet; 21 in. high by 19 in. wide (54 by 49 cm).

E3 A display cabinet, with inlaid carved ivory and wood; 99 in. (250 cm) high.

E4 A fruitwood moon cabinet, carved with dragons, early 20th century; 81 in. (206 cm) high.

Cabinets on European stands

D5 A Chinese Coromandel lacquer cabinet, on carved and silvered stand, Kangxi period.

E6 A Chinese black and gold lacquer cabinet-on-stand, with brass hinges and lockplate, the upper part with ten various-sized drawers, early 18th century; 42 in. (105 cm) wide.

E7 A Chinese polychrome lacquer cabinet, on giltwood stand, enclosing 12 various-sized drawers, early 18th century; 33 in. (84 cm) wide.

E8 A Chinese Coromandel lacquer cabinet, ornately decorated with peonies, chrysanthemums, butterflies, herons and Chinese figures, on carved wood stand, 18th century; 69 in. (175 cm) high.

E9 A Japanese lacquer cabinet-on-stand, the cabinet with brass mounts and handles, decorated in gilt with flowers and foliage on a black ground; 31 in. (78 cm) high.

E10 A Japanese lacquered travelling cabinet-on-stand, the doors enclosing ten drawers, late 18th/early 19th century; 60 in. (152 cm) high.

E11 A Japanese lacquer cabinet on a parcel gilt walnut stand, of George I design, 48 in. high by 27 in. wide (123 by 68 cm); 19th century.

D12 A lacquered cabinet-on-stand, the two door cabinet with large ornate hinges, the stand with griffin supports, 31 in. (78 cm) wide.

E13 A padoukwood collector's cabinet-on-stand, the doors enclosing eight drawers, 53 in. (135 cm) high; c. 1890.

Cabinets on Oriental stands

D 1 A Chinese lacquer cabinet-on-stand, the upper section with two doors with large ornate hinges; 17th-18th century.

E 2 A Chinese export black and gold lacquer cabinet-on-stand, 18th century; 36 in. (92 cm) wide.

D 3 A Chinese black-lacquered cabinet-on-stand, with gilt landscape decoration, the interior fitted as a shrine, 18th century; 39 in. (99 cm) high.

D 4 A Chinese double-doored cabinet-on-stand, with red lacquer, hardstone and ivory decoration, 18th century; 37 in. (92 cm) wide.

D 5 A Chinese black and gold lacquer cabinet, late 18th century; 34 in. (86 cm) wide.

E 6 A lacquer cabinet-on-stand, decorated in gilt and inlaid with mother of pearl, 18 in. (45 cm) wide.

E 7 A small Japanese parquetry cupboard, with two doors each enclosing six small drawers, *c.* 1900; 46 in. by 30 in. (115 by 75 cm).

E 8 A Chinese rosewood and porcelain cabinet-on-stand, of rectangular form, with a pair of Canton famille rose porcelain-panelled doors, painted with figures, 42 in. by 29 in. (107 by 75 cm); 20th century.

CHESTS 1600-1910

As the popularity of early imported lacquer work grew, European middlemen began to commission Chinese craftsmen to produce lacquered pieces in Western styles – among them the domed-top coffer.

Collectors' attention for the last century however has been concentrated on authentic indigenous pieces that were never intended for export. The altar chest is a good example, being admired for its inherent design qualities rather than for an opulent finish.

C 9 A Japanese lacquer coffer, the domed lid and sides decorated with shaped lozenges, inlaid mother of pearl borders, mid-17th century; 50 in. high by 38 in. wide (127 by 96 cm).

C 10 A Japanese lacquer coffer, with moulded lid, decorated in raised silver and gilt, 17th century; 54 in. (137 cm) wide.

C 11 A blond huanghuali altar coffer, with fine-grained top, Ming Dynasty; 34 in. high by 61 in. wide (87 by 156 cm).

D 1 A huanghuali altar chest, the well-figured top with scrolling ends above a pair of doors flanked by rounded rectangular slightly splayed legs, the wood of rich tone, Ming, 17th century; 34 in. high by 47 in. wide (88 by 121 cm).

D 2 A huanghuali altar coffer, the top with bird's tail scrolls supported on four slightly splayed straight legs flanked by brackets, with baitong mounts, 17th century; 31 in. high by 39 in. wide (81 by 100 cm).

D 3 A dark huanghuali small altar chest, the floating grooved plank top above two deep drawers and a pair of doors, the angles with plainly carved scrolling brackets, Ming, 17th century; 32 in. high by 48 in. wide (81 by 122 cm).

E 4 A Chinese black and gold lacquer coffer with moulded lid, decorated in raised gilt, on a William and Mary ebonized stand; 46 in. high by 64 in. wide (116 by 163 cm).

E 5 A Chinese black lacquer coffer, the top and sides decorated in raised gilt, mounted with gilt-brass handles, early 18th century; 62 in. (159 cm) wide.

E 6 A Chinese lacquer coffer with domed lid, on ebonized square-legged stand, 18th century; 39 in. high by 31 in. wide (100 by 79 cm).

E 7 A Chinese black and gold lacquer coffer, early 18th century; 57 in. (145 cm) wide.

E 8 A black and gold dower chest, decorated with intricate riverside scenes, on carved scroll stand; 18th century.

E 9 A brown lacquer chest, with mounted lockplates and handles, 19th century; 13 in. high by 29 in. wide (31 by 74 cm).

E 10 A red lacquer chest, decorated in gilt with flowers, 19th century; 13 in. high by 29 in. wide (31 by 74 cm).

D 11 A carved hongmu altar coffer, 19th century; 34 in. high by 75 in. wide (86 by 190 cm).

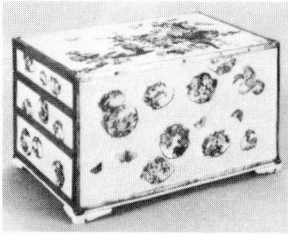

E 12 A shibayama three-drawer chest, 19th century; 10 in. (25 cm) wide.

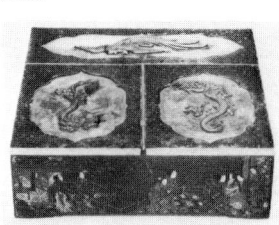

E 13 An export lacquered brass and silver suzuribako, late 19th century; 8 in. (21 cm) square.

Oriental Lacquer Work

There are essentially two types of lacquering, an art that was known in China as early as the Shang Yin period. The first is that in which lacquer is applied and built up to create low-relief scenes, in the second the lacquer is incised. Incised lacquer work is also of two types: polychrome Bantam work and the deep lustrous red of cinnabar lacquer.

The best guide to whether lacquer is of Occidental or Oriental origin is the quality and colour of the ground work. If the quality is high and is backed up by fine rendering of the main features, the work is probably Oriental (much European work was traced from Oriental originals and so loses the finer points). Oriental grounds are usually dark – yellow, blue or green grounds normally signify a piece decorated (and therefore made) in Europe.

E 14 A lacquer kyodai, decorated with jimaki, with brass fittings, Meiji; 26 in. (66 cm) high.

E 15 A Chinese rosewood chest-on-stand, boldly carved, early 20th century; 30 in. high by 31 in. wide (76 by 79 cm).

DESKS
1800-1890

It is fairly safe to assume that Oriental desks are of Chinese origin or, if Japanese, were made for the export market – see no. 4. Some of the quaintest export pieces are those in which colonial influences have been added to pure English or Dutch models, as in no. 1.

An instantly recognizable Oriental model however is no. 3, usually made of polished hardwood, in three or five pieces and folding to make a transportable item.

E1 An export gilt lacquer lady's desk, the medallion-topped pediment above a pair of doors, the fall-flap enclosing a leather-covered angled writing surface, late 18th/early 19th century; 68 in. high by 24 in. wide (172 by 61 cm).

D2 A Chinese scarlet lacquer kneehole desk, decorated in polychrome with mythical beasts, early 19th century; 56 in. (142 cm) wide.

E3 A burlwood and hongmu partners' desk, the top with a hongmu panel, a row of three drawers within the ribbon frame, demountable from the pair of pedestals, 19th century; 33 in. high by 66 in. wide (83 by 170 cm).

E4 A Japanese black and gilt lacquer writing desk, with fitted interior, on a later stand, 66 in. by 31 in. (167 by 77 cm).

E5 A Chinese rosewood and mother of pearl desk, the superstructure with a pair of cupboard doors and divisions, enclosed by an animal carved cresting and ears, flanked on either side by a short drawer above a sloping top, late 19th century; 71 in. high by 56 in. wide (180 by 142 cm).

SCREENS
1700-1900

The description of Oriental screens as Coromandel, though fully acceptable, betrays an ancient misunderstanding, it being thought they came from India, even though their lacquer decoration was described as japanning.

To the Chinese, screens were draught excluders or modesty protectors, whereas to the Japanese they were the (moveable) walls of rooms. The scenes on Japanese screens, which are usually painted paper, are simpler.

B6 One half of a 12-leaf Coromandel screen, one side brilliantly carved, the original gilt and coloured pigments in good condition, with a scene of celebration in the pavilions, terraces and gardens of a large villa, the reverse with a long inscription, Kangxi; 104 in. (265 cm) high.

C7 A Chinese Coromandel lacquer eight-leaf screen, with a central rectangular panel carved with various figures on a brown ground, between multiple upper and lower panels of landscapes and flowering branches, the reverse decorated wtih multiple lobed panels of precious vessels, mountainous landscapes, figures and branches, early 18th century; 122 in. (312 cm) wide.

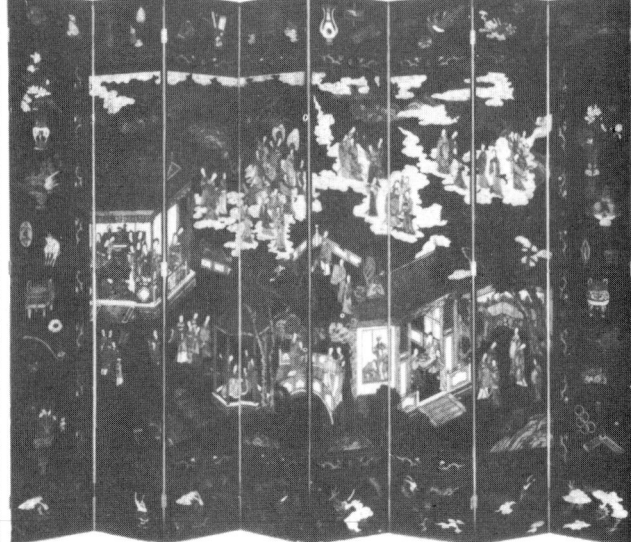

C8 An eight-leaf brown ground Coromandel screen, carved in bas relief and decorated in fresh colours on a deep aubergine-brown ground on one side with Immortals amongst clouds, the reverse with exotic birds, early 18th century; each panel 90 in. high by 16 in. wide (230 by 41 cm).

D 1 A Chinese Coromandel lacquer 12-leaf screen, incised and decorated, an extensive description on the reverse, 18th century; each leaf 112 in. high by 18 in. wide (284 by 48 cm).

D 2 A 12-panel gilt ground Coromandel screen, elaborately carved in crisp low relief with processions of Daoist Immortals, the reverse undecorated black, pin hinges, late 18th century; each panel 93 in. high by 17 in. wide (236 by 43 cm).

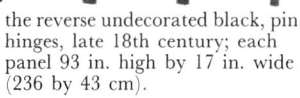

E 3 A Chinese four-fold screen, 18th century; each panel 74 in. high by 16 in. wide (185 by 40 cm).

D 5 A Chinese Coromandel green lacquer four-leaf screen, decorated in colours and carved with various figures, the reverse also decorated, late 18th century; each panel 79 in. high by 16 in. wide (202 by 40 cm).

E 4 A carved jade table screen, spinach green in high relief, Chia Ching period, *c.* 1790; 9 in. (22 cm) wide.

E 6 A Kesi panel, mounted as a table screen, woven with a pair of Daoist Immortals, 18th/19th century; 23 in. (59 cm) high.

D 7 A Chinese export lacquer eight-leaf screen, early 19th century; each leaf 93 in. (237 cm) high.

E 8 A Chinese four-fold lacquered screen, with applied figure in landscape decoration, 19th century; 73 in. (180 cm) high.

E 9 A Chinese two-fold screen, with ornately carved top; *c.* 1900.

E 10 A Chinese hardwood four-fold screen, each fold with moulded pierced scroll cresting, each fold 48 in. high by 32 in. wide (124 by 82 cm); late 19th century.

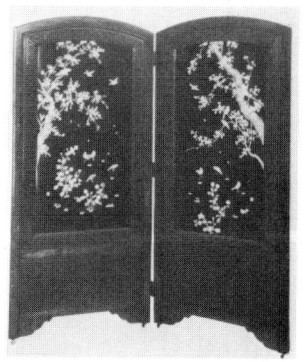

E 11 A Japanese two-fold screen, mounted with bone, ivory and mother of pearl, each leaf 71 in. high by 33 in. wide (182 by 84 cm).

E 12 A Japanese gold ground six-leaf screen, painted with wisteria, azaleas, tree peonies, red and white poppies, iris and other flowering plants beside a stream, late Meiji period; each leaf 63 in. high by 24 in. wide (165 by 64 cm).

613

SEAT FURNITURE 1780-1900

Whereas in Japan it was the custom to kneel on the floor or to squat on cushions, chairs were the rule in China from an early date, both for dining and for relaxing. Chairs with arms were more honorific than those without and both kinds were for men – women sat on stools.

The design of Chinese chairs has been immensely influential in the West, notably the beautifully simple lines of the Ming style (no. 7) but also bamboo export ware (no. 1).

E1 A Chinese export bamboo armchair, with a spindle-fitted arched curved back, filled and geometric patterns, the caned seat with railed frame on clustered legs and stretchers, late 18th century.

E2 A Chinese export bamboo open armchair, the stepped canted back filled with geometric tracery panels with slightly outcurved arms and octagonal rattan seat with squab cushion, on clustered legs and stretchers, headed by key pattern angle brackets; late 18th century.

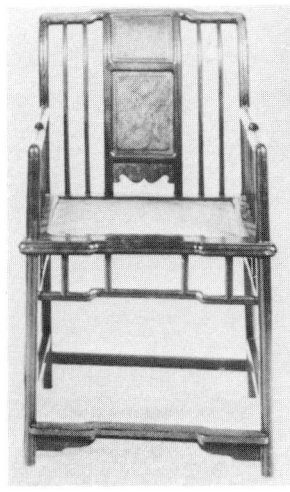

E3 A Ming style hongmu spindle-back chair, the top rail supported on a row of shubei struts, with caned seat, early 19th century; 34 in. (87 cm) high.

E4 A large Chinese teakwood Mandarin chair, magnificently carved with dragons and scales, on scrolling feet; 27 in. (67 cm) wide.

D5 A gilt-decorated low back hongmu armchair, with stepped back, late 18th/early 19th century; 40 in. (101 cm) high.

E6 A carved hongmu armchair, early 19th century; 40 in. (120 cm) high.

E7 A Ming style hongmu armchair, with shaped top rail, 19th century; 42 in. (106 cm) high.

E8 A hongmu square stool, 19th century; 21 in. high by 17 in. square (51 by 44 cm).

E9 A hongmu horseshoe-back chair, with panelled seat, 19th century; 40 in. (120 cm) high.

E10 A Yimu armchair in elmwood, late 19th century; 37 in. (94 cm) high.

E11 A huanghuali armchair, with panelled seat, 36 in. high by 21 in. wide (95 by 53 cm); 19th century.

E12 A Chinese redwood daybed, the back and sides of pierced geometric panels, the apron extensively carved, on curved legs; 19th century; 86 in. (214 cm) wide.

D 13 A pair of Chinese scarlet lacquer folding chairs, with U-shaped top rails, trellis pattern giltwood splats and leather seats on X-frames with folding foot rests, 19th century; 40 in. (103 cm) high.

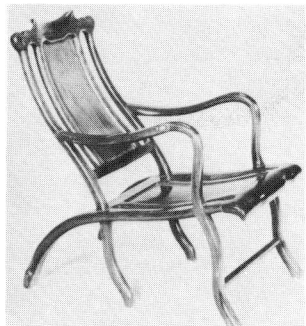

E 14 A huanghuali yoke-back chair, with shaped top rail, 39 in. (100 cm) high.

E 15 A hongmu reclining armchair, with out curving back and similarly formed seat, late 19th century; 33 in. (83 cm) high.

E 16 A marble-inset hongmu expandable daybed, the back-rest a marble landscape panel, late 19th century; 37 in. high by 73 in. wide (94 by 185 cm).

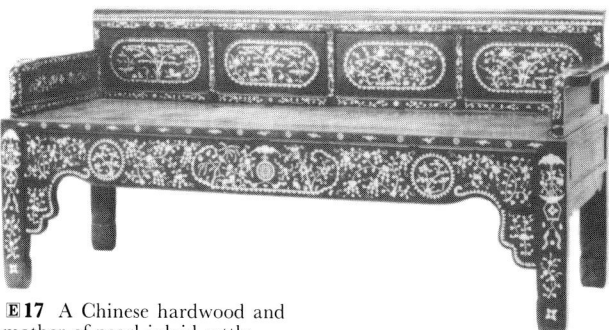

E 17 A Chinese hardwood and mother-of-pearl inlaid settle, 74 in. (188 cm) wide; *c.* 1900.

STANDS 1850-1910

Oriental stands had both secular and sacred uses, but it is the urn stand with its wan-sek marble top and carved frame that comes most immediately to mind. In its later forms the carved urn stand – particularly those made for the export market – became over elaborate and suffered from bulbousness.

Sacred stands being frequently of low table form and therefore not recognizable as stands in the normal sense are shown with tables overleaf.

E 1 A hongmu plant stand, with a square panelled top above a slightly arched apron, 19th century; 34 in. high by 13 in. square (86 by 34 cm).

E 2 A hongmu stand, with a waisted narrow frieze and a bombé apron, 19th century; 32 in. high, 17 in. square (81 by 43 cm).

E 3 A Chinese hardwood urn stand, with a circular marble inset to the square top, late 19th century; 31 in. high by 16 in. wide (77 by 40 cm).

E 4 An elaborately carved dark cinnabar tall square table stand; 35 in. high by 16 in. square (90 by 42 cm).

E 5 A fine padoukwood occasional table, the quatrefoil top decorated with inlaid mother-of-pearl and red marble, 14 in. (35 cm) wide.

E 6 A Chinese rosewood urn stand, with an inset marble top, 20th century; 28 in. high by 21 in. wide (71 by 53 cm).

TABLES
1550-1920

Whereas in Europe the trestle table was abandoned except as a peasant style, in China it remained the object of the finest design and workmanship as an alternative to the conventionally legged table. Tables of full height – as distinct from the low k'ang or platform tables – were made both for dining and as side tables. K'ang tables, usually on the ancient curved leg, were designed for reading, writing and for the support of musical instruments.

D 1 An early huanghuali k'ang table, the apron carved with confronted horned kui dragons, Ming Dynasty; 37 in. (62 cm) wide.

D 2 An early huanghuali Chuan table, with inset small drawer, 20 in. (52 cm) wide; c. 1600.

C 3 A fine Ming huanghuali table, with three tzutan drawers, 17th century; 49 in. (124 cm) wide.

C 4 A fine Ming huali table, above three drawers of laohuali with brass pulls, 17th century; 48 in. (124 cm) wide.

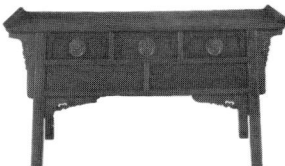

C 5 A fine huanghuali altar table, the drawers carved on three sides with foliage, 17th century; 68 in. (175 cm) wide.

D 6 A huanghuali low table, the floating panel top set on plain legs, later Ming Dynasty; 35 in. (90 cm) wide.

D 7 A small Ming huanghuali table, with figured wood top, early 17th century; 36 in. (91 cm) wide.

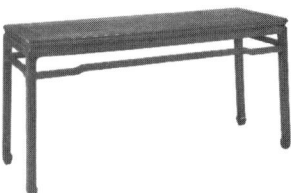

C 8 A fine Ming blond huanghuali painting table, with floating panel top, on straight feet, 17th century; 71 in. (180 cm) wide.

D 9 A huanghuali low table, the floating top with rounded corners, the round legs joined by four curving openwork bar and quatrefoil aprons, c. 1700; 34 in. (88 cm) wide.

C 10 A fine blond huanghuali altar coffer, late 17th/early 18th century; 73 in. (186 cm) wide.

D 11 A rare small huanghuali low table, early 18th century; 32 in. (80 cm) wide.

E 12 A Chinese lacquered table, decorated with flowers on a clear vermilion background, 18th century; 38 in. (95 cm) wide.

E 13 A Chinese lacquer low table, the top with strapwork trellis incised with characters, flowerheads, dragons and Yang and Ying symbols, 18th century; 40 in. (103 cm) wide.

E 14 A small mother-of-pearl inlaid brown lacquer k'ang table, of quatrefoil form, with conforming apron, the top with a scene of figures and landscapes, 18th century; 25 in. (64 cm) wide.

D 15 A huali rectangular table, the floating top supported by double jointed reeded legs, the friezes with confronted archaistic dragons, late 18th century; 49 in. (124 cm) wide.

E 16 A hardwood rectangular table, with two narrow drawers crisply carved with scaly dragons, above a similar frieze of squared scrolls, late 18th century; 33 in. (84 cm) wide.

D 17 A pair of jade inset hongmu altar tables, with ornately carved aprons of bats amidst scrolling clouds holding long cords to celadon jade insets, early 19th century; 43 in. (107 cm) wide.

E1 A Lac Burgaute model of an altar table, the top with upturned scroll ends, with red and green polychrome decoration, 18th/19th century; 16 in. (41 cm) long.

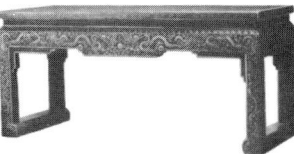

E2 A cinnabar lacquer low table, the apron ornately carved with dragons pursuing flaming pearls, late 19th century; 34 in. (86 cm) wide.

C3 A Chinese scarlet lacquer centre table, the top with inverted corners decorated with birds, butterflies, flowers and foliage, 19th century; 31 in. (80 cm) high.

E4 A huali k'ang table, on four monster mask scroll cabriole legs, joined by an apron of interlocking dragons, 19th century; 26 in. (66 cm) wide.

E5 A Chinese hongmu desk of simple form, the crossbanded rectangular top over three fielded drawers, with panels to the sides, on square legs; 48 in. (122 cm) wide; 19th century.

E6 A marble-topped hongmu small table, stand or stool, the apron carved with scrollwork, on beaded square legs, 19th century.

E7 A Chinese hongmu bench, with cane seat, 19th century; 43 in. (107 cm) wide.

E8 A fine Ming style hongmu centre table, the straight legs joined by an openwork apron, 19th century; 32 in. (82 cm) high.

E9 A cinnabar lacquer low table, the top finely carved with an all-over trellis pattern, *c.* 1860; 33 in. (85 cm) wide.

E10 A Chinese teakwood and rose medallion inlaid centre table, 19th century; 36 in. (90 cm) wide.

E11 A Ming style hongmu altar table, the top with upcurving ends and carved apron, 57 in. (145 cm) wide; 19th century.

E12 A Ming style hongmu altar table, the top with upcurving ends and simple apron, 19th century; 57 in. (145 cm) wide.

E13 A fine Ming style hardwood altar table, the top with scrolling bird's tail ends, on four straight legs, late 19th century; 67 in. (171 cm) wide.

E14 A Chinese carved hardwood altar table, the shaped frieze with star motifs, *c.* 1900; 63 in. (160 cm) wide.

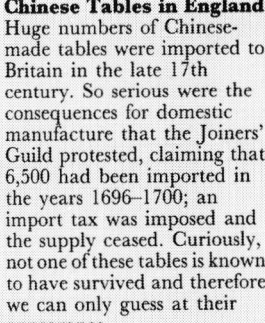

E15 A Chinese rosewood envelope card table, the square top carved with dragons and cloud bands, enclosing baize playing surface and dishes for counters, early 20th century; 22 in. (56 cm) wide.

E16 A Chinese rosewood altar table, the rectangular top with upturned ends above three frieze drawers and a pair of cupboard doors, each carved with entwined dragons and cloud bands, flanked by pierced ear pieces and a frieze, 20th century; 72 in. (183 cm) wide.

Spain & Portugal

The coupling of these two countries is no more than a geographical convenience, for the development of their furniture followed quite different paths. Both countries saw economic and political structures decline in the 17th century, but in Spain, as if to camouflage the demise, furniture was made to bear increasingly ornate decoration. It was inevitable though that the country's condition should show eventually in its artefacts and large amounts of provincial or peasant-class merchandise emerged.

In contrast, Portugal's economic decline was attacked by a programme of austerity. One result of this was the absence of expensive imported craftsmen and thus the 17th century saw the emergence of a distinctly Portuguese style. Naturally, it drew heavily on earlier foreign influences and it is this combination of decorative features that creates the originality of the form. Nowhere else was the Oriental so intriguingly juxtaposed with Italian and North European, and nowhere else was the potential of that wonderful timber, jacaranda, better realized. The strong fibrous grain allowed curvilinear and flamboyant decoration to be created with such delicacy as to appear defiant of use.

CABINETS AND CHESTS

In Spain the chest remained the most important article during and well after the 15th and 16th centuries, Spain's greatest age, and developed into the vargueño and later the papeleira. Both are types of cabinet, the former with a fall front, the latter without, and both were largely replaced by the commode during the 18th century.

Whereas Spain, with its Bourbon rulers, found a natural affinity with France and Italy, Portugal in the first half of the 18th century was hostile to its neighbour and closely allied with England. Thus first Queen Anne and, later, Chippendale chairs are to be found frequently in Portugal, though often in a less imposing form and with more fanciful carving.

In Spain the 19th century saw some ponderous interpretations of the French Directoire and later Empire styles before some political stability was restored in the 1880s, while Portugal and her style became assimilated with Europe and North America as her two-way trade and prosperity grew.

CABINETS 1620-1880

The vargueño or fall-front cabinet is probably the most immediately recognizable type of Spanish furniture. It developed out of ecclesiastical models and is also found as the papeleira, without the fall.

The exteriors are usually fairly similar, decorated with perforated metal plates and nails only, disguising stunningly elaborate interiors.

They are usually set on turned open stands, though some were placed on chests.

E1 A Spanish walnut vargueño, enclosing a well-fitted interior, early 17th century; 41 in. (103 cm) wide.

E2 A Spanish cabinet-on-stand, with carrying handles and ornate brass inlay, 17th century.

E3 A Spanish walnut painted and gilded vargueño, with 11 drawers and two cupboards, 41 in. (104 cm) wide.

E4 A Spanish Renaissance walnut vargueño-on-stand, first half of the 17th century; 54 in. high by 37 in. wide (137 by 92 cm).

E5 A Spanish tortoiseshell cabinet of breakfront architectural form, flanked at each side by three short drawers, first half of the 17th century; 17 in. high by 42 in. wide (43 by 109 cm).

E6 A Spanish marquetry cabinet-on-stand, with an arrangement of 11 drawers, mid 17th century; 60 in. high by 37 in. wide (154 by 95 cm).

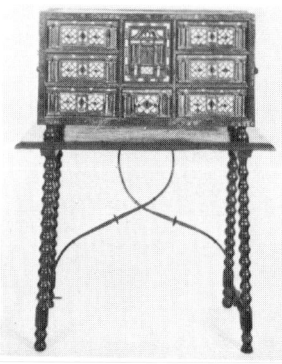

E7 A Spanish Baroque walnut, parcel-gilt and bone parquetry vargueño-on-stand, with central cupboard door, mid 17th century; 42 in. (107 cm) wide.

E1 A rare Spanish verre églomisé cabinet-on-stand, *c.* 1675; 77 in. high by 56 in. wide (195 by 143 cm).

E2 A Spanish tortoiseshell, ebony and rosewood table cabinet, with an architectural cupboard door enclosing four drawers, 17th century; 41 in. (104 cm) wide.

E3 A Portuguese rosewood cabinet-on-stand or contador with ripple moulded cornice, 17th century; 30 in. (77 cm) wide.

E4 A Iberian painted cabinet-on-stand, third quarter of the 17th century; 66 in. high by 44 in. wide (168 by 112 cm).

E5 A Portuguese rosewood chest-on-stand, the front with an arrangement of small drawers, late 17th century; 49 in. high by 31 in. wide (122 by 79 cm).

E6 A Portuguese Baroque parcel-gilt rosewood cabinet-on-stand, with rectangular top above 12 short parcel-gilt ripple drawers mounted with brass interlaced scrolls, the angles mounted with pierced brass scrollwork, above a pierced interlaced foliate apron, late 17th century; 54 in. high by 39 in. wide (137 by 99 cm).

D9 A Spanish ebonized, tortoiseshell and ivory cabinet-on-stand, with a central door inlaid with Solomonic columns and architectural facade, mid 17th century; 69 in. high by 43 in. wide (175 by 110 cm).

E7 A Spanish walnut vargueño, applied on the fall front with pierced iron panels and enclosing an arrangement of 15 drawers painted with scenes of the life of King David, 17th century; 55 in. high by 39 in. wide (140 by 100 cm).

E10 A Portuguese hardwood chest-on-stand, with an arrangement of six short, one long and three deep drawers panelled to resemble sixteen small drawers, late 17th century; 63 in. high by 42 in. wide (161 by 108 cm).

E8 A Spanish bone-inlaid, tortoiseshell-veneered table cabinet, comprising an arrangement of 11 drawers, 19 in. high by 36 in. wide (48 by 93 cm); second half of the 17th century.

E11 A Spanish vargueño on later stand, with rectangular hinged front mounted with pierced strapwork, iron clasps and drop handles, enclosing various arcaded small drawers carved with parcel-gilt strapwork and inlaid with bone roundels, late 17th century; 41 in. (105 cm) wide.

E1 A Spanish fruitwood cabinet, the inverted breakfront moulded cornice with dentil carved decoration above moulded panel doors, on shaped feet, 17th century; 73 in. high by 53 in. wide (185 by 135 cm).

E2 A Portuguese rosewood-veneered cabinet-on-stand, with moulded cornice above short and long drawers, panelled to resemble four rows of short drawers, *c.* 1680; 60 in. (152 cm) high.

D3 A Spanish gilt metal mounted ivory, tortoiseshell and walnut cabinet-on-stand, with mirrored interior flanked by nine various-sized drawers with ebonized moulded borders, inlaid with biblical and mythical scenes, on conforming stand, 48 in. (122 cm) wide.

D4 A Spanish tortoiseshell, bone-inlaid and ebony cabinet-on-stand, late 17th century; 48 in. (122 cm) wide.

E5 An Indo-Portuguese cabinet, in redwood, inlaid with ivory, ebony and mother of pearl; 17th century.

E6 A Spanish rosewood, ebony and ivory marquetry cabinet-on-stand or papeleira, late 17th century; 42 in. (108 cm) wide.

E7 A Spanish Baroque walnut vargueño on stand, 17th century; 44 in. (110 cm) wide.

E8 A Spanish walnut and ivory-inlaid table cabinet, with pierced brass gallery and fitted with eight drawers surrounding a cupboard geometrically inlaid in the Moorish taste, on claw-and-ball feet, late 17th century; 37 in. (95 cm) wide.

E9 A Spanish walnut table cabinet, the panelled doors enclosing a Karelian birch veneered and marquetry cupboard with small drawers, *c.* 1700; 33 in. (84 cm) wide.

E10 A Spanish ivory-inlaid ebony table cabinet, with 12 various-sized drawers and cupboard enclosing short drawers, 48 in. (122 cm) wide.

E1 A Spanish walnut cabinet, with pierced brass gallery, the drawers inlaid in bone, mother of pearl and tortoiseshell, 41 in. (104 cm) wide.

E2 A Portuguese rosewood cabinet-on-stand, with a concave moulded cornice above five coffered drawers simulating nine drawers, the stand with ripple moulding and a scroll-carved apron, on turned spiral twist supports, late 17th/early 18th century; 55 in. (140 cm) high.

E4 An Indo-Portuguese mother of pearl inlaid ebony table cabinet, 18th century; 23 in. (60 cm) wide.

E5 A Spanish walnut and pine standing vargueño, 16th century style; late 19th century.

D3 A Spanish papier peint table cabinet, the front, sides and interior with a variety of alfresco figure subjects, in red and green on pale yellow ground, inscribed Manuel Lopez, 18th century; 23 in. (58 cm) high.

CHAIRS
1650–1880

The most distinctive Spanish chair form is the sillón de fraileros, with its openwork walnut frame and back and seat of embossed leather. First made in the 17th century, it remained popular, with minor decorative changes, for the next 200 years. One attractive variation is that where the arm supports are made wide enough to hold food and drink.

Once the Portuguese had begun to import cane, that material was sometimes used instead of leather or fabric.

E6 A Spanish walnut open armchair, the padded back and seat upholstered in flowered tapestry, with brass studs and gilt finials; 17th century.

E7 A Spanish walnut armchair of sillón de fraileros type (also known as a monk's chair). The finely carved stiles protrude prominently above the upholstery back, their carved ornament matched on the arm supports and echoed in the feet; 17th century.

E8 A Spanish oak dining chair, the back and seat in nailed embossed leather; 17th century.

E9 A Spanish baroque walnut chair, the arched back with studded embossed leather, the front stretcher with shell carving; c. 1680.

E10 A Spanish walnut chair, with solid back and seat on square legs, green squab cushion; c. 1700.

E1 A Spanish walnut armchair, the back carved with a quartered coat-of-arms within an inscribed border, with openwork balustrade beneath; *c.* 1700.

E4 A chair in 18th century Portuguese style, carved with acanthus leaves and upholstered in red leather.

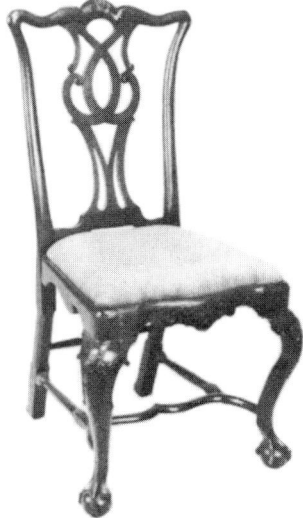

E7 A Portuguese rococo mahogany dining chair, the moulded serpentine crest rail carved with a shell above a pierced interlacing vase-shaped splat; *c.* 1750.

E10 A Portuguese hardwood side chair, with pierced shell-carved arched crest rail; 18th century.

E2 A Spanish walnut fauteuil, the shaped back covered with pressed leather with a coat-of-arms, the sides with brass nails; 18th century.

E5 A Portuguese rococo rosewood and walnut side chair, upholstered in red silk; mid 18th century.

E8 A Portuguese rococo mahogany and parcel-gilt side chair, upholstered in peach velvet; mid 18th century.

E11 A Portuguese padoukwood dining chair, upholstered in crimson linen; mid 18th century.

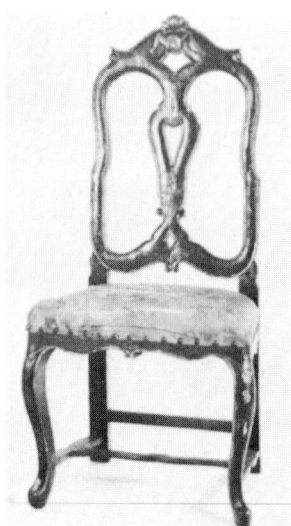

E3 A Portuguese rococo green-painted and parcel-gilt side chair; mid 18th century.

E6 A Portuguese rococo mahogany chair, the waisted open back with pierced strapwork splat; mid 18th century.

E9 A Portuguese rosewood chair, with padded vase splat and stuffed drop-in seat; mid 18th century.

D12 A Portuguese rosewood dining chair, in the Chippendale style; mid 18th century.

E13 A Spanish carved giltwood chair, with guilloche-carved frame, the oval stuffed back headed by fruit, and with an oval seat on fluted tapering legs; *c.* 1780.

E14 A Spanish baroque revival rosewood settee, the ornate backrest with a row of turned finials, upholstered in floral tapestry, mid 19th century; 53 in. high by 46 in. wide (135 by 112 cm)

E15 A Portuguese walnut dining chair, the seat upholstered in pink floral damask, 48 in. (122 cm) high; late 19th century.

CHESTS
1450-1870

Among the finest products of Spanish Renaissance workmanship are the leather-covered domed chests of the period. The fine tooling and colouring of the leather, known as *guadamecil*, was part of the artistic legacy of the Moors.

Another powerful Moorish decorative influence was the Mudejar style, which relies on the use of geometric inlay of ivory or similar material, usually in triangular pieces and similar to the Italian *certosina*.

E1 A Spanish walnut chest, probably 15th century but with later oak top; 33 in. high by 63 in. wide (84 by 160 cm).

E2 A Spanish carved chest, *c.* 1480; 30 in. high by 71 in. long (75 by 180 cm).

E3 A Spanish embossed leather trunk, 17th century; 39 in. (100 cm) wide.

E4 A Spanish coffer, covered in polychrome leather, 17th century; 32 in. (82 cm) wide.

E5 A Spanish walnut food cupboard, with framed knotched foliate borders, and painted in red and green, 25 in. (65 cm) wide.

E6 A heavily carved Spanish oak coffer, the rising lid carved in relief with two siege scene panels, the front having a central panel

C7 A Portuguese rococo yew-wood commode, the serpentine moulded top above three drawers, with brass leaf handles, *c.* 1750; 52 in. (132 cm) wide.

E8 An Iberian transitional breakfront commode, *c.* 1780; 35 in. high by 52 in. wide (89 by 132 cm).

D9 A Spanish neoclassical rosewood and walnut parquetry commode, with rectangular white and grey marble inset top and frieze inlaid with Greek key pattern in stained and engraved woods, with a central rectangular panel depicting a river landscape, *c.* 1800; 51 in. (129 cm) wide.

depicting the Pillars of Hercules with a crown above, set on scrolled and carved feet, late 17th century; 53 in. (134 cm) wide.

E10 A Spanish tortoiseshell-veneered chest, with four drawers, the kingwood-veneered top with bandings of ebony and ivory, the drawers each with two panels applied with tubular tortoiseshell panels within ebony and ivory mouldings and mother of pearl inlaid borders and side pieces, the sides inlaid similarly to the top; 40 in. high by 37 in. wide (103 by 95 cm); third quarter of the 19th century.

SPAIN & PORTUGAL/*TABLES*

TABLES
1630-1850

With the exception of the typically Spanish table with open standard ends held firm by iron bars, one has to go to the Iberian colonies to find table forms significantly different from those of the rest of Europe.

The collapsible trestle table (as no. 1) is a relic of an age when much furniture was made to be transportable, but it continued to be made in this form long after the reason for its structure had disappeared.

E1 A Spanish walnut table, the moulded top on ornate scrolling trestle supports carved with flowerheads and acanthus leaves, 31 in. high by 54 in. wide (79 by 137 cm); early 17th century.

E2 A Spanish walnut side table, with moulded top and frieze drawer, on moulded scrolled legs and shaped stretchers, 38 in. (96 cm) wide; 17th century.

E3 A Spanish chestnut side table, the plain plank top above two fitted drawers, the sturdy turned legs joined by an H-stretcher, 17th century; 61 in. (155 cm) wide.

E4 An Indo-Portuguese style table, in natural wood inlaid with ivory, pewter and copper, the top decorated with panels depicting figures, surrounded by arabesques and geometric motifs, supported by ornate legs with central turned "spinning tops", on ball feet, 17th century; 28 in. (70 cm) high.

E5 A Spanish walnut side table, with rectangular top and two coffered frieze drawers, on shaped trestle ends, joined by turned iron stretchers, late 17th century; 51 in. (130 cm) wide.

E6 A Spanish walnut table, the panelled drawer with iron lockplate and handles, 18th century; 61 in. (154 cm) wide.

E7 A Spanish or Portuguese marquetry games table, the polished interior leather-lined, c. 1790; 39 in. (99 cm).

E8 A Portuguese solid rosewood table, the top with a rose-twist edge, the panelled frieze with three drawers divided by corbels, raised on turned, spiral-twist legs joined by similar stretchers, early 19th century; 32 in. (82 cm) high.

E9 A Portuguese rosewood low table, the top with gadroon-carved edge, the frieze drawer with waved moulding, on turned legs and stretchers, 15 in. high by 24 in. wide (39 by 61 cm); early 18th century.

E10 A Spanish oak table with single plank top, fitted with three frieze drawers with geometric incised mouldings, straight out-turned legs joined by plain stretchers, 24 in. high by 58 in. wide (61 by 147 cm); 19th century.

E11 A Spanish walnut lectern, the moulded book-rest on a turned support and substantial scrolling tripod base, 17th century; 44 in. (112 cm) high.

GLOSSARY

Cross-references within this glossary are shown in SMALL CAPITALS. References to **Periods and Styles** are to the chart on pages 630-631.

A

Acanthus Classical decorative motif based on leaves of the acanthus plant.

Acroterion Pedestal for urn, bust or statue at the apex and lower angles of a pediment.

Adam Classical revival principally inspired by Robert Adam (1728-1792). *See* **Periods and Styles.**

Affleck, Thomas Principal furniture maker from 1740-1795 of the American Philadelphia style.

Amorini/Amoretti Carved or painted small cupid figures common in Italian Renaissance art.

Anthemion Formalized decorative motif based on honeysuckle, particularly popular from the late 18th century.

Arabesque Repetitive, intricate pattern derived from Arab designs based originally on plant and flower motifs.

Arcading Arched decoration applied on panels, used particularly on 16th and 17th century oak English and European chests, presses, court cupboards, etc.

Armada chest Heavy iron chest with system of elaborate locks and bolts on the underside of the lid, made in Flanders, Germany and Austria during the 16th and 17th centuries and imported into England, where they later acquired their rather romantic name.

Armoire A French provincial cupboard of great size, heavily carved and with two doors. The term has more recently been used to describe any French provincial press or cupboard.

Arrow back American term for Windsor chairs or rockers with arrow-shaped spindles filling the hooped back, made extensively in the United States between 1825 and 1850.

Art Nouveau A Victorian English development in design, typified by the sinuous "Liberty look". Allied to the Pre-Raphaelite movement, fostered in the 1880s by William Morris and his followers. *See* **Periods and Styles.**

Astragal Small semi-circular moulding, often used now to describe any glazing bars on furniture.

Atlantes Correct term for carved male figures or half-figures supporting entablatures. *See also* CARYATID.

Auger flame American term for urn-and-flame finials on secretaires, bureaux and longcase clocks. The native American form was less fluid than the English and resembles a straight spiral rather than a flame.

Aumbry Medieval cupboard with pierced doors for ventilation used for storing food, sometimes built into the thickness of a wall, particularly in churches where it housed the sacramental vessels, wine and bread.

Aventurine Properly a form of spangled quartz and glass, the word is also used to describe powdered gold scattered on JAPANNED objects.

B

Bachelor's chest Small chest of drawers with fold-over top supported by slides.

Backstool Term used today to describe pre-18th-century chair construction in which the back supports are a continuation of the back legs. Originally a crude three-legged chair with triangular seat and with the central rear leg continued up to form a back.

Bantam work Originating in the Java province of Bantam from the late 17th century, a technique of INCISED LACQUER also known as "cut work".

Bar-back Shield-shaped open back to chairs or settees with decorative bars curving up from base to cresting.

Baroque *See* **Periods and Styles.**

Basin stand 18th-century term describing a variety of wash stands, basically a tripod stand or small square stand with a moulded ring to hold the basin, small drawers below the frieze and a shelf for a ewer beneath.

Basket stand Variation on a work table, usually a tripod stand with two tiers of open gallery-work for holding nick-nacks.

Basset table Small table for playing bassette, a card game popular in Italy and France in the late 17th century and in England in the early 18th.

Bed steps Two or three steps of solid construction used for getting easily into a high bed from the 18th century. Sometimes they enclosed a fitted space for a bidet or chamber pot. Not to be confused with LIBRARY STEPS.

Bed wagon Hooped wooden frame enclosing a platform for a small charcoal-burning pan. Probably used to air beds, and not as an alternative to a warming pan.

Bergère Upholstered armchair modelled on a French design, fashionable from *c.*1725. Often with canework sides, back and seat.

Biedermeier *See* **Periods and Styles.**

Birdcage A wooden mechanism fitted to the top of some tripod table pillars, allowing the top to be rotated.

Blind fret Fretted decoration applied to the surface of solid wooden furniture.

Block front In England, solid doors of cabinets or secretaires without glazing—"blind" is perhaps the more familiar term. In America, characteristic treatment of 18th-century New England and Philadelphia cabinet and chest furniture, consisting of three vertical panels, the outer two convex, the inner one concave.

Bog oak Oak which has been submerged in peat bogs, attaining an almost black colour, used in 16th- and 17th-century furniture as inlay and decorative detail in imitation of ebony. Bog oak was revived in Victorian England for black-stained rustic-looking oak furniture.

Bois durci Mid-19th-century wood-based substance made from blood and fine sawdust of rosewood, ebony, etc. Very hard and capable of being finely moulded, it was ideally suited for medallions, plaques and other ornament.

Boiserie French term for carved wooden panelling to rooms, including doors, frames, cupboards and shelves which were part of the panelling.

Boulle/Bühl Eponymous term for technique developed by André-Charles Boulle (1642-1732) of inlaying brass with tortoiseshell and, sometimes, pewter, fashionable and highly prized in France throughout the 18th century. Usually made in pairs, the second commode, table or cabinet was in "contre boulle"—the reverse version with tortoiseshell inlaid with brass. English boulle was first popular during the Regency period. Rarely of as high quality as the French, it was increasingly debased as machine techniques enabled a similar effect to be achieved during the Victorian period.

Braganza foot *See* SPANISH FOOT.

Breakfast table In America a Pembroke table, often with the addition of a deep decorative frieze, apron or fretwork stretchers.

Brewster chair Akin to the English THROWN CHAIR but with turned spindles below the seat rail and beneath the armrests. Named after Elder Brewster of the Massachusetts Bay Colony in the 17th century.

Brushing slide A pull-out surface on chests of drawers and dressing furniture, located between the top moulding and the top drawer.

Buffet A 16th-century serving or side table, frequently with two or three tiers, the term often being confused with COURT CUPBOARD. In the late 17th and early 18th centuries there were cupboards beneath the serving surface and an elaborate superstructure above. In general it was superseded by the sideboard, but enjoyed a revival during the Victorian Gothic period.

Bühl *See* BOULLE.

Bureau à cylindre Late 18th-century desk with curved quarter-circle front in solid wood which, when lifted, swung up beneath the underside of the top.

Bureau plat French writing table of substantial proportions: a library table.

Butterfly table Tavern table made in America in the late 17th and 18th centuries. The name arises because of the wing-shaped extended fly-brackets which supported the flaps instead of the more common gateleg. The legs were canted outwards to achieve a more elegant shape.

Cable moulding Originally applied to Norman architectural convex moulding of twisted rope, the theme became a fashionable feature of chair-backs, columns, etc. during the early Regency as a tribute to Nelson's sea victories. *See also* TRAFALGAR CHAIR.

Cabochon Oval convex decorative ornament frequently found on knees of cabriole legs.

Caquetoire A 16th-century armchair in wood with a tall, narrow panelled back, outcurving arms and a seat tapering towards the back.

Carolean *See* **Periods and Styles**.

Cartouche Oval, occasionally rectangular decorative tablet. The term is most frequently used for the decorative surround to an armorial bearing.

Carver (English) Open-armed chair en suite with a set of dining chairs.

Carver chair (American) Armchair, usually of ash or maple, with rush seat and turned uprights, contemporary with BREWSTER CHAIRS. Named after John Carver, Governor of Plymouth and one of the original Pilgrim Fathers (1571-1621).

Caryatid Correct term for carved female figures or half-figures supporting an entablature instead of columns. *See also* ATLANTES.

Cassone Large Italian chest, sometimes carved or painted, made from *c*.1400 onwards.

Cassapanca A cassone with added back and arms.

Cavetto Concave moulding on cornices and pediments.

Cellaret A wine cooler with a lockable lid, usually fitted with a bottle rack.

Champlevé Technique of enamelled decoration where the metal base is channelled or cut out to receive the enamel.

Cheveret A type of small writing desk with pigeonholes or drawers above a writing surface; similar to a bonheur du jour.

Chimera Fabulous animal used in Greek and Roman decoration, revived and much favoured by designers in the Regency period.

Chippendale, Thomas (1718-1779). Furniture designer, cabinet-maker and interior decorator. *See* **Periods and Styles**.

Cloisonné Technique of enamelling using fine strips of metal soldered to the base to divide one colour enamel from another.

Close chair/stool A polite term for a toilet commode, with lifting seat concealing a chamber pot.

Cockbead Plain half-circular moulding used round veneered drawer-fronts from the late 17th century (standard from *c*.1710) projecting slightly and overlapping to protect the veneer on the frame.

Cock-fighting chair A popular name for a chair with a saddle-shaped seat and low circular back, which the sitter straddled, using the back rail as an armrest. It differs from a READING CHAIR or LIBRARY CHAIR in that there is no adjustable bookrest attached to the back.

Confidante A large sofa of French origin, with separate seats at either end, facing diagonally outwards. In the 19th century the term was used for all sorts of seating furniture designed for two or more people.

Connecticut chest A form of MULE CHEST with panels and drawer-fronts carved in low relief, made in 1650-1700 in New England. The most common decorative features were formalized tulips, hearts and flowers, and applied split balusters often decorated the stiles.

Constitution mirror Late 18th-century American mirror in the Chippendale style in mahogany or walnut with much gilding around the frame which was surmounted by a phoenix rising in the centre of a scrolled pediment.

Conversation chair A later version of the cockfighting chair from *c*.1800. The seat was saddle-shaped, the back topped by a wide padded crest rail, and when the occupant sat astride with arms resting on the back, the wide full skirts of his coat hung down behind, uncreased.

Coopered joints Cabinet-maker's term for curved timber joints, as in barrels or tubs, used in making wine cisterns, knife urns, etc.

Corridor stool A long stool or bench with raised ends, made in mahogany from *c*.1800, always without upholstery. Also known as a rout stool.

Corset back American term for an elbow chair with waisted back, popular in the mid-19th century and contemporary with early versions of the English Victorian balloon-backed chair.

Court cupboard Three-tiered open sideboard, dating from the end of the 16th century for the display of plate. Seldom more than four feet tall, the name is believed to be an anglicized version of the French word *court* or short.

Credence table Small serving table or cupboard on legs; contemporary use of the term includes small 16th- and 17th-century flap tables of semi-circular or triangular shape.

Credenza Early Italian serving table or sideboard with canted corners, two or three cupboards in the base and drawers in the frieze. In use from earliest times in Italy, many ornate credenzas were made elsewhere in the 19th century.

Cricket table Term for small plain three-legged country table made from the 17th century onwards.

Crossbanding A strip or band of veneer laid across the grain.

Crossgrained moulding Moulding with the grain running across the width and not down the length, particularly characteristic of walnut furniture at the end of the 17th and early 18th centuries.

Cushion drawer A convex-fronted "secret" drawer beneath the cornice of a chest-on-stand or escritoire, or in the frieze of early walnut side tables, without pulls or handles, and concealed as part of the moulding.

Cyma curve A double curve of two forms: cyma recta or ogee in which the upper part is concave and the lower part convex, and cyma reversa or reverse ogee, which is convex in the upper part and concave below.

Danhauser Leading workshop for Biedermeier furniture 1804-1838. *See* **Periods and Styles**.

Deception table A small table made in the 18th and 19th centuries similar to a Pembroke table but which, upon closer inspection, reveals that the one flap hinges downward and outward to hide a "pot cupboard or any other secret use" (Sheraton, *Cabinet Dictionary*, 1803).

Deudarn A Welsh version of the court cupboard, with two tiers of shelves for plate and with cupboards below.

Diaper Refers today to diamond-shaped ornament or carving in low relief, gesso and inlaid wood. The term originally meant a pattern of lozenges and hence was applied to PARQUETRY.

Directoire *See* **Periods and Styles**.

Dole cupboard A medieval hanging or standing cupboard with railed doors and patterns pierced in the wood for ventilation. In church, food for the poor was kept in such cupboards and "doled out" as a charity.

Duchesse Mid-18th century couch consisting of two bergère chairs facing each other across a central stool.

Eagle In mythology, sacred to Jupiter, sometimes with a thunderbolt in its beak. In England from 1730s, carved and gilded eagles perched on rocks supported console tables, surmounted clocks and looking glasses and decorated central plinths of broken pediments. An eagle with spread wings appeared as the armorial bearing of the Prussian Empire and in France the double-headed eagle was a symbol of the Emperor Napoleon at the end of the 18th century. After the adoption of the Constitution in 1776 the bald-headed eagle became the foremost patriotic symbol of America.

Ebéniste In France, general term for cabinet-maker as opposed to makers of seat furniture. The ancient guild of menuisiers-ébénistes protected their members from cheaper work by foreign craftsmen and from 1741 ordered them to sign their work, which was then passed by the Juré des menuisiers-ébénistes, who approved and stamped each piece "JME".

Ebonizing Close-grained wood, such as beech or birch, stained and polished to resemble ebony, much used in the 18th century, particularly for chairs.

Eclecticism *See* **Periods and Styles.**
Edwardian *See* **Periods and Styles.**
Elbow hinge A brass hinge composed of two straight sections jointed at the centre like the arms of a compass.

Empire *See* **Periods and Styles.**
Enamel *See* CLOISONNE, CHAMPLEVE.
Encoignure French name for a standing corner cupboard, usually made en suite with a commode, with marble top and ormolu or gilt metal mounts.

Etruscan style Style of decoration derived from ancient Greek, Roman and Etruscan ornament, applied to many interiors by ADAM of which the Etruscan Room at Osterley Park, London, is the only remaining intact example.

Farthingale chair 19th-century name for upright chairs without arms and with padded half-backs and seats, widely made and used throughout Europe in the 17th century. As the term was not then in current use, it cannot be confirmed or denied that these chairs were designed to accommodate the huge skirts of Elizabethan and Tudor ladies.

Fauteuil French name for an elegant, comfortable chair with open arms and upholstered back and seat, dating from the mid-18th century and originally covered in silk, satin, velvet or damask, usually replaced in 19th century with tapestry.

Featherbanding A strip or band of veneer laid at approximately 45° to the grain. Sometimes called "herringbone".
Federal *See* **Periods and Styles.**
Fiddleback Correctly, the grain of the mahogany veneer on central splats of bended back chairs which resembles the back of a violin, and not the vase-shaped splat itself.

Figure Generic term for the natural patterns revealed by skilful cutting of veneer e.g. flame grain, Cuban curl, fiddleback, oyster, etc.
Flambeau A torch or flame, sometimes springing from an urn, used as a decorative finial from the end of the 17th century and throughout the 18th.
Florentine mosaic work *See* PIETRA DURA.
Fly bracket The hinged bracket-shaped support that opens out on a table to support the flap.
French chair English 18th-century term for the French FAUTEUIL.
French foot A bracket foot which splays outward and is generally tapering, used frequently on bow-fronted and serpentine-fronted chests (American term).
French stool An upholstered seat, wide enough for two people, with upcurving ends. Otherwise known more prosaically as a window seat.

G

Gadroon/Gadrooning Also called nulling, knurling, lobing. A carved decoration to the edges of tables, desks, shelves, etc., widely used from the 16th century onwards. Properly the term applies to silver, and originated in the shape of clenched knuckles.
Gainsborough chair 18th-century English design for an open armchair of rectangular shape. Also known as a Hogarth chair.
Garde du vin Free-standing cellaret designed en suite with a sideboard beneath which it stood. *See also* WINE CISTERN.
Georgian *See* **Periods and Styles.**
Gesso Paste composed of whiting or finely powdered chalk mixed with linseed oil and size which sets hard and is easy to carve. Used extensively in the 18th century as a base for decorative gilding and embellishment of carved woodwork such as mirror frames.
Gilding Methods of gilding wood have remained unchanged and the two main techniques are still in current use: water gilding, invariably applied to GESSO, is the application of gold leaf, some of which is then burnished. Oil gilding is the application of fine sheets of gold leaf on to a roughened surface, a more lasting process but less lustrous. Gilt-metal and gilded metal are achieved by fire-gilding (also known as mercurial gilding), when an amalgam of mercury is applied to the metal to be gilded, which fuses on being heated.

Giltwood A term applied to carved wood, usually lime, which has been gilded and where no gesso has been used to add embellishment.
Girandole Wall-mounted candelabrum of French inspiration, with one or more candle branches set in a giltwood or gilt-metal frame surrounding a small asymetric or convex mirror to reflect the light of the flame.
Gothic *See* **Periods and Styles.**
Grisaille Decorative monochrome painting in tones of grey, in oil, gouache or tempera, widely used for decorative panels for 18th-century interiors and occasionally for furniture.
Guéridon A general term for a lamp stand in France, used more specifically in England for Moors or Blackamoors holding circular trays, popular until the late 19th century. The "table en guéridon" was a small circular tea table.
Guilloche Decoration consisting of two bands twisted in a continuous figure of eight.

H

Harlequin table In appearance resembling a Pembroke table or small writing table, this ingenious late 18th-century device had a rising section with pigeonholes and drawers, two flaps hinging outward and a deep apron which concealed the rising top when in the lowered position.
Hepplewhite, George (*d.*1786) Cabinet-maker and chair-maker, author of the *Cabinet Maker and Upholsterer's Guide*, 1788, 1789 and 1794. *See* **Periods and Styles**.
Highboy Quite distinct from the English TALLBOY, an American term for a chest-on-stand or high chest derived from William and Mary and Queen Anne furniture, but with more elaborate bonnet top or decorative pediment. Highboys continued to be made until the end of the 19th century.
Hope, Thomas (1770-1831). Architect and furniture designer, and influential leader of the Regency classical revival of the early 19th century. *See* **Periods and Styles**.

Husk Derived from the dry ripe husks of grain, chains of husks were a popular decoration of Adam period painted furniture, as a motif for giltwood and in plasterwork.

Hutch From the French *huche*, a chest. Another medieval food cupboard predating the AUMBRY, with similar usage to the DOLE CUPBOARD, either hanging or standing, with pierced doors for ventilation. In America the term is sometimes used for open dressers.

Incised lacquer Screens or doors of cabinets built up of different coloured layers of lacquer which is then cut through to form patterns from the different layers. *See also* BANTAM WORK.

Intaglio Cutting a figure or design so that it is hollowed out; the opposite of cameo.

Intarsia Inlaid pictorial decoration loosely described as mosaic in wood. The design is cut out of different coloured woods and then inset in panels.

Jacob, Georges (1739-1814) French cabinet-maker and founder of family business with long-lasting influence on French furniture design. Particularly associated with the innovative design of the Louis XVI chair. *See* **Periods and Styles**.

Jacobean *See* **Periods and Styles**.

Japanning In imitation of lacquerwork from Japan and the Far East, a technique used in England from the late 17th century, which was at its height in the late 18th century when the term was usually applied to metal coated with layers of varnish, dried and hardened by heat. Confusingly, "japanning" became interchangeable with LACQUERWORK when applied to wood coated with a form of gesso and then with layers of varnish.

Kas From the Dutch word *kasse*, a chest. A large two-doored cupboard or press made in North America by Dutch settlers in the second half of the 17th century in the old state of the New Netherlands, between the Delaware and Connecticut rivers. Typically the kas has bun feet, two doors, a heavily decorated cornice and grisaille paintings of fruit, flowers, etc. in the panels.

Klismos Elegantly designed chair made by the ancient Greeks, with concave tapered legs and curved back, revived particularly by Thomas Hope during the Regency period.

Knurl *See* GADROON.

Lacquerwork Originating in the Far East, the method consisted of coating wood or papier-mâché with layers of pigmented resin, the surface of which could then be painted. The composition of early European lacquer was different from the Oriental models and the techniques of application and decoration were rarely as fine.

Lannuier, Charles Honoré (1779-1819). Emigré French cabinet-maker working in New York from 1803. *See* **Periods and Styles**.

Lazy Susan Late 18th-century American version of the dumb waiter – a revolving tray sometimes with compartments on a low stand, placed in the centre of a dining table.

Library steps Made in a variety of forms in the 18th century, some resembling BED STEPS but with fitted compartments for books and papers, some as chairs which, with the seat hinged over, transformed into a set of three or four steps. The most ingenious opened like a fan from a single pole into a miniature ladder of three or four treads.

Line inlay American term for STRINGING.

Livery cupboard Domestic cupboard with pierced or openwork door for ventilation, free-standing with a shelf beneath the cupboard. Used to contain bread and victuals, it was a late 15th-century refinement of the AUMBRY but of purely secular use.

Lobing *See* GADROON.

Louis XIV, XV and XVI *See* **Periods and Styles.**

Lowboy In America, term for a dressing table, usually with one long drawer and three short ones, made en suite with a HIGHBOY. The term is also used for English Queen Anne period dressing tables.

Lozenge *See* DIAPER.

Marlborough leg Late 18th-century cabinet-maker's term for a square-sectioned tapered leg.

Marot, Daniel (*c.*1662-1752). French-born designer and architect, greatly influencing Dutch design as architect to William of Orange whom he followed to Hampton Court from 1694-96. *See* **Periods and Styles.**

Marquetry A form of decorative veneering in which exotic and contrasting woods were cut and fitted together like a jigsaw to form intricate patterns which were then applied as panels of veneer. There were basically two types: arabesque or seaweed marquetry using box or holly with walnut, and floral marquetry using fruitwoods, burr-walnut, ivory, ebony, etc.

Marquise chair Broad chair to accommodate two people, made in France towards the end of the 17th century. Similar to the Carolean double-backed settee with cane seat, but with padded seat and arms.

Mule chest Recent term for late 17th-century blanket chests with two or three drawers in the base.

Neoclassical *See* **Periods and Styles**.

Night table/stool 18th-century bedside CLOSE STOOL designed to conceal its function, with tray top and mock drawer supported on two legs which pulled out, accommodating a seat and fitted pan.

Oeben, Jean-Francois (*d.* 1763). Leading cabinet-maker of the Louis XV and French Transitional periods, master of RIESENER.

Ogee Double curved moulding, convex above, concave below. *See* CYMA CURVE.

Omnium Pretentious Victorian name for a whatnot.

Ormolu In France, a highly specialized craftsman-made gilded metal or "bronze dorée" for which special alloys of bronze and brass were made, for furniture mounts, clocks, girandoles, etc. In England ormolu was never considered a great art, and was commonly plain brass, cast and gilded.

Oyster veneer Of Dutch origin, introduced into England in the late 17th century, a form of veneering which used the cross-sections of small branches of walnut, olive, laburnum and other woods cut at 45°.

Overstuffed Chairs and seat furniture with the padding and covering taken over the wooden frame of the seat and seat rails, being more comfortable than padded drop-in seats with the seat frame exposed. *See also* STUFF-OVER.

Palmette Classical motif similar to a fan or stylized palm leaf, often used in conjunction with a lotus.

Parcel gilt Literally partially gilded, the term originally referred to silver, but latterly has been used also of furniture.

Parquetry Decorative geometrical inlay using contrasting grain of different woods. Most prevalent in late 17th century and early 18th century walnut veneered furniture.

Patera Small disc-shaped ornament with formalized flower-head decoration, a Neoclassical feature.

Péché mortel An easy chair made in similar fashion to a DUCHESSE with a bergère chair fastened to a stool of the same height to form a daybed.

Pennsylvania Dutch Plain, sturdy furniture in cherrywood, pine and local woods, often painted with tulips, hearts and birds, made by German and Swiss immigrants to America. "Deutsch" has become corrupted to "Dutch".

Periods and Styles See pages 630-631.

Philadelphia Chippendale A term used for a style of American furniture contemporary with that of Thomas Chippendale, but predominantly a variation made by THOMAS AFFLECK and WILLIAM SAVERY between 1742 and 1795. See **Periods and Styles**.

Phyfe, Duncan (1768-1854). The most fashionable New York cabinet-maker of his day and probably the most influential in America. See **Periods and Styles**.

Pietra dura An inlay of semi-precious stones such as agate, chalcedony, lapis lazuli, porphyry, sardonyx; the technique was at its height in Italy around 1600, but the result was so expensive that the cheaper SCAGLIOLA process came to dominate.

Plum pudding Description of dark-figured mahogany veneer, the darker marks representing fruit in a pudding; also called "plumbago" and "plum mottle".

Pot board Long shelf in the base of a dresser and occasionally between the stretchers of tables made for kitchen use, on which to keep pots and pans.

Pouch table 18th-century needlework or work table with fabric bag, often of pleated silk, hanging below the frame.

Press Term used in America to describe a late 16th-century cupboard similar to a COURT CUPBOARD and known in England as a hall cupboard. Its wider application includes every known kind of cupboard in which linen was kept.

Quadrant drawer Drawer in writing table or desk, in the form of a quarter-circle pivoting out from the frieze, often fitted to take containers for ink, pens, sand and pounce.

Quadrant stay A brass quarter-circle support for fall-fronts, adjustable chair backs etc.

Quartering/Quarter veneer Veneer cut and laid in four pieces, usually with grain at right angles, most frequently found on early English pieces from the end of the 17th century.

Quartetto A nest of small tables fitting one beneath the other, made from the later 18th century onwards.

Quatrefoil Four-leaved.

Queen Anne style See **Periods and Styles**.

Reading chair A chair with a saddle-shaped seat and curved back fitted with adjustable bookrest on which the occupant sat astride. Made from the early 18th century and sometimes called "library chairs" there were sometimes small candle-trays hinged below the arms or attached to the bookrest. A 19th-century version of the reading chair has an adjustable bookrest-cum-writing surface on one arm.

Récamier Directoire chaise longue or daybed in the Grecian manner with upward curving ends.

Régence See **Periods and Styles**.

Regency See **Periods and Styles**.

Riesener, Jean-Henri (1734-1806). Renowned French cabinet-maker and most influential in the spread of the French taste across Europe in the 18th century. See **Periods and Styles**.

Rocaille Term first used to describe the artificial grottoes of Versailles and believed to be the origin of the word "rococo", it is accurately used to describe the shell and rock motifs in rococo ornament.

Rococo See **Periods and Styles**.

Roentgen, Abraham (1711-1793). Cabinet-maker of international repute, father of DAVID ROENTGEN, who opened his workshop in Neuwied in 1750 after working in Holland and England.

Roentgen, David (1743-1801). German cabinet-maker of Europe-wide fame with a particular expertise in metamorphic furniture. Son of ABRAHAM ROENTGEN.

Sabot French term for the metal foot to which casters were affixed.

Saddle seat 1. A seat shaped like an elongated saddle, stuffed with horsehair and covered with leather, as in READING CHAIRS and COCK-FIGHTING CHAIRS. 2. A solid wooden seat with two depressions separated by a small ridge at the front,

used on many versions of Windsor chair.

Savery, William. Philadelphia furniture maker (1721-1788) whose label appears on some of the finest Chippendale period pieces.

Scagliola Imitation marble composed of plaster-of-Paris, isinglass, chips of marble and colouring, most popular in 17th and 18th centuries for console tables, commode tops and small pieces of furniture. See also PIETRA DURA.

Sconce A wall fitting with candle branches made in a wide variety of materials, shapes and designs, in use from medieval times, frequently with polished metal backplates to reflect the light, and later with panels of mirrored glass. See also GIRANDOLE.

Scrutoire Escritoire or scriptoire, an early form of writing cabinet with a fall-front, ancestor of the bureau.

Seaweed marquetry Intricate designs of marquetry using two woods only—box or holly with walnut.

Secrétaire à abattant A French fall-front writing desk.

Seymour, John (1738-1818) and his son **Thomas** (1771-1848). American cabinet-makers working mainly in Boston in the Sheraton style. See **Periods and Styles**.

Sheraton, Thomas (1751-1806). Designer and decorator of furniture with severe lines, frequently multi-purpose pieces of considerable ingenuity. See **Periods and Styles**.

Sheveret See CHEVERET.

Spandrel The space enclosed by two surfaces at right angles, or between an arch and its frame, frequently filled with small fretted ornament or inlaid fans.

Spanish foot A grooved foot ending in a slightly inward curving scroll, found on 17th-century chairs and tables, etc. Also called a "Braganza foot".

Squab seat Loose cushion stuffed with horsehair, used on wooden or cane-seated chairs and armchairs from the end of the 17th century.

Strapwork Interlaced geometric and arabesque decoration in low relief, often applied in fretted strips to Elizabethan and Jacobean furniture and made up from patterns in Dutch pattern books.

Stringing Very narrow strips of inlay, in boxwood, holly, ebony or other contrasting wood on 17th century marquetry, and in satinwood, rosewood and brass in the Regency period. Often called "line inlay" in America.

Stuart See **Periods and Styles**.

Stuff-over Upholsterers' term for the whole frame of a chair or settee being almost completely covered in upholstery. Very often confused with OVERSTUFFED.

Stump work English relief work embroidery, primarily of the 17th century.

Dates	ITALY	FRANCE	LOW COUNTRIES
1450-1500	RENAISSANCE	GOTHIC/RENAISSANCE	GOTHIC
1500-1550	RENAISSANCE	RENAISSANCE	GOTHIC/RENAISSANCE
1550-1600	MANNERISM	RENAISSANCE	FLEMISH RENAISSANCE
1600-1650	BAROQUE	***Louis XIII*** *(1610-1643)*	RENAISSANCE
1650-1700	BAROQUE *Andrea Brustolon*	***Louis XIV*** *(1660-1710)* *Jean Bérain* *Adam Weisweiler* *André-Charles Boulle*	BAROQUE *Daniel Marot*
1700-1730	LATE BAROQUE	REGENCE (1710-1730) *Charles Cressent*	LATE BAROQUE
1730-1770	ROCOCO *Giuseppe Maggiolini* *Pietro Piffetti*	ROCOCO ***Louis XV*** *(1715-1774)* *Bernard van Risenburgh* *Jean-François Oeben* TRANSITIONAL (1755-1770s)	ROCOCO
1770-1800	NEOCLASSICISM	NEOCLASSICISM ***Louis XVI*** *(1774-1792)* *J.H. Riesener* *Georges Jacob* *David Roentgen* DIRECTOIRE (1790s)	NEOCLASSICAL
1800-1830	EMPIRE	EMPIRE (1804-1815) *Jacob-Desmalter*	EMPIRE
1830-1880	ECLECTICISM	ECLECTICISM REVIVALS	LATE EMPIRE/BIEDERMEIER ECLECTICISM
1880-1900	ECLECTICISM	ART NOUVEAU	ART NOUVEAU *Victor Horta* *Van de Velde*
1900-1920	ART NOUVEAU FUTURISM	MODERN MOVEMENT	MODERN MOVEMENT DE STIJL/BAUHAUS

ENGLAND	GERMANY & AUSTRIA	AMERICA	*Dates*
GOTHIC	GOTHIC		*1450-1500*
TUDOR	GOTHIC/RENAISSANCE		*1500-1550*
ELIZABETHAN	RENAISSANCE		*1550-1600*
JACOBEAN STUART	RENAISSANCE		*1600-1650*
CAROLEAN **Charles II** *(1660-1685)* **William and Mary** *(1688-1702)* *Daniel Marot*	RENAISSANCE/BAROQUE	EARLY COLONIAL WILLIAM AND MARY (1680-1720)	*1650-1700*
Queen Anne *(1702-1714)* **George I** *(1714-1727)*	BAROQUE	QUEEN ANNE (1720-1770)	*1700-1730*
BAROQUE **George II** *(1727-1760)* *William Kent* ROCOCO	ROCOCO *Abraham Roentgen* *J.A. Nahl* *J.F. & H.W. Spindler* *François Cuvilliés*	QUEEN ANNE *Townsend Goddard* CHIPPENDALE (from 1750s)	*1730-1770*
ROCOCO **George III** *(1760-1820)* *Thomas Chippendale* NEOCLASSICISM *Robert Adam* *Thomas Sheraton* *George Hepplewhite*	NEOCLASSICISM *David Roentgen*	CHIPPENDALE (to 1790) *Thomas Affleck* *William Savery* NEOCLASSICISM EARLY FEDERAL (from 1790)	*1770-1800*
REGENCY *Henry Holland* *Thomas Hope*	EMPIRE BIEDERMEIER *Josef Danhauser*	EARLY FEDERAL to 1810 *John Seymour* LATER FEDERAL 1810-1820 *Duncan Phyfe* EMPIRE	*1800-1830*
William IV *(1830-1837)* **Victoria** *(1837-1901)* ECLECTICISM	REVIVALS *Michael Thonet*	EMPIRE ECLECTICISM *Shaker furniture*	*1830-1880*
ARTS AND CRAFTS *William Morris* ART NOUVEAU	JUGENDSTIL	ECLECTICISM ARTS AND CRAFTS	*1880-1900*
EDWARDIAN	MODERN MOVEMENT BAUHAUS	ART NOUVEAU MODERN MOVEMENT *Frank Lloyd Wright*	*1900-1920*

Sweep front/Swept front A shallow bow-front, sometimes used in America instead of "bow-front".

Tabouret Low upholstered stool, originally used at court during the 17th and 18th centuries.

Tallboy English chest-on-chest with two small drawers at the top and six wide ones below. Sometimes incorporated a secretaire drawer in the top of the base section. In America its equivalent is the HIGHBOY but the terms are not interchangeable.

Tambour Sliding doors or curving pull-down fronts for desks made from thin reeded convex strips of wood glued to a linen or canvas backing and running in grooves. Used on small night tables, pot cupboards, commodes and later developed into the roll-top for desks.

Tavern table American term for a plain country-made rectangular table with carved support at either end and a stretcher in between, mainly 17th and 18th centuries.

Teapoy A tea caddy on stand, usually fitted to take several different teas.

Term A carved armless figure applied as ornament.

Tête à tête seat Generally describes an S-shaped seat for two people to sit decorously side by side without touching, made in England and America in the 19th century.

Thrown chair Old name for a turned or turner's chair.

Tole/Tole peinte Decorative applied painted metal panels.

Toleware American term for tinplate and tinware.

Townsend Goddard Catch-all abbreviation for two Quaker families making richly decorative American Chippendale furniture. *See* **Periods and Styles**.

Trafalgar chair Made from 1805 onwards, to celebrate Nelson's victory at Trafalgar, generally used to describe a sabre-legged chair with a rope-twist or cable-twist crest rail.

Tridarn Welsh version of the COURT CUPBOARD with three tiers of shelves above a double-doored cupboard.

Trophy Decoration of victory symbols – captured arms and standards – or musical instruments much favoured by Robert Adam and his followers for inlaid panels; also in grisaille with less effect.

Tudor *See* **Periods and Styles**.

Turnip Foot American version of a bun foot, usually with shallow ringed moulding and narrower neck.

Upholder 18th-century version of "upholsterer", used interchangeably in titles of 18th-century pattern books.

Van Risenburgh, Bernard (*d.*1767). Flemish-born ébéniste designing and making furniture of extreme luxury during Louis XV period in France, particularly associated with marquetry, Oriental lacquer and the incorporation of Sèvres plaques into furniture. *See* **Periods and Styles**.

Vargueño Decorative fall-front Spanish chest-on-stand, often with miniature shrine in central recess which was surrounded by small drawers and architectural motifs including arches, pillars and pediments. Without the fall-front it is a papeleira. Made from the 15th to 19th centuries.

Vauxhall glass Early English mirror glass and glass factory, established 1670 and closed in 1780 producing glass with faint blue tinge, usually with wide shallow bevel, known as "Vauxhall bevel".

Vernis Martin Brilliant translucent lacquer technique perfected by the French Martin brothers who were granted a monopoly in 1730 and by mid-century ran three lacquering factories. The family, originally coach painters, produced many variations of lacquerwork, the most highly prized being a green flecked with gold, used on furniture and small decorative objects.

Verre églomisé An ancient technique of painting glass on the underside and backing it with silver or gold-coloured metallic foil. Jean-Baptiste Glomy, collector and art dealer, revived the technique for framing prints in the second half of the 18th century and gave it his name.

Victorian *See* **Periods and Styles**.

Vitruvian scroll Bands of undulating scrolls like waves.

Voider Old word for a large tray with two hand holes, for clearing food and dirty cutlery and plates from the table. Of medieval origin, voiders today are more often called "butlers' trays".

Volute The helix-like ornamental scroll terminating Ionic capitals.

Wave scroll *See* VITRUVIAN SCROLL.

Welsh dresser Recent term for a kitchen dresser that has a rack of shelves over a dresser base that may be variously composed of drawers, cupboards and a potboard. They are by no means all of Welsh origin and many regional versions exist.

William and Mary *See* **Periods and Styles**.

William IV *See* **Periods and Styles**.

Wine cistern A wine cooler, of the open type, to be distinguished from the lockable CELLARET. Also known as a wine cooler.

ACKNOWLEDGMENTS

The editors acknowledge with gratitude the permission of the following individuals and organizations to reproduce their photographs on the pages indicated.

Adams Antiques, London: *267, 287*
Aldridges of Bath: *166, 237, 262, 350, 444, 492, 549*
Ambrose (Auctioneers), Loughton: *117, 341*
Anderson & Garland, Newcastle-upon-Tyne: *124, 133, 134, 140, 145, 160, 163, 244, 255, 273, 282, 333, 347, 418, 552, 578, 607, 615*

Banks & Silvers, Worcester: *396*
Bannister & Co, Haywards Heath: *144*
Bearnes, Torquay: *115, 135, 149, 157, 160, 165-167, 205, 207, 228, 229, 244, 253, 255, 275, 280, 330, 335, 357, 358, 360, 398, 400, 415, 417, 418, 420, 440, 468, 515, 517, 565, 573, 576, 580, 587, 588, 609, 622*
Bell Passage Antiques, Wotton-under-Edge, Glos: *345*
Boardman, Haverhill, Suffolk: *205, 285, 519, 522, 585, 594, 596, 597, 604*
Bonhams, London: *116, 130, 133, 134, 136, 144, 145, 153, 160, 162, 176, 191, 203, 209, 211, 221, 227, 228, 240, 247, 255, 265, 271, 279, 286, 321, 326, 332, 347, 352, 356, 360, 386, 388, 389, 391, 397, 416, 417, 425, 429, 433, 438, 440, 445, 446, 479, 484, 489, 491, 497, 504, 507, 521, 527, 546, 553, 554, 560, 565, 573, 577-579, 588, 590, 593, 601, 607*
William H. Brown, Grantham: *347*
Bruton Knowles, Gloucester: *274, 482*
David E. Burrows, Leicester: *215, 225, 243*
Burrows & Day, Ashford: *262, 284, 285*
Burtenshaw Walker, Lewes: *128, 166, 167, 250, 284, 287, 594, 608*
Butler & Hatch Waterman, Tenterden: *135, 145, 176, 202, 228, 230, 336, 367, 404, 442, 493*

Capes, Dunn & Co, Manchester: *134, 260, 306, 336, 360, 444, 479, 491, 518, 527*
Cheffins, Grain & Chalk, Cambridge: *163, 266, 275, 287*
Christie's & Edmiston's, Glasgow: *210, 262, 265, 272, 277, 283, 307, 309, 323, 334, 340, 364, 394, 404, 427, 491, 512, 548, 579, 608, 609*
Christie, Manson & Woods, Amsterdam: *444, 468, 499, 512, 514, 515, 519-521, 542, 544, 551, 552, 554, 571, 572, 575, 578, 579, 581, 583, 585-588, 594, 596, 598, 601, 603, 605, 607, 609, 611, 617, 622, 624*
Christie, Manson & Woods, London: *64, 112-117, 121-124, 126-129, 131-134, 137-143, 145, 147-155, 157-161, 164, 166, 168-172, 176-181, 184, 185, 187-191, 194, 195, 198-201, 204-208, 210, 211, 213, 214, 216-227, 229, 230, 232, 233, 235, 236, 238-240, 242, 243, 246, 249, 250, 253-259, 264, 266-268, 272-281, 283, 285, 288-294, 296-299, 301, 302, 304-307, 309-311, 313, 314, 316-319, 321-323, 326, 329, 330, 332-335, 337-340, 343-356, 358-360, 362-364, 366, 368-372, 374-376, 378, 379, 381-383, 388-391, 393, 395-399, 401-419, 421, 422, 424, 425, 427, 429, 432, 435, 436, 438-443, 445-451, 456-458, 462, 465, 466, 468-475, 477-490, 493-497, 502, 504-506, 508-512, 514, 516, 517, 519-528, 531-533, 536, 540, 544-550, 555-559, 561-568, 570, 572, 573-576, 577, 579-585, 587-595, 597-604, 608, 610-613, 615, 617-624*
Christie, Manson & Woods, New York: *10-104, 106-113, 118, 121, 122, 124, 125, 127, 128, 131, 135-137, 139, 142, 143, 151, 156, 168-171, 175, 180, 182, 188, 194, 195, 198-204, 206, 209-211, 215-218, 220, 221, 223, 224, 230, 231, 233, 234, 238-240, 246, 248, 253-255, 266, 274-278, 281, 286-288, 290-293, 295-298, 300, 302, 304-306, 309, 311, 313, 315-317, 319-322, 324, 327, 329, 331, 332, 335, 336, 338, 341, 344, 347, 348, 351-354, 363, 366, 370, 372, 373, 375, 379, 380, 382, 383, 386-388, 392, 393, 396, 397, 401, 403, 404, 411, 417, 420,*

422-424, 427, 428, 430, 431, 434, 438, 440, 442-446, 449, 450, 452, 456-461, 465-481, 483-500, 502-506, 508-511, 513, 515-530, 532-536, 539-541, 543, 545-552, 554-558, 560-570, 573-576, 581, 586, 592-595, 600-603, 606-619, 621-623
Christie's Roma, Rome: *371, 535, 537-541, 546-548, 556, 559-562, 564*
Christie's (South Kensington), London: *132, 133, 146, 153, 167, 172, 211, 236, 245, 253, 268, 335, 341, 362, 395, 403, 425, 431, 432, 434, 437, 440, 445, 478, 492, 502, 577, 578, 590, 593, 602-604, 621*
Christie, Manson & Woods (Aust), Sydney: *195, 621*
Christopher Clarke, Stow-on-the-Wold: *140, 230, 249, 305, 318, 404, 420, 421, 434*
Nigel Coleman Antiques, Brasted, Kent: *172, 242, 244, 389*
Coles, Knapp & Kennedy, Ross-on-Wye: *163*
Colliers, Bigwood & Bewlay, Stratford-upon-Avon: *145*
Cooper Hirst, Chelmsford: *433*
Cubbitt & West, Guildford: *202, 208, 392, 550*

Dacre, Son & Hartley, Ilkley, Yorks: *125, 130, 145, 170, 260, 261, 286, 327, 358, 389, 394, 430, 441, 609*
Richard Davidson Antiques, Petworth: *598*
Julian Dawson, Lewes: *57, 146, 202, 228, 236, 244, 270, 311, 324, 397, 398, 409, 436, 605*
Dee & Atkinson, Driffield, Yorks: *264, 336*
Dickinson, Davy & Markham, Brigg, South Humberside: *247, 264, 270, 273, 361, 609*
Dreweatts, Donnington, Newbury: *140, 176, 212, 225-228, 230, 264, 270, 272, 288, 306, 311, 329, 335, 339, 346, 347, 350, 366, 385, 419, 428, 430, 431, 440, 444, 515, 516, 524, 556, 560, 591, 599, 604*
Hy Duke & Son, Dorchester: *275, 324, 489, 492, 520*
Colin Dyte Export, Highbridge, Somerset: *161, 203, 210, 212, 229, 231, 237, 279, 345, 360, 367, 368*

Eatons of Eton, Bucks: *422*
Edwards, Bigwood & Bewlay, Stratford-upon-Avon: *144*
Elliott & Green, Lymington: *323, 437*

John Francis (Thomas Jones & Sons), Carmarthen: *121, 162, 266, 286, 346, 578, 602*
Fryer's Auction Galleries, Bexhill-on-Sea: *267, 592*

Geering & Colyer, Hawkhurst, Kent: *190, 260, 444, 562, 582, 598*
Loth Gijselman, Amsterdam: *583, 590, 591, 597, 613*
Graves Son & Pilcher, Hove: *130, 170, 242, 275, 285, 354, 447, 468, 491, 552, 592, 596*
Gribble, Booth & Taylor, Axminster: *231*

Hallidays Antiques Ltd., Dorchester-on-Thames: *142, 143, 151, 307, 328, 332, 337, 341, 349, 389, 397, 399, 401, 403, 408, 410, 424, 426, 433*
Heath-Bullock, Godalming: *126, 137, 176, 226, 230, 237, 267, 342, 345, 364, 390, 395, 398, 403, 422, 435-437, 441, 445, 479*
Sheila Hines, Petworth: *141, 267, 272, 393, 512, 609*
Humphry Antiques, Petworth: *251*
Huntington Antiques, Stow-on-the-Wold: *114, 197, 216, 239, 240, 251, 261, 262, 281, 283, 284, 286, 342, 343, 393, 423*

Ivy House Antiques, Brasted, Kent: *341*

Tobias Jellinek, London: *343*

G.A. Key, Aylsham, Norfolk: *113, 196*

ACKNOWLEDGMENTS

Lacy Scott, Bury St Edmunds: *363, 422*
Lalonde Bros & Parham, Bristol: *358, 430, 578*
W.H. Lane & Son, Penzance: *134, 145, 146, 196, 239, 278, 324-326, 341, 352, 365-367, 391, 403, 473, 550, 581*
Langlois, St Helier, Jersey: *610*
Lawrences, Crewkerne, Somerset: *116, 122, 129, 130, 133, 138, 143-146, 150, 154, 161-164, 215, 218, 219, 222, 223, 227-229, 232, 242, 244-247, 252, 255, 265-267, 270, 273, 277, 279-281, 283, 286-288, 306, 329, 331-333, 346, 350, 355, 359, 360, 368, 387, 394, 397, 401, 404-406, 415, 417, 418, 424, 427, 431, 434, 441, 444, 468, 470, 475, 513, 579, 588, 590, 591, 593, 597, 598, 605, 610, 613, 621, 623, 624*
Leominster Antiques, Leominster, Herefordshire: *217*
Ann Lingard, Rye: *254, 259*
Lloyd & Greenwood Antiques, Burford: *356*
Locke & England, Leamington Spa: *201, 268, 331, 546*
Thomas Love, Perth: *271*
Lowe of Loughborough: *419*

Mallams, Oxford: *566*
Matsell Antiques, Quorn, Leicester: *237*
Thos. Mawer, Lincoln: *196, 311*
George Mealy & Sons, Castlecomer, Co. Kilkenny: *227, 399, 418, 435*
Messenger, May Baverstock, Godalming: *176, 196, 236, 240, 241, 332, 357, 397, 437, 475, 547, 564, 581, 595, 607*
Miller & Co, Truro: *261, 277, 287, 622*
Morphets of Harrogate: *124, 131, 144, 161, 176, 235, 254, 270, 287, 404, 417, 434, 446*

Neales of Nottingham: *162, 219, 276, 279, 283*
Neale Sons & Fletcher, Woodbridge, Suffolk: *129, 166, 231, 245, 358*
Neumeister, Münchener Kunstauktionshaus, Munich: *512, 521, 523, 527, 528, 566*
North Parade Antiques, Oxford: *345*
Michael Newman, Plymouth: *272, 572*
Edward A. Nowell, Wells: *339*

Olivers, Sudbury, Suffolk: *391 592*
Osmond, Tricks & Son, Bristol: *129, 307, 335, 563, 601, 623*
Outhwaite & Litherland, Liverpool: *116*

J.R. Parkinson, Son & Hamer Auctions, Bury, Lancs: *130, 134, 391*
Parson, Welch & Cowell, Sevenoaks: *122, 133, 142, 147, 149, 164, 167, 236, 240, 248, 266, 281, 286, 330, 336, 337, 347, 389, 392, 419, 490, 492, 520, 523, 572, 588, 592, 610*
Pennard House, Shepton Mallet, Somerset: *133, 213, 215, 227, 228, 230, 236, 312, 337, 367, 392, 422, 437*
Philip, Laney & Jolly, Malvern: *163, 210, 273*
Phillips, London: *135, 138, 144, 175, 206, 274, 275, 329, 349, 402, 422, 439-441, 448, 466, 467, 485, 509, 515, 517, 519, 521-523, 547, 548, 561, 574, 575, 577, 585, 604*
Phillips, New York: *12-14, 16, 18, 41, 43, 47, 48, 52, 54, 55, 57, 61, 81, 83, 87, 95, 98, 111, 152, 161, 271*
Phillips in Scotland, Edinburgh: *274*
Phillips (Knowle), Solihull: *361, 518, 519, 581*
Phillips, Oxford: *117, 144, 246, 268, 269, 425, 434, 521, 558, 592, 598*
Antony Preston Antiques Ltd., Stow-on-the-Wold: *142, 143, 195, 260, 313, 351, 414, 476, 478*

John H. Raby & Son, Manningham, Bradford: *434*
Reeds, Rains, Sale: *123, 144, 146, 202, 215, 231, 236, 271, 307, 407, 433, 435, 597*
Rowland Gorringe, Lewes: *434*
Russell Baldwin & Bright, Leominster, Herefordshire: *159, 196*

Rye Vaults Antiques, Rye: *197, 216, 251, 519, 595*

Daniel Smith, Folkestone, Kent: *316*
Sotheby's Chester: *112, 115, 117, 123, 128, 130, 135, 140, 144, 146, 150, 160, 162, 166, 167, 169, 171, 175, 176, 229, 236, 253-255, 260, 261, 266, 268, 280, 287, 310, 312, 316, 318, 325, 326, 328, 333, 334, 338, 346, 349, 354, 355, 359, 361, 398, 399, 406, 407, 418, 424, 435, 436, 441, 488, 521, 522, 590, 591, 620*
Sotheby's in Ireland: *140, 335, 352, 354, 592, 602*
Sotheby, Parke Bernet, London: *113, 114, 117, 118, 120-126, 128, 129, 131-138, 140, 142-150, 154, 155, 158, 160-168, 170-177, 179-189, 192, 194-213, 216, 217, 219, 221, 222, 224-236, 238-243, 245, 246, 248, 250-255, 257, 259, 260, 262, 264-266, 268-280, 284, 286-290, 299, 300-306, 308, 310-315, 317, 322, 325-327, 329-341, 343, 344, 346-353, 355, 357-364, 366-373, 375, 376, 378-382, 385-388, 390-404, 408, 409, 411-414, 416, 417, 419-431, 433, 435, 436, 438-447, 453, 465-477, 479, 481-497, 500, 501, 503-505, 508, 510, 513, 515-524, 526-531, 534-538, 540-546, 548-556, 558, 562-567, 569, 570, 572-587, 589-593, 595, 597, 601-605, 607, 608, 610-613, 617-619, 622-624*
Sotheby, Parke Bernet, Monaco: *442, 456-461, 465, 470, 473-476, 478, 480, 481, 483, 484, 486, 488, 494, 495, 498, 503, 508, 509, 510, 511, 533, 574*
Sotheby, Parke Bernet, New York: *10, 11, 14, 19, 20, 26-28, 30, 32, 33, 37-43, 47, 48, 50-52, 54-58, 61, 65-83, 87, 90, 92, 93, 94, 96, 97, 100-102, 105-107, 110, 111, 369*
Sotheby's in Sussex: *114, 117, 120, 123, 125-128, 130, 131, 134-137, 141-144, 146, 151, 153-157, 160, 161, 163-168, 171-173, 176, 193, 194, 196, 201, 203, 207-209, 212, 213, 215, 217-220, 222, 227, 228, 232, 233, 238-242, 244, 245, 251-255, 258, 260-262, 268-272, 275, 276, 278, 280-283, 285, 305, 307, 308, 311, 313, 324, 328, 330, 331, 333, 340, 342, 346-352, 361, 364-367, 370, 387, 389-392, 397-399, 402, 410, 414, 416, 418, 419, 421-427, 431-433, 440, 444-448, 466, 468, 473, 484, 486, 491, 492, 497, 507, 513, 517, 523, 525, 545, 556, 557, 561, 563, 565, 572, 577-583, 585-589, 593-595, 599, 601, 602, 604, 608, 609, 615, 617*
Henry Spencer & Sons, Retford, Notts: *144, 162, 220, 510, 575, 592, 602, 614*
Studio Antiques, Bourton-on-the-Water, Glos: *423*
Sutton Valence Antiques, Sutton Valence, Kent: *237*

Louis Taylor & Sons, Hanley, Stoke-on-Trent: *135, 261, 439*
Jeanne Temple Antiques, Milton Keynes: *428, 437*
Tennant's, Leyburn, North Yorks: *112, 203, 234, 262, 621*
Tilings Antiques, Brasted, Kent: *345*
Times Past, Eton, Bucks: *341*

Vidler & Co, Rye: *255*
Village Antiques, Bexhill-on-Sea: *271*
V & V Chattel Auctioneers, Reading: *145, 419, 513*

Ward & Partners, Hythe: *437*
Thomas Watson & Son, Darlington, Co. Durham: *171, 273, 349, 361, 435, 437*
Way, Riddett & Co, Ryde, Isle of Wight: *512*
J.M. Welch & Son, Dunmow, Essex: *176, 229, 307*
The Henry Francis Du Pont Museum, Winterthur: *24, 64*
Woodstock, London: *324, 356, 422*
Woolley & Wallis, Salisbury: *112, 128, 132, 195, 207, 214, 252, 268, 270, 330, 348, 349, 360, 417, 419, 433, 447, 489, 490, 497, 586, 592, 593*
Eldon E. Worrall, Liverpool: *352*
Worsfolds, Canterbury: *163, 166, 175, 271, 336, 576, 611*
Wright-Manley, Nantwich: *139*
Wyatt & Son, Chichester: *145, 160, 166, 267, 586*